SOCIOLOGY 90/91

Editor

Kurt Finsterbusch
University of Maryland, College Park

Kurt Finsterbusch received his bachelor's degree in history from Princeton University in 1957, and his bachelor of divinity degree from Grace Theological Seminary in 1960. His Ph.D. in sociology, from Columbia University, was conferred in 1969. He is the author of several books, including *Understanding Social Impacts* (Sage Publications, 1980), *Social Research for Policy Decisions* (Wadsworth Publishing, 1980, with Annabelle Bender Motz), and *Organizational Change as a Development Strategy* (Lynne Rienner Publishers, 1987, with Jerald Hage). He is currently teaching at the University of Maryland, College Park, and, in addition to serving as editor for *Annual Editions: Sociology*, is also co-editor for The Dushkin Publishing Group's *Taking Sides: Clashing Views on Controversial Social Issues.*

Cover illustration by Mike Eagle

The Dushkin Publishing Group, Inc.
Sluice Dock, Guilford, Connecticut 06437

The Annual Editions Series

Annual Editions is a series of over fifty volumes designed to provide the reader with convenient, low-cost access to a wide range of current, carefully selected articles from some of the most important magazines, newspapers, and journals published today. Annual Editions are updated on an annual basis through a continuous monitoring of over 200 periodical sources. All Annual Editions have a number of features designed to make them particularly useful, including topic guides, annotated tables of contents, unit overviews, and indexes. For the teacher using Annual Editions in the classroom, an Instructor's Resource Guide with test questions is available for each volume.

VOLUMES AVAILABLE

Africa
Aging
American Government
American History, Pre-Civil War
American History, Post-Civil War
Anthropology
Biology
Business and Management
Business Ethics
Canadian Politics
China
Comparative Politics
Computers in Education
Computers in Business
Computers in Society
Criminal Justice
Drugs, Society, and Behavior
Early Childhood Education
Economics
Educating Exceptional Children
Education
Educational Psychology
Environment
Geography
Global Issues
Health
Human Development

Human Resources
Human Sexuality
Latin America
Macroeconomics
Marketing
Marriage and Family
Middle East and the Islamic World
Money and Banking
Nutrition
Personal Growth and Behavior
Psychology
Public Administration
Social Problems
Sociology
Soviet Union and Eastern Europe
State and Local Government
Third World
Urban Society
Violence and Terrorism
Western Civilization,
   Pre-Reformation
Western Civilization,
   Post-Reformation
Western Europe
World History, Pre-Modern
World History, Modern
World Politics

Library of Congress Cataloging in Publication Data
Main entry under title: Annual Editions: Sociology. 1990/91.
        1. Sociology—Periodicals. 2. United States—Social Conditions—1960—Periodicals.
I. Finsterbusch, Kurt, *comp.* II. Title: Sociology.
ISBN 0–87967–855–0   301′.05   72–76876
HM1.A76

Nineteenth Edition

Manufactured by The Banta Company, Harrisonburg, Virginia 22801

Editors/ Advisory Board

To the Reader

In publishing ANNUAL EDITIONS we recognize the enormous role played by the magazines, newspapers, and journals of the *public press* in providing current, first-rate educational information in a broad spectrum of interest areas. Within the articles, the best scientists, practitioners, researchers, and commentators draw issues into new perspective as accepted theories and viewpoints are called into account by new events, recent discoveries change old facts, and fresh debate breaks out over important controversies.

Many of the articles resulting from this enormous editorial effort are appropriate for students, researchers, and professionals seeking accurate, current material to help bridge the gap between principles and theories and the real world. These articles, however, become more useful for study when those of lasting value are carefully *collected, organized, indexed,* and *reproduced* in a *low-cost format,* which provides easy and permanent access when the material is needed. That is the role played by *Annual Editions.*

Under the direction of each volume's *Editor,* who is an expert in the subject area, and with the guidance of an *Advisory Board,* we seek each year to provide in each *ANNUAL EDITION* a current, well-balanced, carefully selected collection of the best of the public press for your study and enjoyment. We think you'll find this volume useful, and we hope you'll take a moment to let us know what you think.

The 1990s inherit from the 1980s crises, changes, and challenges. Crime is running rampant. The public is demanding more police, more jails, and tougher sentences, but less government spending. The economy suffers from foreign competition, trade deficits, budget deficits, and economic uncertainties. Government economic policies seem to create almost as many problems as they solve. Laborers, women, blacks, and many other groups complain of injustices and victimization. The use of toxic chemicals has been blamed for increases in cancer, sterility, and other diseases. Marriage and the family have been transformed, in part, by the women's movement, but new problems are surfacing. Schools, television, and corporations are commonly vilified. Add to this the problems of population growth, ozone depletion, and the greenhouse effect, and it is easy to despair.

The present generation may be the one to determine the course of history for the next 200 years. Great changes are taking place and new solutions are being sought where old answers no longer work. The issues the current generation faces are complex and must be interpreted within a sophisticated framework. The sociological perspective provides such a framework. The articles that follow should help you develop the sociological perspective, which will enable you to determine how the issues of the day relate to the way society is structured. They will provide not only information, but also models of interpretation and analysis which will guide you as you form your own views.

Annual Editions: Sociology 90/91 emphasizes social change, institutional crises, and prospects for the future. It provides an intellectual preparation for acting for the betterment of humanity in times of crucial change. The sociological perspective is needed more than ever as humankind tries to find a way to peace and prosperity. The obstacles that lie in the path of these important goals seem to increase yearly. The goals of this edition are to communicate to students the excitement and importance of the study of the social world, and provoke interest in and enthusiasm for the study of sociology.

Annual Editions depends upon reader response to develop and change. You are encouraged to return the article rating form at the back of the book with your opinions about existing articles, recommendations of articles you think have sociological merit for subsequent editions, and advice on how the anthology can be made more useful as a teaching and learning tool.

Kurt Finsterbusch
Editor

Contents

Introduction

The role of the sociologist and the discipline of sociology are introduced in Berger's article.

Unit 1

Culture

Eight selections consider American values and life-styles, unusual cultures, and ethnic cultures within the United States.

The concepts in bold italics are developed in the article. For further expansion please refer to the Topic Guide, the Index, and the Glossary.

Unit 2

Socialization, Biology, Social Control, and Deviance

Seven articles examine the effects of social influences on childhood, personality, and human behavior with regard to the socialization of the individual.

Unit 3

Groups and Roles in Transition

Seven articles discuss some of the social roles and group relationships that are in transition in today's society. Topics include primary and secondary groups and the reevaluation of social choices.

The concepts in bold italics are developed in the article. For further expansion please refer to the Topic Guide, the Index, and the Glossary.

Unit 4

Social Institutions in Crisis and Change

Ten articles examine several social institutions that are currently in crisis. Selections focus on the political, economic, and social spheres, as well as the overall state of the nation.

The concepts in bold italics are developed in the article. For further expansion please refer to the Topic Guide, the Index, and the Glossary.

Charles Peters identifies is the failure to pass the truth up through the hierarchy. The information that reaches the top is often rosy and biased. The NASA disaster illustrates this problem.

Unit 5

Stratification and Social Inequalities

Six selections discuss the social stratification and inequalities that exist in today's society with regard to the rich, the poor, and blacks.

Unit 6

Social Change and the Future

Six selections discuss the impact that technology, environmental degradation, and changing social values will have on society's future.

The concepts in bold italics are developed in the article. For further expansion please refer to the Topic Guide, the Index, and the Glossary.

Topic Guide

This topic guide suggests how the selections in this book relate to topics of traditional concern to sociology students and professionals. It can be very useful in locating articles which relate to each other for reading and research. The guide is arranged alphabetically according to topic. Articles may, of course, treat topics that do not appear in the topic guide. In turn, entries in the topic guide do not necessarily constitute a comprehensive listing of all the contents of each selection.

TOPIC AREA	TREATED AS AN ISSUE IN:	TOPIC AREA	TREATED AS AN ISSUE IN:
Adults/Adulthood	13. Erik Erikson's Eight Ages of Man	Future	24. Will America Become #2?
			27. Post-Crash Institutions
Blacks	9. Young, Black, Male, and Trapped		43. Third Technological Revolution
	38. Two Black Americas		44. Earth's Vital Signs
			45. America's Rising Sun
Bureaucracy	27. From Ouagadougou to Cape Canaveral		
		Groups	7. What's American About America?
Careers	3. Is Greed Dead?		22. "Sociology of Acceptance"
			23. The Third Age
Children/Childhood	5. The Mountain People		41. Promise of America
	10. Childhood Through the Ages		
	11. Wilding in the Night	Handicapped	20. For Goodness' Sake
	37. Children of the Underclass		22. "Sociology of Acceptance"
Community	20. For Goodness' Sake	Homeless	35. Helping and Hating the Homeless
Competition	24. Will America Become #2?	Leadership	30. Back to Basics
			34. A Talent for Disorder
Crime	11. Wilding in the Night		
	14. Why We're Losing the War on Crime	Leisure	4. How America Has Run Out of Time
	15. Crime in the Suites	Life-styles	2. Why I Love America
Culture	2. Why I Love America		3. Is Greed Dead?
	3. Is Greed Dead?		4. How America Has Run Out of Time
	4. How America Has Run Out of Time		5. The Mountain People
	5. The Mountain People		7. What's American About America?
	6. Shakespeare in the Bush		9. Young, Black, Male, and Trapped
	7. What's American About America?		17. Working Parents
	8. A People's History		18. The Mommy Track
			23. The Third Age
Demography	40. Divided by Demography		
	41. Promise of America	Marriage	See Family/Marriage
Ecology/	5. The Mountain People	Media	33. TV and the Communications
Environment	42. Living Dangerously		Revolution
	44. Earth's Vital Signs		
		Organizations	29. Corporate Teams and Totems
Economy	24. Will America Become #2?		31. How to Kill a Company
	25. As the World Turns		
	26. Post-Crash Institutions	Personality	13. Erik Erikson's Eight Ages of Man
	30. Back to Basics		
	31. How to Kill a Company	Politics/	24. Will America Become #2?
	45. America's Rising Sun	Government	26. Post-Crash Institutions
			27. From Ouagadougou to Cape Canaveral
Education	26. Post-Crash Institutions		28. It's Money That Matters
			34. A Talent for Disorder
Elderly	23. The Third Age		
		Population Growth	40. Divided by Demography
Family/Marriage	3. Is Greed Dead?		41. Promise of America
	5. The Mountain People		
	8. A People's History	Poverty	5. The Mountain People
	10. Childhood Through the Ages		9. Young, Black, Male, and Trapped
	17. Working Parents		20. For Goodness' Sake
	18. The Mommy Track		35. Helping and Hating the Homeless
	19. Changing Role of Fathers		36. What About America's Underclass?
	32. Technology as Destiny		37. Children of the Underclass
	37. Children of the Underclass		38. Two Black Americas
	39. The Global War Against Women		

TOPIC AREA	TREATED AS AN ISSUE IN:	TOPIC AREA	TREATED AS AN ISSUE IN:
Race/Ethnic Relations	7. What's American About America? 8. A People's History 9. Young, Black, Male, and Trapped 41. Promise of America	**Social Movements**	8. A People's History
		Social Relationships	4. How America Has Run Out of Time 5. The Mountain People 39. The Global War Against Women
Roles	10. Childhood Through the Ages		
		Socialization	10. Childhood Through the Ages 11. Wilding in the Night 41. Promise of America
Science/Knowledge	1. Invitation to Sociology 27. From Ouagadougou to Cape Canaveral 42. Living Dangerously 43. Third Technological Revolution		
		Sociological Perspective	1. Invitation to Sociology
Sex Roles	11. Men vs. Women 17. Working Parents 18. The Mommy Track 19. The Changing Role of Fathers	**Technology**	32. Technology as Destiny 42. Living Dangerously 43. Third Technological Revolution
Social Change	3. Is Greed Dead? 4. How America Has Run Out of Time 5. The Mountain People 8. A People's History 10. Childhood Through the Ages 19. The Changing Role of Fathers 23. The Third Age 24. Will America Become #2? 25. As the World Turns 29. Corporate Teams and Totems 30. Back to Basics 32. Technology as Destiny 33. TV and the Communications Revolution 34. A Talent for Disorder 36. What About America's Underclass? 43. Third Technological Revolution 45. America's Rising Sun	**Underclass**	9. Young, Black, Male, and Trapped 35. Helping and Hating the Homeless 36. What About America's Underclass? 37. Children of the Underclass
		Unemployment	*See* Work/Unemployment
		Values	2. Why I Love America 3. Is Greed Dead? 4. How America Has Run Out of Time 5. Mountain People 6. Shakespeare in the Bush 17. Working Parents 18. The Mommy Track 32. Technology as Destiny
		Volunteerism	3. Is Greed Dead? 20. For Goodness' Sake
Social Class/ Stratification	9. Young, Black, Male, and Trapped 25. As the World Turns 34. A Talent for Disorder 35. Helping and Hating the Homeless 36. What About America's Underclass? 38. Two Black Americas	**Women**	8. A People's History 12. Men vs. Women 32. Technology as Destiny 39. The Global War Against Women
Social Control	11. Wilding in the Night 14. Why We're Losing the War on Crime 15. Crime in the Suites 16. Is Rehabilitation a Waste of Time?	**Work/ Unemployment**	17. Working Parents 18. The Mommy Track

Introduction

The study of sociology can be defined as the method by which ordinary people strive to understand what is happening to them and their society. The need for such understanding is urgent at the present historical moment. Change has become so rapid that most people are bewildered and amazed by events over the past two decades: the energy crisis transformed global economics; new technologies changed the workplace; and a complex, interdependent world means that the changes in one country cause changes in other countries.

Most people today are associated with large, complex, and impersonal organizations, which sometimes take actions that disturb our sense of justice. Universities herd students through large classes and seldom create truly joyful intellectual work. The medical system extorts stupendous fees from patients, making them feel like victims. The tobacco industry enthusiastically markets its highly addictive and harmful drug which endangers the health of hundreds of thousands of Americans every year. Corporations close factories in New England and open factories in Taiwan. American banks invest in the Japanese industries which are invading the American market. Is it surprising, then, that individuals often feel powerless against such indignities?

Unprecedented opportunities to build a better world and improve the quality of life for many people lie ahead. The study of sociology can help students figure out how society works and what they can do to change it by developing a sociological imagination and sociological perspective. The article by Peter L. Berger in this introductory section focuses on the common occurrences of everyday life. The author challenges the student to use the sociological perspective to "see," in daily events, the sociological truths which most people miss.

Looking Ahead: Challenge Questions

How can sociology contribute to one's understanding of the contemporary world?

In what ways can the sociological imagination become a significant factor in political policies?

Can sociology contribute to personal growth?

Invitation to Sociology
A Humanistic Perspective

Peter L. Berger

. . . The sociologist, then, is someone concerned with understanding society in a disciplined way. The nature of this discipline is scientific. This means that what the sociologist finds and says about the social phenomena he studies occurs within a certain rather strictly defined frame of reference. One of the main characteristics of this scientific frame of reference is that operations are bound by certain rules of evidence. As a scientist, the sociologist tries to be objective, to control his personal preferences and prejudices, to perceive clearly rather than to judge normatively. This restraint, of course, does not embrace the totality of the sociologist's existence as a human being, but is limited to his operations *qua* sociologist. Nor does the sociologist claim that his frame of reference is the only one within which society can be looked at. For that matter, very few scientists in any field would claim today that one should look at the world only scientifically. The botanist looking at a daffodil has no reason to dispute the right of the poet to look at the same object in a very different manner. There are many ways of playing. The point is not that one denies other people's games but that one is clear about the rules of one's own. The game of the sociologist, then, uses scientific rules. As a result, the sociologist must be clear in his own mind as to the meaning of these rules. That is, he must concern himself with methodological questions. Methodology does not constitute his goal. The latter, let us recall once more, is the attempt to understand society. Methodology helps in reaching this goal. In order to understand society, or that segment of it that he is studying at the moment, the sociologist will use a variety of means. Among these are statistical techniques. Statistics can be very useful in answering certain sociological questions. But statistics does not constitute sociology. As a scientist, the sociologist will have to be concerned with the exact significance of the terms he is using. That is, he will have to be careful about terminology. This does not have to mean that he must invent a new language of his own, but it does mean that he cannot naively use the language of everyday discourse. Finally, the interest of the sociologist is primarily theoretical. That is, he is interested in understanding for its own sake. He may be aware of or even concerned with the practical applicability and consequences of his findings, but at that point he leaves the sociological frame of reference as such and moves into realms of values, beliefs and ideas that he shares with other men who are not sociologists. . . .

We would say then that the sociologist (that is, the one we would really like to invite to our game) is a person intensively, endlessly, shamelessly interested in the doings of men. His natural habitat is all the human gathering places of the world, wherever men come together. The sociologist may be interested in many other things. But his consuming interest remains in the world of men, their institutions, their history, their passions. And since he is interested in men, nothing that men do can be altogether tedious for him. He will naturally be interested in the events that engage men's ultimate beliefs, their moments of tragedy and grandeur and ecstasy. But he will also be fascinated by the commonplace, the everyday. He will know reverence, but this reverence will not prevent him from wanting to see and to understand. He may sometimes feel revulsion or contempt. But this also will not deter him from wanting to have his questions answered. The sociologist, in his quest for understanding, moves through the world of men without respect for the usual lines of demarcation. Nobility and degradation, power and obscurity, intelligence and folly—these are equally *interesting* to him, however unequal they may be in his personal values or tastes. Thus his questions may lead him to all possible levels of society, the best and the least known places, the most respected and the most despised. And, if he is a good sociologist, he will find himself in all these places because his own questions have so taken possession of him that he has little choice but to seek for answers.

It would be possible to say the same things in a lower key. We could say that the sociologist, but for the grace of his academic title, is the man who must listen to gossip despite himself, who is tempted to look through keyholes, to read other people's mail, to open closed cabinets. Before some otherwise unoccupied psychologist sets out now to construct an aptitude test for sociologists on the basis of sublimated voyeurism, let us quickly say that we are speaking merely by way of analogy. Perhaps some little boys consumed with curiosity to watch their maiden aunts in the bathroom later become inveterate sociologists. This is quite uninteresting. What interests us is the curiosity that grips any sociologist in front of a closed door behind which there are human voices. If he is a good sociologist, he will want to open that door, to understand these voices. Behind each closed door he will anticipate some new facet of human life not yet perceived and understood.

The sociologist will occupy himself with matters that others regard as too sacred or as too distasteful for dispassionate investigation. He will find rewarding the company of priests or of prostitutes, depending not on his personal preferences but on the questions he happens to be asking at the moment. He will also concern himself with matters that others may find much too boring. He will be interested in the human interaction that goes with warfare or with great intellectual discoveries, but also in the relations between people employed in a restaurant or between a group of little girls playing with their dolls. His main focus of attention is not the ultimate significance of what men do, but the action in itself, as another example of the infinite richness of human conduct. . . .

Any intellectual activity derives excitement from the moment it becomes a trail of discovery. In some fields of learning this is the discovery of worlds previously unthought and unthinkable. This is the excitement of the astronomer or of the nuclear physicist on the antipodal boundaries of the realities that man is capable of conceiving. But it can also be the excitement of bacteriology or geology. In a different way it can be the excitement of the linguist discovering new realms of human expression or of the anthropologist exploring human customs in faraway countries. In such discovery, when undertaken with passion, a widening of awareness, sometimes a veritable transformation of consciousness, occurs. The universe turns out to be much more wonder-full than one had ever dreamed. The excitement of sociology is usually of a different sort. Sometimes, it is true, the sociologist penetrates into worlds that had previously been quite unknown to him—for instance, the world of crime, or the world of some bizarre religious sect, or the world fashioned by the exclusive concerns of some group such as medical specialists or military leaders or advertising executives. However, much of the time the sociologist moves in sectors of experience that are familiar to him and to most people in his society. He investigates communities, institutions and activities that one can read about every day in the newspapers. Yet there is another excitement of discovery beckoning in his investigations. It is not the excitement of coming upon the totally unfamiliar, but rather the excitement of finding the familiar becoming transformed in its meaning. The fascination of sociology lies in the fact that its perspective makes us see in a new light the very world in which we have lived all our lives. This also constitutes a transformation of consciousness. Moreover, this transformation is more relevant existentially than that of many other intellectual disciplines, because it is more difficult to segregate in some special compartment of the mind. The astronomer does not live in the remote galaxies, and the nuclear physicist can, outside his laboratory, eat and laugh and marry and vote without thinking about the insides of the atom. The geologist looks at rocks only at appropriate times, and the linguist speaks English with his wife. The sociologist lives in society, on the job and off it. His own life, inevitably, is part of his subject matter. Men being what they are, sociologists too manage to segregate their professional insights from their everyday affairs. But it is a rather difficult feat to perform in good faith.

The sociologist moves in the common world of men, close to what most of them would call real. The categories he employs in his analyses are only refinements of the categories by which other men live—power, class, status, race, ethnicity. As a result, there is a deceptive simplicity and obviousness about some sociological investigations.

One reads them, nods at the familiar scene, remarks that one has heard all this before and don't people have better things to do than to waste their time on truisms—until one is suddenly brought up against an insight that radically questions everything one had previously assumed about this familiar scene. This is the point at which one begins to sense the excitement of sociology.

Let us take a specific example. Imagine a sociology class in a Southern college where almost all the students are white Southerners. Imagine a lecture on the subject of the racial system of the South. The lecturer is talking here of matters that have been familiar to his students from the time of their infancy. Indeed, it may be that they are much more familiar with the minutiae of this system than he is. They are quite bored as a result. It seems to them that he is only using more pretentious words to describe what they already know. Thus he may use the term "caste," one commonly used now by American sociologists to describe the Southern racial system. But in explaining the term he shifts to traditional Hindu society, to make it clearer. He then goes on to analyze the magical beliefs inherent in caste tabus, the social dynamics of commensalism and connubium, the economic interests concealed within the system, the way in which religious beliefs relate to the tabus, the effects of the caste system upon the industrial development of the society and vice versa—all in India. But suddenly India is not very far away at all. The lecture then goes back to its Southern theme. The familiar now seems not quite so familiar any more. Questions are raised that are new, perhaps raised angrily, but raised all the same. And at least some of the students have begun to understand that there are functions involved in this business of race that they have not read about in the newspapers (at least not those in their hometowns) and that their parents have not told them—partly, at least, because neither the newspapers nor the parents knew about them.

It can be said that the first wisdom of sociology is this—things are not what they seem. This too is a deceptively simple statement. It ceases to be simple after a while. Social reality turns out to have many layers of meaning. The discovery of each new layer changes the perception of the whole.

Anthropologists use the term "culture shock" to describe the impact of a totally new culture upon a newcomer. In an extreme instance such shock will be experienced by the Western explorer who is told, halfway through dinner, that he is eating the nice old lady he had been chatting with the previous day—a shock with predictable physiological if not moral consequences. Most explorers no longer encounter cannibalism in their travels today. However, the first encounters with polygamy or with puberty rites or even with the way some nations drive their automobiles can be quite a shock to an American visitor. With the shock may go not only disapproval or disgust but a sense of excitement that things can *really* be that different from what they are at home. To some extent, at least, this is the excitement of any first travel abroad. The experience of sociological discovery could be described as "culture shock" minus geographical displacement. In other words, the sociologist travels at home—with shocking results. He is unlikely to find that he is eating a nice old lady for dinner. But the discovery, for instance, that his own church has considerable money invested in the missile industry or that a few blocks from his home there are people who engage in cultic orgies may not be drastically different in emotional impact. Yet we would not want to imply that sociological discoveries are always or even usually outrageous to moral sentiment. Not at all. What they have in common with exploration in distant lands, however, is the sudden illumination of new and unsuspected facets of human existence in society. This is the excitement and, as we shall try to show later, the humanistic justification of sociology.

People who like to avoid shocking discoveries, who prefer to believe that society is just what they were taught in Sunday School, who like the safety of the rules and the maxims of what Alfred Schuetz has called the "world-taken-for-granted," should stay away from sociology. People who feel no temptation before closed doors, who have no curiosity about human beings, who are content to admire scenery without wondering about the people who live in those houses on the other side of that river, should probably also stay away from sociology. They will find it unpleasant or, at any rate, unrewarding. People who are interested in human beings only if they can change, convert or reform them should also be warned, for they will find sociology much less useful than they hoped. And people whose interest is mainly in their own conceptual constructions will do just as well to turn to the study of little white mice. Sociology will be satisfying, in the long run, only to those who can think of nothing more entrancing than to watch men and to understand things human. . . .

Culture

- American Values and Lifestyles (Articles 2-4)
- Unusual Cultures (Articles 5-6)
- Racial and Ethnic Cultures (Articles 7-9)

The ordinary, everyday objects of living and the daily routines of life provide a structure to social existence that is regularly punctuated by festivals and celebrations. Both the routine and special times are the "stuff" of culture, for culture is the sum total of all the pieces of one's social inheritance. Culture includes language, tools, values, habits, literature, and art.

Because culture is often overlooked and taken for granted, it is useful to pause and reflect upon the shared beliefs and relationships that form the foundations of group life. In a similar way, an examination of exotic and different cultures is valuable in helping us recognize how cultural assumptions affect all facets of life. A great deal can be learned by observing how other people treat their elderly or raise their young. Moreover, through such observations, individuals can recognize how misunderstandings begin, and can appreciate the problems of maintaining cultural continuity in a rapidly changing environment. Through an awareness of culture people begin to "know" themselves, for culture lies at the heart of their personal and collective identities. Culture is one of the most powerful and important concepts in sociology.

This section includes articles which look at culture from different perspectives and which portray cultural differences. Often it takes an outsider to see the peculiarities of a group. How do you think Americans look to outsiders? One visitor from England, Henry Fairlie, explains how unusual he thought Americans were because they say "hi" to everyone. From this simple greeting Fairlie learned about American freedom and democracy. He also discusses other peculiarities of America and tells why he loves and adopted this country.

Many of the values that Fairlie describes are deeply rooted in American culture. In contrast, Ronald Henkoff explores recent fads in American values. He argues that the materialism and self-centeredness of the 1980s are waning and the values of saving, nurturing, and sharing are gaining ground. Bush is calling for Americans to serve America, and volunteerism is substantially rising. Henkoff fails to provide a solid explanation for these changes,

which leaves lots of room for readers to speculate on the causes.

The pace of life is an important aspect of culture because it impacts on the way people live and on the values people use to rationalize their lifestyles. According to Nancy Gibbs, time has become much more scarce for the average American. The work week has lengthened, leisure time has shortened, and family life is more hectic. Perhaps people are too ambitious in what they attempt to do. Perhaps people are inundated with information and communications which make it more difficult to keep up. Whatever the reasons, people are exhausted, and the quality of relationships is jeopardized. Stress and health problems result. Some people are dropping out of the rat race, but what is the solution for everyone else?

Specific cultures are shaped by the conditions of life. When those conditions change, the culture will also change over time. Colin Turnbull looks at an African tribe that was moved off its original land and was forced to live in a harsh environment. Literally all aspects of life changed for the tribe's members, in a disturbingly sinister way. The experiences of this tribe lead Turnbull to question some of the individualistic tendencies of America. Laura Bohannan, meanwhile, encountered the barrier of cultural differences while attempting to explain Shakespeare's *Hamlet* to the West African Tiv.

America is a culturally rich nation because many racial, ethnic, and national groups have maintained aspects of their native culture or have developed somewhat unique cultures here. American culture is being created out of many sources and is not strictly a Western culture, according to Ishmael Reed.

Blacks have different experiences from whites in America, and therefore have a different culture. Jill Nelson describes her personal history as a black woman who marched and dreamed with the black movement of the recent past. Her culture did not come ready-made; she had to struggle to create it, and had to find her own answer to the question: What does it mean to be a black woman in America today?

One group in American society that has unusual statistics that need to be explained is that of black men. For example, they have low education and employment and high crime statistics. Patrick Welsh points to prejudice and discrimination as contributing factors, but also discusses the conflict between the feminized culture of the schools and black male culture. He tries to show why it is hard to be a black man in a white society.

Looking Ahead: Challenge Questions

Why do individuals seldom question their cultural values?

What are the boundaries of a culture? How does one cross over boundaries?

What is the relationship between culture and identity?

What might a visitor from a primitive tribe describe as shocking and barbaric about American society?

Why I Love America

Henry Fairlie

I HAD REPORTED from some twenty-four countries before I set foot in America. I will never forget the first shock—even after having been in every country from the Sudan to South Africa—at realizing that I was in another place entirely, a New World. In the casbah of Algiers during the first referendum called by de Gaulle in 1959, when the women hurrying down the steep streets to vote for the first time pulled their yashmaks around their faces as they passed a man (which seemed to me only to make their dark eyes more fascinating), I was still in the Old World, however strange it was. But here in America it was all new.

I had been in the country about eight years, and was living in Houston, when a Texan friend asked me one evening: "Why do you like living in America? I don't mean why you find it interesting—why you want to write about it—but why you *like* living here so much." After only a moment's reflection, I replied, "It's the first time I've felt free." In the nine years that have passed since then, I have often reflected on that answer, and have found no reason to change it. What I mean by it is part of the story to be told here.

Other memories come to mind. One spring day, shortly after my arrival, I was walking down the long, broad street of a suburb, with its sweeping front lawns (all that space), its tall trees (all that sky), and its clumps of azaleas (all that color). The only other person on the street was a small boy on a tricycle. As I passed him, he said "Hi!"—just like that. No four-year-old boy had ever addressed me without an introduction before. Yet here was this one, with his cheerful "Hi!" Recovering from the culture shock, I tried to look down stonily at his flaxen head, but instead, involuntarily, I found myself saying in return: "Well—hi!" He pedaled off, apparently satisfied. He had begun my Americanization.

"Hi!" As I often say—for Americans do not realize it—the word is a democracy. (I come from a country where one can tell someone's class by how they say "Hallo!" or "Hello!" or "Hullo," or whether they say it at all.) But anyone can say "Hi!" Anyone does. Shortly after my encounter with the boy, I called on the then Suffragan Bishop of Washington. Did he greet me as the Archbishop of Canterbury would have done? No. He said, "Hi, Henry!" I put it down to an aberration, an excess of Episcopalian latitudinarianism. But what about my first meeting with Lyndon B. Johnson, the President of the United States, the Emperor of the Free World, before whom, like a Burgher of Calais, a halter round my neck, I would have sunk to my knees, pleading for a loan for my country? He held out the largest hand in Christendom, and said, "Hi, Henry!"

Small anecdotes? But I wish to suggest that it is there, in the small anecdotes, that the secret lies. America has—if one opens oneself to it—a bewitching power. From the very beginning the stranger feels its influence as a loosening. At first this can be disquieting. After all, one is not in an exotic land, where the differences are immediately striking, easy to see, so that one may be fascinated without really being touched by them. Yet from the beginning in America one feels this power, unsettling all that one had thought was familiar, fixed by the ages. To some—I have known them—it is alarming. For there do come moments when one realizes, more than in any other country not one's own, that here one may be being remade. If here history still invents itself, then here also, still, one may invent the future. But suppose that means that one may also invent oneself? Max Ascoli, the Italian Jew who fled from Fascism and founded and edited in America a remarkable magazine, *The Reporter*, once wrote: "It did not cause me any trouble to become an Italian, but my becoming an American is my own work." Every immigrant will know what he means; millions are still working on it in their own lives.

I remember also the time when I still resisted the very power of America to attract. After I had been here in

Washington, D.C., a little while, I noticed one day that all the Americans who had befriended me were preparing to participate in some ritual, and that I was not invited. It was the Fourth of July. I presumed that they were being tactful: How could they ask me to celebrate a British defeat? So I accepted an invitation from Patrick O'Donovan, then the Washington correspondent of *The Observer*. What could we do on the Fourth? We looked at the television listings, and were delighted to find that there was a midday rerun of the original *Scarlet Pimpernel*, with Leslie Howard as Sir Percy Blakeney. We may have been defeated by the Americans, but one Englishman, single-handedly, had outwitted Robespierre's police. So we sat with our elbows on the lunch table, watching Leslie Howard be English, brave, and debonair, and even when the table leaf gave way with a crash, it did not interrupt Sir Percy or our absorption.

Later in the afternoon, Patrick—who had been a strapping young Irish Guards officer during the Second World War, as handsome (as they say) as the devil—opened the screen door into his Georgetown garden, and peed. "It does one good," he proclaimed, "on the Fourth of July, to piss on American soil." But he let in an enormous bug—one of those gigantic bugs that make it all the more inexplicable why Americans like barbecuing on their patios in the fetid summer—which then banged from wall to wall, sometimes wheeling to dive-bomb us. "You shouldn't have pissed on America," I said to Patrick. "George III tried to piss on it, and look what happened to him." But Patrick was by now cowering behing the couch—all six-foot-four Irish Guards of him—shouting to his wife, " 'Mione, 'Mione, HELP!" She came downstairs, took one pitying look at her brave Britishers, got a can of Raid, and destroyed the American intruder. Patrick got up from behind the couch, drew himself up again to his full height, and said as if he were addressing his troops in the desert, "Henry, I cannot *bear* the tropics." By the time the fireworks began on the mall— "More shots to be heard round the world, I suppose," grumbled Patrick—we had the Dutch courage to ignore them. We had drunk our way—what else for exiles to do?—through the Fourth of July.

But as I stayed and felt America drawing me to it, I inevitably began to think of the others who have come. The curiosity about the country which first brought and kept me here scarcely entitles me to claim that I have shared the experience of most immigrants. I have no right to make it seem as if I came here traveling steerage, like the political refugees or those who simply had neither food nor hope in their native lands. But I will say this about the Statue of Liberty. It was an act of imagination, when the French proposed raising the money for it to celebrate the American Revolution, to choose such a site, and not Washington or Mount Vernon or Philadelphia, and to put on it that inscription, recalling nòt the English colonists who made the Revolution, but the millions upon millions of others who have come here since. They were drawn by the promise of this land; the land has performed for many

more of them than it has failed; and they in turn have helped remake the nation. And still they come.

The story of the immigration cannot be told bloodlessly. It cannot be drained of what Osbert Sitwell caught so well, in this hauntingly lovely passage from his *The Four Continents*, published in 1954: "New York, with all its faults, is yet the greatest and the most moving of modern cities . . . built by refugees to shelter and protect their dreams on alien soil. . . . For that is what it is, a metropolis of dreams realized and unrealized . . . dreams of every age and intensity. . . . So when in the small hours you open the window, and the cool of the darkness flows into the heated room, it is on a beautiful and improbable city of dreams that you look, some tragic, some naive, but many of them practicable and to be achieved in the future, near or distant, by the labors of these same dreamers when awake during the working day. Thus in the main the dreams will be fulfilled, and the hopes that prevail over fears are justified." How can one lose the sense that something quite miraculous has happened in the making of one nation from so many different peoples?

No other immigration into any other country has had anything like the same meaning for the rest of the world, for those who did not migrate, lifting the imagination of the world to horizons beyond even the expanse of this continent. The name of America still lends to countless millions its own dreams for them to dream themselves.

An English economist once said that it was America that had taught the world that it need not starve. Consider that. It cannot be denied. The achievements of American agriculture are one of the wonders of the modern world. Americans consume each year only a third of the wheat which American farmers produce; there is no other valley in the world which has been made, by irrigation, as fertile as the Central Valley of California. But it is not only such facts and figures that tell the wonder. One must look down the vastness of the Middle West, as the English poet Louis MacNeice did in 1940, "astonished by its elegance from the air. Elegance is the word for it—enormous plains of beautifully inlaid rectangles, the grain running different ways, walnut, satinwood or oatcake, the whole of it tortoiseshelled with copses and shadows of clouds. . . ." It is common for the American when he is in Europe to gasp at the hedgerows of England or the terraced vineyards of Italy, kept for centuries. But the gasp of the Englishman is no less when he gazes on a continent, immense in scale, still fabulous in its diversity, which not only is cultivated but has by its cultivation been given its own coherence; which unlike Europe has been made one. Who but the Americans would, so early, have made the Great Plains yield so much—those semi-arid lands which even they, at first, called "the Great American Desert"?

But let us return to small things. If America was to produce, it had also to invent. The English critic T. R. Fyvel once told a story of a friend, also English, who had "found himself for a fantastic weekend in a society of Texas millionaires who whizzed around in their private aircraft, dropping in on parties hundreds of miles away."

The friend found this unexpectedly refreshing. He was even more impressed when he saw the children of his host "buzzing around in special little pedal motor cars which were air conditioned." But one night his Texan millionaire host turned to him and said something like: "You know, Bob, I ask myself if our machine civilization isn't shot all to hell." The Englishman, horrified, burst out to his host: "Don't have those decadent thoughts! Don't have any thoughts! Leave them to us—while you stay just as you are!" I understand his response. There seems to be nothing, however fanciful, that the American, with his unflagging inventive genius, will not attempt.

MATTHEW ARNOLD was amazed at the warmth of American houses. "We are full of plans," he wrote to his daughter from Philadelphia in 1883, "for putting an American stove into the Cottage," when he got back to England. In 1912 Arnold Bennett was amazed that, whereas "the European telephone is a toy," in America it was regarded as an indispensable convenience for everyone. In 1942 Sir Philip Biggs was amazed by the supermarket, "where you grab what you want and wheel it to the cashier in steel perambulators made for the purpose," and leave "laden with a variety of food, beyond the range of English households even in peacetimes, from the A & P stores." (Twenty-three years later, on my very first morning in America, the wife of the English friend with whom I was staying took me, not to the Washington Monument, but to a supermarket—just to stare.) In 1963 T. H. White, who made a lecture tour in his old age, accompanied by the eighteen-year-old sister-in-law of Julie Andrews as "my secretary, but really as a protectress," was amazed at the change machine in the automat restaurant on a train: "In went a dollar bill which was inspected and out come [sic] four silver quarters. Why couldn't we put in bits of newspaper cut to the right size?" But he found more to wonder at: "In Long Island fishermen can buy *worms* from slot machines"; and again: "I also learned of *tab-opening cans.* You can open a beer can and, it is to be hoped, you will soon be able to open any can, without a tin opener." They were all responding to something I could not imagine America without.

How I have come to take it all for granted was brought home to me not long ago, when I was sitting in my house with a friend visiting from England. It was a quiet afternoon in early summer, the windows were open, I could hear the birds chirping in the garden. My friend suddenly exclaimed: "How can you bear to live in all this noise?" What noise? "All this noise in the house," he said. "Something is always switching itself off or on, humming or purring." He had destroyed my own peace, for I noticed it from then on. It is no wonder that America consumes so much energy. The electric gadgetry in an American home makes it its own Disney World. But to most Englishmen it is the physical evidence of a society that does not tire of innovation; which by its inventiveness still seems to keep the future open; and in whose inventiveness ordinary people find convenience.

THE INVENTIVENESS and gadgetry of the American reflects the spirit of a society which echoes the song: "It ain't necessarily so." If houses are insufferably cold, you invent a stove, and then you invent central heating; and if anyone writes in to say that the Romans had central heating, the important point is that the common man in Rome did not have it. Ben Franklin invented a prefabricated stove which could be produced for the common man; such a stove in Europe at the time would have been produced by craftsmen for the few. But then it has always been the American way as well, when faced with any injustice or harshness in this society, to say that "it ain't necessarily so," and to do something about it. If ever this spirit is allowed to languish, whether in the invention of things or the improvement of its society, America will have ceased to be what it means to the rest of the world.

When the cafeteria was first invented, the English responded to it with delight, from Clare Sheridan first being taken to one by Upton Sinclair in 1921, when she followed him as "he first took a metal tray from a column of trays," to S.P.B. Mais's description in 1933:

> You put your tray on a slide, help yourself as you rush along to orange juice, puffed rice, eggs, rolls, coffee, marmalade, or whatever it is you eat for breakfast, and when you reach the end of the counter a girl checks your loaded tray with lightning calculation, says "Thirty cents"—or whatever it is—and you take your tray and eat your breakfast at a table. The whole time spent in getting your food is thirty seconds.

The cafeteria has, of course, spread all over the world. But what these first encounters tell, above all, is of their convenience, and the fact that this convenience is liberating, as electrical gadgets (or Clarence Birdseye's invention, frozen foods) are liberating in the home. What they tell secondly is that these conveniences are not for a privileged few. Like the Franklin stove or the Ford Model T, these amenities were meant for all.

What I am trying to show is that, to other Englishmen besides myself, there is a meaning to the material progress of America which has traveled, and is still traveling, to the rest of the world, beyond the physical benefits which it bestows. It was a critic of fastidious taste and judgment, Cyril Connolly, who said in 1952:

> All American influence on Europe, however vulgar, brings with it an improvement in the standard of living and the dissipation of certain age-old desires. Should Europe oppose this influence? Europe, which has destroyed so many exotic civilizations, without even providing them with the democratic optimism which America brings with its films, its gadgets, and its *lingua franca,* the demotic language which obliterates all class distinctions.

BUT CONNOLLY left out the most significant American influence of all: the spread of the manners of a society which has always been more informal, less stiff, less bound by convention, than any other in the world; in which a person is accepted, as Thackeray said during one of his visits, for what he is. The impetus to informality in

America is, at least in part, the source of one of the most striking changes in our century: the change in the relationship between one individual human being and another, and so in their relationship to their society.

The informality is one characteristic which at first both jarred and drew me. By far the most infectious account of this characteristic of America was given by Dom Hubert van Zeller, an English monk who often preached retreats in both countries, and enjoyed America, but was still astonished at this scene:

> In a hall at Denver I had the privilege of being listened to by upwards of six hundred nuns, assembled from different communities, all of whom were eating ices off the ends of sticks. The distribution of the ices, effectively conducted by a member of the home team, took place during the earlier phase of my address, so from the elevated position which I occupied on the platform, I was able to lay bets with myself as to which religious order would finish first.

This is the public informality—often noticed in Congress, in the courts—but the training begins early, with the freedom given the American child.

The children, like the informality, can at first jar. But the true mark of American society is that its informality forms its own patterns and codes. Although the outsider cannot at first detect it, there is a rhythm of American life. This rhythm is a constant improvisation, a flexibility that will accommodate the wishes and whims of every member of the group. No one voice in the typical American family takes precedence over the rest. Someone is always leaving or coming back; someone is always asking if he or she can have the car; someone is always going to the refrigerator for a snack instead of a meal; someone is always arriving late at a meal or leaving it early. The rhythm of the American family is to be found in a system of communications by which the improvised activities of each of its members is made known to all so that they can be taken into account. What holds the home together is a pattern of wires and castings, as hidden from view as the inside of a transistor radio, along which a ceaseless flow of messages is carried, and accommodations made to them. Messages left on the refrigerator door can for days be the only visible form of communication between members of a family who otherwise succeed in never running into each other as they come and go.

This is one reason why Mom and Dad, Lois and Junior, are so noticeable as tourists, and look so uncomfortable. They are not used to doing things as a unit. One can notice this even in an ordinary restaurant in America, when a whole family has for once come out to have dinner together: one by one, each grows restless to get away, and the meal degenerates into a pitiless nagging of the one person (usually, the mother) who is actually having a good time, and so is holding up the rest. What has happened is that they are not using their transistors; since they are all together, the flow of messages has been interrupted; having to do the same thing, at the same time, their common life has lost its rhythm.

I NOTICED AT ONCE the general American aversion to sitting down to a meal, and the time spent, if you are a guest, sitting in an armchair, or a canvas chair on the porch, always with a low table within handy reach. What then happens was perfectly caught in 1952 by the English journalist Mervyn Jones:

> Darting in and out of the kitchen, your hostess keeps the table constantly loaded with sandwiches, plates of cheese, nice little things on crackers, bowls of fruit, nuts, olives, pretzels, rolls, cakes, cookies, and other refreshments. Gin, whisky, beer, and coffee are on tap without a moment's break. You are urged, in case there should be anything you lack, to help yourself from the two or three vast refrigerators. . . . People arrive in cars, sit down, stretch out their hands with the same air of unthinking habit as a horse reaching for a clump of grass, nibble for a while, get into their cars, and go—to be replaced, no matter what the hour, by other nibblers. All sense of time is lost. . . . You have, however, eaten twice as much as though you had sat round the table for three square meals.

The fact is that a wholly different manner of life was invented in America, contrasted with that of Europe (before it began to spread there from America): with more flexibility, more activity, more fragmentation, but still with its own patterns. American society is a kaleidoscope, in which the original pattern is always being rearranged. This is itself freeing, simply in day-to-day behavior, in the opportunities to meet other people, but also in deeper ways.

Though there are classes in America, there is no *class system*. When I answered, "The first time I've felt free," one thing I meant was that I was free of class. How could a class system be fastened onto a shifting kaleidoscope? If you imagine that you have discovered some symmetrical pattern in American society, you have only to change the angle at which you stand to it and the pattern changes. As Martin Green wrote in 1961, "America is not dominated by any single type, much less [a] class-limited one"; and he added, referring to Britain, "In these two ways, America stands for health, and we for sickness." This is strong, but it is just. Class—accent, vocabulary, dress, manners—not only confines the lower class in England, it also confines the upper class. It is much easier to mix here with people who are unlike oneself. To whom can this be more important than the immigrant making his way into the mainstream? Why the barriers remain so difficult for blacks to cross is too large a question to go into here; and the disappointing results so far of the Puerto Rican immigration (of which Nathan Glazer and Daniel Patrick Moynihan expected so much in *Beyond the Melting Pot*) also raise disconcerting questions which are beyond the scope of personal response. I will merely say that the sheer rise of the present colored—Asian, Latin American, Caribbean—immigration seems bound to present challenges which will make Americans again consider the virtues of assimilation.

1. CULTURE: American Values and Lifestyles

OTHER LINES than those of class are also more easily crossed: those of sex, for example, and of age. When the English have come to America they have always written at length about American women. "And what luncheons," exclaimed Clare Sheridan, ". . . and apparently all for themselves. There is never a man. They even pay one another compliments. I wonder if they can be contented." (There has often been this ambivalence in the consistent praise of American women.) I too would comment when I first came here on the numbers of women lunching together in restaurants. But I soon came to believe that it is partly from her associations with other women that the American woman draws, not only a strength and subtlety of feeling for her own existence (a part of her superiority which almost every English visitor has acknowledged), but also her capacity for friendship with men. It is the American man's capacity for friendship with women which is in doubt, and I attribute it to the shallowness of his associations and lack of intimacy with his own sex. In a moment I will show why that last observation is not thrown in just to provoke a riot.

But first I must emphasize what it is in American women which, especially when they began to arrive in England in large numbers a century ago, took the English by storm. In 1907, Lady Dorothy Nevill calling her "bright and vivacious," said, "it is by the American girl we have been conquered." As early as 1864 Lord Bryce, who later married one, thought that American women had "so much more freedom in their manners; . . . the absence of primness was a very agreeable relief." To Rudyard Kipling in 1891, "the girls of America are above and beyond them all. . . . They have societies, and clubs . . . where all the guests are girls. . . ; they understand; they can take care of themselves; they are superbly independent." But the essential point was made by Jerome K. Jerome in 1904: "The American girl has succeeded in freeing European social intercourse from many of its hide-bound conventions. There is still work for her to do. But I have a faith in her."

The barrier of age is also crossed. My first editor in 1945 had lectured to a party of American students on the liner bringing them to observe postwar Europe. He exclaimed to me: "They are so different. They ask questions. They say what they think. They are not afraid to talk." Since I was twenty-one myself, and had never been afraid to talk, I thought he was a little gone in the head. There are few things more delightful than the way in which young Americans all over the country are willing to engage openly and freely in conversation and even friendship with someone perhaps more than twice their age. There is a democracy of manners in America which I would miss terribly if I ever left here.

I have been describing a society that is freeing. But there is no doubt it is also demanding. For if the immigrant feels here that he may invent himself, then is he not in that only being an American already? So much in the Old World is fixed for one: not only one's position but so much of one's

life and even one's self. This is what weighs in the first part of Ascoli's remark: "It did not cause me any trouble to become an Italian." But even for an American born here, is it not his "own work" to become an American? This accounts for the one unease I still feel.

WITH THE CONTRAST I am about to draw, it is worth saying, I know many Americans who agree. It is much easier at first—and it is here that I am thinking of the men—to get to know an American. The welcoming "Hi!," the first names, the ready handshake, the quick generosity. You do not get through these first layers with an Englishman nearly as easily or as quickly. But once through them with an American, you come soon to a dead end, you are not admitted to the core or to any real intimacy. With the Englishman, whereas it is hard to get through the initial reserve, once through those outer layers, all resistance crumbles, and you find that you are sharing a level of extraordinary intimacy.

Julián Marías, the disciple of Ortega y Gasset, who spent much time here in the 1950s and 1960s, observed that although Americans get more mail than any other people in the world, they receive far fewer personal letters. An American friend of mine, Howard Higman, a professor of sociology, makes the point well. A letter from an American is like an itinerary, he says, a letter from an Englishman is like a diary. There is no questioning this, and I have often wondered what it is that Americans fear to expose, even whether they fear that there is nothing at the core to expose at all. But the answer, I believe, is simpler. If there has been so much freedom and informality in which to make oneself, if it really is one's "own work" to be an American, then one is bound to guard jealously a self which must often feel isolated and fragile, far more than in a society where so much of who one is has been determined for one. (For if one has been made by that society, it has made others like oneself, so what is there to fear?) This is the significance of the women's associations on which the English observers at once fixed their attention. The men's associations are far more likely to be centered on some activity—sports, watching football, hunting—anything to avoid having to talk about themselves and bare their souls. This is where one comes to a dead stop. These are the personal letters one misses. Almost all letters from American men are typed, even those from my friends, even those meant to be warmly personal. They might be dictated to a secretary, for the little they dare to say.

There is in all of this one reason why so many American attempts to describe the experience of being an American fall back on myth and metaphor, whereas almost all the English descriptions of what it seems to them to mean to be an American stick to the details and small encounters of everyday life. Americans take too much for granted the details of American life in which may often be found the meaning of the freedom and equality and opportunity which still draw people to it. We all know the wretched side of the life of the immigrants: the rough, menial, even dangerous work; the abysmally low wages; the abject conditions in which they lived, in the notorious dumbbell tenements of New York, for example, honeycombed with tiny rooms. And we know that those wretched conditions, whether in the large cities or in the acres of the Southwest baking under the sun, still exist. Yet there was and is another side. It was not all that long after the Italians began to arrive that, in their communities on the Upper East Side, there were shoulders of meat in the butcher's windows at twelve cents a pound; outside the macaroni shops, under improvised shelters, the macaroni was hung out to dry; along the curbs were the pushcarts with artichokes and asparagus, early melons and tomatoes; and a round of cheese cost twenty-four cents. And although only a third of the Italian immigrants had ever cast a vote in their native country, before the first generation had reached middle age they had politicians courting them; and Fiorello La Guardia was elected to Congress from East Harlem on his second attempt in 1916. As they shopped on their streets, where did their allegiance lie? To Genoa? We can still catch from that picture of their streets the smell of freedom.

As a young officer, George C. Marshall was surprised, when he inspected his troops on landing in France in 1917, at how many of them spoke broken English. But of their stake in America, in its industry, in its freedom, there could be little doubt; this was borne out by the astonishing lack of sedition in America throughout the war. I have tried from my own experience to explain some of the small but revealing reasons why America worked its influence so quickly and so deeply on them. It now seems to be working on some of the new immigrants. In my observa-tion, the East Asians especially (and who would have predicted it?) are responding wholeheartedly to American life—their children are into the Little League almost as soon as they are out of the cradle—as they work their way, often by traditional routes such as running neighborhood stores, into the mainstream. This third wave of immigra-tion is repeating, quite remarkably, many of the charac-teristics of the first two waves. America is still open, and it will be a tragedy if those who wish it to "think small," who will to keep America as a playground for those already here, have their way, and close America down.

I will give the last words to an American. Daniel Patrick Moynihan wrote in 1978: ". . . while the matter has not received much attention, the United States is quietly but rapidly resuming its role as a nation of first- and second-generation immigrants, almost the only one of its kind in the world, incomparably the largest, and for the first time in our history or any other, a nation drawn from the entire world. The Immigration Act of 1965 altered the shape of American immigration and increased its size. . . . Our immigrants in wholly unprecedented proportions come from Asia, South America, and the Caribbean. In fiscal year 1973 the ten top visa-issuing ports were Manila, Monterrey, Seoul, Tijuana, Santo Domingo, Mexico City, Naples, Guadalajara, Toronto, Kingston. I would expect Bombay to make this top ten list before long. . . . In short, by the end of the century, the United States will be a multi-ethnic nation the like of which even we have never imagined."

In this vision, America is still open. And America is about to be remade by its immigrants—again—as they become enthusiastic Americans. And what will the immi-grants write home about? The gadgets, I beg, the gadgets.

IS GREED DEAD?

The party may be over for the Money Society of the 1980s. Flashy spending is out, saving and family are in, and helping has become hip. Credit yuppies in part.

Ronald Henkoff

DON'T DOFF your designer dinner jacket just yet, but be warned: The long, glittery banquet may be coming to a close, the waiters serving the final candied course. The watchwords of the Eighties—make big bucks, borrow, spend, and flaunt—have not disappeared. But new conceits are creeping into the social lexicon, notions like save, nurture, and share. Is greed dead? No, not really. It is—and probably always will be—alive and well in Washington, on Wall Street, even among certain citizens of Small Town U.S.A. But evidence suggests that the great decade-long national binge is beginning to leave a funny taste in the mouth and that America is searching for a more balanced diet.

The conspicuous consumption, cold careerism, and self-centered spirit that made up so much of business as usual in the Eighties now come across as a bit tacky at best, ruinous at worst. Ivan Boesky, the arbitrager who told an applauding Berkeley university audience in 1985 that "greed is healthy," now has time to contemplate ethics at the Lompoc federal prison camp in California. Former House Speaker Jim Wright and Democratic whip Tony Coelho have forfeited the positions they loved, tainted by allegations that they bent the rules to enrich themselves. Michael Milken, high priest of junk bonds and recipient of a $550 million pay package in 1987, has been indicted and let go by his firm. Leona Helmsley, self-styled queen, ends up on trial as a tax cheat of regal proportions.

The forces of reform, moderation, and probity appear to be gaining ground. Rudolph Giuliani, who as federal prosecutor helped bust Boesky, Milken, and assorted mobsters, is running for mayor of New York City—and doing well in the polls. The press voices outrage at exorbitant ex-

REPORTER ASSOCIATE *Rosalind Klein Berlin*

ecutive salaries and investment banking fees, and the public takes up the cry. Jack Kemp vows to clean up an influence-peddling mess at the Department of Housing and Urban Development inherited from the oh-so-fun Reagan years, vowing that future subsidies will help the "needy, not the greedy."

None of these developments point, ipso facto, to a nascent epidemic of piety and altruism. "Conscience," as H. L. Mencken observed, "is the inner voice that warns us someone may be looking." But as the high and mighty tremble and topple, the rest of us *are* pulling back from the excesses of the Eighties. We are buying more temperately, saving more deliberately, and borrowing more prudently.

Three out of four working Americans age 25 to 49 would like "to see our country return to a simpler lifestyle, with less emphasis on material success," according to a poll by Research & Forecasts for Chivas Regal, a Seagram brand. Phony nostalgia? Perhaps a little. But look at the trends: The growth of real per capita consumer spending is down from around 3.5% a year in the mid-Eighties to 1.9% last year. The savings rate bottomed out at 3.2% of disposable personal income in 1987 and has trended slowly upward ever since, reaching 5.2% recently. The growth of per capita consumer debt is down from 9.2% in 1985 to 3.2% last year.

"From now on, any definition of a successful life must include serving others."

**—George Bush
President**

The "national mood," never easy to chart in a country of 249 million, doesn't necessarily change with the passing of a decade or the arrival of a new President. But George Bush does seem to have given voice to a widespread yearning for a shift toward values that aren't calibrated in BMWs, Burberrys, and beach houses. "We

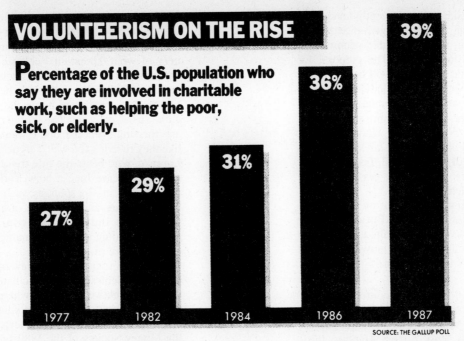

VOLUNTEERISM ON THE RISE

Percentage of the U.S. population who say they are involved in charitable work, such as helping the poor, sick, or elderly.

27% — 1977
29% — 1982
31% — 1984
36% — 1986
39% — 1987

SOURCE: THE GALLUP POLL

are not the sum of our possessions," he said at his inauguration. "We cannot hope only to leave our children a bigger car, a bigger bank account. We must hope to give them a sense of what it means to be a loyal friend; a loving parent; a citizen who leaves his home, his neighborhood, and town better than he found it."

"The 1990s should be the turn for young men and women who came of age in the Kennedy years."
—Arthur Schlesinger, Jr.
Historian

THE AMERICAN FAMILY, sundered, maligned, and neglected for so many years, is edging back toward center stage. Marriage remains popular, the divorce rate hasn't budged since 1986, and the birth rate is rising. For many harried parents, the workaholic ethic of the Eighties has begun to fray some, abraded by a growing desire to spend more time with the kids. When the Chivas Regal poll asked working Americans to identify the most important indicator of success, 62% said "a happy family life." Only 10% said "earning a lot of money."

Across America, volunteerism is thriving. The Gallup organization reports that the proportion of adult Americans devoting time to "charity or social service activities" has grown steadily over the past decade, reaching 39% in 1987, the latest year for which figures are available. Call it a vindication of Reaganomics (a sign that the government can't do everything) or a repudiation of Reaganomics (a sign that the government isn't doing enough). What is incontestable is that helping has become hip, especially among college students and young professionals, groups recently notorious for their selfishness. The Campus Outreach Opportunity League (COOL), founded five years ago to encourage community service, now advises volunteer organizations at 550 colleges and universities.

We can see a modest trend away from the lemming parade of the best business and law graduates heading to high-paying, high-pressure jobs at big-name firms. A few are launching nonprofit organizations to aid the poor, the ill, and the illiterate. "There is a reawakening of the need for public commitment in this country," asserts Michael Brown, Harvard College '84, Harvard Law '88. "It's the end of the 'me decade' and the beginning of the 'we decade.' " Brown, 28, is a co-founder of City Year, a Boston "urban peace corps" run primarily by young professionals and backed by $760,000 in corporate and individual donations.

"People are trying to use ideals to connect with something beyond their bank accounts."

—Douglas Labier
Psychoanalyst

Public service, a concept that not too long ago seemed as anachronistic as pillbox hats and Apollo moon missions, is making a comeback. Federal legislators have introduced no fewer than nine bills calling for government funding of youth service programs. President Bush recently announced his own plan, Youth Engaged in Service to America, or, in the inevitable snappy acronym, YES to America. The proposal for young people age 5 to 25 will be part of the broader Points of Light Initiative, a $25-million-a-year plan to promote community service. The Bush program, says Charles Moskos, a Northwestern University sociologist and author of *A Call to Civic Service*, "is sort of unfocused, but at least it's the first time a President has spoken like that since John Kennedy."

George Bush, to paraphrase Lloyd Bentsen, is no John Kennedy. But clearly there is more than just hot air to the "new breeze" Bush claims is blowing through America. What's going on?

THE MANIFEST contradictions of the decade now ending are finally catching up with us, argues Rosabeth Moss Kanter, Harvard business professor and author of *When Giants Learn to Dance*, a book about management and careers in the Nineties: "The Eighties were a time of incredible prosperity for some but also a time when average family income was flat, when our infrastructure was crumbling and our educational system was deteriorating. It's not surprising that people in the Nineties are waking up."

Waking up may entail a measure of guilt. Says Ginny Blissert, formerly a New York investment banker: "When you live in the lap of luxury and you walk to work past people living in such poverty, you begin to feel that any little thing you can do must somehow make a difference." Blissert is now a student at Northwestern's Kellogg School of Management, where she serves as a co-chair of Business With a Heart, a student-run community services program.

The undulations of the economy in the past two years have persuaded at least some of us that money is a fickle friend. While the October 1987 stock market crash didn't turn out to be the apocalypse many predicted, it did knock a lot of giddiness and hubris out of the system. Following on the heels of the crash, the slowing appreciation of house prices and the job insecurity brought on by takeovers, restructuring, and foreign competition have been enough to send people in search of firmer foundations for their lives. "Tie your self-esteem too narrowly to your paycheck and you'll be in trouble," observes Laurence Shames, author of a new book titled *The Hunger for More: Searching for Values in an Age of Greed*.

It may be too that greed or at least hyperconspicuous consumption has, like many fashions, simply worn itself out. Popular culture no longer glorifies to quite the same extent the acquisitiveness and chicanery of what Thorstein Veblen called the "pecuniary life." *Dynasty* has gone off the air, and *Dallas* has fallen in the ratings. Shows that emphasize home, hearth, and children—*Cosby* and *The Wonder Years*—are thriving. "People don't want to look like they're living too well," argues Ash DeLorenzo, who bears the title trend director at BrainReserve Inc., a New York market consulting firm. Big splurges, such as flashy imported cars and fur coats, are out, he says. Little indulgences—gourmet ice cream, premium vodka, and manicures, for example—are in.

American society, in the view of historian Arthur Schlesinger Jr., oscillates in 30-year cycles between periods where private pursuits and self-interest predominate (the Roaring Twenties, the Eisenhower Years, the Money Society of the 1980s) and periods where activism and common purpose prevail (the Progressive Era at the beginning of the century, the New Deal, the New Frontier of the early 1960s). "There has been a kind of cyclical rhythm," Schlesinger says, "moving from the belief that having everyone make a fast buck for himself was the best way to save the nation to the notion that public service was the best way." The society avidly pursues personal wealth until, with our oft-chronicled propensity for excess, we burn ourselves out. Then the cycle turns, and we pursue commonwealth.

SOCIAL CRITICS can exaggerate the extremes, and may well have done so with the greediness of the Eighties. To begin with, most Americans can't afford to be seriously spendthrift. A study by the Conference Board and the Census Bureau found that only 28.9% of all American households have discretionary income, defined as the money left in the family kitty after taxes and basic everyday expenditures.

But those who do have discretionary income have been anything but discreet. The icon of the Eighties, as raised up by the media, is the young urban professional—the term yuppie first became widespread in 1983. By now we're all numbingly familiar with the habits and appurtenances of the species—their $90 running shoes, $900 briefcases, and $900,000 condos. It's easy to forget how few of these folks there really are. "Only 0.3% of Americans are both younger than age 40 and earn more than $75,000 per year," *American Demographics* magazine pointed out last year.

Still, as the most conspicuous members of the baby-boom generation, yuppies have had a disproportionate impact on society. They have seemed to embody the aspirations of the 78 million Americans born between 1946 and 1964, a generation that has powered the social movements of the past three decades, whether activism, narcissism, careerism, or materialism.

What made the generation that sought nirvana in the Sixties turn to mammon in the Eighties? James Burke, the thoughtful former chief executive of Johnson & Johnson, believes the answer lies in the double failures of the Vietnam war and the Great Society initiatives: "A lot of people may have said, 'The hell with that. I don't want to go to war, and I'm not going to worry about the social problems either.'" Subsequent developments in the public realm, from Watergate to Contragate, only strengthened that resolve.

Douglas LaBier, a Washington psychoanalyst who directs an effort called the Project on Adult Lives, describes the evolution—or failure to evolve—of the boomers' thinking: "The yuppies are direct descendants of the hippies. Among them you find a lot of cynicism and despair over the inability of idealism to coalesce into any kind of social change or political leadership." LaBier interviewed 220 professionals age 25 to 47 for his 1986 book, *Modern Madness: The Hidden Link Between Work and Emotional Conflict.* His subjects, seemingly healthy people, were often troubled by the values they encountered on the job—as reflected in dishonesty, infighting, and self-aggrandizement. Sometimes, says LaBier, they sought an elusive solace in materialism, going on shopping sprees in an attempt to cure depression or to find some sort of fulfillment.

LaBier believes that much of Eighties greed was motivated by fear, by pervasive anxiety about falling behind economically. For many of the younger boomers, the decade was a time of slipping living standards. From 1979 to 1987 median real family income in households headed by people 25 to 34 declined 6.4%, reports the Census Bureau. Back then some of these sliding boomers plunged into debt just to stay even. They bought fancy *objets* to fool the neighbors—and themselves. "Eighties greed," writes author Shames, "was a nervous, twitchy, looking-over-the-shoulder-while-running-full-speed-ahead sort of affair."

The boomers are moving into middle age, and at least in the near term, their economic situation is likely to improve.

This could provide the breathing room they need to embrace new, less frenetic pursuits. More and more of them are getting married, moving to the suburbs, raising kids—in short, settling down. A *Rolling Stone* survey of boomers last year found that 92% had or wanted to have children. Says Peter Meola, 33, a Seagram marketing vice president: "Home life and family have become much more important among the people I associate with. Now it's not so much, 'Let's go to that new restaurant,' or 'Let's see the latest movie,' but, 'Let's get together with our friends and their kids and have a barbecue.'" As the boomers age, predicts Edward Yardeni, chief economist at Prudential-Bache Securities, they will earn more and save more. He thinks they could help boost America's savings rate to 10% over the next five years, a view that other economists find overly optimistic.

Arthur Schlesinger also has great expectations for the older boomers, those born between 1946 and 1957. As they rise to positions of leadership, he predicts, they will bring with them the heady idealism they soaked up during their youth in the Sixties. Critics accuse Democrat stalwart Schlesinger of romanticizing the Sixties: While that turbulent decade did see tremendous advances for minorities and women, it was also a time of assassination, war, and drug abuse. Still, the emotional pull of that era is intense. When the opinion research firm Yankelovich Clancy Shulman asked people in their 30s for their attitudes on the Sixties, 61% viewed it as a constructive period and 51% said they missed the sense of community that existed then.

Maria Foscarinis, a former Wall Street lawyer, carries the banner of the Sixties with her in her new job as director of the National Law Center on Homelessness and Poverty. Foscarinis, 33, has an impeccable yuppie résumé. A graduate of Barnard College and Columbia Law School, she clerked for a federal judge, then joined Sullivan & Cromwell, an elite New York firm. Says she: "That's what you're supposed to do if you want to be successful."

"Child care has become a major issue with so many of the yuppie genre having kids."

—Tod Grantham
Manager

Foscarinis found the work, which included defending an investment bank embroiled in an insider-trading scandal, intellectually stimulating but not particularly fulfilling. "At the end of the day there's something missing," she says. She yearned for a job that would actively advance her ideals—Sixties ideals, as she sees them—"about how the world should be." So in 1985 she took a pay cut from $70,000 to $10,000 a year and opened the Washington, D.C., office of the National Coalition for the Homeless. Since then, the coalition has successfully championed the cause of the homeless in the courts and Congress. In June, Foscarinis left the coalition to start her own organization, one that will focus more broadly on poverty.

NOT MANY PEOPLE are prepared to rearrange their lives so completely, but many well-paid professionals are making more subtle changes. "People are not giving up material goods," observes Douglas LaBier, "but there's more of a letting go of the need to acquire. The desire to have, to get, to possess becomes more in balance with the other aspects of life." Consider the example of Christopher Noon, 39, a Chicago-area developer who donates large amounts of his time and income to Habitat for Humanity International, a Georgia-based organization that builds houses for poor families and counts among its volunteers Jimmy Carter. Says Noon: "The reason we're here on earth is not just to earn money and drive a BMW."

Boston psychotherapist Steven Berglas similarly sees a growing realization that the Eighties' symbols of success—a prestigious and time-consuming job, a six-figure salary, and an abundance of material possessions—is incomplete: "People are saying, 'I've got money and I've got power, but it's worthless unless I can be happy.' You can only collect so many bottles of Pouilly-Fuissé, and then it becomes grape juice." In increasing numbers, says Berglas, his patients are discovering the joy of helping the community—and becoming part of it—through charitable activities.

Employers may want to pick up on the trend: In the Nineties sponsoring volunteer efforts and giving to charity may prove a valuable way to win the good will of the troops. Some 45% of the respondents to the Chivas Regal poll said they would be more loyal to their company if they knew it donated money to a public service cause.

MBA students active in Northwestern's Business With a Heart program say that when they hunt for jobs on graduation, they will seek out firms that do *pro bono* work. Observes Shirley Keller, a senior official at Volunteer—The National Center, an information clearinghouse for charitable activities: "It's just beginning to dawn on some companies that community service can be good for productivity, morale, and loyalty."

COMPANIES HAVE an even bigger lesson to learn for the less greedy Nineties: the increasing importance of the family. You can count on the baby-boomers to force the issue of family vs. work onto the corporate agenda. Fully 73% of all women age 25 to 34 now work for pay, as do half of all women with babies under a year old. For them and their husbands, child care, flexible hours, and job sharing are pressing concerns. Says Dana Friedman, co-president of the New York–based Families and Work Institute: "People have no choice but to bring these problems to the workplace."

When Tod Grantham, 33, a Silicon Valley technical manager with a working wife and baby daughter, went looking for a new job, he had strict criteria: Anybody he would work for had to provide child care, flex-time, and "an understanding that the family was not to be secondary." He received several offers, including one that would have paid $5,000 a year more than the post he ultimately accepted at Oracle Corp., a computer software company in Belmont, California, that met his standards. "The more progressive companies realize that there are families out there that were getting shortchanged," says Grantham. "They're starting to pay more attention to home life." Pushing this change in attitude, says Grantham, are yuppies with children.

Well, there they go again, once more at the forefront of social change. As Grantham points out, families, unlike companies, aren't all that susceptible to hostile takeovers or leveraged buyouts. "A family," he says, "has got a lot more longevity to it, and it's not something you want to ignore for the sake of another fast buck." As social philosophies go, that's a few light years away from the notion that greed is healthy, and a good deal more salubrious. If greed isn't dead, it certainly is hurting.

How America Has Run Out of Time

Workers are weary, parents are frantic and even children haven't a moment to spare: leisure could be to the '90s what money was to the '80s

NANCY GIBBS

All my possessions for a moment of time.
—Queen Elizabeth I, with her dying breath, 1603

If you have a moment to read this story with your feet up, free of interruption, at your leisure . . . put it down. It's not for you. Congratulations.

If, like almost everyone else, you're trying to do something else at the same time—if you are stuck in traffic, waiting in the airport lounge, watching the news, if you're stirring the soup, shining your shoes, drying your hair . . . read on. Or hire someone to read it for you and give you a report.

There was once a time when time was money. Both could be wasted or both well spent, but in the end gold was the richer prize. As with almost any commodity, however, value depends on scarcity. And these are the days of the time famine. Time that once seemed free and elastic has grown tight and elusive, and so our measure of its worth is dramatically changed. In Florida a man bills his ophthalmologist $90 for keeping him waiting an hour. In California a woman hires somebody to do her shopping for her—out of a catalog. Twenty bucks pays someone to pick up the dry cleaning, $250 to cater dinner for four, $1,500 will buy a fax machine for the car. "Time," concludes pollster Louis Harris, who has charted Amer-

ica's loss of it, "may have become the most precious commodity in the land."

This sense of acceleration is not just a vague and spotted impression. According to a Harris survey, the amount of leisure time enjoyed by the average American has shrunk 37% since 1973. Over the same period, the average workweek, including commuting, has jumped from under 41 hours to nearly 47 hours. In some professions, predictably law, finance and medicine, the demands often stretch to 80-plus hours a week. Vacations have shortened to the point where they are frequently no more than long weekends. And the Sabbath is for—what else?—shopping.

If all this continues, time could end up being to the '90s what money was to the '80s. In fact, for the callow yuppies of Wall Street, with their abundant salaries and meager freedom, leisure time is the one thing they find hard to buy. Their lives are so busy that merely to give someone the time of day seems an act of charity. They order gourmet takeout because microwave dinners have become just too much trouble. Canary sales are up (low-maintenance pets); Beaujolais nouveau is booming (a wine one needn't wait for). "I gave up pressure for Lent," says a theater director in Manhattan. If only it were that easy.

More seriously, this shortcut society is changing the way the family functions. Nowhere is the course of the rat race more arduous, for example, than around

the kitchen table. Hallmark, that unerring almanac of American mores, now markets greeting cards for parents to tuck under the Cheerios in the morning ("Have a super day at school," chirps one card) or under the pillow at night ("I wish I were there to tuck you in"). Even parents who like their jobs and love their kids find that the pressure to do justice to both becomes almost unbearable. "As a society," warns Yale University psychology professor Edward Zigler, "we're at the breaking point as far as family is concerned."

The late Will Durant, the Book-of-the-Month Club's ubiquitous historian, once observed that "no man who is in a hurry is quite civilized." Time bestows value because objects reflect the hours they absorb: the hand-carved table, the handwritten letter, every piece of fine craftsmanship, every grace note. But now we have reached the stage at which not only are the luxuries of time disappearing—for reading meaty novels, baking from scratch, learning fugues, traveling by sea rather than air, or by foot rather than wheel—but the necessities of time are also out of reach. Family time. Mealtime. Even mourning time. In 1922 Emily Post instructed that the proper mourning period for a mature widow was three years. Fifty years later, Amy Vanderbilt urged that the bereaved be about their normal business within a week or so.

So how did America become so timeless? Those who can remember washing diapers or dialing phones may recall the silvery vision of a postindustrial age. Computers, satellites, robotics and other wizardries promised to make the American worker so much more efficient that income and GNP would rise while the workweek shrank. In 1967 testimony before a Senate subcommittee indicated that by 1985 people could be working just 22 hours a week or 27 weeks a year or could retire at 38. That would leave only the great challenge of finding a way to enjoy all that leisure.

And not only would the office be transformed. The American household soaked up microwaves, VCRs, blow dryers, mix 'n' eat, the computerized automobile that announces that all systems work and it is getting 23 miles to the gallon. The kitchen was streamlined with so much labor-saving gadgetry that meals could be prepared, served and cleaned up in less time than it took to boil an egg. Thus freed from household chores, Mom could head off to a committee meeting on social justice, while Dad chaired the men's-club clothing drive, and the kids went to bed at 10:30 after watching a PBS special on nuclear physics.

Sure enough, the computers are byting, the satellites spinning, the Cuisinarts whizzing, just as planned. Yet we are ever out of breath. "It is ironic," writes social theorist Jeremy Rifkin in *Time Wars,* "that in a culture so committed to saving time we feel increasingly deprived of the very thing we value." Since leisure is notoriously hard to define and harder to measure, sociologists disagree about just how much of it has disappeared. But they do agree that people *feel* more harried by their life-styles. "People's schedules are more ambitious," says John Robinson, who heads up the Americans' Use of Time project at the University of Maryland. "There just isn't enough time to fit in all the things one feels have to be done."

A poll for TIME and CNN by Yankelovich Clancy Shulman found this sense especially acute among women in two-income families: 73% of the women complain of having too little leisure, as do 51% of the men. Such figures produce no end of questions for sociologists, and everyone else, to stew over. Why do we work so hard? Why do we have so little time to spare? What does this do to us and our children? And what would we give up in order to live a little more peaceably?

Experts tracking the cause and effect are coming to see how progress has carried hidden costs. "Technology is increasing the heartbeat," says Manhattan architect James Trunzo, who designs "automated environments." "We are inundated with information. The mind can't handle it all. The pace is so fast now, I sometimes feel like a gunfighter dodging bullets." In business especially, the world financial markets almost never close, so why should the heavy little eyes of an ambitious baby banker? "There is now a new supercomputer that operates at a trillionth of a second," says Robert Schrank, a management consultant in New York City. "What's a trillionth of a second? Time is being eaten up by all these new inventions. Even leisure is done on schedule. Golfing is done on schedule. My son is on the run all the time. I ask him, 'Are you having fun?' He says, 'Hell, I don't know.'"

The pace of change and the explosion of information mean that professionals are swamped with too many new facts to absorb. Meanwhile, the drill-press operator discovers that the drill comes with a computer attached to it. Workers find that it takes all the energy they have just to remain qualified for their jobs, much less have time to acquire new skills that might allow for promotion. "There is no question that the half-life of most job skills is dropping all the time," says Edward Lawler, University of Southern California professor of management. "People are falling by the wayside, just as companies are."

There is an additional irony: all the time-saving devices may actually make people work harder. Sometime in the early '80s, suggests futurist Selwyn Enzer, Americans came to worship career status as a measure of individual worth, and many were willing to sacrifice any amount of leisure time to get ahead. "Social scientists underestimated the sense of self-esteem that came with having a career," he observes. These days, if an entrepreneur has not made his first million by the time he is 30, his commitment to capital accumulation is suspect. And in the transition from an industrial to a global service economy, many of the white-collar "servants"—lawyers, bankers, accountants—are pushing harder than ever to meet their clients' inexhaustible needs.

For these hardy souls, there is no longer any escape from the office. Simply to remain competitive, professionals find that their lives are one long, continuous workday, bleeding into the wee hours and squeezing out any leisure time. "My wife and I were sitting on the beach in Anguilla on one of our rare vacations," recalls architect Trunzo, "and even there my staff was able to reach me. There are times when our lives are clearly leading us." There are phones in the car, laptops in the den, and the humming fax machine eliminates that once peaceful lull between completing a document and delivering it. "The fax has destroyed any sense of patience or grace that existed," says Hollywood publicist Josh Baron. "People are so crazy now that they call to tell you your fax line is busy."

Add to that a work ethic gone mad. "Work has become trendy," observes Jim Butcher, a management consultant for the Boston Consulting Group. But he and other professionals acknowledge the toll that such a relentless pace takes on creativity. No instrument, no invention, can emit an utterly original thought. "I flew 80,000 miles last year," says economist James Smith of the Rand Corp. "You start losing touch with things. My work is research, which at its best is contemplative. If you get into this mode of running around, you don't have time to reflect."

The risk is that the unexamined life becomes self-sustaining. Attention spans may be richly elastic, but little in this rapid life-style conspires to stretch them. In fact the reverse is true, as TV commercials shrink to 15-second flashes and popular novels contain paragraphs no longer than two sentences. "I do things in a lot of 3½-minute segments," muses UCLA anthropologist Peter Hammond. "Experience just sort of rolls by me. I think it affects the quality of my work."

Technology alone, however, bears only part of the responsibility for the time famine. All the promises of limitless leisure relied on America's retaining its blinding lead in the world's markets and unfolding prosperity at home. No one quite bargained for the Middle-Class Squeeze, what Paula Rayman, a sociologist at Wellesley College's Stone Center, calls "falling behind while getting ahead." The prices of houses have soared, inflation erodes paychecks, wages are stagnant, and medical and tuition costs continue to skyrocket. So now it can take two paychecks to fund what many imagined was a middle-class life. "The American Dream is very much intact," says Rayman. "It's just more expensive."

Keeping a home and raising 2.4 children, as anyone who has ever done it knows, is a full-time job. The increasing rarity of the full-time homemaker has done more to eat away everyone's leisure time than any other factor. If both mother and father are working to make ends meet, as is the case in 57% of U.S. families, someone still has to find the time to make lunches and pediatrician appointments, shop, cook, fix the washer, do the laundry, take the children to choir practice. Single-parent households are squeezed even more.

On the surface, families are coping by teaching children to put the roast in the oven after school, enrolling them in day care, hiring nannies, making play dates, sending out laundry and ordering in pizza. "We spend a lot of time buying time," observes economist Smith. "What we're doing is contracting out for family care," notes Rand demographer Peter Morrison, "but there's a limit. If you contract out everything, you have an enterprise, not a family."

Like the ever expanding white-collar workday, this stage of family evolution defies all the expectations of a generation ago. For years, stress research tended to focus on men, and so the office or factory floor was viewed as the primary source of tension. The home, on the other hand, was a sanctuary, a benign environment in which one recuperated from problems at work. The experts know better now.

Listen to the families:

▶ "Tired is my middle name," says Carol Rohder, 41, a single mother of three in Joliet, Ill. She works days as a medical technician and four nights a week as a waitress. "I'm exhausted all the time. I didn't think it would be this hard on my own. I thought once I was divorced the pressure would be off."

▶ "You get addicted to overworking," says Nancy Baker-Velasquez, a partner in an insurance brokerage in California, whose husband is a sheriff's deputy on the night shift. "At the same time, you have so many more obligations as a parent now. These days, you have to start brushing their teeth even before they have teeth."

▶ "It's not so much that we need to make ends meet," says Jon Hilliard, his three-year-old at his side. Hilliard works for the Street Department in Crown Point, Ind., and as a self-employed carpenter. His wife Sharron is a gym teacher, and together they earn something over $60,000 a year. "It's the way we get extra things. I grew up in a poor family with four kids, and we had no extras. There's no way my kids are going to be like that. We want to make sure that if they're not good athletes or smart academically, they can still go to college."

▶ "The most precious commodity to us is time," agree architect Trunzo and his wife Candace, both 41 and parents of two. "We have tried to simplify our lives as much as possible." Candace believes she and her husband are living "better lives than our parents. More hectic. But fuller." James wonders about that. "It's dangerous to use the word fuller. Where is that sense of spirituality that we talked about in the '60s? Where is the time to go up to the mountaintop? Technology is a diversion from life. You can be transfixed. I'm not sure that technology doesn't remove us from each other, isolate us. In architecture we're seeing demands for media rooms. What ever happened to the kitchen as a gathering place?"

Lynne Meadow and Ron Shechtman, both 42, dote on their son Jonathan, 4. "And there's maybe 30 minutes every day," says Ron, "when we don't discuss having another child. But where would the extra minutes come from?" Lynne runs the red-hot Manhattan Theater Club; Ron is a partner in a midsize law firm. They live in a home where the telephone cords stretch into every room, and the nanny starts work at 7:30 a.m. "You can imagine what getting out the door in the morning is like," says Ron. Are there regrets? He ponders, "Can we take the added pressure that a second child would bring?" For the moment, the answer is no.

Parents know all too vividly the effects of the stress they endure in order to keep up with their lives. Addiction to a speeded-up schedule can lead to a physical breakdown from hypertension, ulcers, heart disease, or dependence on alcohol, cocaine and cigarettes. The effect on the psyche is subtler and more insidious. People find themselves growing impatient and restless, and it seems harder to think logically about a problem. Even if two hours miraculously open up one evening, they may be spent watching TV, since people are too tired to do much else.

More ominous are the effects on children. "Making an appointment is one way to relate to your child," says UCLA anthropologist Hammond, "but it's pretty desiccated. You've got to hang around with your kids." Yet hanging-around time is the first thing to go. The very culture of children, of freedom and fantasy and kids teaching kids to play jacks, is collapsing under the weight of hectic family schedules. "Kids understand that they are being cheated out of childhood," says Edward Zigler at Yale. "Eight-year-olds are taking care of three-year-olds. We're seeing depression in children. We never thought we'd see that 35 years ago. There is a sense that adults don't care about them."

Adults may care a lot, but in ways that are often distorted by their own zealous professional lives. Eager parents arrive home late and pour a day's stored attention onto a child who is more ready to be tucked in than talked at. "It may be that the same loss of leisure among parents produces this pressure for rapid achievement and overprogramming of children," argues Allan Carlson, president of the conservative Rockford Institute, an Illinois think tank. If parents see parenting largely as an investment of their precious time, they may end up viewing children as objects to be improved rather than individuals to be nurtured at their own pace.

Children are scuttling from karate classes to play dates scheduled by Mommy's secretary. Their social lives out of nursery school may rival those of their parents in complexity. Meanwhile, the parents must work even harder to pay for it all. When Arlie Hochschild studied working couples in the San Francisco area for a forthcoming book, *Second Shift,* she found that "a lot of people talked about sleep. They talked about sleep the way a hungry person talks about food."

Thus for many exhausted American families, the premium placed on free time is bringing about both subtle and sweeping changes. In some cases, it means a new division of labor between husband and wife, parents and kids; a search for more flexible professional schedules; or an outright rebellion against the rat race. Any or all of these may force a family to make some hard and intriguing choices. Which is most important? A challenging and fulfilling job? A bigger house? A college education for a gifted child? A life in the big city?

The glib answer most often boils down to women withdrawing from the work force and returning home, thereby easing the time crunch for the whole family. But it is almost never that easy. After 20 years of studying women and stress, Wellesley College researcher Rosalind Barnett has found that alcoholism and depression in women are less frequent among those who work. Nor could most families afford to have one spouse give up working. And the American economy could not stand the hemorrhage of so much talent from its work force.

So the interesting reactions of families and individuals are more daring than simply "dropping out." In 1986 the advertising firm of D'Arcy Masius Benton & Bowles released a poll: If you could have your dream job, it asked, what would it be? The most popular choice among men was to own or manage their own company, followed by being a professional athlete, the head of a large corporation, a forest ranger and a test pilot. The favorite among women? To own and manage their own business, but in their case followed by tour guide, flight attendant, novelist and photographer.

"Running your own business means you are controlling your own destiny," says M.I.T. research director David Birch, who has studied entrepreneurship. While starting a company rarely means more free time, it can promise greater satisfaction, autonomy and flexible working conditions. Freedom-minded men and women alike have recognized that technology and the restructuring of the economy, which so often work against individual peace of mind, can actually work for the small entrepreneur. The same computers and fax machines that torment corporate drudges allow small businesses access to world markets.

Some fast-lane veterans who are fed up with their harried working conditions are trying other escape routes, including climbing down the corporate ladder. Trading in a big salary for a lower-level job with more vacation time, flexible hours, improved maternity or paternity leave, even weekends off may seem a luxury, but it is one that many people are choosing. Dann Pottinger, 42, nephew and grandson of Florida bank presidents, was CEO of Commercial State Bank of Orlando, one of the most profitable independent banks in central Florida. This winter he chaired the search committee to select his replacement. "It is all too time-consuming," he says of his job. Pottinger has spent a total of eight days out of the office in the past year. So he will give up a six-figure salary to go on commission for State Farm Insurance Companies. "I'm not naive enough to say that money doesn't matter," Pottinger says. "But I want my children to know me as something besides their provider."

Such sentiments help explain why the high-draw cities in the U.S. are not the metropolises of New York and Los Angeles but the smaller and more habitable climes of Albuquerque, Fort Worth, Providence and Charlotte, N.C. To many working families, a higher quality of life, and more of it, compensate nicely for the absence of the Metropolitan Opera or the Hollywood Bowl. When Equitable Life Assurance Society summoned Jim Crawford, 43, back to Manhattan from its Des Moines office, he would not relinquish his Iowa life-style. "We based that decision on the quality of the environment," he says. "People do work hard here, and there is a deep appreciation for family life." He traded a higher salary and a two-hour commute for better schools and more free time. "We wonder how we did it, went through the routine," he says now.

For families who cannot handle such a radical departure, there are alternatives. What was once a cottage industry of people providing household services is currently a booming business in cities all across the country. Anyone who can protect a family's free time is a sure success. "The hot new family commodity is 'off time,'" says Heloise, the syndicated oracle of household hints. "If I can give them another 20 minutes, even if it costs them $4 in dry cleaning, then I'm successful."

Four dollars for 20 minutes is cheap. Two corporate dropouts, Glenn Partin and Richard Rogers, founded At Your Service last year in Winter Park, Fla. They are typical of the growing number of entrepreneurs who will perform any service within their expertise, for anywhere between $25 and $50 an hour. They chauffeur people to airports, return video tapes, cater parties. "I can pick up the phone and ask them to do anything," says Debbie Findura, 35, a part-time real estate agent who has called them to fix a light bulb that broke off in the socket, remove a live lizard she found in her oven, and deliver a package of hot-dog buns for one of her family picnics. "We charged $20 to deliver 59¢ worth of hot-dog buns," says Rogers, "but she had them there, and that's what these people expect."

Professional organizers are also in demand. Stephanie Culp of Los Angeles is a pleasant, schoolmarmish woman who seven years ago turned her personal inclinations ("I was neurotically organized") into a career. "If I said I was a professional organizer seven years ago, people would have laughed," she says. "Now the idea is accepted." Culp's golden rule is to set priorities, and she's not kidding. "When you die, what do you want people to say at your funeral?" she asked California businesswoman Baker-Velasquez. Answer: "I didn't want my children to say, 'My mother was a wonderful businesswoman.'"

Among the tactics Culp's clients are testing: watching less TV, shopping by phone, buying low-maintenance clothes and appliances, screening calls on the answering machine and taking a more lax attitude toward housekeeping. "I'm not so immaculate anymore," Baker-Velasquez explains. "There are spots on the carpet, and things are broken. But I'd rather sacrifice my home than my husband's or children's needs."

No combination of innovations, inventions or timely hints will restore the American household to its imagined bygone tranquillity. Only a dramatic change in both attitudes and economics would offer a genuine respite. And, anyway, who hasn't felt the exhilaration of running this race, which many might actually miss if they slowed to a trot. But at some point individuals must find the time to consider the price of their preoccupation and the toll on the spirit exacted by exhaustion. With too little sleep there are too few dreams. And for children, especially, being eight years old should include some long, ice-creamy afternoons of favorite stories and grassy feet. Some things are just worth the time. —*Reported by Marguerite Michaels/ New York and James Willwerth/Los Angeles, with other bureaus*

The Mountain People

Colin M. Turnbull

Anthropologist Colin M. Turnbull, author of The Forest People *and* The Lonely Africans, *went to study the Ik of Uganda, who he believed were still primarily hunters, in order to compare them with other hunting-and-gathering societies he had studied in totally different environments. He was surprised to discover that they were no longer hunters but primarily farmers, well on their way to starvation and something worse in a drought-stricken land.*

In what follows, there will be much to shock, and the reader will be tempted to say, "how primitive, how savage, how disgusting," and, above all, "how inhuman." The first judgments are typical of the kind of ethno- and egocentricism from which we can never quite escape. But "how inhuman" is of a different order and supposes that there are certain values inherent in humanity itself, from which the people described here seem to depart in a most drastic manner. In living the experience, however, and perhaps in reading it, one finds that it is oneself one is looking at and questioning; it is a voyage in quest of the basic human and a discovery of his potential for inhumanity, a potential that lies within us all.

Just before World War II the Ik tribe had been encouraged to settle in northern Uganda, in the mountainous northeast corner bordering on Kenya to the east and Sudan to the north.

Until then they had roamed in nomadic bands, as hunters and gatherers, through a vast region in all three countries. The Kidepo Valley below Mount Morungole was their major hunting territory. After they were confined to a part of their former area, Kidepo was made a national park and they were forbidden to hunt or gather there.

The concept of family in a nomadic society is a broad one; what really counts most in everyday life is community of residence, and those who live close to each other are likely to see each other as effectively related, whether there is any kinship bond or not. Full brothers, on the other hand, who live in different parts of the camp may have little concern for each other.

It is not possible, then, to think of the family as a simple, basic unit. A child is brought up to regard any adult living in the same camp as a parent, and age-mate as a brother or sister. The Ik had this essentially social attitude toward kinship, and it readily

lent itself to the rapid and disastrous changes that took place following the restriction of their movement and hunting activities. The family simply ceased to exist.

It is a mistake to think of small-scale societies as "primitive" or "simple." Hunters and gatherers, most of all, appear simple and straightforward in terms of their social organization, yet that is far from true. If we can learn about the nature of society from a study of small-scale societies, we can also learn about human relationships. The smaller the society, the less emphasis there is on the formal system and the more there is on interpersonal and intergroup relations. Security is seen in terms of these relationships, and so is survival. The result, which appears so deceptively simple, is that hunters frequently display those characteristics that we find so admirable in man: kindness, generosity, consideration, affection, honesty, hospitality, compassion, charity. For them, in their tiny, close-knit society, these are necessities for survival. In our society anyone possessing even half these qualities would find it hard to survive, yet we think these virtues are inherent in man. I took it for granted that the Ik would possess these same qualities. But they were as unfriendly, uncharitable, inhospitable and generally mean as any people can be. For those positive qualities we value so highly are no longer functional for them; even more than in our own society they spell ruin and disaster. It seems that, far from being basic human qualities, they are luxuries we can afford in times of plenty or are mere mechanisms for survival and security. Given the situation in which the Ik found

themselves, man has no time for such luxuries, and a much more basic man appears, using more basic survival tactics.

Turnbull had to wait in Kaabong, a remote administration outpost, for permission from the Uganda government to continue to Pirre, the Ik water hole and police post. While there he began to learn the Ik language and became used to their constant demands for food and tobacco. An official in Kaabong gave him, as a "gift," 20 Ik workers to build a house and a road up to it. When they arrived at Pirre, however, wages for the workers were negotiated by wily Atum, "the senior of all the Ik on Morungole."

The police seemed as glad to see me as I was to see them. They hungrily asked for news of Kaabong, as though it were the hub of the universe. They had a borehole and pump for water, to which they said I was welcome, since the water holes used by the Ik were not fit for drinking or even for washing. The police were not able to tell me much about the Ik, because every time they went to visit an Ik village, there was nobody there. Only in times of real hunger did they see much of the Ik, and then only enough to know that they were hungry.

The next morning I rose early, but even though it was barely daylight, by the time I had washed and dressed, the Ik were already outside. They were sitting silently, staring at the Land Rover. As impassive as they seemed, there was an air of expectancy, and I was reminded that these

were, after all, hunters, and the likelihood was that I was their morning's prey. So I left the Land Rover curtains closed and as silently as possible prepared a frugal breakfast.

Atum was waiting for me. He said that he had told all the Ik that Iciebam [friend of the Ik] had arrived to live with them and that I had given the workers a "holiday" so they could greet me. They were waiting in the villages. They were very hungry, he added, and many were dying. That was probably one of the few true statements he ever made, and I never even considered believing it.

There were seven villages in all. Village Number One was built on a steep slope, and even the houses tilted at a crazy angle. Atum rapped on the outer stockade with his cane and shouted a greeting, but there was no response. This was Giriko's village, he said, and he was one of my workers.

"But I thought you told them to go back to their villages," I said.

"Yes, but you gave them a holiday, so they are probably in their fields," answered Atum, looking me straight in the eye.

At Village Number Two there was indisputably someone inside, for I could hear loud singing. The singing stopped, a pair of hands gripped the stockade and a craggy head rose into view, giving me an undeniably welcoming smile. This was Lokelea. When I asked him what he had been singing about, he answered, "Because I'm hungry."

Village Number Three, the smallest of all, was empty. Village Number Four had only 8 huts, as

against the 12 or so in Lokelea's village and the 18 in Giriko's. The outer stockade was broken in one section, and we walked right in. We ducked through a low opening and entered a compound in which a woman was making pottery. She kept on at her work but gave us a cheery welcome and laughed her head off when I tried to speak in Icietot. She willingly showed me details of her work and did not seem unduly surprised at my interest. She said that everyone else had left for the fields except old Nangoli, who, on hearing her name mentioned, appeared at a hole in the stockade shutting off the next compound. Nangoli mumbled toothlessly at Losike, who told Atum to pour her some water.

As we climbed up to his own village, Number Five, Atum said that Losike never gave anything away. Later I remembered that gift of water to Nangoli. At the time I did not stop to think that in this country a gift of water could be a gift of life.

Atum's village had nearly 50 houses, each within its compound within the stout outer stockade. Atum did not invite me in.

A hundred yards away stood Village Number Six. Kauar, one of the workers, was sitting on a rocky slab just outside the village. He had a smile like Losike's, open and warm, and he said he had been waiting for me all morning. He offered us water and showed me his own small compound and that of his mother.

Coming up from Village Number Seven, at quite a respectable speed, was a blind man. This was Logwara, emaciated but alive and remarkably active. He had heard us and had come to greet me, he said, but he added the inevitable demand for tobacco in the same breath. We sat down in the open sunlight. For a brief moment I felt at peace.

After a short time Atum said we should start back and called over his shoulder to his village. A muffled sound came from within, and he said, "That's my wife, she is very sick—and hungry." I offered to go and see her, but he shook his head. Back at the Land Rover I gave Atum some food and some aspirin, not knowing what else to give him to help his wife.

I was awakened well before dawn by the lowing of cattle. I made an extra pot of tea and let Atum distribute it, and then we divided the workers into two teams. Kauar was to head the team building the house, and Lokelatom, Losike's husband, was to take charge of the road workers.

While the Ik were working, their heads kept turning as though they were expecting something to happen. Every now and again one would stand up and peer into the distance and then take off into the bush for an hour or so. On one such occasion, after the person had been gone two hours, the others started drifting off. By then I knew them better; I looked for a wisp of smoke and followed it to where the road team was cooking a goat. Smoke was a giveaway, though, so they economized on cooking and ate most food nearly raw. It is a curious hangover from what must once have been a moral code that Ik will offer food if surprised in the act of eating, though they now go to enormous pains not to be so surprised.

I was always up before dawn, but by the time I got up to the villages they were always deserted. One morning I followed the little *oror* [gulley] up from *oror a pirre'i* [Ravine of Pirre] while it was still quite dark, and I met Lomeja on his way down. He took me on my first illicit hunt in Kidepo. He told me that if he got anything he would share it with me and with anyone else who managed to join us but that he certainly would not take

anything back to his family. "Each one of them is out seeing what he can get for himself, and do you think they will bring any back for me?"

Lomeja was one of the very few Ik who seemed glad to volunteer information. Unlike many of the others, he did not get up and leave as I approached. Apart from him, I spent most of my time, those days, with Losike, the potter. She told me that Nangoli, the old lady in the adjoining compound, and her husband, Amuarkuar, were rather peculiar.

They helped each other get food and water, and they brought it back to their compound to eat together.

I still do not know how much real hunger there was at that time, for most of the younger people seemed fairly well fed, and the few skinny old people seemed healthy and active. But my laboriously extracted genealogies showed that there were quite a number of old people still alive and allegedly in these villages, though they were never to be seen. Then Atum's wife died.

Atum told me nothing about it but kept up his demands for food and medicine. After a while the beady-eyed Lomongin told me that Atum was selling the medicine I was giving him for his wife. I was not unduly surprised and merely remarked that

that was too bad for his wife. "Oh no," said Lomongin, "she has been dead for weeks."

It must have been then that I began to notice other things that I suppose I had chosen to ignore before. Only a very few of the Ik helped me with the language. Others would understand when it suited them and would pretend they did not understand when they did not want to listen. I began to be forced into a similar isolationist attitude myself, and although I cannot say I enjoyed it, it did make life much easier. I even began to enjoy, in a peculiar way, the company of the silent Ik. And the more I accepted it, the less often people got up and left as I approached. On one occasion I sat on the *di* [sitting place] by Atum's rain tree for three days with a group of Ik, and for three days not one word was exchanged.

The work teams were more lively, but only while working. Kauar always played and joked with the children when they came back from foraging. He used to volunteer to make the two-day walk into Kaabong and the even more tiring two-day climb back to get mail for me or to buy a few things for others. He always asked if he had made the trip more quickly than the last time.

Then one day Kauar went to Kaabong and did not come back. He was found on the last peak of the trail, cold and dead. Those who found him took the things he had been carrying and pushed his body into the bush. I still see his open, laughing face, see him giving precious tidbits to the children, comforting some child who was crying, and watching me read the letters he carried so lovingly for me. And I still think of him probably running up that viciously steep mountainside so he could break his time record and falling dead in his pathetic prime because he was starving.

Once I settled down into my new home, I was able to work more effectively. Having recovered at least some of my anthropological detachment, when I heard the telltale rustling of someone at my stockade, I merely threw a stone. If when out walking I stumbled during a difficult descent and the Ik shrieked with laughter, I no longer even noticed it.

Anyone falling down was good for a laugh, but I never saw anyone actually trip anyone else. The adults were content to let things happen and then enjoy them; it was probably conservation of energy. The children, however, sought their pleasures with vigor. The best game of all, at this time, was teasing poor little Adupa. She was not so little—in fact she should have been an adult, for she was nearly 13 years old—but Adupa was a little mad. Or you might say she was the only sane one, depending on your point of view. Adupa did not jump on other people's play houses, and she lavished enormous care on hers and would curl up inside it. That made it all the more jump-on-able. The other children beat her viciously.

Children are not allowed to sleep in the house after they are "put out," which is at about three years old, four at the latest. From then on they sleep in the open courtyard, taking what shelter they can against the stockade. They may ask for permission to sit in the doorway of their parents' house but may not lie down or sleep there. "The same thing applies to old people," said Atum, "if they can't build a house of their own and, of course, *if* their children let them stay in their compounds."

I saw a few old people, most of whom had taken over abandoned huts. For the first time I realized that there really was starvation and saw why I had never known it before: it was confined to the aged. Down in Giriko's village the old ritual priest, Lolim, confidentially told me that he was sheltering an old man who had been refused shelter by his son. But Lolim did not have enough food for himself, let alone his guest; could I . . . I liked old Lolim, so, not believing that Lolim had a visitor at all, I brought him a double ration that evening. There was a rustling in the back of the hut, and Lolim helped ancient Lomeraniang to the entrance. They shook with delight at the sight of the food.

When the two old men had finished eating, I left; I found a hungry-looking and disapproving little crowd clustered outside. They muttered to each other about wasting food. From then on I brought food daily, but in a very short time Lomeraniang was dead, and his son refused to come down from the village above to bury him. Lolim scratched a hole and covered the body with a pile of stones he carried himself, one by one.

Hunger was indeed more severe than I knew, and, after the old people, the children were the next to go. It was all quite impersonal—even to me, in most cases, since I had been immunized by the Ik themselves against sorrow on their behalf. But Adupa was an exception. Her madness was such that she did not know just how vicious humans could be. Even worse, she thought that parents were for loving, for giving as well as receiving. Her parents were not given to fantasies. When she came for shelter, they drove her out; and when she came because she was hungry, they laughed that Icien laugh, as if she had made them happy.

Adupa's reactions became slower and slower. When she managed to find food—fruit peels, skins, bits of bone, half-eaten berries—she held it in her hand and looked at it with wonder and delight. Her playmates caught on quickly; they put tidbits in her way and watched her simple drawn little face wrinkle in a smile. Then as she raised her hand to her mouth, they set on her with cries of excitement, fun and laughter, beating her savagely over the head. But that is

not how she died. I took to feeding her, which is probably the cruelest thing I could have done, a gross selfishness of my part to try to salve my own rapidly disappearing conscience. I had to protect her, physically, as I fed her. But the others would beat her anyway, and Adupa cried, not because of the pain in her body but because of the pain she felt at the great, vast, empty wasteland where love should have been.

It was *that* that killed her. She demanded that her parents love her. Finally they took her in, and Adupa was happy and stopped crying. She stopped crying forever because her parents went away and closed the door tight behind them, so tight that weak little Adupa could never have moved it.

The Ik seem to tell us that the family is not such a fundamental unit as we usually suppose, that it is not essential to social life. In the crisis of survival facing the Ik, the family was one of the first institutions to go, and the Ik as a society have survived.

The other quality of life that we hold to be necessary for survival—love—the Ik dismiss as idiotic and highly dangerous. But we need to see more of the Ik before their absolute lovelessness becomes truly apparent.

In this curious society there is one common value to which all Ik hold tenaciously. It is *ngag,* "food." That is the one standard by which they measure right and wrong, goodness and badness. The very word for "good" is defined in terms of food. "Goodness" is "the possession of food," or the "*individual* possession of food." If you try to discover their concept of a "good man," you get the truly Icien answer: one who has a full stomach.

We should not be surprised, then, when the mother throws her child out at three years old. At that age a series of *rites de passage* begins. In this environment a child has no chance of survival on his own until he is about 13, so children form age bands. The junior band consists of children between three and seven, the senior of eight- to twelve-year-olds. Within the band each child seeks another close to him in age for defense against the older children. These friendships are temporary, however, and inevitably there comes a time when each turns on the one that up to then had been the closest to him; that is the *rite de passage,* the destruction of that fragile bond called friendship. When this has happened three or four times, the child is ready for the world.

The weakest are soon thinned out, and the strongest survive to achieve leadership of the band. Such a leader is eventually driven out, turned against by his fellow band members. Then the process starts all over again; he joins the senior age band as its most junior member.

The final *rite de passage* is into adulthood, at the age of 12 or 13. By then the candidate has learned the wisdom of acting on his own, for his own good, while acknowledging that on occasion it is profitable to associate temporarily with others.

One year in four the Ik can count on a complete drought. About this time it began to be apparent that there were going to be two consecutive years of drought and famine. Men as well as women took to gathering what wild fruits and berries they could find, digging up roots, cutting grass that was going to seed, threshing and eating the seed.

Old Nangoli went to the other side of Kidepo, where food and water were more plentiful. But she had to leave her husband, Amuarkuar, behind. One day he appeared at my *odok* and asked for water. I gave him some and was going to get him food when Atum came storming over and argued with me about wasting water. In the midst of the dispute Amuarkuar quietly left. He wandered over to a rocky outcrop and lay down there to rest. Nearby was a small bundle of grass that evidently he had cut and had been dragging painfully to the ruins of his village to make a rough shelter. The grass was his supreme effort to keep a home going until Nangoli returned. When I went over to him, he looked up and smiled and said that my water tasted good. He lay back and went to sleep with a smile on his face. That is how Amuarkuar died, happily.

There are measures that can be taken for survival involving the classical institutions of gift and sacrifice. These are weapons, sharp and aggressive. The object is to build up a series of obligations so that in times of crisis you have a number of debts you can recall; with luck one of them may be repaid. To this end, in the circumstances of Ik life, considerable sacrifice would be justified, so you have the odd phenomenon of these otherwise singularly self-interested people going out of their way to "help" each other. Their help may very well be resented in the extreme, but is done in such a way that it cannot be refused, for it has already been given. Someone may hoe another's field in his absence or rebuild his stockade or join in the building of a house.

The danger in this system was that the debtor might not be around when collection was called for and, by the same token, neither might the creditor. The future was too uncertain for this to be anything but one additional survival measure, though some developed it to a fine technique.

There seemed to be increasingly little among the Ik that could by any stretch of the imagination be called social life, let alone social organization. The family does not hold itself together; economic interest is centered on as many stomachs as there are people; and cooperation is merely a device for furthering an interest that is consciously selfish. We often do the same thing in our so-called "altruistic" practices, but we tell ourselves it is for the good of others. The Ik have dispensed with the myth of altruism. Though they have no centralized leadership or means of physical coercion, they do hold together with remarkable tenacity.

In our world, where the family has also lost much of its value as a social unit and where religious belief no longer binds us into communities, we maintain order only through coercive power that is ready to uphold a rigid law and through an equally rigid penal system. The Ik, however, have learned to do without coercion, either

spiritual or physical. It seems that they have come to a recognition of what they accept as man's basic selfishness, of his natural determination to survive as an individual before all else. This they consider to be man's basic right, and they allow others to pursue that right without recrimination.

In large-scale societies such as our own, where members are individual beings rather than social beings, we rely on law for order. The absence of both a common law and a common belief would surely result in lack of any community of behavior; yet Ik society is not anarchical. One might well expect religion, then, to play a powerful role in Icien life, providing a source of unity.

The Ik, as may be expected, do not run true to form. When I arrived, there were still three ritual priests alive. From them and from the few other old people, I learned something of the Ik's belief and practice as they had been before their world was so terribly changed. There had been a powerful unity of belief in Didigwari—a sky god—and a body of ritual practice reinforcing secular behavior that was truly social.

Didigwari himself is too remote to be of much practical significance to the Ik. He created them and abandoned them and retreated into his domain somewhere in the sky. He never came down to earth, but the *abang* [ancestors] have all known life on earth; it is only against them that one can sin and only to them that one can turn for help, through the ritual priest.

While Morungole has no legends attached to it by the Ik, it nonetheless figures in their ideology and is in some ways regarded by them as sacred. I had noticed this by the almost reverential way in which they looked at it—none of the shrewd cunning and cold appraisal with which they regarded the rest of the world. When they talked about it, there was a different quality to their voices. They seemed incapable of talking about Morungole in any other way, which is probably why they talked about it so very seldom. Even that weasel Lomongin became gentle the only time he talked about it to me. He said, "If Atum and I were there, we would not argue. It is a good place." I asked if he meant that it was full of food. He said yes. "Then why do Ik never go there?" "They do go there." "But if hunting is good there, why not live there?" "We don't hunt there, we just go there." "Why?" "I told you, it is a good place." If I did not understand him, that was my fault; for once he was doing his best to communicate something to me. With others it was the same. All agreed that it was "a good place." One added, "That is the Place of God."

Lolim, the oldest and greatest of the ritual priests, was also the last. He was not much in demand any longer, but he was still held in awe, which means kept at a distance. Whenever he approached a *di,* people cleared a space for him, as far away from themselves as possible. The Ik rarely called on his services, for they had little to pay him with, and he had equally little to offer them. The main things they did try to get out of him were certain forms of medicine, both herbal and magical.

Lolim said that he had inherited his power from his father. His father had taught him well but could not give him the power to hear the *abang*—that had to come from the *abang* themselves. He had wanted his oldest son to inherit and had taught him everything he could. But his son, Longoli, was bad, and the *abang* refused to talk to him. They talked instead to his oldest daughter, bald Nangoli. But there soon came the time when all the Ik needed was food in their stomachs, and Lolim could not supply that. The time came when Lolim was too weak to go out and collect the medicines he needed. His children all refused to go except Nangoli, and then she was jailed for gathering in Kidepo Park.

Lolim became ill and had to be protected while eating the food I gave him. Then the children began openly ridiculing him and teasing him, dancing in front of him and kneeling down so that he would trip over them. His grandson used to creep up behind him and with a pair of hard sticks

drum a lively tattoo on the old man's bald head.

I fed him whenever I could, but often he did not want more than a bite. Once I found him rolled up in his protective ball, crying. He had had nothing to eat for four days and no water for two. He had asked his children, who all told him not to come near them.

The next day I saw him leaving Atum's village, where his son Longoli lived. Longoli swore that he had been giving his father food and was looking after him. Lolim was not shuffling away; it was almost a run, the run of a drunken man, staggering from side to side. I called to him, but he made no reply, just a kind of long, continuous and horrible moan. He had been to Longoli to beg him to let him into his compound because he knew he was going to die in a few hours, Longoli calmly told me afterward. Obviously Longoli could not do a thing like that: a man of Lolim's importance would have called for an enormous funeral feast. So he refused. Lolim begged Longoli then to open up Nangoli's *asak* for him so that he could die in *her* compound. But Longoli drove him out, and he died alone.

Atum pulled some stones over the body where it had fallen into a kind of hollow. I saw that the body must have lain parallel with the *oror.* Atum answered without waiting for the question: "He was lying looking up at Mount Meraniang."

Insofar as ritual survived at all, it could hardly be said to be religious, for it did little or nothing to bind Icien society together. But the question still remained: Did this lack of social behavior and communal ritual or religious expression mean that there was no community of belief?

Belief may manifest itself, at either the individual or the communal level, in what we call morality, when we behave according to certain principles supported by our belief even when it seems against our personal interest. When we call ourselves moral, however, we tend to ignore that ultimately our morality benefits us even as individuals, insofar as we are social individuals and live in a

society. In the absence of belief, law takes over and morality has little role. If there was such a thing as an Icien morality, I had not yet perceived it, though traces of a moral past remained. But it still remained a possibility, as did the existence of an unspoken, unmanifest belief that might yet reveal itself and provide a basis for the reintegration of society. I was somewhat encouraged in this hope by the unexpected flight of old Nangoli, widow of Amuarkuar.

When Nangoli returned and found her husband dead, she did an odd thing: she grieved. She tore down what was left of their home, uprooted the stockade, tore up whatever was growing in her little field. Then she fled with a few belongings.

Some weeks later I heard that she and her children had gone over to the Sudan and built a village there. This migration was so unusual that I decided to see whether this runaway village was different.

Lojieri led the way, and Atum came along. One long day's trek got us there. Lojieri pulled part of the brush fence aside, and we went in and wandered around. He and Atum looked inside all the huts, and Lojieri helped himself to tobacco from one and water from another. Surprises were coming thick and fast. That households should be left open and untended with such wealth inside . . . That there should have been such wealth, for as well as tobacco and jars of water there were baskets of food, and meat was drying on racks. There were half a dozen or so compounds, but they were separated from each other only by a short line of sticks and brush. It was a village, and these were homes, the first and last I was to see.

The dusk had already fallen, and Nangoli came in with her children and grandchildren. They had heard us and came in with warm welcomes. There was no hunger here, and in a very short time each kitchen hearth had a pot of food cooking. Then we sat around the central fire and talked until late, and it was another universe.

There was no talk of "how much better it is here than there"; talk revolved around what had happened on the hunt that day. Loron was lying on the ground in front of the fire as his mother made gentle fun of him. His wife, Kinimei, whom I had never even speak to him at Pirre, put a bowl of fresh-cooked berries and fruit in front of him. It was all like a nightmare rather than a fantasy, for it made the reality of Pirre seem all the more frightening.

The unpleasantness of returning was somewhat alleviated by Atum's suffering on the way up the stony trail. Several times he slipped, which made Lojieri and me laugh. It was a pleasure to move rapidly ahead and leave Atum gasping behind so that we could be sitting up on the *di* when he finally appeared and could laugh at his discomfort.

The days of drought wore on into weeks and months and, like everyone else, I became rather bored with sickness and death. I survived rather as did the young adults, by diligent attention to my own needs while ignoring those of others.

More and more it was only the young who could go far from the village as hunger became starvation. Famine relief had been initiated down at Kasile, and those fit enough to make the trip set off. When they came back, the contrast between them and the others was that between life and death. Villages were villages of the dead and dying, and there was little difference between the two. People crawled rather than walked. After a few feet some would lie down to rest, but they could not be sure of ever being able to sit up again, so they mostly stayed upright until they reached their destination. They were going nowhere, these semianimate bags of skin and bone; they just wanted to be with others, and they stopped whenever they met. Perhaps it was the most important demonstration of sociality I ever saw among the Ik. Once they met, they neither spoke nor did anything together.

Early one morning, before dawn, the village moved. In the midst of a hive of activity were the aged and crippled, soon to be abandoned, in danger of being trampled but seemingly unaware of it. Lolim's widow, Lo'ono, whom I had never seen before, also had been abandoned and had tried to make her way down the mountainside. But she was totally blind and had tripped and rolled to the bottom of the *oror a pirre'i;* there she lay on her back, her legs and arms thrashing feebly, while a little crowd laughed.

At this time a colleague was with me. He kept the others away while I ran to get medicine and food and water, for Lo'ono was obviously near dead from hunger and thirst as well as from the fall. We treated her and fed her and asked her to come back with us. But she asked us to point her in the direction of her son's new village. I said I did not think she would get much of a welcome there, and she replied that she knew it but wanted to be near him when she died. So we gave her more food, put her stick in her hand and pointed her the right way. She suddenly cried. She was crying, she said, because we had reminded her that there had been a time when people had helped each other, when people had been kind and good. Still crying, she set off.

The Ik up to this point had been tolerant of my activities, but all this was too much. They said that what we were doing was wrong. Food and medicine were for the living, not the dead. I thought of Lo'ono. And I thought of other old people who had joined in the merriment when they had been teased or had a precious morsel of food taken from their mouths. They knew that it was silly of them to expect to go on living, and, having watched others, they knew that the spectacle really was quite funny. So they joined in the laughter. Perhaps if we had left Lo'ono, she would have died laughing. But we prolonged her misery for no more than a few brief days. Even worse, we reminded her of when things had been different, of days when children had cared for parents and parents for children. She was already dead, and we made her unhappy as well. At the time I was sure we were right, doing the only "human" thing. In a way we *were*—we were making life more comfortable for ourselves. But now I wonder if the Ik way was not right, if I too should not have laughed as Lo'ono flapped about, then left her to die.

Ngorok was a man at 12. Lomer, his older brother, at 15 was showing signs of strain; when he was carrying a load, his face took on a curious expression of pain that was no physical pain. Giriko, at 25 was 40, Atum at 40 was 65, and the very oldest, perhaps a bare 50, were centenarians. And I, at 40, was younger than any of them, for I still enjoyed life, which they had learned was not "adult" when they were 3. But they retained their will to survive and so offered grudging respect to those who had survived for long.

Even in the teasing of the old there was a glimmer of hope. It denoted a certain intimacy that did not exist between adjacent generations. This is quite common in small-scale societies. The very old and the very young look at each other as representing the future and the past. To the child, the aged represent a world that existed before their own birth and the unknown world to come.

And now that all the old are dead, what is left? Every Ik who is old today was thrown out at three and has survived, and in consequence has thrown his own children out and knows that they will not help him in his old age any more than he helped his parents. The system has turned one full cycle and is now self-perpetuating; it has eradicated what we know as "humanity" and has turned the world into a chilly void where man does not seem to care even for himself, but survives. Yet into this hideous world Nangoli and her family quietly returned because they could not bear to be alone.

For the moment abandoning the very old and the very young, the Ik as a whole must be searched for one last lingering trace of humanity. They appear to have disposed of virtually all the qualities that we normally think of as differentiating us from other primates, yet they survive without seeming to be greatly different from ourselves in terms of behavior.

Their behavior is more extreme, for we do not start throwing our children out until kindergarten. We have shifted responsibility from family to state, the Ik have shifted it to the individual.

It has been claimed that human beings are capable of love and, indeed, are dependent upon it for survival and sanity. The Ik offer us an opportunity for testing this cherished notion that love is essential to survival. If it is, the Ik should have it.

Love in human relationships implies mutuality, a willingness to sacrifice the self that springs from a consciousness of identity. This seems to bring us back to the Ik, for it implies that love is self-oriented, that even the supreme sacrifice of one's life is no more than selfishness, for the victim feels amply rewarded by the pleasure he feels in making the sacrifice. The Ik, however, do not value emotion above survival, and they are without love.

But I kept looking, for it was the one thing that could fill the void their survival tactics had created; and if love was not there in some form, it meant that for humanity love is not a necessity at all, but a luxury or an illusion. And if it was not among the Ik, it meant that mankind can lose it.

The only possibility for any discovery of love lay in the realm of interpersonal relationships. But they were, each one, simply alone, and seemingly content to be alone. It was this acceptance of individual isolation that made love almost impossible. Contact, when made, was usually for a specific practical purpose having to do with food and the filling of a stomach, a single stomach. Such contacts did not have anything like the permanence or duration required to develop a situation in which love was possible.

The isolation that made love impossible, however, was not completely proof against loneliness. I no longer noticed normal behavior, such as the way people ate, running as they gobbled, so as to have it all for themselves. But I did notice that when someone was making twine or straightening a spear shaft, the focus

of attention for the spectators was not the person but the action. If they were caught watching by the one being watched and their eyes met, the reaction was a sharp retreat on both sides.

When the rains failed for the second year running, I knew that the Ik as a society were almost certainly finished and that the monster they had created in its place, that passionless, feelingless association of individuals, would spread like a fungus, contaminating all it touched. When I left, I too had been contaminated. I was not upset when I said good-bye to old Loiangorok. I told him I had left a sack of *posho* [ground corn meal] with the police for him, and I said I would send money for more when that ran out. He dragged himself slowly toward the *di* every day, and he always clutched a knife. When he got there, or as far as he could, he squatted down and whittled at some wood, thus proving that he was still alive and able to do things. The *posho* was enough to last him for months, but I felt no emotion when I estimated that he would last one month, even with the *posho* in the hands of the police. I underestimated his son, who within two days had persuaded the police that it would save a lot of bother if he looked after the *posho*. I heard later that Loiangorok died of starvation within two weeks.

So, I departed with a kind of forced gaiety, feeling that I should be glad to be gone but having forgotten how to be glad. I certainly was not thinking of returning within a year, but I did. The following spring I heard that rain had come at last and that the fields of the Ik had never looked so prosperous, nor the country so green and fertile. A few months away had refreshed me, and I wondered if my conclusions had not been excessively pessimistic. So, early that summer, I set off to be present for the first harvests in three years.

I was not surprised too much when two days after my arrival and installation at the police post I found Logwara, the blind man, lying on the roadside bleeding, while a hundred yards up other Ik were squabbling

over the body of a hyena. Logwara had tried to get there ahead of the others to grab the meat and had been trampled on.

First I looked at the villages. The lush outer covering concealed an inner decay. All the villages were like this to some extent, except for Lokelea's. There the tomatoes and pumpkins were carefully pruned and cleaned, so that the fruits were larger and healthier. In what had been my own compound the shade trees had been cut down for firewood, and the lovely hanging nests of the weaver birds were gone.

The fields were even more desolate. Every field without exception had yielded in abundance, and it was a new sensation to have vision cut off by thick crops. But every crop was rotting from sheer neglect.

The Ik said that they had no need to bother guarding the fields. There was so much food they could never eat it all, so why not let the birds and baboons take some? The Ik had full bellies; they were good. The *di* at Atum's village was much the same as usual, people sitting or lying about. People were still stealing from each other's fields, and nobody thought of saving for the future.

It was obvious that nothing had really changed due to the sudden glut of food except that interpersonal relationships had deteriorated still further and that Icien individualism had heightened beyond what I thought even Ik to be capable of.

The Ik had faced a conscious choice between being humans and being parasites and had chosen the latter. When they saw their fields come alive, they were confronted with a problem. If they reaped the harvest, they would have to store grain for eating and planting, and every Ik knew that trying to store anything was a waste of time. Further, if they made their fields look too promising, the government would stop famine relief. So the Ik let their fields rot and continued to draw famine relief.

The Ik were not starving any longer; the old and infirm had all died the previous year, and the younger survivors were doing quite well. But the famine relief was administered in a way that was little short of criminal. As before, only the young and well were able to get down from Pirre to collect the relief; they were given relief for those who could not come and told to take it back. But they never did—they ate it themselves.

The facts are there, though those that can be read here form but a fraction of what one person was able to gather in under two years. There can be no mistaking the direction in which those facts point, and that is the most important thing of all, for it may affect the rest of mankind as it has affected the Ik. The Ik have "progressed," one might say, since the change that has come to them came with the advent of civilization to Africa. They have made of a world that was alive a world that is dead—a cold, dispassionate world that is without ugliness because it is without beauty, without hate because it is without love, and without any realization of truth even, because it simply is. And the symptoms of change in our own society indicate that we are heading in the same direction.

Those values we cherish so highly may indeed be basic to human society but not to humanity, and that means that the Ik show that society itself is not indispensable for man's survival and that man is capable of associating for purposes of survival without being social. The Ik have replaced human society with a mere survival system that does not take human emotion into account. As yet the system if imperfect, for although survival is assured, it is at a minimal level and there is still competition between individuals. With our intellectual sophistication and advanced technology we should be able to perfect the system and eliminate competition, guaranteeing survival for a given number of years for all, reducing the demands made upon us by a social system, abolishing desire and consequently that ever-present and vital gap between desire and achievement, treating us, in a word, as individuals with one basic individual right—the right to survive.

Such interaction as there is within this system is one of mutual exploitation. That is how it already is with the Ik. In our own world the mainstays of a society based on a truly social sense of mutuality are breaking down, indicating that perhaps society as we know it has outworn its usefulness and that by clinging to an outworn system we are bringing about our own destruction. Family, economy, government and religion, the basic categories of social activity and behavior, no longer create any sense of social unity involving a shared and mutual responsibility among all members of our society. At best they enable the individual to survive as an individual. It is the world of the individual, as is the world of the Ik.

The sorry state of society in the civilized world today is in large measure due to the fact that social change has not kept up with technological change. This mad, senseless, unthinking commitment to technological change that we call progress may be sufficient to exterminate the human race in a very short time even without the assistance of nuclear warfare. But since we have already become individualized and desocialized, we say that extermination will not come in our time, which shows about as much sense of family devotion as one might expect from the Ik.

Even supposing that we can avert nuclear holocaust or the almost universal famine that may be expected if population keeps expanding and pollution remains unchecked, what will be the cost if not the same already paid by the Ik? They too were driven by the need to survive, and they succeeded at the cost of their humanity. We are already beginning to pay the same price, but we not only still have the choice (though we may not have the will or courage to make it), we also have the intellectual and technological ability to avert an Icien end. Any change as radical as will be necessary is not likely to bring material benefits to the present generation, but only then will there be a future.

The Ik teach us that our much vaunted human values are not inherent in humanity at all but are associated only with a particular form of survival called society and that all, even society itself, are luxuries that can be dispensed with. That does not make them any less wonderful, and if man has any greatness, it is surely in his ability to maintain these values, even shortening an already pitifully short life rather than sacrifice his humanity. But that too involves choice, and the Ik teach us that man can lose the will to make it. That is the point at which there is an end to truth, to goodness and to beauty, an end to the struggle for their achievement, which gives life to the individual and strength and meaning to society. The Ik have relinquished all luxury in the name of individual survival, and they live on as a people without life, without passion, beyond humanity. We pursue those trivial, idiotic technological encumbrances, and all the time we are losing our potential for social rather than individual survival, for hating as well as loving, losing perhaps our last chance to enjoy life with all the passion that is our nature.

Shakespeare in the Bush

Laura Bohannan

Laura Bohannan is a professor of anthropology at the University of Illinois, at Chicago.

Just before I left Oxford for the Tiv in West Africa, conversation turned to the season at Stratford. "You Americans," said a friend, "often have difficulty with Shakespeare. He was, after all, a very English poet, and one can easily misinterpret the universal by misunderstanding the particular."

I protested that human nature is pretty much the same the whole world over; at least the general plot and motivation of the greater tragedies would always be clear—everywhere—although some details of custom might have to be explained and difficulties of translation might produce other slight changes. To end an argument we could not conclude, my friend gave me a copy of *Hamlet* to study in the African bush: it would, he hoped, lift my mind above its primitive surroundings, and possibly I might, by prolonged meditation, achieve the grace of correct interpretation.

It was my second field trip to that African tribe, and I thought myself ready to live in one of its remote sections—an area difficult to cross even on foot. I eventually settled on the hillock of a very knowledgeable old man, the head of a homestead of some hundred and forty people, all of whom were either his close relatives or their wives and children. Like the other elders of the vicinity, the old man spent most of his time performing ceremonies seldom seen these days in the more accessible parts of the tribe. I was delighted. Soon there would be three months of enforced isolation and leisure, between the harvest that takes place just before the rising of the swamps and the clearing of new farms when the water goes down. Then, I thought, they would have even more time to perform ceremonies and explain them to me.

I was quite mistaken. Most of the ceremonies demanded the presence of elders from several homesteads. As the swamps rose, the old men found it too difficult to walk from one homestead to the next, and the ceremonies gradually ceased. As the swamps rose even higher, all activities but one came to an end. The women brewed beer from maize and millet. Men, women, and children sat on their hillocks and drank it.

People began to drink at dawn. By midmorning the whole homestead was singing, dancing, and drumming. When it rained, people had to sit inside their huts: there they drank and sang or they drank and told stories. In any case, by noon or before, I either had to join the party or retire to my own hut and my books. "One does not discuss serious matters when there is beer. Come, drink with us." Since I lacked their capacity for the thick native beer, I spent more and more time with *Hamlet*. Before the end of the second month, grace descended on me. I was quite sure that *Hamlet* had only one possible interpretation, and that one universally obvious.

Early every morning, in the hope of having some serious talk before the beer party, I used to call on the old man at his reception hut—a circle of posts supporting a thatched roof above a low mud wall to keep out wind and rain. One day I crawled through the low doorway and found most of the men of the homestead sitting huddled in their ragged cloths on stools, low plank beds, and reclining chairs, warming themselves against the chill of the rain around a smoky fire. In the center were three pots of beer. The party had started.

The old man greeted me cordially. "Sit down and drink." I accepted a large calabash full of beer, poured some into a small drinking gourd, and tossed it down. Then I poured some more into the same gourd for the man second in seniority to my host before I handed my calabash over to a young man for further distribution. Important people shouldn't ladle beer themselves.

Reprinted from *Natural History*, August/September 1966 by permission of the author.

"It is better like this," the old man said, looking at me approvingly and plucking at the thatch that had caught in my hair. "You should sit and drink with us more often. Your servants tell me that when you are not with us, you sit inside your hut looking at a paper."

The old man was acquainted with four kinds of "papers": tax receipts, bride price receipts, court fee receipts, and letters. The messenger who brought him letters from the chief used them mainly as a badge of office, for he always knew what was in them and told the old man. Personal letters for the few who had relatives in the government or mission stations were kept until someone went to a large market where there was a letter writer and reader. Since my arrival, letters were brought to me to be read. A few men also brought me bride price receipts, privately, with requests to change the figures to a higher sum. I found moral arguments were of no avail, since in-laws are fair game, and the technical hazards of forgery difficult to explain to an illiterate people. I did not wish them to think me silly enough to look at any such papers for days on end, and I hastily explained that my "paper" was one of the "things of long ago" of my country.

"Ah," said the old man. "Tell us."

I protested that I was not a story-teller. Story telling is a skilled art among them; their standards are high, and the audiences critical—and vocal in their criticism. I protested in vain. This morning they wanted to hear a story while they drank. They threatened to tell me no more stories until I told them one of mine. Finally, the old man promised that no one would criticize my style "for we know you are struggling with our language." "But," put in one of the elders, "you must explain what we do not understand, as we do when we tell you our stories." Realizing that here was my chance to prove *Hamlet* universally intelligible, I agreed.

The old man handed me some more beer to help me on with my story-telling. Men filled their long wooden pipes and knocked coals from the fire to place in the pipe bowls; then, puffing contentedly, they sat back to listen. I began in the proper style, "Not yesterday, not yesterday, but long ago, a thing occurred. One night three men were keeping watch outside the homestead of the great chief, when suddenly they saw the former chief approach them."

"Why was he no longer their chief?"

"He was dead," I explained. "That is why they were troubled and afraid when they saw him."

"Impossible," began one of the elders, handing his pipe on to his neighbor, who interrupted, "Of course it wasn't the dead chief. It was an omen sent by a witch. Go on."

Slightly shaken, I continued. "One of these three was a man who knew things"—the closest translation for scholar, but unfortunately it also meant witch. The second elder looked triumphantly at the first. "So he spoke to the dead chief saying, 'Tell us what we must do so you may rest in your grave,' but the dead chief did not answer. He vanished, and they could see him no more. Then the man who knew things—his name was Horatio—said this event was the affair of the dead chief's son, Hamlet."

There was a general shaking of heads round the circle. "Had the dead chief no living brothers? Or was this son the chief?"

"No," I replied. "That is, he had one living brother who became the chief when the elder brother died."

The old men muttered: such omens were matters for chiefs and elders, not for youngsters; no good could come of going behind a chief's back; clearly Horatio was not a man who knew things.

"Yes, he was," I insisted, shooing a chicken away from my beer. "In our country the son is next to the father. The dead chief's younger brother had become the great chief. He had also married his elder brother's widow only about a month after the funeral."

"He did well," the old man beamed and announced to the others, "I told you that if we knew more about Europeans, we would find they really were very like us. In our country also," he added to me, "the younger brother marries the elder brother's widow and becomes the father of his children. Now, if your uncle, who married your widowed mother, is your father's full brother, then he will be a real father to you. Did Hamlet's father and uncle have one mother?"

His question barely penetrated my mind; I was too upset and thrown too far off balance by having one of the most important elements of *Hamlet* knocked straight out of the picture. Rather uncertainly I said that I thought they had the same mother, but I wasn't sure—the story didn't say. The old man told me severely that these genealogical details made all the difference and that when I got home I must ask the elders about it. He shouted out the door to one of his younger wives to bring his goatskin bag.

Determined to save what I could of the mother motif, I took a deep breath and began again. "The son Hamlet was very sad because his mother had married again so quickly. There was no need for her to do so, and it is our custom for a widow not to go to her next husband until she has mourned for two years."

"Two years is too long," objected the wife, who had appeared with the old man's battered goatskin bag. "Who will hoe your farms for you while you have no husband?"

"Hamlet," I retorted without thinking, "was old enough to hoe his mother's farms himself. There was no need for her to remarry." No one looked convinced. I gave up. "His mother and the great chief told Hamlet not to be sad, for the great chief himself would be a father to Hamlet. Furthermore, Hamlet would be the next chief: therefore he must stay to learn the things of a chief. Hamlet agreed to remain, and all the rest went off to drink beer."

While I paused, perplexed at how to render Hamlet's disgusted soliloquy to an audience convinced that Claudius and Gertrude had behaved in the best possible manner, one of the younger men asked me who had married the other wives of the dead chief.

"He had no other wives," I told him.

"But a chief must have many wives! How else can he brew beer and prepare food for all his guests?"

I said firmly that in our country even chiefs had only one wife, that they had servants to do their work, and that they paid them from tax money.

It was better, they returned, for a chief to have many wives and sons who would help him hoe his farms and feed his people; then everyone loved the chief who gave much and took nothing—taxes were a bad thing.

I agreed with the last comment, but for the rest fell back on their favorite way of fobbing off my questions: "That is the way it is done, so that is how we do it."

I decided to skip the soliloquy. Even if Claudius was here thought quite right to marry his brother's widow, there remained the poison motif, and I knew they would disapprove of fratricide. More hopefully I resumed, "That night Hamlet kept watch with the three who had seen his dead father. The dead chief again appeared, and although the others were afraid, Hamlet followed his dead father off to one side. When they were alone, Hamlet's dead father spoke."

"Omens can't talk!" The old man was emphatic.

"Hamlet's dead father wasn't an omen. Seeing him might have been an omen, but he was not." My audience looked as confused as I sounded. "It *was* Hamlet's dead father. It was a thing we call a 'ghost.' " I had to use the English word, for unlike many of the neighboring tribes, these people didn't believe in the survival after death of any individuating part of the personality.

"What is a 'ghost?' An omen?"

"No, a 'ghost' is someone who is dead but who walks around and can talk, and people can hear him and see him but not touch him."

They objected. "One can touch zombis."

"No, no! It was not a dead body the witches had animated to sacrifice and eat. No one else made Hamlet's dead father walk. He did it himself."

"Dead men can't walk," protested my audience as one man.

I was quite willing to compromise. "A 'ghost' is the dead man's shadow."

But again they objected. "Dead men cast no shadows."

"They do in my country," I snapped.

The old man quelled the babble of disbelief that arose immediately and told me with that insincere, but courteous, agreement one extends to the fancies of the young, ignorant, and superstitious, "No doubt in your country the dead can also walk without being zombis." From the depths of his bag he produced a withered fragment of kola nut, bit off one end to show it wasn't poisoned, and handed me the rest as a peace offering.

"Anyhow," I resumed, "Hamlet's dead father said that his own brother, the one who became chief, had poisoned him. He wanted Hamlet to avenge him. Hamlet believed this in his heart, for he did not like his father's brother." I took another swallow of beer. "In the country of the great chief, living in the same homestead, for it was a very large one, was an important elder who was often with the chief to advise and help him. His name was Polonius. Hamlet was courting his daughter, but her father and her brother . . .[I cast hastily about for some tribal analogy] warned her not to let Hamlet visit her when she was alone on her farm, for he would be a great chief and so could not marry her."

"Why not?" asked the wife, who had settled down on the edge of the old man's chair. He frowned at her for asking stupid questions and growled, "They lived in the same homestead."

"That was not the reason," I informed them. "Polonius was a stranger who lived in the homestead because he helped the chief, not because he was a relative."

"Then why couldn't Hamlet marry her?"

"He could have," I explained, "but Polonius didn't think he would. After all, Hamlet was a man of great importance who ought to marry a chief's daughter, for in his country a man could have only one wife. Polonius was afraid that if Hamlet made love to his daughter, then no one else would give a high price for her."

"That might be true," remarked one of the shrewder elders, "but a chief's son would give his mistress's father enough presents and patronage to more than make up the difference. Polonius sounds like a fool to me."

"Many people think he was," I agreed. "Meanwhile Polonius sent his son Laertes off to Paris to learn the things of that country, for it was the homestead of a very great chief indeed. Because he was afraid that Laertes might waste a lot of money on beer and women and gambling, or get into trouble by fighting, he sent one of his servants to Paris secretly, to spy out what Laertes was doing. One day Hamlet came upon Polonius's daughter Ophelia. He behaved so oddly he frightened her. Indeed"—I was fumbling for words to express the dubious quality of Hamlet's madness—"the chief and many others had also noticed that when Hamlet talked one could understand the words but not what they meant. Many people thought that he had become mad." My audience suddenly became much more attentive. "The great chief wanted to know what was wrong with Hamlet, so he sent for two of Hamlet's age mates [school friends would have taken long explanation] to talk to Hamlet and find out what troubled his heart. Hamlet, seeing that they had been bribed by the chief to betray him, told them nothing. Polonius, however, insisted that Hamlet was mad because he had been forbidden to see Ophelia, whom he loved."

"Why," inquired a bewildered voice, "should anyone bewitch Hamlet on that account?"

"Bewitch him?"

"Yes, only witchcraft can make anyone mad, unless, of course, one sees the beings that lurk in the forest."

I stopped being a storyteller, took out my notebook and demanded to be told more about these two causes of madness. Even while they spoke and I jotted notes, I tried to calculate the effect of this new factor on the plot. Hamlet had not been exposed to the beings that lurk in the forests. Only his relatives in the male line could bewitch him. Barring relatives not mentioned by Shakespeare, it had to be Claudius who was attempting to harm him. And, of course, it was.

For the moment I staved off questions by saying that the great chief also refused to believe that Hamlet was mad for the love of Ophelia and nothing else. "He was sure that something much more important was troubling Hamlet's heart."

"Now Hamlet's age mates," I continued, "had brought with them a famous storyteller. Hamlet decided to have this man tell the chief and all his homestead a story about a man who had poisoned his brother because he desired his brother's wife and wished to be chief himself. Hamlet was sure the great chief could not hear the story without making a sign if he was indeed guilty, and then he would discover whether his dead father had told him the truth."

The old man interrupted, with deep cunning, "Why should a father lie to his son?" he asked.

I hedged: "Hamlet wasn't sure that it really was his dead father." It was impossible to say anything, in that language, about devil-inspired visions.

"You mean," he said, "it actually was an omen, and he knew witches sometimes send false ones. Hamlet was a fool not to go to one skilled in reading omens and divining the truth in the first place. A man-who-sees-the-truth could have told him how his father died, if he really had been poisoned, and if there was witchcraft in it; then Hamlet could have called the elders to settle the matter."

The shrewd elder ventured to disagree. "Because his father's brother was a great chief, one-who-sees-the-truth might therefore have been afraid to tell it. I think it was for that reason that a friend of Hamlet's

father—a witch and an elder—sent an omen so his friend's son would know. Was the omen true?"

"Yes," I said, abandoning ghosts and the devil; a witch-sent omen it would have to be. "It was true, for when the storyteller was telling his tale before all the homestead, the great chief rose in fear. Afraid that Hamlet knew his secret he planned to have him killed."

The stage set of the next bit presented some difficulties of translation. I began cautiously. "The great chief told Hamlet's mother to find out from her son what he knew. But because a woman's children are always first in her heart, he had the important elder Polonius hide behind a cloth that hung against the wall of Hamlet's mother's sleeping hut. Hamlet started to scold his mother for what she had done."

There was a shocked murmur from everyone. A man should never scold his mother.

"She called out in fear, and Polonius moved behind the cloth. Shouting, 'A rat!' Hamlet took his machete and slashed through the cloth." I paused for dramatic effect. "He had killed Polonius!"

The old men looked at each other in supreme disgust. "That Polonius truly was a fool and a man who knew nothing! What child would not know enough to shout, 'It's me!' " With a pang, I remembered that these people are ardent hunters, always armed with bow, arrow, and machete; at the first rustle in the grass an arrow is aimed and ready, and the hunter shouts "Game!" If no human voice answers immediately, the arrow speeds on its way. Like a good hunter Hamlet had shouted, "A rat!"

I rushed in to save Polonius's reputation. "Polonius did speak. Hamlet heard him. But he thought it was the chief and wished to kill him earlier that evening. . . ." I broke down, unable to describe to these pagans, who had no belief in individual afterlife, the difference between dying at one's prayers and dying "unhousel'd, disappointed, unaneled."

This time I had shocked my audience seriously. "For a man to raise his

hand against his father's brother and and the one who has become his father—that is a terrible thing. The elders ought to let such a man be bewitched."

I nibbled at my kola nut in some perplexity, then pointed out that after all the man had killed Hamlet's father.

"No," pronounced the old man, speaking less to me than to the young men sitting behind the elders. "If your father's brother has killed your father, you must appeal to your father's age mates; *they* may avenge him. No man may use violence against his senior relatives." Another thought struck him. "But if his father's brother had indeed been wicked enough to bewitch Hamlet and make him mad that would be a good story indeed, for it would be his fault that Hamlet, being mad, no longer had any sense and thus was ready to kill his father's brother."

There was a murmur of applause. *Hamlet* was again a good story to them, but it no longer seemed quite the same story to me. As I thought over the coming complications of plot and motive, I lost courage and decided to skim over dangerous ground quickly.

"The great chief," I went on, "was not sorry that Hamlet had killed Polonius. It gave him a reason to send Hamlet away, with his two treacherous mates, with letters to a chief of a far country, saying that Hamlet should be killed. But Hamlet changed the writing on their papers, so that the chief killed his age mates instead." I encountered a reproachful glare from one of the men whom I had told undetectable forgery was not merely immoral but beyond human skill. I looked the other way.

"Before Hamlet could return, Laertes came back for his father's funeral. The great chief told him Hamlet had killed Polonius. Laertes swore to kill Hamlet because of this, and because his sister Ophelia, hearing her father had been killed by the man she loved, went mad and drowned in the river."

"Have you already forgotten what we told you?" The old man was re-

1. CULTURE: Unusual Cultures

proachful. "One cannot take vengeance on a madman; Hamlet killed Polonius in his madness. As for the girl, she not only went mad, she was drowned. Only witches can make people drown. Water itself can't hurt anything. It is merely something one drinks and bathes in."

I began to get cross. "If you don't like the story, I'll stop."

The old man made soothing noises and himself poured me some more beer. "You tell the story well, and we are listening. But it is clear that the elders of your country have never told you what the story really means. No, don't interrupt! We believe you when you say your marriage customs are different, or your clothes and weapons. But people are the same everywhere; therefore, there are always witches and it is we, the elders, who know how witches work. We told you it was the great chief who wished to kill Hamlet, and now your own words have proved us right. Who were Ophelia's male relatives?"

"There were only her father and her brother." *Hamlet* was clearly out of my hands.

There must have been many more; this also you must ask of your elders when you get back to your country. From what you tell us, since Polonius was dead, it must have been Laertes who killed Ophelia, although I do not see the reason for it."

We had emptied one pot of beer, and the old men argued the point with slightly tipsy interest. Finally one of them demanded of me, "What did the servant of Polonius say on his return?"

With difficulty I recollected Reynaldo and his mission. "I don't think he did return before Polonius was killed."

"Listen," said the elder, "and I will tell you how it was and how your story will go, then you may tell me if I am right. Polonius knew his son would get into trouble, and so he did. He had many fines to pay for fighting, and debts from gambling. But he had only two ways of getting money quickly. One was to marry off his sister at once, but it is difficult to find a man who will marry a woman desired by the son of a chief. For if the chief's heir commits adultery with your wife, what can you do? Only a fool calls a case against a man who will someday be his judge. Therefore Laertes had to take the second way: he killed his sister by witchcraft, drowning her so he could secretly sell her body to the witches."

I raised an objection. "They found her body and buried it. Indeed Laertes jumped into the grave to see his sister once more—so, you see, the body was truly there. Hamlet, who had just come back, jumped in after him."

"What did I tell you?" The elder appealed to the others. "Laertes was up to no good with his sister's body. Hamlet prevented him, because the chief's heir, like a chief, does not wish any other man to grow rich and powerful. Laertes would be angry, because he would have killed his sister without benefit to himself. In our country he would try to kill Hamlet for that reason. Is this not what happened?"

"More or less," I admitted. "When the great chief found Hamlet was still alive, he encouraged Laertes to try to kill Hamlet and arranged a fight with machetes between them. In the fight both the young men were wounded to death. Hamlet's mother drank the poisoned beer that the chief meant for Hamlet in case he won the fight. When he saw his mother die of poison, Hamlet, dying, managed to kill his father's brother with his machete."

"You see, I was right!" exclaimed the elder.

"That was a very good story," added the old man, "and you told it with very few mistakes. There was just one more error, at the very end. The poison Hamlet's mother drank was obviously meant for the survivor of the fight, whichever it was. If Laertes had won, the great chief would have poisoned him, for no one would know that he arranged Hamlet's death. Then, too, he need not fear Laertes' witchcraft; it takes a strong heart to kill one's only sister by witchcraft.

"Sometime," concluded the old man, gathering his ragged toga about him, "you must tell us some more stories of your country. We, who are elders, will instruct you in their true meaning, so that when you return to your own land your elders will see that you have not been sitting in the bush, but among those who know things and who have taught you wisdom."

What's American about America? Toward claiming our multicultural heritage

ISHMAEL REED

America as the fabled land of immigrants' dreams was a constant refrain in the presidential election last fall. And indeed, no other countries are quite like the U.S. and Canada, where so many people from so many lands have come together. But politicians rarely stop to reflect on what this unique situation means for our culture and our destiny. That is a subject better explored by writers. Novelist Ishmael Reed envisions America as a vast cultural crossroads where the best of all human civilization can interact and take root. Reed, who is known for the fury he brings to literary feuds, also has a few choice words for his fellow writers who feel that U.S. culture should remain a repository for the largely European traditions of Western civilization. Peter Marin, a Harper's Magazine *contributing editor, looks not at what immigrants found in the U.S., but what they lost in leaving their homelands. This experience, he believes, also shapes American culture—affecting each one of us.*

An item from the *New York Times* June 23, 1983: "At the annual Lower East Side Jewish Festival yesterday, a Chinese woman ate a pizza slice in front of Ty Thuan Duc's Vietnamese grocery store. Beside her a Spanish-speaking family patronized a cart with two signs: 'Italian Ices' and 'Kosher by Rabbi Alper.' And after the pastrami ran out, everybody ate knishes."

On the day before Memorial Day, 1983, a poet called me to describe a city he had just visited. He said that one section included mosques, built by the Islamic people who dwelled there. Attending his reading, he said, were large numbers of Hispanic people, 40,000 of whom lived in the same city. He was not talking about a fabled city located in some mysterious region of the world. The city he'd visited was Detroit.

A few months before, as I was visiting Texas, I heard the taped voice used to guide passengers to their connections at the Dallas Airport announcing items in both Spanish and English. This trend is likely to continue; after all, for some southwestern states like Texas, where the largest minority is now Mexican-American, Spanish was the first written language and the Spanish style lives on in the western way of life.

Shortly after my Texas trip, I sat in a campus auditorium at the University of Wisconsin at Milwaukee as a Yale professor—whose original work on the influence of African cultures upon those of the Americas has led to his ostracism from some intellectual circles—walked up and down the aisle like an old-time Southern evangelist, dancing and drumming the top of the lectern, illustrating his points before some Afro-American intellectuals and artists who cheered and applauded his performance. The professor was "white." After his lecture, he conversed with a group of Milwaukeeans—all who spoke Yoruban, though only the professor had ever traveled to Africa.

One of the artists there told me that his paintings, which included African and Afro-American mythological symbols and imagery, were hanging in the local McDonald's restaurant. The next day I went to McDonald's and snapped pictures of smiling youngsters eating hamburgers below paintings that could grace the walls of any of the country's leading museums. The manager of the local McDonald's said, "I don't know what you boys are doing, but I like it," as he commissioned the local painters to exhibit in his restaurant.

From *Utne Reader,* March/April 1989, pp. 100-105. Excerpt from *Writin' Is Fightin'* by Ishmael Reed. © 1988 by Ishmeal Reed.
Reprinted with permission of Atheneum Publishers, an imprint of Macmillan Publishing Company.

Such blurring of cultural styles occurs in everyday life in the United States to a greater extent than anyone can imagine. The result is what the above-mentioned Yale professor, Robert Thompson, referred to as a cultural bouillabaisse. Yet members of the nation's present educational and cultural elect still

---

The nation's present cultural elect still cling to the notion that the United States belongs to some vaguely defined "Western civilization."

---

cling to the notion that the United States belongs to some vaguely defined entity they refer to as "Western civilization," by which they mean, presumably, a civilization created by the people of Europe, as if Europe can even be viewed in monolithic terms. Is Beethoven's Ninth Symphony, which includes Turkish marches, a part of Western civilization? Or the late 19th and 20th century French paintings, whose creators were influenced by Japanese art? And what of the cubists, through whom the influence of African art

changed modern painting? Or the surrealists, who were so impressed with the art of the Pacific Northwest Indians that, in their map of North America, Alaska dwarfs the lower 48 states in size?

Are the Russians, who are often criticized for their adoption of "Western" ways by Tsarist dissidents in exile, members of Western civilization? And what of the millions of Europeans who have black African and Asian ancestry, black Africans having occupied several European countries for hundreds of years? Are these "Europeans" a part of Western civilization? Or the Hungarians, who originated across the Urals in a place called Greater Hungary? Or the Irish, who came from the Iberian Peninsula?

Even the notion that North America is part of Western civilization because our "system of government" is derived from Europe is being challenged by Native American historians who say that the found-

---

Is Beethoven's Ninth Symphony, which includes Turkish marches, a part of Western civilization?

Asians dominate recent immigration trends

During the 1980s legal immigration has averaged 570,000 people a year—30 percent higher than the average for the 1970s and substantially more than in any year from 1924 to 1978. In addition, hundreds of thousands of aliens with non-immigrant status live legally in the United States. These include not only Mexicans, but increasing numbers of other nationalities—Central Americans as well as Irish in New England and Poles in Chicago.

Between 1983 and 1986, Mexican-born immigrants made up the largest share of legal immigrants to the United States—about 60,000 people a year. The Philippines contributed about 46,000 immigrants a year. Immigrants from mainland China, Taiwan, and Hong Kong together account for another 45,000 annually. The next largest groups are Koreans and Vietnamese, with an annual average of nearly 35,000 immigrants each, and Asian Indians and Dominicans, averaging about 25,000 each.

New York City attracts more immigrants than any other metropolitan area—more than 90,000 from 1984 through 1986. The greatest share of these immigrants were born in the Dominican Republic: more than one-sixth of New York City's immigrants come from this small country. Jamaica comes next with more than 10 percent of immigrants.

Los Angeles-Long Beach is second in the numbers of immigrants it attracts. Over one-sixth of new immigrants to this area were born in Mexico, fol-

lowed by Filipinos (12 percent), and Koreans (9 percent).

Chicago gained more than 20,000 legal immigrants a year between 1984 and 1986. Nineteen percent of these newcomers were born in Mexico. Asian Indians account for 11 percent, and Filipinos another 10 percent.

In 1986 and 1987, Korean immigrants settled in large numbers in Baltimore and the Bergen-Passaic area in New Jersey. Immigrants from Mexico and the Philippines have been much more likely to settle in San Diego than in earlier years. Cambodians have been choosing Boston and Atlanta more frequently as destinations.

Smaller cities sometimes also attract many immigrants from a particular nation. Providence, Rhode Island, for example, has attracted many Cambodians. Dominicans make up a considerable share of immigrants to the Lawrence/Haverhill area in Massachusetts. Jamaicans immigrate to Hartford, Connecticut, in substantial numbers, as do Filipinos to Norfolk-Virginia Beach-Newport News, Virginia.

—James P. Allen and Eugene J. Turner
American Demographics

Excerpted with permission from American Demographics *(Sept. 1988). Subscriptions: $58/yr. (12 issues) from American Demographics, Box 50246, Boulder, CO 80321-0246. Back issues: $5 from Box 68, Ithaca, NY 14851.*

ing fathers, Benjamin Franklin especially, were actually influenced by the system of government that had been adopted by the Iroquois hundreds of years prior to the arrival of Europeans.

Western civilization, then, becomes another confusing category—like Third World, or Judeo-Christian culture—as humanity attempts to impose its small-screen view of political and cultural reality upon a complex world. Our most publicized novelist recently said that Western civilization was the greatest achievement of mankind—an attitude that flourishes on the street level as scribbles in public restrooms: "White Power," "Niggers and Spics Suck," or "Hitler was a prophet." Where did such an attitude, which has caused so much misery and depression in our national life, which has tainted even our noblest achievements, begin? An attitude that caused the incarceration of Japanese-American citizens during World War

II, the persecution of Chicanos and Chinese Americans, the near-extermination of the Indians, and the murder and lynchings of thousands of Afro-Americans.

The world has been arriving at these shores for at least 10,000 years from Europe, Africa, and Asia.

The Puritans of New England are idealized in our schoolbooks as the first Americans, "a hardy band" of no-nonsense patriarchs whose discipline

Third World USA

America is becoming more diverse every day because of the unbelievable facility of new Third World immigrants to put a piece of their original culture inside American culture. The notion of a "dominant" American culture is changing every moment. It is incredible coming to America to find you are somewhere else—in Seoul, in Taipei, in Mexico City. You can travel inside Korean culture right on the streets of Los Angeles, for instance.

For an Eastern European, to come to America at the turn of the century was a very strong cultural shock. His connection to home was cut abruptly. Today, immigrants are living in one place physically, but they are sustained culturally from elsewhere. They can watch Mexican soap operas on TV, or regularly fly back and forth to Mexico on the cheap midnight flight out of Los Angeles International Airport. They can read Korean news at the same time it is being read in Seoul, and can take the daily jumbo jets to Korea. The freedom to have this sort of contact is culturally and psychologically healthy. Immigrants don't feel completely cut off from their past the day after their departure from home.

To live here, you don't even need to speak English. In Los Angeles there is an ever-growing sphere where you don't even hear the English language. You don't see it on the commercial signs, in advertising, in the local newspapers. You don't hear it on the radio or on the cable TV channels.

Recently I flew from Toronto to Philadelphia. It was late at night. My plane landed. Other planes were also just landing, from Miami, from Los Angeles. At this airport Cubans and Puerto Ricans were coming to meet the planes with their whole families. Lots of children were playing, slipping down, crying. My luggage was lost. Nobody could find anything. It was hot, crowded, noisy. A mess. There I was in Phil-

adelphia, the historical American town, and I hadn't seen one white face. There was terrible disorder, the lost luggage, the cry of the children, Spanish language only. I said to myself, "I'm at home. I'm in the Third World."

Features of Third World society are penetrating American life. Third World influences—dynamic disorganization, easygoing attitudes, a slower pace of life, a different measurement of time and relations to family—are altering the once dominant northern European ways of putting society together. The sphere of neat, well-organized white society is shrinking.

The wrong angle to approach the new multicultural reality is from the perspective of Western cultural values, including Greek philosophy. Each culture has something to bring to the new pluralistic culture being created.

We can't say Western values are broken down. We are in a period of transition in which the notion of values is broader. We are departing from the time in which we accepted only one set of values as the truthful way of living. We are entering the period in which we will have to accept values that represent other cultures that are not "worse" than our values, but different. This transition is very difficult because our conditioning is ethnocentric. The mind of the future America, however, will be polycentric.

—Ryzsard Kapuscinski
New Perspectives Quarterly

Excerpted with permission from an interview with Polish journalist Ryzsard Kapuscinski conducted by Nathan Gardels in New Perspectives Quarterly (Summer 1988). Subscriptions: $30/yr. (4 issues) from 10951 W. Pico Blvd., 2nd floor, Los Angeles, CA 90064. Back issues: $5 from same address.

razed the forest and brought order to the New World (a term that annoys Native American historians). Industrious, responsible, it was their "Yankee ingenuity" and practicality that created the work ethic.

The Puritans, however, had a mean streak. They hated the theater and banned Christmas. They punished people in a cruel and inhuman manner. They killed children who disobeyed their parents. They exterminated the Indians, who had taught them how to survive in a world unknown to them. And their encounter with calypso culture in the form of a servant from Barbados working in a Salem minister's household, resulted in the witchcraft hysteria.

The Puritan legacy of hard work and meticulous accounting led to the establishment of a great industrial society, but there was the other side—the strange and paranoid attitudes of that society toward those different from the elect.

The cultural attitudes of that early elect continue to be voiced in everyday life in the United States: the president of a distinguished university, writing a letter to the *Times*, belittling the study of African civilizations; the television network that promoted its show on the Vatican art with the boast that this art represented "the finest achievements of the human spirit."

When I heard a schoolteacher warn the other night about the invasion of the American educational system by foreign curricula, I wanted to yell at the television set, "Lady, they're already here." It has already begun because the world is here. The world has been arriving at these shores for at least 10,000 years from Europe, Africa, and Asia. In the late 19th and early 20th centuries, large numbers of Europeans arrived, adding their cultures to those of the European, African, and Asian settlers who were already here, and recently millions have been entering the country from South America and the Caribbean, making Robert Thompson's bouillabaisse richer and thicker.

North America deserves a more exciting destiny than as a repository of "Western civilization." We can become a place where the cultures of the world crisscross. This is possible because the United States and Canada are unique in the world: The world is here.

A People's History, One Child's Future

*As a politically aware black woman, the
author came to believe the struggle,
however necessary, could mean death.
She chose to have a child in the face of
that knowledge.*

JILL NELSON

I was 20 years old when my daughter was born in 1972.
Like mothers of any age, I was ill-prepared for the
responsibilities of parenthood. I wanted to have a baby,
but had no idea what that entailed. The absoluteness of
motherhood. The knowledge that for the rest of my life I
will be inextricably linked to another person. That I will
hear her footsteps when she is hundreds of miles away in
summer camp, walk more carefully in the world because
I know she needs me, think of someone before myself.
At the time she was born, I was caught up in the style
of life more than in its substance. I enjoyed being pregnant the way I enjoyed having an Afro. I gloried in
natural childbirth as I gloried in attending anti-war rallies, screaming, "Nixon, pull out like your father should
have" until I was hoarse. I loved my beautiful baby
daughter as I loved the voice of Marvin Gaye as he
crooned, "Save the babies, oh, save the children."

Growing up in the 1960s, my life had been, to a great
extent, defined by death. The assassinations of John
Kennedy, Malcolm X, Martin Luther King Jr. and Bobby
Kennedy were the benchmarks of my young womanhood.
Struggle, I learned, however necessary, could mean
death. I chose to have a child in the face of this
knowledge. Coupled with the "twoness" of being black
and American that W.E.B. DuBois wrote about was my
own and my daughter's femaleness. Black, female and
American, we inherited a legacy of political, economic
and sexual exploitation, of oppression at work and in the
family—the necessity of behaving as latter-day Harriet
Tubmans in the world and agreeable partners to our men
at home. Our lives, as the lives of all black people, were
and are defined by contradiction, by deep optimism existing side by side with deep cynicism. Just as thousands of
other black women have done throughout history, I chose

life in the face of death, laughing at the devil. Now, I
realize how very young I was. I saw parenting in the abstract, from the outside only, as something I did rather
than something I was. Such a vision of mothering did
not last for long. My daughter and the world made sure
of that.

Long before my daughter's birth, I had read Marx,
repeating hiply, "The only thing constant is change," in
appropriate forums, usually political meetings. But it was
not until my daughter's birth that I came to personally
understand what Marx was talking about. I found myself,
at 20, with a baby, a mate and the responsibility of taking care of them both when I could barely take care of
myself. Frankly I hadn't given the responsibility much
thought. I was, as were many children of the late 1960s,
a woman of selfish impulse: I did what I wanted, when I
wanted, because I wanted to. I gave little thought to what
other, particularly older, people wanted. After all, these
people were the ones who'd put the world in the disastrous condition it was in, people easily dismissed as
"bourgeois running dog lackeys"—as the Black Panther
Party newspaper described them—and ignored. I was
smug in the youthful belief that the revolution was just
around the corner. After all, I told myself, it would be
me and my generation who created a new world, the
past be damned.

Perhaps this way of looking at the world might have
worked had I been living in a vacuum, but I wasn't. I
was living in New York City, where I was born, sur-
rounded by family and friends. My parents, once
dismissed by me as "bougie" because they had the self-
interest and stamina to become professionals—my father
a dentist and my mother a librarian—were now the proud
grandparents of their first grandchild and demanding to

be involved. I was a full-time college student who needed all the help and support I could get.

And I was scared. Having a baby was the first act of my life that was irrevocable, that could not be undone. When I told my father I was pregnant, he was not happy and asked me, "What are you trying to do? Be like Nikki Giovanni?" At the time, I was highly insulted. How dare he suggest that my motives for having a child was inspired by the poems of a black single mother, however much I treasured her books and quoted her obnoxiously at the dinner table? Today, I am willing to acknowledge some truth in my father's accusation: My decision to have a baby was, like Giovanni's early poetry, simplistic. The saving grace is that our children will remain vivid long after Giovanni's poems and my words are forgotten.

During the first years of my daughter's life we lived by the Hudson River. I bought an old rocker and placed it by the window, and this is where my daughter and I spent much of our time, rocking, nursing, watching the water and listening to black music, Bob Marley and Miles Davis in particular. I nursed my baby for a year and a half, embarrassed as she got older by her cries of "Titty! Titty!" on public transportation, but confident that extended breast feeding not only was healthier but would create a bond of intimacy between us like no other.

For those first two years, the three of us—my daughter, her father and I—lived largely alone, in a world of our own definition. We had no television because we believed the images it presented of black Americans were consistently negative. We bought books for my daughter from the Liberation Bookstore on Lenox Avenue and 131st Street, books for and about black children, full of pictures of kids who looked like her. We ate macrobiotically: I ground my own whole wheat flour and became a master of the art of cooking the red, pellet-like aduki beans that are a staple of macrobiotic eating. Ironically, just a few weeks ago, calling home from a long day at work, I suggested to my daughter I make her a hamburger and french fries for dinner. "That's all I've had all week!" she wailed. "You never cook anymore!" Once I got over my anger at being made to feel inadequate as a parent, her words were funny. Couldn't she remember, I wondered, 12 years ago when I cooked three elaborate meals a day, balancing yin and yang as I held her on my hip, laboring long and hard in the vineyards of righteous dieting?

Isolated by motherhood, I read voraciously, often aloud to my uncomprehending toddler. I read fiction, history, biography, political theory—if not by African-Americans, then about them. The complete works of Franz Fanon, some DuBois, most of the writers of the Harlem Renaissance, Rainier Maria Rilke, Tri-Continental (a magazine from Cuba), African novelists, anything by a black woman I could get may hands on. I took a leave from school, did not work and left the house most regularly for the baby's monthly clinic appointments. The walls I papered with images of African-Americans: Tubman, Martin Luther King, Angela Davis, Malcolm X. My baby's father, a longtime partyer turned black nationalist, worked, bringing home soybeans and information from the world outside. We spent most of our time with his

friends—many of whom were Muslims—or my family.

I talked to my daughter constantly, long before she could talk back, trying to tell her everything I knew, to fill her up with a sense not only of her own personal history, but also of her people's. Her bedtime stories came from a book of African mythology or from history, with a liberal dose of my imagination thrown in. I told my daughter stories of Tubman, King, Angela Davis, of kings and queens of Africa. I sang her the traditional lullabies of my childhood and freedom songs from the civil rights movement, and old songs, many of them taught to me by Bernice Reagon, my music teacher during a long-ago summer spent in camp. These were fighting songs, inspirational songs, cautionary tales and oral histories set to music. When at a loss, I wrote short stories just for her. One, "The Loser But Still the Greatest," inspired by Muhammad Ali's 1978 loss to Leon Spinks, became a favorite, a fable about losing and winning at the same time.

I wanted to give her a sense of mission, as I had been given one. Early on, I knew most clearly what I didn't want for my daughter. She would not be a housewife or a girdle saleswoman like her great-grandmothers, or a thwarted businesswoman-turned-librarian-turned-housewife, or a public dependent like her grandmothers. Unlike so many black women, she would not clean other people's toilets, walk their dogs or raise their children.

Gradually, I began to run out of stories to tell my daughter. I did not know enough to teach her what she needed to know about the world in order to positively define herself. I was, to paraphrase Sly Stone, a baby who had made a baby, no sin in itself but a sin of ignorance because of my youth.

I returned to college in 1974, tying my daughter on my back in the African tradition and taking her to classes with me. Initially I maintained the roles of my pre-college days: cooking two big meals a day, taking care of the household and, for the most part, the baby. But as the song goes, "A change is gonna come." It soon became impossible to do it all and have anything left over for me. I was a master at playing the serious sister in the early 1970s: I was political, demurely dressed, could burn in the kitchen and obeyed my man. Outside, we were the perfect couple; inside, I didn't know who I was, but I knew I had to find out. I prioritized and to my child's father's mind, he was the loser. Where, he wondered, was the agreeable and malleable girl of 19 he'd hooked up with? She had disappeared, replaced by a 22-year-old mother struggling to educate her child and herself in tandem. There was not much room left for him. Although I loved him, motherhood had made me fiercely pragmatic. I knew I had to get my own act together so that my daughter could do the same. I owed it to her. Life, once infinite, became finite.

My responsibility was to take care of myself and my child, to educate her to be a black woman capable of moving in this world. I wanted her to have a sense of self along with a sense of politics. I did not want my daughter to be a reactionary, doomed to being only a victim or a victimizer. I wasn't quite sure how to do this, but society solved the problem for me. In December of 1974, I was arrested.

The hospital clinic where my daughter was born and where I took her monthly for checkups had me arrested on a sunny December afternoon after an examination of my daughter. I was charged with prima facie child abuse. The hospital guard would not allow me to take my daughter home. She was physically healthy, mentally alert, potty trained, talking in paragraphs and a few days shy of her second birthday. Her medical history was standard, except, like her father, she was thin. She'd had all kinds of blood tests to determine her state of health and was always fine. At the hospital's insistence, I went regularly to a staff nutritionist to discuss our macrobiotic diet and she felt I was doing a good job. In spite of these facts, for 24 hours I was charged with child abuse, based on the fact that my daughter looked too thin and ate different foods. Punished for not being like everyone else.

Though my daughter has no recollection of the 24 hours she spent as a captive of the hospital, it was a critical event in determining the future course of our lives. Already alienated from the political mainstream and life as a housewife, I was radicalized by my arrest. Clearly, the fact that I was intelligent and in college, came from a middle-class family and had done nothing wrong was irrelevant. What was relevant was that I was black, not legally married and had no health insurance. I was therefore guilty of whatever the hospital said I was until I proved myself innocent. Until then, they would keep my child.

With the assistance of several lawyers, a few judges, some city officials and my family, my daughter was returned to me, unharmed, the following morning. On the outside, life had returned to normal. Inside, everything was different. Forced to accept that I could not protect my daughter from the world, I determined to do everything I could to enable her to protect herself. The incident at the hospital taught me that the arena must be enlarged: It was not enough to sit by the river, rocking, listening to beautiful music, whispering in my baby's ear. My arrest made it horribly clear that, like black women throughout history, I could not enjoy the luxury of simply doing my own thing. My blackness bound me, obliterating any notions of class privilege, to my people. I learned more in those 24 hours than I had in the previous 22 years about what it really means to be a black woman in America. Pushing me closer to myself and other women, this knowledge pushed me away from men, including my baby's father.

That same year, we separated. With me, she became a full-time college student and activist. Many evenings and most weekends we went to political meetings concerning international women's day, the Supreme Court's Bakke decision, housing discrimination against single women in New York, African liberation day. My daughter grew taller and more talkative and made her own friends at the meetings and demonstrations we went to. She still remembers being carried down Pennsylvania Avenue on the shoulders of a tall black man at the anti-Bakke march in 1977 and laughingly recalls the "day care room" provided by most organizations during political meetings.

As much as we were mother and daughter, we were companions growing up together. Maybe we still are.

Such a relationship probably makes parenting more difficult; it fudges the dividing line between parent and child and makes it hard for me to pull rank. I am not a particularly effective disciplinarian. My daughter questions not only my authority, but almost everyone else's, sometimes to her detriment. When she is told to do something, she immediately asks why and will not quit until she is satisfied. She learned this from me. While I am proud that she is a person who questions, I am often exasperated that she is a daughter who does. Occasionally, I hear myself answer her queries of "Why?" with "Because I said so!"—words my own mother said to me, words I swore I would never utter. This does not devastate me as I once thought it would. At best, children provide not only an abstract sense of history but a familial one. I appreciate my parents, my ancestors, more now that I have my daughter. It is their personal and our collective history that is passed on in a phrase, a gesture, an attitude, even the foods we eat.

My daughter's proclivity to question authority has not made her passage through life or performance in school easier. I hope it has afforded her an understanding of the world necessary to survive and change it. My daughter knows that Columbus didn't discover America, that adults often don't know what they're talking about, that presidents, particularly Ronald Reagan, often aren't the president of all the people. She also knows that there's often a difference between what's right and what's true. She is a wonderful girl but not an easy one. I have suffered many moments of doubt, of questioning old decisions to be unequivocally honest with her. I know that honesty is not always the best policy and that the truth hurts, but I believe it will set her free. The rewards have been great. For the past four years it has been my daughter who reminded me that the Monday before Labor Day is Black Solidarity Day and we should participate in a demonstration or cultural activity. It was my 6-year-old daughter who, hearing Gil Scott-Heron's "Johannesburg" blaring from the stereo each morning before we left for school on New York's East Side (where most of the black faces we encountered had on maids' uniforms or were walking poodles), asked, "Is this like Johannesburg?" And it was she who, after reading a story on homeless children in the newspaper, went through both of our closets, filling two plastic bags with unneeded clothing and making sure I delivered the clothes to the children's residence. It was also my daughter who insisted we simply leave the clothing and not stick around to hand it out. "That's obnoxious," she said in her matter-of-fact way. "We're not so great, we just have more than they do."

Before my arrest, I thought that I could raise my daughter in a bell jar, protected from the world and its conflicts by the cocoon of my love, by the few privileges of class afforded me. I believed that my fierce love for her was enough and found out that it wasn't. I came to understand the interminable Sunday-morning breakfasts of my own childhood, at which my father, eschewing organized religion, delivered his own sermon to and concerning his family. These breakfasts were his way of handing down a sense of the past and the future to his children. And although at the time I was more interested in him hurrying up so I could do the Sunday dishes and get out of the house, I still remember many of the things my father said, long after the morning's menu has been forgotten.

Now that my daughter is 14, I know that she thinks I am a bit extreme at times, but she understands why. However, extremism is simply not her method. She reads the newspaper, though, and shares my anger and grief at the deaths of children, the disaster at Chernobyl, the violence of law enforcement officials. While I rant and cry and write, as is my strategy, my daughter watches, listens and thinks ahead. When I write about those issues that impassion me, it is my daughter who first hears the horror stories from my reporting, who lives with me as I live with my work. She has grown up, by necessity, immersed in the world. In some ways, this has been unfair to her. It would be nice if she didn't have to know at age 6 that policemen aren't always her friends, or at 9 that men and women don't always live happily ever after, or at 12 that you can't always get what you want, but life for black women is often not nice. Better, I think, that she learn this from me than from strangers. It is my job, as it has been the job of generations of black mothers, to offer my daughter hope along with a healthy cynicism, optimism along with pessimism.

Somehow, she has managed to avoid or transcend acceptance of much of the negativity that allows racism to work. For her, racism is too absurd to personally buy into. She understands, though, how it influences and rocks the world in which she lives. But her world is defined less by race than by love, compassion and a global sense of family. A minority in America, she knows she is a majority in the world. When my daughter traveled with me to Haiti two months after Duvalier was routed, I was obsessed with the facts of the matter. It was my daughter who made sure to carry coins to give to the begging children, who grinned and blushed when a Haitian boy her age told her in French he loved her and blew her a kiss. She blew one back. I like to think that both her understanding and her transcendence come in some part from the way in which she was raised, from the miles walked at dozens of demonstrations, from the multi-cultural day care room at political meetings, from the dedicated people of many colors she encountered as we grew up together.

In August of 1985 I decided, after much thought and counseling, to travel to South Africa to work on a film about Winnie Mandela. When I told my daughter, the first question she asked was if I would be breaking the cultural boycott. I prepared for the trip with great anticipation and trepidation. I was scared to go, scared not to, worried about what would happen to my daughter if I went and didn't come back. But how could I, having taught my daughter not to fear the unknown, fear it myself?

I went, confident that I would make it back alive, but more confident that if I didn't my daughter would be all right; that she had the foundation she needed not only to survive but to love herself, to paraphrase Yeats, for herself alone, and not for her yellow hair.

Sitting in the garden of Winnie Mandela's house in Soweto several weeks later, the sun scorching and the military surveillance vehicles roaring, Winnie asks if I have family. I tell her about my daughter. Taking leave that evening, Mandela presses a folded sheet of paper into my hand. It is a note to my daughter. It reads, in part:

"Amandla! In the name of my country and all the oppressed people of my land which is your home, I salute you, your mother and your family for caring so much that your mother could come to our country to express her solidarity with us . . . In South Africa we are very proud to be black, we regard our struggle for human dignity as yours too, our freedom will mean your freedom too. We love you and have no doubt we shall overcome soon."

"That's really nice," my daughter said when she read it. "Maybe we can go visit when Winnie's free." Maybe. Maybe my daughter will go alone, after I'm gone. But that's okay. When I gave birth to my daughter 14 years ago, I was a kid myself. I couldn't understand how my parents and others could talk about change, about equal rights for all people and use the phrase, apparently without sadness, "Not in my lifetime." The other night we were talking about police brutality, an ongoing topic in our lives, and I heard myself tell my daughter I was sure it would end—but maybe not in my lifetime. I realize now why my parents, grandparents, Winnie Mandala and even I can say this without sadness. Because we live on, if we are blessed, through our children. As the Rev. Martin Luther King Jr. said several days before he was killed, "I just want to leave a committed life behind . . . then my living will not have been in vain."

Young, Black, Male, and Trapped

Patrick Welsh

Patrick Welsh teaches English at T. C. Williams High School in Alexandria. He is the author of "Tales Out of School."

Last March I dropped in on my daughter's kindergarten class on the morning they happened to be going on a special tour of the White House. Celeste Lenzini, one of Alexandria's top teachers, had them primed. As she asked questions about President Bush and his family, the kids were jumping out of their seats to give answers. None were more enthusiastic than the black male students, most of whom are bused into the school from public housing. They glowed as they fired back the right answers.

That scene still haunts me, for I know that the way things are going, many of those boys will gradually lose ground academically and socially. Their enthusiasm for learning will dim, and they will never come close to reaching the great potential they showed so clearly that morning. Those who do succeed in school will have to struggle for acceptance in a society that will view them with suspicion and hostility.

"Black males—especially teens—are viewed as the most threatening people in our country," says Frank Matthews, publisher of Black Issues in Higher Education. "These guys are stigmatized early and get it everywhere." Matthews, like many other affluent black parents, has witnessed his own 11-year-old son and his black friends going into Fairfax malls and immediately becoming objects of suspicion to sales clerks and security guards. "The assumption is, 'These guys can't have money; they must be here to steal,'" says Matthews, who is a professor at George Mason University.

Imagine, if you can, what it would be like to have achieved what Larry Ward has and yet find yourself shunned solely on the basis of your sex and skin color. One of my all-time favorite students, Larry is now an instructor and counselor at Boston University. Ward says that whenever he goes to a pool to swim laps—be it in Alexandria, Virginia, or Cambridge, Massachusetts—three or four white swimmers will crowd the lanes on either side rather than share his lane. "Can I be that threatening? What could I do to them in a pool?"

Or imagine what it's like to be Dwayne Rawlings, who scored 1400 on his SATs and now, at Brown University, must put up with signs proclaiming "Niggers Go Home," "Put the Kitchen Help Back in the Kitchen" that appeared on the dormitory doors of black students last year.

Painful as they are, the problems of successful young men like Ward and Rawlings pale in comparison with the plight of so many others of their race and sex. Former Howard University dean Douglas Glascoe says that the crisis of the black male is the crisis of the black community. "It is the source of the rage and despair of black women who have been left to raise families alone, of the anger of children who have learned to hate their fathers. It will soon be the biggest crisis in America."

Certainly the statistics are daunting. Glascoe, author of "The Black Underclass," notes that black males are "unchallenged for last place in every important demographic statistic."

For example: Black men make up only 3.5 percent of the college population but 46 percent of the prison population; a black male has a 1-in-23 chance of being murdered before he is 25.

Between 1976 and 1986, college enrollments for black males aged 18 to 24 declined from 35 percent to 28 percent; between 1973 and 1986, the percentage of black men 18 to 29 employed full-time, year-round fell from 44 to 35 percent, and average real earnings for black males fell by 50 percent; since 1970 the number of black households headed by women has more than doubled.

To some extent these statistics become a self-fulfilling prophecy: Society points to the numbers as justification for the low regard and fear in which it holds black men, and many black youths are trapped into playing the destructive roles into which the society has cast them.

1. CULTURE: Racial and Ethnic Cultures

"The presence and very lives of black men are devalued today more than ever. In the days of slavery, they were a resource in the economy; today they are seen as unnecessary," says Lawrence Gary, director of Howard's Center for Urban Studies.

"With humanistic values at an all-time low and materialism at an all-time high, black men are seen as objects to be pushed aside or shipped away to prisons," says Na'im Akbar, past president of the Association of Black Psychologists and author of "Chains and Images of Psychological Slavery."

The problems become evident in the early years. Tony Faulkner, now a sophomore at Madison University, remembers his elementary school friends as "bright guys who got locked out of the game early. No one threw a net out for them. I know I wasn't supposed to make it. My mother was 15 when I was born. I have never known my father. When I was in second grade I was way behind in reading. I could have easily gone down the tubes, but my grandparents, uncles and aunts gathered around me and made me feel I could make it.

"Many of my friends felt they could never win no matter what they did. Somewhere I got my ticket stamped 'smart' and from then on I loved school. I can tell you the name of every teacher I ever had."

An extremely bright black male who recently graduated from T. C. Williams High School but admits working below his ability put it this way: "Early on in grammar school, black guys get the feeling that this is not their arena. The white guys used to get most of the answers right and when I answered something my black friends would say 'Go sit over with those white guys.' I stopped pushing hard because I wanted to fit in with the guys from my neighborhood."

"Teachers overreact to the assertiveness and aggressiveness of young black males," says Akbar. "Schools have been feminized. They demand passivity, non-assertiveness, reflectiveness and non-challenging posture—all the qualities that have been traditionally associated with women. White boys overcome it because they are supported by the many images of white men who have accepted that role and made it. Black guys feel that school forces them to deny both their manhood and their race because they don't know any black men who have accepted the role and gained self respect. Those of us who have done it are regarded as freaks."

For many young blacks, material goods are the only measure of achievement. Douglas Glascoe says that "so much of black life is controlled by a search for, and hope to obtain, society's invidious symbols of achievement. To park a Grand Prix outside of your squalid housing project is a statement: 'While I can't get out of this entrapment, I at least have one symbol of success.' "

Harvey Yancey, a T. C. football star who graduated two years ago, says that his friends who were selling drugs were "ambitious guys who had big dreams and wanted to make it. A lot of them were athletes who turned to drugs after it hit them they weren't going to make the pros. They want to have what their parents didn't have or can't give them. So many of my black friends from grammar school have been in trouble with the law."

I talked to four 17-year-olds being held in the Alexandria jail as adults on drug charges. The stories they tell are now sadly familiar.

Said one, a New Yorker who professed to be making several thousand dollars a week in the drug trade: "For me it was just being out there, the fame and glory—having that feeling that I was 'one cool brother.' I still had a vision of being legitimate; going to college and setting myself up for a career, but when you are in the game for a while, the money becomes an addiction and you can't give it up. You make $150 a week at Roy Rogers, but $150 a minute on the street."

"When you see a friend 'grow'—bust out and buy a new car—you just want to do it. I always had this feeling of missing something: I got desperate to have cars, clothes and guns," said another.

Tony Faulkner buys the materialism argument—but only up to a point. It's true he says that "a white guy will try to dazzle or intimidate by mentioning his father's job, his prep school or the colleges he's applying to. Society waves all this stuff in front our face that we want to have—the BMW, the Jeep Cherokee, the clothes." Still, he adds, "sometimes I feel that's a weak argument—that they [guys selling drugs] are squandering opportunities. My grandfather couldn't go to school with whites and have good books but he made a success of himself. Society doesn't care about excuses, that you had a couple of strikes against you."

Larry Ward worries that some black families may be giving their children excuses not to succeed. "A lot of black parents have tremendous animosity toward white people and it comes across to their kids. My father was the victim of enormous discrimination, but we never got that constant diet of 'look what the white man has done to us' that cripples so many black kids."

The scarcity of practical role models certainly makes it much harder for black adolescents to develop a realistic sense of their own potential. Says Frank Matthews: "If these guys see a white do something, it doesn't ring a bell. But as soon as they see a black, they'll think they can do it. The trouble is they only see the TV roles of athlete, newscaster, entertainer—roles that few can make it in. It's distressing to see so many black communications majors in our colleges; they are going to have trouble getting jobs. But they are there because they've seen guys like Jim Vance and James Brown make it on TV." Matthews says that when young black men meet him they often think of becoming a publisher.

Consultant Jeffery Johnson, who has written extensively on the endangered status of black males, says that these boys "who grow up without males in their lives imagine that black men aren't about anything. These kids are growing up alone and no one is interpreting the world for them." In the Alexandria secondary schools, in fact, there are only two black male guidance counselors. At T. C. Williams there are only 11 black male teachers on a faculty of some 150, and only three teach traditional academic subjects. For the most part, black guys see black males in the roles of custodians, or when they do see black administrators, it's often in the role of a disciplinarian.

Alexandria is mobilizing to address some of these issues. Yesterday there was a city-sponsored "Summit on Youth" involving schools and other city agencies—and not a minute too soon.

There has been an enormous reluctance among both blacks and whites in the school community to talk frankly about the special problems of young black men. One white staff member, who has been active in Alexandria's minority-achievement program says, "Whites don't want to risk being called racists and blacks feel outnumbered and don't want to show their rage. No one will fight it out openly as they did on the sex education program, so not much really happens. There has been no urgency—no sense that people's lives are at stake."

There is hypocrisy and misunderstanding on all sides. White teachers feel guilty about not reaching black males. Some feel that black colleagues blame them while not doing much better themselves.

Black leaders in jurisdictions around the Washington metropolitan area have complained that disproportionate numbers of black males are suspended from schools. But white educators say the problem isn't theirs. "Some of these kids come from the worst environments imaginable," says an elementary school teacher who has been unusually effective with black children. "It's like a dagger through the heart when you find out what some innocent kids have suffered. Tiny malnourished children out walking the streets alone; parents selling or using drugs. They come into school angry and upset because of what goes on at home. You aren't supposed to talk about it publicly, but their behavior can be despicable. It can take a couple of hours of stroking to get them settled down. It's no question that they are the majority of discipline problems, but black teachers and administrators get defensive about these kids."

I have heard white parents and teaches complain when middle-class blacks send their own kids to private schools. "They don't want their own kids' education impeded by the lower class, but they call us racists when we show the same concern about our kids," one white parent told me. And white parents often oppose special efforts to help underachieving black children because they feel this will drain off resources from their children.

Black parents themselves are ambivalent about special help programs. "If a white kid is behind, parents try to get special help, but blacks shy away from special help so the kids often don't get what they need. They want to avoid any kind of label," says the elementary school teacher.

The subject of racism itself—quite apart from any specific instance—can sometimes be a stumbling block in the way of practical progress. Jeffery Johnson says, "Too many blacks harp on racism without doing anything creative to change things. Continually blaming whites is stagnation. Integration has not achieved a genuine and friendly respect. Look at the tensions. Black men want a sense that they have contributed, have been a positive part of the American experience."

But white society has to be more honest, too. It has to stop pretending it is "color-blind." Historically black men have been—and still are—frozen out by the simple fact of their blackness. Asking them simply to fit in is asking them to forget who they are.

Larry Ward's brother Hubert, who now works for a major newspaper, often wonders why blacks haven't "become more mainstream" in America. "The problem is you aren't supposed to be black. So many black guys are confused about themselves. That's why they don't go back to help younger kids. We are not judged on how we compete, but on how well we assimilate. Whites can identify with the dumbest, most violent black athlete but a black guy in academics has to look non-threatening. There is no middle ground. Either you are a good athlete or you have to assimilate. It just takes so much energy to be a black man in a white society."

Socialization, Biology, Social Control, and Deviance

- Childhood (Articles 10-11)
- Influences on Personality and Behavior (Articles 12-13)
- Crime and Social Control (Articles 14-16)

Belonging is as essential to human survival as breathing. Recent studies confirm the threat to health and well-being caused by social isolation. Learning how to belong is one of the most fundamental lessons of socialization; it is a lifelong process of adapting to others and learning what is the expected behavior in particular situations. Through contact with others, one gains self-knowledge. Socialization may take place in many contexts. The most basic socialization takes place in the family, but churches, schools, communities, the media, and workplaces also play major roles in the process.

This section contains articles which deal with the conditions of childhood and both the negative and positive socialization of children. In the first article, Elin McCoy reveals that parents were callous and indifferent toward children hundreds of years ago. Before the eighteenth century, many children were punished severely for trifling offenses, many died in their first year, and many spent little time with their parents.

As all parents know, children resist socialization to some degree. Sometimes the results are shocking, as in the case reported by Nancy Gibbs of six boys brutally beating a woman in a park without any reason. This episode raises questions about what factors are interfering with the positive socialization of children.

The next two articles analyze some of the factors that shape us, including biology, developmental stages, and social pressures. The first article describes the major biological differences between males and females and relates them to findings about sex differences in moral thinking and political attitudes. Men have an edge in spatial relations, math, strength, and aggressiveness, but the edge that women have in human relations and verbal skills may be more important in the post-industrial society.

David Elkind's article "Erik Erikson's Eight Ages of Man," about the stages of psychosocial development, has become a classic. A child learns to be an adult in stages. Erikson identified five stages of childhood and explained what is learned in each stage. If these stages are navigated successfully, the child develops a sense of trust, autonomy, initiative, industry, and identity by age 18. If problems are encountered in any of these stages, the child may develop feelings of mistrust, self-doubt, guilt, inferiority, and role confusion. The final three stages of development are young adulthood, middle age, and advanced middle age or old age. Growth in these stages produces intimacy, generativity, and integrity.

Crime is a leading concern of Americans and law enforcement efforts are being strengthened. Some zones in certain cities are almost completely lawless. News reports are filled with stories of murders. The news is also filled with stories of the poisoning of the environment and accidents at work sites. Many of these are really stories about crimes, but are seldom understood as such. Crimes by corporations victimize millions of people, cost many times the costs of robberies, and injure and kill many people, but little punishment is meted out to the perpetrators. Three articles deal with crime and social control. One describes certain types of law-breaking by corporations. One points out the misconceptions about criminal behavior that underlie the new war on crime, and explains why the war will fail. The last attacks the misconception that rehabilitation of criminals does not work. Together these articles will shake up the reader's perceptions of crime, deviance, social control, and rehabilitation.

Socialization suggests learning and adaptation. It is a dynamic and ever-changing process. In many ways, it is synonymous with living.

Looking Ahead: Challenge Questions

How can the ways in which children are socialized in America be improved?

Why is socialization a lifelong process?

What are the principal factors that make people what they are?

How are girls socialized differently from boys?

Childhood Through the Ages

Elin McCoy

Elin McCoy is the author of "The Incredible Year-Round Playbook" (Random House).

A gentleman-in-waiting and the nurse of little Comte de Marle often amused themselves tossing the swaddled infant back and forth across the sill of an open window. One day one of them failed to catch him, and the infant landed on a stone step and died.

The surgeon of the newborn Louis XIII cut the "fiber" under his tongue a few days after he was born, believing that if it remained uncut, Louis would be unable to suck properly and would eventually stutter.

These aren't atypical examples of child rearing in the past. Recent historical research indicates that for most of the past 2,500 years, childhood was a brief, grim period in most people's lives, especially when judged against contemporary views of child rearing.

A new field—family history.

Through a new field of historical research, known as family history, we now know that family life and childhood in the previous centuries were startlingly different from what most people, including historians, had imagined them to be. Scores of historians are currently probing such questions as: How were children treated in the past? What concept of childhood did people have in different centuries? How important were children to their parents? Is there such a thing as "instinctual" parental behavior? What do the prevailing child-rearing beliefs and practices of the past tell us about the political, social, and psychological ideals of society? And

what kind of adults resulted from such child-rearing practices?

"Family history is the most explosive field of history today," says Professor Lawrence Stone—director of Princeton University's Shelby Cullom Davis Center for Historical Studies—whose 1977 book, *The Family, Sex and Marriage in England 1500–1800,* came out in an abridged paperback last year. "In the 1930s only about 10 scholarly books and articles on the family and childhood in history were published each year, but, incredibly, between 1971 and 1976 over 900 important books and articles were published on that subject, just covering America, England, and France." Two scholarly journals devoted to the subject were also started in the 1970s.

Why, suddenly, have so many historians focused on the family? "A whole series of contemporary anxieties has contributed to this new interest," explains Professor Stone. "General anxiety about the state of the family and whether it's breaking down, concern about the rising divorce rate, anxieties about current permissiveness in raising children, and concern about what effects women's liberation will have on children, the family, and society. And underlying all of these anxieties are two questions: Are we really doing so badly? Was it better in the past?"

In addition, two other trends in historical research have focused attention on childhood and the family. The first is social historians' growing interest in the daily lives of ordinary people in history, which has meant a greater concern with children, parenting, marriage, disease, death, and aging. The second is historians' recent efforts to employ psychological concepts as

a research tool in order to understand human motivations and experiences in the past.

Although all family historians agree that child-rearing patterns influence what happens in history, they disagree about how much and in what precise ways the treatment of children shapes history. Some researchers in the field, like Lloyd deMause, founder of *The Journal of Psychohistory: A Quarterly Journal of Childhood and Psychohistory,* go so far as to say that, in deMause's words, "child-rearing practices have been *the* central force for change in history." Along with some other psychohistorians, deMause believes that "if you want to understand the causes of historical events like the growth of Nazism, you have to look at how the children who became Nazis as adults were treated as children." But many scholars have reservations about attributing the character of a society solely to the relations between parents and children, pointing out that these relations must be understood in the context of the society as a whole and that such factors as economics must also be taken into account.

Surprising discoveries.

Family historians have recently exploded many long-standing myths about childhood and the nature of the family throughout history. It's now clear that the functions and structure of the family have changed continuously over the years and that a variety of family types coexisted in each historical period in different regions and classes. Scholars have found, surprisingly, that the prevailing family mode in America today (the small nuclear family of parents and children living apart from other relatives)—a struc-

From *Parents*, January 1981, pp. 60–65. Reprinted by permission of Elin McCoy and her agents, Raines & Raines, 71 Park Avenue, New York, N.Y. 10016. Copyright © 1981 Elin McCoy.

ture that is under much attack—is not as new to our culture as they had previously thought. Even as long ago as thirteenth-century England, as many as half of all families consisted of only a mother and/or father and two to three children. In fact, the large, loving extended families we tend to picture, with eight to ten children and several generations of relatives living under the same roof, were more the exception than the rule, even in Colonial America.

According to Professor Tamara Hareven—founder and head of the first History of the Family program in the country, at Clark University in Worcester, Massachusetts, and founding editor of the *Journal of Family History*—one of the great surprises for today's historians was "finding out that in the past, the concept of childhood and children was not the same in all centuries, classes, and countries. While the middle classes were 'discovering' childhood and becoming interested in children," she explains, "the working classes still regarded children as small adults with the same responsibilities. And in the past, childhood as we know it lasted for a much shorter time." In medieval England, for example, children as young as seven were sent to live in other households as apprentices, and for peasant children, childhood was even briefer—they joined their parents to work in the fields as soon as they could.

Infants were regarded in medieval times as unimportant, unformed animals, in the sixteenth century as "exasperating parasites," and even as late as the seventeenth century they were not seen as individuals with their own identities. Children were considered interchangeable, and frequently were given the same name as an older sibling who had died. Small children were not even viewed as interesting; Montaigne, the French essayist, summed up the prevailing attitudes of a few hundred years ago when he dismissed infants as having "neither movement in the soul, nor recognizable form in the body by which they could render themselves lovable."

Scholars tell us that infants and small children were important only insofar as they could benefit their parents. Considered possessions with no individual rights, they were used to further adult aims, and they ended up as security for debts, as ways of increasing property holdings through arranged marriages, as political hostages, and even as slaves sold for profit.

Infancy in the past.

Throughout history, parents' treatment of infants and very small children has been characterized by psychological coldness and physical brutality that horrify most of us today. But this behavior becomes at least comprehensible when we realize some of the conditions of people's lives. The physical realities of life were oppressive. And there were severe parental limitations as well: in addition to being influenced by unscientific medical knowledge and religious views about the nature of man, most adults had to concentrate so much of their energy on mere survival that they had little time to care for or worry about infants and small children. Abusive and violent behavior was common among adults and, therefore, not looked on with disapproval when it appeared in the treatment of children.

In view of the following facts, consider what your experience as a parent and your child's experience as an infant would have been if you had lived prior to the eighteenth century.

Your child probably wouldn't have been wanted. Lack of birth control meant that having children was not a choice. For poverty-stricken peasants, an infant meant another mouth to feed—and food was precious—as well as interference with the mother's role as a worker whose contribution was necessary to the family's ability to survive. In all classes, the high risk of maternal mortality made the birth of a child a traumatic event. Even in the relatively healthy conditions enjoyed by the inhabitants of Plymouth Colony, 20 percent of women died from causes related to childbirth (compared with under 1 percent today), and in seventeenth-century England and France, the rates were much higher. It's no wonder that most children were probably unwanted. In fact, Professor Stone suggests that the availability of birth control was probably one of the necessary conditions for the increase in affection for children that began in England and America in the eighteenth century.

Your infant would have had a good chance of dying before his or her first birthday. In medieval England and seventeenth-century France, for example, between 20 and 50 percent of all infants died

within the first year after birth. Complications of childbirth, prematurity, diseases such as smallpox and the plague, and generally unsanitary living conditions, as well as such customs as baptism in icy water in freezing churches, took a heavy toll among vulnerable newborns. America was healthier for infants—in Plymouth Colony, infant mortality was only 10 to 15 percent (which is still ten times higher than it is in America today). The likelihood that one's infants would die discouraged parents from investing much affection or interest in them and from regarding them as special, unique individuals until it appeared more certain that they might live to adulthood.

Illegitimate infants and infants of poverty-stricken parents (and parents who felt they already had enough children) were often the victims of infanticide through deliberate murder, abandonment, or neglect. In ancient Greece, for example, infants who seemed sickly or didn't have a perfect shape or cried too much or too little were "exposed," or abandoned to die, a decision that was made by the father shortly after birth. In mid-eighteenth-century England, so many babies—both legitimate and illegitimate—were abandoned to die in the streets of cities and towns that the first foundling home established in London received several thousand babies a year. In early America, infanticide seems to have affected only illegitimate children.

If you were well-off, your baby probably would have been breast-fed by someone else. In spite of the fact that all medical advice since Roman times had stressed that babies breast-fed by their own mothers had a better chance of survival, for eighteen centuries any woman who could afford it sent her infant to a wet nurse.

Recuperation from a difficult childbirth prevented some women from breast-feeding, but many others thought it too demanding, especially since it was customary for infants to breast-feed for as long as two years. Also, many husbands would not allow their wives to breast-feed, partly because medical opinion held that women who were breast-feeding should not engage in sexual intercourse.

Underlying these reasons may have been parents' desire to distance themselves emotionally from their infants.

51

In Renaissance Italy, middle-class infants were delivered to the *bália*, or wet nurse, immediately after baptism—two or three days after birth—and, if they survived, remained there for two years. Rarely did mothers visit their infants, and thus a baby was returned home at the end of that time to a stranger.

Although some wet nurses moved in with the family, most women left their babies at the wet nurse's home, where the child was often neglected and starved because wet nurses commonly took on too many babies in order to make more money. Frequently wet nurses ran out of milk, and infants had to be sent to a series of different nurses and thus were deprived even of a single surrogate mother.

The first groups of middle-class women to change this 1,800-year-old pattern on a large scale were the Puritans in the seventeenth century. Eventually, in the eighteenth century, there was a widespread cult of maternal breast-feeding in both America and England. Scholars have suggested that this shift may have contributed substantially to the shift in parental feelings for infants that began in the eighteenth century; certainly it reduced infant mortality.

Your infant would have spent little time with you. In the past, parents spent much less time with their children than even working parents do today and clearly did not feel the need to arrange supervision for them. Peasant women commonly left their infants and toddlers alone all day at home while they worked elsewhere. In one area of England during the thirteenth century, for example, half the infant deaths involved infants in cradles being burned while no one was home. Unsupervised toddlers frequently wandered off and drowned. In the middle and upper classes, parental neglect took the form of turning toddlers over to the servants to raise.

Your infant would have been swaddled in tightly bound cloths from birth to as old as eight months. Emotional distancing, economic necessity, and faulty medical knowledge are also evident in another common practice—swaddling. In England this practice continued up to the eighteenth century; in France, the nineteenth century; and in Russia, into the twentieth century. Kept in tightly bound bandages, swaddled infants were totally isolated from their surroundings for the first four months or so. After that, only their legs were bound. They couldn't turn their heads, suck their own thumbs for comfort, or crawl. Swaddling that was too tight occasionally caused suffocation. Although doctors advocated changing the infant two or three times a day, this apparently was uncommon, and even Louis XIII developed severe rashes because of his swaddling bands.

Medical reasons for the practice included the beliefs that if free, the infant might tear off his ears or scratch out his eyes, that swaddling was necessary to keep infants warm in cold, draughty cottages, houses, and castles, and that it ensured that the infant's pliable limbs would grow straight so he would be able to stand erect. Even when the swaddling bands were removed from their legs, children were not allowed to crawl "like an animal," but were forced to stand with the help

Mother's helper: The "roundabout" was a 19th-century gadget designed to keep baby out of mother's way. But it sacrificed a freedom of movement that today we know is crucial to a child's development.

THE BETTMANN ARCHIVE

of bizarre contraptions. Convenience was another reason for swaddling: it caused infants to sleep more and cry less, so they could be left for long periods of time while mothers worked. Also, swaddled infants were easier to carry and could even be hung on a peg on the wall out of the way.

Your infant or child would probably have received harsh beatings regularly—from you or a servant—even for such "normal" behavior as crying or wanting to play. For many centuries, discipline and teaching of the infant and young child concentrated on "breaking the child's will," which meant crushing all assertiveness and instilling complete obedience. This was accomplished through physical and psychological maltreatment that today we would consider "child abuse." Susanna Wesley, mother of John Wesley, the founder of the Methodist Church, records her treatment of her children: "When turned a year old, and some before, they were taught to fear the rod and cry softly." Louis XIII was whipped every morning, starting at the age of two, simply for being "obstinate," and was even whipped on the day of his coronation at the age of nine. The Puritans believed that "the newborn babe is full of the stains and pollutions of sin" and saw the first strivings of a one- and two-year-old to independence—which we now recognize as essential to a child's growing mastery of himself and understanding of the world—as a clear manifestation of that original sin. It was considered the duty of parents to use physical harshness and psychological terrorization—locking children in dark closets for an entire day or frightening them with tales of death and hellfire, for example—to wipe this sin out.

These child-rearing practices, as well as the difficult realities of life in the past, had important psychological effects on children's development. According to Professor Stone, the isolation, sensory deprivation, and lack of physical closeness that resulted from swaddling; the absence of a mother because of death in childbirth or the practice of wet-nursing; the common experience for small children of losing parents and siblings; and the suppression of self-assertion through whipping and other fear-producing techniques all resulted in an "adult world of emotional cripples."

A change for the better.

In the late seventeenth and eighteenth centuries, many of these child-rearing practices began to change among wealthy merchants and other groups in the upper middle classes of England and America. Some changes can be traced to the Puritans, who, even though they advocated harsh disciplinary measures, focused a new attention on children and the importance of their upbringing. By the late eighteenth century, among some groups, methods of contraception were available, swaddling had been abandoned, maternal breast-feeding had become the fashion, and "breaking the will" had given way to affection and a degree of permissiveness that seems extraordinary even by today's standards. In England the indulgent Lord Holland, for example, intent on gratifying his little son Charles's every whim, allowed him to jump and splash in the large bowl of cream intended for dessert at a grand dinner while the guests, a group of foreign ministers, looked on. Many adults feared the effect on society when these spoiled children reached maturity. And in fact, many of them did spend their lives in lifelong dissipation and often became followers of evangelical religions. While the Victorian era varied from harsh to permissive in the treatment of children, by the end of the nineteenth century the child-oriented family became a reality for all classes in Western society.

What it all means for us.

Were childhood and family life better in the past? The answer—obviously—is a resounding no. One is tempted to agree with Lloyd deMause that "the history of childhood is a nightmare from which we have only recently begun to awaken."

Nevertheless, Professor Hareven feels that there *were* some good aspects to childhood in the past, which we can learn from today. "Children were not so segregated from adults and responsibility," she points out. "The historical record shows children grew up in households that included servants, other workers employed by the family, lodgers, visiting relatives, and siblings of widely differing ages, as well as parents. They were exposed to a greater variety of adult roles than children usually are today and they interacted with a greater variety of people of all ages. They also knew more about their parents' work. And unlike today, children were working, contributing members of families and the society from an early age—as they are in contemporary China. Today's child-oriented family and the postponement of responsibility and work limit children's experience. The models are there in history for us to borrow and shape to today's ideals."

Historical research on childhood helps us view our own ideas about parenthood from a perspective in which it is clear that there are no absolutes. The new facts that are available to us show that assumptions behind child rearing change and that what we think of as parents' "instincts" actually depend on the beliefs and experiences of their society. The possessiveness and affection toward infants, which we take for granted, is a recent development. Even the "maternal instinct" to breast-feed one's own child was not instinctive for many women for over 1,800 years.

Family history also gives us an informative view of family structure. Those who are worried about the high divorce rate and the effect of parental separation on children, for example, should realize that in the past, approximately the same percentage of families were separated—only it was by the death of one of the parents instead of by divorce.

Although problems with child rearing will probably always be with us,

"The Human Comedy": That's the name of this 19th-century sketch—but the partially-swaddled child, left alone hanging on a wall, isn't finding anything in his situation to laugh about.

the very existence of family history means that we have come to the point where we are much more self-conscious about how we raise children, and, in turn, this may help us to be more thoughtful about the way we treat them. By examining childhood in the past, we become aware that our own attempts to do things differently—"nonsexist" child rearing, co-parenting, and different mixes of permissiveness and discipline—may have profound effects on society. If we can avoid the mistakes of the past, borrow what was good, and continue to examine our own aims and practices, the society our children make may be a better one than ours.

Wilding in the Night

A brutal gang rape in New York City triggers fears that the U.S. is breeding a generation of merciless children

NANCY GIBBS

From time to time a new word bursts into the lexicon, capturing with shocking force the latent fears of a troubled age. The latest such word is "wilding," the term used by a band of New York City teenagers to describe the mischief they set out to commit on a clear April night in Central Park. Looking, they said, for something to do, they roamed the park's northern reaches, splintering into smaller groups and allegedly assaulting one hapless victim after another. Finally, one pack came upon a 28-year-old woman jogging alone past a grove of sycamore trees. According to police, they chased her into a gully, then spent the next half an hour beating her senseless with a rock and a metal pipe, raping her and leaving her for dead. When she was found three hours later, she had lost three-quarters of her blood and had lapsed into a coma.

By last week the attack had escalated from a local tragedy into a morbid national obsession. Perhaps the story resonated across the country because the victim was a wealthy, white financier with degrees from Wellesley and Yale. Or because the scene was Central Park, the backyard of powerful news media and a symbol of everything Americans most fear about New York City. Or it may have been because of the word wilding, which seemed simultaneously to define and obscure the transformation of a group of teenage boys into a bloodthirsty mob.

Last week six youths were indicted for rape, and two others were indicted for a separate attack on a male jogger. According to investigators, these were not crimes of drugs or race or robbery. Newspapers claimed that the suspects came from stable, working families who provided baseball coaching and music lessons. The youths, some barely into their teens, may not have been altar boys, but they hardly seemed like candidates for a rampage. One was known for helping elderly neighbors at his middle-income Harlem apartment complex. Another was a born-again Christian who had persuaded his mother to join his church. Only one had ever been in trouble with the police.

If children so seemingly normal went so horribly wrong, the obvious question is Why? The youths, described by police as smug and remorseless, have offered only one motive: escape from boredom. "It was fun," detectives quoted one suspect as saying. "It was something to do."

The evidence that youthful offenders are becoming more violent is everywhere. Two Denver students have been charged with stabbing a man to death so they could steal his credit cards and use them to buy camping equipment. At a Los Angeles Greyhound station, a 15-year-old girl was kidnaped at knifepoint by two men, held captive for five days and repeatedly raped. She managed to escape and flagged down a passing car. "Get me out of here!" she begged the three teenagers inside. They did, and took her to a park in East Los Angeles, where the eldest of the boys, 18, allegedly raped her again.

New York Mayor Ed Koch, for one, does not care to hear excuses for the violence of the young. "You name one societal reason," he said, "that would cause people to engage in a wolf-pack operation, looking for victims." Throughout the week sociologists obliged, proffering familiar theories about why many delinquents of this generation do not content themselves with stealing hubcaps and breaking windows. The experts argue that too many families are broken, too many schools and communities are crumbling, too many drugs are available for children to acquire a sturdy sense of mercy or morality to guide their behavior.

Into this vacuum the circuits of popular culture transmit images of brutality without consequences. Children play video games in which they win points for killing the most people. They watch violence-packed cartoons. They listen to songs titled *Be My Slave* and *Scumkill*. Or they are baby-sat by vastly popular movie videotapes like *Splatter University* and *I Spit on Your Grave*. Says sociologist Gail Dines-Levy of Wheelock College in Boston: "What we are doing is training a whole generation of male kids to see sex and violence as inextricably linked."

But such theories, however valid, ring hollow in the face of crimes like the Central Park attack. Pornography, even the most gruesome kind, is commonplace in countries where the level of violence does not approach that in the U.S. The impulses behind the most brutal attacks are extremely complicated. "What we're seeing is a real distortion in personality development," says Michael Nelson, professor of psychology at Xavier University in Cincinnati. "It's not nice little neurotic people acting out problems."

If a culture of violence can corrupt affluent suburban adolescents, it plays special havoc when mixed with the pathology of the ghetto, where danger surrounds children every day, sometimes inside their homes, always outside. At least one of the Central Park suspects was sexually assaulted when he was a child, and the private histories of the others are still a mystery. In such brutal conditions, a youngster's peers can become his family, and wilding can be a way to prove his masculinity. "Kids who roam in groups gain a sense of power that they do not have individually," says Elijah Anderson, professor of sociology at the University of Pennsylvania. Caught in a mob frenzy, each boy believes he is the only one hesitant to go ahead with a destructive act, and will not resist or show remorse out of fear that the others in the group will think him a coward.

As the explanations and indictments rolled in last week, the New York City case continued to feed a debate about freedom and fear, anarchy and obligation. "Blaming society, parents, poverty, racism, school systems and neighborhoods for teenage violence is too easy," said Dr. Edward Shaw, director of mental health for the New York State division of youth. "It does not answer the question Why do some teenagers in the same environment get into trouble and others do not?" There were those still willing to look for the hard answers last week. But others could only watch a woman in a coma, hear the noises of the city and wonder what might come next.

—Reported by Mary Cronin/ New York and Melissa Ludtke/Boston

MEN VS. WOMEN

Biology may not be destiny, but these days researchers are finding some significant differences between the sexes–and, in many ways, women are coming out ahead

 There was a time, not so long ago, when all the answers seemed clear. Everyone *knew* which was the weaker sex: Analyzed in terms of political power and bodily brawn, wasn't it obvious? Turn-of-the-century scientists produced learned tracts solemnly warning against an excess of exercise or education for girls: Too much activity—or thinking—would divert needed blood from their reproductive systems. Pseudoscientists meticulously measured human brains and found women's wanting (along with those of blacks and Irishmen). And when the new science of intelligence testing turned up repeated and systematic superiority among girls, researchers kept tinkering with the tests until they produced the "right" results.

We've come a long way since those bad old days. We have also moved beyond a backlash of 1970s feminist scholarship, which insisted with equal ideological fervor that apart from the obvious dimorphism of human beings, there were *no* real differences between the sexes—that seeming disparities in mental abilities, emotional makeup, attitudes and even many physical skills were merely the product of centuries of male domination and male-dominated interpretation.

Lately, in bits and pieces that are still the subject of lively debate, science has been learning more about the fine points of how men and women differ—more about their physiology, their psychology, the interplay between the two and the subtle ways society influences both. Among the questions these studies may help answer:

■ Are more women doomed to die of heart attacks as they rise to positions of power in the work world? Or are they peculiarly protected from the stresses that beleaguer modern men? Is there something to be learned from female longevity that might help improve and prolong the lives of men?

■ Are boys always going to be better at math than girls? And why is it that there have been relatively few women of acknowledged artistic genius?

■ Are men, by nature, better suited than women to lead and manage other people? Or is it possible that society would be better off with women's ways in the board rooms, female fingers near the nuclear buttons?

The old answers, once so sure, just won't do any more. In *The Myth of Two Minds,* her provocative 1987 book analyzing findings on sex differences, Beryl Lieff Benderly put the argument succinctly: "Who had the stronger shoulders, who might unpredictably become pregnant, clearly meant a great deal when work and warfare ran on muscle power and conception lay as far beyond human control as the weather. But now, when every American fingertip commands horsepower by the thousands, when the neighborhood drugstore and clinic offer freedom from fertility, those two great physical differences weigh very lightly indeed in the social balance."

While scientists still have a long way to go, research in a dozen disciplines—from neurology, endocrinology and sports medicine to psychology, anthropology and sociology—is beginning to point in the same direction: There are differences between the sexes beyond their reproductive functions, the pitch of their voices, the curves of elbows and knees, the fecundity of hair follicles. Many of these differences suggest that women are at least as well equipped as men for life in the modern world—and that in some ways they are, in fact, the stronger sex.

DIVERGING PATHS
Differences appear as early as six weeks after conception

FETUS At first, the embryo has all the equipment to become either sex. The only clue to its destiny is buried deep in the genetic code, in the 23rd chromosome pair. In the sixth week of development, if the embryo has inherited a Y chromosome from its father, a gene signals the start of male development. In both sexes, hormones begin to prepare the brain for the changes of puberty a dozen years away.

INFANT At birth, the skeletons of girls are slightly more mature than those of boys. Some studies have suggested that newborn girls are slightly more responsive to touch and that infant boys spend more time awake. There is also evidence that boy infants respond somewhat earlier to visual stimuli, girls to sounds and smells.

TODDLER Boys gain and pass girls in skeletal maturity by the end of the first year. At the age of 2, boys begin to show signs of greater aggressiveness. At 3, a slight, early female edge in verbal ability disappears—but by 10 or 11, it is back. Boys begin to show superiority in spatial skills at the age of 8 or so, and at 10 or 11, they start outperforming girls in math.

ADOLESCENT Girls begin to fall behind in body strength. In both male and female, reproductive organs develop rapidly. Both spurt in height; when it is over, the average male will be 10 percent taller than the female. Meanwhile, the female superiority in verbal skills increases. So does the male edge in spatial skills and math.

ADULT The mature woman carries twice as much body fat as a man. And the man carries 1½ times as much muscle and bone. Because of the female hormone estrogen, which works to keep women's bodies in peak childbearing condition, women have some built-in health advantages—including more-pliable blood vessels and the ability to process fat more efficiently—and safely—than men.

OLD AGE After menopause, estrogen production drops off, and women lose some of the protection the hormone formerly provided. Even so, the advantages of her fertile decades persist for at least 15 years: Only slowly, for example, do the blood vessels become more rigid. The male can continue spermatogenesis into the late 80s and early 90s.

BODY

The distinctions are more than just skin-deep

If God created man first, He or She apparently took advantage of hindsight when it came to woman. Except for the moment of conception (when 13 to 15 males are conceived for every 10 females), the distaff side simply has a better chance at survival. Spontaneous abortions of boys outnumber those of girls. More males than females die during infancy, youth and adulthood. In every country in the world where childbirth itself no longer poses mortal danger to women, the life expectancy of females exceeds that of males. And in the United States, the gap is growing. A baby girl born today can look forward to nearly 79 years—seven more than a baby boy.

Why? Some of the answers seem to lie deep in the genes. Others doubtless float in the hormones that carry messages from organ to organ, even, some researchers believe, "imprinting" each human brain with patterns that can affect the ways it responds to injury and disease. The research suggests that females start out with some distinct biological advantages. Among them:

■ **THE GENETIC CODE.** Genesis was wrong: Women came first—embryologically speaking, at least. Genetically, the female is the basic pattern of the species; maleness is superimposed on that. And this peculiarity of nature has the side effect of making males more vulnerable to a number of inherited disorders.

The reason lies in the way our genes determine who's a male and who's a female. A normal embryo inherits 23 chromosomes from the mother and 23 from the father. One of these chromosome pairs, the 23rd, determines what sex the baby will be. From the mother, the embryo always receives an X chromosome. From the father, it receives either an X, creating a female, or a Y, creating a male.

The Y chromosome carries little more than the genetic signal that, in the sixth week of development, first defeminizes the embryo, then starts the masculinization process. In a female, the X chromosome supplied by the father duplicates much of the genetic information supplied by the mother. Thus, if there are potentially deadly genetic anomalies on one of the female's X chromosomes, the other may cancel their effects. But the male embryo has no such protection: What's written on his sole X chromosome rules the day. Among the X-linked troubles he is more likely to inherit: Colorblindness, hemophilia, leukemia and dyslexia.

■ **THE ESTROGEN FACTOR.** The main task of the female sex hormones, or estrogens, is to keep the female body prepared to carry and care for offspring. But as it turns out, what's good for female reproduction is also good for the arteries. One effect of estrogens, for example, is to keep blood vessels pliable in order to accommodate extra blood volume during pregnancy. That also reduces the risk of atherosclerosis. And because a developing fetus needs lots of carbohydrates but is unable to use much fat, the mother's body must be able to break down the extra fat left behind after the fetus's demands are met. Estrogen makes this happen by stimulating the liver to produce high-density lipoproteins (HDL), which allow the body to make more efficient use of fat—and help to keep arteries cleared of cholesterol.

The male hormone testosterone, by contrast, causes men to have a far higher concentration of *low*-density lipoprotein. "LDL forms and fixes in large amounts to the lining of the blood vessels," explains endocrinologist Estelle Ramey. "They become narrower and more fragile." That didn't matter 2 million years ago, when men were far more physically active: Exercise lowers the LDL count.

Long after menopause, when estrogen production drops dramatically, women maintain the cardiovascular advantages built up during their childbearing years. The Framingham study, a 24-year examination of the health of almost 6,000 men and women between the ages of 30 and 59, found approximately twice the incidence of coronary heart disease in men as in women, even in the upper age

REMARKABLE DIFFERENCES

Between 130 and 150 males are conceived for every 100 females. About 105 boys are born for every 100 girls. But by the time they reach the age of 20, there are only about 98 males per 100 females. And among those 65 and older, just 68 men survive for every 100 women.

Females have a better sense of smell than males from birth onward. They are also more sensitive to loud sounds. But males are more sensitive to bright light—and can detect more subtle differences in light.

It is physiologically more difficult for women than for men to maintain a desirable weight and still meet their nutritional needs.

Women on average spend 40 percent more days sick in bed than do men.

Sexual perversions—foot fetishes, for instance—are an almost exclusively male phenomenon.

Boys get more than 90 percent of all perfect scores of 800 on the math section of the Scholastic Aptitude Test. And the gap between SAT math scores for boys and girls is greatest—about 60 points higher for males—among students who are in the top 10 percent of their class.

Infant girls show a strong, early response to human faces—at a time when infant boys are just as likely to smile and coo at inanimate objects and blinking lights.

Boys are far more likely than girls to be left-handed, nearsighted and dyslexic (more than 3 to 1). Males under 40 are also more likely than females to suffer from allergies and hiccups.

range. And in an analysis of the health patterns of 122,000 U.S. nurses, Graham Colditz, assistant professor at Harvard Medical School, has found that women who use estrogen supplements after menopause cut their risk of heart attacks by a third.

So—would men live longer if they took doses of estrogens? So far, the answer is a resounding no. In experiments where men received estrogen supplements, "they dropped like flies," says Elaine Eaker, an epidemiologist at the National Institutes of Health—from heart attacks. Eaker speculates that men don't have the proper receptor sites for estrogen.

But there may be hope for greater longevity in highly experimental work on macrophages, cells that form part of the immune system. Macrophages, Ramey explains, "gobble up" unmetabolized glucose that randomly affixes itself to DNA—and would eventually cause damage. As people age, the macrophage system slows, and the damage gets worse. "Macrophage activity in females, because of estrogen, is much higher," says Ramey. It's the hope of researchers that they can find a way to increase and prolong that activity in both sexes.

■ **THE STRESS SYNDROME.** "Women," Ramey declares flatly, "respond better to stress." Although the evidence on how stress hurts the human body is still equivocal, there are two main hypotheses. The first is mechanical: Elevation of heart rate and blood pressure due to stress promotes damage to the inner lining of the artery wall, laying the groundwork for heart disease. The second is chemical: Increased production of stress hormones promotes arterial damage.

Ramey is one scientist who is convinced that stress does damage. And she puts the blame squarely on testosterone—and the fact that while the world has changed substantially, men's bodies have not. In the world where primitive man evolved, "testosterone is the perfect hormone." In effect, it orders neuroreceptors in the brain to drop everything else and react as quickly as possible to a release of stress hormones. This greater reaction to stress may be damaging in the long run, but the short-term benefits were much more important in an age when "the life expectancy was about 23," says Ramey. Today, when the average man is less likely to be threatened by a saber-toothed tiger than by a corporate barracuda, his stress reaction is exactly the same—and just as damaging to long-term health.

Perhaps because testosterone isn't egging them on, women seem to respond to stressful situations more slowly, and with less of a surge of blood pressure and stress hormones. Some researchers suspect that psychosocial factors also play a big role.

Dr. Kathleen Light, a specialist in behavioral medicine at the University of North Carolina, thinks women may have a different perception of just what situations are threatening. Women show much less stress than men, for instance, when asked to solve an arithmetic problem. But Light's preliminary data in a study of public speaking show that women experience about the same surge in blood pressure as men. "Women may respond more selectively than men," she suggests. "We think this reflects learned experience."

But Karen Matthews is not so sure. Postmenopausal women, she observes, show higher heart rates and produce more stress hormones than women who are still menstruating. This leads her back to the reproductive hormones. One possible conclusion: Estrogens may be better adapted than testosterone for the flight-or-fight situations of modern life.

■ **THE BRAIN PLAN.** Men's and women's brains really are different. Over the last decade, researchers have discovered that in women, functions such as language ability appear to be more evenly divided between the left and right halves of the brain; in men, they are much more localized in the left half. After strokes or injuries to the left hemisphere, women are three times less likely than men to suffer language deficits.

What accounts for these differences in brain organization? One clue: The central section of the corpus callosum, a nerve cable connecting the left and right halves of the brain, seems to be thicker in women than in men, perhaps allowing more right-brain-left-brain communication.

Many researchers think that sex hormones produced early in fetal development—as well as after birth—literally "sex" the brain. In young animals, says neuroendocrinologist Bruce McEwen of New York's Rockefeller University, "the brain cells respond to testosterone by becoming larger and developing different kinds of connections."

These changes add up to big behavioral differences. Inject a female rat pup with testicular hormones, for instance, and it will mount other females just like a male. And it's not just a matter of mating. Male rat pups deprived of testicular hormones perform more poorly on maze tests than normal males; young females injected with testicular hormones do better. Many researchers are convinced that hormones have similar effects on human brains. Males produce testosterone from the third to the sixth month of gestation. Another burst is released just after birth, and then one final spurt at the onset of puberty—roughly coinciding with the time boys begin to surpass girls in math. What's more, males with an abnormality that makes their cells insensitive to testosterone's effects have cognitive profiles identical to girls: Their verbal IQ is higher than in normal males and their "performance" IQ (correlated with mechanical ability) is inferior to that of normal males.

Such findings are highly controversial. Feminist scholars, in particular, fear that they will give new life to the notion that biology is destiny—and that females just aren't the equal of men at certain tasks. But biodeterminists tend to ignore a critical difference between humans and other animals: The hugely complex human brain is not simply the sum of its synapses. There are other factors at play.

MIND

Different ways of thinking, from math to morals

Declare that women are more sensitive to the color red, and you get a few raised eyebrows. Argue that females are—by nature—not as good as males at mathematics, and you'll get outrage. Not surprisingly, intellectual ability is the arena in which sex differences are most hotly disputed. The stakes are high: Research findings can influence funding and policy decisions in everything from education to employment.

Most of the controversy over sex differences has focused on the longstanding male edge on tests of math aptitude. And it was further fueled in 1980, when Johns Hopkins University researchers Camilla Benbow and Julian Stanley reported on a study of 10,200 gifted junior-high students who took the Scholastic Aptitude Test between 1972 and 1979. Their conclusion: Boys were far more likely than girls to be mathematically talented. The researchers went on to speculate that there may be 13 male math geniuses for every female with such talent—and that the sex differences in math are the result of biological factors, perhaps exposure to the male sex hormone testosterone.

The Johns Hopkins studies were savagely attacked from the moment they were released. For one thing, the SAT's regularly have shown wider differences in male-female scores than other math tests. And the population that Benbow and Stanley studied is by definition exceptional: Its performance does not necessarily mean anything about boys and girls in general.

MATTERS OF LIFE AND DEATH

About 60 percent of the gap in mortality rates between the sexes is the result of increased social risks for men—smoking, drinking and fatal accidents; some demographers expect women will lose some of that advantage soon, as the rise of female smoking during the 1950s begins to show up in the statistics. The other 40 percent seems rooted in biology. Women are sick more often than men and more likely to suffer from chronic conditions. But men are more likely to suffer from killers like heart disease. The bottom line: The risk of death is higher for males of all ages—and for every leading cause of death.

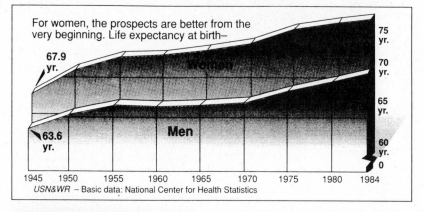

For women, the prospects are better from the very beginning. Life expectancy at birth—

67.9 yr. / 63.6 yr.

75 yr. / 70 yr. / 65 yr. / 60 yr. / 0

1945 1950 1955 1960 1965 1970 1975 1980 1984

USN&WR – Basic data: National Center for Health Statistics

WOMEN
Chronic conditions that afflict women between the ages of 45 and 64 more often than they appear in men of the same age group. The percentages indicate the higher prevalence of each disorder among women, as compared with its rate among men

Nonfatal	
Thyroid diseases	551%
Bladder infection, disorders	382%
Anemias	378%
Bunions	335%
Spastic colon	305%
Frequent constipation	253%
Varicose veins	233%
Migraine headaches	175%
Diverticulitis of intestines	152%
Chronic enteritis and colitis	111%
Sciatica	85%
Trouble with corns, calluses	82%
Neuralgia and neuritis	79%
Gallstones	64%
Arthritis	59%
Dermatitis	59%
Gastritis and duodenitis	54%
Heart rhythm disorders	43%
Diseases of retina	32%
Fatal	
Asthma	41%
High blood pressure*	8%

MEN
Chronic conditions that afflict men between the ages of 45 and 64 more often than they appear in women of the same age group. Percentages indicate the higher prevalence of each disorder among men, as compared with its rate among women

Nonfatal	
Visual impairments	49%
Hearing impairments	46%
Paralysis, complete or partial	25%
Tinnitus	21%
Hernia of abdominal cavity	18%
Intervertebral disk disorders	14%
Hemorrhoids	5%
Fatal	
Emphysema	59%
Atherosclerosis	54%
Ischemic heart disease	51%
Cerebrovascular disease	32%
Liver disease including cirrhosis	23%
Other selected heart diseases	3%
Ulcer of stomach, duodenum	3%

* A risk factor for fatal circulatory diseases. Women's higher prevalence rates are thought to reflect earlier diagnosis and control, compared with men. For younger, premenopausal women, high blood pressure is less common than among men, and more men die from the disease because of damage done to their blood vessels at the younger age, when they do contract it in higher proportions.
USN&WR—Basic data: Lois Verbrugge of University of Michigan and unpublished data from the National Health Interview Surveys, 1983-85

But many other tests have consistently turned up a male superiority in math as well. And the explanation of the results offered by critics—that boys traditionally have been *expected* to do better at math, so they got more encouragement from parents and teachers—doesn't quite wash, either. Girls get better average *grades* in math at every level.

Lately, some researchers have found hints that testosterone plays a role in enhancing math aptitude: Girls who have received abnormal doses of it in the womb seem to do better than average on the tests.

Whatever the explanation, however, the gap is narrowing. According to psychologist Janet Hyde of the University of Wisconsin, a preliminary analysis of dozens of studies of sex differences suggests that the gap has been cut in half in the past seven years.

But on another cognitive front—visual-spatial ability—males still hold an undisputed edge. The male advantage begins to show up around the age of 8, and it persists into old age.

Some simple explanations are tempting: A few researchers have even suggested that a single, sex-linked gene is responsible for the male edge in analyzing and mentally manipulating three-dimensional objects. Like hemophilia, such a sex-linked trait could be carried by both men and women but would become active in a woman only rarely—when both of her X chromosomes carried the gene. Men, who have only one X chromosome, would by contrast need only a single copy of the gene to acquire the ability.

But there are no rigorous data to support the idea: No gene has been identified, nor has anyone been able to trace the inheritance of an enhanced spatial ability from mothers to sons—as has been done extensively in the case of hemophilia. Moreover, most researchers are skeptical that such a complex ability as spatial reasoning could possibly rest in a single gene.

Many researchers are thus beginning to suspect that the male superiority is the product of a combination of factors—genetic, hormonal and cultural—with roots deep in humanity's hunting-gathering past.

Nature vs. nurture

Separating out those various factors is a daunting task. One promising approach is to study sex differences as they develop, rather than merely focusing on aptitude-test scores. Among the recent findings:

■ Females are more attracted to people and males to objects.

Numerous studies show that girl infants between 5 and 6 months detect differences in photographs of human faces, while males of the same age do not. In addition, writes psychologist Diane McGuinness, studies on very young infants show that "females smile and vocalize only to faces, whereas males are just as likely to smile and vocalize to inanimate objects and blinking lights." McGuinness concludes that there probably is a biological predisposition in females to caretaking behavior that is later reinforced by observing adults.

■ Boys have a shorter attention span.

McGuinness has conducted a series of studies of sex differences in preschool children. Her results are intriguing: In a given 20-minute interval, boys did an average of 4.5 different activities, while girls concentrated on 2.5. Girls started and finished more projects than the boys. Boys were more distractible, interrupting their play to look at something else almost four times as often as girls—and they also spent more time in general watching other kids. Why the difference? "Maybe boys are just more visually oriented, and they learn by watching," McGuinness suggests.

■ Boys and girls differ in their approach to moral problems.

The pioneering work in the study of moral development was carried out 20 years ago by Harvard psychologist Law-

---

Are males better at math? Try it yourself

Tests of cognitive ability have long shown a male edge in mathematics and visual-spatial skills and a female advantage in work needing verbal aptitude

Mathematical

A kindergarten class wants to buy a $77 tropical tree for the school. If the teacher agrees to pay twice as much as the class and the administration promises to pay four times as much as the class, how much should the teacher pay?

(A) $11.00   (C) $22.00
(B) $15.40   (D) $25.70
                (E) $38.50

Answer: C

If x, y and z are three positive whole numbers and $x > y > z$, then, of the following, which is closest to the product xyz?

(A) (x-1)yz   (C) xy(z-1)
(B) x(y-1)z   (D) x(y+1)z
                 (E) xy(z+1)

Answer: A

Boys and girls do about equally well at arithmetic-problem solving. But when it comes to higher mathematics, boys have long shown a distinct advantage on average—even over girls who have taken comparable courses.

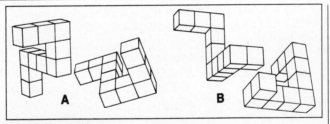

Spatial-visual

Can these pairs of three-dimensional objects be superimposed by rotation?

Answers: A yes; B yes

Males consistently outscore females in spatial-visual-abilities tests. At a young age, they are better on mazes; later, they show particular talent on exercises requiring mental manipulation of three-dimensional "objects" like those in the drawing above. The average 12-year-old boy knows that the water level remains horizontal in both glasses, but about half of college women get the answer wrong.

Assume that these glasses are half filled with water. Draw a line to indicate the top of the waterline in each.

Verbal

Five girls are sitting side by side on a bench. Jane is in the middle, and Betty sits next to her on the right. Alice is beside Betty, and Dale is beside Ellen, who sits next to Jane. Who are sitting on the ends?

Answer: Dale and Alice

Mark the "word" that *best* fills the blank:

A gelish lob relled perfully.

I grolled the _____ meglessly.

(A) gelish (B) lob (C) relled (D) perfully

Answer: B

During early adolescence, girls begin to outperform boys on tests of verbal ability, including questions designed to measure their understanding of logical relationships. The female edge persists into adulthood.

Sources: *Bias in Mental Testing*, by Arthur R. Jensen (the Free Press); *The Psychology of Sex Differences*, by Eleanor Emmons Maccoby and Carol Nagy Jacklin (Stanford University Press); *Sex Differences in Cognitive Abilities*, by Diane F. Halpern (Lawrence Erlbaum Associates); College Entrance Examination Board

rence Kohlberg. But as one of his former students, Carol Gilligan, notes, Kohlberg's research seemed to assume that "females simply do not exist": He studied 44 boys over 20 years, but no girls.

Gilligan has retraced some of Kohlberg's steps, including girls this time, and found some highly interesting differences between the sexes. One example: Gilligan posed one of the "moral dilemmas" Kohlberg used in his studies to a boy and a girl, both 11 years old. The dilemma involves the case of "Heinz," who faces the choice of stealing a drug his wife needs to stay alive but which he cannot afford, or obeying the law and letting her die. Jake, the boy, thought Heinz should steal the drug because a life is worth more than property. Amy, the girl, argued that the problem was more complicated: "I think there might be other ways besides stealing it, like if he could borrow the money or make a loan or something. If he stole the drug, he might save his wife then, but if he did, he might have to go to jail, and then his wife might get sicker again and he couldn't get more of the drug."

In Gilligan's analysis, Amy sees the moral problem in terms of "a narrative of relationships that extend over time." Jake, by contrast, sees a "math problem."

Even a few years ago, research on sex differences still met enormous resistance from feminists and others who believed that merely posing the question was unscientific at best, politically inspired at worst. Diane McGuinness recalls the rejection she received once from a scientific journal when she submitted a paper on cognitive processes in males and females. One of the scientific referees who reviewed the paper wrote: "The author *purports* to find sex differences. Who cares!"

That attitude is beginning to change. "As time passes, people are less frightened and less rigid," says Grace Baruch, associate director of the Center for Research on Women at Wellesley College. Scholars are finding that a focus on "female" psychology and behavior can add much to a body of knowledge built almost exclusively upon studies of males. And new statistical techniques have also made the investigation of sex differences more reliable.

The new wave of results has even made converts of researchers who were skeptical that sex differences existed. "I've had to revise my view considerably," confesses Purdue University social psychologist Alice Eagly. Still, she adds, "the public needs to be warned that knowing a person's sex doesn't allow you to predict much of anything about him or her." The overlap between men and women is still much greater than their average differences. There are males who

are every bit as adept at verbal skills as even the best females—and women who are better at math than most men.

ATTITUDE

In politics and management, the "gender gap" is real

There is one difference between the sexes on which virtually every expert and study agree: Men are more aggressive than women. It shows up in 2-year-olds. It continues through school days and persists into adulthood. It is even constant across cultures. And there is little doubt that it is rooted in biology—in the male sex hormone testosterone.

If there's a feminine trait that's the counterpart of male aggressiveness, it's what social scientists awkwardly refer to as "nurturance." Feminists have argued that the nurturing nature of women is not biological in origin, but rather has been drummed into women by a society that wanted to keep them in the home. But the signs that it is at least partly inborn are too numerous to ignore. Just as tiny infant girls respond more readily to human faces, female toddlers learn much faster than males how to pick up nonverbal cues from others. And grown women are far more adept than men at interpreting facial expressions: A recent study by University of Pennsylvania brain researcher Ruben Gur showed that they easily read emotions such as anger, sadness and fear. The only such emotion men could pick up was disgust.

What difference do such differences make in the real world? Among other things, women appear to be somewhat less competitive—or at least competitive in different ways—than men. At the Harvard Law School, for instance, female students enter with credentials just as outstanding as those of their male peers. But they don't qualify for the prestigious *Law Review* in proportionate

---

A DIFFERENCE OF OPINION

Percentage-point margins by which women adopt these positions more than men. (Negative numbers indicate men agree more than women.)

	1964-71	1972-76	1977-83	1984-88
Oppose–				
Use of force	12.2%	8.3%	8.4%	9.0%
Strong defense	7.2%	5.7%	5.9%	1.1%
Support–				
Spending on social programs	3.2%	2.2%	4.1%	3.6%
Government regulation	3.0%	4.9%	7.2%	-1.1%
Traditional values	-0.9%	2.2%	3.6%	5.4%
Women's rights	-3.6%	-2.1%	-2.3%	-3.7%

USN&WR–Basic data: Study by Robert Y. Shapiro and Harpreet Mahajan and Roper Center for Public Opinion Research at Univ. of Connecticut

Gender gap in action

Share of men and women surveyed who would vote for–

■ Bush   ▦ Dukakis

Women: 34% / 58%   Men: 40% / 50%

USN&WR–Basic data: Gallup Poll on July 22-24, 1988, of 1,001 registered voters

Share of men and women surveyed who feel the following descriptions apply to Bush or Dukakis–

Strong leader
Women: 43% / 57%   Men: 50% / 52%

Cares about people
Women: 51% / 70%   Men: 50% / 68%

Has a vision for the future
Women: 59% / 72%   Men: 63% / 66%

CHART BY SARAH SHAW—USN&WR

USN&WR–Basic data: *Washington Post*-ABC News Poll May 19-25, 1988, of 1,172 registered voters

numbers, a fact some school officials attribute to women's discomfort in the incredibly competitive atmosphere.

Students of management styles have found fewer differences than they expected between men and women who reach leadership positions, perhaps because many successful women deliberately imitate masculine ways. But an analysis by Purdue social psychologist Alice Eagly of 166 studies of leadership style did find one consistent difference: Men tend to be more "autocratic"—making decisions on their own—while women tend to consult colleagues and subordinates more often.

Studies of behavior in small groups turn up even more differences. Men will typically dominate the discussion, says University of Toronto psychologist Kenneth Dion, spending more time talking and less time listening.

Political fallout

The aggression-nurturance gulf even shows up in politics. The "gender gap" in polling is real and enduring: Men are far more prone to support a strong defense and tough law-and-order measures such as capital punishment, for instance, while women are more likely to approve of higher spending to solve domestic social problems such as poverty and inequality. Interestingly, there is virtually no gender gap on "women's issues," such as abortion and day care; in fact, men support them slightly *more* than women.

That fact might serve as a lesson in this year's election campaign. Alarmed at George Bush's low marks among women, his strategists have aimed their candidate directly at the "women's issues." It may be the wrong tactic. A close look at recent polls suggests that it's not the specifics of his programs, but a far bigger problem—his weak image in terms of strength, compassion and vision—that bothers women voters about Bush. And there's a political foot-note to the differences between the sexes in the Democratic camp. Veteran strategist Kirk O'Donnell, a top adviser to Michael Dukakis, says flatly that his is one of the best campaign organizations he has ever observed—with a remarkable lack of intramural squabbling, which O'Donnell attributes squarely to the unusually high number of women in senior positions.

Applied to the female of the species, the word "different" has, for centuries, been read to mean "inferior." At last, that is beginning to change. And in the end, of course, it's not a question of better or worse. The obvious point—long lost in a miasma of ideology—is that each sex brings strengths and weaknesses that may check and balance the other; each is half of the human whole.

---

by Merrill McLoughlin with Tracy L. Shryer, Erica E. Goode and Kathleen McAuliffe

Erik Erikson's Eight Ages of Man

*One man in his time plays
many psychosocial parts*

David Elkind

DAVID ELKIND *is professor of psychology and psychiatry at the
University of Rochester.*

At a recent faculty reception I happened to join a small group in which a young mother was talking about her "identity crisis." She and her husband, she said, had decided not to have any more children and she was depressed at the thought of being past the child-bearing stage. It was as if, she continued, she had been robbed of some part of herself and now needed to find a new function to replace the old one.

When I remarked that her story sounded like a case history from a book by Erik Erikson, she replied, "Who's Erikson?" It is a reflection on the intellectual modesty and literary decorum of Erik H. Erikson, psychoanalyst and professor of developmental psychology at Harvard, that so

few of the many people who today talk about the "identity crisis" know anthing of the man who pointed out its pervasiveness as a problem in contemporary society two decades ago.

Erikson has, however, contributed more to social science than his delineation of identity problems in modern man. His descriptions of the stages of the life cycle, for example, have advanced psychoanalytic theory to the point where it can now describe the development of the healthy personality on its own terms and not merely as the opposite of a sick one. Likewise, Erikson's emphasis upon the problems unique to adolescents and adults living in today's society has helped to rectify the one-sided emphasis on childhood as the beginning and end of personality development.

Finally, in his biographical studies, such as "Young Man Luther" and "Gandhi's Truth" (which has just won a

National Book Award in philosophy and religion), Erikson emphasizes the inherent strengths of the human personality by showing how individuals can use their neurotic symptoms and conflicts for creative and constructive social purposes while healing themselves in the process.

It is important to emphasize that Erikson's contributions are genuine advances in psychoanalysis in the sense that Erikson accepts and builds upon many of the basic tenets of Freudian theory. In this regard, Erikson differs from Freud's early co-workers such as Jung and Adler who, when they broke with Freud, rejected his theories and substituted their own.

Likewise, Erikson also differs from the so-called neo-Freudians such as Horney, Kardiner and Sullivan who (mistakenly, as it turned out) assumed that Freudian theory had nothing to say about man's relation to reality and to his culture. While it is true that Freud emphasized, even mythologized, sexuality, he did so to counteract the rigid sexual taboos of his time, which, at that point in history, were frequently the cause of neuroses. In his later writings, however, Freud began to concern himself with the executive agency of the personality, namely the ego, which is also the repository of the individual's attitudes and concepts about himself and his world.

It is with the psychosocial development of the ego that Erikson's observations and theoretical constructions are primarily concerned. Erikson has thus been able to introduce innovations into psychoanalytic theory without either rejecting or ignoring Freud's monumental contribution.

The man who has accomplished this notable feat is a handsome Dane, whose white hair, mustache, resonant accent and gentle manner are reminiscent of actors like Jean Hersholt and Paul Muni. Although he is warm and outgoing with friends, Erikson is a rather shy man who is uncomfortable in the spotlight of public recognition. This trait, together with his ethical reservations about making public even disguised case material, may help to account for Erikson's reluctance to publish his observations and conceptions (his first book appeared in 1950, when he was 48).

In recent years this reluctance to publish has diminished and he has been appearing in print at an increasing pace. Since 1960 he has published three books, "Insight and Responsibility," "Identity: Youth and Crisis" and "Gandhi's Truth," as well as editing a fourth, "Youth: Change ·and Challenge." Despite the accolades and recognition these books have won for him, both in America and abroad, Erikson is still surprised at the popular interest they have generated and is a little troubled about the possibility of being misunderstood and misinterpreted. While he would prefer that his books spoke for themselves and that he was left out of the picture, he has had to accede to popular demand for more information about himself and his work.

The course of Erikson's professional career has been as diverse as it has been unconventional. He was born in Frankfurt, Germany, in 1902 of Danish parents. Not long after his birth his father died, and his mother later married the pediatrician who had cured her son of a childhood illness. Erikson's stepfather urged him to become a physician, but the boy declined and became an artist instead—an artist who did portraits of children. Erikson says of his post-adolescent years, "I was an artist then, which in Europe is a euphemism for a young man with some talent and nowhere to go." During this period he settled in Vienna and worked as a tutor in a family friendly with Freud's. He met Freud on informal occasions when the families went on outings together.

These encounters may have been the impetus to accept a teaching appointment at an American school in Vienna founded by Dorothy Burlingham and directed by Peter Blos (both now well known on the American psychiatric scene). During these years (the late nineteen-twenties) he also undertook and completed psychoanalytic training with Anna Freud and August Aichhorn. Even at the outset of his career, Erikson gave evidence of the breadth of his interests and activities by being trained and certified as a Montessori teacher. Not surprisingly, in view of that training, Erikson's first articles dealt with psychoanalysis and education.

It was while in Vienna that Erikson met and married Joan Mowat Serson, an American artist of Canadian descent. They came to America in 1933, when Erikson was invited to practice and teach in Boston. Erikson was, in fact, one of the first if not the first child-analyst in the Boston area. During the next two decades he held clinical and academic appointments at Harvard, Yale and Berkeley. In 1951 he joined a group of psychiatrists and psychologists who moved to Stockbridge, Mass., to start a new program at the Austen Riggs Center, a private residential treatment center for disturbed young people. Erikson remained at Riggs until 1961, when he was appointed professor of human development and lecturer on psychiatry at Harvard. Throughout his career he has always held two or three appointments simultaneously and has traveled extensively.

Perhaps because he had been an artist first, Erikson has never been a conventional psychoanalyst. When he was treating children, for example, he always insisted on visiting his young patients' homes and on having dinner with the families. Likewise in the nineteen-thirties, when anthropological investigation was described to him by his friends Scudder McKeel, Alfred Kroeber and Margaret Mead, he decided to do field work on an Indian reservation. "When I realized that Sioux is the name which we [in Europe] pronounced "See us" and which for us was *the* American Indian, I could not resist." Erikson thus antedated the anthropologists who swept over the Indian reservations in the post-Depression years. (So numerous were the field workers at that time that the stock joke was that an Indian family could be defined as a mother, a father, children and an anthropologist.)

Erikson did field work not only with the Oglala Sioux of Pine Ridge, S. D. (the tribe that slew Custer and was in turn slaughtered at the Battle of Wounded Knee), but also with the salmon-fishing Yurok of Northern California. His reports on these experiences revealed his special gift for sensing and entering into the world views and modes of thinking of cultures other than his own.

It was while he was working with the Indians that Erikson began to note syndromes which he could not explain within the confines of traditional psychoanalytic theory. Central to many an adult Indian's emotional problems seemed to be his sense of uprootedness and lack of continuity between his present life-style and that portrayed in tribal history. Not only did the Indian sense a break with the past, but he could not identify with a future requiring assimilation of the white culture's values. The problems faced by such men, Erikson recognized, had to do with the ego and with culture and only incidentally with sexual drives.

The impressions Erikson gained on the reservations were reinforced during World War II when he worked at a veterans' rehabilitation center at Mount Zion Hospital in San Francisco. Many of the soldiers he and his colleagues saw seemed not to fit the traditional "shell shock" or "malingerer" cases of World War I. Rather, it seemed to Erikson that many of these men had lost the sense of who and what they were. They were having trouble reconciling their activities, attitudes and feelings as soldiers with the activities, attitudes and feelings they had known before the war. Accordingly, while these men may well have had difficulties with repressed or conflicted drives, their main problem seemed to be, as Erikson came to speak of it at the time, "identity confusion."

It was almost a decade before Erikson set forth the implications of his clinical observations in "Childhood and Society." In that book, the summation and integration of 15 years of research, he made three major contributions to the study of the human ego. He posited (1) that, side by side with the stages of psychosexual development described by Freud (the oral, anal, phallic, genital, Oedipal and pubertal), were psychosocial stages of ego development, in which the individual had to establish new basic orientations to himself and his social world; (2) that personality development continued throughout the whole life cycle; and (3) that each stage had a positive *as well* as a negative component.

Much about these contributions—and about Erikson's way of thinking—can be understood by looking at his scheme of life stages. Erikson identifies eight stages in the human life cycle, in each of which a new dimension of "social interaction" becomes possible—that is, a new dimension in a person's interaction with himself, and with his social environment.

TRUST vs. MISTRUST

The first stage corresponds to the oral stage in classical psychoanalytic theory and usually extends through the first year of life. In Erikson's view, the new dimension of social interaction that emerges during this period involves basic *trust* at the one extreme, and *mistrust* at the other. The degree to which the child comes to trust the world, other people and himself depends to a considerable extent upon the quality of the care that he receives. The infant whose needs are met when they arise, whose discomforts are quickly removed, who is cuddled, fondled, played with and talked to, develops a sense of the world as a safe place to be and of people as helpful and dependable. When, however, the care is inconsistent, inadequate and rejecting, it fosters a basic mistrust, an attitude of fear and

suspicion on the part of the infant toward the world in general and people in particular that will carry through to later stages of development.

It should be said at this point that the problem of basic trust-versus-mistrust (as is true for all the later dimensions) is not resolved once and for all during the first year of life; it arises again at each successive stage of development. There is both hope and danger in this. The child who enters school with a sense of mistrust may come to trust a particular teacher who has taken the trouble to make herself trustworthy; with this second chance, he overcomes his early mistrust. On the other hand, the child who comes through infancy with a vital sense of trust can still have his sense of mistrust activated at a later stage if, say, his parents are divorced and separated under acrimonious circumstances.

This point was brought home to me in a very direct way by a 4-year-old patient I saw in a court clinic. He was being seen at the court clinic because his adoptive parents, who had had him for six months, now wanted to give him back to the agency. They claimed that he was cold and unloving, took things and could not be trusted. He was indeed a cold and apathetic boy, but with good reason. About a year after his illegitimate birth, he was taken away from his mother, who had a drinking problem, and was shunted back and forth among several foster homes. Initially he had tried to relate to the persons in the foster homes, but the relationships never had a chance to develop becuase he was moved at just the wrong times. In the end he gave up trying to reach out to others, because the inevitable separations hurt too much.

Like the burned child who dreads the flame, this emotionally burned child shunned the pain of emotional involvement. He had trusted his mother, but now he trusted no one. Only years of devoted care and patience could now undo the damage that had been done to this child's sense of trust.

AUTONOMY vs. DOUBT

Stage Two spans the second and third years of life, the period which Freudian theory calls the anal stage. Erikson sees here the emergence of *autonomy*. This autonomy dimension builds upon the child's new motor and mental abilities. At this stage the child can not only walk but also climb, open and close, drop, push and pull, hold and let go. The child takes pride in these new accomplishments and wants to do everything himself, whether it be pulling the wrapper off a piece of candy, selecting the vitamin out of the bottle or flushing the toilet. If parents recognize the young child's need to do what he is capable of doing at his own pace and in his own time, then he develops a sense that he is able to control his muscles, his impulses, himself and, not insignificantly, his environment—the sense of autonomy.

When, however, his caretakers are impatient and do for him what he is capable of doing himself, they reinforce a sense of shame and doubt. To be sure, every parent has rushed a child at times and children are hardy enough to endure such lapses. It is only when caretaking is consistently overprotective and criticism of "accidents" (whether these be wetting, soiling, spilling or breaking things) is harsh and unthinking that the child develops an excessive sense of shame with respect to other people and an excessive sense of doubt about own abilities to control his world and himself.

If the child leaves this stage with less autonomy than shame or doubt, he will be handicapped in his attempts to achieve autonomy in adolescence and adulthood. Contrariwise, the child who moves through this stage with his sense of autonomy buoyantly outbalancing his feelings of shame and doubt is well prepared to be autonomous at later phases in the life cycle. Again, however, the balance of autonomy to shame and doubt set up during this period can be changed in either positive or negative directions by later events.

It might be well to note, in addition, that too much autonomy can be as harmful as too little. I have in mind a patient of 7 who had a heart condition. He had learned very quickly how terrified his parents were of any signs in him of cardiac difficulty. With the psychological acuity given to children, he soon ruled the household. The family could not go shopping, or for a drive, or on a holiday if he did not approve. On those rare occasions when the parents had had enough and defied him, he would get angry and his purple hue and gagging would frighten them into submission.

Actually, this boy was frightened of this power (as all children would be) and was really eager to give it up. When the parents and the boy came to realize this, and to recognize that a little shame and doubt were a healthy counterpoise to an inflated sense of autonomy, the three of them could once again assume their normal roles.

INITIATIVE vs. GUILT

In this stage (the genital stage of classical psychoanalysis) the child, age 4 to 5, is pretty much master of his body and can ride a tricycle, run, cut and hit. He can thus initiate motor activities of various sorts on his own and no longer merely responds to or imitates the actions of other children. The same holds true for his language and fantasy activities. Accordingly, Erikson argues that the social dimension that appears at this stage has *initiative* at one of its poles and *guilt* at the other.

Whether the child will leave this stage with his sense of initiative far outbalancing his sense of guilt depends to a considerable extent upon how parents respond to his self-initiated activities. Children who are given much freedom and opportunity to initiate motor play such as running, bike riding, sliding, skating, tussling and wrestling have their sense of initiative reinforced. Initiative is also reinforced when parents answer their children's questions (intellectual initiative) and do not deride or inhibit fantasy or play activity. On the other hand, if the child is made to feel that his motor activity is bad, that his questions are a nuisance and that his play is silly and stupid, then he may develop a sense of guilt over self-initiated activities in general that will persist through later life stages.

INDUSTRY vs. INFERIORITY

Stage Four is the age period from 6 to 11, the elementary school years (described by classical psychoanalysis as the *latency phase*). It is a time during which the child's love for the parent of the opposite sex and rivalry with the same sexed parent (elements in the so-called family romance) are quiescent. It is also a period during which the child becomes capable of deductive reasoning, and of playing and learning by rules. It is not until this period, for example, that children can really play marbles, checkers and other "take turn" games that require obedience to rules. Erikson argues that the psychosocial dimension that emerges during this period has a sense of *industry* at one extreme and a sense of *inferiority* at the other.

The term industry nicely captures a dominant theme of this period during which the concern with how things are made, how they work and what they do predominates. It is the Robinson Crusoe age in the sense that the enthusiasm and minute detail with which Crusoe describes his activities appeals to the child's own budding sense of industry. When children are encouraged in their efforts to make, do, or build practical things (whether it be to construct creepy crawlers, tree houses, or airplane models—or to cook, bake or sew), are allowed to finish their products, and are praised and rewarded for the results, then the sense of industry is enhanced. But parents who see their children's efforts at making and doing as "mischief," and as simply "making a mess," help to encourage in children a sense of inferiority.

During these elementary-school years, however, the child's world includes more than the home. Now social institutions other than the family come to play a central role in the developmental crisis of the individual. (Here Erikson introduced still another advance in psychoanalytic theory, which heretofore concerned itself only with the effects of the parents' behavior upon the child's development.)

A child's school experiences affect his industry-inferiority balance. The child, for example, with an I.Q. of 80 to 90 has a particularly traumatic school experience, even when his sense of industry is rewarded and encouraged at home. He is "too bright" to be in special classes, but "too slow" to compete with children of average ability. Consequently he experiences constant failures in his academic efforts that reinforces a sense of inferiority.

On the other hand, the child who had his sense of industry derogated at home can have it revitalized at school through the offices of a sensitive and committed teacher. Whether the child develops a sense of industry or inferiority, therefore, no longer depends solely on the caretaking efforts of the parents but on the actions and offices of other adults as well.

IDENTITY vs. ROLE CONFUSION

When the child moves into adolescence (Stage Five— roughly the ages 12-18), he encounters, according to traditional psychoanalytic theory, a reawakening of the family-romance problem of early childhood. His means of resolving the problem is to seek and find a romantic partner of his own generation. While Erikson does not deny this aspect of adolescence, he points out that there are other problems as well. The adolescent matures mentally as well as physio-logically and, in addition to the new feelings, sensations and desires he experiences as a result of changes in his body, he develops a multitude of new ways of looking at and thinking about the world. Among other things, those in adolescence can now think about other people's thinking and wonder about what other people think of them. They can also conceive of ideal families, religions and societies which they then compare with the imperfect families, religions and societies of their own experience. Finally, adolescents become capable of constructing theories ahd philosophies designed to bring all the varied and conflicting aspects of society into a working, harmonious and peaceful whole. The adolescent, in a word, is an impatient idealist who believes that it is as easy to realize an ideal as it is to imagine it.

Erikson believes that the new interpersonal dimension which emerges during this period has to do with a sense of *ego identity* at the positive end and a sense of *role confusion* at the negative end. That is to say, given the adolescent's newfound integrative abilities, his task is to bring together all of the things he has learned about himself as a son, student, athlete, friend, Scout, newspaper boy, and so on, and integrate these different images of himself into a whole that makes sense and that shows continuity with the past while preparing for the future. To the extent that the young person succeeds in this endeavor, he arrives at a sense of psychosocial identity, a sense of who he is, where he has been and where he is going.

In contrast to the earlier stages, where parents play a more or less direct role in the determination of the result of the developmental crises, the influence of parents during this stage is much more indirect. If the young person reaches adolescence with, thanks to his parents, a vital sense of trust, autonomy, initiative and industry, then his chances of arriving at a meaningful sense of ego identity are much enhanced. The reverse, of course, holds true for the young person who enters adolescence with considerable mistrust, shame, doubt, guilt and inferiority. Preparation for a successful adolescence, and the attainment of an integrated psychosocial identity must, therefore, begin in the cradle.

Over and above what the individual brings with him from his childhood, the attainment of a sense of personal identity depends upon the social milieu in which he or she grows up. For example, in a society where women are to some extent second-class citizens, it may be harder for females to arrive at a sense of psychosocial identity. Likewise at times, such as the present, when rapid social and technological change breaks down many traditional values, it may be more difficult for young people to find continuity between what they learned and experienced as children and what they learn and experience as adolescents. At such times young people often seek causes that give their lives meaning and direction. The activism of the current generation of young people may well stem, in part at least, from this search.

When the young person cannot attain a sense of personal identity, either because of an unfortunate childhood or difficult social circumstances, he shows a certain amount of *role confusion*—a sense of not knowing what he is, where he belongs or whom he belongs to. Such confusion is a frequent symptom in delinquent young people. Promiscuous adolescent girls, for example, often seem to have a fragmented sense of ego identity. Some young people seek a "negative identity," an identity opposite to the one prescribed for them by their family and friends. Having an identity as a "delinquent," or as a "hippie," or even as an "acid head," may sometimes be preferable to having no identity at all.

In some cases young people do not seek a negative identity so much as they have it thrust upon them. I remember another court case in which the defendant was an attractive 16-year-old girl who had been found "tricking it" in a trailer located just outside the grounds of an Air Force base. From about the age of 12, her mother had encouraged her to dress seductively and to go out with boys. When she returned from dates, her sexually frustrated mother demanded a kiss-by-kiss, caress-by-caress description of the evening's activities. After the mother had vicariously satisfied her sexual needs, she proceeded to call her daughter a "whore" and a "dirty tramp." As the girl told me, "Hell, I have the name, so I might as well play the role."

Failure to establish a clear sense of personal identity at adolescence does not guarantee perpetual failure. And the person who attains a working sense of ego identity in adolescence will of necessity encounter challenges and threats to that identity as he moves through life. Erikson, perhaps more than any other personality theorist, has emphasized that life is constant change and that confronting problems at one stage in life is not a guarantee against the reappearance of these problems at later stages, or against the finding of new solutions to them.

INTIMACY vs. ISOLATION

Stage Six in the life cycle is young adulthood; roughly the period of courtship and early family life that extends from late adolescence till early middle age. For this stage, and the stages described hereafter, classical psychoanalysis has nothing new or major to say. For Erikson, however, the previous attainment of a sense of personal identity and the engagement in productive work that marks this period gives rise to a new interpersonal dimension of *intimacy* at the one extreme and *isolation* at the other.

When Erikson speaks of intimacy he means much more than love-making alone; he means the ability to share with and care about another person without fear of losing oneself in the process. In the case of intimacy, as in the case of identity, success or failure no longer depends directly upon the parents but only indirectly as they have contributed to the individual's success or failure at the earlier stages. Here, too, as in the case of identity, social conditions may help or hinder the establishment of a sense of intimacy. Likewise, intimacy need not involve sexuality; it includes the relationship between friends. Soldiers who have served together under the most dangerous circumstances often develop a sense of commitment to one another that exemplifies intimacy in its broadest sense. If a sense of intimacy is not established with friends or a marriage partner, the result, in Erikson's view, is a sense of isolation—of being alone without anyone to share with or care for.

GENERATIVITY vs. SELF-ABSORPTION

This stage—middle age—brings with it what Erikson speaks of as either *generativity or self-absorption*, and stagnation. What Erikson means by generativity is that the person begins to be concerned with others beyond his immediate family, with future generations and the nature of the society and world in which those generations will live. Generativity does not reside only in parents; it can be found in any individual who actively concerns himself with the welfare of young people and with making the world a better place for them to live and to work.

Those who fail to establish a sense of generativity fall into a state of self-absorption in which their personal needs and comforts are of predominant concern. A fictional case of self-absorption is Dickens's Scrooge in "A Christmas Carol." In his one-sided concern with money and in his disregard for the interests and welfare of his young employee, Bob Cratchit, Scrooge exemplifies the self-absorbed, embittered (the two often go together) old man. Dickens also illustrated, however, what Erikson points out: namely, that unhappy solutions to life's crises are not irreversible. Scrooge, at the end of the tale, manifested both a sense of generativity and of intimacy which he had not experienced before.

INTEGRITY vs. DESPAIR

Stage Eight in the Eriksonian scheme corresponds roughly to the period when the individual's major efforts are nearing completion and when there is time for reflection—and for the enjoyment of grandchildren, if any. The psychosocial dimension that comes into prominence now has *integrity* on one hand and *despair* on the other.

The sense of integrity arises from the individual's ability to look back on his life with satisfaction. At the other extreme is the individual who looks back upon his life as a series of missed opportunities and missed directions; now in the twilight years he realizes that it is too late to start again. For such a person the inevitable result is a sense of despair at what might have been.

These, then, are the major stages in the life cycle as described by Erikson. Their presentation, for one thing, frees the clinician to treat adult emotional problems as failures (in part at least) to solve genuinely adult personality crises and not, as heretofore, as mere residuals of infantile frustrations and conflicts. This view of personality growth, moreover, takes some of the onus off parents and takes account of the role which society and the person himself play in the formation of an individual personality. Finally, Erikson has offered hope for us all by demonstrating that each phase of growth has its strengths as well as its weaknesses and that failures at one stage of development can be rectified by successes at later stages.

The reason that these ideas, which sound so agreeable to "common sense," are in fact so revolutionary has a lot to do with the state of psychoanalysis in America. As formulated by Freud, psychoanalysis encompassed a theory of personality development, a method of studying the human mind and, finally, procedures for treating troubled and unhappy people. Freud viewed this system as a scientific one, open to revision as new facts and observations accumulated.

The system was, however, so vehemently attacked that Freud's followers were constantly in the position of having to defend Freud's views. Perhaps because of this situation, Freud's system became, in the hands of some of his followers

and defenders, a dogma upon which all theoretical innovation, clinical observation and therapeutic practice had to be grounded. That this attitude persists is evidenced in the recent remark by a psychoanalyst that he believed psychotic patients could not be treated by psychoanalysis because "Freud said so." Such attitudes, in which Freud's authority rather than observation and data is the basis of deciding what is true and what is false, has contributed to the disrepute in which psychoanalysis is widely held today.

Erik Erikson has broken out of this scholasticism and has had the courage to say that Freud's discoveries and practices were the start and not the end of the study and treatment of the human personality. In addition to advocating the modifications of psychoanalytic theory outlined above, Erikson has also suggested modifications in therapeutic practice, particularly in the treatment of young patients. "Young people in severe trouble are not fit for the couch," he writes. "They want to face you, and they want you to face them, not a facsimile of a parent, or wearing the mask of a professional helper, but as a kind of over-all individual a young person can live with or despair of."

Erikson has had the boldness to remark on some of the negative effects that distorted notions of psychoanalysis have had on society at large. Psychoanalysis, he says, has contributed to a widespread fatalism—"even as we were trying to devise, with scientific determinism, a therapy for the few, we were led to promote an ethical disease among the many."

Perhaps Erikson's innovations in psychoanalytic theory are best exemplified in his psycho-historical writings, in which he combines psychoanalytic insight with a true historical imagination. After the publication of "Childhood and Society," Erikson undertook the application of his scheme of the human life cycle to the study of historical persons. He wrote a series of brilliant essays on men as varied as Maxim Gorky, George Bernard Shaw and Freud himself. These studies were not narrow case histories but rather reflected Erikson's remarkable grasp of Europe's social and political history, as well as of its literature. (His mastery of American folklore, history and literature is equally remarkable.)

While Erikson's major biographical studies were yet to come, these early essays already revealed his unique psycho-history method. For one thing, Erikson always chose men whose lives fascinated him in one way or another, perhaps because of some conscious or unconscious affinity with them. Erikson thus had a sense of community with his subjects which he adroitly used (he calls it *disciplined subjectivity)* to take his subject's point of view and to experience the world as that person might.

Secondly, Erikson chose to elaborate a particular crisis or episode in the individual's life which seemed to crystallize a life-theme that united the activities of his past and gave direction to his activities for the future. Then, much as an artist might, Erikson proceeded to fill in the background of the episode and add social and historical perspective. In a very real sense Erikson's biographical sketches are like paintings which direct the viewer's gaze from a focal point of attention to background and back again, so that one's appreciation of the focal area is enriched by having pursued the picture in its entirety.

This method was given its first major test in Erikson's study

Erikson in a seminar at his Stockbridge, Mass., home.

"Young analysts are today proclaiming a 'new freedom' to see Freud in historical perspective, which reflects the Eriksonian view that one can recognize Freud's greatness without bowing to conceptual precedent."

of "Young Man Luther." Originally, Erikson planned only a brief study of Luther, but "Luther proved too bulky a man to be merely a chapter in a book." Erikson's involvement with Luther dated from his youth, when, as a wandering artist, he happened to hear the Lord's Prayer in Luther's German. "Never knowingly having heard it, I had the experience, as seldom before or after, of a wholeness captured in a few simple words, of poetry fusing the esthetic and the moral; those who have suddenly 'heard' the Gettysburg Address will know what I mean."

Erikson's interest in Luther may have had other roots as well. In some ways, Luther's unhappiness with the papal intermediaries of Christianity resembled on a grand scale Erikson's own dissatisfaction with the intermediaries of Freud's system. In both cases some of the intermediaries had so distorted the original teachings that what was being preached in the name of the master came close to being the opposite of what he had himself proclaimed. While it is not possible to describe Erikson's treatment of Luther here, one can get some feeling for Erikson's brand of historical analysis from his sketch of Luther:

"Luther was a very troubled and a very gifted young man who had to create his own cause on which to focus his fidelity in the Roman Catholic world as it was then. . . . He first became a monk and tried to solve his scruples by being an exceptionally good monk. But even his superiors thought that he tried much too hard. He felt himself to be such a sinner that he began to lose faith in the charity of God and his superiors told him, 'Look, God doesn't hate you, you hate God or else you would trust Him to accept your prayers.' But I would like to make it clear that someone like Luther becomes a historical person only because he also has an acute understanding of historical actuality and knows how to 'speak to the condition' of his times. Only then do inner struggles become representative of those of a large number of vigorous and sincere young people—and begin to interest some troublemakers and hangers-on."

After Erikson's study of "Young Man Luther" (1958), he turned his attention to "middle-aged" Gandhi. As did Luther, Gandhi evoked for Erikson childhood memories. Gandhi led his first nonviolent protest in India in 1918 on behalf of some mill workers, and Erikson, then a young man of 16, had read glowing accounts of the event. Almost a half a century later Erikson was invited to Ahmedabad, an industrial city in western India, to give a seminar on the human life cycle. Erikson discovered that Ahmedabad was the city in which

Gandhi had led the demonstration about which Erikson had read as a youth. Indeed, Erikson's host was none other than Ambalal Sarabahai, the benevolent industrialist who had been Gandhi's host—as well as antagonist—in the 1918 wage dispute. Throughout his stay in Ahmedabad, Erikson continued to encounter people and places that were related to Gandhi's initial experiments with nonviolent techniques.

The more Erikson learned about the event at Ahmedabad, the more intrigued he became with its pivotal importance in Gandhi's career. It seemed to be the historical moment upon which all the earlier events of Gandhi's life converged and from which diverged all of his later endeavors. So captured was Erikson by the event at Ahmedabad, that he returned the following year to research a book on Gandhi in which the event would serve as a fulcrum.

At least part of Erikson's interest in Gandhi may have stemmed from certain parallels in their lives. The 1918 event marked Gandhi's emergence as a national political leader. He was 48 at the time, and had become involved reluctantly, not so much out of a need for power or fame as out of a genuine conviction that something had to be done about the disintegration of Indian culture. Coincidentally, Erikson's book "Childhood and Society," appeared in 1950 when Erikson was 48, and it is that book which brought him national prominence in the mental health field. Like Gandhi, too, Erikson reluctantly did what he felt he had to do (namely, publish his observations and conclusions) for the benefit of his ailing profession and for the patients treated by its practitioners. So while Erikson's affinity with Luther seemed to derive from comparable professional identity crises, his affinity for Gandhi appears to derive from a parallel crisis of generativity. A passage from "Gandhi's Truth" (from a chapter wherein Erikson addresses himself directly to his subject) helps to convey Erikson's feeling for his subject.

"So far, I have followed you through the loneliness of your childhood and through the experiments and the scruples of your youth. I have affirmed my belief in your ceaseless endeavor to perfect yourself as a man who came to feel that he was the only one available to reverse India's fate. You experimented with what to you were debilitating temptations and you did gain vigor and agility from your victories over yourself. Your identity could be no less than that of universal man, although you had to become an Indian—and one close to the masses—first."

The following passage speaks to Erikson's belief in the general significance of Gandhi's efforts:

"We have seen in Gandhi's development the strong attraction of one of those more inclusive identities: that of an enlightened citizen of the British Empire. In proving himself willing neither to abandon vital ties to his native tradition nor to sacrifice lightly a Western education which eventually contributed to his ability to help defeat British hegemony—in all of these seeming contradictions Gandhi showed himself on intimate terms with the actualities of his era. For in all parts of the world, the struggle now is for *the anticipatory development of more inclusive identities* . . . I submit then, that Gandhi, in his immense intuition for historical actuality and his capacity to assume leadership in 'truth in action,' may have created a ritualization through which men, equipped with both realism and strength, can face each other with mutual confidence."

There is now more and more teaching of Erikson's concepts in psychiatry, psychology, education and social work in America and in other parts of the world. His description of the stages of the life cycle are summarized in major textbooks in all of these fields and clinicians are increasingly looking at their cases in Eriksonian terms.

Research investigators have, however, found Erikson's formulations somewhat difficult to test. This is not surprising, inasmuch as Erikson's conceptions, like Freud's, take into account the infinite complexity of the human personality. Current research methodologies are, by and large, still not able to deal with these complexities at their own level, and distortions are inevitable when such concepts as "identity" come to be defined in terms of responses to a questionnaire.

Likewise, although Erikson's life-stages have an intuitive "rightness" about them, not everyone agrees with his

Freud's "Ages of Man"

Erik Erikson's definition of the "eight ages of man" is a work of synthesis and insight by a psychoanalytically trained and worldly mind. Sigmund Freud's description of human phases stems from his epic psychological discoveries and centers almost exclusively on the early years of life. A brief summary of the phases posited by Freud:

Oral stage—roughly the first year of life, the period during which the mouth region provides the greatest sensual satisfaction. Some derivative behavioral traits which may be seen at this time are *incorporativeness* (first six months of life) and *aggressiveness* (second six months of life).

Anal stage—roughly the second and third years of life. During this period the site of greatest sensual pleasure shifts to the anal and urethral areas. Derivative behavioral traits are *retentiveness* and *expulsiveness*.

Phallic stage—roughly the third and fourth years of life. The site of greatest sensual pleasure during this stage is the genital region. Behavior traits derived from this period include *intrusiveness* (male) and *receptiveness* (female).

Oedipal stage—roughly the fourth and fifth years of life. At this stage the young person takes the parent of the opposite sex as the object or provider of sensual satisfaction and regards the same-sexed parent as a rival. (The "family romance.") Behavior traits originating in this period are *seductiveness* and *competitiveness*.

Latency stage—roughly the years from age 6 to 11. The child resolves the Oedipus conflict by identifying with the parent of the opposite sex and by so doing satisfies sensual needs vicariously. Behavior traits developed during this period include *conscience* (or the internalization of parental moral and ethical demands).

Puberty stage—roughly 11 to 14. During this period there is an integration and subordination of oral, anal and phallic sensuality to an overriding and unitary genital *sexuality*. The genital sexuality of puberty has another young person of the opposite sex as its object, and discharge (at least for boys) as its aim. Derivative behavior traits (associated with the control and regulation of genital sexuality) are *intellectualization* and *estheticism*.

—D.E.

formulations. Douvan and Adelson in their book, "The Adolescent Experience," argue that while his identity theory may hold true for boys, it doesn't for girls. This argument is based on findings which suggest that girls postpone identity consolidation until after marriage (and intimacy) have been established. Such postponement occurs, says Douvan and Adelson, because a woman's identity is partially defined by the identity of the man whom she marries. This view does not really contradict Erikson's, since he recognizes that later events, such as marriage, can help to resolve both current and past developmental crises. For the woman, but not for the man, the problems of identity and intimacy may be solved concurrently.

Objections to Erikson's formulations have come from other directions as well. Robert W. White, Erikson's good friend and colleague at Harvard, has a long standing (and warm-hearted) debate with Erikson over his life-stages. White believes that his own theory of "competence motivation," a theory which has received wide recognition, can account for the phenomena of ego development much more economically than can Erikson's stages. Erikson has, however, little interest in debating the validity of the stages he has described. As an artist he recognizes that there are many different ways to view one and the same phenomenon and that a perspective that is congenial to one person will be repugnant to another. He offers his stage-wise description of the life cycle for those who find such perspectives congenial and not as a world view that everyone should adopt.

It is this lack of dogmatism and sensitivity to the diversity and complexity of the human personality which help to account for the growing recognition of Erikson's contribution within as well as without the helping professions. Indeed, his psycho-historical investigations have originated a whole new field of study which has caught the interest of historians and political scientists alike. (It has also intrigued his wife, Joan, who has published pieces on Eleanor Roosevelt and who has a book on Saint Francis in press.) A recent issue of Daedalus, the journal for the American Academy of Arts and Sciences,

was entirely devoted to psycho-historical and psycho-political investigations of creative leaders by authors from diverse disciplines who have been stimulated by Erikson's work.

Now in his 68th year, Erikson maintains the pattern of multiple activities and appointments which has characterized his entire career. He spends the fall in Cambridge, Mass., where he teaches a large course on "the human life cycle" for Harvard seniors. The spring semester is spent at his home in Stockbridge, Mass., where he participates in case conferences and staff seminars at the Austen Riggs Center. His summers are spent on Cape Cod. Although Erikson's major commitment these days is to his psycho-historical investigation, he is embarking on a study of preschool children's play constructions in different settings and countries, a follow-up of some research he conducted with preadolescents more than a quarter-century ago. He is also planning to review other early observations in the light of contemporary change. In his approach to his work, Erikson appears neither drawn nor driven, but rather to be following an inner schedule as natural as the life cycle itself.

Although Erikson, during his decade of college teaching, has not seen any patients or taught at psychoanalytic institutes, he maintains his dedication to psychoanalysis and views his psycho-historical investigations as an applied branch of that discipline. While some older analysts continue to ignore Erikson's work, there is increasing evidence (including a recent poll of psychiatrists and psychoanalysts) that he is having a rejuvenating influence upon a discipline which many regard as dead or dying. Young analysts are today proclaiming a "new freedom" to see Freud in historical perspective—which reflects the Eriksonian view that one can recognize Freud's greatness without bowing to conceptual precedent.

Accordingly, the reports of the demise of psychoanalysis may have been somewhat premature. In the work of Erik Erikson, at any rate, psychoanalysis lives and continues to beget life.

Why We're Losing the War on Crime

**Michael Gottfredson
and Travis Hirschi**

President Bush's long-awaited national strategy to combat the drug problem puts great faith in the potential of conventional law-enforcement strategies and governmental intervention. The Democrats' response differs chiefly in degree, not in kind, with the high ground seeming to belong to those who would spend more.

But the hard-line programs proposed by the president—more prisons, more prosecutors, more hardware for the border patrol, more law enforcement officials, more drug testers—taken together, will have little impact on the crime rate or the drug problem.

The $8 billion earmarked by President Bush for the New War on Drugs would go atop the $44 billion already spent each year at all levels of government for police and prisons—along with tens of billions more for customs agents, judges, probation and parole officers.

Since the early '70s and the backlash against Great Society programs, everyone seems to agree that the key to crime and drug abuse is to be found in the criminal justice system—in the workings of the police, courts and prisons—and not in economic or social conditions. This consensus has powered the immense growth in law-enforcement organizations, anti-crime programs (e.g., drug testing, "career-criminal" units, mandatory sentencing), and the number of people in jails and prisons.

According to the federal Bureau of Justice Statistics, expenditures for criminal justice in the last few years have increased four times as rapidly as for education, and twice as rapidly as for health and hospitals. Since 1980, the number of adults behind bars has doubled. As of January, 627,000 adults were incarcerated in federal and state prisons. The latest figures show that 1 adult in 55 is under some form of correctional supervision.

But all the effort and money have not bought relief from crime. According to FBI figures, the crime rate peaked about 1980, declined for a few years, and then increased for the past four years. (The mild downturn of the early '80s resulted from the aging of baby-boomers. The peak age of incarceration comes a few years after the peak age of crime. [See illustration.] This fact, coupled with tougher sentencing policies, accounts for the increase in the numbers incarcerated.)

No one can substantiate the slightest reduction in drug use or the rate of crime as a consequence of increases in expenditures in the '80s, and there is no reason to think these failed government programs will now work simply because even more money is thrown their way. In fact, there are good reasons to believe otherwise. The latest scientific research on crime and drug use does not accord with the law-enforcement image of criminals and drug dealers as sophisticated, cunning, persistent and highly organized. Nor does it support the view that strengthening the crime-control apparatus is our only hope.

In fact, the research paints quite a different picture. Studies of the most common criminal events show that they are generally acts of force, fraud or mood enhancement in the pursuit of immediate self-interest. The typical burglary or robbery takes little effort, little time and little skill.

The typical burglar takes advantage of opportunities of the moment; he lives in the neighborhood and victimizes easy targets—such as houses with unlocked doors—carrying away whatever seems of value. The typical car thief finds a car with the keys in the ignition and drives until the gas tank is empty. The typical drug user is satisfied with whatever drug is available at a suitable price. Consequently, most lavish police operations involving costly high-tech hardware are irrelevant to reducing the number of typical crimes. Solid research studies show that most ordinary crimes can be prevented by the presence of even the most minor obstacles: locks on doors, keys taken out of ignitions, reduced late-night hours for convenience stores, and the like.

Nor do the crime data indicate that putting more cops on the street will decrease the frequency of offenses. Daily life presents practically limitless opportunities for crime or drug use. As a result, prevention by policing is nearly impossible. In fact, a growing body of research documents the negligible impact of police patrols in lowering the crime rate.

2. SOCIALIZATION AND BIOLOGY: Crime and Social Control

Moreover, it is becoming clear that criminals and drug abusers are also less complex and less driven than current policies suggest. Indeed, two facts about offenders are directly at odds with the assumptions found in law-enforcement policies. Unless these misconceptions are corrected, there is little hope for efficient and realistic crime policy.

RANDOM PATTERNS

The first fact is this: Offenders are extraordinarily versatile in their choice of criminal and deviant acts. That is, the same people who use drugs also steal cars, commit burglaries, assault and rob others and drive recklessly. Indeed, they are so versatile that knowing their prior offenses does not permit us to predict what crimes they will commit in the future. Despite decades

of study, criminologists have failed to discover meaningful numbers of criminal specialists—people who commit particular crimes to the exclusion of others.

For example, when researchers at the University of Pennsylvania followed to age 30 nearly 10,000 boys born in 1945, they discovered virtually no pattern or specialization in each individual's offenses recorded in police files.

The versatility of offenders goes beyond conventional crime categories to include alcohol abuse, spouse and child abuse, accidents, truancy from school and work, and sexual promiscuity. Research repeatedly shows that these behaviors are consistently found together in the same people. A celebrated study by Lee Robins at Washington University tracked over 500 children referred to a guidance clinic over the course of 30 years, comparing them with a control group. As

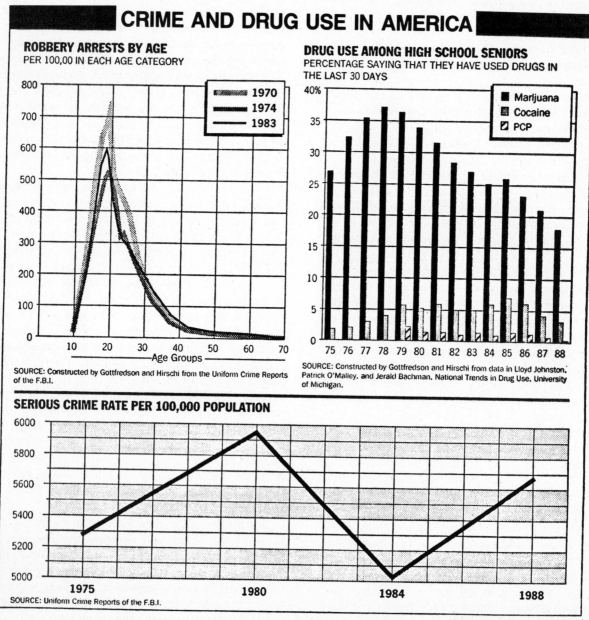

CRIME AND DRUG USE IN AMERICA

ROBBERY ARRESTS BY AGE
PER 100,00 IN EACH AGE CATEGORY

SOURCE: Constructed by Gottfredson and Hirschi from the Uniform Crime Reports of the F.B.I.

DRUG USE AMONG HIGH SCHOOL SENIORS
PERCENTAGE SAYING THAT THEY HAVE USED DRUGS IN THE LAST 30 DAYS

SOURCE: Constructed by Gottfredson and Hirschi from data in Lloyd Johnston, Patrick O'Malley, and Jerald Bachman, National Trends in Drug Use, University of Michigan.

SERIOUS CRIME RATE PER 100,000 POPULATION

SOURCE: Uniform Crime Reports of the F.B.I.

MICHAEL DREW FOR THE WASHINGTON POST

Getting Straight

Recent statistics from the National Institute of Drug Abuse—the same data cited repeatedly by William Bennett and President Bush—show that the rate of illegal drug use peaked in the late 1970s (at about the same time the overall crime rate peaked) and has since continuously declined.

Survey data show that the demand for drugs of all kinds—legal and illegal—is at its lowest point in many years. Americans are drinking less, smoking less and using fewer illicit drugs. Every year since the middle '70s, researchers at the University of Michigan have measured the recent use of a wide variety of drugs in a national sample of high school seniors, the age group at greatest risk. For the most part, drug use by these teen-agers peaked in the late 1970s and has declined substantially since then. The percentage reporting using marijuana in the previous month in 1988 was 18, half the percentage reporting such use in 1979. Hard drugs, too, are down. PCP use has declined from a rate of 24 per thousand in 1979 to 3 per thousand in 1988. The use of cocaine, the drug featured in the president's proposals, declined by 50 percent between 1985 and 1988, from 6.7 percent of seniors to 3.4 percent. And heavy smokers of cigarettes are only half as plentiful today as 10 years ago.

Nor are these trends confined to teen-agers: the Michigan data show the same results for marijuana and cocaine use among those aged 19–22.

Other surveys confirm the move away from drugs in American society. The National Restaurant Association reports that alcohol consumption in restaurants dropped 17 percent between 1980 and 1987. During the same period beer consumption was down by 7 percent, wine consumption by 14, and distilled spirits by 23.

While law-enforcement and political groups portray an ever-worsening crisis (predictably suggesting that drug gangs are spreading the epidemic to the suburbs, to rural areas and to previously unaffected groups), the facts suggest that America's drug problem is being blown out of proportion, that our fear of drugs is generated more by drug fighters than drug users.

The reason that both drug use and crime have declined from their peaks early in the decade has more to do with the aging of the population than with government crime-control policies. The decline also reflects a major shift in attitudes toward drug use in the United States, as documented by the Michigan researchers. They report that the proportion of high-school seniors approving of marijuana use has declined by two-thirds since 1980, and the number thinking that marijuana carries little physical risk has been halved in the same period. These radical changes in attitude and behavior began well before—and thus could not have resulted from—the war on drugs or the current emphasis on lengthier prison terms.

—Michael Gottfredson and Travis Hirschi

adults, the clinic children were more likely to be arrested for a wide variety of offenses, more likely to be divorced, to be unemployed, to be on welfare, to use alcohol excessively and to be hospitalized for psychiatric problems.

What explains this amazingly dependable correlation among such diverse acts? We believe it is a common element: All of them produce immediate pleasure without regard to potential long-term consequences. This general tendency to engage in such acts we call "low self-control."

Indeed, recent research into offender motivation casts doubt on the standard explanations of drug use and criminal behavior, and on the supposed connection between them. It suggests instead that when adolescents use drugs they are merely seeking an immediate good feeling—and that no deeper social, psychological or economic motives are involved.

Thus, in committing auto theft, the offender is not pursuing upward mobility, doing what his culture requires him to do or pondering the possibility that a third felony on his record will make him eligible for career criminal sentencing. Instead, he is merely seeking easy transportation in a good looking car. If auto theft and drug use go together, it is not because one is the cause of the other, but because both produce immediate benefits for an offender who pays little attention to long-term costs. This directly contradicts two basic assumptions of contemporary law enforcement: that fear of lengthy prison terms deters offenders from their acts; and that a war on drugs can be separated from a war on crime in general.

A TIME FOR EVERY PURPOSE

The second problematic fact about criminal behavior is that all forms of drug use and crime decline sharply as offenders grow older. This phenomenon has proven astonishingly stable through time. Early in this century, the British criminologist Charles Goring reported that age statistics of conviction "obey natural laws of frequency." [See illustration.]

Current research reaffirms Goring's findings: The age-distribution curve of crime in the United States today is virtually identical to the one produced by English convicts over three-quarters of a century ago. That is, the propensity to commit crime increases very rapidly throughout adolescence, peaks in the late teens, then declines quickly and steadily throughout adulthood.

The implications for current drug and crime policy are profound. The decline in crime and drug use with age is so steep that it overwhelms most crime-control strategies that focus on the offender, such as incarceration and rehabilitation. After all, if the vast majority of offenders are teenagers, and if they rapidly quit using drugs and committing crimes of their own accord, what is the point of incarcerating them well into adulthood, or, for that matter, treating them after the problem is over? The present fascination with ever-longer sentences and abolition of parole implies enormous expenditures for almost no payoff in terms of crime reduction.

The age effect is so strong and so obvious to correctional officials that it tends to undermine the resolve to hold prisoners "for the rest of their natural lives." After 30 years in prison, what danger does the 50-year-old "career robber" pose to society? The rate of robbery in that age group is one-fiftieth the rate for 17-year-olds. More to the point of the proposed drug sentencing policies (and arguments about large financial benefit from imprisonment), what can be the advantage of adding 10 years to sentences that already exceed the active life of the typical offender? Why lock up drug offenders well beyond the age of active substance abuse? Taxpayers may be fooled into thinking they are safer with longer sentences, but when these sentences keep offenders behind bars into middle age (at an average cost, per year, of $25,000 per offender), they should keep their hands more firmly on their wallets.

BRINGING THE WAR HOME

Any potentially successful plan to combat crime must acknowledge that individual differences in the tendency to commit crimes and use drugs remain reasonably stable over the life course. People who do these things when they are very young tend to do them as adolescents, and to have higher rates than others as adults. People who abstain as adolescents, on the other hand, tend to abstain throughout life. Even when the "crime years" are essentially over, those active as adolescents will be found to have relatively high rates of noncriminal deviant behavior—such as excessive drinking, marital problems and employment instability. For example, psychologists studying aggression have discovered that differences in the rate of pushing, shoving, and disobedience at age 8 are reasonably good predictors of criminal convictions at age 30.

The president's drug plan conspicuously ignores the notion of prevention. Yet the stability of differences from early childhood suggests that any worthwhile crime or drug policy must focus on the early years of life; that wars on crime and drugs, if they are to be successful, must target children.

Research clearly demonstrates that children who are taught early to respect the property of others, to delay gratifications of the moment if they conflict with long-term goals and to understand the negative consequences of drug and alcohol abuse are unlikely to abuse drugs or commit criminal acts, no matter what the criminal justice system looks like. The same research shows that children not taught these things are likely to run into trouble with the law.

Parents, not police, are the key to the drug crisis. Today, drug and crime policies focus on the wrong institution of social control (the government), treat an inappropriate age category (adults), falsely assume specialization of offenders, falsely assume a causal connection between drug use and criminal acts, and misperceive the motives of offenders. As long as this continues, no amount of taxpayer's money will win the war on crime.

CRIME in the suites

Russell Mokhiber

Russell Mokhiber is a lawyer and author of Corporate Crime and Violence: Big Business Power and the Abuse of the Public Trust *(Sierra Club Books, 1989). He is currently editor of* The Corporate Crime Reporter, *a weekly newsletter based in Washington, D.C.*

One June 6, 70 federal agents raided the Rocky Flats nuclear weapons facility in Colorado. The decision to invade the bomb plant came on the heels of a lengthy investigation described in FBI agent Jon S. Lipsky's 116-page affidavit, which convinced a federal judge to unleash the agents. In his report, Lipsky accused Rockwell International and the U.S. Department of Energy (DOE) of "knowingly and falsely" stating that the plutonium-processing plant complied with this country's environmental laws. In doing so, the contractor and its government client concealed "serious contamination" at the site. Lipsky charged that Rockwell and DOE secretly dumped hazardous waste into public drinking water and surreptitiously operated an incinerator they said had been shut down.

While scandal at nuclear weapons plants seems almost a regular news feature of late, the capacity demonstrated by the Justice Department in Colorado to deploy an environmental police force—replete with FBI agents, investigators, prosecutors, wiretaps and aerial surveillance—is in fact an unusual thing. The government rarely flexes its legal muscle to prosecute major environmental crimes or, for that matter, corporate crimes generally. For every Rocky Flats, there are dozens of corporate environmental crimes that go undetected, unprosecuted and unpunished.

"Crime is a sociopolitical artifact, not a natural phenomenon," writes legal scholar Herbert Packer in *The Limits of the Criminal Law.* "We can have as much or as little crime as we please, depending on what we choose to count as criminal." In this country, we have chosen to have very little corporate crime. Most corporate wrongs against humans and the environment are not considered criminal in the traditional sense—that is, activity that is prohibited by the state and prosecuted to conviction. While corporations like Rockwell International can be criminally prosecuted for serious violations of environmental laws, they usually face less demanding and less visible civil procedures.

On the face of it, this leniency is grossly out of proportion to the effects of the corporate crime wave. Every year, roughly 28,000 deaths and 130,000 serious injuries are caused by dangerous products. At least 100,000 workers die from exposure to deadly chemicals and other safety hazards. Workplace carcinogens are estimated to cause between 23 and 38 percent of all cancer deaths. More than 45,000 Americans die in automobile crashes every year. Many of those deaths either are caused by defects or are easily preventable by a simple redesign.

The financial cost to society is staggering. The National Association of Attorneys General reports that fraud costs the nation's businesses and indiviudals upwards of $100 billion each year. The Senate Judiciary Committee has estimated that faulty goods, monopolistic practices and other such violations annually cost consumers $174 to $231 billion. Added to this is the $10 to $20 billion a year the Justice Department says taxpayers lose when corporations violate federal regulations. As a rule of thumb, the Bureau of National Affairs estimates that the dollar cost of corporate crime in the United States is more than 10 times greater than the combined total from larcenies, robberies, burglaries and auto thefts committed by individuals.

The full extent of the corporate crime wave is hidden. Although the federal government tracks street crime month by month, city by city through the FBI's Uniform Crime Reports, it does not track corporate crime. So the government can tell the public whether burglary is up or down in Los Angeles for any given month, but it cannot say the same about insider trading, midnight dumping, consumer defrauding or illegal polluting.

Still, we do know that corporate crime is pervasive. A 1979 Justice Department study, "Illegal Corporate Behavior," found that 582 corporations surveyed racked up a total of 1,554 law violations in just two years. A 1980 *Fortune* magazine survey revealed that 11 percent of 1,043 large companies had been convicted on criminal charges or consent decrees for five offenses: bribery, criminal fraud, illegal political contributions, tax evasion and criminal antitrust. A *U.S. News & World Report* study of the 500 largest corporations found that "115 have been convicted in the last decade of at least one major crime or have paid civil penalties for serious misbehavior" in excess of $50,000. And in 1985, George Washington University Professor Amitai Etzioni found that roughly two-thirds of America's 500 largest companies were involved to some extent in illegal behavior over the preceding 10 years.

By the mid-1930s, evidence was mounting that exposure to asbestos was a threat to human health. In 1982, the Manville Corporation (previously Johns Manville), the nation's largest manufacturer of asbestos, filed for bankruptcy to shelter its assets from 16,500 personal injury lawsuits. In the

From *Greenpeace*, Vol. 14, No. 5, September/October 1989, pp. 14-17. *Greenpeace*, 1436 U Street, NW, Washington, DC 20009.

CORPORATE CRIME-BUSTING: SOME LEGAL AND SOCIAL REMEDIES

✗ Congress should pass an executive responsibility statute making it a criminal offense for a corporate supervisor willfully or recklessly to fail to oversee an assigned activity that results in criminal conduct. The globe-trotting chief executive, like Exxon's Lawrence G. Rawl, would have a new incentive to monitor the safe conduct of his corporation.

✗ Corporate managers should be required to report to federal authorities a product or process that may cause death or serious injury. This would ensure that R&D departments keep worker health and safety in mind. A bill to this effect, introduced by Representative George Miller (D-CA) in 1979, was defeated thanks in part to corporate lobbying.

✗ Congress should require publicly held corporations to report their litigation records—indictments, convictions, sentences, fines and product-liability lawsuits—to the FBI. This corporate crime database could then be used by communities and prosecutors to inform their fights against criminally inclined companies.

✗ At the local level, corporate crime-watch committees should be formed to keep an eye on the activities of neighboring corporations and to keep police and prosecutors on their toes. Victims of corporate crime, such as those who have been injured by the Dalkon Shield, Agent Orange and asbestos, have formed organizations to lobby for just compensation, strong laws and, where applicable, effective prosecution and strict sentences.

✗ Creative penalties should be devised, such as court-ordered adverse publicity. As a condition of probation, for example, a judge could order a company to take out network television advertisements telling viewers about its long criminal record.

✗ More than anything else, corporate criminals should do time. They should be jailed alongside the mugger and drug dealer, not in the posh "Club Feds" usually reserved for white-collar crooks.

in 1963, "it is felt that he should not be told of his condition so that he can live and work in peace, and the company can benefit from his many years of experience."

Over the next 30 years, 240,000 people—8,000 per year, almost one every hour on average—will die from asbestos-related cancer. The company will pay some $2.5 billion to its victims, a hefty civil penalty. But no asbestos executive has ever been prosecuted for reckless homicide.

Likewise, it was not a "crime," in the traditional sense of the word, for Union Carbide's Bhopal, India, subsidiary to operate a pesticide manufacturing plant so incompetently that in 1984, clouds of deadly methyl isocyanate gas escaped, killing 2,000 to 5,000 persons and injuring 200,000.

And it is not a "crime" for the tobacco companies knowingly to market a highly addictive drug that kills more than 365,000 Americans a year, 1,000 every day. This toll is higher than the number of Americans killed annually by AIDS, heroin, crack, alcohol, car accidents, fire and murder combined.

And it is not a "crime" to market known cancer-causing pesticides such as Alar. Nor is it a "crime" to dump toxins into the air and water. General Motors (GM), among others, has been campaigning actively against public health for decades. In 1949, the company was convicted of conspiracy to destroy the nation's mass transit systems by buying up and then dismantling electrical transit systems in urban areas around the country.

The environmental consequences of this crime are still felt today. Los Angeles, which in the 1930s boasted an efficient system of electrified public transit that served 56 cities, saw the system destroyed and replaced with diesel buses and a freeway network for GM's cars. The city now has one of the worst air pollution problems in the country, and the Bush administration has proposed exempting it from some provisions of the Clean Air Act.

"What is good for General Motors is not necessary good for the country," former San Francisco Mayor Joe Alioto told senators in a hearing about the destruction of the electric transit system in the Bay Area. "In the field of transportation, what has been good for General Motors has, in fact, been very, very bad for the country."

With the enormous resources available to them, companies like General Motors can ensure that the laws protecting us from them remain weak. During the last decade, for example, General Motors has successfully op-

posed amendments that would strengthen federal clean air and federal fuel-efficiency standards. GM has spent more than $1.8 billion lobbying Congress against clean air amendments since 1981, the year the Clean Air Act came due for reauthorization. In addition, GM's political action committee made more than $750,000 in campaign contributions, much of it to legislators who sit on committees with jurisdiction over clean air issues.

Lack of accountability is deeply embedded in the concept of the corporation. Shareholders' liability is limited to the amount of money they invest. Managers' liability is limited to what they choose to know about the operations of the company. And the coporation's liability is limited by Congress (the Price-Anderson Act, for example, caps the liability of nuclear power companies in the aftermath of a nuclear disaster), by insurance and by laws allowing corporations to duck liability by altering their corporate structure (the Manville bankruptcy dodge, for example).

In addition, since the turn of the century, most laws governing corporate behavior give regulators the option of avoiding criminal charges and proceeding with less burdensome and less noticeable civil enforcement. In this way, corporations avoid either admitting or denying that they violated the law and are let off with slap-on-the-wrist fines and consent decrees. For environmental, labor, securities, energy, and food and drug violations, the civil injunction is today the primary method of enforcing the law against big business.

Fines, dismissed by criminologists as "license fees to violate the law," are the customary civil penalty for corporate wrong-doing. "One jail sentence is worth 100 consent decrees," said one federal judge. "Fines are meaningless because the defendant in the end is always reimbursed by the proceeds of his wrongdoing or by his company."

Under civil enforcement, the executives of criminal corporations are freed from the stigma of prosecution and possible jail sentences. "The violations of these laws are crimes," wrote Edwin Sutherland in his 1949 classic, *White-Collar Crime*, "but they are treated as though they are not crimes, with the effect and probably the intention of eliminating the stigma of crime."

Sanctions for egregious corporate crimes rarely match the gravity of the offense, nor do they compare well with the punishment meted out for common street crimes. Not one corporate executive went to jail for marketing thalidomide, a drug that caused severe birth defects in 8,000 babies during the

intervening 50 years, the corporation actively suppressed asbestos studies and hid information from its employees on the dangers of working with asbestos. They even cut workers off from their own health records. "As long as [the employee] is not disabled," rationalized the company's medical director

1960s, but Wallace Richard Stewart of Kentucky was sentenced in July 1983 to 10 years in prison for stealing a pizza. Not one Hooker Chemical manager went to jail, nor was Hooker charged with a criminal offense after the company exposed its workers and Love Canal neighbors to toxics, but under a Texas habitual offenders statute, William Rummel was sentenced to life in prison for stealing a total of $229.11 over a period of nine years. And General Motors was fined a mere $5,000 for its mass transit conspiracy, which set back the country's environmental standards for decades.

"No amount of money paid out of corporate assets can address the wrongful acts of the individuals responsible within the organization," says Kenneth Oden, a District Attorney in Austin who has prosecuted a number of occupational homicide cases. "Sometimes the boss needs to be placed in handcuffs and taken to jail." While incarceration of street criminals may have a limited deterrent effect, jail time for corporate executives has a markedly different impact. "I would starve before I would do it again," said one General Electric official, convicted and jailed in a price-fixing scandal.

In February 1983, a worker at Film Recovery Systems' silver extraction plant became nauseated while working in a room with open vats of hydrogen cyanide. He staggered outside the plant, collapsed and died. The medical examiner reported that he died of "acute cyanide toxicity." A month later the state attorney for Cook County, Chicago, charged three executives of Film Recovery Systems with homicide.

Prosecutors argued that plant employees were forced to work in the equivalent of a huge gas chamber, that the company hired mostly illegal aliens who spoke little English, that the company had scraped skull and crossbones

warnings off the side of the cyanide drums, and that ventilation was so inadequate that a thick yellow haze hung inside the plant.

After a two-month trial, each of the three executives was found guilty of murder and reckless conduct, fined $10,000 and sentenced to 25 years in prison for murder and 364 days for reckless conduct. Two operating corporations were found guilty of reckless conduct and involuntary manslaughter and fined $11,000 each.

The Film Recovery Systems case represents the first time a corporate executive has been found guilty of murder in an occupational death case, and public sentiment seems to be calling for more such legal actions. Earlier this year in Torrance, California, the city attorney, citing the fear of a "disaster of Bhopal-like proportions," filed an unusual lawsuit against Mobil Oil. He sought to have Mobil's giant Torrance refinery declared a public nuisance, thus giving the city the authority to regulate it. The lawsuit cites the plant's appalling safety record—127 accidents at the refinery since December 1979, including the fiery deaths of three persons, among them a passing motorist, in an explosion and fire at the tank farm.

The district attorney (DA) for Los Angeles County requires prosecutors to investigate the circumstances of every occupational death or serious injury on the job. In the past four years, the DA has investigated more than 100 such cases and has brought criminal charges in more than two dozen cases. And in Austin, Milwaukee and New York City, activist prosecutors are hitting employers with homicide charges for death on the job.

In early 1989, the Commonwealth of Massachusetts announced the creation of a statewide Environmental Crimes Task Force that will use prosecutors, scientists, investigators and police offi-

cers to target high-priority threats to public health and natural resources. The 34-member strike force will specialize in major cases involving threats to drinking water supplies, harm to wetlands, illegal dumping and toxic discharges into sewage systems.

"This should send a clear message to everyone across the state: If you pollute, we're going to catch you and you'll pay the price," said Massachusetts Environmental Affairs Secretary John DeVillars. "Poisoning someone's water supply or illegally dumping material isn't a victimless crime. It's a costly crime that has a major impact on individuals whose health may suffer. It damages our quality of life."

At the federal level, the Justice Department's Environmental Crimes Section, which was created in 1983, has recorded 520 indictments and more than 400 convictions, bringing in $22 million in fines and more than 240 years of actual jail time. Earlier this year, Ashland Oil was found guilty of violating federal environmental laws in connection with the collapse of an Ashland storage tank that spilled more than 500,000 gallons of oil into the Monongahela River outside of Pittsburgh on January 2, 1988.

The developments described above point to a new willingness on the part of the public and the judicial system to see corporate crime punished fairly. Until now, the law has taught that if you are strong, rich and corporate, you can inflict the most egregious wrongs on society and continue business as usual. There is no reason why this cannot change. In a just society, the criminal law should also teach that those who poison the air, water and land, injure and kill others, or inflict cancer and birth defects are criminals and should be justly punished.

Is Rehabilitation a Waste of Time?

Jerome Miller

Late one gloomy winter afternoon in 1980, New York sociologist Robert Martinson hurled himself through a ninth-floor window of his Manhattan apartment while his teen-age son looked on. Martinson had become the leading debunker of the idea that society could "rehabilitate" criminals. His melancholy suicide was to be a metaphor for what would follow in American corrections.

The question that obsessed Martinson still haunts debate on the purposes of corrections. It surfaced recently in the controversy over Maryland's Patuxent Institution; and it underlies drug czar William Bennett's plan for more prisons and Mayor Marion Barry's call for 2,000 more cells. They embody the now-popular assumption that rehabilitation is pointless. Policy initiatives emphasize more cells for more inmates, and the main federal "message" to cities, as Attorney General Richard Thornburgh succinctly put it, is: "Do the crime, you do the time."

But the present fixation on punishment and deterrence may prove a costly mistake. In fact, there is considerable evidence that rehabilitation which adheres to certain principles can be dramatically successful [see box.] And we'd better start learning what those standards are. The currently fashionable notion of more "hard time" for more offenders could bankrupt many state and local budgets while guaranteeing even higher recidivism rates.

Martinson's skepticism about rehabilitation derived from his role in co-authoring a 1975 survey of 231 studies on offender rehabilitation spanning the previous 30 years. Titled "The Effectiveness of Correctional Treatment," it became the most politically influential criminological study of the past half century.

The time was ripe: From 1963 to 1973, murder, assault and burglary rates doubled while robberies tripled. Martinson's views were enthusiastically embraced by the national media, often under the headline, "Nothing Works!" Yet curiously, all the *sturm und drang* was over something that scarcely existed. Even at the height of the so-called "rehabilitative era," a corrections department spending more than 2 percent of its budget on treatment was unusual. But the attack was taken up by liberals and conservatives alike—many of whom felt that belief in rehabilitation, as Harvard's James Q. Wilson put it, "requires not merely optimistic but heroic assumptions about the nature of man."

But as Berkeley criminologist Elliott Currie would later explain, "programs cited by Martinson and other critics as evidence that rehabilitation did not work were often not only underfunded and understaffed, but typically staffed by poorly trained and often unmotivated people. These early critics of rehabilitation made little effort to separate reasonably serious and intensive programs from those—vastly more common—that at best offered minimal counseling or tutoring to people who were otherwise allowed to languish in the enforced bleakness of institutions or in the shattered, dead-end communities from which they had come."

The classic 30-year "Cambridge-Somerville Youth Study" is a premier example. In the Harvard-sponsored program begun in 1937, researchers followed 320 boys for 30 years. The boys were assigned to 10 "counselors" who had no training in mental health or psychotherapy and were told to do "whatever they thought best." Each youth was seen only five times annually during the early years of the project. Not surprisingly, the program had little effect on subsequent criminal behavior.

Problems of Perspective

Part of the problem in evaluating rehabilitation is deciding what constitutes success. For example, in studying the effectiveness of family therapy with hard-core delinquents (each having 20 or more previous convictions), one survey found that after 15 months, 60 percent of those in therapy had re-offended. However, 93 percent of the matched "non-therapy" control group re-offended. A medical procedure that suppressed symptoms in 40 percent of a group of chronically ill patients, 93 percent of whom deteriorate without treatment, would be seen as a virtual triumph. In corrections, however, such results are usually regarded as failure.

Moreover, simply residing in some communities increases the likelihood of being labeled a recidivist. Nearly half (46 percent) of the boys in some areas will appear in juvenile court during their teen years. Among young black men in certain parts of the country, seven out of 10 can anticipate being arrested at least once. Though this may suggest failure, it may not measure individual criminal behavior. Indeed, among chronic delinquents the simple fact of rearrest may be less important than whether the young offender is winding down his criminal activity.

But the biggest problem in getting a fair hearing for rehabilitation is that so many efforts have failed spectacularly. A team of researchers from the Academy for Contemporary Problems found that the "velocity of recidivism" among youthful offenders actually increased with each trip to a state reform school for rehabilitation. Rand Corp. researchers reported similar patterns among adults.

Nonetheless, some theorists maintain that the very fact that a prison is dangerous and violent makes it rehabilitative. It's a variation on the "Scared Straight" theory. Unfortunately, repeated studies have shown that it doesn't work.

The Incapacitation Gambit

So runs the presently popular notion, if we can't get a complete "cure," why not simply lock up all offenders? Simon Dinitz from the Academy for Contemporary Problems' "Dangerous Offenders Project" considered this Draconian option. He estimates that incarcerating every first-time felony offender for five years would likely yield no more than a modest 7.3 percent decrease in crime rates. But U.S. prisons (already overcrowded) would have to increase their populations 300 to 500 percent, entailing construction costs of $130 billion and increasing annual operating budgets from $12 billion to between $36 billion and $60 billion. And even that would not guarantee that crime rates would stay down for long. Those in prison are often replaced by others waiting in the wings (particularly among drug offenders). More ominously, such a policy would yield 3 to 5 million slightly more hardened ex-convicts dumped into the streets every five years.

The most unusual case for incapacitation was made late last year by Richard B. Abell, an assistant attorney general in the Justice Department. Writing in Policy Review, and using figures compiled by a Justice economist, Abell concluded that we save $40 million annually in crime costs for every 100 offenders we incarcerate—based on the extraordinary assumption that a typical offender commits 187 crimes per year at an average $2,300 per crime, or $430,100 annually.

Calling these estimates "not merely wrong, but ludicrously wrong," University of California researchers Franklin Zimring and Gordon Hawkins noted that at a rate of 187 crimes per offender per year, putting a half-million more persons in prison would lower the number of crimes nationally by almost 50 million—thus making the nation crime-free, since there are about 45 million crimes reported annually. By Abell's calculations, in fact, crime must have disappeared sometime in late 1985 as a result of the doubling of prison and jail populations from approximately 300,000 in 1978 to about 800,000 in 1986. Nonetheless, President Bush—who pledged during the campaign to double the federal prison-building budget over four years—has used the same argument.

All this suggests that we are willing to invest large sums in variations on themes of retribution and deterrence. Yet Canadian psychologist Paul Gendreau and University of Ottawa sociologist Robert Ross, citing sophisticated new mathematical analyses of the data on rehabilitation, concluded that "the (substantiated) claims for effective rehabilitation of offenders far outdistanced those of the major competing ideology: applied deterrence or punishment."

Actually, Something Works

As early as 1976, a Rand Corp. report had suggested that the "nothing works" conclusion was probably premature. Three years later, a National Academy of Sciences panel concluded that "when it is asserted that 'nothing works,' the panel is uncertain as to just what has been given a fair trial." And now, in their latest survey of the rehabilitative literature, from 1980 to 1987, Gendreau and Ross found "reductions in recidivism, sometimes as substantial as 80 percent had been achieved in a considerable number of well-controlled studies. Effective programs were conducted in a variety of community and (to a lesser degree) institutional settings, involving pre-delinquents, hard-core adolescent offenders and recidivistic adult offenders, including criminal heroin addicts."

The literature of the '80s demonstrates that a number of techniques can reduce recidivism among both property and violent offenders. These include substance-abuse treatment (combining intensive counseling with drug screening), family therapy, individual therapy stressing support rather than pathology and punishment, and—particularly with young offenders—assigning "advocates" to work with individuals on a daily basis, including crisis intervention at odd hours. In Massachusetts, Harvard researchers found that reconvictions fell among older former reform-school youth when a range of such alternatives was available. In those regions of the state where no such array existed, recidivism remained the same or increased.

Educational programs for hard-core adult offenders have also shown promising results. Inmates of a Canadian federal prison, many with long and serious criminal histories, were assigned randomly either to normal prison routine, or to a special humanities program stressing individual tutoring using Socratic dialogue. In a report prepared for the Canadian government, psychologist D. J. Ayers and his colleagues found that after 20 months of post-prison follow-up, the recidivism rate of those in the program was 14 percent as compared to a 52-percent rate for those randomly assigned to prison routines.

Discovering what works is less a matter of deciding on a specific treatment technique than of creating programs that are intensive, taken seriously, last a reasonable period of time and focus on high-risk offenders. (In fact, programs directed at low-risk offenders can sometimes be counterproductive if they are allowed to pick up antisocial skills and attitudes from higher-risk persons.) Canadian psychologists D. A. Andrews and J. Keissling found that effective therapy promoted prosocial attitudes, rewarded non-criminal pursuits, made use of a wide range of community resources, taught skills for handling relapse and treated the offender with respect and empathy—many of the very qualities that characterize effective psychotherapy with non-offenders.

Ironically, even Martinson himself changed his mind on the efficacy of rehabilitation. In a 1979 article in the Hofstra Law Review, he wrote that "startling results are found again and again . . . for treatment programs as diverse as individual psychotherapy, group counseling, intensive supervision and what we have called individual help." The man who started it all had come full circle. But by then no one was listening.

And apparently they still aren't. On Jan. 18, the U.S. Supreme Court confirmed the abandonment of rehabilitation. In Mistretta v. U.S., the Court upheld federal sentencing guidelines which all but remove rehabilitation from serious consideration. The dissonant reverberation from a decade earlier has become the national anthem. As a result, federal prison populations are expected to double.

Thus contemporary corrections theory offers a choice between equally unattractive extremes: ineffective probation/parole or debilitating prisons. Finding help is akin to asking a doctor for headache relief and being told there are only two treatments—an aspirin or a lobotomy. Harsher sentences, warehouse prisons and an ideology which militantly rejects the idea of salvaging offenders are the rule of the land. Meanwhile, violent crime surges. We must now wait for the swing of the pendulum. It may be a long wait.

Groups and Roles in Transition

- **Work-Family Dynamics (Articles 17-19)**
- **Community Action (Articles 20-21)**
- **Changing Situation of Special Groups (Articles 22-23)**

Primary groups are small, intimate, spontaneous, and personal. In contrast, secondary groups are large, formal, and impersonal. Often primary groups are formed within a factory, school, or business. Primary groups are the main source that the individual draws upon in developing values and an identity. The family, couples, gangs, cliques, teams, and small tribes or rural villages are examples of primary groups. Secondary groups include most of the organizations and bureaucracies in a modern society, and carry out most of its instrumental functions.

Urbanization, geographic mobility, centralization, bureaucratization, and other aspects of modernization have had an impact on the nature of groups, the quality of the relationships between people, and individuals' feelings of belonging. The family in particular is undergoing radical transformation. The greatly increased participation of women in the paid labor force and increased careerism among women have caused severe strains between their work and family roles. Two articles explore this issue. T. Berry Brazelton has counseled many women in these crosscurrents, and conveys his understanding of the problems and offers methods for dealing with them. The most painful issue is turning young children over to other care providers. Mothers are haunted by guilt and anxiety. One way to deal with this is to work fewer hours or drop out of work until the children are older. In the corporate world this practice is called the "mommy track." The next article discusses the mommy track pattern and the forces that have created it. Corporations have demanded that employees put work ahead of family so they are reluctant to provide a mommy track. Nevertheless, they are being forced to adopt new policies in order to retain female employees that they badly need.

If mother roles are changing, so are the roles of fathers. Roger Barkin documents some of these changes and the impacts they are having on the children. Shared parenting improves relationships with both children and spouse. Children develop more intellectually, relate better to peers, and are better able to deal with strange situations.

The next subsection deals with communities and community action. Until recently the community or the neighborhood were major foci for sociological research because they were the important context for people's lives. Today people's social ties are less community or neighborhood based. Nevertheless, social disorganization is so great in some parts of many cities that community vitality must be regained or life becomes terror,

despair, and defeat. Nancy Gibbs's article is less focused on geographically based community action and more focused on people mobilizing to meet some public need. Volunteerism in its many forms is needed even in wealthy America to care for many human needs that would otherwise go unattended to. David Osborne describes the wonderful accomplishments of the people of a public housing project who have taken over its management, cleaned it up, made it safe, and launched programs to improve the lives of the residents.

The last two articles consider two groups that are rapidly redefining their places in American society. Howard Schwartz argues that the handicapped have achieved a high level of social acceptance and in some ways are valued more highly than non-handicapped persons. Public opinion has improved considerably in recent years, as Schwartz demonstrates in his study of attitudes toward a handicapped person being the subject of a Playboy photo layout. His analysis has implications for the sociology of deviance.

The last article focuses on the elderly and considers how the older years can be a time of growth and development. Even while the body powers decline, the interior life can grow and flower. "The third age [over 60] is also a period for giving back to society the lessons, resources, and experiences accumulated over a lifetime." Many changes are required in society to fully achieve this possibility. The authors' vision of these possibilities deserves thoughtful examination.

Looking Ahead: Challenge Questions

How can women balance family and career? What changes are needed in the work world to accommodate two-career families? How can these changes be brought about?

Will the mommy track provide an excuse to keep women from competing with men?

Why have fathers and husbands changed so little while women have changed so much in respect to responsibilities in the home?

What factors are needed to make self-help work? Why are disadvantaged groups so infrequently mobilized?

If the government initiates more social programs, will volunteerism recede dramatically?

How do the disabled want to be treated? Give examples. How do the elderly want to be treated?

Working Parents

One of America's leading pediatricians tells how to cope with the stresses of jobs and family life

DR. T. BERRY BRAZELTON

The question I'm asked most frequently these days is, "Has child rearing changed since you started working with families in the 1950s?" I become almost speechless. The changes have been so great, and the new stresses on families so real and so apparent. What hasn't changed is the passion that parents have for doing a good job in raising their children. We in the '50s were passionate. But we were somber, undecided, retiring. We turned for advice to Dr. Spock. We brooded about whether we were doing the right things for our children.

The degree of stress that new parents feel about child rearing hasn't changed, but the focus for their anxiety has. We are in a period of real pressure on families. Parents have as much concern today about keeping the family together as in doing well by their children. At a time when nearly 50 percent of all marriages end up in divorce, maintaining family life is a high-risk venture. Single parents struggle against the dual demands of providing financial and emotional support for their children. Two-career couples face the conflicts of trying to balance work and family life—and trying to do both well.

These "new" families are searching for guidelines for rearing their children. As I talk with working parents around the country, they ask similar questions about how to cope with work and home—how to care for their children in a changing world, how to deal with the limited time they have for family life, how to live with the anxieties they have about child care, how to handle the inevitable

competition they feel with their mates and caregivers. Yet for all their doubts and fears, there is a new force in the air that I feel in my contact with young families. The parents of this generation are beginning to feel empowered. They are asking hard questions, demanding answers, and they are ready to fight for what they need for their children and for themselves. "Parent power" is the new catch phrase.

Roles and Rivalries

In our culture, we live with a deep-seated view that a woman's role is in the home. She should be there for her children, so the theory goes, and both she and they will suffer if she's not. I felt that way for a long time myself, and it took constant badgering from my three militant daughters, who all work, as well as from a whole succession of working parents in my practice, to disabuse me of my set of mind. This bias prevents us from giving working women the support they need. It keeps us from realizing that 52 percent of women whose children are under 3 are in the work force, and it prevents us from providing them with choices for adequate child care. Many working women have no alternative but to leave their infants and small children in conditions none of us would trust. These women are as certain as you and I that their babies are at risk. But they have no choice.

Because of their double roles, women face a costly, necessary split within themselves. Can they invest themselves in a successful career and still be able to nurture a family? Can they cope with the guilt and the grief that they feel when they leave their children every day? Will women feel threatened as men get closer to the children? Their worries are understandable. A parent who must leave her small baby before she has completed her own work of attaching to him can't help but grieve. It's hard to free up energy for the workplace if a mother spends her time wondering whether her child is being adequately cared for. Women who choose to stay home with their children are equally conflicted. They wonder whether they should continue their careers out of self-protection—and whether the family can manage on one salary instead of two.

Upsetting as they may be, such concerns can be put to positive use. Women should allow themselves to feel anxious and guilty about leaving their children—those feelings will press them to find the best substitute care. Women can also find strength in their double roles. Lois Hoffman, a professor at the University of Michigan, has demonstrated in a study that working mothers who feel confident and fulfilled in their jobs bring that sense of competence home to their children.

For men, greater involvement in the work of family life has forced them to confront the same conflicts women do—trying to balance working and caring. And as fathers accept nurturing roles within the family, competition with women is bound to emerge. There is an inevitable rivalry for the baby that will spring up between caring parents. Women may unconsciously act

From *Newsweek*, February 13, 1989, pp. 66-70. Copyright © 1989 by T. Berry Brazelton.

Bringing up Baby: A Doctor's Prescription for Busy Parents

Juggling work and family life can often seem overwhelming. Dr. Brazelton offers some practical advice for easing the strain on harried parents:

1 Learn to compartmentalize—when you work, be there, and when you are at home, be at home.

2 Prepare yourself for separating each day. Then prepare the child. Accompany him to his caregiver.

3 Allow yourself to grieve about leaving your baby—it will help you find the best substitute care, and you'll leave the child with a passionate parting.

4 Let yourself feel guilty. Guilt is a powerful force for finding solutions.

5 Find others to share your stress—peer or family resource groups.

6 Include your spouse in the work of the family.

7 Face the reality of working and caring. No supermom or superbaby fantasies.

8 Learn to save up energy in the workplace to be ready for homecoming.

9 Investigate all the options available at your workplace—on-site or nearby day care, shared-job options, flexible-time arrangements, sick leave if your child is ill.

10 Plan for children to fall apart when you arrive home after work. They've saved up their strongest feelings all day.

11 Gather the entire family when you walk in. Sit in a big rocking chair until everyone is close again. When the children squirm to get down, you can turn to chores and housework.

12 Take children along as you do chores. Teach them to help with the housework, and give them approval when they do.

13 Each parent should have a special time alone with each child every week. Even an hour will do.

14 Don't let yourself be overwhelmed by stress. Instead, enjoy the pleasures of solving problems together. You can establish a pattern of working as a team.

like "gatekeepers," excluding men from their babies' care. A new mother will say to her inexperienced, vulnerable husband, "Darling, that's not the way you diaper a baby!" or "You hold a baby *this* way." Working families need to be aware of this competition, which can disrupt family ties unless it is recognized. If parents can discuss it, the rivalry can motivate each person to become a better parent.

How can working men and women make the time they have with their children "quality time"? It's difficult when parents see their children for only an hour or two in the morning and a few hours in the evening. The whole concept of quality time can feel like a pressure. But if parents can concentrate on getting close to their children as soon as they walk in the door, then everything that follows becomes family time—working, playing, talking. Parents can involve children in their chores, teaching them to share the housework. Children who participate in the family's solutions will be competent to handle the stresses of their own generation. Even if time is short during workdays, parents can set aside time on the weekend for family celebration. Each parent should have a special time alone with each child at least once a week. An hour will do. But talk about it all week to remind the child—and yourself—that you will have a chance to cement your special relationship.

Conflicts

All parents worry about the same kinds of problems—sleep, feeding, toilet training, sibling rivalry. But there are some issues that seem especially troublesome for working parents, in part because the limited time they have with their children makes each problem seem twice as difficult. Some of the more perplexing issues—and suggestions for coping with them:

Going back to work: I am often asked when women should go back to work. I don't like to advocate one period of time over another, because for economic reasons some women don't have a choice about how long they can stay home. I am fighting for a four-month period of unpaid parental leave for both fathers and mothers, however, because I believe we must provide parents with the time to learn how to attach both to the baby and to each other. By 4 months, when colic has ended, and when the baby and parent know how to produce smiles and to vocalize for each other, the baby feels secure enough to begin turning away to look at other adults and to play with his own feet and his own toys. For the parent, it is marked by the sure knowledge that "he knows *me*. He will smile or vocalize at *me*."

Rx: Regardless of how much time new parents can take off from work, it's important to recognize that the process of learning to attach to a new infant is not a simple

one. Everyone who holds a new baby falls in love. But while falling in love is easy, staying in love takes commitment. A newborn demands an inordinate amount of time and energy. He needs to be fed, changed, cuddled, carried and played with over endless 24-hour periods. He is likely to cry inconsolably every evening for the first 12 weeks. Much of the time his depressed, frightened parents are at a loss about what to do for him. A new mother will be dogged by postpartum blues; a new father is likely to feel helpless and want to run away. Their failures in this period are a major part of the process of learning to care. When new parents do not have the time and freedom to face this process and live through it successfully, they may indeed escape emotionally. In running away, they may miss the opportunity to develop a secure attachment to their baby—and never get to know themselves as real parents.

Separation: Leave-taking in the morning can be a problem. Children will dawdle. They won't get dressed and they won't eat. Parents feel under pressure to get going; children resist this pressure. Everything goes to pot. The parent is faced with leaving a screaming child, and ends up feeling miserable all day.

Rx: Get up earlier. Sit down to talk or get close with the children before urging them to get dressed. Help them choose their clothes. Talk out the separation ahead. Remind them of the reunion at the end of the day. When you're ready to go, gather them up. Don't expect cooperation—the child is bound to be angry that you're leaving. And don't sneak out: always tell a child when you're going. Say goodbye and don't prolong your departure.

Discipline: The second most important parental job is discipline. Love comes first, but firm limits come second. A working parent feels too guilty and too tired to want to be tough at the end of the day. Of course parents would rather dodge the issue of being tough. But a child's agenda is likely to be different. When a child is falling apart, as children tend to do at the end of the day, he needs you most. He gets more frantic, searching for limits. Children need the security of boundaries, of knowing where they must stop.

Rx: Discipline should be seen as teaching rather than punishment. Taking time out, physically restraining and holding the child or isolating him for a brief period breaks the cycle. Immediately afterward parents can sit down and discuss the limits with firm assurance. No discipline works magically. Every episode is an opportunity to teach—but to teach *over time*. Working families need more organization than other families to make things work, and discipline gives a child a sense of being part of that organization.

Sleep issues: Separation during the day is

A child can adjust to two or more styles of child rearing if each of the adults cares about him as an individual

so painful for working parents that separating at night becomes an even bigger issue, and putting their children to bed is fraught with difficulty. The normal teasing any child does about staying up is so stressful that working parents find it tough to be firm. Then a child's light-sleep episodes, which occur every three or five hours, become added conflicts. If the child cries out, parents often think they must go in to help her get back into a deep sleep. But learning to sleep through the night is important for the child's own sense of independence.

Rx: Teaching the child to get to sleep is the first goal. A child is likely to need a "lovey" or a comfort object, an independent resource to help her break the day-to-night transition. Learning to get herself to sleep means having a bedtime ritual that is soothing and comforting. But a child shouldn't fall asleep in her parent's arms; if she does, then the parents have made themselves part of the child's sleep ritual. Instead, after she's quiet, put her in bed with her lovey and pat her down to sleep. When she rouses every four hours, give her no more than five minutes to scrabble around in bed. Then go in and show her how to find her own comfort pattern for herself.

Feeding: Parents often believe that feeding is the major responsibility they have in taking care of their children. "If a child doesn't eat properly, it's the parent's fault," goes the myth. "A good parent gets a well-rounded diet into a child." Yet this myth ignores the child's need for autonomy in feeding. Each burst of independence hits feeding headlong, and food becomes a major issue. But because they are away most of the day, parents feel a need to become close to their children at mealtimes.

Rx: Try to ease up on the struggle. Leave as much as possible to the child. Steps to create autonomy in feeding: start finger-feeding at 8 months. Let her make all of her own choices about what she'll eat by 1 year. Expect her to tease with food in the 2nd year. Set yourself easily attainable goals. If a child won't eat vegetables, give her a multivitamin every day. A simple amount of milk and protein covers her other needs for the short run. Most important, don't make food an issue. When parents come home from work in the evening, family time should emphasize sharing the experiences of the day, not eating. Your relationship is more important than the quantities of food consumed.

Competition with the caregiver: Every important area in child rearing—eating, discipline, toilet training—is likely to be a source of conflict between parents and caregivers. Both must recognize that the child's issues are ones of independence; the caregiver's, ones of control.

℞: Conflict is inevitable. A child can adjust to two or even three different styles of child rearing if each of the adults really cares about him as an individual—and if parents and caregivers are in basic agreement on important issues. Differences in technique don't confuse a child—differences in basic values do.

Supermom and superbaby: People in conflict or under pressure dream about perfectionism. But trying to be perfect creates its own stresses. Any working mother is bound to blame any inadequacy in her own or her child's life on the fact that she's working. Being a perfect parent is not only an impossibility—it would be a disaster. Learning to be a parent is learning from mistakes.

℞ : Understand that there is no perfect way to be a parent. The myth of the supermom serves no real purpose except to increase the parent's guilt. And for children in working families, the pressures are already great. To expect them to be superbabies adds more pressure than they can face. Respect the child by understanding the demands she already faces in the normal stages of growing up. Teaching a child too early deprives her of her childhood. Play is the way a child learns and the way she sorts out what works for her. When she finds it on her own she gains a sense of competence.

Support Systems

We need a cushion for parents who are learning about their new job, to replace the role of the extended family when it is not available. When young parents are under stress—the normal stresses of childbearing and child rearing—they often don't know whom to turn to for help. If possible, I would prefer that grandparents be nearby and available. They can offer their own children a sense of security and support, which comes in handy at each new stress point. But parents often hesitate to turn to grand-

parents for advice. "They would tell me what to do, and I'd never do it that way" is a refrain I hear. My response is: "But if you know you'd 'never do it their way,' then you'd have a simpler decision to make."

Working men and women can also turn to other parents for support. Childbirth-education classes have been enormously valuable in helping parents face pregnancy and delivery successfully. Peer groups that provide support systems for parents are building on this model. Since its start 10 years ago, for example, The Family Resource Coalition in Chicago has been a drop-in center for single parents trying to raise their children alone in poorer sections of Chicago. There are similar centers across the United States for parents of all circumstances. Memberships in these groups can be counted in the hundreds of thousands. Special peer-support groups have been formed for parents of premature and high-risk babies; others have formed for the parents of almost every kind of impaired child.

What Can Be Done

Why haven't we done more as a nation to help working parents face the stresses of family life? We seem to be dominated by a bias left over from our pioneering ancestors: "Families should be self-sufficient. If they're not, they should suffer for it." Ironically, government help seems to increase families' dependency and insufficiency. As they are now configured, our government programs are available only to those who are willing to label themselves as failures—poor, hungry, uneducated, unmarried, single parents. This labeling produced the effect of giving up one's self-image. Labeled families become a self-fulfilling prophecy. We are reinforcing people not for success, but for failure.

Several of us have just formed a new grass-roots organization in Washington called Parent Action. This is a lobbying organization to demonstrate the energy that parents have. The organization of the American Association of Retired Persons has been successful in lobbying for the elderly. We want to push the concerns of families to the forefront of our nation's conscience.

So far, we in the United States have not even begun to address the burgeoning need for quality care for the children of working parents. We are the only industrialized country (aside from South Africa) that has not faced up to what is happening to young families as they try to cope with working and raising children. Indeed, our disappointing record in supporting families and children suggests that we are one

of the least child-oriented societies in the world. The recent failure of the Alliance for Better Child Care, a bill sponsored by the Children's Defense Fund, a Washington-based advocacy group, represents just such an example. It would have provided national funds to increase the salaries of child-care workers so that trained personnel would have an incentive to care for infants and small children.

In order to pay for the kind of care that every child deserves, the cost could be amortized four ways: by federal and state governments, by individual businesses and by the individual family. Business can play a key role. Offering employees parental leave, flexible work schedules and on-site or nearby day care would assure companies of a kind of allegiance that can be seen in European and Asian countries. Businesses that pay attention to the family concerns of their employees are already reaping rewards. Studies demonstrate that employees of such firms display less burnout, less absenteeism, more loyalty to the company and significantly more interest in their jobs.

As a nation, we have two choices. One is to continue to let our biases dominate our behavior as a society. The other is to see that we are a nation in crisis. We are spending billions of dollars to protect our families from outside enemies, imagined and real. But we do not have even 50 percent of the quality child care we need, and what we do have is neither affordable nor available to most families. These conditions exist in the face of all we know about the effects of emotional deprivation in early childhood. The rise in teenage suicide, pregnancies and crime should warn us that we are paying a dreadful price for not facing the needs of families early on. We are endangering both the present and the next generation.

Improving conditions for working parents has a visible payoff. When parents have options and can make their own choices, they feel respected and secure. I can tell when working parents are successfully sharing the day-to-day work of the family. Men walk differently as they enter my office. A father who is participating actively in his child's care walks straighter, has a more jaunty air, and he can't wait to tell me about each of his baby's successes. A working mother who has found a balance between her work and her family speaks more decisively. She handles her baby with assurance, and she is eager to include her solutions in our discussion of her child's progress. These parents are empowered. Helping others to feel the way they do is an investment in the future.

THE MOMMY TRACK

JUGGLING KIDS AND CAREERS IN CORPORATE AMERICA TAKES A CONTROVERSIAL TURN

On Monday, Tuesday, and Wednesday, Anne Keller, middle manager, revels in corporate life. As a marketing analyst at Digital Equipment Corp.'s worldwide field headquarters in Stowe, Mass., she is a liaison between the company's far-flung sales force and its engineering department. Keller has new-product introductions to follow up on and technical work to review. There are memos and meetings. Deadlines. Day care.

Then it stops. Thursday mornings, as PCs boot up, and fax machines all over American begin to hum, you can find Anne Keller, mom, down at the neighborhood diner. She orders eggs and hash browns for her two children, 16-month-old Nicholas and Cara, 4. After breakfast, it's grocery shopping and play dates. She pours countless drinks of juice and wipes up spills . . . until Monday morning, when reality shifts again.

INSIDIOUS. "I'm neither fish nor fowl," says Keller. But her kind is multiplying. Across the country, female managers and professionals with young families are leaving the fast track for the mommy track. They are searching for new ways to balance career goals and mothering—a human place to stand, if you will, between Superwoman and June Cleaver. Their employers, worried about losing top performers and attracting talented women in years to come, are beginning to help. They are offering alternative work patterns, from flexible hours to job sharing to telecommuting. In the process, they may be changing the nature of work for men and women.

Reshaping work to help a woman raise a family is alien to corporate orthodoxy. To reach the top, many executives have sacrificed their "outside" lives. Managers, often wedded to bureaucratic ways of assigning work and evaluating it, may resist new work styles. But adapt they must. Between now and the end of the century, women will make up 65% of the new entrants into the work force. They will bring more of the skills employers need: Among new graduates, women now account for 13% of all engineers, 39% of all lawyers, and 31% of all MBAS. The choice is clear: either "flex" to accommodate women's needs or lose some of the best women to those who do.

The numbers are small, but employers are moving to protect their investment in top-flight women. In accounting, law, and consulting, part-time options and slower

ON THE MOMMY TRACK: WHERE

ALTERNATIVE CAREER PATHS

Attorneys at Skadden Arps can work part-time, be associates or "special counsels." They work for a salary and may lower their odds of becoming partners. At Arthur Andersen, accountants who want to become partners in the firm receive credit for part-time work.

EXTENDED LEAVE

One of the most generous employers in this area is IBM, where employees can take up to three years off—with benefits and the guarantee of a comparable job on return. One requirement: Leave-takers must be on call for part-time work during two of the three years.

FLEXIBLE SCHEDULING

This often happens ad hoc, but at NCNB it's official. Employees create customized schedules and work at home. Most who chose to cut their hours work two-thirds time and are paid pro rata. New mothers can "phase in" after six months maternity leave.

Reprinted from March 20, 1989 issue of *Business Week*, pp. 126-129, 132, 134 by special permission. Copyright © 1989 by McGraw-Hill, Inc.

tracks to coveted partnerships are becoming established options. At some of the largest corporations, managers and professionals are experimenting with part-time work. Hundreds of companies let employees begin and end the workday earlier or later than the norm. Telecommuting—staying in touch via phone and modem—has taken off in Southern California, where just getting to work and back can use up three hours a day.

Many women believe they can slow down at work for a few years, get their kids launched, and come back with renewed zest. But even if more corporations accept that notion, the implications are not to everyone's taste. Opponents see something insidious: a mommy track, separate and unequal, that will permanently derail women's careers, making them second-class citizens at work and confirming the prejudices of male executives.

The mommy tracker "puts up a sign: Don't consider me for promotions now," says Betty Lehan Harragan, author of *Games Mother Never Taught You.* Feminists believe that raising children should not be solely a woman's concern. The mommy track, they argue, means giving up the good fight—for social and family changes that would help mothers have full careers while fathers share more nurturing responsibilities.

Felice N. Schwartz has set the controversy boiling. In a recent *Harvard Business Review* article, Schwartz, the founder and president of Catalyst, an advisory group on women's leadership, set out what some see as a justification for second-class treatment of mothers. Employers, she argued, should identify and nurture two separate groups. Treat high-potential "career-primary" women, most of whom will be childless, just as if they were talented men. Then help "career-and-family" women be productive—but probably not upwardly mobile—by supporting their need for child care and flexible hours.

"The high-performing woman who does want to participate in the rearing of her children and is willing to trade off some career growth and remuneration for the freedom to do so will be happy at middle management for a significant period of her life," Schwartz says. She insists that having talented, committed women at those levels—working and not competing—"will also serve to upgrade middle management."

The notion of two classes of corporate women, only one of which makes it to the top, doesn't sit well with Faith A. Wohl, a director of employee relations at Du Pont Co. "I'm not sure we should honor lack of family as a criterion and value women who are willing to put it aside," says Wohl. She argues that in this day of two-earner households, with more fathers taking responsibility for home and children, the nature of corporate careers has to change for everyone. Du Pont is trying to remold its culture along these lines, says Wohl.

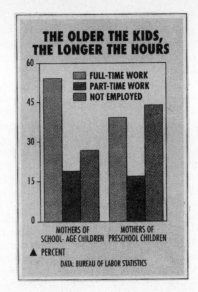

THE OLDER THE KIDS, THE LONGER THE HOURS

DATA: BUREAU OF LABOR STATISTICS

"Do we need as many relocations as we've always thought, for example? Can a person have a period of part-time work—and still be considered for promotions?"

Equity, not mommy tracks, should be the goal, says Wohl. Critics also see favoritism: So far, most companies make such special arrangements only for a few, highly valued managers and professionals. Indeed, many companies refuse to publicize their policies for this reason.

There is no question that good child care, decent maternity leave, and partners who pull their weight at home are essential for working mothers and wives. Social support for single parents is more critical still. But there are other issues: time, which is finite, and the emotional pull of parenthood, which is not. And a woman's expectations of what it means to be a good mother are highly individual and can't always be separated from her own upbringing. The result can be conflict.

Consider Katie Glockner, 31. A brand manager at Quaker Oats Co., she barely missed a beat at work when her son Thaddeus G. Seymour Jr.—T. G. for short—was born in 1986. But by the following year, Glockner had had enough of long hours and weekends. She asked to go part-time. "I loved my job. I was always career-oriented. But I had forgotten the fact that you fall in love with these little people, and I didn't feel comfortable giving up so much of the care," Glockner says.

MORE MATURE. Chicago-based Quaker had moved a few women from line to staff positions in the past, cutting their hours on the way, but a part-time brand manager? "I was the guinea pig," says Glockner. Quaker turned her request into a pilot program. She worked with higher-ups to set objectives. There were quarterly reviews. Personnel documented everything. Now, Glockner tends fewer brands and makes less money, but she has Mondays and

---

SOME EMPLOYERS ARE HEADED

FLEXTIME

Less innovative than flexible scheduling, this is the most widely accepted Mommy Track reform. Any employee has the right to shift the standard workday forward or back by one hour. Thousands of public and private employers now allow such flexibility.

JOB SHARING

Not for everyone, but in some ways the most creative Mommy Track solution. At Steelcase, for example, two employees can share title, work load, salary, health benefits, and vacation. So far, the program is experimental and most participants are clerical.

TELECOMMUTING

The high-tech answer to being a working Mom. Some employers such as Pacific Telesis allow employees to limit the time they spend in the office by using personal computers, fax machines, and electronic mail at home. Perfect for many number-crunching jobs.

Fridays free for T. G. Two other brand managers have followed her lead.

Role-conflict blues never bothered Margaret M. Hovell, a director in the personal systems line of business at IBM, in White Plains, N.Y. "I tell the children one of the things mommy likes to do is work. That has gone over very well," she says. Hovell joined IBM as a programmer right out of college in 1963. She followed a classic career path of transfers and new assignments. She waited until age 38 to start a family, taking the standard maternity leave after each of her two kids was born. Away from home 11 hours a day, she manages well—thanks to a live-in nanny and a paragon of a husband who "also gives 100%."

But in 1986, there was one little problem. "My son needed his mother as he entered school," Hovell says. After 23 years with the company, she gave up her senior-level job as a divisional director of information systems and took a leave of absence for 18 months. Such departures may soon be more common: IBM recently announced that it will offer all employees up to three years of personal leave with paid benefits and a job when they come back. The "quintessential fast track," says Hovell, "has given way to a "much more mature and balanced view."

In 1985, Christina Ling, 38, left the corporate world after she and her husband, a city planner, spent three years juggling sitters. A former manager of financial planning and analysis at SmithKline Beckman Corp.'s Allergan Inc. division, Ling—who used to do grocery shopping on her lunch breaks—reflects: "I knew I couldn't keep working nights and weekends and seeing my child 45 minutes a day just to get the positions I wanted before."

CHANGING PRIORITIES. It's not that most women in management and professions are bailing out. Many view work as an integral part of their identities, just as men do. And most must work to maintain a certain standard of living. In fact, women with highly paid jobs and good benefits are more likely than others to return to work after giving birth.

Ling, however, now is running a home-based business—a well-trodden "outside" route for ambitious women. Still, it's second-best. "I want to return to a corporate job but without getting back into that rat race again," she says. "I think I could only make a three-quarter commitment."

As the new demographics force change, even the old prejudice against rehiring corporate dropouts is fading away. In 1982, Corning Glass Works lost Bonnie L. Milliman, a 26-year-old engineering supervisor. A new mother, Milliman balked at returning to 50-to-70 hour weeks overseeing 15 engineers, so she quit. "I knew I'd be splitting my priorities too often," she recalls.

Eventually, priorities changed at Corning. In 1986, a company survey revealed that women were not becoming top managers and that they were twice as likely to leave as men. Just replacing them cost more than $2 million a year. Corning's isolated location in upstate New York was a factor, but its maximum-devotion work ethic made things worse. "A new mother was really kind of stuck," says human resources head Thomas E. Blumer. Now Corning offers all salaried employees the option of working part-time or flexible hours. Twenty-five women signed on in the program's first year.

Milliman, now the mother of two girls, aged 7 and 4, was lured back to Corning in 1987. She is a project engineer, at the same level as the job she left, but she works only two days a week. Her husband, Bruce, is manager of office systems at Corning, and she is completing an executive MBA at Syracuse University, at company expense. "When she left us, she was touted as a high-potential, senior-level manager," says Blumer. "Hopefully, she still can be."

Can she? That question is at the heart of the mommy-track debate. On one side, is Catalyst's Felice Schwartz, who argues that a few years on the slow boat shouldn't matter. Even if a female manager drops out for five years when her children are small, argues Schwartz, she would work 38 years as opposed to the typical man's 43 years—a barely perceptible difference. Indeed, a mother with school-aged children tends to be the most stable employee of all, says executive mobility expert Eugene Jennings at Michigan State University. "She's already gone through a lot of what causes women to leave," he explains.

Pacific Telesis Group, a company that has a tradition of lifetime employment—and a work force that's half female—takes the long view. "In the course of 32 years, an absence of two or three years is not the end of the world, and it's fairly common," says Jim R. Moberg, executive vice-president of human resources. "These people are going to be with us for a long time. I can't imagine being so rigid that you didn't understand that."

At Pacific Telesis, extended leaves of absence are more common than part-time jobs for managers. Still, after her first child was born in 1982 and her maternity leave was over, Linda E. Chinn arranged for eight months of part-time work. That helped her reorganize herself as a working mother for the long haul, she says.

'MARTYR SYNDROME.' But Chinn, now an assistant vice-president for finance, felt that continuing part-time work would compromise her future. She chose instead what she calls "the martyr syndrome,"

returning to 12-hour workdays, which she sometimes starts at 5 a.m. to have evenings at home. Chinn's husband, an emergency-room physician, works long hours, too. "My challenge is to demonstrate that women can be women and be mothers and make it into the executive ranks," says Chinn.

And there's the rub. Baby-boom women who entered the work force 10 to 20 years ago are approaching their 40s—exactly when their male peers are making the big push into senior positions. Add to that the so-called glass ceiling—a cultural barrier many believe keeps women from the top. "First of all, a woman's going to have a harder time because the playing field's not level. The second issue is that she wants to take a few years off," says Mary Anne Devanna, who directs executive education at Columbia University's business school. "I think you'd be better off if you had your kids at 21, got them into school, and then went to work. If you want to be chairman of the board, your mid-30s are critical," Devanna maintains.

Only about 2% of corporate officers at major public companies are women. About 60% of top female executives do not have children, while 95% of the men do. The message seems clear: If you're a mother, don't bother.

DADDY TRACK. Men who made it to the upper ranks have done so by relying on their wives to raise the kids and take full responsibility at home. A fast-track woman with an equally ambitious mate gets caught in a time and energy crunch, even if both parents are equal partners at home. "I really think somebody has to cut back when the kids are small," says Gail Deegan, mother of five- and seven-year-old sons, and chief financial officer of Eastern Gas & Fuel Associates in Weston, Mass. True, a full-time housekeeper gets dinner on her family's table. But her husband, William R. Huddleston, a clinical psychologist, also has reduced his sessions with clients to 20 hours a week at home. You might say he's on the daddy track.

Few men have been willing to buck cultural norms to that degree. And that leads some critics to believe that men will simply leave the mommy trackers in the dust. "In most organizations, the mommy track is a millstone around your neck," says Richard Belous, an economist at the National Planning Assn. In his recent study of 50 management and professional women who went part-time, Belous had to promise anonymity: Participants were nervous that just identifying themselves could hurt their careers. "CEOs and rainmakers don't come out of the mommy track," he warns. "If you go part-time, you're signaling to your employer you're on the B-team."

Sometimes work places make that message explicit. At some elite law firms and Big Eight accounting firms, "permanent associate" jobs have been designed to halt the exodus of those who fail to make partner—and to accommodate women's needs. The new positions are more secure than the all-or-nothing gamble of traditional partnership tracks, and there's nothing to stop men from applying. But such jobs can relegate women to the least interesting cases and the fringes of power. Partners, of course, also earn far more.

But Miriam V. Gold, 39, a division counsel at the U.S. headquarters of Ciba-Geigy Corp., insists she "really wasn't penalized" for her mommy-track years. An attorney and mother of three, Gold started at Ciba in 1977, cut her hours to three days a week in 1981, and recently returned full-time—for a promotion. As counsel to three large divisions and an operating unit, she works at home one day a week. Similar deals have been cut for only six Ciba managers—top performers whom the company didn't want to lose. "Miriam Gold is an exceptional lawyer," says Stanton Goldberg, Ciba's human resources director. Such arrangements, he believes, "should be restricted to high-quality employees."

Most companies also say that flexible schedules must be custom-tailored to work well. Some tasks can be done partly at home. Others may allow a shorter workday. Quite a few positions lend themselves to job sharing. At office-furniture maker Steelcase Inc., two women are sharing a dealer service representative job. They split salary, vacation, and benefits, working alternate weeks. Managers like the way job-sharing cuts down on absenteeism and helps fill the gaps during vacation time.

NEW YARDSTICKS. There is general agreement that jobs that can be done on a project basis are best suited to mommy tracks. Information-based jobs, where the files and the referencing system are stored in someone's head, are a lot tougher. And the consensus is that managing people cannot be done well at all. That's bad news for women, since corporations have traditionally measured career progress by how many bodies inhabit one's fiefdom.

This yardstick may now be outmoded, though. Downsizing has flattened many work organizations, with more people managing projects than supervising peo-

ple. And even people managers often handle more than one department or delegate responsibility when they travel, which suggests that these functions can be segmented or shared. "What's the difference whether you're in Cleveland or at home with your family?" asks Corning's Blumer.

WOMEN ARE LANDING BETTER JOBS...

	Woman as percent of total 15 years ago	Now
MANAGERS & ADMINISTRATORS	20	40
GRADUATING ENGINEERS	1	13
GRADUATING LAWYERS	5	39
GRADUATING MBAS	4	31

DATA: NATIONAL PLANNING ASSN., BUREAU OF LABOR STATISTICS

...BUT FEW MOTHERS HAVE REACHED THE TOP
FEMALE EXECUTIVES

MARRIED, NO CHILDREN 9%
39% MARRIED OR DIVORCED, WITH CHILDREN
52% SINGLE

DATA: KORN/FERRY INTERNATIONAL

Moreover, an individual whose life is narrowly focused on work may not be the best manager of people, particularly in a time of growing work force diversity. Women's socialization, on the other hand, is precisely about getting along with other people. "When you're a mother or a father, you have to get everybody going in a constructive direction every morning. You have to have a sense of humor and keep your cool. Those things are very helpful in business life," says Ellen R. Gordon, who has four grown daughters and is president of $114 million Tootsie Roll Corp.

Male-dominated institutions have never valued these skills. But as companies live with more women managers, they will have to examine the values they do hold. The question, really, is whether mommy trackers lose critical experiences and competence—or whether they simply break the organization's cherished rules.

Given the opportunity to experiment, managers may come up with their own solutions. Last year, NCNB Corp., a bank holding company based in Charlotte, N.C.,

made an extraordinary offer to accommodate family needs with flexible schedules for each of its 14,000 employees. No men have applied. But Vice-President Patricia Goolsby, 39, who oversees corporate cash management services, jumped at the chance.

She reorganized her 11-person staff into independent teams so that they would not need constant access to their boss. Goolsby began leaving at noon on Thursdays and Fridays. That gave her time to get her daughters, ages 5 and 8, to Girl Scouts and dance classes, and to volunteer tutor the older girl's classmates in math. She must sometimes put in extra hours, but only after the kids are asleep. NCNB's program "is going to give us a clear recruiting edge," says career development director Karen Geiger. "Other companies are starting to do it, because they know we'll take their people."

The new work styles have their problems. Part-time professionals often find the hours stretching into full-time and are less likely to get "invaluable" sponsorship from higher-ups. Working at home is no panacea either: Even with a computer in your den, you still need a baby-sitter. It's hard to be all business when your child gets on the phone with a client and says anything from " 'the washing machine's overflowing' to 'I have diarrhea,' " adds Claudia Wyatt, who takes calls at home two days a week as a Chicago consultant (no relation) at Wyatt Co.

Wyatt, a compensation and benefits consulting firm, recently offered a part-time path—with the option of returning to the fast track. One of the first to request a reduced schedule was a new father whose wife had just delivered twins.

That just might be what the future will look like. For there is another side to the demographics that are reshaping the world of work. The 1980s saw the ethic of long hours escalate in corporations and professions, partly because the baby-boom generation was competing for career advancement.

As the boomers age, more men as well as women may trade the next rung on the ladder for other rewards—more time, the ability to try something new, or a better quality of life. The challenge for companies is to provide flexibility and a rainbow of options so both men and women can raise their families as they see fit and still contribute.

By Elizabeth Ehrlich in New York, with bureau reports

The Changing Role of FATHERS

The stereotypical role of the father has evolved into a shared partnership with the mother. Today, he brings the children to day care, stays home when someone is sick, and even may take a paternity leave.

Roger M. Barkin

Dr. Barkin is chairman of the Department of Pediatrics, Rose Medical Center, Denver, Colo., and author of The Father's Guide: Raising a Healthy Child *(Fulcrum, Inc.).*

IT'S official—fathers are no longer the invisible parent. Changes in American society have initiated a new family structure. More fathers now are assuming an equal partnership to raise children, an increased involvement that crosses all cultural and socioeconomic classes. Indeed, in many families, fathers have assumed a major role in shared parenting or become the primary care-giver when divorce or death intervenes. These enormous changes in the family present a challenging opportunity that few fathers had in the past.

Historically, men have been considered to possess minimal child-raising skills, a notion that obviously has proven untrue. Stereotyping of our sociocultural and economic environment has led to distinct role identification that is passe. Traditional concepts of parenting derived from our own fathers have changed. In every setting where it has been tested, men quickly acquire the skills and sensitivity necessary for nurturing. Increasingly, elementary and

secondary school education is providing children with an earlier understanding of the changing role of men in society. Evolving attitudes toward the balance of family and work have produced a marked rethinking of roles.

Mothers no longer are stereotyped as the only parent raising the children and fathers as the career-minded disciplinarian. Bringing home a paycheck and periodically reading an obligatory bedtime story is not the model for today's fathers.

Now, fathers are involved more intimately in the parenting process. Once banned to the waiting room, fathers participate during childbirth and are present in the delivery room at the cherished moment. Only 25% of fathers attended deliveries in the early 1970's; this recently has escalated to over 75%.

Fathers continue to be involved in all aspects of nurturing children, whether it is cradling an infant, changing diapers, giving bottles, going shopping, or a variety of

other activities on a constant basis. These changes are evident in daily life and even are reflected in advertising messages for infant products—men changing diapers, giving baths, and feeding children. Fathers share car-pooling responsibilities, take children to day care, attend school on parents' day stay home when someone is sick, and accompany their children to the doctor's office for regular check-ups. Coaching a soccer team, leading a scout troop, and helping with gymnastics or dance are all joint activities. Some fathers may become the primary care-giver, raising children as a single parent or with joint custody.

Shared parenting has been shown to improve relationships with children and spouse. Mothers and fathers each contribute in distinct ways to the cognitive development of their children. Mothers tend to stimulate children by talking, demonstrating new toys and activities, and encouraging warmth and affection. Fathers often spend more time playing with their children and are more likely to roughhouse with them and engage in physically stimulating activities such as peek-a-boo and ball toss. Fathers are less verbal, but more tactile, especially with their sons. Interactions with their daughters involve more verbal stimulation—conversations, praise, and compliments. These differences may serve as an early basis of traditional sex-appropriate behavior. Fathers' expectations for daughters probably will evolve with changing values and increasing participation of women in the workplace. Encouraging them to get involved in traditional "male" activities, such as fixing the car, making house repairs, or throwing a football, develops self-confidence and a broader definition of "being female." Fathers should learn to feel at ease when discussing sensitive topics and educate themselves about medical issues unique to children of each gender.

A father's wonderful, positive impact extends beyond intellectual development. Children growing up in households where parenting is a shared concept are more likely to develop solid peer relationships and the ability to confront strange situations. They have more secure self-images and are less apt to stereotype others in future work-related and personal roles.

The increasing number of women in the workforce has produced changes in the role a father plays. Now, 48% of U.S. women with children under the age of one have jobs, compared with only 33% of this group in 1975. Sixty-three percent of mothers with children four-five years old presently have jobs, up from 45% in 1975.

This increased maternal employment is a result of a greater acceptance of women in the workforce, diminished harassment, and women's escalating interest in developing pursuits and a career independent of home and hearth. The financial reality that two incomes often are required to maintain a desired standard of living is, of course, a dominant factor. In some families where finances are not paramount, the mother actually may not begin a new career or return to work, but she becomes increasingly involved with a community or civic organization as a key volunteer, which leads to significant time commitments outside the home.

Is there an ideal time for mothers to begin a new career or return to work? Fathers now are asking similar questions. There is clearly not one answer. The decision must reflect the children's adjustment and development, financial and personal priorities, employment flexibility, and maternal health. Working parents often worry about missing important moments—like the baby's first step—but evidence suggests that this is not necessarily a problem if spending time with children is valued. They daily can spend an average of four to six hours if this is made a priority during leisure time.

The impact of maternal employment on children has been studied in great depth. The findings have not been uniform, but the impact has been consistent. Infants and young children do not suffer from the absence of a working parent if day care arrangements are high quality and provide significant ongoing social interaction in a positive, productive environment. Attachments to care-givers do not interfere with the primary parent relationship. Children of working parents actually may become well-adjusted and demonstrate high intellectual abilities. The mother-child relationship will remain strong if it constantly is supported, strengthened, and remains a primary focus of family activity.

When mothers work

School-aged daughters of employed mothers tend to have consistently high academic performance. They also tend to develop close relationships with their fathers if they are warm, supportive, and participate actively in parenting. School-aged sons tend to have better social and personality adjustments as well as higher academic achievement if their mothers work outside the home. However, sons of lower socioeconomic families with a working mother may be less admiring of their fathers, perhaps because of the perceived notion of economic failure on their part.

Adolescents benefit when their mothers work. Employed women (or those with significant interests or activities outside the home) usually are happier, more satisfied, and more likely to encourage their children to be independent. Sons tend to demonstrate better social and personal adjustments at school, and daughters tend to be more outgoing, independent, motivated, and better adjusted to their environment. Children of working mothers also are less likely to have stereotyped perceptions of life roles on the basis of being male or female.

The newly evolved role of fathers and the concept of shared parenting have led some corporations to develop paternity-leave policies, but fewer than one percent of eligible men make use of them. Barriers include the financial burden on the family from loss of income and the subtle psychological pressure that defines work as the highest priority for men. Federal legislation has been introduced to guarantee paternity leave with provisions for reinstatement to the same job without loss of seniority and with protection from harassment.

Families in which both parents work or actively are involved in outside activities must recognize the potential for additional stress. Fathers who share the responsibilities of child-rearing help to minimize this stress, while fulfilling their desire to develop a more significant role in raising their children. This comes from a mutual understanding of the shared nature of bringing up children. When men are supportive of their wives, marital stress decreases and the relationship functions better. Although this is certainly a worthwhile and important goal, it requires commitment and hard work.

Burdens of time and priorities have an impact on the family unit. Indeed, compromises constantly are made. Work schedules often must be altered, when possible, to increase flexibility of hours, vacation, travel time, patterns of delegation, and assumption of responsibilities. Organization is essential to reducing stress and can be achieved by simplifying activities and establishing specific blocks of time for the family. Delegating routine chores to others and even omitting some activities often is helpful. After all, time is ultimately the most precious commodity.

With more contemporary models of parenting providing greater choices and opportunities, men are able to share and become better partners in raising their children. By prioritizing time, responsibilities, and commitments, mother and father can enjoy the valuable nurturing experience. Parenting *should* be shared and savored. Children grow up fast. The magic moments of infancy quickly are lost as the independence of childhood and adolescence grows.

Children should be raised on love and quality time. Expectations according to age should be gauged consistently. Communications must be open and honest. In this environment, men will evolve more rapidly into their new expanded role of father, and mothers can enjoy their relationship with their children and husbands even more.

For Goodness' Sake

What Americans do when they see a crying need

NANCY GIBBS

Kenny spent his first two Christmases in the Harlem hospital where his mother abandoned him, in a roomful of babies with AIDS. His third Christmas he spent in an Albany children's home. There he had the luck to meet his first angel.

Gertrude Lewis spent her days driving a city bus and, every other Saturday, volunteering at the Albany home. "I saw this boy with these beautiful eyes," she recalls, "just looking up and smiling." She was 47 years old, had never married, never had a family of her own. She decided then and there she would become a foster mother.

Now Kenny lies in his crib upstairs in her home, in a house she shares on a tree-lined street, where her heart prepared him room. This nursery is merry with orange walls and pictures and 27 watchful stuffed animals. "It's going to be hard to lose him," says Gertrude.

What are we to make of a woman willing to take to heart a baby she knows is likely to die? Surely, she confounds all descriptions of the roaring '80s as a morally chintzy stretch of history, where such problems as Kenny's are greeted with more petulance than pity. In an age of toxic cynicism, Gertrude is a Samaritan: a woman who, in the spacious privacy of her life, went out of her way to help a child who needed her. She is not running for office, not running charity balls and not running away. Perhaps she seems a rare heroine at an end of a decade when the rich got greedier, the poor got needier, and everyone else tended to his own shiny self-interest.

But the redeeming truth, to our own surprise, is that Gertrude is in vast company. Last March, Independent Sector, a Washington research and lobbying group, commissioned a Gallup poll to plumb the depths of our charity: What do we give, and why, and who does the giving, and how much? It turns out that almost half of all American adults offer their time to a cause, an astounding figure even allowing for the number of people who lie to pollsters. And most are giving more time than

ever. These are commitments, not gestures. The average volunteer offers nearly five hours a week, for a total of 19.5 billion hours in 1987—the equal, roughly, of 10 million full-time employees. There is something infectious about mercy.

And so it is that George Bush, the heir-elect, looks out over the nation and raptly muses about a thousand points of light, savoring the phrase, if not quite understanding it. He did not add that the lights are shining into corners that have grown bleak and dim in the past eight years. And he got the numbers wrong. Out of sight of the Rose Garden, something like 80 million individuals are doing whatever they can to address the problems that politicians are fleeing.

Try to draw a profile of the typical do-gooder, and the only thing certain is that it is probably wrong. Volunteer work is not the sole province of the housewives holding Christmas fairs, the idle rich sponsoring benefits and the young selling cookies. The aggressive, entrepreneurial cast of much modern charity reflects the fact that the largest number of volunteers, according to a J.C. Penney survey, are between the ages of 35 and 49.

Certainly the most eager and conspicuous new recruits are the yuppies. Since they absorb much of the blame for the moral defoliation of the '80s, they deserve some recognition for their redemption. "We're trying to break the cycle of you get up, you go to work, step over a homeless person on the way to the subway, go to the gym, go to the sushi bar, go home and fall asleep," says Kenneth Adams, executive director of New York Cares, a sort of charitable clearinghouse for yuppies that has recruited 600 young volunteers to tutor dropouts, serve in soup kitchens, renovate housing and visit the elderly. "The Me generation is dying," says Adams, "and New York Cares is one example of how it's being put to rest." Call it yuppie love.

But even that is not the whole story. For all the flood of new professionals into charity work, more than a quarter of all volunteers still come from households

with incomes of $20,000 or less. Families earning less than $10,000 a year give more of their income to charity than individuals earning more than $100,000. Since the less rich families in this country rub more intimately against its sores, they are often the first to offer their money and time. "You feel the pain, you feel the hurt," says Wilfred Schill, a North Dakota farmer who with his wife counsels couples who fear foreclosure. "It gives you the greatest incentive to do something like this."

Gallup's evidence defies our low expectations. We are, perhaps, a little better than we think, though maybe not as good as we'd like. If 80 million adults are volunteering, then there may be 80 million impulses for doing so—whether political, professional, spiritual or personal. The precise mixture is measured from needs within and needs without. In the end, the decision to volunteer usually occurs at a crossroads, where moral indignation and moral responsibility meet.

In both the cities and the farmlands, the indignation of the moment is palpable. The Reagan Administration did not invent the poor, but it has largely ignored them. "We've dug deep pits in this country in the past eight years," says Tanya Tull, a Los Angeles housewife who founded Para Los Niños, a family-service facility on Skid Row. "People are falling into them—and we've taken away the ladders too." Reagan's policies, argues Marian Wright Edelman of the Children's Defense Fund, have "created a set of social problems that simply were not there in 1980. We're going to be paying for them for a long time."

Hence the sheer volume of volunteers: an overwhelming majority of Americans believe that charities are needed more now than they were just five or ten years ago. In New York City there are about 35,000 people living on the streets, compared with 500 a decade ago. AIDS, which alone has pulled thousands of people into action, did not exist. Crack, which has perhaps done more to ruin children than any other drug, did not exist. "Volunteerism is as old as the nation," says Winifred Brown, executive director of New York City's Voluntary Action Center, "and it's as new as today's headlines."

But it is not just that the needs are greater. In the minds of many Americans, the weight of moral responsibility shifted, publicly and dramatically, somewhere between Jimmy Carter's "malaise" days in 1979 and the Hands Across America hoopla of 1986. "Government has a lot of money but doesn't know how to take care of people," says banker Peter Flanigan, founder of the Student/Sponsor Partnership, which helps shepherd poor kids through Catholic schools in New York City. "That revives the latent feeling in people that they should do it themselves."

Democracy does demand shared responsibility, not only for our governance but for our welfare as well. Yet each generation weaves its own mythology of philanthropy. Ours in the '80s owes most to the lessons of the 1960s and the heady afternoons of the Great Society. For a time it looked as though Washington would take care of everything: it was government as

governess. Caseworkers trooped through the ghettos and housing projects promising advocacy, access and opportunity for the dispossessed. For many, it was a dream that came true. But too often the army hunkered down into an occupying, rather than a liberating, force.

The lasting accomplishments of the Great Society have been challenged by some who believed in it deeply. But beginning in 1981, the very premises of activist government came under attack as Reagan lashed the "welfare queen" and extolled "neighborliness." By the time Charles Murray published *Losing Ground* in 1984, his argument that the War on Poverty had wounded more people than it had saved was poised to become conventional wisdom. "Whatever our political persuasion," says Independent Sector president Brian O'Connell, "we all understand the practical limitations of Big Government, and very often that means setting up alternative organizations."

In place of a waning welfare state, Reagan promised that enterprise freed would bring prosperity for all. A surging

economy with low inflation and high employment would do more to help the poor than a raft of welfare programs. As for solving the particular problems of the poor, that was best left to states and towns and, above all, individuals who knew better. This transfer of responsibility camouflaged the neglect of vital programs, particularly subsidized housing and programs for children. "When voluntary action is translated to national policy, it assumes that communities have the ability to pull themselves up by the bootstraps," observes Barry Checkoway, professor of social work at the University of Michigan. "Some of them don't even have boots."

One reason Reagan got away with the cuts was that he so cannily persuaded people that they could do it better themselves. And indeed, individuals began to step in the minute government backed off. "My personal motivation," says Talmage Newton III, 44, a St. Louis advertising executive who chairs Operation Food Search, an organization to distribute food to the poor, "was a belief that any citizens' group can perform any function better than any government, with the exception

Planting Trees of Life

"I don't like the title Dreamer . . . That tends to mean nondeliverer"

Andy Lipkis, 34, a bearded, boyish, homespun half saint, knows something about delivering dreams. His life is a demonstration in respectable alchemy, creating gold from nothing. Inspired by the belief that planting trees can reduce smog, protect the ozone layer, feed hungry people and, when all is said and done and planted, save the planet, Lipkis has become a global Johnny Appleseed. The organization he founded 15 years ago, TreePeople, is directly or indirectly responsible for planting more than 170 million trees around the world. At the center of TreePeople's mission is the belief that people can save themselves by saving the land.

Lipkis' ideas about voluntarism have a certain earthy logic. "Scientists define pollution as energy waste. Sewage is pollution when you dump it in the ocean—yet it's so loaded with nutrients that it could enrich any soil it is put into," he explains. "It's the same with humans. People have an immense amount of energy, but for the most part it isn't being used. The result is a kind of pollution: frustration, depression, rage, crime. Society needs that energy, and nobody is making the connection."

Lipkis' revelation came 18 years ago at summer camp, where he planted his first smog-resistant trees. "It was backbreaking work that required all of our creativity," he recalls. "For me, it was a life-altering experience." Lipkis went on to study ecology and search for ways to encourage more people to plant more trees. "I started a long process of trying and failing," he remembers, as he sought to enlist

public and private support for his cause. "Being able to fail is a key to the volunteer process," he adds now. "In their jobs, people aren't allowed to do that. The real joy of being a volunteer is the freedom to express yourself without fear that it will be held against you."

Lipkis emerged from his trials and errors a resourceful man, in the most literal sense of the word. Since founding TreePeople, he has enlisted volunteers everywhere, from senior citizens' homes to grade schools, to plant millions upon millions of trees. He has persuaded nurseries to donate unsold seedlings they would otherwise have destroyed. He has coaxed the California National Guard ("all those empty trucks and planes sitting around") into helping transport the trees. He once even persuaded Club Med to rescue and care for two exhausted TreePeople volunteers in Senegal who had fallen ill while planting fruit trees in famine-stricken African countries. "I don't know how many bureaucrats have laughed us off over the years," he muses. "Then one person says, 'Maybe we can help you.' That's vital to voluntarism."

Nowadays, after a year of ecological nightmares, Lipkis is promoting tree planting as the easiest solution to the greenhouse effect, the buildup of CO_2 that has environmentalists warning of a disastrous global warming trend. Trees absorb as much as 48 lbs. of carbon dioxide per year each. Guided by the success of Lipkis' volunteer efforts, the American Forestry Association announced in October a citizens' campaign to plant 100 million trees around the country.

Lipkis manages all this on an annual budget of half a million dollars, raised entirely by donations. His "save our planet earth" pitch is not merely fund-raising rhetoric. It has been his goal all along. "Our message is so far beyond trees," he says. "If the idea of voluntarism can be presented in the right way, I think it has the potential for healing everything."

of national defense."

Reagan's vision of America not only altered what Americans expect of government; it also played deftly on what we expect from ourselves. We are all to some extent tending to our character, trying to turn efforts of will into habits of mind in the hope that generosity will one day come easily. People of all faiths find in charity a chance for thanks, praise and obedience. "What doth the Lord require of thee," asks Micha, "but to do justly, and to love mercy, and to walk humbly with thy God?" To borrow from the Quakers, many volunteers believe that when the worship is over, the service begins.

To be sure, there are also plenty of self-serving reasons to serve: glamour seeking, résumé padding and networking. "There is usually an opening in your life when you decide to volunteer," says Core Trowbridge, 26, volunteer coordinator for TreePeople in Los Angeles. "Young people come here, treating this as a singles' scene. Old people who've retired but not run out of energy come." But when researchers inquire further into motives, the most common reason cited is a desire to do something useful. To comfort a child, succor a patient, rescue a school or salvage a neighborhood gives volunteers a sense of success that few jobs can match. The chance to create and control a daring solution is irresistible and restorative. Attorney Tom Petersen is on leave from the Dade County state attorney's office to establish, among other community programs, Teen Cuisine, which teaches culinary skills to teenage mothers. "We discovered almost by accident," he says, "that creative economic incentives can be much more effective in changing the girls' behavior than traditional counseling."

That sparkle of individual ingenuity sets many new volunteer efforts apart from the huge corporate rescue missions that define much American charity. While the United Way, the American Red Cross and the American Cancer Society serve vast needs and do great good, they are to charity what GM is to industry. Charity too needs its entrepreneurs, dreaming on a different scale, and perhaps genius ripens most fruitfully in a free and private space. That may explain why 105,000 new service organizations were born between 1982 and 1987. "Volunteers are now expected to *solve* problems," says Jerri Spoehel of the Volunteer Center of San Fernando Valley, Calif., "not just stuff envelopes."

When, as now, there is hope ready for harvesting, excellent ideas become especially fertile. The examples of some national heroes—Candy Lightner, founder of Mothers Against Drunk Driving; Bruce Ritter, father of Covenant House for kids in trouble; and Eugene Lang, whose I Have a Dream program has spawned innumerable imitations—all proved what extraordinary good can be reaped from one person's crusade. Faced with a desperate need, many new volunteers see not only a moral challenge but also a tactical one: to do as much as possible with as little as possible, and then share the idea, to allow it to spread.

Take Chris Renner, 26, who helped create Food Partnership Inc. outside Los Angeles. It troubled him that food banks were spending a fortune in transport fees to collect donations. With the help of the California Trucking Association and United Way, he worked out a method for trucks to transport food between donors and food banks when they were returning empty from a long haul. So far, the program has carried nearly 4 million lbs. of food and saved the food banks $55,000 in trucking fees.

Or Pedro José Greer, a Miami physician who found his calling not only in hospitals but also under bridges and highways, where many of the city's homeless live. Four years ago, "Dr. Joe," 32, opened a clinic next to a shelter called Camillus House. He now has 130 volunteer doctors and medical personnel working on 40 patients a day. "There is so much talent among the poor, we must help them no matter what," he says. "We lose so much when we lose the people from the inner cities." At the University of Miami medical school, where he is a fellow in hepatology, there is a three-month waiting list for the "homeless elective" for medical students.

Or Suzanne Firtko, an architectural historian in New York City who invented the Street Sheet, instructions that direct homeless people to the nearest soup kitchens and clothes banks. She persuaded Du Pont to donate water-proof, tear-resistant paper, and designed the sheets with easy-to-understand graphics so the disoriented and illiterate could use them. The entire operation that first year cost $1,800. "Projects like mine become very expensive when they're done by established agencies," she says. "It's very cheap when you're doing it at your kitchen table."

The efforts of American Samaritans, in short, reflect a new frame of mind in which sympathy complements competence but does not replace it: wide-eyed but hard-nosed. Private charity cannot and should not replace public policy. It can, however, set standards, set priorities and set an example for the best use of resources. Throwing money at a problem may be just the easiest way to attack it, not the wisest. The more effective forces, it seems, are harder to marshal: vision, tenacity, patience and courage.

In the Bible, Samaritans were viewed with contempt until Jesus' tale of how one of their community showed great mercy to a stranger redeemed them for history. Perhaps the generation that closes the millennium will find the same vindication. The unheralded gestures of gracious individuals may in the end outlast and belie the labels hung on the Me generation. And government, in the meantime, could take some lessons from the most creative of these very private enterprises. Good ideas need money and leadership as well as light and oxygen to brighten and spread. In the process, we might even discover that this is already a kinder, gentler nation than we ever imagined. —*Reported by Janice C. Simpson/ New York and James Willwerth/Los Angeles*

'THEY CAN'T STOP US NOW'

Kimi Gray and the other residents of D.C.'s Kenilworth-Parkside complex
have overcome poverty, crime, drugs and innumerable layers of public housing
bureaucracy—not to mention charges that they're just cogs in Jack Kemp's
propaganda machine. Their goal? To take control of their own lives

DAVID OSBORNE

David Osborne is the author of Laboratories of Democracy, *which examined social and economic policy innovations in state government in the 1980s.*

IT WAS AUTUMN 1986, AND AFTER THREE YEARS OF WAIT-ing, Kimi Gray was about to get her first glimpse of the city's plans to renovate her home. In 1983, the federal Department of Housing and Urban Development had awarded the city a grant to modernize the 464-unit Kenilworth-Parkside public housing complex in Northeast Washington. After dragging its feet for years, the city had hired an architectural firm. But when Kimi and her staff had asked to meet with the firm to explain what they wanted done—as required by HUD—the architects had repeatedly demurred. It wasn't time yet, they said. They weren't ready. Apparently, they did not relish the prospect of planning a major renovation project with a roomful of poor black women.

Finally they had agreed to a meeting. As they unfolded their sketches and presented their plans, Kimi's anger grew. Where were the plans for a new heating plant? What about the under-ground water pipes that kept bursting? What about the plumb-ing? These were pretty colored drawings, but they were fluff. They had nothing to do with Kenilworth's real problems.

Michael Price was the first to speak. A decade earlier, Price had been a high school dropout, hanging out on the streets. Kimi had convinced him to go back to school, then sent him to college through her College Here We Come program. Now a professional architect, he was repaying his debt, helping the Resident Management Corp. negotiate the renovation plans.

Price asked about the heating plant, the plumbing, the pipes.

"I was shocked, because they knew that half of that stuff I would catch," he says. "I guess they banked on me just letting it ride—being polite and not saying anything. But I got quite angry."

Other residents picked up on his anger. Finally, their board chairman stood up and walked slowly to the front of the room. "No hard feelings against you all," Kimi said, "but your super-visors sent you down here to get your asses kicked. And that's exactly what we're going to do tonight." She proceeded to take apart the drawings in harsh language and great detail. Other residents joined in.

After 45 minutes, Kimi entertained a motion to adjourn. "You just pack up and go home," she told the architects. "We'll deal with it."

And deal with it they did. Kimi went to HUD and demanded that the agency refuse to reimburse the $500,000 the city had already paid the architects. By failing to consult with the tenants, she argued, the architects had broken their contract. HUD agreed, and the city was out $500,000.

It's Economics, That's What It's All About'

It was not the first time the irresistible force of Kimi Gray had met the immovable object of the city bureaucracy. And it was not the first time the irresistible force had won.

A massive figure with short cropped hair, large earrings and several pounds of jewelry around her neck and wrists, Kimi—as virtually everyone calls her—patrols the Kenilworth-Parkside development like a mother bear circling her cubs. Her voice erupts out of her slow-moving body like a volcano: one moment soft and low, the next exploding in a shout, the next dissolving in deep, rich laughter.

Sitting at her desk or behind the wheel of her ubiquitous van, wearing her jewelry and her bright yellow dresses, she brings the full force of her personality to bear on everyone who crosses her path.

Whether it is a child who needs discipline: "What you doing, girl? Why aren't you in school?"

Or an employee who deserves her praise: "I want to thank you so much, Lonnie. I understand the parade was *excellent*."

Or a teenager with a wad of bills: "Little boys went out two Sundays ago, they came back, they had a knot. I said, 'Where's that money from, boy?' They say, 'Kimi, we worked!' They go over to the Eastern Market and sell tie-dye shirts they made—they work about three or four hours, they make about $75 or $80."

Or a D.C. police officer who neglected to invite her to his backyard barbecue: "Okay, do me a favor. You put a message on the board, in dark Magic Marker print. Tell him I got a CON-TRACT on his head, for not inviting me to his damn cookout Saturday! And tell him I say when he gets off work at 3:30, report to my office! Immediately! Underline immediately!" Her voice returns to velvet: "Thank you, my love. Bye bye."

Kimi's desk sits where a receptionist would normally be, right by the front door, so the residents can always find her. Her assistants work upstairs, away from the constant stream of visitors. They field the calls, slip her messages, bring her paperwork to sign between sentences. This is a woman who has won award after award, who has been invited to the White House, who has preached her message from Paris to Seoul. But when a resident comes in, she drops everything.

"The only way that you'll truly get my time is getting me away from this property," she tells the public housing director of Alaska, who wants her help. " 'Cause if a resident walks through this door with me, I don't care who's here, he's my first priority. And I won't try and make believe it's no different, okay?" Reporters wait hours for an interview, weeks for a return phone call. Jack Kemp recently waited an hour and a half for a photo session at her office; finally, he gave up.

Somehow, through it all, things get done. It is easy to exaggerate the accomplishments of Kenilworth-Parkside, and Kimi Gray's supporters have often done so. Kenilworth residents are still poor: Many are single mothers, some are on welfare. Drug use is still widespread. This is still public housing, and though the grass gets cut, it still has that public housing shagginess around the edges. Twenty-five percent of the rent money still goes uncollected. All that said, there is no denying that a remarkable transformation has taken place.

The drug dealers who once used Kenilworth-Parkside as an open-air market are gone.

Teenage pregnancies have fallen.

Residents who once lived with gunfire now walk the project streets in safety. The crime rate has fallen from 12 to 15 reported crimes a month—one of the highest levels in the city—to 2, according to the police.

In the 15 years since Kimi founded College Here We Come, according to her records, more than 600 residents have gone to college. In the previous 15 years, two had.

In 1986, the accounting firm Coopers & Lybrand released an audit of Kenilworth-Parkside. During the four years that Kenilworth had been managed by its tenants, the firm reported, rent collections increased 77 percent—seven times the increase at public housing citywide. Vacancy rates fell from 18 percent—then the citywide average—to 5.4 percent. The Kenilworth-Parkside Resident Management Corp. helped at least 132 residents get off welfare: It hired 10 as staff and 92 to run the businesses it started, while its employment office found training and jobs for 30 more. (Others received part-time jobs.)

Overall, Coopers & Lybrand estimated, four years of resident management had saved the city at least $785,000. If trends continued over the next six years, it would save $3.7 million more. (The federal government would reap additional savings.)

Since the Coopers & Lybrand audit, a complete renovation of Kenilworth has begun under HUD's normal renovation program. (Hence only about 70 units are now occupied; more than 300 families have been temporarily relocated.) The most amazing moment will come next year, if the renovation is completed on schedule: The residents will buy the development from the city for $1. A community of 3,000, once characterized largely by families on welfare, will have become a community of homeowners, the majority of whom work.

It is an incredible story, but not a unique one. Residents in a handful of other public housing complexes around the nation have similar stories to tell. They are testaments to the power of empowerment—vivid demonstrations of what happens when ownership of public services is pulled out of the hands of bureaucrats and put in the hands of those receiving the services. They are living proof that when people are treated as clients for whom decisions must be made, they will learn dependency; but when they are given control over their destinies, they will learn independence.

These stories are also tales of salvation through self-help, rather than salvation through politics. "Self-sufficiency" is the driving theme at Kenilworth-Parkside; one hears the phrase constantly, from all sides. "It's economics, that's what it's all about," says Kimi Gray. "We can talk racism and all this and that, but it's economics. If you got some money, you can buy a lot of this stuff we're talking about begging for, okay?"

Finally, the story of tenant management and tenant ownership is a story of extraordinary political role reversals. Empowerment of poor people was a theme close to the heart of the New Left, carried forward into populist citizens' organizations with fanciful acronyms: ACORN, COPS, BUILD. But in Washington, conservatives like Jack Kemp and Stuart Butler, director of domestic policy studies at the Heritage Foundation, led the charge for tenant management and ownership—and they convinced Ronald Reagan and George Bush to come along.

Low-income housing activists have supported tenant management for two decades. But when Reagan and then-Congressman Kemp picked up the cause—and added the wrinkle of *selling* public housing to its tenants—red flags went up throughout the liberal community. Reagan cut federal funding for low-income housing from $24 billion to $8 billion a year. He slowed construction of public housing from more than 30,000 units a year to fewer than 5,000. And Jack Kemp voted with him. To many liberals, Kemp's talk of tenant management, his constant invocation of Kenilworth-Parkside and Kimi Gray, are political cover for a devastating retreat from federal commitments to the poor. Worse, they say, proposals to sell public housing to tenants are a ploy to get the federal government out of the housing business.

"Mr. Bush projects a gentler, kinder nation," says Maxine Green, chairperson of the National Tenants Organization. "Fine. Let the tenants have a kinder, gentler position, with the funds that are required to make that kind of a nation. But don't go into the capital, where you have 59 public housing developments, and sing about one.

"Kimi Gray was an active member of the National Tenants Organization," Green adds. "I give myself credit for sitting with her and giving her a direction. And now Kimi has joined, to my understanding, the Heritage Foundation."

A lifelong Democrat, Kimi does not let such suspicions worry her. She is a savvy politician who uses her relationship with Jack Kemp to the advantage of her residents—just as she does her relationship with Democrat Marion Barry. She understands that Kemp and Barry will use her in turn. (Kemp is so eager to be identified with Gray and tenant management that his staff volunteered an interview for this article without being asked.)

For Kimi Gray, economic self-sufficiency for her residents overrides all other goals. "I've been approached by some people who say, 'Well, Kimi, now you're a Republican,' " she explains. "And I say, 'No, I'm a dollar bill. And on each bill there's a different president. My family was poor when we had Roosevelt in the White House, we were poor when we had Kennedy, we were poor when we had Nixon and Ford and Carter. And we're no richer now.' "

'The System Penalizes Performance'

Kimi Odesser Houston was born January 1, 1945. She was raised in the Frederick Douglass public housing project in Southeast Washington by her mother and grandmother. Her father died when she was 7.

"Odesser's my grandmother's name," Kimi says. "She and I did not see eye to eye, not one day of her life. Now I know why, because we are identical. She was a strong-willed old southern lady who had a lot of morals and principles, and she didn't tolerate bad behavior.

"When I was young my grandma told me, 'No, babe, you cannot be *as good as* him, you gotta be *better* than he is.' When I ran track, I didn't want to run with the girls, 'cause I knew I could beat them. I wanted to run against the boys, okay? You can't be as good as them, you got to be better than them—as long as you keep thinking that way, that's what you'll be. And that's what I tell all my kids."

Kimi was an organizer from the start. In first grade, she got her first formal assignment: Her teacher made her substitute teacher—"and I just took over." When she was 11, she was elected citywide chairman of the youth section of the Junior Police and Citizen Corps.

But Kimi's energy was not always channeled into civic duty. "I put the J in juvenile delinquent myself," she says today. When she was 14, she had her first child. When she was 16, expecting her third, she married. At 19, with five children, she separated from her husband and went on welfare. She was 21 and miserable, living with her five children in a tiny apartment, when she got an apartment at Kenilworth. It was "1966, December the third, on a Wednesday," she says. "That's how happy I was to get this unit out here."

A complex of 37 low-rise buildings, Kenilworth-Parkside is sandwiched between the Anacostia River and I-295 hard by the Maryland line. It opened in 1959, about the time public housing began its downward spiral. The federal program had been launched during the New Deal as transitional housing for working people who hit hard times. Once constructed, units were not subsidized: Local public housing authorities charged enough rent to cover their operating costs. They screened carefully, and their standards were rigid. Parents had to be married. Many authorities excluded people on welfare. And if residents found better jobs and could afford to move out, they had to.

The program worked well for two decades, but during the boom times of the 1950s, the middle class headed for the suburbs, working families moved out of public housing, and poor migrants from the South poured in. Urban renewal hastened the process: When redevelopment agencies needed to move poor people out of the way of their bulldozers, they pressured

the housing authorities to take them—regardless of their incomes, moral standards or presence on the welfare rolls.

Public housing's new residents were poorer; many had trouble coping with life in urban high-rise apartments; and many were black—which often meant they were ignored. Yet as this radically different population moved in, few housing authorities did anything to address its problems.

Meanwhile, early public housing developments were beginning to exhaust their 30-year life cycles. Yet because tenants' incomes were falling behind expenses, housing authorities were burning up the reserves they needed for renovation. When they raised rents to cope with the squeeze, Congress slapped them back, limiting rents to 25 percent of family income.

Soon Congress had to provide an operating subsidy. With Washington making up the difference between expenses and income, local housing authorities now had little incentive to run businesslike operations. If they saved money or increased their income, Washington gave them smaller subsidies. As a spokesman for the Council of Large Public Housing Authorities put it, "The system penalizes performance." To make matters worse, until 1980, Congress provided no capital budget to finance renovation.

Welfare policy also undermined public housing. Congress decided to deny welfare to most families if the father was present—which drove many fathers away. Meanwhile, welfare mothers in public housing got subsidized rent, which meant that if they left welfare to work, their rent often tripled or quadrupled.

In some cities, including New York, dedicated housing authorities made the program work against all odds. But in others, many of the largest, most congested public housing developments sank into a vicious cycle of drugs, crime, violence, teenage pregnancy and welfare dependency. The crisis earned its most enduring symbol in 1972, when the St. Louis housing authority quit trying to rescue a 15-year-old, 43-building development called Pruitt-Igoe, and simply blew it up.

In Washington, the housing authority lost virtually all ability to respond to its 50,000 customers. The director of a 1987 blue ribbon commission that investigated the system described it to The Washington Post as "total chaos." Drugs and crime were rampant; half the residents were not paying rent; repairs were so slow that the vacancy rate was approaching 20 percent; and the vast majority of eviction notices were never even served. Then-public housing director Alphonso Jackson described an agency riddled with employees "who are not capable of doing their jobs," property managers who "just sat in their offices all day," engineers who were "creating havoc in our boiler rooms" and administrators who regularly submitted reports full of inaccurate data.

College Here We Come

KIMI GRAY STARTED ORGANIZING VIRTUALLY THE DAY SHE arrived at Kenilworth-Parkside. She got training and then a job with a federally funded social services organization, working with delinquent youth. (Today, her only income is from her $22,000-a-year job with the D.C. Department of Recreation as a counselor to troubled youth. She receives no salary as Kenilworth board chairman and says she donates all speaking honoraria to College Here We Come.) In the early '70s, she began trying to breathe new life into Kenilworth's moribund residents council. Then in 1974, "Some students came to me and said, 'Miss Kimi, we want to go to college.' What the hell did I know about going to college? Well, I've always worked with young people—always—because they have their dreams, and they're our future. So I said, 'Let me check it out.' "

With help from the local Community Action agency and the city's resident services staff, she gathered information on colleges and financial aid and set up a regular Tuesday meeting with the kids. Soon she and her helpers were tutoring them, bringing in black college graduates to talk, drumming up scholarship money, helping kids find summer and part-time jobs and helping them fill out applications.

With the money from their jobs, the students opened bank accounts. After all the scholarships and loans and work-study jobs had been hustled, if a student still needed $600 or $1,000, College Here We Come kicked in the rest—much of it raised from bake sales and raffles.

To make the program intriguing, Kimi took her students out to play tennis, had birthday parties for them and took them on weekend trips to visit colleges. "That brought about a lot of unity among them," she says, "till it became a family. So we went through the winter and the summer together, and when it was time for our first group to go away, we cried. The hardest job was us departing from one another. When you would go to the bus station, we all would pile in the car."

When kids started actually leaving for college, word spread quickly: "Man, this stuff is real! People really going to college! These children couldn't believe that. Poor people, from public housing, their mothers on welfare, absent fathers, going to college?

"Seventeen kids went to school the first August. That first semester when they came back, we must not have slept for two days. They had so much to tell us. Kids were out West, down South, up North, they were everywhere. They couldn't believe it! They were sharing experiences: 'Well, let me tell you about this!' 'Well, did you know this?' 'Well, it's nothing like this.' "

Nine of the original 17 graduated, and four went on to graduate school. Of the 600 Kimi says have gone to college since, she guesses 75 percent have graduated. (There is no way to independently verify such numbers, and Kimi has been known to exaggerate. But graduates of the program back up the figures.)

Whatever the numbers, College Here We Come is clearly an in thing to do at Kenilworth. Even 16-year-old boys who hang out on street corners look up to those in the program. Every year, Kimi asks graduates to come back and share their experiences with the younger kids. "That's all I ask of 'em: 'Come back and share something. Pass it on.' "

Michael Price was in one of the early groups. When Kimi first asked him what he wanted to do with his life, he told her he wanted to go back to school and become a draftsman. "No," she said. "You don't want to be a draftsman. You want to be an architect. That's where the money is." She helped him earn his high school degree, then sent him off to Paine College in Georgia. He lasted a semester.

"Kimi was very disappointed and angry at me," Price remembers. "But during the winter of '77, I said, 'Look, I want to try it again.' " This time he attended Elizabeth City State University in North Carolina. After a shaky start, he earned a high enough grade point average to transfer to the architecture program at Howard University.

"It was difficult," he says. "I'd call Kimi, and sometimes I'd cry, and she'd cuss me out. She'd tell me, 'Yeah, you're not going to succeed. You're not going to make it.' I'd be so angry, I'd sit back down at my drawing board, at 3 o'clock in the morning, and I'd say, 'I'm going to make it. You think I'm going to quit, but I'm not.' She used reverse psychology on me, and it worked.

"At other times, she would be just as gentle as could be.

Kenilworth-Parkside and the Politics of Public Housing

THE DAY KENILWORTH-PARKSIDE RESIDENTS ANNOUNCED the deal designed to turn them into homeowners, Jesse Jackson and D.C. Del. Walter Fauntroy held a "counter event." Though the sale would not take place for another two years, the Reagan administration had scheduled the announcement for 10 days before the 1988 election.

"This administration is having a housing press conference instead of a housing policy," Jackson declared. "My fear is that an uncritical media will let them have this photo opportunity and escape responsibility for the fact that they have cut the federal housing budget by 75 percent, at a time when 7.7 million people are in inadequate housing, when 5.4 million needy families receive no housing assistance, when 3 million to 5 million Americans are homeless."

So it was that Jackson, the Democrat most admired by poor blacks, and Fauntroy, the Democratic sponsor of a bill enabling Kenilworth residents to buy their homes, came together to denounce the sale. If ever one scene could capture the bizarre politics surrounding Kimi Gray and Kenilworth-Parkside, it happened on that chilly October afternoon. Few issues so disorient the political gyroscopes of Washingtonians as tenant management and ownership of public housing.

Neither issue is new. Tenants in Boston's Bromley-Heath project pioneered tenant management back in 1973, after crime got so bad that stores wouldn't deliver and taxis wouldn't drive into the area. Residents of St. Louis's Cochran Gardens tried it three years later. Born of crisis, both efforts achieved startling results: Crime rates dropped, vacant apartments were renovated, jobs were created, and residents were hired. Today, 13 public housing developments are managed by their residents.

Local housing authorities have been selling units to tenants even longer. Most such "turnkey" sales have involved single-family homes or small apartment buildings, sold to handpicked tenants with decent incomes; efforts to sell larger complexes have generally failed. There have been exceptions: Louisville recently sold a 100-unit complex to its residents as condos. But most turnkey sales of large projects have faltered because the tenants did not go through the process of organizing and taking control of their community.

"The psychological transformation doesn't happen when today I'm a renter and tomorrow I'm an owner," says David Freed, a consultant who specializes in low-income tenant buyouts. "It happens when there is a process that renters go through together, and there is a change in people's view of themselves and their neighbors. I see it again and again: It's that conversion experience."

The Kimi Grays of the world understand this. Several years ago, Robert Woodson of the National Center for Neighborhood Enterprise asked public housing tenant leaders to draw up a list of policy changes that would remove barriers to their success. Based on that list, they developed seven amendments to federal housing legislation. Woodson took them to then-U.S. Rep. Jack Kemp and recruited Fauntroy to co-sponsor the bill. Their 1987 legislation specifically targeted the transformation process: It gave resident councils the right to manage their own developments; it gave them priority for HUD renovation grants; it set up procedures by which they could buy their projects after three years of successful self-management; and it appropriated $5 million to train residents in self-management at 50 projects.

As HUD secretary, Kemp says, he would like to provide training grants to several hundred more groups during the next four years, help perhaps 50 of them begin managing their own developments and see perhaps half of those push on to financial ownership. He has already persuaded President Bush to support a $44 million home-ownership fund to help this "urban homesteading" along.

"I'm not suggesting that we're going to force it down people's throats, or that everybody should be treated in exactly the same manner," Kemp says. "But I at least want the opportunity out there for everybody." He promises to support the kinds of subsidies provided at Kenilworth-Parkside.

Kemp's strategy has sown confusion and anger among liberals, who often find their enthusiasm for tenant empowerment overwhelmed by their distrust of conservative motives. Liberal critics articulate three basic criticisms of the strategy:

1. It won't work. Specifically, critics argue that management of large properties is too difficult for most tenants; that ownership is too expensive for the poor; and that there are too few leaders like Kimi Gray to make it widely replicable.

This line of reasoning simply misses the point, supporters retort. Yes, self-management is difficult, they agree, but where tenants do not want management responsibilities, other tactics are available: Some resident councils have significant input into housing authority decisions; some hire and fire their own private management companies; some create partnerships with private management firms. The point is to empower residents, by whatever means they choose.

When tenants are powerless, advocates argue, they become dependent. "Bureaucratic, command-control approaches transfer the will for self-achievement away from local people, to bureaucracies," says Robert Woodson. Look at most D.C. public housing projects: Residents have no power to police their communities to enforce standards of behavior, to evict criminals. If someone deals drugs out of the apartment next door, they can complain, but the system rarely responds. So they give up.

As with self-management, empowerment advocates do not argue that ownership is for all tenants; even Kemp envisions a limited number of sales. They understand that most tenant groups could not afford to pay even the operating expenses on their apartments. But as Robert Woodson and Kimi Gray point out, resident management corporations do not just do housing; they do *economic development*. They create jobs, provide training and raise incomes. Where they succeed, ownership can become realistic.

Are there enough Kimi Grays out there to replicate the Kenilworth-Parkside story a thousand times? Woodson points out that every vital organization—whether Kenilworth-Parkside or IBM—owes its start to a strong leader. So why not create more opportunities in poor communities, and see how many leaders emerge?

2. The dwindling stock of public housing should be preserved for the poor. At the insistence of liberals, the Kemp-Fauntroy bill required that housing authorities replace any unit sold with a new unit of public housing. It also stipulated that any unit later resold had to go—for a limited price—to a low-income person, a resident management corporation or a housing author-

ity. Some liberal critics want more, insisting that if buyers rise to middle-income status, they be forced to sell and move out.

In fact, tenants are no longer evicted from public housing when their incomes rise—their rents simply go up, remaining at 30 percent of their incomes. So even under current circumstances, some units are "lost" to middle-income people. But even if this were not the case, supporters ask, what is wrong with "losing" public housing units, if the people in them make the jump into the middle class? Public housing and welfare operate as traps, creating powerful incentives to remain poor and dependent. Should they not be redesigned to function as ladders out of poverty?

Besides, doesn't the current system guarantee the loss of thousands of units every year? Today, 78,000 of the nation's 1.4 million public housing units are vacant, ripe for decay and eventual destruction. Many will be lost forever—added to the thousands already "deprogrammed."

What we need, argues Woodson, is a new system: "If 20 percent of public housing was under the management of residents, we could save $5 billion a year."

"We are dealing with social behavior," adds Bertha Gilkey, who led the tenant takeover at Cochran Gardens. "You can spend $22 million on fixing up those buildings. You can spend $32 million. But unless you change the behavior of the people who live there, they're still going to tear them up." If Gilkey's experience is any indication, empowering tenants can not only change that behavior, it can actually *increase* the supply of low-income housing. Cochran Gardens has already developed 1,300 units of new housing, in partnership with private development firms.

3. Unless it is accompanied by significant new funding for low-income housing, the Reagan-Bush embrace of Kimi Gray is a political sideshow designed to distract voters from the appalling homelessness that is the real result of conservative housing policy. Gordon Cavanaugh, a spokesman for the Coalition of Large Public Housing Authorities, pulls no punches: "I think the conservative agenda is ending public ownership of public housing, and they cloak that agenda in the rhetoric of empowerment. I mean, this is the same crowd that killed HUD's 235 program, which was designed to subsidize low-income people into ownership. This is the same administration that is trying to kill the Farmers Home program that does much the same thing. Why wouldn't I be skeptical about what we're about here? We've had an administration which for eight years fought to kill all the programs that provided low-income home ownership, and all during that time we had this thing waved in our faces."

Jack Kemp responds that many federal housing programs deserved to be eliminated, because—like public housing—they flushed enormous sums down the toilet. "But what I want to do is not just curse the darkness," he is quick to add. "I want to light some candles." And candles, he agrees, cost money.

This is Kemp's quandary: Until George Bush is willing to propose significant new funding for urban homesteading, Kemp will face a political stalemate. Liberals will continue to distrust conservatives because they have gutted funding for housing. Conservatives will continue to distrust liberals because they are unwilling to restructure programs that waste billions of dollars every year. To break the logjam, Bush will have to demonstrate a commitment to both restructuring *and* investment. Kemp understands this, and says he has made it plain to the president. "The jury's out," he acknowledges, "but I'm confident we can get a program."—D.O.

She'd say, 'I know it's hard, but you gotta hang in there, Mike. You know what our dream is.' " From the beginning, she had told him, "'Mike, you go to school and become the architect, and I'll stay home and do the legwork, and together we're going to do Kenilworth.' And we did it." After five years as an architect—including his stint at Kenilworth—Price is now a construction superintendent for the Temple Group Inc. "I just thank God that Kimi was there for me," he says. "She's a beautiful person." He pauses, and laughs. "And she can be a *dangerous* person."

The Force of Peer Pressure

DESPITE THE STUDENTS' SUCCESS, CONDITIONS WERE STILL going downhill at Kenilworth. The resident council seized on a HUD program through which a private management company ran the project, but things went from bad to worse. The roofs started to leak. There was no grass left, no fences. Rubbish was rarely picked up; rats infested the buildings. Drug dealers were common, and the management company put a bulletproof barrier around its office. For three years, residents often went without heat or hot water.

Not long after Mayor Marion Barry took office in 1979, Kimi told him her residents wanted to manage Kenilworth themselves. He agreed. The tenants wrote their own constitution and bylaws, their own personnel and policy procedures, their own job descriptions. The bureaucrats "*could not* believe it," Kimi says. "Public housing residents? I said, 'The worst it can do is have wrong grammar in it.' But at least we would understand and we would know clearly what was in it, right? So therefore we could enforce what we knew we had written." Besides, if HUD wrote it, there would be 10 lawyers in the room, writing "rules for things that don't even exist."

Knowing tenant management was on the way, Kimi says, the private management company left Kenilworth-Parkside on December 31, 1981. "It was the coldest winter since 1949," she remembers. "I'll never forget it: We were having a New Year's Eve party, and it seemed like every pipe on our property started bursting. The Lord had seen fit for us to take on this, and He said, 'I'll really give you a challenge.' " It was the perfect metaphor for the way D.C. spends money on public housing—people shivering while hot water ran down the middle of the street.

The residents patched the pipes with rubber hoses, put their own staff in place and got the housing authority to start replacing pipes. On March 1, 1982, the Kenilworth-Parkside Resident Management Corp.—a nonprofit organization—signed a contract to manage the property. Its elected board of residents, chaired by Kimi Gray, held monthly meetings of all tenants. They hired and trained residents to manage the property and do the maintenance. In what Kimi dubbed a "Bring the Fathers Out of the Closets" campaign, they hired absentee fathers. They set up fines for violating the rules—littering, loitering in hallways, sitting on fences, not cutting your grass—and created a system of elected building captains and court captains to enforce them. They created mandatory Sunday classes to teach housekeeping, budgeting, home repair and parenting. And they began to bend the force of peer pressure toward their own ends.

"The only way you can make a change is through peer pressure," says Kimi. "Rules can't be enforced if you have to go through judiciary proceedings." For instance, "If your momma was a bad housekeeper, and if her stove broke down, we would put the old dirty range out in front of her house, so everybody could see it. Leave it there *all day long*. Go get the brand-new stove, in the carton so everybody could see it, have it brought

down, but not to your house." Instead it would go to a good housekeeper, whose old stove would go to the bad housekeeper. "Now when your momma learns to keep the stove clean, she'll get a brand-new one."

The Resident Management Corp. limited use of the day-care center to mothers who worked, went to school or were in training. As demand rose, they trained residents to provide day-care in their apartments. They had their college students do a "needs survey" to find out what people wanted. Based on the results, they created an after-school homework and tutorial program for kids whose mothers worked full time. They set up courses to help adults get their high school degrees. They contracted with a doctor and a dentist to set up part-time office hours and make house calls at the development. They set up an employment office to help people find training and jobs. And they began to create their own businesses, to keep money and jobs within the community.

The first was a shop to replace windows, screens and doors, owned by a young man who could neither read nor count. In return for a start-up loan from the resident council, he trained 10 students, who went on to market their skills elsewhere in Washington. The board fired the garbage collection service and contracted with another young man, on condition he hire Kenilworth-Parkside residents. At one time or another over the next five years, Kenilworth had a cooperative store, a snack bar, two laundromats, a beauty salon, a barber shop, a clothes boutique, a thrift shop, a catering service, a moving company, and a construction company that helped renovate vacant apartments. All employed residents, and all were required to hire young people to work with the adults. Before relocation of several thousand residents during the renovation shut most of the businesses down, 120 residents had jobs at Kenilworth-Parkside.

Gradually, maintenance improved as well. If something needed repairing, the managers and maintenance men lived on the property. "It has to be someone who's there all the time, on the property," says Renee Sims, head teacher at the Learning Center. "Because if you have someone outside managing it, and a pipe bursts over the weekend, you're not going to get it done."

Kimi and her managers estimate that in 1982, when they took over, less than half the rent was being collected. There was no heat or hot water, few other services, and people had caught on that if they didn't pay, there were no penalties. Resident manager Gladys Roy and her assistants began going door to door, serving 30-day eviction notices. They explained that if people didn't pay the rent, they couldn't afford the repairs people needed. If people did not have the cash, they worked out payment plans or collected what they could. As services improved and the managers kept up their door-to-door rounds, rent collections gradually improved. They were up to 75 percent by late 1987, according to Dennis Eisen, a real estate consultant hired to prepare a financial plan for tenant ownership.

'My Fear Was Drugs and Crime'

Denise Yates moved to Kenilworth with her parents in 1979. She was 22, unmarried, with one child. Their new apartment was "depressing," she says. "The roof leaked terribly. There was no heat for weeks at a time, no hot water. The grounds weren't kept up. Cars were parked up on your lawn. There were burglaries, there were rapes, there were drugs, there were shootouts. The person who lived there before was selling drugs out of the house, so we had a problem with people constantly knocking on the door at night."

Yates had never lived in public housing, never been on welfare. Now she was doing both: "Sitting at home, nothing to look forward to but the monthly check. I knew I was worth more than that." A high school graduate and a good typist, she enrolled in a shorthand program to become a steno clerk. She took a civil service exam. And then she waited. No job offer came from the city, and when she looked elsewhere she could find nothing.

"When we moved into public housing," she says, "my fear was drugs and crime." Her fears came true when one of her sisters was raped. "From that point on, all our thoughts were negative. We basically stayed to ourselves." She was afraid to let her kids—she had two now—play outside alone, because of the drug dealers. She was trapped.

In 1982, the Resident Management Corp. hired Denise as a clerk typist. She began to understand that she was not alone, and she began to find her voice. BY 1985, she had been promoted to assistant manager. But the job did nothing to change her fears: If anything, the drug dealing intensified. Hundreds of dealers lined Quarles Street every night, selling to people who pulled off I-295, a block away. Mothers kept their children barricaded indoors.

Many of the worst offenders lived at Kenilworth. "These guys were not cream puffs," says Sgt. Robert L. Prout Jr. of the Sixth District police. "We had people here wanted for bank robbery, very serious crimes. And we were somewhat reluctant to come over here because the citizens were hostile to the police."

Even when they came, they had trouble making a dent in the drug problem. "Drug dealers are a lot smarter than we give them credit for," says Prout. "What they would do is stash their drugs in various locations. We would confront them, and they wouldn't have any drugs on them."

Finally Kimi called a meeting and invited the police. At first, most residents wouldn't come. "They thought if the police were there, the people that attended were gonna snitch on other residents, or on kids of other residents, and get them arrested," says Prout. "It took a long time for them to develop confidence in us."

The residents first asked for foot patrols at Kenilworth. Then they suggested a temporary station—a trailer—right on the grounds. The police agreed. "By putting guys over there, on a regular basis, they began slowly to develop a sense of trust in us," Prout explains. "And they began to give us information. At first it was channeled through Miss Roy or Kimi or one of the other people who worked for her. Then it became a thing where people were not afraid to be seen talking to us right on the street. We would tell them who we were looking for. And little by little, people would call up on the phone and give us information, and we'd come over. We would ask the residents to tell us where the stash was—if it's in a trash can, or hanging from a tree, or whatever. And they would. And now it's got to the point where we have mothers that have sons that if they're wanted for something, they'll pick up the phone and call us."

Kimi remained the role model. She turned in anyone who was selling drugs—even members of her beloved College Here We Come. Her own son was arrested for dealing in Southwest D.C. "I'm not cold, now, I'm a loving mother," she says. "But my son was 26, living in his own apartment, and he chose that as his way of life. After I spent my money to send him to college for two years, he decided that he wanted to be a hustler. So I figured he must have wanted to go to jail to see what that experience was like too. He's home now. Don't smoke, drink or nothing, works two jobs. He learned his lesson. The best thing I think I did was I didn't cater to him while he was incarcerated. I was hurt. But my momma and my grandma always said to me, 'You make your bed hard, you got to lay in it.' "

Every household in which someone was dealing got a 30-day eviction notice. The message was for the others: "Put him out, or lose your place." If nothing happened, "We got with the attorney down at the Housing Department, and we wore 'em to death, till we got them to take our cases to court. Now once we got to court, we were all right, because we would take residents with us down to court to say, 'No, your honor, that fella cannot stay in our community any longer.' " Four families were evicted, Kimi says. "That's all it took. People seen, 'Hey, they serious.' "

Evictions did not stop the dealers who lived elsewhere, of course. Finally, in 1984, the residents decided to confront them head on. "We got together and we marched," says Denise Yates. "Day after day, and in the evening too. We marched up and down the street with our signs. We had the police back us. Maybe half the community would march. A lot of teenagers and little kids, in addition to mothers."

At first the dealers assumed it was a temporary nuisance. But after several weeks of disrupted business, they began to drift away. That was the turning point. Today "there's very little crime" at Kenilworth, says Prout. "We have almost no break-ins. We still have a little minor drug traffic. What that is, that's your 15- and 16-year-olds that still live here, who try to do what they say their friends do. But it's nothing like it was."

Making the change was not easy. Residents were threatened. Someone cut the brake lines in Kimi's car, put sugar in her gas tank, slashed her tires. "They cut the brand-new tires," Kimi says. "That's when I got angry. I knew the guy that was the main guy, that I figured paid somebody to do it. I said, 'You went a tad too goddam far! You know how much those four tires cost me to go on that van? More than the damn van cost!' I said, 'Now I'm goin' to cut your damn tires up!' " For good measure, she threatened to send her brother, who stands 6-foot-3, to call. "And he's been nice to me ever since"—until he left for jail, that is.

Kimi's confidence rubbed off. "When people saw she didn't show any fear of being seen with the police, or riding through the neighborhood with us, then they more or less followed suit," says Prout.

The lesson is clear: The police can make raid after raid, but only if a community decides to take responsibility for its own safety can the police be truly effective. "We tell them, 'The police can't be here all the time,' " says Prout. " 'You live here, you know more about what goes on, you know who does what. It's just a matter of whether you want your community, or whether you want them to have your community.' "

Carrots and Sticks

Weeding out drug dealers is not the same as ending drug abuse, of course. Dr. Alice Murray, a psychologist who runs Kenilworth's Substance Abuse Prevention project ("SAP, because you're a sap if you take drugs") believes that "a large percentage of the families" still at Kenilworth have at least one family member with a drug problem. She helps an average of two people a month get into treatment. "Crack is the problem at the moment," she says. "They experiment with it for six months, and then they're really into it. It is highly addictive."

Murray and her staff of six have a budget of $300,000 from the city. They attack the drug problem in a dozen different ways. Narcotics Anonymous meets every noon. A "Chief Executive Officers" program puts young mothers through 15 weeks of training—three days a week, six hours a day—in everything from child rearing to personal responsibility. The Teen Council (a youth version of the Residents Council) operates a Youth

Enterprise Program—"to get young people to understand how they can take their skills of hustling on the street and use them in a positive way, the way people make money in America." In addition to running their tie-dye clothing business, the kids design, produce and sell greeting cards, and they bake and sell

cookies. They are paid wages, returning the rest of their earnings to the program.

During the summer, Murray's staff operates two "academies," one for 5- to 9-year-olds, another for teenagers. "We call it an academy, not a camp, because though it's play, we want

How Not to Manage Public Housing

Getting accurate information from the city about Kenilworth-Parkside's finances is a bit like getting a straight answer from the Cheshire Cat. The D.C. Department of Public and Assisted Housing (DPAH), which runs Washington's 59 public housing projects, makes Alice's Wonderland look absolutely straightforward. How much of Kenilworth's operating expenses are covered by rental income? DPAH doesn't know. "We looked for that," says Alphonso Jackson, who ran DPAH for 18 months before leaving last December in frustration. (He now runs the Dallas Housing Authority.) "Those records were nowhere to be found."

DPAH does not keep separate accounts for each of its public housing developments, so it cannot say how much rent is coming from each. You want to know how much resident management at Kenilworth has saved (or cost) the city? Sorry, DPAH doesn't know. You want to compare expenses and rental income at Kenilworth with those at other developments? "I think even the GAO gave up on that," says Valerie Holt, DPAH's deputy director for finance and subsidized housing. (The General Accounting Office is conducting a study of Kenilworth-Parkside for the Senate Subcommittee on Housing and Urban Affairs.)

Within the fog of nonexistent and often-conflicting numbers, however, a few things are clear:

•DPAH signs an annual contract under which the Kenilworth-Parkside Resident Management Corp. handles all expenses save utilities. In 1987 and 1988, DPAH provided just over $1 million a year.

•DPAH in turn receives an operating subsidy from HUD. Again, it is impossible to isolate Kenilworth's share from that of the 58 other projects. But when HUD required a figure in planning for the sale of Kenilworth, Jackson "guesstimated" it at $1.7 million to $1.8 million. He added that DPAH absorbed about a third of the total in overhead.

•Several programs at Kenilworth are subsidized separately. For instance, the Substance Abuse Prevention project receives $300,000 a year, half from DPAH, half from another city agency.

•DPAH has received roughly $23 million from HUD to renovate Kenilworth-Parkside under the federal modernization program. This translates into nearly $50,000 per unit—double the average cost in neighboring Baltimore, though the renovation required may be less extensive there. The whopping price tag has led some critics to charge that the Reagan administration shoveled money to Kenilworth far in excess of what other projects received. The administration did insist that a renovation grant go to Kenilworth to support tenant management and to pave the way for ownership. But the cost per unit is so high mainly because DPAH manages renovation so ham-handedly. Other DPAH renovation projects have cost even more—and contractors' bids today are coming in at *$80,000* to *$90,000* per unit.

According to virtually all knowledgeable observers, DPAH is a textbook case of how not to manage public housing. "I've been chairman of the Committee on Housing and Economic Development since 1981," says D.C. Council member Charlene Drew Jarvis. "Since then, there have been eight heads of the department. The department has suffered from a lack of continuity of leadership, a problem with timely contracting, a relative absence of contract monitoring and an absence of skilled workers. The simple tracking of work orders has even been a problem."

The problems were exacerbated in Kenilworth's case, Jarvis adds, by "tension" between DPAH and HUD after HUD insisted that a renovation grant go to Kenilworth.

"They said to me, 'This wasn't one we'd planned to do, so we'll just have to get to it when we do,' " explains Margaret White, manager of HUD's D.C. field office. "We could not get the housing authority to send the paperwork to us. It was as though there was a concerted effort to delay, to drag it out, to obfuscate, to pull red herrings across the trail."

White, as it happens, was on temporary reassignment as this article went to press, pending the investigation of management failures in *her* office. Part of the nationwide HUD scandal probe, the D.C. investigation focuses on the theft by private escrow agents of proceeds from the sale of foreclosed properties. So far, it is unrelated to public housing.

Still, if one did want to examine problems in D.C. public housing, DPAH would be an obvious place to start. The problems at Kenilworth have been endless.

After two years of inaction by DPAH, leaking roofs threatened to make Kenilworth unsalvageable. To save it, White finally ordered that the roofs be done separately, driving costs up. Then the architects' drawings turned out to be "inadequate," to use Jackson's phrase, because "DPAH did not hold the architects and engineering firms accountable." While units stood vacant, pipes and other equipment were vandalized. DPAH finally fired the original contractor, and HUD has threatened to do the same with the second. With so many complications, the original $13.2 million renovation grant ran out, and DPAH went back to HUD for $9 million more.

"My honest perspective on it," says Jackson, "is that it was incompetence on the part of DPAH that took so long to get that project started. What I had in D.C. was unorganized chaos."

Roland Turpin, who succeeded Jackson at DPAH a few months ago, declined to be interviewed for this story. Instead, he provided a statement: "We are fully aware that there are problems, but we are firmly committed to this home ownership conversion for the residents of Kenilworth-Parkside, and we'll do whatever is appropriate to see that it becomes a reality."

Meanwhile, most Kenilworth residents are stuck in other public housing projects, where they were relocated several years ago. "I tell you, every time I ride by that place, I get totally infuriated," says for Kenilworth resident and architect Michael Price. "The people downtown go home every night to their plush homes in the suburbs or wherever, and the residents are in housing projects like Kenilworth was back in the 1970s. They weathered that storm, and it's not fair for them to be moved into a brand-new storm. The people in that bureaucracy ought to be horsewhipped."

—D.O.

them to maintain their academic skills," Murray explains. Virtually all the children at Kenilworth participate. They play, do arts and crafts, take trips, work on academics and receive substance abuse education—all with a heavy stress on emotional and family health.

Other efforts include a mandatory eight-hour substance abuse prevention program for new residents; counseling for addicts and their families; referrals to in-patient and out-patient care; follow-up with families after treatment; a program to help parents work with the public schools; and a teen pregnancy prevention program.

"What we're working for is a change of behavior and attitude," says Murray. In the case of teen pregnancy, it appears to be working. Accurate numbers are hard to come by at Kenilworth (when asked how much welfare dependency had been reduced, for instance, Kimi Gray and her top two managers gave wildly different figures). But all sources agree that teenage pregnancy—once the norm—has dropped significantly.

"One of the things that this community has brought back is a kind of old-fashioned shunning," says Murray, "a way of saying, 'This behavior we will not tolerate. Should it happen, then we put you through all the services, but we don't expect it to happen ever again.' It's done in a very kind and gentle and loving way, but there's shame when it occurs—which is not the case in the outside community."

By shunning negative behavior, supporting constructive behavior and offering treatment for people with drug problems, Kenilworth's leaders are trying to build a viable culture. It is a constant effort, using both carrots and sticks. Mothers turn children in for drug dealing: College Here We Come attends every high school graduation to cheer its members on.

"Development begins with a belief system," says Robert Woodson, whose National Center for Neighborhood Enterprise has worked with Kenilworth since 1981. "What Kimi and other tenant leaders have done is just self-confidence, and they've passed that self-confidence on to others. Only when you overcome the crisis of self-confidence can opportunity make a difference in your life. But we act with programs as if opportunity carries with it elements of self-confidence. And it does not."

This is where ownership comes in. Kimi and her colleagues believe that when they become property owners, the process of building self-confidence and opportunity will take another quantum leap. Late next year, if the schedule holds, the last family will move back into the renovated development (courtesy of a HUD grant of roughly $23 million). Not only that, they will own the place. The experience cannot help but send a powerful message.

It will not be easy. It costs close to $400 per unit per month simply to maintain and operate the complex. Federal subsidies will continue for five more years, probably somewhere between $1.2 million and $1.7 million a year, but that will not be enough. At some point, the Resident Management Corp. plans to sell shares in a limited equity co-op for perhaps $10,000 per unit—though details are still sketchy and no one knows what kind of down payment, if any, will be required. The residents also hope to borrow $1.75 million, to put in air conditioning, dishwashers, a community cafeteria, tennis courts, racquetball courts, a locker room and a swimming pool. Financial plans are still extremely tentative. But one recent version called for Kenilworth to raise rent collections from 75 percent to 92.5 percent by 1995, drive residents' average income ($10,200 by 1987, at least for reported income) up 6 percent annually and put $500,000 of the HUD subsidy in the bank every year—just to stay afloat when the subsidy ends.

The strategy is ambitious and the assumptions optimistic, but according to experts on co-op conversions, it is not impossible. It will require a more businesslike operation, particularly when Kenilworth becomes dependent on bankers rather than bureaucrats. "It will require strong property management, fiscal oversight and also very good tenant education," says David Freed, a real estate consultant who specializes in low-income co-op conversions in D.C. "The key to good cooperative ownership conversion is the quality of the leadership. And they have superb leadership."

'The Door Is Open'

Kimi Gray is not worried about whether her residents will be able to afford ownership. She's got bigger plans than that.

There's the reverse commute program—from inner city to suburbs—that she's working on with a grant from the Department of Transportation. And the shopping mall she wants to build next to Kenilworth. And the self-help credit union, and the industrial facility and the construction company. There are two buildings she is trying to buy and renovate—to train her construction company and house her college students. There's a building she plans to put up for senior citizens. And there are the condos she wants to develop, so the most successful Kenilworth residents can move up without leaving the community.

On a recent Monday, Kimi spent an entire afternoon at the D.C. Department of Public and Assisted Housing—cajoling the director, talking to his lawyer, rounding up the right people and shepherding them back to the director's office, all to get title to land Kenilworth will own in a year anyway, so she can start building her senior housing now. After three hours of tireless and expert manipulation, she still did not have what she wanted.

"You know," she said as she left the building, "every time I get the runaround, I think about the same thing. They have to deal with me, 'cause I've got all this publicity, and this is how they treat me. How the hell do you think they treat Mrs. Jones?"

There is no time to be bitter, however, There is too much to do. It is 1989, and the dam is finally breaking. "Folk want freedom," Kimi says, as she climbs back into her van and heads for one more meeting. "Folk want power. The door is open— they can't stop us now."

Further Thoughts on a "Sociology of Acceptance" for Disabled People

Howard D. Schwartz

HOWARD D. SCHWARTZ is professor of sociology at Radford University.

Social scientists studying the relationship between people with disabilities and the larger society, in recent years and with increasing intensity, have been waging a frontal assault against the dominant conceptual model of disability as deviance. A central tenet of the critics is that the deviance perspective leads to a predetermined view of people with disabilities as negatively valued by, and socially isolated from, the rest of society.

To be found among the growing number of critical voices are Robert Bogdan and Steven Taylor (1987) who call for the development of a "sociology of acceptance" through which to view people with disabilities. In proposing this, Bogdan and Taylor do not totally reject the deviance approach. Rather, they point to the need for adding a complementary perspective to accommodate those instances when the disabled person is accepted rather than rejected by others. While this contention seems legitimate and important, the informality of their presentation makes their argument less persuasive than it might be.

In the first place, and Bogdan and Taylor recognize this, the supporting data they present are less than satisfactory. Drawn ad hoc from their 15 years of clinical work in human services, the evidence is more suggestive than confirmatory regarding societal acceptance of people with disabilities.

Second, the authors talk about two different accepting public postures without, unfortunately, providing anything more than a preliminary discus-

> **There is clear evidence of a change toward a far more favorable public opinion of the disabled.**

sion of either posture or the difference between them. On the one hand, they speak of the kind of acceptance found in the seminal work of Nora Groce's *Everyone Here Spoke Sign Language* (1985). Analyzing the position of the deaf in the community of Martha's Vineyard up to the first part of this century, Groce concludes that "they were just like everyone else" (which is, in fact, the title of the first chapter). In a community where everyone was bilingual in English and sign language, the deaf were simply seen as equal to the hearing, no better, no worse.

On the other hand, Bogdan and Taylor consider acceptance in terms of disabled persons being viewed by others as "special, more interesting, more stimulating, more challenging, more appreciative." The example of a caseworker and his mentally retarded client is used to show the disabled person in this favored-status role. After a while, the caseworker came to value as special his disabled friend's candor, which included the ability to express feelings and show emotions.

For conceptual clarity, the term *acceptance* will be used here to define relationships between disabled and able-bodied persons in which all partici-

pants are viewed as equals. The term *advocacy* will be employed where those with disabilities are given favored status. It thus becomes the positive counterpart of rejection in a continuum of public postures that includes rejection, acceptance, and advocacy.

With these comments about the Bogdan and Taylor argument in mind, what emerges from the recent empirical research, including my own, is admittedly limited, but clear evidence of a change toward a far more favorable public opinion of disabled persons.

EVIDENCE FOR A "SOCIOLOGY OF ACCEPTANCE"

In 1986, in a paper that received considerable attention, Katz, Kravetz, and Karlinsky reported the results of a study comparing the attitudes of high school seniors in Berkeley, Calif., toward disabled and nondisabled people. According to the authors, what was notable about the study results was that they were not consistent with those of many earlier research results, since they seemed "to imply that the disabled person is viewed more positively than the nondisabled one in the United States."

The students had been presented with videotapes of a man who was variously identified as being a civilian or in the military, disabled or able-bodied. The respondents rated, on intelligence, vocational (work) competence, morality, and sociability, the individual that they viewed. After an overall rating score was calculated for each student, it was found that the av-

From *Social Policy,* Fall 1988, pp. 36-39. Copyright 1989 by Social Policy Corporation. *Social Policy,* published by Social Policy Corporation, New York, New York 10036.

erage score for the disabled person was significantly higher than the average score for the ablebodied one.

The researchers speculate that an explanation of their results might be found in the unique nature of Berkeley. As an archtypical academic environment, it contains a substantial disabled population affected by mainstreaming and other educational innovations aimed at changing public attitudes toward persons with a disability. Consequently, "the nondisabled population is exposed to persons with disabilities who cope and live within the community" and "get to know them and their abilities beyond the disability."

While Katz and his colleagues are correct in their assessment of the atypical character of their study findings, they are not the only ones to have identified public advocacy of disabled people. Several studies, also using student respondents, have found that, on several key dimensions, disabled people are rated higher than the ablebodied as potential employees.

In one study, Siegfried and Toner (1981) asked college students to rate two target subjects: a potential coworker and a potential supervisor. One-half of the students thought these people were disabled due to an automobile accident, and the other half were presented with the identical description except that there was no mention of a disability. For 11 of the 16 dependent measures, covering a wide range of work-related behaviors (e.g., professional competence, missing work, successful performance, and ability to travel), the disabled and ablebodied target subjects were rated equally. On those five factors for which significant differences were found, the disabled person was rated higher. He or she was seen as more likely to be approached with a personal problem, more likely to be asked a favor of, less likely to upset co-workers, and less likely to need special assistance.

In a similar vein, in a study published earlier by Krefting and Brief (1976), college students rated a disabled person (a paraplegic using a wheelchair) equal to an ablebodied person on most job-related measures, but higher on work motivation and likelihood of being a long-term employee.

THE *PLAYBOY* STUDY

My own research, carried out in the fall of 1987, can now be added to this body of literature (Schwartz, 1988). While similar to the aforementioned studies in its use of student respondents, a wheelchair-user target subject, and the same kind of experimental technique, it differed in an important way. The target subject was neither a military man nor a potential employee, but Ellen Stohl, the first disabled woman to be the subject of a *Playboy* (1987) photo layout.

As explained in the story accompanying the pictures, Ms. Stohl, who had a spinal-cord injury, offered to pose for *Playboy* as a way of demonstrating that people with disabilities can also be sexy. In the letter in which she asked the magazine for the opportunity to pose, she wrote, "Sexuality is the hardest thing for disabled persons

Several studies have found that the disabled are rated higher than the ablebodied as potential employees.

to hold onto," and that she wanted to "teach society that being disabled does not make a difference."

Irving Kenneth Zola (1987), a sociologist writing about disability in America, views "the right to be sexy" as a central item on the agenda related to the psychological and social liberation of people with disabilities. Harlan Hahn (1988) has touched on the same issue in his article, "Can Disability Be Beautiful?" Nevertheless, there seem to be limited opportunities for disabled people to assert their claim to sexuality, particularly through the media of popular culture. The *Playboy* article is unique in providing such a forum. It also offered the possibility of research to ascertain how, in a sexual context, the public evaluates the disabled person compared to the ablebodied one, and the disabled versus the ablebodied person's "right to be sexy."

The study was carried out at a medium-sized state university in Virginia, with a total enrollment of about 8,000. The majority of students come from urban centers within a 500-mile radius of the university such as Washington, D.C., with about one-third coming from more rural areas in the general vicinity of the university. Ten percent are from out of state.

The respondents were all of the students taking introductory sociology. Each student was shown one of two pictures of Ellen Stohl that had appeared in *Playboy*: one showed Stohl's face in closeup and shoulder partially bare; the other, providing a higher level of sexual display, had a partially-nude Stohl sitting on a couch with her legs tucked under her and wearing a negligee open in the front exposing a breast and her midriff. An additional aspect of the research design was that each student was given only one of two versions of whichever picture he or she received. An ablebodied version included, along with the picture, a biographical sketch which noted that Stohl was a college student and that the pictures had appeared in a national magazine with a readership of over 3 million. A second, disabled version had the identical biography except that Stohl was identified as spinal-cord injured, and a smaller picture of her fully clothed in a wheelchair was presented along with the larger picture. The analysis centered on comparing, for each picture, the responses of the students receiving the two versions.

The almost 700 respondents (80 students who had seen the pictures in *Playboy* or had heard about them were excluded) were asked to look at the photo of Stohl and rate her on six personal characteristics and on six factors concerned with conjectured success-failure or satisfaction-dissatisfaction in present or future life situations.

Regardless of the picture seen (the specific picture viewed had no effect in any of the comparisons), the disabled Stohl was rated equal to the ablebodied Stohl on sociability, intelligence, physical attractiveness, and the likelihood of having a fulfilling life.

Most interestingly, for five of the eight dependent measures for which a significant difference was found, Stohl was rated higher when presented as disabled than when presented as ablebodied. When identified as spinal-cord injured, she was seen as having greater strength of character, sensitivity to others, and competence at work, more likelihood of being a good parent, and less likelihood of getting divorced. The disabled Stohl's perceived relative superiority on these factors seems to confirm the finding of the previously cited studies which used the same or similar dependent measures that a disabled person is seen as better than one who is not disabled. Put another way, there is the strong hint of the disabled person's being viewed as a "paragon of virtue."

For two of the three measures on which the disabled Stohl was rated lower—the likelihood of getting married and satisfaction with life—the differences, while statistically significant, were so small as to be negligible. On the third, sexual appeal (the only measure to show a gender difference), the women saw no difference between the disabled and ablebodied Stohl while the men favored the latter. Yet, as far as the response of the male students is concerned, this is somewhat misleading. In fact, while both the men and women rated the disabled Stohl's sexual appeal as very high, the men rated it higher than the women did. In absolute terms, the men rated Stohl when disabled as "very sexually appealing," the second highest response on the 6-point Likert item.

Taken together, the ratings on sexual appeal and the equal ratings on physical attractiveness lead us to conclude that disability did very little, if anything, to diminish Stohl's physical appeal in the eyes of respondents.

In addition to rating Stohl on this array of measures, respondents were asked, "In your opinion, was it appropriate for this woman to pose for this picture?" (The respondents could answer "yes," "no," or "undecided".) The results show unequivocally that it was deemed more appropriate for the disabled Stohl to pose.

In all but one group comparison (over 80 percent of the men who viewed Stohl's face in closeup approved of her posing), a significantly higher percentage of those who saw the disabled Stohl approved of her posing. For example, of those shown the partially-nude picture, 55 percent with the disabled version approved compared to 36.4 percent with the ablebodied version. For men alone, the corresponding percentages were 75 percent versus 52.1 percent, and for women, 43.2 percent to 30.6 percent.

THE RIGHT TO BE SEXY
Analysis of the open-ended responses of those who, upon viewing the disabled Stohl, approved of her posing can better help us to understand the distinction between acceptance and advocacy of the disabled person's "right to be sexy." Grouping respondents according to the reasons given for approval allows us to differentiate those reasons in terms of whether they are likely to lead to one or the other positive postures.

Acceptance would seem to be a logical outcome of the responses of two groups. The first group gave what might be called "disabled-blind" explanations ("Why not? An honest way to make a dollar"). The common factor here was the absence of any recognition of the disability. A second group did take account of Stohl's disability,

Educational institutions may now constitute enabling environments.

couching their approval in terms of the very basic theme of equal rights ("She has as much right as anyone to pose for this picture").

Advocacy would likely follow from the responses of three other groups. A good number of respondents saw Stohl as an example or role model representing to the public and/or other disabled people the ability of the disabled to succeed in endeavors in which they have not, historically, had the opportunity to participate ("Maybe her doing so will show other handicapped people that they are beautiful and show the general public the same. Good for her"). The responses of a second group expressed admiration for the disabled person having to overcome much more than others to achieve a goal ("With her disability it is a great step and very courageous. She is doing things in her life."). The underlying theme in the responses of the third group was the unique social-psychological benefits that a disabled person would derive from this experience ("If it makes her feel more 'complete' or happier why not?").

Assuming that the above speculation about the link between response type and the two positive public postures has validity, the difference between acceptance and advocacy is that in the case of advocacy there exists the perception of a greater urgency, sali-

ence, or merit related to the disabled person's "right to be sexy." This is most evident in the statements of those students who held a double standard, resulting in a type of "reverse discrimination" on behalf of the disabled. As one respondent put it, "Normally, I'm *very* against people posing in these pornographic pictures, but in this case I feel she made a statement that she is comfortable with, and I can't help but admire her reasons for it. She's trying to convey that handicapped people can be human, they are sexually attractive, and they are in control of their lives."

DISABLED PERSONS IN SOCIETY
The data presented provide support, and the beginnings of an empirical database, for social scientists like Bogdan and Taylor, who insist that there is a need to augment the conceptual and theoretical arsenal used in assessing the role of disability and disabled people in society. The finding of overwhelmingly favorable student attitudes toward an individual who uses a wheelchair raises doubts about the relevance of the deviance perspective to specific instances of disability. Maybe most striking is the absence in my research of any evidence of what Hahn has argued is discrimination toward disabled people based on aesthetic criteria. Not only was the disabled Stohl seen as physically attractive as her ablebodied counterpart, but also her disability did not lead to the imputation of "sexlessness," a causal sequence taken as a given in the literature. Quite to the contrary, the disabled Stohl was perceived as a woman with considerable sexual appeal.

Exploration of the origins and implications of the view of the disabled individual as a "paragon of virtue" is called for. Bogdan and Taylor see this perception as arising from the particular character of a specific one-to-one relationship between a disabled and nondisabled individual. While they may be correct on this score, the new research points to the existence of a more generalized notion that may involve a cultural stereotyping of disabled people in this way. Future research can provide important answers as to why they are seen as more likely to fulfill normatively-defined role obligations in circumstances ranging from friend to parent, spouse and employee. It is worth cautioning that, although obviously there is nothing inherently wrong with being viewed as a good person, there is always the possibility that this kind of stereotype could lead to unrealistic and unfair expectations concerning what disabled people are like and how they are likely to behave.

The limited purview of the studies presented precludes any grandiose claims about how far society has come in the way it perceives and treats people with disabilities. For example, the target subjects were all physically-disabled wheelchair users. And the literature shows that, in general, the physically disabled evoke more positive reactions from ablebodied people than do those with emotional and cognitive impairments (Bordieri and Drehmer, 1987). Despite this, the data presented do underscore the need to refrain from viewing all disabled people as occupying a unitary social status. One would hope that a new generation of writers will avoid describing all those with disabilities as "stigmatized" (Goffman, 1963) or as "outsiders" inhabiting the "other side" (Becker, 1963, 1964). It is time for works of quality that deal with how the various public postures — that is, rejection, acceptance, and advocacy — are distributed over the broad range of disabled persons.

A theoretical perspective that needs to be exploited in the future is one implied by Bogdan and Taylor and explicated most clearly by those taking a "minority group" approach to disabled people. It would replace the focus on disabled versus nondisabled individuals with one on disabling and enabling environments. The research cited here suggests that, as with the contexts of family and friends discussed by Bogdan and Taylor, educational institutions may now constitute enabling environments.

This was a position taken by Katz and his colleagues to explain the Berkeley high school students' favorable perception of disabled people. It is also compatible with my impression of the social milieu at the site of my study. There, over the last decade, disabled people have become an increasingly visible and prominent segment of the campus community.

Student attitudes in the studies discussed may also be a consequence of a more favorable climate toward disabled people in the society at large. In this regard, I cannot help but make mention of the recent, and very striking, events that took place at Gallaudet University in the spring of 1988. The unexpected force of public support — both immediate and seemingly unanimous — for the student body seeking deaf leadership may have been the critical factor in the swift capitulation of the powers-that-were. As the board of trustees' choice for the presidency of the university declared when she resigned, "I was swayed by the groundswell across the nation that it is time for a deaf president."

Finally, something must be said about the relevance of what has been discussed to the very practical issue of the employment of the disabled. When *Playboy* decided to publish pictures of Ellen Stohl, the mass media reported that the editorial staff was strongly divided on the wisdom of that decision and that those who held the negative opinion felt that the public was not ready for it. As my data show, they needn't have worried. Moreover, insofar as employers are reluctant to hire disabled people for fear of an unaccepting public, the data from all four studies show that they may be misreading public opinion. The dissemination

of social scientific research and perspectives relating to the acceptance and advocacy of people with disabilities would seem an important step in any process that is to have the capability of leading to their full integration into the larger society.

REFERENCES

Becker, Howard S., *Outsiders: Studies in the Sociology of Deviance* (New York: The Free Press. 1963).

___. *The Other Side: Perspectives on Deviance* (New York: The Free Press, 1964).

Bogdan, Robert and Steven Taylor, "Toward a Sociology of Acceptance: The Other Side of the Study of Deviance," *Social Policy* (Fall 1987), pp. 34-39.

Bordieri, James W. and David E. Drehmer, "Attribution of Responsibility and Predicted Social Acceptance of Disabled Workers," *Rehabilitation and Counseling Bulletin* (June 1987), pp. 219-26.

Groce, Nora, *Everyone Here Spoke Sign Language: Hereditary Deafness on Martha's Vineyard* (Cambridge: Harvard University Press, 1985).

Goffman, Erving, *Stigma: Notes on the Management of Spoiled Identity* (Englewood Cliffs, NJ: Prentice-Hall, 1963).

Hahn, Harlan, "Can Disability be Beautiful?" *Social Policy* (Winter 1988), pp. 26-31.

Katz, Shlomo, Shlomo Kravetz, and Mickey Karlinsky, "Attitudes of High School Students in the United States Regarding Disability: A Replication of an Israeli Study," *Rehabilitation Counseling Bulletin* (December 1986), pp. 102-9.

Krefting, Linda A. and Arthur P. Brief, "The Impact of Applicant Disability on Evaluative Judgments in the Selection Process," *Academy of Management Journal* (December 1976), pp. 675-80.

"Meet Ellen Stohl," *Playboy* (July 1987), pp. 16-18.

Schwartz, Howard D., "Disability and Sexual Display: Empirical Evidence of Public Advocacy for Disabled People and the Disabled Person's Right to be 'Sexy.'" Paper presented at the annual meeting of the American Sociological Association, Atlanta, August 28, 1988.

Siegfried, William D. and Ignatius J. Toner, "Students' Attitudes toward Physical Disability in Prospective Co-Workers and Supervisors," *Rehabilitation Counseling Bulletin* (September 1987), pp. 20-25.

Zola, Irving Kenneth, "Neither Defiant nor Cheering," *Disability Rag* (September/October 1987), pp. 16-18.

THE THIRD AGE

As the baby boomers careen toward fortysomething, America is on the crest of a demographic wave that promises to transform our bodies, minds, and spirits.

Ken Dychtwald
with Joe Flower

Ken Dychtwald, the president of Age Wave, Inc., is a consultant to government and private industry on issues of aging. He is the author of Bodymind *and five other books. Joe Flower is a free-lance writer whose articles have appeared in* Esquire, The New York Times, Playboy, *and other publications.*

ABOUT TEN YEARS AGO, I was invited to speak to a group of nearly a thousand religious leaders about the increasing health, vigor, and beauty we could expect to see among the "new" elderly in the years ahead. The talk went very well, and at its conclusion a wave of applause filled the room.

Filled with the exhilaration of having delivered a well-received program, I sat down at the head table and turned to chat with the gentleman sitting next to me, the prominent religious leader and gerontologist Monsignor Charles Fahey. "Well," I said, "what did you think of my presentation?"

"Very exciting talk," he said.

I thanked him.

"But, Ken," he went on, "I'm sorry to tell you that I think you may be missing the most important point of the entire subject."

I felt suddenly deflated. I asked him to explain.

"If the entire purpose of old age is to be just like we were when we were young, for several more decades," he began, "what's the value of that?"

Should the primary goal of childhood be an attempt to be an infant as long as possible? Is prolonging adolescence for a few more years the purpose of young adulthood? I think not. I sure hope not!

"Think about it," he continued. "We know that even with the best of care overall fitness will decline gradually with the years. While the strength of the senses is weakening, what if the powers of the mind, the heart, and the spirit are rising? If life offers the ongoing opportunity for increased awareness and personal growth, think of how far we could evolve, given the advantage of several extra decades of life!"

Monsignor Fahey's comments struck me very deeply. Until that moment, I had believed that the inner life was essentially like a flower that blossomed in youth. Throughout the rest of life, the task was to try to keep the petals from falling off. What Fahey was proposing was that, although our bodies may decline somewhat with age, our spirits have the capability of soaring to new heights in our later years. In fact, he suggested that the growth and evolution of the inner life may be the unique and special opportunity that the aging of America will bring.

AMERICA IS AGING. The nation that was founded on young backs, on the strength, impetuosity, and hope of youth, is growing more mature, steadier, deeper—even, one may hope, wiser.

The Population Reference Bureau, a nonprofit demographics study group in Washington, D.C., has projected that by the year 2025 Americans over sixty-five will outnumber teenagers by more than two to one. According to the Census Bureau, by 2030 the median age is expected to have reached forty-one. By 2050, it's likely that as many as one in four Americans will be over sixty-five. Many demographers consider these projections to be very conservative: By some estimates, the median age will eventually reach fifty.

Three separate and unprecedented demographic phenomena are converging to produce the coming "Age Wave":

•**The Senior Boom.** Americans are living longer than ever before, and older Americans are healthier, more active, more vigorous, and more influential than any other older generation in history.

•**The Birth Dearth.** A decade ago, the birth rate in the United States plummeted to its lowest point ever. It has been hovering there ever since, and it's not likely to change. The great population of elders is not being offset by an explosion of children.

•**The Aging of the Baby Boom.** The leading edge of the boomer generation has now passed forty. As the boomers approach fifty and pass it, their numbers will combine with the first two major demographic changes to produce a historic shift in the concerns, structure, and style of America.

Our concept of marriage will change, as "till-death-do-us-part" unions give way to serial monogamy. In the era of longer life, some people will have marriages that last seventy-five years, while others will have different mates for each major stage of life.

The child-focused nuclear family will increasingly be replaced by the "matrix" family, an adult-centered, transgenerational unit bound together

From *New Age Journal*, January/February 1989, pp. 50-54, 56. Excerpt from *Age Wave* by Ken Dychtwald. Copyright © 1989 by Ken Dychtwald. Reprinted by permission of Bantam Books, publisher.

What Monsignor Fahey caused me to realize was that there are special human qualities and abilities that can come to full blossom only with age.

by friendship and choice as well as by blood and obligation.

More people will work into their seventies and eighties; many will "retire" several times during their lives in order to raise a second (or third) family, enter a new business, or simply take a couple of years off to travel and enjoy themselves.

Even the physical environment will change. To fit the pace, physiology, and style of a population predominantly in the middle and later years of life, the typeface in books will get larger and traffic lights will change more slowly. Steps will be lower, bathtubs less slippery, chairs more comfortable, reading lights brighter. Neighborhoods will be safer. Food will be more nutritious.

But the aging of America will affect more than just our institutions, lifestyles, and surroundings. The outer demographic changes that are rearranging our society are also touching our most personal inner thoughts, hopes, and plans. The gift of longevity will cause us to rethink the pace and tempo of our lives as well as the relative purposes, goals, and challenges of life's various stages.

The topic of how best to fulfill the opportunity of long life has been explored in tales and folklore throughout history. For example, in J.R.R. Tolkein's *The Lord of the Rings*, the hobbit Smaegol discovers a magic ring that renders him both invisible and immortal. The catch is that the ring does not bring greater "quality" to his life; it just stretches out his life. As Smaegol lives longer and longer, he loses the positive attributes of life—a feeling of purpose, attachments to others, a sense of wonder. His skin becomes waxy and pale. His voice sinks to a gravelly whisper, and he speaks only to himself. Finally, he retreats to an island in an underground lake, where he lives in darkness. By the time we meet him, he is an attenuated, whimpering, wraithlike being who goes by the name of Gollum. He has been drained of his life force: A slave to the ring, he is hundreds of years old and unable to die.

The image is poetic, but very real. Until now, history has been filled with men and women who died *before* their time. With longer life expectancy, we increasingly meet people who seem to be living *beyond* their time, people who have outlived the purpose they established for themselves in youth and who now merely exist, in an empty old age. We see it all around us: men and women, however fit they may be, who have grown old with no new goals or dreams, no useful identity for their later years, but only memories of who they "used to be."

On the other hand, a "Dorian Gray" life of unending youth may not be fulfilling, either. Although most of us would hope for some measure of energy and vitality in our later years, being trapped forever in the body and spirit of youth without ever being able to mature or age has its own nightmarish qualities.

What Monsignor Fahey caused me to realize was that there are special human qualities and abilities that can come to full blossom only with age—for example, mature wisdom, experienced leadership, the ability to give back to society the lessons and resources that have been harvested over a lifetime. And if these deeper, greater qualities were to be associated with age, then we might think of the evolution from young to old as an *ascending*, not *descending* passage. On the other hand, if we evaluate the worth and value of age through the criteria of youth, the later years will fare poorly. By aiming at the wrong target, we will always be yearning for what we, too, "used to be."

MODERN WESTERN psychology, molded as it was on the inner wars of childhood, has done little to date in the way of providing a clear blueprint for who we can become in our later years. Freud, for all his brilliance and innovation, did not even believe in adult development. He thought of childhood as the essential shaper of the psyche. He did not expect adults to grow in new directions, and he was reluctant to work with patients over fifty. Of course, in Freud's era, fifty was considered very old, not the mid-life point it is becoming today.

Perhaps the first organized investigation into the ascending psychological concerns of later life was offered by Erik Erikson, the "father of adult development." In his 1950 landmark work, *Childhood and Society*, Erikson insightfully outlined eight stages of human development, based on his clinical psychoanalytic research and his Freudian-oriented psychological training. He suggested that each life stage is marked by a developmental task or challenge, usually presented as a dichotomy, which the individual must successfully resolve in order to move on to the next, more mature level of development.

According to Erikson, the key inner themes of late adulthood are not focused around the challenges of youth—issues of autonomy and the basic formulation of personal identity. Rather, the transformational turmoil of the later years is much more likely to center on two qualities: generativity (that is, the concern with how to pass along to future generations what one has gathered in life) and ego integrity (the achievement of a sense of personal wholeness in life's final stages). The practical meaning of this viewpoint was captured perfectly by Gray Panthers founder Maggie Kuhn when she commented, "I continue to realize that old age is a time of great fulfillment, when all the loose ends of life can be gathered together."

Erikson, himself now approaching his ninetieth birthday, has recently amended his earlier theories to include the achievement of wisdom as the ultimate stage of emotional maturation. According to Erikson, "Wisdom comes from life experience, well-digested. It's not what comes from reading great books. When it comes to understanding life, experiential learning is the only worthwhile kind." However, even in Erikson's now-classic eight stages of development, the greatest emphasis remains on youth, not age: Five of the eight developmental stages take place in childhood.

In some ways, it was the pioneering work of psychologist Abraham Maslow in the late '50s that offered the first guide to understanding the special purposes and opportunities offered by long life. In his well-known hierarchy of needs, Maslow proposed that some of our drives have precedence over others. The most basic needs are physiological—hunger and thirst, for instance. Next come concerns pertaining to safety, security, and stability. Above these are the needs for belonging and love and for affection and identification; then come concerns related to self-esteem, prestige, and self-respect. Finally, at the very top of the hierarchy, is the desire for self-actualization—that is, for realizing all of one's latent awareness and capabilities. Maslow thus suggested that this last need is the ultimate goal and purpose of human existence.

This concept of an ascending hierarchy—in which one must come to terms with one level of needs before one is free to tackle the next—is in contrast to Freud's and other homeostatic theories, which propose no goal for adult human life beyond "adjusting" to reality and coming to terms with one's childhood influences. According to Maslow's view, the extra time and experience that come with growing older would seem to afford a historically unprecedented opportunity to come to terms with life's larger and more profound questions. However, influenced as he was by the youth-oriented perspective of the '50s and '60s, Maslow himself did not relate his theories to human aging.

IT IS FROM OUTSIDE the realm of traditional psychology that we find a new perspective on the inner possibilities of old age. A compelling philosophy has recently emerged from the European tradition of adult education that provides a simple, yet visionary orientation to this issue. Referred to as *Le troisième age*—"The third age"—this point of view proposes that there are three "ages" of man, each with its special focus, challenge, and opportunity.

In the first age, from birth to approximately twenty-five years of age, the primary tasks of life center around biological development, learning, and survival. During the early years of history, the average life expectancy of most men and women wasn't much higher than the end of the first age, and as a result the entire thrust of society was oriented toward these most basic drives.

In the second age, from about twenty-six to sixty, the concerns of adult life focus on issues pertaining to the formation of family, parenting, and productive work. The years taken up by the second age are very busy and are filled with social activity; the lessons gathered during the first age are applied to the social and professional responsibilities of the second. Until several decades ago, most people couldn't expect to live much beyond the second age, and society at that time was thus centered on the concerns of this age.

Now, however, a new era of human evolution is unfolding: the third age of man. The purpose of the third age is twofold. First, with the children grown and many of life's basic adult tasks either well under way or already accomplished, this less pressured, more reflective period allows the further development of the interior life of the intellect, memory, and imagination, of emotional maturity, and of one's own personal sense of spiritual identity.

The third age is also a period for giving back to society the lessons, resources, and experiences accumulated over a lifetime. From this perspective, the elderly are seen not as social outcasts, but as a living bridge between yesterday, today, and tomorrow—a critical evolutionary role that no other age group can perform. According to Monsignor Fahey, who serves as director of Fordham University's Third Age Center, "People in the third age should be the glue of society, not its ashes."

Of course, this is not a new or novel perspective, just one that years of youth focus have obscured. In other cultures and at other times, the elderly have been revered for their wisdom, power, and spiritual force. In ancient China, for example, the highest attainment in mystical Taoism was long life and the wisdom that came with the passing of years. According to social historian Simone de Beauvoir, "Lao-tse's teaching sets the age of sixty as the moment at which a man may free himself from his body and become a holy being. Old age was therefore life in its very highest form."

Among the Aranda, hunters and gatherers of the Australian forests, extreme old age brings with it a transition to near-supernatural status: "The man whom age has already brought close to the other world is the best mediator between this and the next. It is the old people who direct the Arandas' religious life—a life that underlies the whole of their social existence."

In contemporary Japanese culture, a high value is placed on the unique opportunities for spiritual development offered by old age. According to Japanese culture expert Thomas Rohlen:

"What is significant in Japanese spiritualism is the promise itself, for it clearly lends meaning, integrity, and joy to many lives, especially as the nature of adult existence unfolds. It fits the physical process of aging. It recognizes the inherent value of experience. It reinforces the notion that social structure is justifiably gerontocratic. And for all its emphasis on social responsibility, discipline, and perseverance in the middle years, it encourages these as a means to a final state of spiritual freedom, ease, and universal belonging. . . . Here is a philosophy seemingly made for adulthood—giving it stature, movement, and optimism."

Even in the United States, before modernization shifted our interest from the old to the young, the elderly were the focus of great reverence. In the early 1840s, Reverend Cortlandt van Rensselaer captured this viewpoint in the following excerpt from a sermon: "What a blessed influence the old exert in cherishing feelings of reverence, affection, and subordination in families; in detailing the results of experience; in importing judicious counsel in church and State and private life."

According to Calvinist doctrine, which was profoundly influential during this period, living to a great age was taken as a sign of God's special favor. The more spiritually evolved elder was considered one of the elect, and therefore worthy of veneration. In keeping with this point of view, old age was highly honored and revered in all social rituals and on all public occasions. According to social historian David Hackett Fischer: "The most important and solemn public gatherings in a New England town were the moments when the people met to worship together. In their meetinghouse they were carefully assigned seats of different degrees of dignity. The most honorable places did not go to the richest or strongest, but to the oldest."

And as influential leader Increase Mather commented in the late eighteenth century, "If a man is favored with long life . . . it is God that has lengthened his days." The soul, the Puritans believed, grew like the body, reaching its highest earthly perfection in old age.

IF WE ARE TO LIVE longer, on the average, than humans have ever lived before, and if our culture's center of gravity is to shift from youth to age, should this be regarded as good news or bad?

It depends on whether our society can make the following changes:

•uproot the ageism and gerontophobia that cloud our hopes for the future and replace them with a new, more positive view of aging;

• replace the limiting confines of the linear life plan with a flexible, cyclic plan, which is more appropriate to the shifting needs of a longer life;

• create a new spectrum of family relationships that takes into account the sexual, companionship, and friendship needs of adults;

• discover ways to grow old well, in the absence of debilitating disease;

• provide products and services that will offer older men and women comfort, convenience, and pleasure; and

• achieve cooperation among Americans of all ages in creating a social system that is fair and equitable for everyone.

For us as individuals, whether an aged America turns out to be good or bad news will depend on whether we can grow beyond the values and expectations of youth to discover a positive and expanded vision of who we might become in our later years. Ultimately, it will not be the number of years that determines whether we live a "great age," but the wisdom, richness, and quality that we bring to those years.

And, in the further discovery and expansion of the self that the precious extra years of life will make possible, we may realize that there is both more that we can be and more that we can give to society. We will have the maturity of vision and power that the young are too inexperienced to possess and that middle-

aged adults are usually too busy to actualize.

In the past, older members of society were revered for their great wisdom and the mature perspective they could bring to social problems and crises. But historically, the children far outnumbered the few long-lived sages. We are now quickly heading for a time when tens of millions of us will have experienced the depth and perspective of age.

As a result, more and more of us will have not merely the opportunity to live well and to live long, drawing much from life, but the time and energy to give more back, enriching society with the special qualities and deep experiences of long life. When this happens, we will truly live to a great age.

Social Institutions in Crisis and Change

- Various Views of the State of the Nation (Articles 24-26)
- The Political Sphere (Articles 27-28)
- The Economic Sphere (Articles 29-31)
- The Social Sphere (Articles 32-33)

Social institutions are the building blocks of social structure. They represent the ways in which the important tasks of society are accomplished. The regulation of reproduction, socialization of children, production and distribution of economic goods, law enforcement and social control, and organization of religion and other value systems are examples of social tasks performed by social institutions.

Social institutions are not rigid arrangements; they reflect changing social conditions. Institutions generally change slowly. At the present time, however, many of the social institutions in the United States are in a state of crisis and are undergoing rapid change. The political system is ineffective; it does not generate great leaders. The public consensus seems to be "the less government intervention, the better." American foreign policy sometimes appears to be guided more by fear than by reason. The United States economy is on shaky ground. The management of American businesses has been blamed for the decline in productivity. Medical care in some cases is uncaring. Institutional crisis is found everywhere. Even the family as an institution is under attack. Critics of the system complain that social institutions are not meeting the needs of society. Whether this is because institutions are changing too rapidly or too slowly will continue to be debated. However, in order to appreciate how social institutions endure, it is necessary to understand the development and process of such changes.

The first section of this unit presents three contrasting views of the overall state of the nation. In general, are the institutions of the United States healthy or sick, appropriate or inappropriate for changing conditions, bringing about progress or decline? Abu Selimuddin observes that America has lost its substantial lead over other nations and will slip to number two by the end of the century unless it changes its ways. Specifically, it must increase its savings, investments, and productivity. It is time to produce more and spend less, but will America do so? Robert Reich also focuses on the world economy, but argues that America's merging with the global economy is helping the rich but hurting the poor. The world economy pays unskilled labor little and "symbolic analysts" much. The most thorough critique, however, is by Richard Lamm, who predicts traumatic crises ahead unless many of our institutions are completely overhauled.

Americans have much to be proud of in the political sphere, from human rights and civil liberties to democratic processes and the rule of law. Nevertheless, the polity also has its warts, as the next two selections point out. Charles Peters focuses on a major flaw of bureaucracies: the fact that within them, bad news is screened out as information is passed up to the top. Ed Garvey then complains that money wins elections because it buys the TV time that is the only way to reach most of the voters.

In the economic sphere, dramatic changes are taking place. Organizations are radically restructuring away from hierarchy to networks, as Edgar Schein explains. Inventions, in which America still leads, are spurring many of the changes in the economy. America, however, is far behind Japan in translating inventions into products for the market. Another new development in the economy is the leveraged buyout. Max Holland argues that this is a negative development.

The social sphere is also very dynamic. Jean Bethke Elshtain analyzes some of the issues arising from the new technologies of reproduction. She is most concerned about the commercialization of reproduction. The final article analyzes how TV has homogenized America by breaking down class and regional boundaries. It has also made it more difficult for leaders to lead.

Looking Ahead: Challenge Questions

Why is it important to preserve some continuity in institutions?

Can institutions outlive their usefulness?

Why are institutions so difficult to change? Cite examples where changes are instituted from the top down, and others where they are instituted from the bottom up. Do you see a similar pattern of development for these types of change?

WILL AMERICA BECOME #2?

"If the U.S. does not meet the challenge of new competition, it surely will lose its leadership to the East and slip to number two in the world economy by the end of this century."

Abu K. Selimuddin

Mr. Selimuddin is associate professor of business, Berkshire (Mass.) Community College.

WORLD War II radically altered the fate and future of many countries. Nations that were once the strongest, such as Great Britain and France, came out of the war weakened economically and militarily. Their colonies, from which they previously derived economic power and strength, won independence. Japan and Germany lost the war, which left them in ruins. In contrast, it helped free America from the terrible grip of the Great Depression, which had lasted over a decade.

At the end of World War II, America emerged as the economic leader of the free world economy and has remained the undisputed champion since. In the 1950's and 1960's, the U.S. virtually had faced no fearful challenger. It was the number-one GNP producer in the world economy, and Americans enjoyed the highest standard of living, made possible by the largest per capita income in the world. In international commerce, it enjoyed an absolute monopoly of market share by leading in world manufacturing exports. Trade deficit, national debt, and inflation were not

the critical concerns worrying Americans then. The U.S. was also the biggest creditor and net exporter of capital across the globe. For example, through the Marshall Plan, America provided a total of $12,000,000,000 to the non-communist countries of Europe. Another $3,000,000,-000 in grants and trade credits went to Japan to rebuild its war-devastated economy between 1945 and 1955. Encouraged by the success in Western Europe and Japan, the U.S. turned its attention to helping the Third World countries of Africa, Asia, and Latin America by becoming the most generous aid donor to the capital-poor countries of the free world.

Today's global economy is much more competitive. Nations of the East—such as Japan and Asia's four "little dragons" (South Korea, Taiwan, Singapore, and Hong Kong)—and West have closed the gigantic lead in economic power once held by the U.S. America's domination of manufacturing exports and world market share is long gone. The U.S. now feels threatened by the shrinkage in its economic

clout, which has been eroding since 1970.

In contrast, Japan already is enjoying the fruit of its "economic miracle" by being able to produce 70% of America's GNP. Most economic historians predict that Japan's per capita income will surpass America's by 20% at the turn of the century. By the 1980's, Japan's GNP was higher than the combined GNP's of Britain and France, and it outproduced Britain in 1966 and France and Germany in 1967. Tokyo's stock exchange is the largest in the world, and most of the top banks in the world are situated in Japan. It is now the largest exporter of capital, made possible by its $1,000,000,000-a-day saving rate and trade surpluses estimated at $85,000,000,000 annually.

War-devastated West Germany also has made a comeback with strength and vigor. Its per capita income has risen to about $14,000, which is about 84% of America's, up from 40% in 1950. Germany enjoys a high saving rate and the second largest trade surplus after Japan.

The European Economic Community in

its report, "The Economics of 1992," predicts a six percent growth in the Common Market's GNP. According to the experts, the elimination of internal barriers among EEC nations will make European products more attractive to their consumers than imports. American companies, which sell more to Europe than Japanese firms, are bound to experience more serious losses.

Asia's "little dragons" have gotten bigger, better, and richer. They have high levels of education to absorb sophisticated technology; their growth rate averaged an impressive eight percent in the last five years, causing some shift of economic weight to the East; they are among the top 20% of manufacturing exporters in the world; and their total exports equal 80% of Japan's. Japan now imports from the "little dragons" twice what she did in the early part of this decade. All of them enjoy trade surpluses with America. They also have accumulated huge surpluses of yen, whose dramatic appreciation should give them extra impetus to enhance their competitive position relative to the U.S.

Thailand, China, India, and Indonesia also have great potential. Many other developing countries have projected annual growth rates of more than five percent. By contrast, in 1980, America exported $26,000,000,000 more to newly industrialized nations than it imported; in 1986, it imported $28,000,000,000 more than it exported.

What is also profoundly different today is the speed and scope of growth in world markets. Cheaper and faster transportation and information systems have expanded trade and travel. Interdependence among countries has been accelerated by a boom in foreign direct investment. Third World nations have been drawing increasing attention from Japan and America as cheap labor sources and consumer markets. Japan is making eyes at Asia's sleeping giant, China, by offering the Chinese a loan of over $5,000,000,000 to finance economic projects in the next five years. Japan and China can derive enormous strength from each other by building an economic bridge between the world's most dynamic economy and the largest reservoir of labor and consumer market.

In the global competition of market-grabbing, the rise of the East may mean less economic security for the West.

Forty years ago, who would have imagined that America, the biggest and the best, would have to worry about its industrial competitiveness and ability to hold on to the number-one spot in the world economy? Yet, many experts, including the President's Commission on Industrial Competitiveness, have concluded that its capacity to compete in the world market is eroding.

"We are still number one, but we have come down a notch or two. The fear is that we may fall even further," warns Alan Greenspan, chairman of the Federal Reserve System. Several facts support this view:
• While the U.S. share of global GNP has been falling since 1972, other countries, such as Japan, Germany, and Asia's "little dragons," were increasing theirs. In annual per capita income gain, Japan and Germany averaged 4.3% and 2.5%, respectively, over the last eight years, while Asia's "little dragons" averaged a very impressive eight percent. In contrast, the U.S. had a 1.8% average increase during the same period.
• America is turning into a capital-poor country because of a dismally low rate of domestic saving. In 1986 and 1987, Americans saved only 2-2.5% of their disposable income. In contrast, Great Britain saved five percent, major industrialized nations averaged 10%, and the Japanese banked about 18%. America's capital-crunch is forcing the U.S. to sign more IOU's to get loans from Japan and others in order to keep the current expansion going.
• U.S. investment in plant and equipment during the 1980's was less than in the 1950's, 1960's, or 1970's, and its capital-labor ratio grew less quickly than any of America's major competitor nations.
• America is losing ground in manufacturing productivity to Japan and Germany. Its annual growth rate in manufacturing averaged 0.3% in the last five years, compared with 7.8% and 0.8%, respectively, for Japan and Germany.
• Japan is able to introduce new products faster than its competitors, constantly improve their quality, and adapt them to changing market environments. American firms do not make innovations incrementally. Instead, they tend to move from one production plateau to another. As a consequence, change takes more time and involves more risk.
• America's rising propensity to import and lack of competitiveness in exports have caused a mountainous deficit in trade balance—a negative export-import balance of 6.2%, while Japan and Germany grew 2.1% and 1.3%, respectively. Among the top 15 key manufacturing exportables, Japan led in automobiles, steel, telecommunication, instruments, textiles, semiconductors, and machine tools. Germany was first in petrochemicals, plastics, pharmaceuticals, and aluminum. In contrast, America led only in aircraft and computers, and its market share in the latter is down by seven percent since 1980. Blue-collar and rural employment are falling, partly as a consequence of the loss in manufacturing production and export.
• The U.S. is exporting jobs overseas.

For example, in 1980, 6.9% of domestic consumer goods were imported, up from 5.4% in 1975; by 1987, 11.6% were imports. In capital goods, America imported 15% in 1980, compared with eight percent in 1975; by 1987, imports reached nearly 40% of total consumer products.
• America rapidly is losing its semiconductor market share to Japan. The takeover of semiconductor chip production raises the fear that the Pentagon may have to depend entirely on the Japanese for its needed chips for weapons. For example, six of the world's 10 largest semiconductor producers are now Japanese; a decade ago, only two were. Since 1980, America's share of the world semiconductor market has declined from 60% to 40%, while Japan has doubled its share to 50%.
• Japanese auto makers are more cost efficient and productive than the U.S.'s. For example, the cost difference between an average American and a comparable Japanese car is now over $600. American man hours per car is 150, in comparison to 100 man hours in Japan. By 1995, the U.S. expects to reduce the man hours per car from 150 to 100, while Japan hopes to reduce it to 80.
• Japanese manufacturing facilities are newer and more modernized than American plants—10 years old, on average, as compared to 20 years in the U.S.

Living beyond our means

U.S. consumers and corporations are living beyond their means because exports are not paying for the surge of imports. America's trade deficit, which reflects consumers' and businesses' debt, reached an all-time high of $175,000,000,000 in 1987. In contrast, Japan and Germany enjoyed surpluses of $75,000,000,000 and $45,000,000,000, respectively. These countries are recycling their accumulated trade surpluses by lending to American consumers, corporations, and government. They also are using these surpluses in buying pieces of America. Foreign investment in the U.S. amounted to $260,000,000,000 in 1987. By 1990, the estimated foreign ownership of America could stand at 10%, up by six percent from 1988. More foreign ownership will mean more influence on America's economic and political policymaking. The U.S. also will lose more economic clout in the world economy.

Other bleak facts lead to prospects of a continuing decline:
• American workers put in less work-hours and are less productive than their counterparts in Japan and Germany. During the last decade, American labor productivity gain was 40% of Japan's and 60% of Germany's. Annual work hours per American are 1,700, compared to 2,400 in Japan.

4. SOCIAL INSTITUTIONS: The State of the Nation

● U.S. factory workers are the world's highest paid. In contrast, Koreans earn 15%, Taiwanese 17%, Brazilians 11%, and Japanese 70% of what Americans receive. Low hourly compensation, combined with productivity levels that match those in America, partly explains why the newly industrialized countries are gaining in competitiveness. In contrast, higher labor costs and lower productivity are pushing a number of U.S. manufacturing firms to move production overseas, causing loss of jobs and income at home.

● Japan's top manufacturing firms perform admirably in cutting costs and producing quality, partly as a consequence of their using many more industrial robots than American companies. For example, Japanese utilize over 67,000 industrial robots in producing autos, home appliances, and other goods, in comparison to 14,000-plus in America.

● In the U.S., Federal debt has doubled in the last eight years to a mind-boggling $2.8 trillion. The ratio of debt to GNP rose from 34.21% in 1980 to 55% in 1988. Interest fees on national debt is now three percent of GNP. This is dangerous for America's wealth. The stock market crash in October, 1987, with the Dow Jones industrial average falling 508 points, partly was a consequence of overweight Federal debts and the inability of American government to put itself on a diet. Some $500,000,000,000 in paper value, a sum equal to the entire GNP of France, vanished into thin air. The crash also sent a signal

that America no longer could disguise its illusion of prosperity.

● Long the world's largest creditor and capital exporter, the U.S. is now the largest debtor in the global economy. America's net foreign debt is equivalent to seven percent of 1988's GNP. In the same year, Japan and Germany had net foreign assets of 8.5% and 10.5% of their respective GNP's. The power of Japan's growing economic might is well-demonstrated by its having budgeted $10,000,000,000 on foreign aid this year, displacing America, which committed $9,500,000,000, as the world's number-one aid donor.

● The U.S. school system is at risk. "American public schools are producing an army of illiterates. Of 4,000,000 18-year-old Americans in 1988, 700,000 could not read their high school diplomas," reports *Fortune* magazine. "Public education has put this country at a terrible competitive disadvantage . . . if current trends continue, American business will have to hire a million new workers a year who can't read, write or count," says Xerox Corporation CEO David T. Kearns.

To fix the system, some radical and fundamental changes would be required. "What we need is something approaching a revolution," says former Secretary of Education William Bennett. Japan, on the other hand, has produced a 99% literacy rate. In math and basic science skills, Japanese students are at the head of the class.

● America has fallen behind the Japanese in the global financial race. For example,

the biggest Japanese investment bank, Nomura, has $1,000,000,000 more equity and 10 times more market value than America's largest, Merrill Lynch. Among the world's biggest commercial banks, the first four are Japanese-owned; the biggest U.S. commercial bank, Citicorp, is number five. International assets of American banks total $580,000,000,000, while Japan's are $640,000,000,000.

America has lost some business battles in the world economy, but not yet the major war. "The United States still earns and enjoys the world's highest real income per capita. If we call the U.S. level 100, . . . Canada is next to us, in the high 90's. Norway, West Germany, Sweden, and Switzerland are all below 90. Japan is scarcely yet at 80. . . . The Soviet Union is below 50," observes Nobel Laureate in Economics Paul A. Samuelson. Since 1973, the U.S. has added 35,000,000 new jobs; in contrast, the entire Common Market has created about 6,000,000 during the same time. Despite everything, America is still the locomotive to the free world economy.

However, one must not take comfort in thinking that the U.S. always will be number one. What America needs to do—and do quickly—is sharpen its competitiveness in the global marketplace. If the U.S. does not meet the challenge of new competition, it surely will lose its leadership to the East and slip to number two in the world economy by the end of this century.

U.S. income inequality keeps on rising.

As THE WORLD TURNS

Robert B. Reich

Between 1978 and 1987, the poorest fifth of American families became eight percent poorer, and the richest fifth became 13 percent richer. That leaves the poorest fifth with less than five percent of the nation's income, and the richest fifth with more than 40 percent. This widening gap can't be blamed on the growth in single-parent lower-income families, which in fact slowed markedly after the late 1970s. Nor is it due mainly to the stingy social policy of the Reagan years. Granted, Food Stamp benefits have dropped in real terms by about 13 percent since 1981, and many states have failed to raise benefits for the poor and unemployed to keep up with inflation. But this doesn't come close to accounting for the growing inequality. Rather, the trend is connected to a profound change in the American economy as it merges with the global economy. And because the merging is far from complete, this trend will not stop of its own accord anytime soon.

It is significant that the growth of inequality shows up most strikingly among Americans who have jobs. Through most of the postwar era, the wages of Americans at different income levels rose at about the same pace. Although different workers occupied different steps on the escalator, everyone moved up together. In those days poverty was the condition of *jobless* Americans, and the major economic challenge was to create enough jobs for everyone. Once people were safely on the work force escalator, their problems were assumed to be over. Thus "full employment" became a liberal rallying cry, while conservatives fretted over the inflationary tendencies of a full-employment economy.

In recent years working Americans have been traveling on two escalators—one going up, the other going down. In 1987 the average hourly earnings of nonsupervisory workers, adjusted for inflation, were lower than in any year since 1966. Middle-level managers fared much better, although their median real earnings were only slightly above the levels of the 1970s. Executives, however, did spectacularly well. In 1988 alone, CEOs of the hundred largest publicly held industrial corporations received raises averaging almost 12 percent. The remunerations of lesser executives rose almost as much, and executives of smaller companies followed close behind.

Between 1978 and 1987, as the real earnings of unskilled workers were declining, the real incomes of workers in the securities industry (investment bankers, arbitrageurs, and brokers) rose 21 percent. Few investment bankers pocket anything near the $50 million lavished yearly upon the partners of Kohlberg, Kravis, Roberts & Company, or the $550 million commandeered last year by Michael Milken, but it is not unusual for a run-of-the-mill investment banker to bring home comfortably over a million dollars. Partners in America's largest corporate law firms are comparatively deprived, enjoying average yearly earnings of only $400,000 to $1.2 million.

Meanwhile, the number of impoverished *working* Americans climbed by nearly two million, or 23 percent, between 1978 and 1987. The number who worked full time and year round but were poor climbed faster, by 43 percent. Nearly 60 percent of the 20 million people who now fall below the Census Bureau's poverty line are from families with at least one member in full-time or part-time work.

The American economy, in short, is creating a wider range of earnings than at any other time in the postwar era. The most basic reason, put simply, is that America itself is ceasing to exist as a system of production and exchange separate from the rest of the world. One can no more meaningfully speak of an "American economy" than of a "Delaware economy." We are becoming but a region—albeit still a relatively wealthy region—of a global economy, whose technologies, savings, and investments move effortlessly across borders, making it harder for individual nations to control their economic destinies.

By now Washington officials well understand that the

nation's fiscal and monetary policies cannot be set without taking account of the savings that will slosh in or slosh out of the nation in consequence. Less understood is the speed and ease with which new technologies now spread across the globe, from computers in, say, San Jose, to satellite, and then back down to computers in Taiwan. (America's efforts to stop the Japanese from copying our commercial designs and the Soviets from copying our military designs are about equally doomed.) And we have yet to come to terms with the rise of the global corporation, whose managers, shareholders, and employees span the world. Our debates over the future of American jobs still focus on topics like the competitiveness of the American automobile industry or the future of American manufacturing. But these categories are increasingly irrelevant. They assume the existence of a separate American economy in which all the jobs associated with a particular industry, or even more generally with a particular sector, are bound together, facing a common fate.

New technologies of worldwide communication and transportation have redrawn the playing field. American industries no longer compete against Japanese or European industries. Rather, a company with headquarters in the United States, production facilities in Taiwan, and a marketing force spread across many nations competes with another, similarly ecumenical company. So when General Motors, say, is doing well, that probably is good news for a lot of executives in Detroit, and for GM shareholders across the globe, but it isn't necessarily good news for a lot of assembly-line workers in Detroit, because there may, in fact, be very few GM assembly-line workers in Detroit, or anywhere else in America. The welfare of assembly-line workers in Detroit may depend, instead, on the health of corporations based in Japan or Canada.

More to the point: even if those Canadian and Japanese corporations are doing well, these workers may be in trouble. For they are increasingly part of an international labor market, encompassing Asia, Africa, Western Europe—and perhaps, before long, Eastern Europe. Corporations can with relative ease relocate their production centers, and alter their international lines of communication and transportation accordingly, to take advantage of low wages. So American workers find themselves settling for low wages in order to hold on to their jobs. More and more, your "competitiveness" as a worker depends not on the fortunes of any American corporation, or of any American industry, but on what function you serve within the global economy. GM executives are becoming more "competitive" even as GM production workers become less so, because the functions that GM executives perform are more highly valued in the world market than the functions that GM production workers perform.

In order to see in greater detail what is happening to American jobs, it helps to view the work Americans do in terms of functional categories that reflect the real competitive positions of workers in the global economy. Essentially, three broad categories are emerging. Call them symbolic-analytic services, routine produc-

tion services, and routine personal services.

1. *Symbolic-analytic services* are based on the manipulation of information: data, words, and oral and visual symbols. Symbolic analysis comprises some (but by no means all) of the work undertaken by people who call themselves lawyers, investment bankers, commercial bankers, management consultants, research scientists, academics, public-relations executives, real estate developers, and even a few creative accountants. Also: advertising and marketing specialists, art directors, design engineers, architects, writers and editors, musicians, and television and film producers. Some of the manipulations performed by symbolic analysts reveal ways of more efficiently deploying resources or shifting financial assets, or of otherwise saving time and energy. Other manipulations grab money from people who are too slow or naive to protect themselves by manipulation in response. Still others serve to entertain the recipients.

Most symbolic analysts work alone or in small teams. If they work with others, they often have partners rather than bosses or supervisors, and their yearly income is variable, depending on how much value they add to the business. Their work environments tend to be quiet and tastefully decorated, often within tall steel-and-glass buildings. They rarely come in direct contact with the ultimate beneficiaries of their work. When they are not analyzing, designing, or strategizing, they are in meetings or on the telephone—giving advice or making deals. Many of them spend inordinate time in jet planes and hotels. They are articulate and well groomed. The vast majority are white males.

Symbolic analysis now accounts for more than 40 percent of America's gross national product, and almost 20 percent of our jobs. Within what we still term our "manufacturing sector," symbolic-analytic jobs have been increasing at a rate almost three times that of total manufacturing employment in the United States, as routine manufacturing jobs have drifted overseas or been mastered by machines.

The services performed by America's symbolic analysts are in high demand around the world, regardless of whether the symbolic analysts provide them in person or transmit them via satellite and fiber-optic cable. The Japanese are buying up the insights and inventions of America's scientists and engineers (who are only too happy to sell them at a fat profit). The Europeans, meanwhile, are hiring our management consultants, business strategists, and investment bankers. Developing nations are hiring our civil and design engineers; and almost everyone is buying the output of our pop musicians, television stars, and film producers.

It is the same with the global corporation. The central offices of these sprawling entities, headquartered in America, are filled with symbolic analysts who manipulate information and then export their insights via the corporation's far-flung enterprise. IBM doesn't export machines from the United States; it makes machines all over the globe, and services them on the spot. IBM world headquarters, in Armonk, New York, just exports strategic planning and related management services.

Thus has the standard of living of America's symbolic

analysts risen. They increasingly find themselves part of a global labor market, not a national one. And because the United States has a highly developed economy, and an excellent university system, they find that the services they have to offer are quite scarce in the context of the whole world. So elementary laws of supply and demand ensure that their salaries are quite high.

These salaries are likely to go even higher in the years ahead, as the world market for symbolic analysis continues to grow. Foreigners are trying to learn these skills and techniques, to be sure, but they still have a long way to go. No other country does a better job of preparing its most fortunate citizens for symbolic analysis than does the United States. None has surpassed America in providing experience and training, often with entire regions specializing in one or another kind of symbolic analysis (New York and Chicago for finance, Los Angeles for music and film, the San Francisco Bay area and greater Boston for science and engineering). In this we can take pride. But for the second major category of American workers—the providers of routine production services—the laws of supply and demand don't bode well.

2. *Routine production services* involve tasks that are repeated over and over, as one step in a sequence of steps for producing a finished product. Although we tend to associate these jobs with manufacturing, they are becoming common in the storage and retrieval of information. Banking, insurance, wholesaling, retailing, health care—all employ hordes of people who spend their days processing data, often putting information into computers or taking it out.

Most providers of routine production services work with many other people who do similar work within large, centralized facilities. They are overseen by supervisors, who in turn are monitored by more senior supervisors. They are usually paid an hourly wage. Their jobs are monotonous. Most of these people do not have a college education; they need only be able to take directions and, occasionally, undertake simple computations. Those who deal with metal are mostly white males; those who deal with fabrics or information tend to be female and/or minorities.

Decades ago, jobs like these were relatively well paid. Henry Ford gave his early production workers five dollars a day, a remarkable sum for the time, in the (correct) belief that they and their neighbors would be among the major buyers of Fords. But in recent years America's providers of routine-production services have found themselves in direct competition with millions of foreign workers, most of whom are eager to work for a fraction of the pay of American workers. Through the miracle of satellite transmission, even routine data-processing can now be undertaken in relatively poor nations, thousands of miles away from the skyscrapers where the data are finally used. This fact has given management-level symbolic analysts ever greater bargaining leverage. If routine producers living in America don't agree to reduce their wages, then the work will go abroad.

And it has. In 1950 routine production services constituted about 30 percent of our national product and well over half of American jobs. Today such services represent about 20 percent of national product and one-fourth of jobs. And the scattering of foreign-owned factories placed here to circumvent American protectionism isn't going to reverse the trend. So the standard of living of America's routine production workers will likely keep declining. The dynamics behind the wage concessions, plant closings, and union-busting that have become commonplace are not likely to change.

3. *Routine personal services* also entail simple, repetitive work, but, unlike routine production services, they are provided in person. Their immediate objects are specific customers rather than streams of metal, fabric, or data. Included in this employment category are restaurant and hotel workers, barbers and beauticians, retail sales personnel, cabdrivers, household cleaners, daycare workers, hospital attendants and orderlies, truck drivers, and—among the fastest-growing of all—custodians and security guards.

Like production workers, providers of personal services are usually paid by the hour, are carefully supervised, and rarely have more than a high school education. But unlike people in the other two categories of work, these people are in direct contact with the ultimate beneficiaries of what they do. And the companies they work for are often small. In fact, some routine personal-service workers turn entrepreneurial. (Most new businesses and new jobs in America come from this sector—now constituting about 20 percent of GNP and 30 percent of jobs.) Women and minorities make up the bulk of routine personal-service workers.

Apart from the small number who strike out on their own, these workers are paid poorly. They are sheltered from the direct effects of global competition, but not the indirect effects. They often compete with illegal aliens willing to work for low wages, or with former or would-be production workers who can't find well-paying production jobs, or with labor-saving machinery (automated tellers, self-service gas pumps, computerized cashiers) dreamed up by symbolic analysts in America and manufactured in Asia. And because they tend to be unskilled and dispersed among small businesses, personal-service workers rarely have a union or a powerful lobby group to stand up for their interests. When the economy turns sour, they are among the first to feel the effects. These workers will continue to have jobs in the years ahead and may experience some small increase in real wages. They will have demographics on their side, as the American work force shrinks. But for all the foregoing reasons, the gap between their earnings and those of the symbolic analysts will continue to grow.

These three functional categories—symbolic analysis, routine production, and routine personal service—cover at least three out of four American jobs. The rest of the nation's work force consists mainly of government employees (including public school teachers), employees in regulated industries (like utility workers), and government-financed workers (engineers working on defense weapons systems), many of whom are sheltered from global competition. One further clarification:

some traditional job categories overlap with several functional categories. People called "secretaries," for example, include those who actually spend their time doing symbolic-analytic work closely allied to what their bosses do; those who do routine data entry or retrieval of a sort that will eventually be automated or done overseas; and those who provide routine personal services.

The important point is that workers in these three functional categories are coming to have a different competitive position in the world economy. Symbolic analysts hold a commanding position in an increasingly global labor market. Routine production workers hold a relatively weak position in an increasingly global labor market. Personal-service workers still find themselves in a national labor market, but for various reasons they suffer the indirect effects of competition from workers abroad.

How should we respond to these trends? One response is to accept them as inevitable consequences of change, but try to offset their polarizing effects through a truly progressive income tax, coupled with more generous income assistance—including health insurance—for poor working Americans. (For a start, we might reverse the extraordinarily regressive Social Security amendments of 1983, through which poor working Americans are now financing the federal budget deficit, often paying more in payroll taxes than in income taxes.)

A more ambitious response would be to guard against class rigidities by ensuring that any talented American kid can become a symbolic analyst—regardless of family income or race. Here we see the upside of a globalized economy. Unlike America's old vertically integrated economy, whose white-collar jobs were necessarily limited in proportion to the number of blue-collar jobs beneath them, the global economy imposes no particular limit upon the number of Americans who can sell symbolic-analytic services. In principle, all of America's routine production workers could become symbolic analysts and let their old jobs drift overseas. In practice, of course, we can't even inch toward such a state anytime soon. Not even America's gifted but poor children can aspire to such jobs until the government spends substantially more than it does now to ensure excellent public schools in every city and region to which talented children can go, and ample financial help when they are ready to attend college.

Of course, it isn't clear that even under those circumstances there would be radical growth in the number of Americans who became research scientists, design engineers, musicians, management consultants, or (even if the world needed them) investment bankers and lawyers. So other responses are also needed. Perhaps the most ambitious would be to increase the numbers of Americans who could apply symbolic analysis to production and to personal services.

There is ample evidence, for example, that access to computerized information can enrich production jobs by enabling workers to alter the flow of materials and components in ways that generate new efficiencies. (Shoshana Zuboff's recent book *In the Age of the Smart Machine* carefully documents these possibilities.) Production workers who thus have broader responsibilities and more control over how production is organized cease to be "routine" workers—becoming, in effect, symbolic analysts at a level very close to the production process. The same transformation can occur in personal-service jobs. Consider, for example, the checkout clerk whose computer enables her to control inventory and decide when to reorder items from the factory.

The number of such technologically empowered jobs, of course, is limited by the ability of workers to learn on the job. That means a far greater number of Americans will need good health care (including prenatal and postnatal) and also a good grounding in mathematics, basic science, and reading and communicating. So once again, comfortably integrating the American work force into the new world economy turns out to rest heavily on education.

Education and health care for poor children are apt to be costly. Since poorer working Americans, already under a heavy tax load, can't afford it, the cost would have to be borne by wealthier Americans—who also would have to bear the cost of any income redistribution plans designed to neutralize the polarizing domestic effects of a globalized economy. Thus a central question is the willingness of the more fortunate American citizens—especially symbolic analysts, who constitute the most fortunate fifth, with 40 percent of the nation's income—to bear the burden. But here lies a Catch-22. For as our economic fates diverge, the top fifth may be losing the sense of connectedness with the bottom fifth, or even the bottom half, that would elicit such generosity.

The conservative tide that has swept the land during the last decade surely has many causes, but these economic fundamentals should not be discounted. It is now possible for the most fortunate fifth to sell their expertise directly in the global market, and thus maintain and enhance their standard of living and that of their children, even as that of other Americans declines. There is less and less basis for a strong sense of interclass interdependence. Meanwhile, the fortunate fifth have also been able to insulate themselves from the less fortunate, by living in suburban enclaves far removed from the effects of poverty. Neither patriotism nor altruism may be sufficient to overcome these realities. Yet without the active support of the fortunate fifth, it will be difficult to muster the political will necessary for change.

George Bush speaks eloquently of "a thousand points of light" and of the importance of generosity. But so far his administration has set a poor example. A minuscule sum has been budgeted for education, training, and health care for the poor. The president says we can't afford any more. Meanwhile, he pushes a reduction in the capital gains tax rate—another boon to the fortunate fifth.

On withdrawing from the presidential race of 1988, Paul Simon of Illinois said, "Americans instinctively know that we are one nation, one family, and when anyone in that family hurts, all of us hurt." Sadly, that is coming to be less and less the case.

POST-CRASH INSTITUTIONS

Richard D. Lamm

Richard D. Lamm, former governor of Colorado, is partner in the Denver law firm of O'Connor and Hannan. He is also the Leo Block Fellow at the University of Denver and head of the Center for Public Policy and Contemporary Issues. His last article for THE FUTURIST, "Copernican Politics: It's Time to Ask Heretical Questions," appeared in October 1983. His address is University of Denver, University Park, Denver, Colorado 80208.

Last year's stock-market crash warns of a serious economic trauma that could expand into social and political upheaval. Wasteful and ineffectual institutions must be overhauled, and new priorities must be set to stave off another great depression.

Let me disclose my viewpoint up front. I do not believe that we in the United States live in a sustainable society. We are heading for trauma. I suspect that it will start with an economic trauma and quickly expand into social and political trauma. It may start with a serious deflation, or it could start with inflation as monetary and fiscal policy react to a recession. The scenarios are many, but the chances of avoiding economic turmoil are few. Pipers must be paid.

The United States is spending more than it saves and importing far more than it exports. The nation is consuming more than it produces and spending more public monies than it takes in as taxes. When the world's largest debtor nation has the lowest rate of productivity growth in the industrialized world, it should start looking to post-crash scenarios.

An albatross of debt hangs around America's neck: farm debt, corporate debt, individual debt. The federal government borrows 20¢ out of every dollar it spends, and the political system has balanced only *one* budget in the last 28 years. There is something fundamentally unsustainable about an economy that, by the early 1990s, will have to spend 40% of the new wealth it produces abroad to pay the interest on recent borrowing. In a myriad of ways, the United States is defying the laws of economic gravity.

Whole books have been written about how America's problems are outrunning its solutions. Suffice it to say that it is time to start a dialogue on what institutional and structural changes will be needed after the crash to put the country back together.

The stakes are high. Economic chaos preceded Lenin's Russia, Mussolini's Italy, and Hitler's Germany. There is a certain Russian roulette in economic chaos: You may get a Roosevelt or you may get a Hitler. People who love freedom and respect democracy must start now to postulate how we are to put together a new economic order if and when the economy collapses. Economic chaos is profoundly destabilizing. Not only is leadership up in the air, but so is the very form of government. No "solution" is so extreme that it will not find adherents.

The next economic crisis will be worldwide, and to some extent the scenario in the United States will be a function of worldwide pressures. But looking at the possible steps to stabilize the U.S. economy in a time of crisis, we soon see that some of the alternatives available in the 1929 crisis are no longer available.

In 1929, the United States had little federal debt and a great ability to stimulate the economy by Keynesian measures. But this alternative has been foolishly wasted. Keynes never postulated that a nation could continue to borrow indefinitely. He felt that a country could fight a war or a depression on borrowed money but that during times of prosperity debt would be reduced in preparation for the next crisis.

But the United States has allowed deficit spending to become a way of life and a way of government. Neither political party has the backbone to come close to balancing the budget. Today, the United States devotes almost 20% of all federal spending to interest on the $2.4-trillion federal debt. It is doubtful that much deficit spending will be available in the next crisis without making the problem worse.

From *The Futurist*, July/August 1988, pp. 8-12. The Futurist, published by the World Future Society, 4916 St. Elmo Avenue, Bethesda, MD 20814.

4. SOCIAL INSTITUTIONS: The State of the Nation

In 1929, the United States was a large creditor nation. It did not have to export to pay its international obligations. Today, the United States is the world's largest debtor nation, and, at the current rate, sometime in the 1990s, it will owe more to foreign creditors than *all* the rest of the world combined. When (if) the economy collapses, it will be much harder to find palatable solutions. We will pass through a long, hard "winter of discontent."

America will be much more susceptible to the siren songs of the demagogue. "Hair shirt" solutions involving sacrifice and hard work will pale beside those offered by the left and right, who will suggest easy solutions and convenient scapegoats. America will find it hard to accept that it has been living beyond its means and that prosperity was not written into the U.S. Constitution.

I thus suggest that the first challenge of the post-crash world is to find a democratic leader who will restore hope and faith to a traumatized nation. Simply avoiding the natural temptation to succumb to those offering convenient scapegoats and demagogic solutions will be a major hurdle for a nation in turmoil. America will need the functional equivalent of a Winston Churchill — a leader who can call for sacrifice while promising only "blood, sweat, and tears." It is only such a leader who holds the promise of restoring the nation to greatness rather than leading it down the path toward greater despair.

Reprioritizing Government

One of the major challenges of government in a post-crash era will be to maintain the safety-net programs that keep people from tearing the system apart. If there is another depression in the United States, people would be far less likely to suffer in silence, as they did in the 1930s.

Ironically, we may consider it a stroke of luck that there is a degree of waste and inefficiency in government that will be relatively easy to cut. The U.S. government delivers its benefits in a very inefficient

way. Agriculture supports are given to corporate farmers; Medicare is given to wealthy retirees; Social Security is paid to millionaires.

There *are* ways of compassionately shrinking the federal budget. Instead of incurring even larger deficits in a time of economic crisis, the government can rethink many of its priorities. Through taxing Social Security benefits, Medicare, and other programs that are distributed without regard to need, a significant amount of money can be redirected to meet more-pressing needs. Beyond that, the option of "means testing" some, or all, entitlements could save substantial resources. The overwhelming majority of entitlements are paid not to the poor, but to the middle class. New money to meet emergency needs can be found in old excesses. Simply going through existing government programs and distributing them on the basis of need would free up significant resources.

There are a myriad of long-term structural changes that can better focus resources if Congress is scared enough to use them. For example, it is difficult to justify maintaining more than 3,000 military bases when the military itself says it doesn't need more than 300 to defend the nation. If military installations were maintained on the basis of national-security needs, rather than political considerations, the defense budget could be cut in a way that even the Pentagon agrees would not compromise the U.S. defense posture.

Additionally, reform of systems like military and federal civil-service pensions is long overdue. These are programs that were overly generous even in times of economic prosperity and will be unaffordable in an era of economic decline. In order to balance the interests of future taxpayers and future retirees, all federal pension systems will need to incorporate the Social Security system into their base and eliminate "double dipping" — retirees collecting two (or even three) federal pensions.

Other duplicative programs will also need to be reevaluated. A gov-

ernment that already has a Medicare system for the elderly could undoubtedly do without a duplicate system of care for elderly veterans. It is difficult to justify why a nation that, on any given day, has 200,000–300,000 surplus hospital beds is dipping into depleted public coffers to build new Veterans Administration hospitals.

New taxes may be needed, though they are unwise at times of economic crisis. But not all taxes are created equal. Depending on who, what, and how we tax, the results could vary greatly. Ultimately, the United States should recognize that, while its economic competitors encourage savings and tax consumption, the United States does the opposite. A $1 tax on gasoline, for example, could help solve two problems: reduce the deficit and reduce dependency on foreign oil. In the long run, the United States must be less profligate with its diminishing resources. An oil-import tax could be a win–win proposition: If Americans choose to continue consuming large amounts of foreign oil, at least the national treasury would benefit. If it results in conservation, America reduces its dependency on unreliable foreign oil. Rational tax systems are an integral part of economic competitiveness.

The above are just examples of the types of reform that could be available when economic conditions override selfish political considerations. It is clear that the inadequacies in some parts of the system can be funded by the excesses in other parts of the system.

Unfortunately, the steps I have outlined to this point are limited to ideas about how to redistribute the economic pie. None of these ideas is new. Over the past eight years of record deficit spending, the debate has not been over how much to spend, but rather *where* to spend. Democrats and Republicans have not been arguing over the size of the budget; most of the quibbling has come over whether to increase entitlements or increase defense spending. Regardless of where one thinks America's budget priorities should be, the inescapable conclusion is that the nation is spending too much and/or taxing too little.

Ultimately, in my opinion, the United States will have to adopt a balanced-budget amendment. The political risk is too great at this point for either political party to balance the budget. New discipline must be brought to a system now out of control; a balanced-budget amendment, and possibly a line-item veto (which most governors have), while not ideal, can restore stability to the federal system.

Long-Term Institutional Reform

The United States, however, must do more than eliminate government inefficiency and waste if it expects to regain its economic position in the world. It must also reform many of its societal institutions. Ultimately, it is not companies that compete in the international market, but societies. A society whose basic institutions have become wasteful and inefficient will not remain competitive over the long term. Securing the nation's economic future will require more than modernization of plants and equipment — it will demand basic institutional reforms.

America's education, health care, and legal systems are examples of institutions that are no longer part of the solution, but rather have become millstones on the system.

No nation spends more money to educate its children than the United States, yet on all international aptitude tests U.S. children score in the lower third, compared with other industrialized nations. No one spends more money on health care than Americans, yet America has a shorter life expectancy and higher infant mortality than many societies that spend far less on health care. Americans spend more time in court litigating their grievances, while the nation has the lowest rate of productivity growth in the industrialized world. America is filled with dysfunctional institutions that must be reformed and revitalized if it is to regain its international competitiveness.

Faced with an increasingly complex and technological world, the U.S. educational system turns out a bumper crop of lawyers every year, while the nation's economic competitors train engineers. As it becomes increasingly evident that future American prosperity will depend on a populace that can master complex technologies, one in five Americans can barely read a menu. We can no longer educate simply for the sake of education. Public education must be geared toward meeting the educational requirements of the twenty-first century. An education system that turns its best minds into litigators and other assorted paper pushers will inevitably lose out to societies that produce scientists and engineers.

The American educational system, however, is merely a reflection of a misplaced national value system. A society that rewards people who can float junk bonds and think up new ways to put together corporate mergers is one that encourages its best people to pursue MBAs and law degrees. A society that rewards people for turning ideas into useful products is one that produces innovators and entrepreneurs. It doesn't take a genius to figure out which society will enjoy long-term success.

The American health-care system is yet another example of an institution that is inefficient and uncompetitive. Health care has become a fiscal black hole down which America is pouring a greater and greater share of its wealth. With an annual price tag of $511 billion — more than 11% of the gross national product — America has a system that produces medical miracles for a few, denies basic and preventive health care to many, and makes American products uncompetitive on the world market. When the Big Three automakers spend more on health-care coverage for their employees than they do for steel, it is hard to see how they can compete with foreign manufacturers who spend only a fraction of what the United States does on health care.

Perhaps if the enormous U.S. medical bill translated into better health for Americans, these expenditures could be justified. But Americans are not healthier than societies that spend far less on health care. When the average American male can expect to live no longer than the average Cuban male, the United States must question whether it is buying the most health for the buck. Does it really make sense for the same government to spend millions of Medicare dollars on heart transplants while it spends millions more subsidizing tobacco growers? Where is the logic to a system that spends endless resources caring for premature and low-birthweight babies, but cannot find funds to provide prenatal care to poor women?

Health care in America is provided on an ad hoc basis. It is an enormous white elephant that provides heroic medicine to treat emergencies, but has no vision of how to meet the overall health needs of the nation. Health-care costs have become a built-in disadvantage that contributes to the nation's declining competitiveness.

The United States has a legal system that is more adept at producing income for lawyers than it is at administering justice for its citizens. A society that litigates every dispute and expends enormous amounts of time and energy insulating itself against lawsuits is bound to be less productive and less innovative than a society that resolves its differences more efficiently. A nation that has only 5% of the world's population but two-thirds of all the lawyers on the planet cannot operate efficiently. The American legal system has become another institutional impediment to competitiveness.

These are but a few of the institutional dinosaurs that are weighing down the U.S. economy. The new world economy requires efficient and effective institutions, and America has neither. The United States is now in an international economy where an economic Darwinism is weeding out not just uncompetitive industries, but also uncompetitive countries. The future will belong to those countries that can adapt to the new conditions of international competition; those that don't will become extinct.

Dysfunctional Social Systems

Reforming dysfunctional institutions alone will not be enough, however. Many of America's social systems are in disarray and also need mending. These present a far more perplexing problem because they cannot be corrected legislatively — they require fundamental changes in personal behavior and attitudes.

The United States has the highest illegitimacy rate in the industrialized world and one of the highest divorce rates. The high-school dropout, drug addiction, and violent crime rates far exceed the levels found in countries with which the United States is trying to compete. These problems are all interrelated and are all contributing to America's economic decline and will greatly impede the nation's recovery in a post-crash era.

In 1929, when U.S. economic institutions crashed, America still had strong societal institutions — like family, church, and community — to sustain its citizens. A society that lacks that sort of basic stability will not have the fortitude to overcome the hard times. No amount of public spending can keep a child in school if education is not encouraged in the home. No laws will prevent people from sticking needles in their arms or engaging in criminal activities if they don't have the skills to make it in society.

The realities that will exist when (if) the next crash occurs will make these problems far more intractable. It is difficult to be optimistic about an economic renaissance when one out of four children lives in poverty, 14% are children of teenage mothers, 14% are children of unmarried parents, 40% will live in a broken home before they are 18 years old, 30% will be on welfare for all or part of their first 18 years, 30% will never finish high school, and up to 15% do not even speak English.

Unassimilated minorities, selfish special interests, and regional tensions have all contributed to a Balkanizing of America. The United States is a much less homogeneous country than it was in the 1930s. Large numbers of immigrants remain outside the cultural, linguistic, and economic mainstream. The social glue that will be needed to hold the society together in a time of turmoil will be much more difficult to find.

These are problems government alone cannot solve. The role of government is to provide leadership, motivation, and assistance. That leadership is sorely lacking, however. Americans like politicians who tell them what they want to hear; there is little incentive for elected representatives to call upon citizens for discipline and sacrifice to achieve national goals. No institution seems to have the legitimacy to rally the public toward given goals. Nihilism, alienation, distrust, cynicism abound. Coming at a time of economic testing, such social conditions will be doubly disturbing. In the words of an ancient philosopher, "Anyone can hold the helm when the sea is calm," but will we be able to produce the kind of leadership to guide us through the storm?

The Dysfunctional Nature Of American Culture

Winston Churchill once said, "We build our buildings and then they build us." A society's success is ultimately based on its culture. A society whose culture builds productivity, hard work, education, and scientific research will build wealth. A culture that encourages hedonism, sloppy work, poor worker motivation, and illiteracy will be eclipsed. A nation whose culture easily obtains from its citizens cooperation, discipline, and self-sacrifice has a cultural foundation much firmer than those countries whose work ethic has been eroded, whose sense of mission is undercut, and whose destiny is less manifest.

America's work ethic is not competitive with that of its international competitors. Roman satirist Juvenal warned that luxury is more ruthless than war; perhaps Americans have become victims of their own prosperity. The average Korean worker works 54.4 hours per week, while the average Japanese works 44.8 hours and the average American works 35.3 hours.

A nation's success is built on the bedrock of its workers' motivation. America's high absenteeism rate and labor unrest are both a cause and a symptom of declining competitiveness. The President's Commission on Industrial Competitiveness has found that the United States loses 813 days per 1,000 workers to industrial unrest, compared with 31 days for Japan and six days for West Germany. U.S. employee motivation is constantly below that of their international competitors.

U.S. workers do not work at or near their full potential. Three-quarters of U.S. employees believe that there is little connection between their level of pay and the quality of their performance. A mere 9% of U.S. employees believe they would benefit from increased productivity, while 93% of Japanese workers believe an increase in the productivity of their employer will personally benefit them. Eerily, Americans' attitudes seem to have reached a stage where they are more in tune with Soviet socialism than American capitalism.

Not only the work ethic, but the civic ethic has changed as well. Men who risked their lives in World War II now cheat on their income taxes and won't walk to the local schoolhouse to vote. A nation of concerned citizens can claw its way out of its difficulties; an apathetic one will be fertile ground for demagogues.

The United States is living through the Indian summer of its affluence. The nation is not taking the minimum steps necessary to keep the economy or the country together. Americans must start evaluating which institutions need to be revitalized and which ones eliminated.

That Americans have been living far beyond their means for some time is no longer a matter of conjecture. Few experts would disagree that we will pay for our profligacy somewhere down the road. The only question is how far down the road and how severe the price. Ignoring this reality will only compound our foolishness. Americans must start to debate and decide on what post-crash institutions will rebuild the nation. We must prepare for the worst, hope for the best, and begin laying the groundwork for a new, more sustainable future.

FROM OUAGADOUGOU TO CAPE CANAVERAL:
WHY THE BAD NEWS DOESN'T TRAVEL UP

Charles Peters

Charles Peters is editor-in-chief of The Washington Monthly.

Everyone is asking why the top NASA officials who decided to launch the fatal Challenger flight had not been told of the concerns of people down below, like Allan McDonald and the other worried engineers at Morton Thiokol.

In the first issue of *The Washington Monthly*, Russell Baker and I wrote, "In any reasonably large government organization, there exists an elaborate system of information cutoffs, comparable to that by which city water systems shut off large water-main breaks, closing down, first small feeder pipes, then larger and larger valves. The object is to prevent information, particularly of an unpleasant character, from rising to the top of the agency, where it may produce results unpleasant to the lower ranks.

"Thus, the executive at or near the top lives in constant danger of not knowing, until he reads it on Page One some morning, that his department is hip-deep in disaster."

This seemed to us to be a serious problem for government, not only because the people at the top didn't know but because the same system of cut-offs operated to keep Congress, the press, and the public in the dark. (Often it also would operate to keep in the dark people within the organization but outside the immediate chain of command—this happened with the astronauts, who were not told about the concern with the O-rings.)

I first became aware of this during the sixties, when I worked at the Peace Corps. Repeatedly

I would find that a problem that was well-known by people at lower and middle levels of the organization, whose responsibility it was, would be unknown at the top of the chain of command or by anyone outside.

The most serious problems of the Peace Corps had their origins in Sargent Shriver's desire to get the organization moving. He did not want it to become mired in feasibility studies, he wanted to get volunteers overseas and into action fast. To fulfill his wishes, corners were cut. Training was usually inadequate in language, culture, and technical skills. Volunteers were selected who were not suited to their assignments. For example, the country then known as Tanganyika asked for surveyors, and we sent them people whose only connection with surveying had been holding the rod and chain while the surveyor sighted through his gizmo. Worse, volunteers were sent to places where no job at all awaited them. These fictitious assignments were motivated sometimes by the host official's desire to please the brother-in-law of the president of the United States and sometimes by the official's ignorance of what was going on at the lower levels of his own bureaucracy.

But subordinates would not tell Shriver about the problems. There were two reasons for this. One was fear. They knew that he wanted action, not excuses, and they suspected that their careers would suffer if he heard too many of the latter. The other reason was that they felt it was their job to solve problems, not burden the boss with them. They and Shriver shared the view expressed by Deke Slayton, the former astronaut, when he

Reprinted with permission from *The Washington Monthly*, April 1986, pp. 27-31. Copyright by THE WASHINGTON MONTHLY CO., 1711 Connecticut Avenue, NW, Washington, D.C. 20009. (202) 462-0128.

was asked about the failure of middle-level managers to tell top NASA officials about the problems they were encountering:

"You depend on managers to make a decision based on the information they have. If they had to transmit all the fine detail to the top people, it wouldn't get launched but once every ten years."

The point is not without merit. It is easy for large organizations to fall into "once every ten years" habits. Leaders who want to avoid that danger learn to set goals and communicate a sense of urgency about meeting them. But what many of them never learn is that once you set those goals you have to guard against the tendency of those down below to spare you not only "all the fine detail" but essential facts about significant problems.

For instance, when Jimmy Carter gave the Pentagon the goal of rescuing the Iranian hostages, he relied on the chain of command to tell him if there were any problems. So he did not find out until after the disaster at Desert One that the Delta Commandos thought the Marine pilots assigned to fly the helicopters were incompetent.

In NASA's case chances have been taken with the shuttle from the beginning—the insulating thermal tiles had not gone through a reentry test before the first shuttle crew risked their lives to try them out—but in recent years the pressure to cut corners has increased markedly. Competition with the European Ariane rocket and the Reagan administration's desire to see agencies like NASA run as if they were private businesses have led to a speedup in the launch schedule, with a goal of 14 this year and 24 by 1988.

"The game NASA is playing is the maximum tonnage per year at the minimum costs possible," says Paul Cloutier, a professor of space physics. "Some high officials don't want to hear about problems," reports *Newsweek*, "especially if fixing them will cost money."

Under pressures like these, the NASA launch team watched Columbia, after seven delays, fall about a month behind schedule and then saw Challenger delayed, first by bad weather, then by damaged door handles, and then by bad weather again. Little wonder that Lawrence Mulloy, when he heard the warnings from the Thiokol engineers, burst out: "My God, Thiokol, when do you want me to launch? Next April?"

Mulloy may be one of the villains of this story, but it is important to realize that you need Lawrence Mulloys to get things done. It is also important to realize that, if you have a Lawrence Mulloy, you must protect yourself against what he might fail to do or what he might do wrong in his enthusiastic rush to get the job done.

And you can't just ask him if he has any doubts. If he's a gung-ho type, he's going to suppress the negatives. When Jimmy Carter asked General David Jones to check out the Iran rescue

plan, Jones said to Colonel Beckwith: "Charlie, tell me what you really think about the mission. Be straight with me."

"Sir, we're going to do it!" Beckwith replied. "We want to do it, and we're ready."

John Kennedy received similar confident reports from the chain of command about the readiness of the CIA's Cuban Brigade to charge ashore at the Bay of Pigs and overthrow Fidel Castro. And Sargent Shriver had every reason to believe that the Peace Corps was getting off to a fabulous start, based on what his chain of command was telling him.

With Shriver, as with NASA's senior officials, the conviction that everything was A-OK was fortified by skillful public relations. Bill Moyers was only one of the geniuses involved in this side of the Peace Corps. At NASA, Julian Scheer began a tradition of inspired PR that endured until Challenger. These were men who could sell air conditioning in Murmansk. The trouble is they also sold their bosses the same air conditioning. Every organization has a tendency to believe its own PR—NASA's walls are lined with glamorizing posters and photographs of the shuttle and other space machines—and usually the top man is the most thoroughly seduced because, after all, it reflects the most glory on him.

Favorable publicity and how to get it is therefore the dominant subject of Washington staff meetings. The minutes of the Nuclear Regulatory Commission show that when the reactor was about to melt down at Three Mile Island, the commissioners were worried less about what to do to fix the reactor than they were about what they were going to say to the press.

One of the hottest rumors around Washington is that the White House had put pressure on NASA to launch so that the president could point with pride to the teacher in space during his State of the Union speech. The White House denies this story, and my sources tell me the denial is true. But NASA had—and this is fact, not rumor—put pressure on *itself* by asking the president to mention Christa McAuliffe. In a memorandum dated January 8, NASA proposed that the president say:

"Tonight while I am speaking to you, a young elementary school teacher from Concord, New Hampshire, is taking us all on the ultimate field trip as she orbits the earth as the first citizen passenger on the space shuttle. Christa McAuliffe's journey is a prelude to the journeys of other Americans living and working together in a permanently manned space station in the mid-1990s. Mrs. McAuliffe's week in space is just one of the achievements in space we have planned for the coming year."

The flight was scheduled for January 23. It was postponed and postponed again. Now it was January 28, the morning of the day the speech was to be delivered, the last chance for the launch

When NASA's George Hardy told Thiokol engineers that he was appalled by their verbal recommendation that the launch be postponed and asked Thiokol to reconsider and make another recommendation, he was telling them, "Don't tell me," or "Don't tell me officially so that I won't have to pass bad news along to my bosses."

to take place in time to have it mentioned by the president. NASA officials must have feared they were about to lose a PR opportunity of stunning magnitude, an opportunity to impress not only the media and the public but the agency's two most important constituencies, the White House and the Congress. Wouldn't you feel pressure to get that launch off this morning so that the president could talk about it tonight?

NASA's sensitivity to the media in regard to the launch schedule was nothing short of unreal. Here is what Richard G. Smith, the director of the Kennedy Space Center, had to say about it after the disaster:

"Every time there was a delay, the press would say, 'Look, there's another delay....here's a bunch of idiots who can't even handle a launch schedule.' You think that doesn't have an impact? If you think it doesn't, you're stupid."

I do not recall seeing a single story like those Smith describes. Perhaps there were a few. The point, however, is to realize how large even a little bit of press criticism loomed in NASA's thinking.

Sargent Shriver liked good press as much as, if not more than, the next man. But he also had an instinct that the ultimate bad press would come if the world found out about your disaster before you had a chance to do something to prevent it. He and an assistant named William Haddad decided to make sure that Shriver got the bad news first. Who was going to find it out for them? Me.

It was July 1961. They decided to call me an evaluator and send me out to our domestic training programs and later overseas to find out what was really going on. My first stop was the University of California at Berkeley where our Ghana project was being trained. Fortunately, except for grossly inadequate language instruction, this program was excellent. But soon I began finding serious deficiencies in other training programs and in our projects abroad.

Shriver was not always delighted by these reports. Indeed, at one point I heard I was going to be fired. I liked my job, and I knew that the reports that I and the other evaluators who had joined me were writing were true. I didn't want to be fired. What could I do?

I knew he was planning to visit our projects in Africa. So I prepared a memorandum that contrasted what the chain of command was saying with what I and my associates were reporting. Shriver left for Africa. I heard nothing for several weeks. Then came a cable from Somalia: "Tell Peters his reports are right." I knew then that, however much Shriver wanted to hear the good news and get good publicity, he could take the bad news. The fact that he could take the bad news meant that the Peace Corps began to face its problems and do something about them before they became a scandal.

NASA did the opposite. A 1983 reorganization shifted the responsibility for monitoring flight safety from the chief engineer in Washington to the field. This may sound good. "We're not going to micromanage," said James M. Beggs, then the NASA administrator. But the catch is that if you decentralize, you must maintain the flow of information from the field to the top so that the organization's leader will know what those decentralized managers are doing. What NASA's reorganization did, according to safety engineers who talked to Mark Tapscott of *The Washington Times*, was to close off "an independent channel with authority to make things happen at the top."

I suspect what happened is that the top NASA administrators, who were pushing employees down below to dramatically increase the number of launches, either consciously or unconsciously did not want to be confronted with the dangers they were thereby risking.

This is what distinguishes the bad leaders from the good. The good leader, realizing that there is a natural human tendency to avoid bad news, traps himself into having to face it. He encourages whistleblowers instead of firing them. He visits the field himself and talks to the privates and lieutenants as well as the generals to find out the real problems. He can use others to do this for him, as Shriver used me, or as Franklin Roosevelt used his wife Eleanor and Harry Hopkins, and as they in turn used Lorena Hickock* to find out what the New Deal was really accomplishing. But he must have some independent knowledge of what's going on down below in order to have a feel for whether the chain of command is giving him the straight dope.

What most often happens, of course, is that the boss, if he goes to the field at all, talks only to the colonels and generals. Sometimes he doesn't want to know what the privates know. He may be hoping that the lid can be kept on whatever problems are developing, at least until his watch is over, so that he won't be blamed when they finally surface. Or he may have a very good idea that bad things are being done and simply wants to retain "deniability," meaning that the deed cannot be traced to him. The story of Watergate is filled with "Don't tell me" and "I don't want to know."

When NASA's George Hardy told Thiokol engineers that he was appalled by their verbal recommendation that the launch be postponed and asked Thiokol to reconsider and make another recommendation, Thiokol, which Hardy well knew was worried about losing its shuttle contract, was in effect being told, "Don't tell me" or "Don't tell me officially so I won't have to pass bad news along and my bosses will have deniability."

In addition to the leader himself, others must be concerned with making him face the bad news. This includes subordinates. Their having the courage to speak out about what is wrong is crucial, and people like Bruce Cook of NASA and Allan McDonald of Thiokol deserve great credit for having done so. But it is a fact that none of the subordinates who knew the danger to the shuttle took the next step and resigned in protest so that the public could find out what was going on in time to prevent disaster. The almost univer-

*See Political Booknotes, May 1981, page 58. Other articles concerned with the issues raised here: "The Shriver Prescription: How Government Can Find Out What It's Doing," November 1972; "How Carter Can Find Out What the Government Is Doing," January 1977; "Blind Ambition in the White House," March 1977; "The Prince and His Courtiers," March 1971; "Why the White House Press Didn't Get the Watergate Story," July/August 1973. The latter two are included in the fourth edition of Inside the System (Holt Rinehart), the foreword of which, by Richard Rovere, describes evaluation in the Peace Corps. More about Peace Corps evaluation can be found in A Moment in History, by Brent Ashabranner (Doubleday) and The Bold Experiment, by Gerard Rice (Notre Dame). Blowing the Whistle (Praeger) is a collection of Washington Monthly articles dealing with employees who speak up. Also see The Culture of Bureaucracy, (Holt Rinehart) and How Washington Really Works (Addison-Wesley).

sal tendency to place one's own career above one's moral responsibility to take a stand on matters like these has to be one of the most depressing facts about bureaucratic culture today.

Even when the issue was simply providing facts for an internal NASA investigation after the disaster, here is the state of mind Bruce Cook describes in a recent article in The Washington Post:

"Another [NASA employee] told me to step away from his doorway while he searched for a document in his filing cabinet so that no one would see me in his office and suspect that he'd been the one I'd gotten it from."

It may be illuminating to note here that at the Peace Corps I found my most candid informants were the volunteers. They had no career stake in the organization—they were in for just two years—and thus had no reason to fear the results of their candor. Doesn't this suggest that we might be better off with more short-term employees in the government, people who are planning to leave anyway and thus have no hesitation to blow the whistle when necessary?

Certainly the process of getting bad news from the bottom to the top can be helped by institutionalizing it, as it was in the case of the Peace Corps Evaluation Division, and by hiring to perform it employees who have demonstrated courage and independence as well as the ability to elicit the truth and report it clearly.

Two other institutions that can help this process are the Congress and the White House. But the staff they have to perform this function is tiny. The White House depends on the OMB to tell it what the executive branch is doing. Before the Challenger exploded, the OMB had four examiners to cover science and space. The Senate subcommmittee on Space, Science and Technology had a staff of three. Needless to say, they had not heard about the O-rings.

Another problem is lack of experience. Too few congressmen and too few of their staff have enough experience serving in the executive branch to have a sense of the right question to ask. OMB examiners usually come aboard straight from graduate school, totally innocent of practical experience in government.

The press shares this innocence. Only a handful of journalists have worked in the bureaucracy. Like the members of Congress, they treat policy formulation as the ultimate reality: Congress passed this bill today; the president signed that bill. That's what the TV reporters on the Capitol steps and the White House lawn tell us about. But suppose the legislation in question concerns coal mine safety. Nobody is going to know what it all adds up to until some members of Congress and some members of the press go down into the coal mine to find out if conditions actually are safer or if only more crazy regulations have been added.

Unfortunately, neither the congressmen nor the press display much enthusiasm for visits to the mines. Yet this is what I found to be the key to getting the real story about the Peace Corps. I had to go to Ouagadougou and talk to the volunteers at their sites before I could really know what the Peace Corps was doing and what its problems were. I wasn't going to find out by asking the public affairs office.

But that's where most reporters go and sit all day—outside Larry Speakes's office or its equivalent throughout the government.

Because the reporters don't know any better, they don't press the Congress to do any better. What journalists could do is make the public aware of how little attention Congress devotes to what is called "oversight," i.e., finding out what the programs it has authorized are actually doing. If the press would publicize the nonperformance of this function, it is at least possible that the public would begin to reward the congressmen who perform it consistently and punish those who ignore it by not reelecting them.

But the press will never do this until it gets itself out of Larry Speakes's office. Woodward and Bernstein didn't get the Watergate story by talking to Ron Ziegler, or, for that matter, by using other reportorial techniques favored by the media elite, like questioning Richard Nixon at a press conference or interviewing other administration luminaries at fancy restaurants. They had to find lower-level sources like Hugh Sloan, just as the reporters who finally got the NASA story had to find the Richard Cooks and Allan McDonalds.

Eileen Shanahan, a former reporter for *The New York Times* and a former assistant secretary of HEW, recently wrote "of the many times I tried, during my tenure in the Department of Health, Education and Welfare, to interest distinguished reporters from distinguished publications in the effort the department was making to find out whether its billion-dollar programs actually were reaching the intended beneficiaries and doing any good. Their eyes glazed over."

I have had a similar experience with reporters during my 25 years in Washington. For most of that time they have seemed to think they knew everything about bureaucracy because they had read a Kafka novel and stood in line at the post office. In their ignorance, they adopted a kind of wise-guy, world-weary fatalism that said nothing could be done about bureaucratic problems. They had little or no sense about how to approach organizations with an anthropologist's feel for the interaction of atttitudes, values, and institutional pressures.

There are a couple of reasons, however, to hope that the performance of the press will improve. The coverage of business news has become increasingly sophisticated about the way institutional pressures affect executive and corporate behavior, mainly because the comparison of our economy with Japan's made the importance of cultural factors so obvious. And on defense issues, visits to the field are increasingly common as reporters attempt to find out whether this or that weapon works.

But these are mere beachheads. They need to be radically expanded to include the coverage of all the institutions that affect our lives, especially government. This may seem unlikely, but if the press studies the Challenger case, I do not see how it can avoid perceiving the critical role bureaucratic pressure played in bringing about the disaster. What the press must then realize is that similar pressures vitally influence almost everything this government does, and that we will never understand why government fails until we understand those pressures and how human beings in public office react to them.

It's Money That Matters

A candidate looks back in anger

ED GARVEY

Ed Garvey teaches law at the University of Wisconsin, Madison. He was a Democratic candidate for the U.S. Senate in 1986 and for the Democratic Senatorial nomination in 1988.

You'll need some background if you want to understand why I plunged into one race for the United States Senate in 1986 and another in 1988:

I was raised in a small Wisconsin town by parents who assured me that every boy could grow up to become President of the United States. They taught me that it was a great country because it wasn't just for the rich: Everyone with an education had an equal chance to succeed.

In those days, our state legislators were from the people and decidedly part-time. They were farmers, small businessmen, town lawyers. They went to the Capitol in Madison, did their business without staff, and then came home to earn a living. When I was growing up, we sometimes heard stories about too much drinking at some of the legislators' favorite bars—but that was about the extent of any scandal.

When state or national politicians passed through town, we had breakfast gatherings at a local hotel. The cost was what breakfast cost on any other morning. Sometimes there were political bean feeds; the $5 went to pay for the beans, and any profit went to the local party. If anyone had invited my father to a $100-a-plate dinner, he would have asked, "What in the world could they serve for that amount of money?"

Our Senator, Bill Proxmire, had made a career of running for office without spending any money. Election campaigns were based on ideas and personal contact. Any candidate who didn't get around the state to the small communities had a pretty good chance of losing.

So when a group met to discuss the possibility of my running in 1986 against Wisconsin's Republican Senator, Robert Kasten, I was excited. Kasten stood for almost everything I have opposed in a lifetime of activism—from student-body president at the University of Wisconsin to board member of the Student Nonviolent Coordinating Committee and union leader taking on the National Football League.

Kasten is a big-business Republican who has rarely disagreed with his most reactionary Senate colleagues, Jesse Helms and Orrin Hatch. I was eager to take him on and articulate my progressive agenda: Stop funding the contras; tie aid to El Salvador to the peace process; stop nuclear testing and Star Wars research; bring U.S. troops home from Asia and Europe so that we could spend the money to build adequate housing for all our citizens; enact national health-care legislation, and pursue excellence in education the way Ronald Reagan pursued military spending.

God, it would be exhilarating, I thought, to revive progressive politics in Wisconsin.

Right after I decided to make the race, I had a talk with a farmer—one of the old LaFollette progressives you still find in Wisconsin. He told me that the most important thing I could do as a candidate was educate the voters. "After all," he said, "few people have the chance to learn what you've learned. So, like Bob LaFollette, you should judge your campaign on how well you teach, not on the number of votes you get."

It was basic progressive doctrine. LaFollette, Wisconsin's great progressive Governor and Senator, had pushed the open primary so that people would be able to choose from candidates who addressed the issues, not from those selected for them by the lumber barons and railroad magnates who dominated the state's economy in his time.

And *I* would wage a campaign on the issues. My first step would be to assemble the best minds in the state to help figure out solutions to the problems facing us. During a long campaign trip for Walter Mondale in 1984, I had become conscious of the fact that I wasn't talking about what Mondale was for—because I didn't know. Maybe he didn't know. *My* campaign would offer specific answers. The press would criticize my answers, my opponent would accuse me of advocating too much spending, but all that would just stimulate debate. I couldn't wait.

I knew I would need help with "the media"—everyone agrees this is the television era, but most of us don't know how to use television—so I went looking in Washington, where I had lived for thirteen years. I talked with the Democratic Senate Campaign Committee, but it showed no interest in me. The committee wanted winners, and incumbent office-holders are more likely to win.

My first contacts with professional campaign consultants were more encouraging; they thought I could win—with their help. I assumed that their confidence in me was based on a calculation that the sun was setting on the Reagan years and it was time for a return to progressive politics. Not so. They didn't *care* about my politics. The only thing that mattered, they said, was how much money I could raise. One consultant, an old friend, put it this way: "Your job is to raise money. I want you to spend 75 per cent of your time raising money and the rest of the time on the campaign."

"Look," I said, "I'm running because I have a mission to educate, not just to win an election." And I added, "In Wisconsin we don't have expensive races, and anyone who spent a lot of money would lose." The consultants told me that Wisconsin was no different from any other state, and that every first-time candidate said what I was saying.

Reprinted by permission from *The Progressive*, March 1989, pp. 17-21. *The Progressive*, 409 East Main Street, Madison, WI 53703.

'No longer can any boy or girl aspire to the Presidency, or to a seat of Congress. No longer can a rational stand on the issues determine whether a candidate wins or loses.'

So we began with a basic conflict: My campaign director and our consultant wanted me to spend at least five hours a day on the telephone, raising money, while I wanted to visit every senior home, union hall, church, and public forum in the state. I instructed my scheduler to accept every speaking invitation, even if it meant driving across the state on two-lane highways in a single day—never, never to pass up a student audience, a peace group, an opportunity to debate. But soon I was being given three-by-five cards with names and telephone numbers to call between speeches and news conferences.

I tried it. I would place a credit-card call to someone in California or New York, introduce myself, explain how I got the potential contributor's name, and ask for $1,000. Imagine that: I had grown up with the conviction that money and politics didn't mix, that $5 bean feeds were the guts of Democratic politics, and here I was calling strangers from pay phones in restaurants and filling stations, asking for thousand-dollar contributions to my Senatorial campaign.

The notion my parents had drilled into me was, "The Garveys don't ask for things. We earn our way by working hard. We give; we don't ask." But now, at the age of forty-six, I was asking people I didn't even know to help me get elected. And who were these strangers? What did they do for a living? Where did they get their money? Would I be embarrassed if a newspaper ran an exposé of the contributors to the Garvey campaign? There were no answers to these questions. There was no time to ask them. The names came from one or another liberal group, one or another candidate. We assumed they were okay. If not, we could always return their contributions later, but right now we needed the money.

And what did the strangers ask of me when I called? Were they concerned about El Salvador or Star Wars? No—what they wanted to know was how I stood in the polls. When I answered that we had no poll results yet, there was usually no way to persuade them to write a check. It's as simple as that: Out-of-state people who give to candidates for the House and Senate want a good investment, not a long shot. As a rule, they will only contribute to an incumbent—especially in the primaries. "Call me after the primary," 150 or so strangers told me.

What is true for individual givers is doubly true for political-action committees. Individuals might be persuaded by a friend or a particular argument, but PACs pride themselves on "smart giving," and it just isn't smart to give to a candidate challenging an incumbent or to a progressive in a primary fight. The line I heard *ad nauseam* was, "We have too many friends in the race."

Senator Kasten spent about $4 million in his successful bid for reelection in 1986. In 1988, my successful opponent spent $4.25 million in the Democratic primary, and 90 per cent of that was his own money. Bear in mind that an individual may contribute no more than $1,000 to someone else's primary campaign and another $1,000 in a general election, and that PAC contributions are limited to $5,000 per contest. So where is a progressive candidate supposed to find his campaign funds?

I was certain I'd be able to raise all I needed because I had headed a union of football players for thirteen years, had brought it into the AFL-CIO, and had lots of friends in the labor movement. My stand on peace issues was sure to bring me contributions from peace PACs. And because I had been deeply involved in protecting the environment while running the Wisconsin Department of Justice, support from environmental groups would be there for the asking.

I was wrong across the board.

Labor unions rarely get involved in primaries; they usually wait to support the official Democratic candidate—even if he's lukewarm or worse on issues affecting union members. If the state AFL-CIO breaks with tradition and endorses you in the primary, that does not bind any of the international unions and their political directors, who control the money. As a general rule, you must spend hundreds of hours with the state board, attend the AFL-CIO annual meeting in Florida, have coffee with the union political directors, and convince John Perkins, who heads the AFL-CIO Committee on Political Education (COPE), that you could win.

Even if you turn out to be labor's perfect candidate, are running against an antilabor "new Democrat," can show poll results predicting that you will win the primary, and receive every penny any union can afford to put into your campaign, you

wind up with contributions totaling no more than $200,000. In the 1988 primary campaign, my successful opponent wrote out personal checks for more than that every week for three months.

What about the peace groups? I remember my meeting with peace PACs at a small restaurant on Capitol Hill in 1986. On the way to the session, I said to my campaign manager, "It sure will be refreshing to talk issues instead of money, polls, and why this or that group can't support anyone in a primary campaign."

After a round of introductions and handshakes and a quick sandwich order, we got down to business. The first question put to me was, "What do the polls show?" For an hour we talked about the polls, whether I could raise enough money, who my media consultants were, and whether I could use the organizations' membership lists. When the meeting broke up, we hadn't spent five minutes on the issues; no one there could have explained to any member why he or she should back Ed Garvey for the Senate. As for money, they didn't have any.

You may have the ardent support of every environmentalist in your state, but environmental groups won't contribute to primary campaigns and often they stay away from a challenger even if the incumbent's record is bad on everything except Brazilian rain forests. The environmental lobbyists want to preserve their access to the bad guys—but they'll give you lots of nice words.

And women's groups? After all, my 1986 Republican opponent was against *Roe v. Wade*, against the Equal Rights Amendment, bad on comparable worth and day care—a real Neanderthal. I received the state endorsement of the National Organization for Women, and no money.

How do you cope? You have no income because you and your spouse have been campaigning full time, but you give another personal loan to the campaign so the staff can get paid and a mailing can go out. You spend a lot of time at fund-raising parties that may generate, if they're great, as much as $5,000. The all-wise media consultant calls to find out how the money is coming in. Your campaign manager asks, "Did you make your calls?" Nobody asks, nobody cares how you feel about anything—labor-law reform, comparable worth, Star Wars research,

'We should select a national coroner to determine whether the print media are brain-dead and whether the electronic media were born brainless.'

right-to-work, minimum wage, El Salvador, Nicaragua.

But somehow, friends of twenty years, campaign volunteers, staff members come through and some money starts coming in. You can pay the staff, pay for the direct mail, pay for the posters, yard signs, issue papers, bumper stickers. You even have some money for television—not much, but you are on the air. You win the primary—and now you're really up against it, because an incumbent Republican Senator will get all the money he needs. So you go back to the same strangers, the same unions, the same peace groups, and you say, "Okay, I won the primary, now it is safe to give." And it *is* easier: They still ask, "What do the polls show?" but they're more likely to give *something*. And invariably they say, "Call me in late October when we should have more money," which means, "If you have a real chance we'll send more and if not, forget it."

If you score every possible endorsement, you can add another $100,000 or so from peace PACs, women's organizations, environmentalists, and liberal groups to your $200,000 from labor. Then the Democratic Senate Campaign Committee will kick in with an amount scaled to the size of your state and the amount of money you have raised for the DSCC—so you get to go back to all of your new "friends" and ask them to send contributions off to the DSCC in Washington.

I wound up with $290,000 from the DSCC and a total of less than $600,000 from all identifiable Democratic or progressive-liberal sources—a small fraction of the campaign funds at my opponent's disposal. It suddenly hit me that I was way over my head in a high-stakes poker game. All I could do was hope for miracles.

One miracle is the availability of "free media time." You know that you're better on television than your opponent, that you can kill him in debates, that you can outperform him at news conferences, that you have clearly defined positions while he doesn't know where he stands on anything. You'll make the most of free media opportunities and win on the issues.

But the reality is that your opponent won't debate, won't hold news conferences, won't attend candidate forums, won't talk about the issues—and the media will let him get away with all that. Campaigns aren't won today by use of the free media.

Campaigns are won today by paid thirty-second television spots. Your opponent's message reaches every voter in the state two, three, five, ten times a day. His name becomes a household word. Suddenly, he's a celebrity, recognized on the streets. He's Vanna White, Pat Sajak, Oprah, Donahue.

Your staff becomes demoralized. They, too, watch your opponent's television spots and get the feeling that you have lost momentum. People ask, "When are *you* going on TV?" You may just have received a standing ovation for the best speech you've ever delivered on health care, but suddenly you feel you've let down your staff and your volunteers. You haven't raised enough money. You ask yourself, "Should I have made more calls and fewer speeches?"

It hit me when I had just finished shaking hands outside a Packers football game on a cold October Sunday. I had been there from 10 A.M. to 1 P.M., had shaken 2,000 or 3,000 hands, had received lots of encouraging comments. It was hard work, but it was fun, too. As the game started, we went across the street to relax—and there on the television screen was Kasten, attacking me for spreading false rumors and using "Watergate tactics." I realized that if I could have shaken the hands of all 53,000 people entering Lambeau Field that day, I wouldn't have reached a tenth of the people watching that commercial at that moment. I did some quick arithmetic on my pocket calculator: If I averaged 2,000 handshakes a day—a practical impossibility, what with fund-raising trips and calls—it would take me 1,600 days to reach the 3.2 million potential voters in Wisconsin. One television spot could reach them all in a day—not once but over and over again.

And still, our private poll showed me slightly ahead of Kasten in early October. He must have known it too, because suddenly his campaign started a television blitz to tell Wisconsin voters that $750,000 had vanished from the NFL Players Association treasury when I headed the union, and "Ed Garvey didn't know where it went." The implication that I was a thief—or, at best, an incompetent—had incredible impact. My family and I were stunned, and my friends in the Players Association (where no money was missing) were furious.

I said I would sue for libel, and counted on the free media to set the record straight.

They didn't; the electronic media continued to take in thousands of dollars a day for running the false commercial while refusing to comment on it in their newscasts, and the print media ignored it altogether. The voters had it driven home that Garvey was a crook. In the polls, we dropped thirteen to fifteen points within one week. And when those strangers who were getting my fund-raising calls heard about the decline in the polls, the money stopped coming. And that was that.

My 1988 campaign was different. I wasn't up against a right-wing Republican with lots of money and no scruples who waged a negative campaign filled with libelous television spots. Instead, I faced a political unknown who announced, "I will spend whatever it takes to win." And he did. And he won. In a state with only 4.8 million people, he spent $6.1 million of his own money, and today they call him Senator.

When Herb Kohl, the multimillionaire owner of the Milwaukee Bucks basketball team, announced he would seek the Democratic nomination for the Senate seat Bill Proxmire was vacating, the chairwoman of the Wisconsin Democratic Party was elated. "This proves that rich people can be Democrats," she proudly exclaimed. It was a comment that reflected the attitude that prevails today in the higher reaches of the Democratic Party: At last we've gotten out of the union halls, out of the soup kitchens, and into the better restaurants. If it takes lots of money to get elected, how sweet to have a candidate who has lots of money to spend.

Kohl, too, ran a campaign based on thirty-second spots. First, his pollsters determined what people wanted to hear him say. Then his media consultants produced commercials in which he said it. Like Kasten in 1986, he refused to attend all but a handful of candidate forums and participated only in the most tightly structured League of Women Voters debate, while I took part in more than sixty forums and debates and gave hundreds of speeches. Even the thousands of people I met and talked with were more impressed by the thirty-second spots that bombarded them hour after hour, day after day, than by a quick handshake with a live candidate. And, predictably, as Kohl rose in the polls, our money dried up.

Kohl won the primary in a walk. He

'The current leadership of the Democratic Party won't be content until it finds a candidate so far to the Right that he can accuse the Republicans of being liberals.'

won in a landslide. He carried almost every county in the state. When my campaign manager asked, "How could an entire county of Native Americans vote for Kohl?" I replied, "They watch television, too."

This is what I learned: The rules now make it ever more likely that our choice for high offices will be between multimillionaire Democrats and corporate-sponsored Republicans. Senate seats have become so expensive that only incumbents or the wealthy can hope to hold them. Many races for the House of Representatives already cost more than $1 million, and in California Tom Hayden spent that much to win a seat in the state assembly.

The money is spent on thirty-second television spots. That's no way to educate the voters, but it *is* the way to get elected. Once again, as in the days when Bob LaFollette and the progressives recognized that the wealthy were dominating both political parties, money is the way to win public office. No longer can any boy or girl aspire to the Presidency, or to a seat in Congress. No longer can a rational stand on the issues determine whether a candidate wins or loses.

Friends tell me, "So what? Money has always dominated American politics," to which I reply, (1) not to the extent it does today, (2) that doesn't mean we have to accept it, and (3) television has changed all the rules. The thirty-second spot means more than the "walking-around money" politicians used to dispense on election day, more than the money that used to buy posters and fliers and phone banks; it means absolute control over the electoral system.

That message has not yet hit home. Right now, two state senators in Wisconsin are telling their friends that they will soon start campaigning for the nomination to oppose Senator Kasten in 1992. They seem to believe that if they start three years ahead of time, raise money, get around the state, meet people, they'll be able to overcome the media blitz. I can imagine what these would-be candidates are telling their friends:

"If Garvey could meet 300,000 people in eighteen months, I can meet 600,000 in thirty-six months, and that will assure me of winning the primary."

They haven't figured it out yet: If another millionaire decides to spend "whatever it takes," they will not get the early endorsements from labor, peace, environ-mental, and women's groups—and even if they do, they'll lose. You can't raise $5 million or more even if you start five years in advance; the big boys won't give serious money to a progressive candidate in a race against a right-wing incumbent. And if you work eighteen hours a day shaking hands and giving speeches, the television spots will still make the voters forget everything you said.

Well, maybe the television networks will all be cooperatives by 1992, and the newspapers will be devoted to the people's agenda, and miracles will happen. . . .

Do we just give up? I must admit the thought has occurred to me. But I'm not willing to throw in the towel. I want my children and their friends to be able to run for office in the next century. And I believe we will lose on all the other issues we care about unless we deal with the electoral crisis. So long as 99 per cent of the members of the House of Representatives are reelected—mostly because of the large PAC donations they receive—Congress will not give us a progressive income tax; we'll get higher gas taxes instead. Congress will not deal with minimum wages; it will take care of its own wages. Congress will not get serious about the state of the environment so long as the chemical industry pours millions of PAC dollars into the Democratic Party.

And what happens in Washington filters down to the state houses. No longer does Wisconsin have a legislature made up of small-town lawyers, farmers, and small-business proprietors who travel to Madison, transact their business, and then go home to earn a living. Now we have full-time legislators with large staffs, computers, pollsters, media consultants, legislative committees to help with re-election efforts. They cozy up to the lobbyists and PACs just like their big brothers in Washington. And they almost never lose.

If we're going to change the system, we must start some place other than Congress or the legislatures. And we must not be fooled by phony "reform" efforts like the pending bill to limit PAC contributions to $3,000 rather than $5,000. Real reform will require a great public outcry, referenda, talk shows, letters to the editor, demonstrations, and anything else you can think of. Groups considering endorsements ought to demand a written commitment from every candidate on a specific public-funding plank, elimination of PACs, and a limit on individual spending. No commitment, no endorsement.

We should outlaw thirty-second television spots. If the constitutional lawyers say that can't be done, we should push for public financing and an absolute ban on expenditures that exceed the limit. And if we must have television spots, let's have a public Panel of Fairness that can point out that $750,000 wasn't missing from the Football Players Association, that George Bush's Willie Horton spot was filmed in Utah, that the scenes of polluted Boston Harbor didn't show Boston Harbor. Simple fair comment from an independent body will go a long way toward cleaning up the mess we have.

We should select a national coroner to determine whether the print media are brain-dead and whether the electronic media were born brainless. In Wisconsin's largest city, one monopoly owns the two daily newspapers, the largest television station, and the number one AM and FM radio stations. Their coverage of politics is abysmally bad. They trumpet poll results but ignore the fact that those results have been bought by thirty-second spots.

My low point came in Green Bay, our state's second-largest media market. I had scheduled a news conference on the Friday preceding the Tuesday primary, but one of the local television stations refused to cover it; they said it was too close to election day. However, they offered to sell me some commercial time.

We must get a handle on this monster we call television. We must do more than fine-tune the picture; we must change the channel. If we allow the present system to continue, our choices are bound to become worse and worse. Last year, Michael Dukakis became the Democratic Presidential candidate because he had more money than any other Democrat seeking the nomination. George Bush had more money than any of his Republican rivals. In 1992, the Democrats will nominate Sam Nunn or Chuck Robb, depending on whom the big-money people prefer. The current leadership of the Democratic Party won't be content until it finds a candidate so far to the Right that he can accuse the Republicans of being liberals.

But this is no time for despair, nor is it time to start arguing about 1992. It is time for action. Let's stop the show before Vanna White gets elected President.

CORPORATE TEAMS AND TOTEMS

While groping toward new organizational forms, we remain haunted by hierarchies, and belief in the "divine rights" of managers.

Edgar H. Schein

Edgar H. Schein is Sloan Fellows Professor at the Sloan School of Management, Massachusetts Institute of Technology.

We are at the beginning of a major organizational revolution, one that has been commented on by many observers. Peter Drucker has said that organizations will be more information based, flatter, more task oriented, driven more by professional specialists, and more dependent upon clearly focused missions. Some scholars have gone beyond our present concepts and talk of "heterarchies" or "multigons." They point toward models of organization that are more like holograms, in which each part of the organization contains enough information to recreate the whole. Common cultural assumptions in an organization could be thought of as equivalent to genetic codes that permit reconstruction of the whole from any one part. Other metaphors for the evolving workplace include "harmonies of dissimilar elements" or "controlled diversity."

Our thinking about these matters is hampered by one major, deeply embedded cultural assumption so taken for granted that it is difficult even to articulate. This is the assumption that all organizations are fundamentally hierarchical in nature, and that the management process is fundamentally hierarchical. We need new models, but we may have difficulty inventing them because of the automatic tendency to think hierarchically.

Two concrete examples will illustrate the kinds of dilemmas that arise when hierarchy is taken for granted. The first involves some consulting work I did recently with a multinational financial services institution. One group was trying to replace various specialists in tasks such as money transfer and letters of credit with highly sophisticated workstations that would permit an operator to do a range of tasks for a range of customers; most of the tasks' technical aspects could be built into the workstation in the form of expert systems.

What was now an army of specialists would be replaced ultimately with a small number of sophisticated professionals who would work at these "smart machines," thereby increasing productivity, reducing costs, and improving customer service.

In the midst of designing an organization to fulfill this vision, we came upon an unexpected problem. Who would supervise such people? How should the supervisory job be designed? What title should the job be given, and what kind of career path would lead into and out of it? Would operators spend their whole careers at the terminals, or would they become supervisors and ultimately higher-level managers?

Many ideas were proposed—they could be team leaders, consultants, or service managers. But as I listened to the discussion, I reached a terrifying conclusion—neither my clients nor I had the faintest idea of what this job would really be like, what kind of people should occupy it, or how such people should be selected, trained, and managed in terms of rewards, controls, and career paths. Even more striking, it did not occur to any of us that such professionals might not need any kind of supervisor. We had fallen into the trap of hierarchical thinking.

From *Across the Board*, May 1989, pp. 12-17. Reprinted from *Sloan Management Review*, Winter 1989.

A second example comes from the seminal research of Shoshana Zuboff at Harvard University and Larry Hirschhorn at the University of Pennsylvania. Both are interested in the nature of "postindustrial work": What will really happen in the age of the smart machine?

Zuboff shows convincingly that, as information technology not only automates but "informates," operators at all levels learn how things really work and consequently no longer need their supervisors. Coordinating can be done by them and by the information system. In the short run, this will lead to all sorts of transition problems; management will try to protect its position and reassert its prerogative to "run the place." But it seems clear that, in the long run, competitive pressures will force more and more layers of management into roles other than the traditional supervisory ones. Layers of management will either disappear altogether, or else smaller numbers of managers will do different tasks at "headquarters."

This scenario sounds reasonable until one examines the implications of Hirschhorn's findings. He observes that informated operators in the new, networked organizations are subjected to new kinds and levels of anxiety, for the following reasons: They have much higher levels of responsibility; they worked in organizations such as nuclear plants, automated refineries, or chemical plants that often have much greater danger associated with them; and the boundaries of their roles are much more ambiguous and fluid.

Under the old system, line supervisors provided support when crises arose. The hierarchy functioned not only as a coordination mechanism, but also a psychological defense against anxiety. In this capacity, it served workers and managers alike, which may account for the difficulty of imagining work systems without hierarchy.

If such managerial roles disappear, the informated worker must find other sources of support or develop other psychological defenses against anxiety. Such defenses, as Hirschhorn shows, may paradoxically undermine the very efficiencies the technology is designed to create. The worker will routinize and bureaucratize the job, undermining the flexibility designed into the system. Or, worse, he will misread dials that indicate dangerous conditions, because of a need to deny the reality that things really could go wrong. In some cases, workers will display a puzzling degree of boredom, failing to be alert when danger arises, because it is not possible to remain highly alert indefinitely during periods when things are routine.

Perhaps some hypothetical worker of the future will be adjusted to the anxiety levels of modern, technologically sophisticated workplaces, but in the meantime, how do we manage the anxious workers of today? Do we give them new authority figures and thereby reinforce the hierarchy?

Let me begin to answer that question by describing another consulting experience. I recently visited the large auto manufacturing plant at Trollhattan, Sweden, run by Saab-Scania A.B., and I was impressed by the large number of fully functioning robots and autonomous work groups. The group members were all highly trained technicians who could run the robots, fix them, or replace them if they broke down. If these groups had managers, nothing was ever said about them. Group members controlled entry and exit into the group, job assignments, and working style. The overall technological design and strategy of the plant controlled the speed of the line, the product mix, and even the quality with automated checking stations that insured correct assembly.

I was reminded of a theme that surfaced strongly during a visit to Norway in the 1970s. I was told when preparing for a lecture series that I should stress the role of management, because Norwegians assumed that if you had enough good engineers and planners, you did not really need managers. This seemed like an absurd position at the time, but now I wonder if the Norwegians were not simply way ahead of their time.

Their vision of autonomous workers becomes more explicit if we extrapolate from the work of some of my colleagues at the Massachusetts Institute of Technology. Tom Malone, a social psychologist, information technologist, computer scientist, and organization theorist all rolled into one, speculates that future organizations may well be networks in which hierarchy either disappears altogether or plays a far less important role than other forms of coordination and integration.

Malone is developing a coordination theory, which he distinguishes from traditional organization and management theory because he regards those as too mired in traditional hierarchical models. Perhaps the organization of the future will be more like a giant, complex seesaw in which everyone must contribute to effective coordination; management as it exists today will be either invisible or nonexistent, according to this theory.

What I am trying to bring out is that we are on the brink of an organizational revolution that will not simply cut out layers of management or reduce costs or force greater levels of worker participation. Something far more profound may happen that has not yet been fully grasped because, like Hirschhorn's workers, we are probably too anxious to fully understand all of its implications.

What may well happen is that management as

·a traditionally conceived, hierarchical function will disappear altogether, to be replaced with concepts that we have not yet developed. If that happens, of course, our traditional concepts of educating and developing managers will disappear as well, to be replaced with models that do not yet exist.

Our challenge in the next few decades will be to develop these new concepts and educational strategies, but I see some severe difficulties; these stem from the implicit assumption that organizations are fundamentally hierarchical. I hypothesize that we have great difficulty even imagining, much less designing, nonhierarchical or even less hierarchical systems.

The clearest evidence for this hypothesis comes from managers' belief in their divine right to manage. One observes this phenomenon in labor-management negotiations, when a manager argues that union proposals infringe on managerial prerogatives. The basis of these alleged prerogatives is seldom spelled out—and there is an assumption that it need not be.

To illustrate what I mean, I must first make a theoretical point. Organization theory has always stressed that power, authority, influence, and leadership are complex psychological concepts that cannot be understood without analyzing the relationship between superior and subordinate. Employees in an organization do what they are supposed to do for one of several reasons:

Nonlegitimate authority. The person is coerced into doing something because someone with the capacity to reward or punish orders it. This form of organization, symbolized by prisons or slave-labor camps, has drawbacks too obvious to dwell on.

Charismatic authority. One person is so prominent and emotionally powerful that others go along because of complete faith in and admiration for the person. This kind of authority is wonderful if such a person exists and if what that person wants to do happens to fit the needs of the group. It is not a form of authority that can be planned for, and charismatic leaders are not easy to find.

Tradition-based authority. The person does what he or she is told to do by those who have acquired a traditional right to give orders. This model underlies monarchies and empires once they have evolved away from coerciveness and acquired legitimacy through some claim such as the divine right of kings. This kind of claim works in a society where there is religious consensus.

Rational-legal authority. As society evolved toward more democratic forms, organizations developed a new principle of authority, the consent of the governed. Competent people are to be promoted into positions of authority; authority resides in those positions; if the authority of the position is abused, the subordinate has legal recourse through some form of due process. Subordinates give the boss the "right" to give orders, because they accept the system by which supervisory positions are filled.

This form of authority is presumed to underlie the modern, bureaucratic organization and is the principle on which corporations are supposed to operate. The rights and prerogatives of managers at each level are supposed to be spelled out and to reside in the offices. The system is supposed to be rational to the extent that the most competent people get promoted or appointed to the managerial positions. As we all know, the system does not usually work as designed because of power politics, intergroup conflicts, and various other emotional factors.

Purely rational authority. The only reason for following someone's orders, within this model, is that the person is more expert at whatever work needs to be done. Authority is defined by task requirements and individual expertise. It no longer resides in the position but in the person, and only in the person to the extent that he has specific areas of competence. Thus we obey the pilot while the plane is in the air, but we obey the survival expert if the plane crashes in the jungle.

As we contemplate the future of organizations, it seems reasonable to suppose that authority should be based on the purely rational model, but most organizations and schools appear to operate as if the only principles of authority that exist are the coercive, charismatic, traditional, and rational-legal ones.

Clearly, we support hierarchy as a primary legitimation of authority. We may also unwittingly be supporting the divine right of managers to define for themselves what their prerogatives are, and to defend those prerogatives solely on the basis that "it has always been this way" or that "it" is somehow intrinsic to the free-market system.

What is my evidence for this conclusion? Let us look at some examples.

The management-labor metaphor. When proposals are made to share ownership with employees, we treat that request seriously and rationally as a legitimate economic issue to be examined. But when it is proposed that workers be put on the board of directors, there is immediately a level of resistance in senior management that has a moral overtone: "It is not their right to have a say in the running of the company; that is management's prerogative."

A particularly pernicious form of this assumption is expressed metaphorically. When Eastern Airlines first experimented with employee ownership, giving workers stock increased productivity and reduced costs. Some years later, when a new financial crises hit the company, its president at the time, Frank Borman, suggested cutting labor costs, which led to a union counterproposal that would guarantee productivity gains if management would both increase the employee-ownership share and let employees have a voice in management. Borman was quoted as responding to this proposal with the remark, "Oh, so now the monkeys want to run the zoo."

We have allowed ourselves to think of organizations as two-tiered systems—management and labor—and we have allowed a metaphor to illustrate this system: Labor is the animal and management is the keeper. Or, laborers are children and managers are parents. Typically, a company's early years are dominated by paternalistic thinking; possibly such thinking leads quite naturally to the idea that it is the right and even the obligation of management to take care of the "corporate family." The notion of laborers and managers being adults on a par with each other is undermined not only by rank and status but by the socio-economic class distinctions that are frequently correlated with rank.

And I see nothing in our university industrial-relations curricula that serves to undo these terrible stereotypes. By arguing for improvements in the labor-management negotiation system, we are reinforcing the system rather than looking for ways to reconceptualize what organizations need to be in the 21st century.

Hierarchical teams. We glorify teamwork, but our most popular sports analogy is football—a sport in which there is a hierarchy of coaches and positions on the field, with special attention and status attached to the quarterback. In fact, when we select managers we often look for people who have been quarterbacks or team captains. We say we are looking for leadership capabilities, but in fact we are looking for people who have experience working within a hierarchical structure. Yet, it may be that the complex, differentiated, interdependent work of future organizations will require the skills more associated with basketball, hockey, and soccer, in which team performance is dependent on the players' ability to coordinate their own moves with the moves of others and to make reliable autonomous decisions within a broad strategic framework.

The degree to which we are caught up in the unconscious assumptions of hierarchy is further illustrated by Peter Drucker's recent call for flatter organizations; he used the analogy of the orchestra. Orchestras are actually an example of extreme hierarchy in the service of a high degree of coordination. Typically, conductors are highly autocratic; under them are principal soloists, lead players, and sections. Orchestra members are highly conscious—and often resentful—of their positions in the hierarchy; it is only their extraordinary skill, plus the conductor's ear and precise feedback, that produces the perfection we attribute to teamwork. A first-rate orchestra can in fact perform without a conductor because its members are so competent, but it is interesting to note that few orchestras are ever given that license. We seem to believe that the conductor is necessary, and we exaggerate the degree to which this powerful position is the source of the team's greatness.

Performance-appraisal and reward systems. My colleague Lotte Bailyn notes that the seemingly egalitarian and fair concept of merit pay, or pay for performance, actually forces the organization to rank people into a hierarchy that may damage morale and performance.

Even as a concept, merit pay is difficult to defend. There is growing evidence that interdependence in most organizational situations is so high that one can only measure output reliably across organizational units that have clearly defined and relatively autonomous tasks. Yet note how obsessed organizations and managers are with ranking people and differentiating performance, on the incorrect assumption that people's performance can be improved if they are told that they are not as good as someone else. In fact, the only reliable way to improve performance is to give performance feedback whenever possible; giving feedback has nothing to do with ranking or merit pay or other systems of differentiating people. Let me offer a simple analogy. My tennis game will not improve because I am told that I am not as good as someone else. It will only improve if a coach, or a videotape, or my own self-observation shows me what I am doing wrong and how I could do it better.

The degree to which our performance-appraisal systems emphasize differentiating people illustrates how deeply embedded our hierarchical assumptions are. Some systems even require rank ordering everyone in a given category of position.

Senior managers believe such systems are needed because they are the only way to guarantee that the best performers will be rewarded and that poor performers will be terminated. But embedded in that notion is the idea that people are in fact doing similar things. In reality, each employee can be judged based on performance or nonperformance of a given task, and nonperformers can be appraised, trained, or fired. Nothing requires that they be compared with others or differentially rewarded. In fact, there is a growing trend to pay production workers for the number of skills they possess, not for their performance relative to other workers.

Job classification and grading. Why do we have such difficulty instituting a dual ladder for individual technical and professional contributors? Why is there an almost automatic assumption that it is more important to identify managerial potential early in the career? Why do we think in terms of moving potential managers up the ladder rapidly, whereas professional careers are seen as more level? Why are managers typically paid more than individual contributors? Why do job-grading systems almost automatically give higher grades to jobs that involve supervision and measure job level by the number of people supervised?

Why do we have difficulty conceiving of organizations as networks in which "higher" or "lower" makes no sense? After all, we know that in many kinds of work situations—in project teams, in professional offices and partnerships, and in university departments, to name a few—there is a constant, active effort to reduce the hierarchy to the absolute minimum required.

The culture of management. I recently asked a group of high-potential middle managers to identify the critical underlying assumptions of the occupation of management. Several assumptions emerged: Management means working extremely hard to achieve results; management means supervising others; and management means occupying a position in an organizational hierarchy. In fact, the managers' response was that management means hierarchy.

Management and business curricula. I have not done a detailed analysis, so I may be unfair in this area, but it seems to me that our business-management textbooks and courses emphasize the traditional hierarchical form of organization. We teach our students how to wield authority, and we make it clear that career success is making it to the top.

We may not say this out loud, but it is implied even in the concept of higher education; with a degree one can enter the system at a higher level and aspire more immediately to a position of authority. Alumni often complain that they did not get a position of responsibility soon enough; usually they mean they did not get enough authority. Calling the shots is good, something to be aspired to. Invisible contribution to a team effort does not count. Reality is hierarchy, so to get as high as possible is the obvious, valid goal.

We encourage comparative performance rather than individual competence by noting how much our alumni make in their first jobs. We are obsessed with ranking our schools on a hierarchy of overall excellence that has prestige value but little meaning in terms of the actual content of the education; the ratings are not based on a detailed analysis of what actually goes on in the various management schools.

In summary, I believe we take hierarchy for granted and that we have failed to realize how the assumptions underlying hierarchy pervade our thinking both in schools and in the workplace. If it is true that organizations will be flat networks in the future, then we must give serious thought to the following questions:

☐ What do we mean when we say "management"?

☐ Will management reside in individual managers, or will it be distributed as a function in networks and working teams?

☐ Can managers as such be selected, trained, and developed?

☐ Will our models for educating managers continue to have relevance? Will we have to invent wholly new concepts of what individuals must learn in order to coordinate work?

☐ Most important, will we have to abandon hierarchy as an organizing principle and invent new concepts of coordination and control that will generate new kinds of developmental requirements?

BACK TO BASICS

U.S. COMPANIES FORGOT THAT INNOVATION MEANS SMALL BUT STEADY IMPROVEMENTS—NOT JUST BIG BREAKTHROUGHS. NOW THAT'S CHANGING

JAMES FALLOWS, AN AMERICAN AUTHOR living in Japan, was having a convivial beer with an English friend. After taking a long drink, Fallows' companion put down his glass and said: "Why don't you just face the fact that you're second-raters, like us?"

That question reveals just how far the U.S. has slipped in the eyes of the world. Even the British are wondering if the time has come for their former colony to pass the baton—to Japan. Incredulous at the U.S. retreat in market after market for the last two decades, other countries have come to believe that America has lost its spirit of enterprise. Today, as Fallows notes in his new book, *More Like Us: Making America Great Again*, the phrase "lazy American" has become a cliché.

What happened to the mighty U.S. innovation machine? This is the system that invented the phonograph, the color television, the tape recorder (audio and video), the telephone, and the integrated circuit, to name a few milestone products. Yet today, U.S. producers account for only a small percentage of the U.S. market for most of those products—and an even smaller share of the world market.

For the past two years, the Tokyo government has been prodding companies and consumers to buy more imported goods. Purchases of European products have jumped substantially. But not American imports. The Japanese, it seems, have no more use for things stamped "Made in the USA" than Americans did for the knickknacks exported by Japan in the 1950s.

Laziness seems the only logical explanation to many people in Asia and Europe. By nearly all measures, the U.S. should be unbeatable. America has 15 million companies; no other nation comes close. It has 5.5 million scientists and engineers—double the number in Japan—and they have won more Nobel prizes than the rest of the world put together. Plus, the U.S. spends almost twice as much on research and development as Japan and Germany combined.

There's more: Students from around the globe flock here for the world's best training in advanced science, mathematics, and engineering.

The U.S. remains a hothouse of ideas and technology: California's Silicon Valley and Boston's Route 128 serve as perennial models for other governments' thrusts into high tech. And America's venture-capital and job-generating engines are the envy of the world. "We have everything in spades—if we can just get our act together," says D. Bruce Merrifield, until recently the Assistant Secretary of Commerce for Productivity, Technology & Innovation.

But as is now painfully clear, there's more to innovation than Nobel prizes and fat R&D budgets. "The Japanese would gladly give us all the Nobel prizes," says H. John Caulfield, director of the Center for Applied Optics at the University of Alabama in Huntsville. "They're not worth a damn thing unless they're converted into products."

THE PROBLEM IS THAT MOST AMERICANS, including managers and government leaders, believe that invention and innovation are synonymous—or at least that one flows inevitably from the other. That is reflected in Washington's standard recipe for boosting innovation and competitiveness: Throw more resources into basic research and education.

But this knee-jerk response is "a devastating error," says Rustum Roy, director of the Science, Technology & Society Program at Pennsylvania State University. In April, he told a congressional committee that Japan's "awesome machine for converting new scientific discovery into marketable products is living proof of that." Roy's discouraging conclusion: The more inventive ideas the U.S. dreams up, the farther it will fall behind. Each one will be just another opportunity for a foreign rival to out-innovate a U.S. company in producing it.

So the crux of America's problem is manufacturing—translating ideas into products good enough to be sold on international markets to pay the country's import bills. "American companies don't like to build things—they like to make deals," says C. Gordon Bell, R&D vice-president of Ardent Computer Corp. and formerly with Digital Equipment Corp., where he engineered the hugely successful line of Vax minicomputers. "Our large organizations have become purchasing agents."

It wasn't always so. Before World War II, the factory was the cornerstone of American industry. But U.S. managers started to ignore manufacturing in the postwar years, when companies sold everything they could produce. The U.S. had no competition then, so the job of running the factory could safely be delegated to second-rate managers. Just keep the plant churning out widgets, they were told, and don't fix anything that works.

In that static environment, manufacturing quickly ceased to be a source of innovation. Companies began to focus all of their creative support on product designers. Those technicians knew nothing about production and therefore focused on developing brand-new products from scratch. Unfortunately, of the two main routes to innovation, that's the less fertile one.

That kind of product innovation tends to be like a ladder, says Ralph E. Gomory, formerly IBM's chief scientist and now president of the Alfred P. Sloan Foundation. Climb, and you acquire new knowledge that confers a competitive advantage—but only until rivals join you at the top. Then you have to build a new ladder—a very slow and expensive process.

A more productive route, called process-oriented innovation, resembles the wheel in a hamster cage—a ladder wrapped into a cylinder, with no beginning and no end. Each turn of the wheel improves an existing product and its production methods. Year after year, the company unveils not-entirely-new products that keep getting better, more reliable, and cheaper. "It sounds dull," Gomory admits, but the cumulative effect can be exhilarating. It was constant cyclical refinements, for example, that took the semiconductor and computer industries from memory chips that stored 1 bit of data each to today's 4-million-bit designs.

Similarly, auto makers don't try to reinvent totally new forms of transportation every year. It was incremental innovation that replaced manual transmissions with automatics and resulted in power steering and power brakes. "The cumulation of a large number of small improvements is the surest path, in most industries, to increasing your competitive advantage," says John P. McTague, research vice-president at Ford Motor Co.

The Japanese have become masters at that. When they were preparing their assault on the U.S. market, they spotted a glaring weakness in U.S. manufacturing. Because it depended on economies of scale from long production runs, it was vulnerable to a system that could whip out a constant barrage of incrementally better products. Even today, "we put twice the resources into product innovation as we do into process innovation," notes Arden L. Bement Jr., TRW Inc.'s vice-president of technical resources. "Japan does the opposite."

Japan's strategy was brilliant: It yanked the economic rug from under U.S. industry. It has been so successful that U.S. manufacturers still find themselves unable to compete, even with lower-cost labor. "Over half of our trade deficit now comes from foreign industries that pay their workers higher wages than we do," emphasizes Ira Magaziner, a Providence management consultant. "They don't beat us with cheap labor. They beat us with technology and skilled labor."

The results are glaringly apparent in America's balance of trade. Since 1980, the U.S. has sunk from a positive trade balance to the world's biggest debtor. And no end is in sight. DRI/McGraw-Hill Inc. projects that the trade deficit will ease just slightly in coming years, dipping from 1987's $154 billion to "only" $111 billion in 1995. Then, with a united Europe flexing its new-found economic muscle, the deficit could head upward again, hitting an all-time high—$160 billion—in the year 2000. "It really threatens our future," said U.S. Trade Representative Carla A. Hills at a recent Senate hearing.

Plot almost any index of national well-being, from adult literacy to per-capita gross national product, and the U.S. trails its major competitors. Take the rates for savings and fixed investment: During the 1980s, Japan and Germany have been outstripping America by two, three, four, or five to one. Even in the bellwether area of industrial research, Japan has been progressively outspending the U.S. (as a percentage of GNP) since 1971. By 1985, the disparity had swollen to 47% (1.9% of GNP for the U.S. vs. 2.8% for Japan). And the U.S. no longer has the world's highest per-capita GNP.

It has taken a long time, but America's leaders are finally beginning to see that manufacturing is indispensable. Several studies have detailed the reasons why, the latest being *Made in America*, conducted by the Commission on Industrial Productivity at Massachusetts Institute of Technology. It points out that the U.S. consumed roughly $1 trillion in manufactured goods in 1987, while total exports of services that year amounted to only $57 billion. Thus, if the U.S. imported half of its manufactured items, exports of services would have to increase nearly 10 times to pay the bills.

THAT IS HIGHLY UNLIKELY. EXPERIENCE shows that when manufacturing moves offshore, many related services soon follow, including high-value-added functions such as design and engineering. Moreover, manufacturers account for virtually all of the basic research sponsored by industry. This generates the bulk of the technological innovation that fuels long-term economic growth, inside and outside the industries that funded the research.

Even the business schools now recognize that the U.S. cannot go on ceding markets to foreign competitors. "We've got to fight it out in the trenches," says Lester C. Thurow, dean of MIT's Sloan School of Management. "Once you start retreating, you end up retreating into oblivion."

That's quite a turnaround. After World War II, when the U.S. was unconcerned about overseas competition, Harvard and other business schools

INVENTED HERE, MADE ELSEWHERE

U.S.-invented technology	1987 market size (millions $)	U.S. producers' share of domestic market (%)			
		1970	1975	1980	1987
PHONOGRAPHS	$630	90%	40%	30%	1%
COLOR TVS	14,050	90	80	60	10
AUDIOTAPE RECORDERS	500	40	10	10	0
VIDEOTAPE RECORDERS	2,895	10	10	1	1
MACHINE TOOL CENTERS	485	99	97	79	35
TELEPHONES	2,000	99	95	88	25
SEMICONDUCTORS	19,100	89	71	65	64
COMPUTERS	53,500	N.A.	97	96	74

DATA: COUNCIL ON COMPETITIVENESS, COMMERCE DEPT.

introduced portfolio theory to contend with vacillations in the domestic market. The idea was to diversify into counter-cyclical businesses so total profits wouldn't be dragged down by a slump—or intense price competition—in one market.

But diversification meant that top management could no longer be intimately familiar with all its businesses. So the schools devised various manage-by-the-numbers formulas that supposedly enabled an executive to run any business. As a result, U.S. industry today is saddled with people in important positions who don't understand technology, notes Richard M. Cyert, president of Carnegie Mellon university.

To corporate technologists, the financial guidelines imposed by these managers seem designed mainly "to tell you why what you need to do won't pay," says Robert A. Frosch, vice-president for research at General Motors Corp.. "I'm not a big booster of the MBA analysis system," he adds.

Because the bean counters impose such high payback expectations on capital investments, research departments feel forced to swing for home runs rather than slap singles. And since the payoff from basic research rarely falls through to the bottom line in fewer than six or seven years—too long to be factored into Wall Street valuations—most companies have stopped doing it altogether.

But the top brass and Wall Street are not solely to blame. There's also the high cost of U.S. capital, says Joseph P. Martino, senior research scientist at the University of Dayton Research Institute. The difference between a long-term interest rate of 11% in the U.S. and 4.5% in Japan, compounded for 5 to 10 years, becomes a high hurdle. "So it's easy to see why Japanese industrialists look farther ahead," says Martino. "They can afford to."

Another factor is the soaring cost of doing leading-edge research. Just to develop the next-generation chipmaking method, which will use X-rays instead of light to "print" circuit patterns on silicon, IBM is spending $435 million, according to recently named President Jack D.

Kuehler. Tack on the cost of production equipment, and that price tag will more than double.

How many other U.S. chipmakers will be able to afford similar programs? Only a handful—five at most. Yet in Japan, 19 such projects are already under way. Suggesting that typical U.S. companies can compete on their own against the likes of Hitachi, Matsushita, Sumitomo, and Toshiba "brings only a wan smile" to anyone who knows the current state of industrial research on both sides of the Pacific, says Penn State's Roy.

Don't write off America as a rust-bucket case just yet, however. There are signs of brighter days ahead. Harvard business school, for example, is trying to shift gears, says Thomas R. Piper, senior associate dean for educational programs. "In the past three or four years, there has been a change to where faculty are raising public-policy questions on takeovers, leveraged buyouts, and the short-term focus of management." And the school no longer requires students to take a course in quantitative management.

Companies are struggling to do a better job of managing innovation, and more products are being designed with an eye to manufacturability. In many industries, competitors big and small are banding together into research consortiums—and pushing for changes in antitrust laws so they can collaborate on manufacturing as well. While they are asking for government support, it's not a handout, says Robert N. Noyce, chairman of Sematech, the semiconductor consortium. If it helps the U.S. chip industry grow just 5%, he says, corporate taxes on those added revenues will repay the investment.

Size needn't be a prerequisite for competing with Japan's huge conglomerates. "The Germans and Italians do it well without being raised on a sushi diet," quips John Zysman, co-director of the Berkeley Roundtable on the International Economy. There are standout performers in the U.S., too. The MIT productivity commission found one or two in every industry it studied. "So why don't more companies copy what the good performers are doing?" asks commission Chairman Michael L. Dertouzos.

One reason, he says, is that it calls for a disruptive, wrenching restructuring of the entire corporation, from the very top on down. Organizing for innovation means flattening the heirarchy, giving more responsibility to the lower levels, and scuttling discipline-oriented departments in favor of ad hoc mission-team groups. "Forget the organizational structure we've used for 300 years," says Robert L. Callahan, president of Ingersoll Engineers Inc. "Simply put together people who can get the job done, regardless of their function." He terms it "swarming."

So far, only a few American producers—perhaps a half-percent—are swarming to embrace such drastic overhauls. They include Motorola, Hewlett-Packard, Deere, Caterpillar, and Carrier. But it may soon become a matter of necessity as competition heats up still more.

Tearing down internal walls could also have a spinoff benefit: People accustomed to working in a free-form environment should perform better in outside collaborations, too. The upshot: Japanese-style intra-company teamwork spiced with American superstar researchers and Yankee entrepreneurs. "The U.S. is extremely good at blending cooperation and individualism," says MIT's Dertouzos. "Look at professional sports." So with any luck, when Technology Superbowl 2000 rolls around, Team America may be in fitter form than ever.

By Otis Port in New York, with bureau reports

HOW TO KILL A COMPANY

Anatomy of a Leveraged Buyout

Max Holland

Max Holland is the author of "When the Machine Stopped," a case study about a machine-tool division of Houdaille, published this month by Harvard Business School Press.

Phil O'Reilly recognized that his company, Houdaille Industries, was taking a gamble when it underwent a leveraged buyout in 1979. A bad year or two could suck the Florida-based conglomerate into a whirlpool of debt. Ultimately, it might have to sell off its most attractive assets to satisfy creditors and buyout investors.

But if nothing untoward happened, if Houdaille managed to service its debt, then O'Reilly knew that by 1984 a "pot of gold" awaited him and other equity investors. This is the moment when a private, leveraged company, having whittled its debt-to-equity ratio down to acceptable proportions, returns to the stock market. Equity investors then reap a huge reward, as much as 10 or 20 times their original investment.

A buyout is a Faustian deal because it flouts a cardinal rule of management: Don't bet the business. Houdaille's executives did, and lost. Today Houdaille (pronounced WHO-dye) doesn't exist anymore as an industrial manufacturer.

The debate over the business wisdom of LBOs cannot be decided by the fate of one company. Buyout artists point out, and rightly so, that there are lots of "bad" deals to go along with the "good" ones. But interestingly, the investment bankers who engineered the Houdaille deal, Kohlberg, Kravis, Roberts & Co., tout it as a success despite the conglomerate's demise.

More disinterested observers might consider it an object lesson in what's wrong with leveraged buyouts.

Houdaille Industries, took its name from Maurice Houdaille, the Frenchman who invented recoilless artillery during World War I. After the war, a U.S. corporation bought the name and the rights to the rotary shock absorber Houdaille patented. By the 1930s, Houdaille Industries was one of the largest auto-

parts subcontractors in Detroit and the premier U. S. manufacturer of shock absorbers. It was not unusual for a car owner to walk into a garage and ask for a new set of "Houdailles."

When national security warranted, Houdaille also manufactured more sophisticated products. During World War II, it participated in the Manhattan Project to develop the atomic bomb. But the modern era for Houdaille began in the mid-1950s, when it found itself being squeezed out as the number of automakers shrank and the survivors moved parts production in-house. To survive, Houdaille was forced to diversify. By the late 1960s, it had become a high-flying conglomerate, with interests in construction materials, industrial products, pumps and machine tools. In fact, its stable of machine tool companies made it one of the top U.S. builders of the "mother" machines which make all machines.

In the winter of 1978, Houdaille common stock was selling for around $14.50 a share, well below the conglomerate's book value. A depressed stock price was a familiar problem for Houdaille—as for many other industrial conglomerates in the stagflation-prone '70s. Houdaille had a more immediate problem as well: The conglomerate's longtime CEO, Jerry Saltarelli, wanted to retire. But passing the baton, while keeping Houdaille independent, was not going to be easy. Speculators noticed that Houdaille was simultaneously debt-free and cash-rich, making it a likely takeover candidate. Funny things—and heavy trading—began to occur in Houdaille stock.

The prospect of an unfriendly takeover worried Saltarelli. For his energetic lieutenant, Phil O'Reilly, it posed an even greater threat. Taking a leaf from his days as a star football lineman at Purdue, O'Reilly had worked long and hard to overcome every obstacle in the way of his becoming CEO. But now, on the verge of success, Houdaille stood to lose its independence.

Just when there seemed to be no good solution, Houdaille's financial advisers passed along a message from a

then-obscure trio of bankers named Jerome Kohlberg, Henry Kravis and George Roberts. Kohlberg, Kravis, Roberts & Co. suggested that Houdaille could have its cake and eat it too. Saltarelli could liquidate his stake in Houdaille and keep it intact for his chosen successor. There would also be frosting on the cake for holdover management—an opportunity to reap large profits in just a few years. All Houdaille had to do was undergo a leveraged buyout.

At a meeting in Florida, KKR explained the deal. A small group of investors, primarily KKR and holdover Houdaille management, would acquire all the conglomerate's public shares. The cash necessary for the buyout would be borrowed primarily from institutional investors, which would lend the money based on Houdaille's assets. Saltarelli and O'Reilly were mystified by one thing. Where was Houdaille going to get all the cash to pay off the high-interest, or junk-bond, debt incurred as a result of the buyout? At this juncture KKR introduced the Houdaille executives to their silent but consenting partner in the deal: Uncle Sam.

Stripped of all the complicating factors, KKR could offer an unheard-of $40 per share for Houdaille stock, leverage the company to the hilt and then cash in four or five years down the line—all because of Uncle Sam's largesse when it came to the redepreciation of capital assets and interest write-offs. In effect, a leveraged Houdaille would have to pay little, if any, corporate income tax for the life of the buyout. Thus, the same stream of corporate income would suddenly provide an extra 30–40 percent in cash, enabling Houdaille to service its massive debt—courtesy of Uncle Sam. As Treasure Secretary Nicholas Brady observed some years later, "The substitution of [deductible] interest charges for [taxable] income is the mill in which the grist of takeover premiums is ground." Or as buyout artists like to put it, the process "unlocks hidden value."

KKR hastened to add that managing for cash flow, rather than quarterly profits, would not be easy. But other managers had proved that it could be done. And if Houdaille executives could to it too, they would enjoy a financial windfall when the firm went back to the stock market in four or five years—not to mention immediate profits from the $40 buyout and the hefty raises promised if the LBO was consummated. Phil O'Reilly, for one, was promised a raise from $110,000 to $200,000, exclusive of bonuses. Little wonder that wags on Wall Street soon took to calling LBOs the "kiss which turns the frog into a handsome prince."

In May 1979, Houdaille became the first large industrial corporation to undergo a leveraged buyout. The deal was a milestone. No corporation worth more than $100 million had ever been leveraged, and the Houdaille deal was worth $390 million. Wall Street immediately recognized that the financial rules were no longer the same. "The public documents on that deal were grabbed up by every firm on Wall Street," one buyout artist, Frank Richardson, recalled several years later. "We all said, 'Holy mackerel, look at this!'"

On the day that he finally assumed the top spot at Houdaille, Phil O'Reilly, a new millionaire, told *The New York Times*, "We're looking forward to working with KKR. Their experience in finance coupled with our experience in manufacturing and marketing will make a very complementary group." He indicated that Houdaille retained its appetite for growth through acquisition, but for the time being that aim had to take a back seat to a more pressing concern. "We're highly leveraged right now, so our first goal is to pay off some of the debt."

A large chunk of Houdaille's savings, $35 million, was immediately used to retire some debt. In addition, the new, privately-owned Houdaille liquidated the balance of its interests in construction materials, which had not been profitable since 1973. Another product line also underwent abrupt changes as automakers' demand for chrome-plated bumpers—which as recently as 1976 had accounted for more than half of Houdaille's profits—evaporated in 1980 as Detroit turned toward plastic bumpers.

But the acquisition of John Crane in 1981, a company two-thirds the size of Houdaille, more than compensated for these divestitures. John Crane was an Illinois-based maker of mechanical seals used to prevent leaks around rotating parts and enjoyed more than 40 percent of the domestic market and 30 percent of the global markets for seals. By any measure the $204-million acquisition (via debt financing) was a busi-

ness coup, putting the conglomerate exclusively in the business of manufacturing high value-added goods. Some two years after the buyout, Phil O'Reilly had every reason to be ecstatic. Houdaille had been able to restructure, and the pot of gold was within sight.

But then the unexpected happened, or perhaps more accurately, the expected. For surely what makes running a business or corporation so invigorating is the almost constant need to cope with challenges, be they economic or technological. Normally, however, a corporation the size of Houdaille has a comfortable cushion—its own equity—to fall back on. It can suspend dividend payments if need be, or borrow against its equity if new investment is needed. But a leveraged company has only one option: service the debt even if it means breaking up the company.

The unexpected came in the form of a recession and foreign competition. Nothing like the deep 1981–1982 recession had been forecast when Houdaille underwent its LBO in 1979. As if that wasn't enough, seemingly overnight Houdaille was also facing the specter of fierce competition in a business segment that was supposed to be a safe niche: machine tools. The Japanese were making startling inroads into the American market, long the almost exclusive preserve of U.S. builders like Houdaille.

Two years after the buyout, Houdaille was caught in a triple bind of debt, recession, and competition. The first was a given, and the second Houdaille could do nothing about. O'Reilly believed that the last problem, foreign competition, might be amenable to a Washington cure. He hired a savvy lawyer, Richard Copaken, to press Houdaille's case for import protection in Washington. But Copaken's case did not adequately support Houdaille's thesis: that Japan's Ministry of International Trade and Industry had commanded a machine-tool cartel bent on carving up the U.S. market.

After spending $1.5 million on the trade petition, O'Reilly was naturally bitter about losing. The stakes could not have been higher. The hemorrhaging of Houdaille's machine-tool group, which typically accounted for about 25 percent of Houdaille's revenues and profits, subverted the entire buyout because it pushed the pot of gold out of sight. Instead of shrinking as planned, Houdaille's debt was actually increasing: from 107 percent of total capitalization in 1983 to nearly 113 percent in 1984, the year by which equity investors had been promised the pot of gold.

In the always-revealing vernacular of Wall Street, the Houdaille buyout had

become a "dog." Yet Phil O'Reilly was still publicly praising leveraged buyouts. Among the joys cited by O'Reilly was that as CEO of a private company, answerable only to select institutional investors, he could "look out at a longer horizon."

After vigorous but vain attempts to find a buyer for its machine-tool group, Houdaille announced a "business restructuring program" in late 1985, thereby "reducing its interest expense and enhancing its future." The divestiture was a complicated one. All told, seven divisions were split off from the conglomerate, including its entire machine-tool group. Phil O'Reilly blamed the Japanese, and then the Reagan administration, for the 2,200 highly-skilled, high-paying jobs that were lost as a result. But the real significance of Houdaille's demise as a major machine-tool builder was that the Japanese were handed a still greater share of the U.S. and world markets in an industry that remains central to the health of any industrial economy.

The restructuring greatly reduced Houdaille's junk-bond debt, but investors clamored for more. Consequently, one year later Houdaille underwent another leveraged buyout, or what might be more accurately called a recapitalization. Its main purpose was to cash out those equity investors who wanted out of the deal after seven years. These investors, who paid $2.52 per share for their stock in 1979, received $11 per share.

But "quieting the natives" came at a very high cost. Whereas the 1979 deal had been constructed with a pot of gold in mind, the recapitalization piled debt upon debt and put Houdaille on a precipice from which there was no escape, save dismemberment. Debt leverage soared from 103 percent to 152 percent of capitalization. Houdaille's newly-issued junk bonds were rated CCC (a D rating means bankruptcy), and the conglomerate was forced to pay junk bondholders 13.875 percent interest at a time when interest rates were less than 10 percent. "Cash interest coverage and debt service coverage are very thin," noted a Standard & Poor's analyst in a report analyzing Houdaille's new junk bonds. Little wonder that Houdaille's rate of capital investment, as a percentage of revenues, was now less than half of the rate prior to the buyout.

Less than a year after the recapitalization, Houdaille announced that Phil O'Reilly was retiring from active management, effective immediately. His abrupt departure caught industry observers by surprise. Few CEOs were more vigorous than O'Reilly, and at age 61 he was well short of normal retirement. No explanation was given out by Houdaille, but three weeks later, the shoe dropped. A British conglomerate, Tube Investments Group, announced that it was taking Houdaille over. TI intended to keep only one Houdaille division—John Crane—and dispose of the rest.

Houdaille had passed into oblivion as an industrial manufacturer, a classic example of the consequences when debt is more profitable than equity, speculation more lucrative than enterprise.

Ten years after the Houdaille LBO,

the elaborate financial engineering pioneered in that deal has become commonplace, and LBOs are fundamentally restructuring corporate America. In the wake of KKR's unprecedented $25-billion RJR Nabisco deal, Congress decided it was finally time to take a closer look at what Wall Street was up to.

KKR promptly commissioned the accounting firm of Deloitte Haskins & Sells to prepare a study on LBOs. The 32-page report, naturally, extols the virtues of LBOs, or at least some of those engineered by KKR. More to the point,

the last two pages describe the Houdaille success story. "All of the Houdaille 'constituents' . . . fared well in the LBO," says the report. Houdaille never fell behind on its debt service. And far from weakening the conglomerate, the LBO "improved management's flexibility in dealing with the severe, rapid and adverse changes in the company's operating environment." As the result, "not only were all creditors paid in full . . . but superior returns were *realized* [emphasis in the original] by investors."

TECHNOLOGY AS DESTINY

JEAN BETHKE ELSHTAIN

Jean Bethke Elshtain is the Centennial Professor of Political Science at Vanderbilt University and a member of The Progressive's Editorial Advisory Board. Her most recent book is "Women and War," published by Basic Books.

Almost every day, strange newspaper headlines trumpet even stranger content:

MAN FILES TEST-TUBE EMBRYO SUIT. In this bizarre case, a Tennessean divorcing his wife went to court to stop her from becoming pregnant with fertilized eggs they had put in frozen storage as a couple. Decision pending.

YALE RESEARCHERS TO TEST TRANSPLANTS OF FETAL TISSUE. Shorthand for this technique might be, "Parkinson's is the disease; abortion is the cure." The procedure in question involves transplanting brain cells from aborted fetuses into patients with Parkinson's to stem the degenerative course of the disease. For some, this is a potentially marvelous medical advance; for others, a morally sordid situation that raises the specter of pregnancy-for-hire to "harvest" fetal tissue from aborted fetuses for a variety of purposes.

HOSPITAL PUTS INFANT IN ORGAN DONOR WARD. The hospital in question, Loma Linda in Los Angeles, seems to specialize in the macabre, having pioneered the unsuccessful transplant of a chimpanzee heart into a baby. The latest twist is to keep anencephalic newborns alive in order to "harvest" their organs.

Each of the articles detailing these late-breaking developments indicates that they raise "profound" and "troubling" ethical questions. This follows a course that has become almost routine: First, certain techniques are perfected or modeled; then, we consult professional ethicists to advise us on whether we ought to be doing what we are, in fact, already doing.

Ethics has a kind of desperate post-hoc character these days. Biomedical technology, on the other hand, is preemptive, aggressive, on-the-move—and searching for big profits. Reproduction is shaping up as a kind of industrial production: the manufacture of particular goods for a price. The names that genetic-engineering firms choose for themselves tell the tale: Select Embryos; Quality Embryo Transfer Company, Ltd.; Sunshine Genetics; Reproduction Enterprises, Inc.; Treasure Valley Transplants.

What are the implications when life becomes a commodity? Who become our candidates for what was tagged, in Nazi biopolitics, "life unworthy of life"? We don't call it eugenics anymore, because the biopolitics of the Nazi regime gave that word a bad name. But the new eugenics is here.

To be sure, we have a long way to go before we approach the ruthless rules of Nazi biopolitics, which required eliminating unworthies of all sorts—the physically and mentally handicapped, inferior races, and the useless elderly, among others. But we have gone farther down this road than most Americans realize or want to acknowledge.

It has all come to us in the guise of "quality of life," and "reproductive choice." And, of course, it has a lofty rationale: to "free" women of "unwanted" fetuses (unwanted because they are defective or, increasingly, because they are of the wrong sex), or to "free" women to have babies by means of highly touted, enormously expensive, rarely successful methods such as in-vitro fertilization or through the costly but physically painless route of surrogacy, where another woman's body labors.

In this brave new world, who speaks, or claims to speak, *for* women? This is an issue on which feminism surely ought to be heard, raising the alarm against a clear and present danger. But matters are by no means so clear-cut. Feminist discourse since the mid-1960s has been lodged securely, with few dissenting voices, in the notion of reproductive freedom.

Until recently, mainstream feminism paid little attention to newer technologies for controlling human reproduction, except when it came to issuing briefs in behalf of a 100 per cent safe and effective contraceptive and in defense of abortion-on-demand. The voices within the feminist camp that questioned arguments for abortion couched *exclusively* in the language of absolute freedom of choice, or in terms of contractual rights to control one's own body, did not prevail in the debates. Those voices now seem to have astutely anticipated the past decade's runaway developments in reproductive technology and genetic engineering.

In-vitro fertilization, embryo flushing, surrogate embryo transfer, surrogate motherhood, sex preselection, clon-

Reprinted by permission from *The Progressive*, June 1989, pp. 19-23. *The Progressive*, 409 East Main Street, Madison, WI 53703.

ing—the entire panoply of real or potentially realizable techniques for manipulating, redirecting, controlling, and altering human reproduction are upon us *now*. Radical intrusion into human biology is an especially vexing issue for feminists because most of these techniques take place in, or are practiced upon, or require the use of the female body.

Feminist philosopher Anne Donchin contends that feminists have sorted themselves out into three major, conflicting positions on the matter of reproductive technology and its mind-boggling implications: pro-interventionists, who celebrate techniques that sever women from "biological determinism"; anti-interventionists, who oppose the new reproductive technologies as an intensification of patriarchal control over women and nature; and those who share bits and pieces of both the pro- and anti-interventionist positions.

For the radical pro-interventionists, the new eugenics presents no problem so long as it can be wrested from male control. They regard that as the only political dilemma, and assess all moral questions with reference to women's freedom. And that means freeing women from what has been tagged as "biological tyranny" in the interventionist credo.

Once women have been liberated from biological tyranny, the pro-interventionists assert, all systems of oppression—the economy, the state, religion, and the law—will erode and collapse. Deploying rhetoric dominated by market metaphors, strong pro-interventionists seek an end to the "barbarism" of biological reproduction and foresee a feminist utopia to come when every aspect of human life rests in the beneficent hands of a "new elite of engineers, cyberneticians"—the words of Shulamith Firestone, who set the tone for interventionist feminism.

Feminist interventionists share an overall world view with the new eugenicists for they, too, believe that nature must be overcome and that human beings should aspire to godlike power. Those who see only our animal origins and patriarchal control in women's links to biology, birth, and nurture are bound to applaud anything that breaks those links. The feminist revolution, in this scheme of things, is a technological solution to women's "control deficit."

The pro-interventionists, whose voices once tended to dominate the movement, are now on the defensive. A powerful feminist anti-interventionist presence has taken center stage in current debates, conjuring up nightmarish worst-case scenarios of the eugenically engineered world to come. As they continue to demand the right to choose, noninterventionists ponder the many "coercive choices" the new reproductive technology seems to entail.

For example, is amniocentesis really a free choice or is it more and more a manipulated, subtly coercive procedure with only one *correct* outcome—to abort if the fetus is "defective"? As younger and younger women submit to amniocentesis, physicians speak of "maternal anxiety" as the motivation. In the words of one thirty-two-year-old woman, "Having a baby isn't like buying a car, but in a way, he [her husband] wanted to know what he was getting. . . ." So, it seems, did she as she embraced the ever more common "perfect-baby syndrome."

But how liberally are we to define "defect"? And what about the much proclaimed "right" to bear a child—is this not another imposition of a male-dominant society upon women who see themselves as "failures" if they cannot get pregnant and are thus driven to place themselves in the hands of "techno-docs" (Gena Corea's term) to try to rectify their failure?

According to anti-interventionists, all modern technology is designed to deepen and extend patriarchal control. They are deeply skeptical that *this* technology can be turned to good purpose. Radical anti-interventionists insist that just as males moved successfully to control female "sex parts" through various forms of prostitution (including marriage), so they now seek a new reality: the reproductive brothel.

Writes Andrea Dworkin, "Women can sell reproductive capacities the same way old-time prostitutes sold sexual ones. . . . While sexual prostitutes sell vagina, rectum, and mouth, reproductive prostitutes will sell other body parts: Wombs. Ovaries. Eggs."

Not all statements of anti-interventionists are so extreme. Many of the scenarios conjured up by Gena Corea in her book *The Mother Machine* are genuinely frightening, showing how methods first developed as part of animal husbandry—to control the reproduction of non-human animals—are making their way into human lives.

But the anti-interventionist position unravels philosophically—and politically—where one finds assertions of an absolute right to choose, but only so long as the choices are "true," not "false," according to ideologically correct doctrine.

Thus, some feminists claim that the lesbian who wants to assert her right to "independent motherhood" is entitled both to artificial insemination and to sex selection as a basis for abortion should the fetus turn out to be male when she wants a female. But the woman in a heterosexual relationship who, with her husband, opts for in-vitro fertilization is viewed as a hapless dupe of patriarchal wiles. And, should she choose sex selection as a basis for abortion because she and her husband want a male child, that suddenly becomes "feticide" rather than the "right to choose."

This won't do. To offer a genuinely compelling argument, the anti-interventionists would have to extend their opposition to eugenics to include gender preselection on the part of female as well as male-female couples going through artificial insemination by donor. Either one does or does not have moral permission to eliminate the unborn solely on the basis of gender. But for some anti-interventionists, a preferential option for the female fetus is part of the arsenal of weapons to fight patriarchal society.

By sanctioning sex selection of the "right sort" as the basis for abortion, radical feminists are playing with fire—and with social reality. Especially poignant for women is the fact that female fetuses are prime candidates for our version of what might be called "life less worthy of life." There is no doubt that the modern technology of sex preselection will result in a higher proportionate destruction of female fetuses—at least for the *first* birth.

A recent *New York Times* piece proclaimed, "In a major change in medical attitudes and practice, many doctors are providing prenatal diagnoses to pregnant woman who want to abort a fetus on the basis of sex alone." We have reached the point of disrupting the "natural lottery"—the fact that no human being can control whether he or she is white or black, male or female, a Down's syndrome child or a musical prodigy. When we do that, we undermine the very basis of human equality. The *Times* piece goes on to note that it is only "in very rare instances" that "there is a valid medical reason for sex selection." The reasons are social and political.

The erosion of human equality—the fragile insistence that each of us has an ontological dignity that we did not create and over which society has no control—requires that we accept and welcome life in all its variety. Once we claim that we do, in fact, have such control—that we can ensure more males and fewer females, that we can prevent the appearance of the Down's syndrome child and, maybe, in the even braver new world to come, manipulate genes to get the musical prodigy—we pave the way for nightmarish biological totalitarianism.

At that sorry point, some among us—"perfect" white males—will have been given top priority by a three-to-two majority, if current studies are any indication. Others will be inferior, having been placed lower on the preference list. And still others will be disallowed life at all. Should any of this last sort sneak through, there will be no moral basis for insisting that they be given decent treatment as members of the human community since, if the controls had been working right, they wouldn't be here in the first place.

The radical interventionists are right to insist that technical progress is never neutral. But to counterpose good female values (feminism rightly understood) to bad male values gets us nowhere. There are women as well as men who support these technologies—some in the name of feminism.

To insist, as does anti-interventionist Maria Mies, that the "so-called new technology does not bring us and our children any kind of qualitative or quantitative improvement in our lives; it solves none of our basic problems; it will advance even more the exploitation and humiliation of women; therefore we do not need it," strikes a sympathetic chord with many, myself included, who do not share the full range of anti-interventionist assumptions. And warning flags are going up in unexpected places, including *The Village Voice*, which featured a piece on "the selling of in-vitro fertilization" in which the author, Andrea Boroff Eagan, indicated that "tears of gratitude" sprang to her eyes when a Catholic priest on an ethics panel mentioned "conjugal intimacy"—the only person to do so in a week-long discussion of reproduction that was otherwise "desexed, disembodied, dehumanized."

Most feminists and, I would guess, most people generally belong somewhere between the radical pro- and anti-interventionist positions, hoping that real help might come to infertile couples but in ways that seem human and humane; concerned to "do something" about human suffering but worried about eliminating human beings according to someone else's definition of suffering. (The decision to withhold treatment and nourishment from imperfect newborns is usually directly traceable to the premises of a eugenics politics that dictates that a handicap devalues life and undermines any right to it.)

Most people support contraception and do not want abortion made illegal—but neither are they "pro-abortion." Studies consistently find a shaky combination of "yes" and "no" answers to the vast array of powers and projects currently, and dubiously, lumped under the heading of "reproductive freedom."

The Baby M. case crystallized this queasiness and prompted further elaboration of what might be called the moderate position. Here was a situation in which biological motherhood and social parenting were severed—as feminists had long claimed they should be. Here was a situation in which a biological father insisted he wanted to assume the responsibilities of fatherhood—as feminists had long claimed men ought to want to do. Here was a case in which everyone "freely" agreed to a contract. Yet as the case unraveled, more and more feminists expressed opposition to commercial surrogacy and outrage at the initial court decision, which got all woozy over the man's desire for genetic offspring while dismissing Mary Beth Whitehead's frenzied struggle to keep the child to which she had given birth.

The case demonstrated, at times with almost unbearable pathos, the inadequacy of such terms as "procreative liberty," "gestational hostess," "womb rental," "risk pay for pregnancy services," and the host of other depersonalizing euphemisms which seek to transform childbearing into a morally and emotionally neutral activity. As Betty Friedan pointed out, the initial decision denying Whitehead *any* claim—she was no mother of any kind in any way—had "frightening implications for women" because it was a "terrifying denial of what should be basic rights for women, an utter denial of the personhood of women, the complete dehumanization of women. It is an important human-rights case. To put it on the level of contract law is to dehumanize women and the human bond between mother and child."

Yet the business of surrogacy had, in fact, taken off as a venture at the furthest frontiers of reproductive freedom—and, of course, of profit. To condemn the latter required a critical look at the former and at what was now being done under the banner of individualist versions of such freedom.

Some feminists did point to the fine print in the surrogacy contract: Whitehead was to abort on William Stern's demand should the fetus show any signs of "physiological abnormality" following amniocentesis. Many found this repugnant, even immoral, because the male got to order it, not because such abortion is dubious on principle.

Feminists aroused by this case circled around a vital point—that, in Friedan's words, "the claim of the woman who has carried the baby for nine months should take precedence over the claim of the man who has donated one of his fifty million sperm." When Lee Salk, noted psychologist, called Whitehead a "rented uterus" in his testimony in behalf of the Sterns, he earned a permanent place in the rogue's gallery. The most eloquent statement of feminist outrage came from Katha Pollitt who wrote, in *The Nation*, "What William Stern wanted, however, was not just a perfect baby; the Sterns did not, in fact, seriously investigate adoption. He wanted a perfect baby with his genes and a medically vetted mother who would get out of his life forever immediately after giving birth."

Surrogacy and other new eugenics questions bring us back, inevitably, to concerns about the nature of human intimacy and the family. That is as it should be. The new eugenics cannot be separated from the wider cultural and social environment.

All approaches to eugenics with which I am familiar—from Plato's elegant *Republic* to Hitler's vulgar *Reich*—aimed to eliminate, undermine, or leap-frog over the family to achieve their aims. To modern eugenicists, too, the family and "traditional morality" are obstacles in the path of radical social and genetic engineering. As the surrogacy case demonstrated, women's attachment to their own children is a problem. It would be far easier if natural pregnancy could somehow be phased out. But, in the meantime, newer and better ways to convince people to participate in eugenics (under other names, of course) must be devised.

Paradoxically, the new eugenics, operating under the umbrella of reproductive freedom, may have opened women's lives to more invasive forms of control. The search for intervention in human reproduction comes, at least initially, from those able to command the resources of genetic engineers and medical experts. They are prepared to accept a remarkable degree of surveillance and manipulation of their lives to satisfy their demand that babies be made (or unmade) whenever they want and as soon as a "valid contract" can be drafted.

In this way, human procreation is transformed into a technical operation. Writes social critic Jeanne Schuler, "Reproductive liberty sounds as if it was written for women but it signals a new level of alienated sexuality.... Behind the effort to make all things equal in the realm of reproduction figures a new form of discrimination. The hazards of reproductive freedom are not easily visible to liberal politics.... However, liberalism nurtures freedom without cultivating a vision of family, let alone community. Thus it is easily drafted to the side of the status quo, once so-called negative liberties are intact."

Many feminists are troubled by the Frankenstein monster we seem to be unleashing. All women are affected by these developments. The political battles over definitions of motherhood—and, indeed, of human life itself—are only beginning. The new eugenics, in the meantime, has passed one green light after another and is rolling at breakneck speed, claiming "gender equality" and "freedom" on its side.

Erecting a stop sign at future intersections requires that we reject the view that freedom can be narrowed to contractual terms, that human bodies can be bartered, that we have a "right" to eliminate those human beings who don't look or act like our perfect image of ourselves. And it requires that we forge alliances, however fragile, to preserve human dignity, which must be the basis for any genuine project of human equality and justice.

Television and the Communications Revolution

Stanley Rothman and Robert Lerner

Stanley Rothman is Mary Huggins Gamble Professor of Government at Smith College and director of the Center for the Study of Social and Political Change. He is author or coauthor of ninety articles and seven books, including The Media Elite *and* The IQ Controversy, The Media and Public Policy.

Robert Lerner is assistant director of the Center for the Study of Social and Political Change. He has written a number of articles and monographs on the media and on American leadership groups. His latest essay, "Marginality and Liberalism among Jewish Elites," coauthored with Althea Nagai and Stanley Rothman, was published in spring 1989 in the Public Opinion Quarterly.

In the wake of disclosures about Senator Joseph R. Biden plagiarizing a speech by British Labour party leader Neil Kinnock, the *New York Times,* on September 27, 1987, contemplated the at-least temporary end of Biden's presidential aspirations. The *Times* pointed out that in the past thirty years television has fundamentally changed the structure of political campaigns. In the 1950s, indiscretions like Biden's and Gary Hart's would have probably been ignored by the media, taking their cue from party leaders. Now matters are different. The media have taken over the job of judging candidates, and television tapes from vast libraries actually showing Biden aping Kinnock in a New Hampshire living room were powerful images indeed. In addition, television comedians are now in a position to destroy political candidates. As the *Times* pointed out:

It could even be argued that once flaws are revealed they are distributed most efficiently, and decline is most rapidly accelerated, by the television comedians. In Joe Biden's week of agony, he was the favorite topic of Johnny Carson and David Letterman. Once he becomes the butt of a hundred jokes heard in a million bedrooms. . . . it is hard for any politician to survive.

The *Times* is belatedly recognizing that a revolution has taken place in the nature and impact of the mass media in the United States, and in other advanced industrial societies, in the past thirty years or so. Television's impact continued through the 1988 primaries. Observers detected little evidence of bias in the horse-race treatment of candidates, with one exception. Jesse Jackson was undoubtedly helped by the favorable and respectable attention he received in the national media. In addition, both he and the media were responsible for bringing the drug issue front and center and persuading the public, justifiably or not, that the Reagans' efforts in this area had failed.

These events make clear that a revolution has indeed taken place. However, the incidents only deal with the proverbial tip of the iceberg. This article is about the rest of it, that is, some far more important implications of the media revolution. To understand these we must first understand what life was like before the revolution occurred.

American Media: Free and Different

The notion of a free and uncensored media had its origins in Europe and the United States, and it is still largely if not exclusively confined to those areas of the world. In most other parts of the globe, the media remain under tight control of those wielding political power. It is no accident that America, despite its relatively short history, took the lead even among European countries in establishing a relatively free press. The rapid democra-

Published by permission of Transaction Publishers, from *Society,* Vol. 26, No. 1, November/December 1988, pp. 64-70.

tization of American life, under the aegis of the liberal ideology that defined the nation at its founding, certainly played a key role in that process. It is also partly responsible for the fact that journalism for the masses first developed in the United States, followed closely by England and other Western European countries.

The absence of sharp class prejudices and divisions in America as compared to Europe made it easier to envisage a mass press. Further, the United States pioneered the technology of the mass press, just as it was to lead the world in the development of the mass-produced automobile and of television for the masses. By 1910, some 24 million issues of daily newspapers were being published in this country, compared to about 2 million in England.

Europe and America have been the home of a free—that is, freely competitive—press, but the American media (both newspapers and television) have always differed from the Western European and English media for reasons having to do with cultural, economic, and political variables as well as with the sheer size of the United States. Some of these differences are of diminishing importance, but they are relevant to an examination of the changes that have taken place in the United States during the past thirty years.

The mass media in the United States have been and still are primarily privately owned businesses, even though radio and television operate within the framework of public regulation of a sort. In most European countries, on the other hand, both radio and television have been primarily public enterprises. Even where private enterprise has recently come to play a more significant role, it is far less important than in this country.

Newspapers in the United States and Europe are privately owned enterprises, but the historical tradition in the United States has been different from that of Europe. On the European continent a great many newspapers and magazines began as the organs of political parties and remained closely affiliated with them. Newspapers tended to represent various ideological perspectives, some of which were hostile to existing regimes. Thus in many European countries, Socialist and Communist parties published successful daily and weekly journals. Leading journalists were often important intellectuals.

The American pattern was quite different. Throughout most of its history America has been characterized by an ideological consensus, which assumed the truth of both democracy and capitalism. Reporters were not intellectuals, and their aim by the late nineteenth century was to accurately report facts which they assumed had an objective existence.

The best European journalists, writing in societies rent by more or less severe ideological social class conflicts and political parties based upon them, were far more aware that perceptions of social action were at least partly a function of the assumptions that were brought to them. These historical differences still influence the manner in which American and European newspaper people ap-

proach the news. Despite their greater sophistication today, American journalists, for the most part, still find it difficult to recognize that the facts are not merely givens but are, at least to some extent, determined by the ideology one brings to them.

European countries cannot all be lumped together. In their relative freedom from censorship and belief in the possibility of objective reportage of the news, British journalists have historically more closely resembled their American counterparts than journalists in France, Germany, or Italy. The differences between Europe (including England) and America, however, are significant. Quality European newspapers have been and still are far more interested in broader theoretical and ideological issues of public policy. American journalists, while not uninterested in policy concerns, are less self-conscious about ideology and often seek to win their spurs by uncovering mis or malfeasance in office. This emphasis, to some extent, serves as a substitute for ideological concerns. It also reflects a powerful populist strain in American liberalism. Americans may have traditionally felt a strong attachment to their sociopolitical system, but they have always been wary of those to whom they have delegated political power.

Reflecting this tradition and contributing to it, libel laws in this country were generally far less rigorous than those in most European democracies. This was true even before Supreme Court decisions made it all but impossible for a public figure to successfully sue newspapers or television stations. Unlike most European countries, the United States has never boasted the equivalent of an official secrets act. In England, the publication of the Pentagon papers could have—probably would have—led to very long jail sentences for the staff of any newspaper that dared to publish them. Indeed it is unlikely that the material would have been published.

In England, until very recently, those elected to office were supposed to govern. They might be turned out eventually, but while governing they were given wide latitude. This was far less true in continental Europe, given the sharpness of ideological divisions, but even there the gap in status between news people and leading political figures was always considerable, and the leeway permitted to government in preventing the publication of items "essential to the national security" was much greater. Although the pattern is changing rapidly, many European commentators still regard American political life as taking place in a fishbowl.

Unlike most Western European countries, America has historically lacked a national press. There were magazines with national circulations (by the 1930s this included *Time* and *Life*), growing newspaper chains, and, even before World War II, a very few prestigious newspapers such as the *New York Times,* which boasted a national infuence; however, localism was the dominant theme. The 1920s may have roared in some cosmopolitan centers like New York and, to a lesser extent, Chicago, but local standards dominated Main Street in most cities around the country, including the ethnic enclaves of metropolitan areas. In the short run, at least, most Americans remained relatively unaffected by the middle- and upper-class culture of the few large cities that counted.

All these features of the American media predominated until the post-World War II period. Even in the midst of the Great Depression, most Americans were not especially conscious of New York or even Washington. Most also accepted the basic cultural and social parameters of their society as good and right, and thought that those who wished to change them radically were either odd or evil. This world view was reinforced by the images obtained from the newspapers, radio, and Hollywood. Newspaper publishers were relatively conservative, as were those who controlled the airwaves and motion pictures. Especially in the radio and movie industries, executives were primarily concerned with entertaining the public and making profits. They were not by any means all Republicans. Many supported Franklin D. Roosevelt

---

Ronald Reagan foiled the attempts of media critics to diminish his popularity.

---

and the New Deal, but their aim was to reform and save capitalism, and their products by and large reinforced the American liberal Protestant consensus.

The working press was probably more liberal than were publishers, and some newsmen were even radicals. But the reins of authority were in the hands of the publishers, and reporters who wanted to keep their jobs stayed in line. Publishers and network officials also actively catered to the preferences of their advertisers. After all, many, if not all, radio programs were directly controlled by the advertisers who sponsored them.

For the most part, the threat of economic pressure was not the major force behind the media's conservatism. News and entertainment took the view they did largely because publishers and most reporters believed that was the way it was and should be. Key elites in American society accepted the broad framework of the American liberal consensus, and most did not even realize that there might be other ways to look at the world.

National Media Network

In the meantime the nature of the American mass media was changing. As in so many areas, the changes were a function of both technology and affluence. Improvements in communication led to the development of journals with large national audiences, even as the development of the jet airplane, universal automobile

ownership, and a national highway system all contributed to the breakdown of regional differences and isolation.

Radio had developed national audiences, and, by the 1930s, newspaper chains were spreading and national magazines with large circulations wre changing the consciousness of Americans. *Time* magazine was for a long time the prime, in fact the only, exemplar of the trend. Founded in 1923 by Henry Luce and Briton Hadden, its circulation had reached about half a million by 1936, prompting Luce to follow through with his long-held plan to create a photo magazine. Within a short time *Life* far outstripped *Time*, made Luce one of the most powerful forces in American journalism, and prompted, as had *Time*, a series of imitators. The United States was beginning to develop a national media network. A relatively small group of media outlets was increasingly determining the manner in which the world was being presented to Americans. This group of media outlets was largely centered in New York, secondarily in Los Angeles, and, for political news, in Washington.

The trend did not come to fruition until the late 1950s and early 1960s, with the emergence of television. By 1958 the number of television sets just about equaled the number of American homes, and the age of television really began, dominated immediately by the three major networks centered in New York. Given the expense of producing programs, including news programs and television specials, local network affiliates came to depend upon the networks for both entertainment and news programs. They still do. While some things have changed, the decisions about nationwide news and entertainment are made by relatively few persons in a few key cities. Cable television may yet change this pattern, but so far it has not succeeded in doing so.

The New Sensibility

By its very nature, television added new dimensions to the communication of information and radically changed the rules of the game. One does not have to accept Marshall McLuhan's hyperbole to recognize these profound effects on American life. By the middle 1960s television was already transforming America. Adults and children were watching television programs six-to-seven hours a day. Television had become an integral part of American life.

Television is a major business in a competitive capitalist society, and, whatever the social and political views of those who make decisions, it has been and is capturing attention and increasing the size of audiences. This produces profits and insures solvency.

Given the nature of network television and its need for mass audiences, and the nature of the medium and the information it conveys, the emphasis of television news is bound to center on the personal and the dramatic rather than upon the abstract and discursive. It is hard to see how this emphasis can be avoided except in a society, such as the Soviet Union, in which television is tightly controlled. Even in the Soviet Union, attempts have been made in recent years to follow a similar pattern in an effort to enlarge audiences.

The charge made by scholars and others that television news necessarily emphasizes entertainment may not be true on the conscious level. Herbert Gans argues, for example, that newsmen do not let questions of audience appeal determine coverage. However, it is bound to play some role. Anchormen, producers, and directors want audiences to tune in, not to tune off. Ratings are closely monitored and affect news judgment, as do time and financial constraints and the availability of staff.

Decisions as to what will capture the attention of audiences are often based on instinctive readings of audiences by those in charge of production. Thus, the values of such people come into play in a hit-or-miss pattern of decision making. Indeed they have more leeway than they realize. Audiences are not turned off or on as quickly or easily as is assumed. At one time, for example, it was thought that television reporters had to be male WASPS if they were to capture audiences. This has now changed as more and more Jews, women, blacks, Hispanics, and Asians are in front of the camera without apparent loss of audience attention.

It is difficult to separate out the effects of television as an instrument of communication from the fact that it is a commercial enterprise, but the consequences for certain aspects of American life are clear. Far more than newspapers, radio, or movies, television provides its audience with a sense that what it views is the truth. Viewers see events taking place in their living rooms. Stories, documentaries, even drama take on a reality with which other media cannot compete. Events are seen "as they happen." The written word can be discounted, as can the spoken word, but pictures seen in the privacy of our homes are too compelling. Even if we know that what we see may have been spliced together and, conceivably, may not be accurate, it is hard to escape the perception that we are viewing reality.

Television has broken down class and regional boundaries to a far greater extent than other media. Books and newspapers are segregated by area and readership. Only the well-educated can read serious books, and the style of the *New York Times* can appeal only to those with a certain level of education and affluence. Thus, to some extent, newspapers and books encourage the segregation of knowledge. Radio begins to break down that segregation. Television goes much further. There are programs that cater to more elite audiences and are watched only by them, but insofar as television seeks the lowest common denominator and finds it, Americans as a group are introduced to the same themes in the same way. "Roots" and other docudramas, as well as the six o'clock news, are watched by millions of Americans of all educational and social backgrounds; they see the same pictures and receive the same information.

Television breaks down regional boundaries in infor-

mation retrieval as well. The same voices, the same accents, and the same life-style reach rural areas in Arkansas as readily as the upper east side of New York. Insofar as those who live on New York's upper east side or in Los Angeles help create the reality that America sees, those voices help change the expectations and views of Americans.

At one point, a young person from a rural background or a small town experienced a genuine culture shock when he or she enrolled in an eastern elite college or even a major state university, experiencing new and different life-styles for the first time. The cultural gap between rural America, the main streets of small-town America, and urban metropolitan areas has been considerably narrowed. The effects of new metropolitan styles created in New York or Los Angeles now spread far more rapidly than they once did.

The process begins early in childhood. As Joshua Meyrowitz points out, cultures in which knowledge is dependent on the ability to read require substantial preparation before one can penetrate many of the secrets of adult life. Television has broken that barrier. Children can and do watch television programs that tell them about the off-stage behavior of parents, and introduce them to themes they would otherwise not encounter until much later in life. Young children are exposed to the news almost every day along with their parents. Most so-called family programs deal with themes with which children would not have been familiar even twenty-five years ago. Millions of children are still awake at hours when more "mature" television programs are shown. As Meyrowitz points out in *No Sense of Place*:

> It is difficult for parents to control their children's viewing of the television without limiting their own viewing as well. While a child has very limited access to the content of books and newspapers being read by adults in the same room, a television program being watched by adults is accessible to any child in the same space. Many children are exposed to adult news, for example, because their parents watch the news during dinner.

> With book reading, a family can stay together in a single room and yet be divided into different households. In multiple-set television households, children and adults can be in different rooms and still be united into a single informational network. "Roots," "Mash," "Dallas," the Vietnam War, and 1960s urban riots were seen by millions of children under ten years old.

All of this has played an important role, along with other factors, in weakening traditional ties of church, ethnic group, and neighborhood. Television has contributed to American social and geographic mobility as much as the revolution in transportation, in part because it has enabled Americans to feel almost equally at home in Oshkosh, New York, or Dallas. It has homogenized American culture and nationalized it.

It is impossible to understand the revolution that took place in American values and attitudes during the 1960s and 1970s without taking into account the influence of television on American life, including its breaking down of old barriers and its weakening of old ties. In the 1920s, the new therapeutic ethic of self-realization had only permeated a small section of America's metropolitan upper middle class. By the 1970s it was rapidly becoming accepted by most Americans. Not surprisingly, few realize how rapid the pace of change has been. The events of the 1960s, including the rapid loss of faith in American institutions, and the legitimation of once deviant life-styles, could not have occurred in a pretelevision age.

America has become a loosely bounded culture. Americans' primordial ties to family, locality, church, and what is considered appropriate behavior have eroded, and Americans have lost their sense of place. They are not alone in this. The experience is increasingly shared by Europeans, Japanese, and, perhaps, even Russians; and certainly mass television is not the only factor at work. The revolution is real, and the epoch we live in is new.

Working-class parochials may continue to identify with those they know, those who work and live in their neighborhoods; but public reality is now such that we also know and develop intimate and intense relationships with public figures of all kinds, to a far greater extent than we once did. The stars of television—from anchormen to rock performers to politicians—have become pseudointimate acquaintances.

The impact of television on the substance of politics has been at least as great as it has been on our personal life. Seeing political events, the expressions on faces, and the use of hands or eyes during an interview adds a concrete dimension to political figures, even as it may reduce the abstract elements in the message conveyed. Politicians who sweat on television (as Richard Nixon did in the 1960s television debates) lose points as compared to those who do not. The camera can make a political figure look as if he or she is evading a question or is stammering and confused, and materials which might never appear in print, or at least would not have the same impact (such as Edmund Muskie crying in response to an insult to his wife), routinely appear on television.

Television has changed the very structure of political discourse. Political figures could once issue carefully written pronouncements to the newspapers. They now appear on television interviews—warts, stutters, and all. Spoken communication, after all, is rarely grammatical. We rely on all sorts of cues to get our message across. These cues work well in the lecture hall but not as part of a permanent television record.

Politicians and others are caught exhibiting behavior on-stage which in other epochs would have occurred only off-stage, thus breaking down the barrier between the two realms. In print, for example, politicians and others can set their thoughts down carefully. They conceal their doubts, their boredom, their prejudices when they present public statements. The same is true of doctors or lawyers. In the age of television, this is far more difficult, especially in time of crisis. As television becomes more and more ubiquitous, we all have increasing access to backstage behavior. The paradigmatic case is probably the Nixon tapes, although this owed little to television per se. As Meyrowitz points out, Nixon and his colleagues were often engaging in just the kinds of obscenity and gratuitous insults that one finds in the backstage behavior of politicians, or, for that matter, academics. We hardly realize it is present, because it rarely comes to the front of the stage. Most of us could not easily survive the monitoring of our conversations about other colleagues and groups with close friends; nor would we be terribly proud of our diction.

Americans and others long for great leaders. Yet, such is their ambivalence toward authority that they also revel in their weaknesses. Television inevitably caters to that second wish. In so doing, it reduces our power to produce great leaders.

The television revolution has affected newspapers and news magazines. In part, it has forced them to turn to in-depth reportage of the kind that television handles much less effectively. On the other hand, it has encouraged them, partly for competitive reasons, and partly because television has created a new atmosphere, to seek out the same dramatic off-stage exposés that television can achieve. Vietnam and Watergate may have contributed to the development of an adversary press, but so did the changing assumptions of media personnel as to what constitutes news and how one deals with political figures. It was television reportage, too, which gave journalists the sense that they could make the news as well as report it, although many of them continue to deny that they do so.

Ronald Reagan's success during most of his presidency had at least something to do with his previous career. Given his involvement in the media, including television, he was able to develop a style that enabled him almost always to provide newsmen with an on-stage performance—a style that looked as if it were off-stage and thus appeared even more genuine. An accomplished television performer, Reagan foiled the attempts of media critics to diminish his popularity.

Journalists sometimes claimed that they had been too easy on Reagan. Nothing could be further from the truth. They could not touch him, until the Iran-*contra* affair, because as long as he could retain reasonable control of the circumstances under which he appeared on television he gave the impression of being, at one and the same time, a sympathetic ordinary person and yet a strong leader. He could compete effectively with all the other celebrities, including anchormen, who now appear regularly on television—an ability lacked by the three presidents who preceded him. However once the Iran-*contra* affair came to light, plus a host of other revelations, Reagan's style was no longer sufficient; his popularity rapidly declined despite a series of what could be interpreted as foreign policy successes.

During the 1960s and 1970s the influence of television continued to grow. Limited at one time by large-scale equipment needs, technological change increasingly permitted television to cover the whole world on the fly, and to transmit images almost instantaneously from and to all portions of the globe.

As the ubiquity of television increased, its credibility grew. It could tap experts, and, indeed, it created experts by defining them as such on television news and talk shows. Television was used by various groups, including terrorist groups, to attract national and even worldwide attention and hence to gain influence. It could and did legitimize terrorists by presenting events from their perspective. Again and again it set agendas by defining issues as important. It even established the parameters within which issues would be discussed.

Television's Impact

Paradoxically, the advent of television increased the influence of a few eastern print media outlets such as the *New York Times, Time, Newsweek,* and, to a lesser extent, the *Washington Post* and the *Wall Street Journal.* With the sources of political news increasingly centered in New York and Washington, and those responsible for producing, directing, and reporting the news increasingly literate, key newspapers and magazines on the east coast took on new importance.

What television had done was to nationalize and standardize communication to an extent never before achieved in the United States. New York and Washington styles and modes now became national styles and modes. If the *New York Times* was read by New York and Washington elites, and those who produced the news for the television networks, it would also be read elsewhere. Even if it were not read, the issues that it considered important and the approach it took to them would become national currency. The same is true of the *Washington Post* and a number of other media outlets, which share with television the ability to set agendas and even to strongly influence the framework within which political and social issues are debated.

Even as the role and influence of the media, and television in particular, grew, the nature of the journalistic community was changing, as was the relationship of journalists to those who owned newspapers or mass news journals or those who controlled the television networks. In the old days, the days of *The Front Page,* journalists, like most Americans, went to work after graduating from high school or even before. While some journalists and excutives on leading papers were from upper middle-class backgrounds, journalism was most often a source of social mobility for working-class and lower middle-class youth. The generally Democratic sympathies of working

reporters in the 1930s was partly a function of their class background.

After World War II the pattern changed. Increasing numbers of young men and women from upper middle-class backgrounds began to seek jobs in journalism and in television as a way of partaking of an exciting and creative career and having an impact on society.

Journalists who work for the key national media today are far more likely than businessmen to have come from relatively affluent backgrounds and to have graduated from elite universities. Our study of the staffs of leading media outlets reveals that 45 percent remember their parents' income as above average as compared to 31 percent of a sample of business executives at major firms. In our study, we ranked the status of schools attended from 1 (lowest) to 7 (highest) based on such factors as endowment and student SAT scores. The average rating of undergraduate institutions attended by journalists was 5.56 as against 4.77 for businessmen.

Given that most of them have married professional women, and that the salaries of television reporters and anchor persons now reach astronomical figures, their incomes compare favorably with those of the business elite. In short, they are highly educated and fairly well-to-do individuals. They can enjoy the good things of life. Journalism is no longer a source of social mobility for most. Indeed it is less so than business. A much larger proportion of business executives in major firms come from working-class backgrounds than do elite journalists (28 percent as against 12 percent).

Journalists do stand at the cutting edge of our loosely bounded culture. As many studies demonstrate, they are both the products and the creators of the new American and international culture. They are liberal and cosmopolitan in outlook and not unaware, despite ritual denials, of the influence that they have acquired. Their loyalty to the transmission of news increasingly transcends previously narrowly defined standards of national interest. They tend also to move on the surface of events, and the judgments they present to the public on television or in the press are often based on shallow knowledge of the subjects with which they deal. They were educated at elite universities, but they are not scholars, and their careers discourage scholarly activity. They do not have time to read many books or to think issues through carefully.

Journalists learn by reading newspapers and journals and, more importantly, by picking the brains of those they interview to develop a superficial sophistication about issues that face the country. This is partly a matter of temperament and choice, and explains why they are journalists rather than scholars, but it is also a function of their work. Operating under rigid schedules, and forced to deal with one breaking story after another, they do not have time to investigate material in depth. Nevertheless, an underlying skepticism toward traditional institutions and authority and toward traditional groups leads them almost instinctively to credit certain groups and individuals above others. They are more likely to trust women

starved of talent. The Japanese-born scientist who won last year's Nobel Prize for medicine delivered a similar denunciation of Japanese research as soon as his selection was announced. Japanese science was suffocating beneath the weight of a settled, seniority-based Establishment, he said. It stifled new talent and forced him to America and Europe to do the research that won the prize. The best positive example of Olson's analysis is probably South Korea, where a high proportion of entrepreneurs and go-getters fled as refugees from North Korea or arose from the chaos after the Korean War.

Most stagnating societies, Olson said, had to fall back on the South Korean cure for a sclerotic Establishment. It took wartime defeat (Japan, Germany), bloody revolution (18th-century France) or generalized carnage (Korea) to break up old, corrupt power and give new talent a chance. But the U.S., almost uniquely, could hope to invigorate its society through less drastic means. Its basic principles provided for a number of sources of self-renewal. Immigration is the most obvious, but there are others: Americans' habit of moving from place to place, the country's general disdain for tradition, and the occasional government steps, such as the GI Bill or civil-rights legislation, that bring new players into the game. Canada, Australia and a handful of other societies can afford to expose themselves to similar nonrevolutionary change. Most other countries would find it too traumatic—and even for us it's hard.

Hard it may be, but making room for new establishments is more necessary now than ever before, since other peculiarities of American culture make us fundamentally unfit for modern international competition. We're all familiar with one kind of handicap: America is vastly richer than the Soviet Union but the Russians can probably win any peacetime military-spending race, since they're not so bogged down by dissent and consumer demands. Nor can we ever keep secrets as well as the Soviet police state. These are handicaps, but we'd rather live with them than change.

Our handicaps in economic competition are, if anything, more profound. Although the Japanese, Koreans and Taiwanese learned many manufacturing skills by imitating Americans, it is much harder for Americans to profit by imitating them. Their economic success is based on cultural fundamentals totally different from ours. Japan, especially, depends on an ethic of national/racial solidarity that is utterly contrary to America's nation-of-immigrants belief. When in 1986, then Prime Minister Nakasone made his notorious statement that the level of education and intellect in the U.S. was low because of its large black and Hispanic populations, he was really trying to explain how much easier it is to run a country when everyone feels a "racial purity" family tie to everyone else. Not since World War II or, perhaps, the week after John Kennedy's assassination has America displayed the unity that Japan enjoys, automatically, every day.

Some scholars contend that Confucian-based societies, such as those in East Asia, should be failures in capitalist competition rather than the runaway successes they've proved to be. After all, Confucianism teaches reverence for tradition and horror of rapid change—all in all, not the formula for aggressive market penetration and growing trade surpluses. But other Confucian habits are very useful and very hard for us to imitate—for instance, the ingrained willingness to obey superiors and to loyally wait one's turn before moving ahead.

If America cozies up to a permanent Establishment, it will be throwing away its most distinctive strength. Seeing if we can run a society as organized and harmonious as Japan's is like trying to outsacrifice and outconceal the Russians. It can't be done, and we'd be crazy to try. What has brought America this far is its talent for *dis*order, its ability to get surprising results from average people—the ones that Conant called "least capable"—by putting them in situations where old rules and limits don't apply. That's the meaning of immigration, of the frontier, of leaving the farm for the big city, of going to college to make a new start. No other society has managed disorder so well: none of our competitors needs to keep promoting disorder, by endlessly rotating establishments, as much as we do.

In a tart, insightful book called *Shadows of the Rising Sun*, Jared Taylor, who grew up in Japan as a missionary's son, considered the argument that America should revive itself by "being more like them," emulating the Japanese. It's the other way around, he said; we need to be "more like us," doing the things American society can do best. We are most like ourselves when, as this issue shows we are, we are in flux.

HELPING AND HATING THE HOMELESS

The struggle at the margins of America

Peter Marin

Peter Marin is a contributing editor of Harper's Magazine. *He is currently completing a book about homelessness.*

When I was a child, I had a recurring vision of how I would end as an old man: alone, in a sparsely furnished second-story room I could picture quite precisely, in a walk-up on Fourth Avenue in New York, where the secondhand bookstores then were. It was not a picture which frightened me. I liked it. The idea of anonymity and solitude and marginality must have seemed to me, back then, for reasons I do not care to remember, both inviting and inevitable. Later, out of college, I took to the road, hitchhiking and traveling on freights, doing odd jobs here and there, crisscrossing the country. I liked that too: the anonymity and the absence of constraint and the rough community I sometimes found. I felt at home on the road, perhaps because I felt at home nowhere else, and periodically, for years, I would return to that world, always with a sense of relief and release.

I have been thinking a lot about that these days, now that transience and homelessness have made their way into the national consciousness, and especially since the town I live in, Santa Barbara, has become well known because of the recent successful campaign to do away with the meanest aspects of its "sleeping ordinances"—a set of foolish laws making it illegal for the homeless to sleep at night in public places. During that campaign I got to know many of the homeless men and women in Santa Barbara, who tend to gather, night and day, in a small park at the lower end of town, not far from the tracks and the harbor, under the rooflike, overarching branches of a gigantic fig tree, said to be the oldest on the continent. There one enters much the same world I thought, as a child, I would die in, and the one in which I traveled as a young man: a "marginal" world inhabited by all those unable to find a place in "our" world. Sometimes, standing on the tracks close to the park, you can sense in the wind, or in the smell of tar and ties, the presence and age of that marginal world: the way it stretches backward and inevitably forward in time, parallel to our own world, always present, always close, and yet separated from us—at least in the mind—by a gulf few of us are interested in crossing.

Late last summer, at a city council meeting here in Santa Barbara, I saw,

The word 'homeless' is applied to so many different kinds of people, with so many different histories, that it is almost meaningless

close up, the consequences of that strange combination of proximity and distance. The council was meeting to vote on the repeal of the sleeping ordinances, though not out of any sudden sense of compassion or justice. Council members had been pressured into it by the threat of massive demonstrations—"The Selma of the Eighties" was the slogan one heard among the homeless. But this threat that frightened the council enraged the town's citizens. Hundreds of them turned out for the meeting. One by one they filed to the microphone to curse the council and castigate the homeless. Drinking, doping, loitering, panhandling, defecating, urinating, molesting, stealing—the litany went on and on, was repeated over and over, accompanied by fantasies of disaster: the barbarian hordes at the gates, civilization ended.

What astonished me about the meeting was not what was said; one could have predicted that. It was the power and depth of the emotion revealed: the mindlessness of the fear, the vengefulness of the fury. Also, almost none of what was said had anything to do with the homeless people I know—not the ones I once traveled with, not the ones in town. They, the actual homeless men and women, might not have existed at all.

If I write about Santa Barbara, it is not because I think the attitudes at work here are unique. They are not. You find them everywhere in America. In the last few months I have visited several cities around the country, and in each of them I have found the same thing: more and more people in the streets, more and more suffering. (There are at least 350,000 homeless people in the country, perhaps as many as 3 million.) And, in talking to the good citizens of these cities, I found, almost always, the same thing: confusion and ignorance, or simple indifference, but anger too, and fear.

What follows here is an attempt to explain at least some of that anger and fear, to clear up some of the confusion, to chip away at the indifference. It is not meant to be definitive; how could it be? The point is to try to illuminate some of the darker corners of homelessness, those we ordinarily ignore, and those in which the keys to much that is now going on may be hidden.

The trouble begins with the word "homeless." It has become such an abstraction, and is applied to so many different kinds of people, with so many different histories and problems, that it is almost meaningless.

Homelessness, in itself, is nothing more than a condition visited upon men and women (and, increasingly, children) as the final stage of a variety of problems about which the word "homelessness" tells us almost nothing. Or, to put it another way, it is a catch basin into which pour all of the people disenfranchised or marginalized or scared off by processes beyond their control, those which lie close to the heart of American life. Here are the groups packed into the single category of "the homeless":

☐ Veterans, mainly from the war in Vietnam. In many American cities, vets make up close to 50 percent of all homeless males.

☐ The mentally ill. In some parts of the country, roughly a quarter of the homeless would, a couple of decades ago, have been institutionalized.

☐ The physically disabled or chronically ill, who do not receive any benefits or whose benefits do not enable them to afford permanent shelter.

☐ The elderly on fixed incomes whose funds are no longer sufficient for their needs.

☐ Men, women, and whole families pauperized by the loss of a job.

☐ Single parents, usually women, without the resources or skills to establish new lives.

☐ Runaway children, many of whom have been abused.

☐ Alcoholics and those in trouble with drugs (whose troubles often begin with one of the other conditions listed here).

☐ Immigrants, both legal and illegal, who often are not counted among the homeless because they constitute a "problem" in their own right.

☐ Traditional tramps, hobos, and transients, who have taken to the road or the streets for a variety of reasons and who prefer to be there.

You can quickly learn two things about the homeless from this list. First, you can learn that many of the homeless, before they were homeless, were people more or less like ourselves: members of the working or middle class. And you can learn that the world of the homeless has its roots in various policies, events, and ways of life for which some of us are responsible and from which some of us actually prosper.

We decide, as a people, to go to war, we ask our children to kill and to die, and the result, years later, is grown men homeless on the street.

We change, with the best intentions, the laws pertaining to the mentally ill, and then, without intention, neglect to provide them with services; and the result, in our streets, drives some of us crazy with rage.

We cut taxes and prune budgets, we modernize industry and shift the balance of trade, and the result of all these actions and errors can be read, sleeping form by sleeping form, on our city streets.

The liberals cannot blame the conservatives. The conservatives cannot blame the liberals. Homelessness is the *sum total* of our dreams, policies, intentions, errors, omissions, cruelties, kindnesses, all of it recorded, in flesh, in the life of the streets.

You can also learn from this list one of the most important things there is to know about the homeless—that they can be roughly divided into two groups: those who have had homelessness forced upon them and want nothing more than to escape it; and those who have at least in part *chosen* it for themselves, and now accept, or in some cases, embrace it.

I understand how dangerous it is to introduce the idea of choice into a discussion of homelessness. It can all too easily be used to justify indifference or brutality toward the homeless, or to argue that they are only getting what they "deserve." And yet it seems to me that it is only by taking choice into account, in all of the intricacies of its various forms and expressions, that one can really understand certain kinds of homelessness.

The fact is, many of the homeless are not only hapless victims but voluntary exiles, "domestic refugees," people who have turned not against life itself but against *us*, our life, American life. Look for a moment at the vets. The price of returning to America was to forget what they had seen or learned in Vietnam, to "put it behind them." But some could not do that, and the stress of trying showed up as alcoholism, broken marriages, drug addiction, crime. And it showed up too as life on the street, which was for some vets a desperate choice made in the name of life—the best they could manage. It was a way of avoiding what might have occurred had they stayed where they were: suicide, or violence done to others.

We must learn to accept that there may indeed be people, and not only vets, who have seen so much of our world, or seen it so clearly, that to live in it becomes impossible. Here, for example, is the story of Alice, a homeless middle-aged woman in Los Angeles, where there are, perhaps, 50,000 homeless people. It was set down a few months ago by one of my students at the University of California, Santa Barbara, where I taught for a semester. I had encouraged them to go find the homeless and listen to their stories. And so, one day, when this student saw Alice foraging in a dumpster outside a McDonald's, he stopped and talked to her:

> She told me she had led a pretty normal life as she grew up and eventually went to college. From there she went on to Chicago to teach school. She was single and lived in a small apartment.
>
> One night, after she got off the train after school, a man began to follow her to her apartment building. When she got to her door she saw a knife and the man hovering behind her. She had no choice but to let him in. The man raped her.
>
> After that, things got steadily worse. She had a nervous breakdown. She went to a mental institution for three months, and when she went back to her apartment she found her belongings gone. The landlord had sold them to cover the rent she hadn't paid.
>
> She had no place to go and no job because the school had terminated her

We must learn to accept that there may be people who have seen so much of our world that to live in it becomes impossible

The homeless reduce their world to a small area, and thereby protect themselves from a world that might otherwise be too much to bear

employment. She slipped into depression. She lived with friends until she could muster enough money for a ticket to Los Angeles. She said she no longer wanted to burden her friends, and that if she had to live outside, at least Los Angeles was warmer than Chicago.

It is as if she began back then to take on the mentality of a street person. She resolved herself to homelessness. She's been out West since 1980, without a home or job. She seems happy, with her best friend being her cat. But the scars of memories still haunt her, and she is running from them, or should I say *him*.

This is, in essence, the same story one hears over and over again on the street. You begin with an ordinary life; then an event occurs—traumatic, catastrophic; smaller events follow, each one deepening the original wound; finally, homelessness becomes inevitable, or begins to *seem* inevitable to the person involved—the only way out of an intolerable situation. You are struck continually, hearing these stories, by something seemingly unique in American life, the absolute isolation involved. In what other culture would there be such an absence or failure of support from familial, social, or institutional sources? Even more disturbing is the fact that it is often our supposed sources of support—family, friends, government organizations—that have caused the problem in the first place.

Everything that happened to Alice—the rape, the loss of job and apartment, the breakdown—was part and parcel of a world gone radically wrong, a world, for Alice, no longer to be counted on, no longer worth living in. Her homelessness can be seen as flight, as failure of will or nerve, even, perhaps, as *disease*. But it can also be seen as a mute, furious refusal, a self-imposed exile far less appealing to the rest of us than ordinary life, but *better*, in Alice's terms.

We like to think, in America, that everything is redeemable, that everything broken can be magically made whole again, and that what has been "dirtied" can be cleansed. Recently I saw on television that one of the soaps had introduced the character of a homeless old woman. A woman in her thirties discovers that her long-lost mother has appeared in town, on the streets. After much searching the mother is located and identified and embraced; and then she is scrubbed and dressed in style, restored in a matter of days to her former upper-class habits and role.

A triumph—but one more likely to occur on television than in real life. Yes, many of those on the streets could be transformed, rehabilitated. But there are others whose lives have been irrevocably changed, damaged beyond repair, and who no longer want help, who no longer recognize the *need* for help, and whose experience in our world has made them want only to be left alone. How, for instance, would one restore Alice's life, or reshape it in a way that would satisfy *our* notion of what a life should be? What would it take to return her to the fold? How to erase the four years of homelessness, which have become as familiar to her, and as much a home, as her "normal" life once was? Whatever we think of the way in which she has resolved her difficulties, it constitutes a sad peace made with the world. Intruding ourselves upon it in the name of redemption is by no means as simple a task—or as justifiable a task—as one might think.

It is important to understand too that however disorderly and dirty and unmanageable the world of homeless men and women like Alice appears to us, it is not without its significance, and its rules and rituals. The homeless in our cities mark out for themselves particular neighborhoods, blocks, buildings, doorways. They impose on themselves often obsessively strict routines. They reduce their world to a small area, and thereby protect themselves from a world that might otherwise be too much to bear.

Pavlov, the Russian psychologist, once theorized that the two most fundamental reflexes in all animals, including humans, are those involving freedom and orientation. Grab any animal, he said, and it will immediately struggle to accomplish two things: to break free and to orient itself. And this is what one sees in so many of the homeless. Having been stripped of all other forms of connection, and of most kinds of social identity, they are left only with this: the raw stuff of nature, something encoded in the cells—the desire to be free, the need for familiar space. Perhaps this is why so many of them struggle so vehemently against us when we offer them aid. They are clinging to their freedom and their space, and they do not believe that this is what we, with our programs and our shelters, mean to allow them.

Years ago, when I first came to California, bumming my way west, the marginal world, and the lives of those in it, were very different from what they are now. In those days I spent much of my time in hobo jungles or on the skid rows of various cities, and just as it was easier back then to "get by" in the easygoing beach towns on the California coast, or in the bohemian and artistic worlds in San Francisco or Los Angeles or New York, it was also far easier than it is now to survive in the marginal world.

It is important to remember this—important to recognize the immensity of the changes that have occurred in the marginal world in the past twenty years. Whole sections of many cities—the Bowery in New York, the Tenderloin in San Francisco—were once ceded to the transient. In every skid-row area in America you could find what you needed to survive: hash houses, saloons offering free lunches, pawnshops, surplus-clothing stores, and, most important of all, cheap hotels and flophouses and two-bit employment agencies specializing in the kinds of labor (seasonal, shape-up) transients have always done.

It was by no means a wonderful world. But it *was* a world. Its rituals were spelled out in ways most of the participants understood. In hobo jungles up and down the tracks, whatever there was to eat went into a common pot and was divided equally. Late at night, in empties crisscrossing the country, men would speak with a certain anonymous openness, as if the shared condition of transience created among them a kind of civility.

What most people in that world wanted was simply to be left alone. Some of them had been on the road for years, itinerant workers. Others were recuperating from wounds they could never quite explain. There were young men and a few women with nothing better to do, and older men who had no families or had lost their jobs or wives, or for whom the rigor and pressure of life had proved too demanding. The marginal world offered them a respite from the other world, a world grown too much for them.

But things have changed. There began to pour into the marginal world—slowly in the sixties, a bit faster in the seventies, and then faster still in the eighties—more and more people who neither belonged nor knew how to survive there. The sixties brought the counterculture and drugs; the streets filled with young dropouts. Changes in the law loosed upon the streets mentally ill men and women. Inflation took its toll, then recession. Working-class and even middle-class men and women—entire families—began to fall into a world they did not understand.

At the same time the transient world was being inundated by new inhabitants, its landscape, its economy, was shrinking radically. Jobs became harder to find. Modernization had something to do with it; machines took the place of men and women. And the influx of workers from Mexico and points farther south created a class of semipermanent workers who took the place of casual transient labor. More important, perhaps, was the fact that the forgotten parts of many cities began to attract attention. Downtown areas were redeveloped, reclaimed. The skid-row sections of smaller cities were turned into "old townes." The old hotels that once catered to transients were upgraded or torn down or became warehouses for welfare families—an arrangement far more profitable to the owners. The price of housing increased; evictions increased. The mentally ill, who once could afford to house themselves in cheap rooms, the alcoholics, who once would drink themselves to sleep at night in their cheap hotels, were out on the street—exposed to the weather and to danger, and also in plain and public view: "problems" to be dealt with.

The old hotels that once catered to transients have been upgraded or torn down. Jobs become harder to find

Our response to the homeless is fed by a complex set of cultural attitudes, habits of thought, and fantasies and fears

Nor was it only cheap shelter that disappeared. It was also those "open" spaces that had once been available to those without other shelter. As property rose in value, the nooks and crannies in which the homeless had been able to hide became more visible. Doorways, alleys, abandoned buildings, vacant lots—these "holes" in the cityscape, these gaps in public consciousness, became *real estate*. The homeless, who had been there all the time, were overtaken by economic progress, and they became intruders.

You cannot help thinking, as you watch this process, of what happened in parts of Europe in the eighteenth and nineteenth centuries: the effects of the enclosure laws, which eliminated the "commons" in the countryside and drove the rural poor, now homeless, into the cities. The centuries-old tradition of common access and usage was swept away by the beginnings of industrialism; land became *privatized*, a commodity. At the same time something occurred in the cultural psyche. The world itself, space itself, was subtly altered. It was no longer merely to be lived in; it was now to be owned. What was enclosed was not only the land. It was also *the flesh itself*; it was cut off from, denied access to, the physical world.

And one thinks too, when thinking of the homeless, of the American past, the settlement of the "new" world which occurred at precisely the same time that the commons disappeared. The dream of freedom and equality that brought men and women here had something to do with *space*, as if the wilderness itself conferred upon those arriving here a new beginning: the Eden that had been lost. Once God had sent Christ to redeem men; now he provided a new world. Men discovered, or believed, that this world, and perhaps time itself, had no edge, no limit. Space was a sign of God's magnanimity. It was a kind of grace.

Somehow, it is all this that is folded into the sad shapes of the homeless. In their mute presence one can sense, however faintly, the dreams of a world gone aglimmering, and the presence of our failed hopes. A kind of claim is made, silently, an ethic is proffered, or, if you will, a whole cosmology, one older than our own ideas of privilege and property. It is as if flesh itself were seeking, this one last time, the home in the world it has been denied.

Daily the city eddies around the homeless. The crowds flowing past leave a few feet, a gap. We do not touch the homeless world. Perhaps we cannot touch it. It remains separate even as the city surrounds it.

The homeless, simply because they are homeless, are strangers, alien—and therefore a threat. Their presence, in itself, comes to constitute a kind of violence; it deprives us of our sense of safety. Let me use myself as an example. I know, and respect, many of those now homeless on the streets of Santa Barbara. Twenty years ago, some of them would have been my companions and friends. And yet, these days, if I walk through the park near my home and see strangers bedding down for the night, my first reaction, if not fear, is a sense of annoyance and intrusion, of worry and alarm. I think of my teenage daughter, who often walks through the park, and then of my house, a hundred yards away, and I am tempted—only tempted, but tempted, still—to call the "proper" authorities to have the strangers moved on. Out of sight, out of mind.

Notice: I do not bring them food. I do not offer them shelter or a shower in the morning. I do not even stop to talk. Instead, I think: my daughter, my house, my privacy. What moves me is not the threat of *danger*—nothing as animal as that. Instead there pops up inside of me, neatly in a row, a set of anxieties, ones you might arrange in a dollhouse living room and label: Family of bourgeois fears. The point is this: our response to the homeless is fed by a complex set of cultural attitudes, habits of thought, and fantasies and fears so familiar to us, so common, that they have become a *second* nature and might as well be instinctive, for all the control we have over them. And it is by no means easy to untangle this snarl of responses. What does seem clear is that the homeless embody all that bourgeois cul-

Order, ordure—this is, in essence, the tension at the heart of bourgeois culture

ture has for centuries tried to eradicate and destroy.

If you look to the history of Europe you find that homelessness first appears (or is first acknowledged) at the very same moment that bourgeois culture begins to appear. The same processes produced them both: the breakup of feudalism, the rise of commerce and cities, the combined triumphs of capitalism, industrialism, and individualism. The historian Fernand Braudel, in *The Wheels of Commerce*, describes, for instance, the armies of impoverished men and women who began to haunt Europe as far back as the eleventh century. And the makeup of these masses? Essentially the same then as it is now: the unfortunates, the throwaways, the misfits, the deviants.

> In the eighteenth century, all sorts and conditions were to be found in this human dross . . . widows, orphans, cripples. . . journeymen who had broken their contracts, out-of-work labourers, homeless priests with no living, old men, fire victims . . . war victims, deserters, discharged soldiers, would-be vendors of useless articles, vagrant preachers with or without licenses, "pregnant servant-girls and unmarried mothers driven from home," children sent out "to find bread or to maraud."

Then, as now, distinctions were made between the "homeless" and the supposedly "deserving" poor, those who knew their place and willingly sustained, with their labors, the emergent bourgeois world.

> The good paupers were accepted, lined up and registered on the official list; they had a right to public charity and were sometimes allowed to solicit it outside churches in prosperous districts, when the congregation came out, or in market places. . . .
>
> When it comes to beggars and vagrants, it is a very different story, and different pictures meet the eye: crowds, mobs, processions, sometimes mass emigrations, "along the country highways or the streets of the Towns and Villages," by beggars "whom hunger and nakedness has driven from home." . . . The towns dreaded these alarming visitors and drove them out as soon as they appeared on the horizon.

And just as the distinctions made about these masses were the same then as they are now, so too was the way society saw them. They seemed to bourgeois eyes (as they still do) the one segment of society that remained resistant to progress, unassimilable and incorrigible, inimical to all order.

It is in the nineteenth century, in the Victorian era, that you can find the beginnings of our modern strategies for dealing with the homeless: the notion that they should be controlled and perhaps eliminated through "help." With the Victorians we begin to see the entangling of self-protection with social obligation, the strategy of masking self-interest and the urge to control as *moral duty*. Michel Foucault has spelled this out in his books on madness and punishment: the zeal with which the overseers of early bourgeois culture tried to purge, improve, and purify all of urban civilization—whether through schools and prisons, or, quite literally, with public baths and massive new water and sewage systems. Order, ordure—this is, in essence, the tension at the heart of bourgeois culture, and it was the singular genius of the Victorians to make it the main component of their medical, aesthetic, *and* moral systems. It was not a sense of justice or even empathy which called for charity or new attitudes toward the poor; it was *hygiene*. The very same attitudes appear in nineteenth-century America. Charles Loring Brace, in an essay on homeless and vagrant children written in 1876, described the treatment of delinquents in this way: "Many of their vices drop from them like the old and verminous clothing they left behind. . . . The entire change of circumstances seems to cleanse them of bad habits." Here you have it all: *vices, verminous clothing, cleansing them of bad habits*—the triple association of poverty with vice with dirt, an equation in which each term comes to stand for all of them.

These attitudes are with us still; that is the point. In our own century the person who has written most revealingly about such things is George Orwell, who tried to analyze his own middle-class attitudes toward the poor. In 1933, in *Down and Out in Paris and London*, he wrote about tramps:

> In childhood we are taught that tramps are blackguards . . . a repulsive, rather dangerous creature, who would rather die than work or wash, and wants nothing but to beg, drink or rob hen-houses. The tramp monster is no truer to life than the sinister Chinaman of the magazines, but he is very hard to get rid of. The very word "tramp" evokes his image.

All of this is still true in America, though now it is not the word "tramp" but the word "homeless" that evokes the images we fear. It is the homeless who smell. Here, for instance, is part of a paper a student of mine wrote about her first visit to a Rescue Mission on skid row.

> The sermon began. The room was stuffy and smelly. The mixture of body odors and cooking was nauseating. I remember thinking: how can these people share this facility? They must be repulsed by each other. They had strange habits and dispositions. They were a group of dirty, dishonored, weird people to me.
>
> When it was over I ran to my car, went home, and took a shower. I felt extremely dirty. Through the day I would get flashes of that disgusting smell.

To put it as bluntly as I can, for many of us the homeless are *shit*. And our policies toward them, our spontaneous sense of disgust and horror, our wish to be rid of them—all of this has hidden in it, close to its heart, our feelings about excrement. Even Marx, that most bourgeois of revolutionaries, described the deviant *lumpen* in *The Eighteenth Brumaire of Louis Bonaparte* as "scum, offal, refuse of all classes." These days, in puritanical Marxist nations, they are called "parasites"—a word, perhaps not incidentally, one also associates with human waste.

What I am getting at here is the *nature* of the desire to help the homeless—what is hidden behind it and why it so often does harm. Every government program, almost every private project, is geared as much to the needs of those giving help as it is to the needs of the homeless. Go to any government agency, or, for that matter, to most private charities, and you will find yourself enmeshed, at once, in a bureaucracy so tangled and oppressive, or confronted with so much moral arrogance and contempt, that you will be driven back out into the streets for relief.

Santa Barbara, where I live, is as good an example as any. There are three main shelters in the city—all of them private. Between them they provide fewer than a hundred beds a night for the homeless. Two of the three shelters are religious in nature: the Rescue Mission and the Salvation Army. In the mission, as in most places in the country, there are elaborate and stringent rules. Beds go first to those who have not been there for two months, and you can stay for only two nights in any two-month period. No shelter is given to those who are not sober. Even if you go to the mission only for a meal, you are required to listen to sermons and participate in prayer, and you are regularly proselytized—sometimes overtly, sometimes subtly. There are obligatory, regimented showers. You go to bed precisely at ten: lights out, no reading, no talking. After the lights go out you will find fifteen men in a room with double-decker bunks. As the night progresses the room grows stuffier and hotter. Men toss, turn, cough, and moan. In the morning you are awakened precisely at five forty-five. Then breakfast. At seven-thirty you are back on the street.

The town's newest shelter was opened almost a year ago by a consortium of local churches. Families and those who are employed have first call on the beds—a policy which excludes the congenitally homeless. Alcohol is not simply forbidden *in* the shelter; those with a history of alcoholism must sign a "contract" pledging to remain sober and chemical-free. Finally, in a paroxysm of therapeutic bullying, the shelter has added a new wrinkle: if you stay more than two days you are required to fill out and then discuss with a social worker a complex form listing what you perceive as your personal failings, goals, and strategies—all of this for men and women who simply want a place to lie down out of the rain!

Every government program is geared as much to the needs of those giving help as it is to the needs of the homeless

5. SOCIAL INEQUALITIES: The Rich and Poor

A society owes its members whatever it takes for them to regain their places in the social order

It is these attitudes, in various forms and permutations, that you find repeated endlessly in America. We are moved either to "redeem" the homeless or to punish them. Perhaps there is nothing consciously hostile about it. Perhaps it is simply that as the machinery of bureaucracy cranks itself up to deal with these problems, attitudes assert themselves automatically. But whatever the case, the fact remains that almost every one of our strategies for helping the homeless is simply an attempt to rearrange the world *cosmetically*, in terms of how it looks and smells to *us*. Compassion is little more than the passion for control.

The central question emerging from all this is, What does a society owe to its members in trouble, and *how* is that debt to be paid? It is a question which must be answered in two parts: first, in relation to the men and women who have been marginalized against their will, and then, in a slightly different way, in relation to those who have chosen (or accept or even prize) their marginality.

As for those who have been marginalized against their wills, I think the general answer is obvious: A society owes its members whatever it takes for them to regain their places in the social order. And when it comes to specific remedies, one need only read backward the various processes which have created homelessness and then figure out where help is likely to do the most good. But the real point here is not the specific remedies required—affordable housing, say—but the basis upon which they must be offered, the necessary underlying ethical notion we seem in this nation unable to grasp: that those who are the inevitable casualties of modern industrial capitalism and the free-market system are entitled, *by right*, and by the simple virtue of their participation in that system, to whatever help they need. They are entitled to help to find and hold their places in the society whose social contract they have, in effect, signed and observed.

Look at that for just a moment: the notion of a contract. The majority of homeless Americans have kept, insofar as they could, to the terms of that contract. In any shelter these days you can find men and women who have worked ten, twenty, forty years, and whose lives have nonetheless come to nothing. These are people who cannot afford a place in the world they helped create. And in return? Is it life on the street they have earned? Or the cruel charity we so grudgingly grant them?

But those marginalized against their will are only half the problem. There remains, still, the question of whether we owe anything to those who are voluntarily marginal. What about them: the street people, the rebels, and the recalcitrants, those who have torn up their social contracts or returned them unsigned?

I was in Las Vegas last fall, and I went out to the Rescue Mission at the lower end of town, on the edge of the black ghetto, where I first stayed years ago on my way west. It was twilight, still hot; in the vacant lot next-door to the mission 200 men were lining up for supper. A warm wind blew along the street lined with small houses and salvage yards, and in the distance I could see the desert's edge and the smudge of low hills in the fading light. There were elderly alcoholics in line, and derelicts, but mainly the men were the same sort I had seen here years ago: youngish, out of work, restless and talkative, the drifters and wanderers for whom the word "wanderlust" was invented.

At supper—long communal tables, thin gruel, stale sweet rolls, ice water—a huge black man in his twenties, fierce and muscular, sat across from me. "I'm from the Coast, man," he said. "Never been away from home before. Ain't sure I like it. Sure don't like *this* place. But I lost my job back home a couple of weeks ago and figured, why wait around for another. I thought I'd come out here, see me something of the world."

After supper, a squat Portuguese man in his mid-thirties, hunkered down against the mission wall, offered me a smoke and told me: "Been sleeping in my car, up the street, for a week. Had my own business back in Omaha. But

I got bored, man. Sold everything, got a little dough, came out here. Thought I'd work construction. Let me tell you, this is one tough town."

In a world better than ours, I suppose, men (or women) like this might not exist. Conservatives seem to have no trouble imagining a society so well disciplined and moral that deviance of this kind would disappear. And leftists envision a world so just, so generous, that deviance would vanish along with inequity. But I suspect that there will always be something at work in some men and women to make them restless with the systems others devise for them, and to move them outward toward the edges of the world, where life is always riskier, less organized, and easier going.

Do we owe anything to these men and women, who reject our company and what we offer and yet nonetheless seem to demand *something* from us?

We owe them, I think, at least a place to exist, a way to exist. That may not be a *moral* obligation, in the sense that our obligation to the involuntarily marginal is clearly a moral one, but it is an obligation nevertheless, one you might call an existential obligation.

Of course, it may be that I think we owe these men something because I have liked men like them, and because I want their world to be there always, as a place to hide or rest. But there is more to it than that. I think we as a society need men like these. A society needs its margins as much as it needs art and literature. It needs holes and gaps, *breathing spaces*, let us say, into which men and women can escape and live, when necessary, in ways otherwise denied them. Margins guarantee to society a flexibility, an elasticity, and allow it to accommodate itself to the natures and needs of its members. When margins vanish, society becomes too rigid, too oppressive by far, and therefore inimical to life.

It is for such reasons that, in cultures like our own, marginal men and women take on a special significance. They are all we have left to remind us of the narrowness of the received truths we take for granted. "Beyond the pale," they somehow redefine the pale, or remind us, at least, that *something* is still out there, beyond the pale. They preserve, perhaps unconsciously, a dream that would otherwise cease to exist, the dream of having a place in the world, and of being *left alone*.

Quixotic? Infantile? Perhaps. But remember Pavlov and his reflexes coded in the flesh: animal, and therefore as if given by God. What we are talking about here is *freedom*, and with it, perhaps, an echo of the dream men brought, long ago, to wilderness America. I use the word "freedom" gingerly, in relation to lives like these: skewed, crippled, emptied of everything we associate with a full, or realized, freedom. But perhaps this is the condition into which freedom has fallen among us. Art has been "appreciated" out of existence; literature has become an extension of the university, replete with tenure and pensions; and as for politics, the ideologies which ring us round seem too silly or shrill by far to speak for life. What is left, then, is this mute and intransigent independence, this "waste" of life which refuses even interpretation, and which cannot be assimilated to any ideology, and which therefore can be put to no one's use. In its crippled innocence and the perfection of its superfluity it amounts, almost, to a rebellion against history, and that is no small thing.

Let me put it as simply as I can: what we see on the streets of our cities are two dramas, both of which cut to the troubled heart of the culture and demand from us a response we may not be able to make. There is the drama of those struggling to survive by regaining their place in the social order. And there is the drama of those struggling to survive outside of it.

The resolution of both struggles depends on a third drama occurring at the heart of the culture: the tension and contention between the magnanimity we owe to life and the darker tendings of the human psyche: our fear of strangeness, our hatred of deviance, our love of order and control. How we mediate by default or design between those contrary forces will determine not only the destinies of the homeless but also something crucial about the nation, and perhaps—let me say it—about our own souls.

A society needs its margins, its holes and gaps, into which men and women can escape and live, when necessary

What About America's Underclass?

Integrating a growing underclass into the mainstream will be a major challenge of the '90s. We have to bolster families, put people into jobs, and break the intergenerational cycle of poverty through education.

ISABEL V. SAWHILL

Isabel V. Sawhill is a senior fellow of The Urban Institute and codirector of the Changing Domestic Priorities project there.

Poverty has been surprisingly persistent in the United States. Despite considerable efforts to reduce it, the incidence of poverty in 1986 was as high as it had been in the late 1960s. It was also higher than the rate in most other industrial countries for which comparable data are available. This much poverty in one of the world's wealthiest democracies invites notice.

Not only has poverty not declined significantly over the past twenty years, but the composition of the poverty population has shifted toward groups about whom the public feels ambivalent—if not downright disapproving. When the typical poor person was an elderly widow, rather than an unwed mother, it was easier for society to act compassionately, and providing income seemed the obvious solution. Now, with the perception that a rising proportion of the poor are concentrated in inner-city areas where crime, teenage pregnancies, and welfare dependency are common, there is talk of a growing underclass in American society. New data presented here confirm that it is indeed growing rapidly.

The next generation of antipoverty policies is likely to be strongly influenced by this development. Whereas the older War on Poverty relied heavily (if unintentionally) on providing income to the poor and succeeded in substantially reducing poverty among groups

such as the elderly and disabled, it did little to stem the growth of chronic poverty among the able-bodied, nonelderly population or to prevent the spread of antisocial behavior within this group. The major challenge for the next decade will be to integrate this growing underclass back into the mainstream by strengthening family responsibilities, putting people to work, and breaking the intergenerational cycle of poverty through education. What will be the shape of these new, nonwelfare strategies—and to what extent are they likely to succeed?

Profile of the poor

The 32 million poor people in the United States are a diverse group. One way to characterize the poverty population is to divide it into five mutually exclusive groups according to the major reason for the low income of the head of the household in which these people live (as reported to the census):

• The elderly and disabled, a set of people who are not generally able to work and for whom direct income assistance is probably the most appropriate form of aid.

From *Challenge*, May/June 1988, pp. 27-36. This article was excerpted from the chapter on "Poverty and the Underclass" in *Challenge to Leadership: Economic and Social Issues for the Next Decade* (The Urban Institute Press, Washington, D.C., 1988).

• Single parents, most of them women, whose child-care responsibilities make it difficult for them to work, especially full-time.

• The "underemployed poor," those who report that they are poor because they are unemployed or unable to find sufficient work.

• The "hardworking poor," those who work all year at a full-time job but still do not earn enough to escape from poverty.

• A residual that includes students, early retirees, and homemakers (without minor children). Because all the members of this last group are able-bodied and do not report having any difficulty finding work, it seems likely that they are only temporarily poor or that they represent statistical anomalies.

As indicated in Figure 1 on page 176, among the total poverty population, approximately one in three persons lives in a household headed by someone who is elderly or disabled. One in five lives in a household headed by a single parent; one in six, by someone who is underemployed; one in eight, by a low-wage, full-time worker; and one in six by someone in the residual category. Ironically, the homeless are not even counted among the "official" poor, because the Census Bureau surveys households only.

Ideally, it would be helpful to know, in addition to why people are poor, how long they remain poor. Not all the people who report themselves as poor to the census have chronically low incomes. Indeed, considerable turnover is evident within the poverty population. Many people suffer temporary drops in income because of the loss of a job, a divorce, or a period of illness, and then later regain their previous standard of living. As a result, only about one-half of the census poor who are not elderly are likely to remain poor for eight years or more.

Still a third way to characterize the poor is by where they live. A little over half live in a big city, where they tend to be concentrated in downtown rather than suburban areas. Very few live in what might be called urban slums. In 1980, 7 percent lived in big-city neighborhoods where the poverty rate was 40 percent or higher.

In sum, the poverty population—defined by annual income alone—is large and diverse. About one-third are elderly and disabled. Another one-third are likely to remain poor only temporarily. The remaining one-third might be called the ' 'core' poor—those working-age, able-bodied family heads and their dependents who have chronically low incomes. If there is an underclass in this country, it is drawn from this third group.

Is there an underclass?

Recent journalistic accounts paint a picture that leaves little doubt that an underclass exists. This picture includes young men who father children with little or no expectation of supporting them. It includes unmarried women on welfare, raising children at taxpayers' expense and passing a life of poverty on to the next generation. It includes men who spurn regular work in favor of more lucrative but less legitimate or conventional means of earning a living, and alienated teenagers who drop out of school and remain semiliterate into their adult years. Whatever its contents, the picture is usually framed by a depressed urban landscape, and most of the faces are black.

Research confirms that there is an urban underclass in the United States and that it is growing. Estimates of the size of the underclass vary with the definition chosen to describe it. Some researchers have equated the underclass with the able-bodied, persistently poor, a group estimated to number around eight million people in the mid–1980s. Others have defined the underclass as people living in areas of concentrated poverty, a definition that yields considerably lower estimates. For example, in 1980, 2.4 million poor people lived in neighborhoods where the poverty rate was above 40 percent.

Recent work at The Urban Institute has taken still another approach, focusing on behavior rather than income as the distinguishing characteristic of the underclass. In this work, the underclass is defined as people who live in neighborhoods where welfare dependency, female-headed families, male joblessness, and dropping out of high school are all common occurrences. Although not all the people in these neighborhoods are poor (in part, because some obtain income illegally and in part because many are employed, albeit erratically), given the environment in which they live, they are all at risk of being dragged into the underclass.

The size of this "at risk" group was 2.5 million people in 1980, of which 1.1 million also had poverty-level incomes. The group is disproportionately concentrated in large northeastern or midwestern cities such as New York or Chicago. A majority of the residents of these neighborhoods are black or Hispanic, and more than three-fifths of the adults have less than a high school education. In addition, the majority of men in these communities are not regularly employed, three-fifths of the households are headed by women, and about a third of the households are dependent on public assistance (Table 1). Although the problems in these neighborhoods are serious, the proportion of the total poverty population living in such areas is only 4

Table 1   **Estimated Size and Composition**
of the Underclass, 1980

Characteristic	Living in:	
	Underclass areas	United States
Total population	2,483,676	226,545,805
Total poverty population	1,065,952	26,072,000
Percentage[a] of total population that is		
Urban	99%	77%
In Northeast	36	25
In North Central	27	24
In South	26	30
In West	11	21
White	28	82
Black	59	12
Hispanic	20	03
Children (under age 19)	34	30
Adult with less than a high school education	63	31
Families headed by women, with children	60	19
High school dropouts, ages 16 to 19	36	13
Adult men not regularly employed	56	31
Families with public assistance income	34	08
Ratio of women to men	1.2:1	1.05:1

Source: Urban Institute analysis of the 1980 census.

a. Percentages are from unpublished data and do not include untracted areas in either the numerator or denominator.

percent (1.1 million divided by a total of 26.1 million poor in 1980). And although 59 percent of the underclass is black, according to these estimates, stereotypes that imply that being black and being a member of the underclass are synonymous are clearly misleading. Less than 6 percent of the black population and less than one-fifth of the black poverty population live in such areas.

The substantial attention paid to the underclass, despite its small size, undoubtedly reflects the serious social consequences that most people attach to its existence and possible continued growth. Such growth is disturbing and raises compelling questions about the dynamics of the process. It may be that some inner-city areas become so devoid of stable families, well-functioning schools, and employed adults that they make "escape" into the middle class extremely difficult and thereby become breeding grounds for another generation of poor people with little hope of becoming part of the mainstream.

The limited evidence that exists suggests that this group, though small, is growing quite rapidly. Between 1970 and 1980, although the overall poverty population grew by 8 percent, the number of people

living in underclass areas grew from 752,000 to 2,484,000—230 percent—according to Urban Institute estimates. Although neighborhood-level data are available only from the decennial censuses, making it difficult to know what has happened since 1980, a good guess is that this group has continued to expand.

Broadly defined then, the underclass is the approximately eight million people living in households headed by able-bodied, chronically poor adults. More narrowly defined, it is the two to three million people living in neighborhoods where mainstream behavior patterns and lifestyles have all but disappeared. Any definition, like the definition of poverty itself, is inherently arbitrary, and it is perhaps best to think in terms of a continuum of disadvantages linked to income, behavior, and neighborhood environment.

Priorities for the next decade

The nation's top priority should be to stem the growth of chronic poverty and the underclass. The costs of allowing the underclass to grow unchecked include more crime, greater welfare dependency, and lower productivity among the working-age population. Children growing up in chronically poor families, and especially those living in troubled neighborhoods, may—in the absence of intervention—be doomed to repeat their parents' lives. And the emergence of such a permanent underclass damages the social fabric. That damage is compounded when a majority of this population consists of minorities who are not being effectively integrated into the larger society.

The objective of moving this group of chronically poor, able-bodied adults toward self-sufficiency will not be easy to achieve but is probably best advanced through policies that strengthen parents' responsibility for their children, encourage work, and improve education.

Re-establishing parents' responsibility

The incidence of poverty among female-headed families with children has always been very high. Roughly half of them are poor, and this statistic has changed little over the past half-century. However, 50 years ago there were far fewer such women, many more of them were widows, and they were generally not expected to work. Under the circumstances, public support for poor women and their children was neither very expensive nor particularly controversial.

Today, in contrast, as the result of higher divorce rates and more out-of-wedlock childbearing, more than one in every five children lives in a female-headed family, up from one in ten in 1960. In nine out of ten cases, these children have a living, if absent, father who can be presumed capable of providing some support to his children. Moreover, virtually all the parents of these children came of age during a period when effective contraception was widely available and most middle-class couples were limiting the size of their families as one means of maintaining their standard of living. Finally, employment has become commonplace for women.

Less early widowhood, more control over family size, and more employment opportunities for women might have been expected to reduce the dependency of children on government assistance. Yet the proportion of all children under age 18 dependent on AFDC rose from around 3 percent in 1960 to approximately 11 percent in 1985. These developments have produced a new interest in re-establishing the primacy of parental financial responsibility for children.

This overall objective can be furthered in three ways: 1) by discouraging childbearing among people not yet prepared to take on this responsibility (usually teenagers); 2) by requiring that absent parents (usually fathers) contribute to the support of children already born; and 3) by requiring or encouraging welfare mothers to work.

As indicated in Table 2, these three factors together are potentially responsible for most of the poverty among female-headed families with children. Thirty-seven percent of these mothers had their first child as a teenager, 79 percent are receiving no assistance from the child's father, and 34 percent are not themselves contributing to the financial support of the family. The proportion of female-headed families who have poverty-level incomes despite the facts that they delayed childbearing and that both parents contribute something to the support of their children is only 10 percent.

Preventing Early Childbearing. Teenage pregnancy rates have increased about 20 percent since 1972 in the United States—the only developed country to have experienced such a rise. The rate of births to teenagers has actually fallen somewhat over this same period, because a rising proportion of all adolescent pregnancies (almost half in recent years) are terminated by abortion. Research has shown that the life chances of teenage mothers and their children are severely limited; that about two-thirds of them spend some time on welfare; that they are responsible for at least half of total AFDC expenditures; and that they cost the nation an estimated $17 billion a year in welfare, food stamps, and Medicaid benefits.

Table 2 — **Poor Female-Headed Families, by Reasons for Their Low Incomes, 1986**

Category	Number	Percentage
Total, poor female-headed families	2,039,171	100.0
Mother bore first child as a teenager	754,276	37.0
Father does not provide support	1,608,574	78.9
Mother is not employed	689,700	33.8
All three problems[a]	182,172	8.9
None of above problems[b]	198,449	9.7

Source: Urban Institute tabulations from the March 1987 Current Population Survey.

a. Poor female-headed families in which the mother bore children as a teenager, the father does not pay child support, and the mother does not work.
b. Poor female-headed families in which the mother delayed childbearing, the mother is employed, and the father pays child support.

Solutions to this problem remain elusive in part because of deeply held views on such questions as sexuality, family planning, and abortion—and in part because we do not know much about the motivations of teenagers or ways to affect them. However, research on adolescent pregnancy and childbearing indicates some areas that could be addressed in formulating more effective policies:

• Sex education has been found to be associated with lower pregnancy rates. Although sex education courses are widely available in large city schools, most districts do not introduce the most relevant or essential information early enough (i.e., before the ninth grade).

• The availability of family-planning services in a community is associated with lower teenage birthrates. A promising, though controversial, new approach is school-based health clinics that provide both information and access to contraceptives.

• Providing family-planning services to teenagers who are already mothers may help to prevent second or third births (the evidence is mixed).

• The potential role of the media in affecting the attitudes and contraceptive behavior of teenagers has not been exploited. Teenagers watch approximately 24 hours of TV each week and listen to the radio 18 hours a week.

• The availability of abortion is currently preventing about 675,000 first births among unmarried women each year in the United States. If access to legal abortion were restricted by, say, a constitutional amendment, some of these women would undoubtedly take greater precautions to avoid pregnancy and some would marry the child's father or put the baby up for adoption. But the available evidence suggests that the majority would simply resort to illegal abortions and that a significant minority—probably the most disadvantaged— would become unwed mothers. One estimate puts the additional growth in such families that would be occasioned by a constitutional amendment at roughly 80,000 a year. Because the number of female-headed families with children has been growing, on average, at a rate of 113,000 a year since 1980, a restriction on legal abortion would mean an estimated 70 percent increase in the number of such families being formed each year.

Collecting Child Support. Teenage pregnancy is only one of the reasons for the high incidence of poverty among single-parent families. Another important reason is that the children in such families are receiving inadequate levels of support from their fathers. As we have seen in Table 2, four-fifths of poor mothers heading families from which the father is absent receive no help from their children's fathers. Although it is often assumed that absent parents either cannot afford to support their children or cannot be identified or located, what information is available (and it is inadequate) suggests that these may be false assumptions. Specifically:

• Divorced and separated fathers do not appear to have lower incomes than other men.

• Several studies of the fathers of AFDC children show that they have average incomes of between $13,986 and $18,143 (1986 dollars).

• A survey of a matched sample of 203 custodial and noncustodial parents in Florida and Ohio found that the median income of the noncustodial parents was $13,394, whereas the median income of the custodial parents was $7,411 (1986 dollars). The incidence of poverty was 31 percent among the noncustodial parents and 57 percent among the custodial parents.

• Although many young men father a child when they are still in school or unemployed, this does not mean that they will have no income to contribute to their children for 18 years. Furthermore, in cases where the age of the father is known, 70 percent of the babies born to teenage mothers were fathered by men over the age of 20. Men of all ages may take a greater interest in pregnancy prevention if they know there are future financial consequences.

• About one-fifth of all women eligible to receive child support have never been married, and this group is growing far more rapidly than the ever-married group. These women are much less likely to receive child support than ever-married women, in part because the establishment of paternity in the case of out-of-wedlock births has not been vigorously pursued. In 1981 only about one-quarter of women who gave birth out of wedlock had paternity adjudicated. The technical means to do so exists, and other countries have far better records. In Sweden, for example, paternity is established in more than 90 percent of cases. The best approach appears to be through the health care system—that is, securing voluntary acknowledgment of paternity at the time of birth.

• In a pretest of a national survey of absent parents, researchers at The Urban Institute and the National Opinion Research Center were able to locate 84 percent of all absent parents, a far higher proportion than had been anticipated.

Numerous recent studies show that if child support awards were more prevalent, more generous, or better enforced, poverty and welfare costs could be substantially reduced. For example, it is estimated that the kind of child support system now being tested in Wisconsin could reduce the amount of poverty among female-headed families with children by about 40 percent and AFDC caseloads by nearly 50 percent, with savings to the governments of over $2 billion a year. Although these estimates are probably too optimistic, because they assume 100 percent compliance with the relatively generous Wisconsin standard, they underscore the potential of this strategy and suggest that it is particularly important to review current and proposed policies in this area.

The 1984 Child Support Enforcement Amendments were an important step in the right direction. Under this law, states are required to withhold child support payments from an absent parent's wages after one month of delinquency, are encouraged to establish statewide child support standards, and are given financial incentives to collect support on behalf of non-AFDC as well as AFDC mothers. Because the law has been in effect only since late 1985, it is too early to tell what effects it will have. However, the Census Bureau estimates that only $7 billion out of the $10 billion of child support currently due is being collected, and a number of studies indicate that tougher enforcement at the state level increases the amount collected.

Although better enforcement of existing awards is important, the potentially most significant feature of the 1984 law is the encouragement provided to the states to establish more adequate child support standards. Some research suggests that it is higher standards, rather than better enforcement alone, that are most likely to reduce poverty and welfare dependency.

Expecting Welfare Mothers to Work. According to the new social contract, it is not only fathers that should be asked to help support their children but mothers as well. Now that 67 percent of all mothers in the United States are employed, almost half of them year-round and full-time, the right of poor mothers to stay home with their children at taxpayers' expense is being questioned. Somewhat surprisingly, a similarly high proportion of poor women are employed, although fewer work full-time. Only one-third are not employed at all. However, a large proportion (64 percent) of these nonemployed mothers are dependent on public assistance.

Studies of welfare recipients suggest that they want to work, but they apparently need more encouragement and assistance in preparing for and finding jobs as well as help with child care. Where such assistance has been provided, as in some earlier federal jobs programs and in many of the programs initiated by the states since 1981, the results have been somewhat encouraging.

In evaluating employment programs for welfare recipients in San Diego, Baltimore, Arkansas, Virginia, and West Virginia recently, the Manpower Demonstration Research Corporation found that these programs increase the employment and earnings of participants and reduce welfare costs for taxpayers. Employment rates for participants in the programs were three to six percentage points higher than for other welfare recipients, and the proportion of participants receiving any AFDC declined by one to five percentage points. Thus, the effects, although positive, are generally small. Extrapolating to the nation as a whole, at best, employment rates among women on welfare might increase from 52 to 58 percent, and the proportion of poor female-headed households dependent on welfare might decline from 46 to 41 percent.

It is not yet clear what mix of program services or work requirements best achieves these results. However, job search assistance and training probably need to be part of the package. Workfare alone (that is, requiring people to perform unpaid work in entry-level clerical, maintenance, and human service jobs in the community in return for their welfare benefits) may not be sufficient. Workfare does provide useful public services. In West Virginia, the productivity of workfare participants was judged to be higher, on average, than that of regular workers doing the same jobs, and the state was able to provide some public services that it otherwise could not have afforded. Moreover, working for one's benefits may be deemed an appropriate obligation by taxpayers and welfare recipients alike. Surveys of workfare participants indicate that the great majority of them consider a work requirement fair. However, at present, there is no evidence that workfare discourages people from applying for wel-

fare or helps them to move toward greater self-sufficiency.

Assuming job search assistance, training, education, child care, and other services are required to move welfare recipients into regular jobs, an up-front investment will be needed to accomplish this goal. The hope is that over the longer run these investments will more than pay for themselves by reducing welfare and related public assistance costs and increasing revenues as more people are productively employed. In the five demonstration programs mentioned earlier, the costs of the up-front investment varied from $200 to $1,000 per participant. Thus, a program that attempted to serve all welfare mothers with no children under six could cost between $78 million and $388 million per year. The evaluations of the demonstration programs suggest that such an investment would pay for itself within five years. However, these estimates are based on a variety of assumptions about the extent to which any earnings and employment gains persist into the future and the extent to which welfare recipients displace other workers in the job market, thereby decreasing the latter's net contribution to public revenues.

A program that failed to pay for itself in narrow fiscal terms would not necessarily be a bad investment for society as a whole. To the extent that more people were productively employed, that they felt better about themselves, and that their children were not harmed in the process, it would have been a worthwhile effort.

Encouraging work:
the broader challenge

The recent interest in substituting work for welfare among single parents is understandable given the drain of AFDC outlays on public treasuries, the persistence of poverty among this group, and the evidence that they can be helped by work-related programs. In other respects, however, the emphasis may be misplaced. First, nonemployed women on welfare represent only 15 percent of all those working-age, able-bodied household heads who are poor because they are not working enough. Targeting exclusively on welfare recipients may put them in competition with other poor people for existing jobs, leading to a reshuffling of the poverty population that penalizes poor people who have not applied for welfare. Second, such proposals—by focusing almost exclusively on unemployed women while ignoring unemployed men—may contribute to the growth of female-headed families and the poverty that is associated with it.

These considerations suggest that work-related pro-

5. SOCIAL INEQUALITIES: The Rich and Poor

Figure 1

A Profile of the Poor
(percentages)

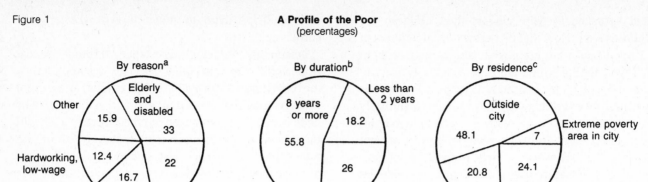

a. Percentages based on number of individuals living in households where the head is in one of these categories; b. Includes nonelderly poor only; c. City refers to one of the 100 largest standard metropolitan statistical areas.

Sources: Urban Institute tabulations from the March 1987 Current Population Survey; U.S. Bureau of the Census, *Money Income, and Poverty Status for Families and Persons in the U.S.: 1985 Current Population Reports,* p. 60, no. 154, tables 19 and 20; Mary Jo Bane and David T. Ellwood, "Slipping Into and Out of Poverty: The Dynamics of Spells," *Journal of Human Resources,* 21, no. 1:1-23, Winter 1983, table 2; and U.S. Bureau of the Census, *Poverty Areas in Large Cities,* vol. 2, Subject Reports, PC80-2-8D, February 1985.

grams for welfare recipients, although potentially valuable, must be seen not as the centerpiece of efforts to reduce poverty and dependency but as one potentially valuable element in a broader strategy of moving people toward self-support. Doing this will require both increasing employment and rewarding work more adequately.

Increasing Employment. A large number of the heads of poor households are not working or are working irregularly, and they report that the reason is their inability to find work (see Figure 1). It is hard to distinguish the extent to which jobs are really unavailable and the extent to which people are using this answer as a socially acceptable cover for their own lack of interest in working—at least in the kinds of jobs that are available to them. It *is* clear that when the overall unemployment rate drops, so does the incidence of poverty, especially the proportion of the poverty population that consists of household heads looking for work.

Even when the economy has enough jobs for everybody, there may be a mismatch between the skills or location of jobs and job seekers. Some evidence suggests that this mismatch is particularly serious in the large cities of the Northeast and Midwest. These cities have many people with little education; recall that 63 percent of the adults in "underclass areas" have less than a high school education. These people typically do not qualify for jobs in the growing service and information-based sectors of the nation's major metropolitan centers. For example, between 1970 and 1984, the number of jobs in New York City that required less than a high school education declined by 34 percent, while those requiring some higher education increased

by 24 percent. Similar figures apply to other northern cities.

The fact that jobs are more difficult to get when unemployment is high or when the structure of the economy changes does not mean that there are no jobs available. Help-wanted signs, the classified ads, the flow of immigrants into the U.S. labor market, and the large increase in total employment over the past decade all testify to the contrary. Even the most disadvantaged may have some job opportunities. A 1979–80 survey of young black men living in poverty areas in Boston, Chicago, and Philadelphia found that 71 percent of nonemployed, out-of-school youths thought they could obtain a minimum-wage job either very or somewhat easily. Alternative sources of income such as crime or hustling may keep these young men from accepting very low-paid jobs, and alternative sources of labor such as women and immigrants may keep employers from offering higher pay.

Other workers, with fewer disadvantages than those associated with inner-city black youths, may be unemployed for similar reasons—their inability to locate quickly a job that meets their requirements in terms of wages, location, and type of work. Whether these requirements are viewed as reasonable is debatable. The reality is that a low-paid job is no guarantee of escape from poverty, that community norms about what is and is not "acceptable work" matter to most people, and that a temporary bout of joblessness and poverty may be the price of holding out for a job that promises better long-term prospects. In some cases, child care or transportation expenses may loom large relative to prospective wages.

Rewarding Work. Moving unemployed people

into jobs is no guarantee that poverty will be ended. As indicated in Figure 1, the number of people who are poor despite rather strenuous efforts to earn a living is not large; but the significance of this group probably should not be judged by its size alone (and it would be larger if employed single parents were included).

In 1987, a full-time, year-round, minimum-wage job produced an income of just under $7,000 a year. Although this is enough income to move a single person above the poverty line, it is not enough for an adult with even one dependent. (It is also lower than the combined AFDC and food stamp benefits available to a mother and two children in 15 states. In addition, unlike most low-paid jobs, welfare automatically provides health care benefits through Medicaid and involves no payroll taxes and no child care or other work-related expenses.) Two adults, one working full-time and the other half-time, can earn $10,500 a year—still not enough to support a couple with two children above the poverty line. Thus, for young people who do not yet have any dependents, working at a minimum wage job is not a disaster. But for adults with family responsibilities, it is a recipe for poverty.

The best long-term strategy for the ''hardworking'' poor is more schooling to prepare them for higher-paying jobs. In the interim—and for those whose productivity may always be low—the options include raising the minimum wage, or supplementing the earnings of the poor through wage subsidies or refundable tax credits (a variant of a negative income tax).

Other changes that might benefit the working poor include allowing welfare recipients with inadequate earnings to keep a larger portion of their grant, making the tax credit for child care and dependent care refundable, raising state income tax thresholds above the poverty line (as was done for federal income tax thresholds in 1986), and extending health care protection to the working poor so that they will not be worse off than welfare recipients who automatically qualify for Medicaid. (In 1984, roughly three-quarters of workers from poor families worked in jobs that did not offer group health insurance.) None of these policies is cheap, but all are designed to make work more attractive than welfare and to reward the efforts of people who are trying to support themselves and their families by working at relatively low-paid jobs.

Investing in education

Although efforts to strengthen family responsibilities and make people self-supporting through work are important, they do not tackle one of the root causes of poverty: a lack of education or basic skills. In 1986,

half of the heads of poor families had less than a high school education compared with about a quarter of all family heads. Equally striking is the association between deficiencies in basic skills and such problems as becoming an unwed parent, dropping out of school, welfare dependency, unemployment, and crime (see Table 3).

Table 3   **Persons 18 to 23 Years Old in Bottom Fifth of Basic Skills Distribution**

Category[a]	Percentage
All persons 18 to 23 years old	20
In a poor household	46
Unwed parent	59
Welfare dependent	53
School dropout	52
Not working	40
Arrested	37

Source: Gordon Berlin and Andrew Sum, ''Toward a More Perfect Union: Basic Skills, Poor Families, and Our Economic Future,'' based on a speech delivered by Gordon Berlin at a Conference of School and Employment and Training Officials sponsored by the National Governors' Association and the Chief State School Officers, December 1986.

Note: Based on scores on the Armed Forces Qualification test, which measures reading and mathematical skills and has been administered to a representative national sample of youth, interviewed annually from 1979 to 1985 as part of the National Longitudinal Survey of Youth Labor Market Experience.

a. All categories except the first exclude persons attending college from the base used to calculate percentage.

Education has always been the route to upward social mobility in the United States. Although education is one vehicle by which relatively advantaged parents pass on these advantages to their children, it is also the chief way to break the cycle of poverty between generations. Children from low-income families are more likely to end up poor as adults than are children from high-income families; but more than half of those whose families were in the bottom one-fifth of the income distribution when they were growing up end up in a higher income group after establishing their own households. The evidence also suggests that overall social mobility has increased since the early 1960s. It is less clear whether these findings extend to people with the most disadvantaged backgrounds, such as children being raised in ''underclass areas'' where poor schools and a high incidence of crime and drug abuse make learning difficult and where racial discrimination compounds the problems. Indeed, the very growth of the underclass could be interpreted as suggesting that upward mobility for children born into chronically poor families living in distressed neighborhoods has all but ceased.

5. SOCIAL INEQUALITIES: The Rich and Poor

In other respects, this conclusion is too pessimistic. Intergenerational mobility is a long-term process. Thus, even if social mobility were to have improved for the generations born after the civil rights revolution and the start of the War on Poverty, we would not yet have seen it in the data, because these children are only now entering adulthood. The more direct evidence on their educational experiences is encouraging. Overall educational attainment has gone up, and the gap between minority and nonminority students has narrowed substantially. Moreover, contrary to popular impression, average test scores for persons born after the mid–1960s have improved—with the gains being particularly large for minorities, students from schools in disadvantaged urban communities, and those whose parents did not graduate from high school.

For example, the proportion of blacks, ages 22 to 24, who were high school dropouts declined from 38 percent in 1970 to 18 percent in 1985 (versus a decline from 16.3 to 13.3 percent for whites). At the same time, the mean reading proficiency scores of black 17-year-olds increased by 10 percent (versus a 1 percent improvement for whites). In general, whether the test scores are examined by race, by parent's education, or by type of school attended, the differences have narrowed over this period. Thus, clear progress has been made in reducing the dependence of education on race, family background, or neighborhood and in improving educational outcomes for those most at risk of being poor.

Despite this progress, an educational underclass remains. In 1985, one-fifth of Americans 21 to 25 years old (and almost half of the blacks this age) were reading below the eighth-grade level. Large gaps in schooling and test scores remain between students from different backgrounds. The reading scores of 17-year-olds who are black, come from disadvantaged urban communities, or have parents without a high school degree are no higher than the reading scores of 13-year-olds who are white, come from advantaged urban communities, or have parents with at least some college education.

These educational deficiencies are interacting with an economy that increasingly demands or requires higher levels of literacy. Currently, 18 percent of all jobs require less than a high school education, but it is conservatively estimated that not more than 14 percent of the jobs created between now and the year 2000 will fall into this category. Furthermore, according to detailed analysis by the U.S. Department of Labor, the most rapidly growing occupations are those that require the highest levels of language, math, and reasoning skills.

What can be done to raise the levels of education and literacy? A number of existing programs have proved reasonably successful and would seem to be candidates for further expansion: Head Start for disadvantaged preschoolers, compensatory education under Chapter One of the Education Consolidation and Improvement Act for grade-school youth, and the Jobs Corps for school dropouts.

Preschool programs appear to have been especially effective. Early childhood education has an immediate, positive effect on a child's intellectual performance, and although the gains in IQ fade after a few years, the programs have a more lasting effect on school performance. The most plausible interpretation of these results is that the programs give children the confidence that they can succeed. Success in the early years then has a cumulative impact, establishing the basis for further learning at each stage in the educational process. The best programs typically work with parents as well as children, thereby changing the entire family's attitudes toward education.

In the Perry Preschool program of Ypsilanti, Michigan, where 123 children were randomly assigned either to an experimental or to a control group in the early 1960s, and their progress was followed until they were age 19, quite dramatic findings have been reported. The group attending preschool was much more likely to be employed, to have graduated from high school, and to be enrolled in further education or training. They were also less likely to have become pregnant or to have been arrested. For each dollar invested in the program, $4.75 was saved because of lower costs for special education, public assistance, and crime. Although it is not clear that such high-quality programs can be replicated nationally, the attempt to do so would appear to be extremely worthwhile. Currently, less than one-fifth of the children eligible for Head Start are enrolled in the program.

The Job Corps is another successful, largely residential program for extremely disadvantaged out-of-school youths, ages 14 to 21. Virtually all enrollees are from poor or welfare-dependent families, and the average participant enters the program reading at about the sixth-grade level. The program provides a range of services including remedial education, vocational training, and health care; the cost can be as high as $15,000 per person per year. However, careful evaluations of the program indicate that it improves health and educational outcomes and increases annual earnings by about 28 percent, an increase that is sustained for at least four years after the end of the program. And despite the high cost of the program, its estimated social benefits exceed its costs by 46 percent.

The results achieved from these and similar education and training programs—along with the post-1960s gains in educational attainment and test scores cited earlier—suggest that intergenerational mobility and equality of opportunity can be enhanced by investments in children. Early, intensive interventions that involve parents as well as children, and build self-esteem as well as skills, appear to be the most promising approaches.

The need: tough-minded compassion

The debate about how much poverty exists in the United States and what to do about it will undoubtedly continue. Conservatives will emphasize the responsibility of the poor for their own fate, and liberals will bemoan the shortcomings of our social and economic system. Although these ideological differences will never be fully resolved, there are signs of an emerging maturity in our public debates, one that accepts that both systemic and individual factors play a role, often interacting with one another in complex ways.

Accompanying this more balanced, less simplistic view of the causes of poverty may be a new realism about the role of government in responding to the problem. If it was naive to believe that antipoverty programs would accomplish as much as some of the architects of the War on Poverty had hoped, it is equally naive to believe that these programs have been as counterproductive as some conservatives have recently argued. The nation seems to be groping for a new middle ground, one based on a compassion tempered by concern about the willingness of the poor to help themselves, the cost of any new effort, and its likely effectiveness.

Making progress against persistent poverty is likely to be a long, difficult, and expensive process. It would be far easier to treat the symptoms than to cure the disease. But a sensible strategy would go after root causes: weak families, substantial joblessness, and poor education. Although there should be no expectation of early success, a society that does not even try to reduce poverty and bring members of the underclass back into the mainstream cannot feel very good about itself.

CHILDREN
OF THE
UNDERCLASS

This story was reported by Vern E. Smith, Howard Manly and David L. Gonzalez. It was written by Tom Morganthau.

Felix and his friends are hanging out at 19th and Susquehanna, waiting for something. Everybody knows Felix: at 17, he runs one of the more successful crack franchises in north Philadelphia. Today, a rainy Saturday, Felix is wearing a black baseball cap and an expensive-looking black raincoat. He is scowling: anyone can see he's taking care of business. Thirty minutes go by before Silk comes up the block. Silk is carrying an umbrella, and he looks nervous. Felix and his friends meet Silk in the middle of the intersection. There is a sudden argument, and two of Felix's friends hit Silk with a flurry of quick body punches. Silk's umbrella goes flying and he falls to the rain-slick pavement; he lies there, defenseless and unresisting. "I *TOLD* you not to mess with my *MONEY!*" Felix yells, standing over Silk. Then he and his friends saunter away. A message has been delivered, and everyone on the block will hear it.

It is late afternoon when Miss Nee comes home with the clothes for her foster child Joe: two pairs of shorts and two T shirts, bought at the secondhand store for less than $5. "I just didn't want him to have to put up with people talking about him," she says. "You know how kids are. If you don't look just right, they're going to

make fun of you." It's a slow afternoon in midsummer, oppressively hot on North 19th Street. Down the block, near Susquehanna Avenue, three teenagers are shooting craps in the doorway of Craig's Laundromat. Toddlers race up and down the sidewalk, playing noisy baby games, and older kids are lining up at Jewel's Store, around the corner on Susquehanna, for flavored water ice. Up on Diamond Street, at the other end of the block, a group of men nurse 40-ounce bottles of beer called 4-0s in brown paper bags.

Miss Nee's house stands near the north end of the block, on the west side of 19th Street. Owned by the Philadelphia Housing Authority, it is flanked on both sides by boarded-up buildings and it is almost barren inside. Officially, at least, Miss Nee, Joe, Kita and Yvonne are the only occupants, although on any given night Miss Nee, who is well known for her open-door policy, plays hostess for up to a dozen neighborhood kids. Miss Nee—Geneva Leaks, 52—has been rearing children all of her life. She raised her younger brothers and sisters and five kids of her own—and if she now takes no sass from Joe, Yvonne and Kita, she clearly understands their need for mothering. Joe Rut-

ling is 14, and he has been living with Miss Nee for slightly more than a year. Okita (Kita) Allen, 15, moved in four years ago. Yvonne Williams, who is 14, has been in Miss Nee's care since she was 5 years old. None is related to Miss Nee by blood or marriage.

Miss Nee's neighborhood is in serious trouble, and the reason is crack cocaine. Crack is more than just the latest drug to hit the American underclass. Since its appearance on inner-city streets three to five years ago, it has proven to be an illicit bonanza for those who sell it and a curse on those who use it. Unlike heroin, crack is widely used by women. That fact alone has disastrous consequences for low-income families. If single-parent households have contributed to the intractability of poverty in the past, no-parent households may be poverty's appalling future. And crack is a catastrophe for the young. It has touched off an explosive increase in birth defects and an epidemic of child abuse and parental neglect. Its profits, in neighborhoods where the standard of living is very low, have led or forced thousands of inner-city youngsters into hard-core crime, and many others into addictions from which they may never recover. It has bankrupted parental authority and it is destroying the fraying social fabric of inner-city neighborhoods all over the United States.

Miss Nee and her neighbors are under siege every day, but they have by no means surrendered to crack. The neighborhood, just west of Temple University and only 15 blocks from Philadelphia's glossy downtown, is a mixture of middle-income and low-income residents. The 2100 block of North 19th Street, where Miss Nee lives, includes a church, a vest-pocket city park and 34 brick row houses. Many are owned by the Philadelphia Housing Authority and rented to low-income tenants. The residents take part in a neighborhood crimewatch program, and a clear majority want no part of drugs or drug dealing. Jewel Williams, the unofficial mayor of the Susquehanna Avenue area, has been fighting for his neighborhood for years. He has more than once considered pulling out. "But every time I get ready to pack up and leave I think, 'How can I escape this?'" he says. "I've got to do something for these babies, for these kids. Somebody's got to save the ones that are salvageable."

Partners in austerity, Miss Nee and her kids make do on food stamps and $474 a month from the government. There is government-surplus rice, plenty of spaghetti and sometimes a little meat; the meat man, who drives through the neighborhood in his car once a week, sells to regular customers like Miss Nee on credit. Until this year, Miss Nee supplemented her income by taking her charges over to New Jersey to do daywork in the blueberry fields. The work was hard—all day in the sun at the minimum wage—but they needed the money and she wanted to teach the kids the value of a dollar. "What you get," Miss Nee likes to say, "is what you sweat for." Last spring, however, the social worker discovered that Yvonne's brother had earned $69 for two days' work in a packing plant: under welfare rules, that amount was deducted from Miss Nee's food-stamp allotment. "They say, 'Try to get your kids a summer job'," Miss Nee says now, "but I'm not taking no chances."

Yvonne, Kita and Joe treat Miss Nee with respect and a hint of wariness: she is a tough lady, but she is the rock of stability in their young lives. All three have seen their families fall apart in recent years, and for practical purposes they are Miss Nee's kids now. Yvonne, whose four brothers and three sisters are scattered among different relatives and foster homes across the city, sees her father only occasionally; she sees her mother, Alberta Williams, somewhat more often. "She goes off on her own a lot," Yvonne says of her mother. "Sometimes she walks in the streets by herself." Alberta Williams, who says children "get on her nerves," has been hospitalized several times for nervous breakdowns. She says her doctor has prescribed Thorazine, a

powerful antipsychotic drug, for her problems, but admits she rarely takes it. "Yeah, I drink," she says, "but so does everybody." Yvonne says her mother "was having problems" and couldn't take care of the family. "I used to cry a lot," she says. "I still love her, even though she can't take care of us. I love my mother and Nee equally."

Kita, still tomboyish in her jeans, is pregnant at the age of 15—"babies having babies," people on the block say, shaking their heads. Kita is laconic about her pregnancy—"it just came about," she shrugs—but Miss Nee says Kita wanted the child. "Kita knows how to raise kids," Miss Nee says. "She's going to be a very good mother. She's been cooking since she was 5 years old, and she took care of her two brothers." Kita's brothers now live with their grandmother, and her family has ceased to exist. Her father was killed in a gang feud before she was born, and though Kita will not talk about it much, her mother has a history of cocaine abuse. "I was a junkie," Kita's mother, Cookie Allen, says. "I was selling drugs out of my house." Allen says she has been homeless since her family broke up two years ago. Asked about her relationship with Kita, Allen says "that's none of your —ing business."

Joe Rutling doesn't talk about his family much either. His father has been in trouble with the law and his mother is down in Virginia, getting away from whatever happened in Philadelphia. When his mother asked him if he wanted to move in with Miss Nee last year, Joe saw his chance and took it. He's a quiet kid who does well in school, and he keeps a certain distance from the other teenagers on the block. Joe sees the devastation crack has brought to north Philadelphia, and he is adamantly opposed to drugs. "I taught *myself* that drugs were bad," he says firmly. "Sometimes, when people start talking about drugs, I just leave. It's hard to tell people that stuff is bad for you—they don't listen." Joe says his father talks to him "every now and then" and that he thinks about his mother "all the time." He likes Miss Nee and he's grateful for her help, but he has come to hate the neighborhood. "I see how it is here," he says tonelessly. "It's evil."

They call it "clocking" in north Philadelphia, and it has nothing to do with punching a time clock. Clocking means getting a pack of cocaine from somebody like Felix, then standing on a street corner to hand off caps of crack to the pipers and users who drift by. The rules are well established: don't let the police catch you holding too much cocaine, don't use it yourself and don't stiff the dealer when it comes time to pay up. (That was Silk's mistake.) The clockers are all juveniles, and one of them,

a boy named Bobby, is only 10 years old. Some of them wear tiny gold charms that look like miniature watch faces—a dealer's trademark, which is probably where the term clocking came from. Everyone on 19th Street knows about clocking, and many of the boys do it. "It's messed up around here," says Kevin Abbott, who is 14. "You can buy about anything for $5."

"It's about *subliminal seduction,*" says Pimpin' Sam. Pimpin' Sam is in his mid-20s—a heroin user, but one of many north Philadelphia addicts who has shifted to speedballing, injecting a combination of heroin and cocaine. Sam went to college for a while, and he uses high-powered terms like "subliminal seduction" to explain the basic appeal of clocking, which is money. "It's like the sneaker commercials on TV that say they can make you run faster and jump higher," he says. "The kids all want them. But basically, they all come from single-parent homes. Some of the parents are on welfare, others work. You got, say, 10 hungry kids that are willing to sell drugs all night and all day to get some Adidases or some other name-brand stuff. This is the only way they're going to get it.

"The dealer takes advantage of that, you understand what I'm sayin'? He flashes the money in their face and says, 'You can have this, you can have that. All you got to do is clock, work on the corner.' And they think that's the way out, they think it's cool. So automatically, they grab hold to it—it's fast money, you know what I'm sayin'? So they're hooked to the drug-dealing lifestyle. They think it's cool to wear gold and name-brand stuff, not being aware that they should be trying to get their education.

"My generation, what we were instilled on was morals, values and respect," Sam says. "If I disrespected your mother, she would beat me, and when I got home my mother would beat me, too. Respect played a bigger part. Now the new generation—what's being cool to them is being a hustler. It's got a lot to do with TV, parents, babies having babies. When you're young, you're gonna do what your parents do, [and] if your mother is on the pipe, you're going to be on the pipe." He hobbles away on crutches—Sam got his leg broken recently in some mysterious street-corner dispute—heading for the shooting gallery they call the Chateau Luzerne. As he walks up Susquehanna Avenue, two boys coming the other way take care to give him plenty of room.

Like any poet, Kevin Abbott writes about what he knows best. This is his rap song about north Philadelphia.

"I grew up in a neighborhood drug-infested.

All these situations, only once arrested.

I saw my people fall and rise, rise and fall

In this short life I've seen it all.

'I saw my people fall and rise, rise and fall, in this short life I've seen it all'

I saw my people selling smoke, and they're sniffing

It was like a dream, but the dream was drifting

So if you're not doing drugs, raise your hand.

'Cause you will be rewarded LIFE in the end."

A girl on the block is talking about her boyfriend. On Mother's Day, she says, her boyfriend wanted to buy his mother a present, but he had no money. So he decided to sell some powder. "I told him that if he wanted to be with me, he couldn't be involved with no drugs," she says. "He didn't have to do it. He never had any problems. He was getting good grades in school. But he was trying to be like the big boys. Earlier in the day, he wanted me to come around and visit him, but I told him no because he had all those drugs on him. I knew something was wrong. I could feel it." He called that

night from jail, she says, busted on his first time out clocking.

Miss Doris Jackson—frail, arthritic and spirited—has lived on 19th Street for 50 years, and she is a pillar of the community. "Don't you care about yourself?" she says to the kids, shaking her cane. "Don't you know your body is a temple?" Neighbors laugh about the time Miss Doris marveled that a newborn child was so small. "Don't you know she's a crack baby, Miss Doris?" someone said. "Don't you know nothing?"

Early one morning Miss Doris got up to investigate loud voices on the street outside her house. It was Felix and his friends.

"You know you ain't supposed to do what you're doing," Miss Doris said.

"What am I doing, Miss Doris?" Felix said, grinning.

"Do you really want me to say it?" she asked.

"No, Miss Doris," Felix said.

"All right, now you know you done wrong," Miss Doris said, satisfied.

"Aww, Miss Doris," Felix said, retreating toward the avenue.

Almost everyone on the block has had some kind of confrontation with the clockers and pipers who infest the neighborhood. The Rev. Al Blasingame, who makes a brave stand for the straight and narrow at Faith Tabernacle Baptist Church just across Susquehanna Avenue, had his moment last spring when someone broke into the church and stole the telephone, some hand tools and his prized pastoral vestments. Furious, the Reverend Al offered a $50 reward for information and got a tip that he ought to check out the clientele at a crack house half a block away. Enlisting Jewel Williams as a backup, Blasingame marched across the street to the crack house and, to the amazement of those inside, kicked in the door. "I'm going to get my stuff back or I'm going to throw each one of you out the window!" he said. "I'll give you three days to get my stuff back or you can prepare to go to war. Do you understand what I'm saying? I want my cape back."

The telephone and the hand tools were returned within the day—but the missing cape, which is what really got the Reverend Al going, turned out to be at the dry cleaner's. Only then did Blasingame realize what he had done. "There were four of them," he says now. "They could have killed me."

The crack house, one of the many city-owned abandoned buildings on the block, suffered a mysterious fire a few weeks later. Whoever did it was kind enough to warn the dopers and the next-door neighbors that it would be wise to go somewhere else that night, and the fire broke out after midnight. A crowd gathered quickly, though it was more than a few minutes before anyone called 911. The building, already stripped of its plumbing and wiring, was gutted so completely that even the crackheads were forced to move on. "Spiritual justice was done," one of the neighbors says.

Torching the building made little difference to the neighborhood. There are three other crack houses within easy walking distance and kids are still clocking along Susquehanna Avenue. The lookouts—little boys, some as young as 6—yell warnings as the police drive by, and the clockers run away through a maze of alleys. Like Vietnam, the Philadelphia drug war is a war with no front line: crack's real damage is within the family.

No one knows it better than Jewel Williams. Jewel is 32—stocky, muscular, perpetually alert, an omnipresent figure in the neighborhood. He owns the tiny convenience store on Susquehanna Avenue, and he is president of the Susquehanna Neighborhood Advisory Council, a city-funded uplift agency that maintains a scruffy set of offices down the avenue from his store. By night Jewel is a campus police officer at Temple University and he has a license to carry a pistol, a Smith & Wesson automatic. It is always there, holstered on his right hip, a symbol of his status as protector and ombudsman for the neighborhood. Jewel is married with three children of his own, and his wife, Bernice, thinks he spends too much time on the block. "My wife gives me hell sometimes because I spend more time with other kids than I do my own," he says.

But Jewel, convinced that "we've lost three generations already," is determined to do all he can. The Neighborhood Advisory Council, called "the NAC," started out as a campaign against blighted housing. But crack's arrival in the north Philadelphia ghetto has changed everything, and Jewel and his staff of three now provide recreation programs, summer jobs, counseling and emergency food supplies, all on a shoestring budget. The common denominator is saving kids. "While we were out fixing up houses," Jewel says, "we found out it was our youth that was deteriorating." He estimates that at least 5,000 children under the age of 14 live within the NAC boundaries, many of them with surrogate mothers like Miss Nee.

One shelf in the NAC office is filled with boxes of infant formula for emergency cases. "We have families who are going hungry because the mother or father is on crack," he says. "They spend the money on drugs and then come here begging for food. Most of the crack mothers drop their babies off on the grandmother. Then we get the grandmothers calling us for milk to feed the newborns." In one case, he says, a woman addict locked up her children in the house while she went out for drugs. "The kids were in there for two days," he says. "Their Pampers had maggots in them. When you see something like that you say to yourself, 'Stop worrying about the 18-year-olds who're getting high and start paying attention to the little kids and the babies'."

He could start with Lucas and Bobby. Bobby is a big kid who looks much older than his real age, which is 10. His mother, so addicted that she is slowly becoming emaciated, spent the welfare checks on crack, and Bobby and his sister lived in an abandoned house with no electricity and no running water. When Bobby's grandmother bought him clothes, his mother sold them to get more crack. Finally Bobby went to a dealer he knew and began clocking on Susquehanna Avenue, hanging out all night until his pack of "nickel powders" was sold. "His mother don't care, as long as he's giving her some," says Lucas, who is 15. Lucas's mother is a crack addict, too. "I talk to her every day," he says. "If I tell her to leave it alone, she'll stop for about three weeks, then go behind my back." When he grows up and gets a job, Lucas says, "I'm gonna take her to a rehab place where she can get herself back together, and then I'm going to take her far, far away and let her live by herself. I love her."

It's not the kids, Renee Johnson says, it's the parents. "If the mother's sitting there selling [crack], what's that telling the child? If the son's out there selling it and the mother's sitting there holding it, what good is that gonna do? ... The mothers know the kids are making money, and they're getting some of the money so they're happy." The kids aren't bad, she says, "they just don't have no discipline. They figure if their mother's doing it, hell, I can go do it, too. That's why I watch the ones whose mothers are on drugs. I sit there and wonder, what're y'all thinking about?"

One reason Renee thinks about the kids so much is that she is a crack user, too—and she has a 13-year-old daughter, a beautiful girl named Kaneesha. Renee says a boyfriend turned her on to crack several years ago and that she became a closet addict. "She's never seen me do it. I used to go to work, come home and go straight to the room. I would never go outside until I came down," she says. Renee's mother persuaded her to enter a residential drug-treatment program in upstate Pennsylvania, but the stay there did not end her addiction. Now, she says, the thought that Kaneesha might try drugs is forcing her to try to set a better example. "What if Kaneesha was to smoke a joint? What could I say? What right would I have to say anything about her when I do it? It made me really slow down," Renee says.

Kaneesha is going to summer school this year, and she has an afternoon summer job as well. She thinks she wants to be a nurse, but she dreams of becoming a model. Renee, watching and worrying for any sign of involvement in drugs, thinks about getting family counseling or sending Kaneesha to Baltimore to live with her uncle. "Kaneesha can't understand why I stay on her the way I do," she says. "But I don't want her to go through the same things I went through when I was coming up. I wasn't taught the way I'm trying to teach her, put it that way, and I don't want to see her follow in my footsteps."

There is a girl in the neighborhood who knows about another crack-house arson. The girl's mother was an addict, and she sold and used crack in the home. The family was in chaos and the children were going hungry. The girl tried to stop her mother's drug abuse many times and failed. Finally the girl said, "If I can't get the drugs out of the house, I can make it so no one gets drugs here." The girl burned down the family's house. She was 12 years old.

Children in this neighborhood are so exposed to drugs that teachers at the Head Start school at 18th and Diamond streets have begun teaching their students about crack before they begin the usual pre-reading program. "They can identify crack caps and vials as young as 4," says one teacher. "We've had to adjust our entire approach to what's important to these children."

Grade-school kids are introduced to cocaine along with marijuana. "It's called a turbocharge," Jewel Williams says. "They think turbo is not addicting, so they start sucking on a joint at 10, 11 or 12. Before they know it, they don't want the weed. They've got to get that charge. So they go and buy a cap and then they're hooked up. They'll take anything and make a pipe out of it—a tin can, a broken car antenna." Kevin Abbott, the neighborhood poet, says younger addicts "know what's happening, but they just don't care."

5. SOCIAL INEQUALITIES: The Rich and Poor

Five years ago a no-name north Philadelphia welterweight named Kevin Howard stunned the boxing world by decking Sugar Ray Leonard in what was supposed to be an easy bout. Leonard survived, winning the fight in a ninth-round TKO, but Howard became an instant hero for the homeboys on the block—another Smokin' Joe Frazier, the pride of black Philadelphia. "Just like I'm talking with you, I was talking with Sugar," Howard says now. "We had lunch together, we had dinner together, we went out together. He said to me, 'There's something about you I like. You ain't like all the other fighters. You ain't talking about killing me or knocking my eye out.' I said, 'It's not like that. This is a business. But believe this: if there's a fight, I'm going to try to take your ass out.' I mean, I showed no fear."

Howard lost it all in a blur of fast living. His last fight was three years ago, and he was knocked out in the seventh round. Today, he lives in a dilapidated row house and spends his days shuffling around the neighborhood with a brokendown shopping cart looking for salvageable trash. "He used to be a bad dude," one of the neighborhood boys says. "But now, Kevin is like, 'Can I have a quarter or something?' "

"It doesn't make me feel good to know what I'm doing out here in the streets and know that kids still look up to me," Howard says. "The No. 1 thing I tell them is, 'Don't let nobody influence you into something wrong' .... It's not only 'caine, it's alcohol, too. It's marijuana. These things are a downfall. I'm talking from experience."

Howard, who is only 28, says it would be "best for me to get out of the neighborhood so I can stay on top." He still thinks he will be "the spoiler of the '90s."

"Man up!" the lookouts shout as plain-clothes officers Jeff Ziernicki and Harold Braxton creep up Susquehanna Avenue in their boxy blue Plymouth. Braxton and Ziernicki work the Double Deuce—the 22nd police district, one of the busiest in Philadelphia. Some 60,000 people live within the 22nd's two square miles, and police work there is a never-ending round of narcotics enforcement and domestic disputes that often involve crack. Drug arrests for adults and juveniles are sharply up in the past two years; last year the 22nd district seized drugs, cars and cash totaling nearly $2 million. The cops see the social causes—the accelerating breakdown of the family, the lack of positive role models and economic opportunity for youth—but they see the pure viciousness, too. In one case, a year and a half ago, two brothers 9 and 12 were murdered when their mother, who was an addict, stole the stash they were holding for a dealer. "We absolutely have to target the real young kids," says Philadelphia Police Commissioner Willie Williams, a veteran of the Double Deuce. "Completely educate them about drugs, sex and how to protect themselves from family members leading them to drugs."

With the city hall in a perennial budget crunch, street manpower is already stretched thin. That means cops like Braxton and Ziernicki spend their shifts jumping from one radio call to another—investigating burglaries, chasing clockers down the alleys, handling domestic disputes. Check day, when the welfare checks arrive, brings an avalanche of 911 calls for drug and alcohol emergencies; because crack abusers tend to be wired and hyperactive, even routine family arguments can erupt in violence. The reports of missing and abandoned children start the following day, when relatives and neighbors realize that the toddlers next door have no one to look after them. "We have to be marriage coun-selors, taxi drivers, referees, babysitters—everything," says Jeanette Barnes, a victim-assistance officer for the 22nd.

Capt. Al Lewis, the 22nd district commander, is trying to promote community-action projects like offering reading classes at the station house. He is also well aware that residents of the Double Deuce "desire nothing less than people in middle-class neighborhoods," which means protecting them from the drug trade and the drug-related crime that is all around them. But the beat cops are not optimistic. "Can this neighborhood be brought back?" one officer asks rhetorically. "No. We lost this generation."

Police veterans and longtime residents are nostalgic about the good old days of heroin, PCP and gang wars—nothing, they say, compares with the social consequences of crack. "I've been through pot, white lady and blue lady [forms of synthetic heroin], and I can't go through this much more," says Jean Hobson, who has lived in north Philly for 40 years. "I'd rather see gang warfare come back. Now you don't have protection from nothing or nobody. When they get on that stuff, they don't know their own mother." Hobson, like Geneva Leaks, is famous in the neighborhood for rescuing unwanted children, and she is shaken by the fact that younger and younger children are being drawn into dealing and using crack. "The little kids are starting—kids 6, 8 years old," she says. "They get the thrill and then they're hooked. [Dealers] use them to carry drugs, because the man ain't gonna bother them. They're kids—kids you never thought would be caught up in this," she says. "My God, they were such good kids."

The names Felix, Silk, Bobby and Lucas used in this article are pseudonyms.

Bush's most urgent policy problem.

THE TWO BLACK AMERICAS

MORTON M. KONDRACKE

THE NEWS from black America—what you read in your newspaper and see on television—is almost always bad. It isn't wrong, either. The portion of blacks living in poverty in 1987, 33 percent, was three times the white rate and was higher than in 1969. Forty-five percent of black children are poor, compared with 15 percent of white children. Blacks constitute 12 percent of the U.S. population, but they made up 46 percent of the inmates in U.S. prisons in 1985 and 60 percent of those arrested for murder in U.S. cities in 1987. The national crime figures for 1988 almost surely will be even worse, thanks largely to drugs. Inner-city cocaine wars helped raise the murder rate in Washington, D.C., by 65 percent last year, even as the city's black mayor was discovered consorting with a drug suspect, yet again.

Of young black men aged 20 to 24 who weren't in school—those who should be just beginning their working careers—17 percent worked not at all during 1987, at least not in the regular economy. A dispute has raged for nearly a decade now over whether, as liberals contend, these men are "structurally unemployed," meaning that jobs in the modern economy increasingly require education and skills they don't have; or whether, as conservatives believe, these men are products of an "underclass culture," where honest work is not valued because hustling, drug dealing, and theft pay better—and where, anyway, people lack even the minimal tools for employment, such as punctuality, courtesy, and elementary verbal skills. The latest evidence seems to favor the second theory: even as the overall economy approaches full employment, and positions in fast-food restaurants and construction companies go unfilled, the black unemployment rate remains in double digits, at 11.6 percent, and the black teenage rate hovers at 30 percent. And these numbers don't count those "not in the work force"—i.e., not looking for jobs.

The good news you occasionally hear from black America is also accurate. Depressing aggregate statistics conceal significant success stories among middle- and upper-class blacks. Nearly ten percent of black families had incomes above $50,000 (in real dollars) in both 1986 and 1987, the highest percentage ever. The average black family in which both husband and wife work now makes 88 percent of the income of a similar white family, when taxes and government benefits are taken into account.

AND YET, even within the black middle class, all is not right. Although middle-class blacks have seen their fortunes rise markedly since the Reagan recovery began in 1982, most are still not back to the levels of the late 1970s, before the Reagan recession. The median income for blacks in 1987 was 57.1 percent of that for whites, lower than in any year of the 1970s. Besides, gains in income are diluted by the fact that, as the Urban League's John Jacob puts it, most blacks, lacking a large savings, "are 26 weeks away from poverty." In 1984 the median net worth of black households was just $3,397, *nine percent* of the white average. Finally, the source of much black middle-class income is in some ways ominous. Fully half of all black managers and professionals are government workers, while the more lucrative jobs in private business are overwhelmingly white. Black business executives tend to be disproportionately lodged in equal-employment opportunity and community-relations posts, and are disproportionately laid off in corporate restructurings.

The prospects for improvement in these trends are clouded by the decline in the fraction of black high school graduates going on to college, from 34 percent in 1976 to 26 percent in 1985, a numerical drop of 15,000 students. The 1980s shift in federal aid from grants to loans seems partly responsible—and suggests one of the many steps George Bush could take to bolster black America. Only 42 percent of those who do go to college graduate. The days are long gone when a high school degree was a ticket out of poverty; 27 percent of black high school graduates were poor in 1987. (And bear in mind, the poverty line is $9,000 per year for a family of three, and life even well above that is scarcely "middle class.") Despite affirmative action, there has also been a decline in the number of black college graduates who go on to graduate and professional studies. All of this bodes especially ill in view of the growing demand for scientifically literate workers.

Much of the anecdotal evidence from the black middle class is also dispiriting. When Jesse Jackson proposed that blacks henceforth be officially called "African-Americans," black columnist William Raspberry found it evidence of "despair" and a "renewed sense of our outsidedness." Raspberry says that the black middle class "feels tenuous about its middle-classedness," fearful that its kids may get dragged into drugs and crime, and also senses "a new line of racism popping up" as evidenced in the Howard Beach incident, various outbreaks of racial hostility on college campuses, and the continued failure of blacks and whites to have much to do with each other outside work. Census studies show that residential segregation is diminishing for Asians and Hispanics, but hardly at all for blacks, even the middle class.

There certainly is hope to be found in the fact that blacks are achieving a new level of prominence, and yet even this is not unalloyed. A sharecropper's son, Jesse Jackson, finished second in the Democratic presidential race last year and may be front-runner for the 1992 nomination. Three hundred cities have black mayors. Toni Morrison, a black author, won the Pulitzer Prize for fiction last year. But an argument could be made that at least some of this is tokenism, an expression of unease about the overall slow rate of progress for blacks. And there is an obvious downside to the growing number of black mayors: they win elections largely because black voters can't afford to follow white voters in fleeing the cities.

BUT WHATEVER troubles beset the black middle class, they are mild compared with those afflicting the underclass, which is relatively small, but by all indications is growing and deepening in its social pathology. It is hard to say how big it is, since statistical definitions of it are highly arbitrary. By one geographic definition, it's estimated that about 2.5 million people live in the most poverty-ridden census tracts of U.S. industrial cities. By one income definition, it's estimated that about four million blacks have lived for ten years below the poverty line. A slightly larger number, 4.3 million, lived in 1987 in families that could be termed "the poorest of the poor"—with an income below $4,528, half the poverty level. Either estimate could be low because of chronic undercounting of the poor, but either way, analysts put the size of the underclass at no more than 15 percent of the nation's 29 million blacks, and usually less.

By all accounts, though, the underclass is growing as a percentage of all blacks, and by most accounts it is growing in absolute terms. The source of the growth is not precisely clear: to what extent are more blacks being absorbed into the underclass as they become poorer and are caught up in the culture of illegitimacy, drugs, and joblessness, and to what extent are children simply being born into the underclass and failing to escape? The two are interconnected.

One thing that a hard core of idle young men seem willing and able to do is have sex with poor young women, who—for reasons that are in dispute—often choose to have babies and not marry.

The problem actually is not that the rate of such births is growing. Black teens, for example, are having babies at a lower rate than they did in 1970 or 1980 (though still at a depressing rate). Rather, the problem is that births in the black underclass are growing as a percentage of black births. Especially significant is the collapse of the birth rate among married, middle-class black women (due partly to a soaring abortion rate). During the 12 months ending in mid-1987, black married women with incomes over $15,000 had fewer than 165,000 babies. During the same period, black unwed women with household incomes under $10,000 (including welfare and other government transfer payments) had 177,000 babies. Last year 61 percent of all black babies were born to unwed mothers. Nearly 25 years after Daniel Patrick Moynihan was pilloried for saying so, it is universally accepted that black poverty is heavily the result of family breakdown.

Children's Defense Fund president Marian Wright Edelman, for example, says that the illegitimacy rate "practically guarantees the poverty of the next generation of black children." At present rates, she says, it will be less than ten years before more than half of all black children are living in poverty. Edelman just got back from a trip to Atlanta, where she found that half of the babies in the neonatal unit of a huge city hospital were drug-addicted, and where workers in a day-care center for homeless children discovered a four-year-old performing oral sex on a three-year-old and were not surprised. "That's what the kids see in the shelters," she said. "We are creating a new kind of monster there."

Besides abysmal education, illegitimacy, welfare-dependency, unemployment, bad housing, insufficient health care, and crime, the black underclass is being raked by drugs and AIDS, and an upsurge in child abuse connected to drug addiction. The director of one Boston-area settlement house says that the incidence of child sexual abuse in underclass families—black and white—is "nearly 100 percent." There was a 28 percent increase in the number of child abuse deaths reported between 1985 and 1986.

HOW THE underclass developed and what should be done about it are two of the most fiercely contested issues in social science and public policy. There are basically three schools of thought—the "welfare school" led by conservative Charles Murray of the Manhattan Institute, the "structural unemployment/social isolation" school led by black liberal Professor William Julius Wilson of the University of Chicago, and the "culture of poverty" school led by Professor Glenn Loury of Harvard, a black who is either a neoliberal or a conservative, depending on who's labeling him and the nuances of his most recent pronouncements.

Murray, the darling of the Reagan right, argued in the 1984 book *Losing Ground* that liberal policies of the 1960s—

notably increases in social spending, loosening of welfare regulations, Warren Court crime rulings, and the lowering of academic standards and discipline in public schools— encouraged young ghetto women to have babies, destroyed the work ethic, made crime pay, and made it harder for poor blacks to learn their way out of poverty. At the heart of Murray's argument was the observation that the percentage of black babies born to unmarried women began its steep climb in the mid-1960s, coinciding with the acceleration of social spending. In 1960, 22 percent of all black babies were born to unwed mothers; in 1970, the figure was 35 percent; in 1980, 55 percent. (For whites, the corresponding figures were two percent, six, and 11.)

Liberals claim that subsequent research, especially by Harvard's David Ellwood, has exploded Murray's thesis by demonstrating that illegitimacy continued to climb in the 1970s and 1980s even though welfare benefits failed to keep pace with inflation, and by showing that there is no state-by-state correlation between out-of-wedlock births and welfare levels. Murray now says what he really meant all along was that welfare, Medicaid, and other benefits enabled (rather than caused) ghetto girls to have children and no jobs and still get by, which they did.

Liberals prefer William Julius Wilson's thesis—advanced in the 1987 book *The Truly Disadvantaged*—that the deindustrialization of the American economy, which started in the early 1970s, and the movement of available jobs to the suburbs left unskilled young ghetto males increasingly unemployable and undesirable as prospects for marriage. According to an earlier Wilson book, *The Declining Significance of Race*, the ability of stable, middle-class and working-class blacks to move out of the inner city left the ghettos increasingly occupied by the poor and the unemployed. So "the communities of the underclass are plagued by massive joblessness, flagrant and open lawlessness, and low-achieving schools . . . the residents of these areas, whether women and children of welfare families or aggressive street criminals, have become increasingly socially isolated from mainstream patterns of behavior."

Wilson's description of a self-perpetuating hell in the modern ghetto is not much different from that advanced by the "culture of poverty" school, but Loury thinks that both Wilson and Murray put too much emphasis on economic determinism and not enough on a breakdown of values in the ghetto and the failure of prominent blacks to help restore them. "Status is awarded for dope-dealing and for a woman to say, 'I'm a mother now,' " said Loury. "There are no centers of authority, public or private, saying, 'No, wait. What it means to be cool is not this.' "

William Raspberry agrees. He says prominent blacks who command the attention of ghetto kids have reinforced "the sense that there's no future for them, nothing worth postponing pleasure for. . . . I think we'd be much better to say, 'A lot can happen to you.' That is what we say to our own flesh and blood." The problem, Raspberry says, is that influential blacks naturally try to foster sympathy for the underclass, especially among policy-makers. Loury thinks

Jesse Jackson is a good example of the resulting contradiction. "On the one hand, he preaches values in his exhortations that 'we can transform ourselves if we but will.' On the other hand, he wants to blame the callous Reagan administration and the retreat of government for our problems. One mode of rhetoric tends to crowd out the other. I've yet to hear him resolve the tension between them."

THIS SAME PROBLEM—the perniciousness of the victim-of-society mentality, however well grounded in fact it may be—afflicts some in the middle class. According to Loury, "race is really very important" in the lives of successful blacks, who feel that "the vicissitudes of life, the slights, the failure to get a job or the rude word from a supervisor, all are due to race. Success has not brought relief from that sense of doubt, that mild sense of paranoia." Loury says he finds the tendency widespread among black college students. "These kids feel embattled. They carry this anger." He suspects this attitude may be unwittingly fostered by college administrators "who respond to every complaint by showing how sympathetic they are."

Which of the three schools of thought has it right? Probably all of them, in some measure. Murray and Wilson seem to have valid explanations for the underclass culture that Loury laments: the perverse incentives of the welfare system and the desertion of the cities by heavy industry, along with their desertion by more affluent blacks, conspired to help create the culture of poverty. It's certain, of course, that raw racism played a part, and it's likely that it continues to. Given the choice of hiring a black male from the ghetto or somebody else, many white employers may well choose somebody else. The danger, as the culture of poverty deepens, is that this increasingly will be a sound economic decision on their part.

SO WHAT'S to be done about the black underclass? As a "thought experiment," Murray proposed in *Losing Ground* "scrapping the entire federal welfare and income-support structure for working-aged persons, including AFDC, Medicaid, food stamps, unemployment insurance, worker's compensation, subsidized housing, disability insurance, and the rest." He said, "It would leave the working-aged person with no recourse whatever except the job market, family members, friends, and public or private locally funded services. It is the Alexandrian solution: cut the knot, for there is no way to untie it."

Murray says he never really meant that, and knew it was politically unrealistic. His point, he says, is that no one knows how really to help the underclass and that federal efforts often end up doing more harm than good. Murray thinks that the continuing idleness among ghetto men during the economic recovery shows that lack of jobs is not their problem. "A different reality has been out there all along, it has been resolutely ignored, and it is finally beginning to intrude," Murray wrote last September in *Commentary*. "Liberals will increasingly be hearing themselves saying, 'Those people just don't want to work.' "

Murray thinks that drugs, AIDS, and crime are going to discourage even liberals from trying to solve the underclass problem, and make them settle for containment—establishing what he calls "custodial democracy" in which the poor simply will be provided with medical care, food, housing, and other social services "much as we currently do for American Indians who live on reservations."

If that's where things are heading, fortunately they have not arrived there yet. Liberals such as Wilson and Edelman still are proposing major programs to employ, educate, and otherwise help the underclass. Edelman's annual Children's Defense Budget contains programs in education, family planning, child care, job training, and employment to help the poor. Wilson says that increases in black male employment in Boston's tight labor market indicate that economic growth can help blacks, and he says that a new survey of 2,500 ghetto residents in Chicago indicates that they would work if they could find jobs, but are cut off from information about where the jobs are. "There is no absence of a work ethic," he said. He also cited a new University of Chicago study showing that a ghetto man who is employed is twice as likely to marry the mother of his children as one who is unemployed. Wilson doesn't deny that culture plays a role in keeping the underclass down, "but that's different from saying that these patterns are so deeply internalized that they won't respond to changed circumstances."

Loury says he favors an amalgam of liberal and conservative ideas—plus increased efforts by black authority figures and ordinary middle-class blacks to work with ghetto youngsters and inculcate middle-class values. There is talk of an expanded Head Start program, of kindergarten beginning at age three, and of various other attempts to get young poor blacks out of the house as early and often as possible and into a more constructive environment.

WHAT GEORGE BUSH can do will be limited by resources, and the crisis of the underclass is so great that probably nothing short of a spiritual renewal in black America would really solve the problem. (The Black Muslims, whatever else one thinks of them, do set crooked people straight. So does Alcoholics Anonymous.) Still, there are worthwhile public policy ideas around. Welfare re-reform is one, as proposed in these pages in 1986 by Mickey Kaus (see "The Work Ethic State," TNR, July 7, 1986), who calls for a synthesis of left and right that would provide both the carrot and the stick: guaranteed jobs and day care along with the elimination of welfare. Opinion has moved in this general direction of late, but only slowly. The "workfare" bill passed by Congress last year barely qualifies for the term. It requires work only if there is adequate state funding to provide guaranteed jobs and child care, and in most states there isn't. Someday, adequate funding will have to be provided.

Another idea is educational reform that would make every school a potential magnet school, giving ambitious ghetto parents the chance to transfer their children to good schools outside the neighborhood. The agenda of Secretary of Housing and Urban Development Jack Kemp, Bush's poverty czar, includes tax breaks to attract jobs and industries to the ghetto, an increase in the earned income tax credit to help the working poor, and opportunities for public housing residents to buy their homes and run their housing projects as cooperatives. (See "The Poverty Thing" by Fred Barnes, TNR, January 30.) Clearly, Bush also should vigorously enforce anti-discrimination laws in a way that the Reagan Justice Department did not.

Finally, there is Bush's "thousand points of light" writ large. With presidential leadership—starting with the Bush family and the White House staff—every business, church, civic group, social organization, government office, and country club in America could be encouraged to tutor kids, adopt schools, fund settlement houses, staff recreation centers, and otherwise rescue the rescuable. Bush could do for voluntary service what John F. Kennedy did for public service, though the effort has to be sustained, lest tutoring become the equivalent of 50-mile hikes, the short-lived fad of Kennedy's era. Bush claimed during the presidential campaign that he was "haunted by the lives lived by the children of our inner cities." He now has a chance to ease his pain. He should light a million points of light, and build to ten million.

THE GLOBAL WAR AGAINST WOMEN

Lori Heise

Lori Heise is a senior researcher at the Worldwatch Institute. She prepared a recent report on this subject for World Watch *magazine.*

Violence against women—including assault, mutilation, murder, infanticide, rape and cruel neglect—is perhaps the most pervasive yet least recognized human-rights issue in the world. It is also a profound health problem sapping women's physical and emotional vitality and undermining their confidence—both vital to achieving widely held goals for human progress, especially in the Third World.

Despite its invisibility, the dimensions of the problem are vast. In Bangkok, Thailand, a reported 50 percent of married women are beaten regularly by their husbands. In the barrios of Quito, Ecuador, 80 percent of women are said to have been physically abused. And in Nicaragua, 44 percent of men admit to beating their wives or girlfriends. Equally shocking statistics can be found in the industrial world.

Then there are the less recognized forms of violence. In Nepal, female babies die from neglect because parents value sons over daughters; in Sudan, girls' genitals are mutilated to ensure virginity until marriage; and in India, young brides are murdered by their husbands when parents fail to provide enough dowry.

In all these instances, women are targets of violence because of their sex. This is not random violence. The risk factor is being female.

Most of these abuses have been reported in one or another country, at one or another time. But it is only when you begin to amass statistics and reports from international organizations and countries around the world that the horrifying dimensions of this global war on women come into focus. For me the revelation came only recently after talking with scores of village women throughout the world.

I never intended to investigate violence; I was researching maternal and child health issues overseas. But I would commonly begin my interviews with a simple question: What is your biggest problem? With unnerving frequency, the answer came back: "My husband beats me."

These are women who daily have to walk four hours to gather enough wood for the evening meal, whose children commonly die of treatable illnesses, whose security can be wiped out with one failed rain. Yet when defining their own concerns, they see violence as their

greatest dilemma. Those dedicated to helping Third World women would do well to listen.

More than simply a "women's issue," violence could thwart other widely held goals for human progress in the Third World. Study after study has shown that maternal education is the single most effective way to reduce child mortality—not because it imparts new knowledge or skills related to health, but because it erodes fatalism, improves self-confidence and changes the power balance within the family.

In effect, these studies say that women's sense of self is critical to reducing infant mortality. Yet acts of violence and society's tacit acceptance of them stand as constant reminders to women of their low worth. Where women's status is critical to achieving a development goal—such as controlling fertility and improving child survival—violence will remain a powerful obstacle to progress.

Measured by its human costs alone, female-focused violence is worthy of international attention and action. But it has seldom been raised at that level, much less addressed. Millions of dollars are spent each year to protect the human rights of fetuses. It is time to stand up for the human rights of women.

The Indian subcontinent is home to one of the most pernicious forms of wife abuse, known locally as "bride-burning" or "dowry deaths." Decades ago dowry referred to the gifts that a woman received from her parents upon marriage. Now dowry has become an important part of premarital negotiations and refers to the wealth that the bride's parents must pay the groom as part of the marriage settlement.

Once a gesture of love, ever-escalating dowry now represents a real financial burden to the parents of unwed daughters. Increasingly, dowry is being seen as a "get rich quick" scheme by prospective husbands, with young brides suffering severe abuse if promised money or goods do not materialize. In its most severe form, dowry harassment ends in suicide or murder, freeing the husband to pursue a more lucrative arrangement.

Dowry deaths are notoriously undercounted, largely because the husband and his relatives frequently try to disguise the murder as a suicide or an accident and the police are loathe to get involved. A frequent scam is to set the women alight with kerosene, and then claim she died in a kitchen accident—hence the term "bride-burning." In 1987 the police official recorded 1,786 dowry deaths in all of India, but the Ahmedabad Women's Action Group estimates that 1,000 women may have been burned alive that year in Gujurat State alone.

5. SOCIAL INEQUALITIES: Racial and Sexual Inequalities

A quick look at mortality data from India reveals the reasonableness of this claim. In both urban Maharashtra and greater Bombay, 19 percent of all deaths among women 15 to 44 years old are due to "accidental burns." In other Third World countries, such as Guatemala, Ecuador and Chile, the same statistic is less 1 percent.

Elsewhere in the world, the marriage transaction is reversed, with prospective husbands paying "bridewealth" to secure a woman's hand in marriage. In many cultures—especially in Africa—the exchange has become so commercialized that inflated bridewealth leaves the man with the distinct impression that he has "purchased" his wife.

The notion that bridewealth confers ownership was clearly depicted during recent parliamentary debates in Papua New Guinea over whether wife-beating should be made illegal. Transcripts show that most ministers were violently against the idea of parliament interfering in "traditional family life." Minister William Wi of North Waghi argued that wife-beating "is an accepted custom and we are wasting our time debating the issue." Another parliamentarian added: "I paid for my wife, so she should not overrule my decisions, because I am the head of the family."

It is this unequal power balance—institutionalized in the structure of the patriarchal family—that is at the root of wife-beating. As Cheryl Bernard, director of Austria's Ludwig Boltzmann Institute of Politics, notes: "Violence against women in the family takes place because the perpetrators feel, and their environment encourages them to feel, that this is an acceptable exercise of male prerogative, a legitimate and appropriate way to relieve their own tension in conditions of stress, to sanction female behavior . . . or just to enjoy a feeling of supremacy."

While stress and alcohol may increase the likelihood of violence, they do not "cause" it. Rather, it is the belief that violence is an acceptable way to resolve conflict, and that women are "appropriate" and "safe" targets for abuse, that leads to battering.

Today's cultures have strong historical, religious and legal legacies that reinforce the legitimacy of wife-beating. Under English common law, for example, a husband had the legal right to discipline his wife—subject to a "rule of thumb" that barred him from using a stick broader than his thumb. Judicial decisions in England and the United States upheld this right until well into the 19th century. Only last week, a New York judge let off with only five years' probation a Chinese immigrant who admitted bludgeoning his wife to death. The judge justified the light sentence partly by reference to traditional Chinese attitudes toward female adultery.

While less overt, the preference for male offspring in many cultures can be as damaging and potentially fatal to females as rape or assault. The same sentiment that once motivated infanticide is now expressed in the systematic neglect of daughters—a neglect so severe in some countries that girls aged 2 to 4 die at nearly twice the rate of boys.

"Let it be late, but let it be a son," goes a saying in Nepal, a country that shares its strong preference for male children with the rest of the Indian subcontinent, as well as China, South Korea and Taiwan. In these cultures and others, sons are highly valued because only they can perpetuate the family line and perform certain religious rituals. Even more important, sons represent an economic asset to the family and a source of security for parents in their old age.

Studies confirm that where the preference for sons is strong, girls receive inferior medical care and education, and less food. In Punjab, India, for example, parents spend more than twice as much on medical care for boy infants as for girls.

In fact, the pressure to bear sons is so great in India and China that women have begun using amniocentesis as a sex identification test to selectively abort female fetuses. Until protests forced them to stop, Indian sex detection clinics boldly advertised it was better to spend $38 now on terminating a girl than $3,800 later on her dowry. Of 8,000 fetuses examined at six abortion clinics in Bombay, 7,999 were found to be female.

In parts of Africa and the Middle East, young girls suffer another form of violence, euphemistically known as female circumcision. More accurately, this operation—which removes all or part of the external female genitalia, including the clitoris—is a life-threatening form of mutilation. According to the World Health Organization, more than 80 million women have undergone sexual surgery in Africa alone.

While female circumcision has its origin in the male desire to control female sexuality, today a host of other superstitions and beliefs sustains the practice. Some Moslem groups mistakenly believe that it is demanded by the Islamic faith, although it has no basis in the Koran. Others believe the operation will increase fertility, affirm femininity or prevent still births. Yet ultimately what drives the tradition is that men will not marry uncircumcised women, believing them to be promiscuous, unclean and sexually untrustworthy.

The medical complications of circumcision are severe. Immediate risks include hemorrhage, tetanus and blood poisoning from unsterile and often primitive cutting implements (knife, razor blade or broken glass), and shock from the pain of the operation, which is carried out without anesthesia. Not uncommonly, these complications result in death.

The long-term effects, in addition to loss of all sexual feeling, include chronic urinary tract infections, pelvic infections that can lead to infertility, painful intercourse and severe scarring that can cause tearing of tissue and hemorrhage during childbirth. In fact, women who are infibulated—the most severe form of circumcision—must be cut open on their wedding night to make intercourse possible, and more cuts are necessary for delivery of a child.

Despite these horrific health effects, many still oppose the eradication of this practice. As late as June 1988, Muslim religious scholars in Somalia argued that milder forms of circumcision should be maintained to temper female sexuality. Others defend circumcision as an "important African tradition." But as the Kenyan women's magazine *Viva* observes: "There is nothing 'African' about injustice or violence, whether it takes the form of mistreated wives and mothers, or slums or circumcision. Often the very men who . . . excuse injustice to women with the phrase 'it is African' are wearing three-piece pin-striped suits and shiny shoes."

Fortunately, women have not sat idle in the face of such abuse. Around the world they are organizing shelters, lobbying for legal reform and fighting the sexism that underlies violence.

Most industrial countries and at least a dozen developing nations now have shelter movements to provide refuge for abused women and their children. Brazil has established almost 30 all-female police stations for victims of rape, battering and incest. And in Africa, women are organizing education campaigns to combat sexual surgery.

Elsewhere women have organized in their own defense. In San Juan de Miraflores, a shantytown of Lima, Peru, women carry whistles that they use to summon other women in case of attack.

Yet it will take more than the dedicated action of a few women to end crimes of gender. Most important is for women worldwide to recognize their common oppression. Violence against women cuts across all cultures and all socioeconomic groups. Indeed, we in America live in our own glass house: In the United States a woman is beaten every 15 seconds, and each day four women are killed by their batterers.

Such statistics are as important as they are shocking. Violence persists in part because it is hidden. If governments and women's groups can expose violence through surveys and better documentation, then ignorance will no longer be an excuse for inaction.

Also critical is challenging the legal framework that undergirds male violence, such as unequal inheritance, discriminatory family laws and a husband's right to chastise. Especially important are the social inequities and cultural beliefs that leave women economically dependent on men. As long as women must marry to survive, they will do whatever they must to secure a husband—including tolerating abuse and submitting themselves and their daughters to sexual surgery.

Action against violence, however, must proceed from the international community down as well as from the grass roots up. Where governments tacitly condone violence through their silence, or worse yet, legitimize it through discriminatory laws and customs, international pressure can be an important impetus for reform. Putting violence against women high on the world agenda is not appeasing a "special interest" group. It is restoring the birthright of half of humanity.

Social Change and the Future

- New Population Issues (Articles 40-41)
- New Technology Issues (Articles 42-43)
- Choices Ahead (Articles 44-45)

Fascination with the future is an enduring theme in literature, art, poetry, and religion. Human beings are anxious to know if tomorrow will be different from today and in what ways it might differ. Coping with change has become a top priority in the lives of many. One result of change is stress. When the future is uncertain and the individual appears to have little control over what happens, stress can be a serious problem. On the other hand, stress can have positive effects on people's lives if the changes can be perceived as challenges and opportunities.

Any discussion of the future must begin with a look at basic demographic trends and then a consideration of how new technologies will affect these and other trends. This section begins by describing demographic trends worldwide and in the United States. Next, some of the problems caused by new technologies are discussed. Finally, two efforts to identify some of the crucial choices that will confront future generations are addressed.

Around 1850 there were only 1 billion people on the earth. Today, less than a century and a half later, there are about 5 1/2 billion, and over 85 million are added each year. At the International Conference on Population held in Mexico City in 1984, most of the countries of the world expressed alarm at the troublesome impacts of the population explosion. Lester Brown points out that "living conditions are deteriorating or in imminent danger of doing so" where the population is growing rapidly. Life support systems could collapse in many densely populated areas if additional population pressures force even more intense use of them. Population growth is also increasing rural landlessness and political and social conflict in Third World countries.

Immigration contributes significantly to population growth in the United States. William Broyles, Jr., tells the glorious story of immigration, symbolized by the Statue of Liberty. America was built by immigrants and Broyles sees much evidence that today's immigrants will contribute greatly to the continued building of America.

Technology is a dynamic force which influences the course of history and the shape of tomorrow. The next two articles discuss new technologies and their environmental impacts. The first article focuses on the dangerous side of technology. In a short period Chernobyl erupted and three spacecraft, including the Challenger, exploded. The chemical industry leaves a trail of death, and biological technology has the potential to accidentally kill millions. Next, Daniel Bell warns us that the third technological revolution is in progress. Computers, telecommunications and other new technologies are revolutionizing economies and societies. The point that Bell dramatically illustrates is that scientific breakthroughs eventually result in profound social changes.

The last two articles consider worldwide environmental and institutional problems and grope for solutions. Lester Brown prescribes population control, soil conservation, reforestation, and strong conservation measures as medicine for our sick planet. The final selection by Joel Kotkin ends on a high note. Kotkin believes that America is currently in decline, as other readings have shown, but it will rise because it has a good resource base, and is dynamic and creative due to immigration and an entrepreneurial economy. If so, it will be the task of this generation of college students to carry out the revival.

Looking Ahead: Challenge Questions

What are the significant factors bringing about social change at the present time?

In what ways will social change accelerate? How can it slow down?

What are some ways to deal with social change?

Unit 6

DIVIDED BY DEMOGRAPHY
ANALYZING THE DEMOGRAPHIC TRAP

LESTER R. BROWN
Mr. Brown is president of the Worldwatch Institute.

In 1945, the eminent demographer Frank Notestein outlined a theory of demographic change based on the effect of economic and social progress on population growth. His theory, known as the demographic transition, classified all societies into one of three stages. Drawing heavily on the European experience, it has provided the conceptual framework for demographic research ever since.

During the first stage of the demographic transition, which characterizes pre-modern societies, both birth and death rates are high and population grows slowly, if at all. In the second stage, living conditions improve as public health measures, including mass immunizations, are introduced and food production expands. Birth rates remain high, but death rates fall and population grows rapidly. The third stage follows when economic and social gains, combined with lower infant mortality rates, reduce the desire for large families. As in the first stage, birth rates and death rates are in equilibrium, but at a much lower level.

A WATERSHED PERIOD

This remarkably useful conceptualization has been widely used by demographers to explain differential rates of growth and to project national and global populations. But as we approach the end of the twentieth century, a gap has emerged in the analysis. The theorists did not say what happens when developing countries get trapped in the second stage, unable to achieve the economic and social gains that are counted upon to reduce births. Nor does the theory explain what happens when second-stage population growth rates of 3 percent per year—which means a twentyfold increase per century—continue indefinitely and begin to overwhelm local life-support systems.

Once incomes begin to rise and birth rates begin declining, the process feeds on itself and countries can quickly move to the equilibrium of the demographic transition's third stage. Unfortunately, these self-reinforcing trends also hold for the forces that lead to ecological deterioration and economic decline: Once populations expand to the point where their demands begin to exceed the sustainable yield of local forests, grasslands, croplands, or aquifers, they begin directly or indirectly to consume the resource base itself. Forests and grasslands disappear, soils erode, land productivity declines, water tables fall, or wells go dry. This in turn reduces food production and incomes, triggering a downward spiral.

A DEMOGRAPHICALLY DIVIDED WORLD

Close to a generation ago, countries were conveniently classified as developed or developing based strictly on economic criteria. Roughly one fifth of the world was classified as developed and four fifths as developing. Whether living standards are improving or deteriorating may be a more useful indicator than the differences in living standards among countries. By this measure, polarized population growth rates are driving roughly half the world toward a better future and half toward ecological deterioration and economic decline.

As the nineties approach, new demographic criteria are needed. The world is dividing largely into countries where population growth is slow or nonexistent and where living conditions are improving, and those where population growth is rapid and living conditions are deteriorating or in imminent danger of doing so. In the second group are countries now in or entering their fourth decade of rapid population growth. Not only have they failed to complete the demographic transition, but the deteriorating relationship between people and ecological support systems is lowering living standards in many of these countries, making it difficult for them to do so.

The risk in some countries is that death rates will begin to rise in response to declining living standards, pushing countries back into the first stage. In 1963, Frank Notestein pointed out that "such a rise in mortality would demonstrate the bankruptcy of all our [development] efforts." For a number of countries, that specter of bankruptcy is growing uncomfortably close.

Grouping geographic regions according to the rate of population growth shows five of them, containing 2.3 billion people, in the slow growth category. (See Table 2-1.) Bracketed by Western Europe, which is on the verge of reaching zero population growth, and by populous East Asia, which grown 1.0 percent annually, this group has a collective growth rate of 0.8 percent per year. In these societies, rising living standards and low fertility rates reinforce each other.

The other five geographic regions are in the rapid growth group, which contains 2.6 billion people—just over half the world's total. This group is growing at 2.5 percent per year, three times as fast as the slowly expanding half. In actual numbers, the slow growth half adds 19 million people each year while the rapid growth group adds 64 million, more than three times as many. For many countries in this latter group, rapid population growth and falling incomes are now reinforcing each other. Many others, such as India and Zaire, are still registering increases in per capita incomes, but they risk a reversal in this trend if they do not slow population growth soon.

These numbers signal just how demographically divided the world has become. The demographic middle ground has almost disappeared. All regions are either growing slowly—at 1 percent per year or less—or rapidly—at 2.2 percent or more. Although a few specific coun-

tries in the rapid growth regions are approaching or have reached the third stage of the demographic transition, such as Argentina, Cuba, and Uruguay in Latin America, their populations are not large enough to markedly influence regional trends.

Southeast Asia, home to some 414 million people, is probably the best candidate for joining the slow growth group in the foreseeable future. Two countries in this region, Thailand and Indonesia, have good family planning programs and rapidly falling fertility. They may well follow China into the small family category. By contrast, the Philippines and Vietnam, with high birth rates and falling living standards, are unlikely to make the breakthrough to low fertility in the near future.

Long-term population projections dramatize the diverging prospects for countries in the slow and rapid growth categories. (See Table 2-2.) The population of the United Kingdom, for example, is expected to level off at 59 million, just 5 percent above the current level. West Germany's population is expected to stabilize at 52 million, some 15 percent below the current population. For the United States, population growth is expected to halt at 289 million, roughly one fifth larger than in 1986.

In stark contrast, Nigeria's population, now just over 100 million, is projected to reach 532 million before it stops growing toward the middle of the next century. If this were to happen, Nigeria would then have within its borders nearly as many people as in all of Africa today, a sobering picture to say the least. Kenya's population is projected to more than quintuple before stabilizing, as is Ethiopia's, where a

Table 2-1. World Population Growth by Geographic Region, 1986

Region	Population (million)	Population Growth Rate (percent)	Annual Increment (million)
Slow Growth Regions			
Western Europe	381	0.2	0.8
North America	267	0.7	1.9
E. Eur. and Soviet Union	392	0.8	3.1
Australia and New Zeal.	19	0.8	0.1
East Asia[1]	1,263	1.0	12.6
Total	2,322	0.8	18.6
Rapid Growth Regions			
Southeast Asia[2]	414	2.2	9.1
Latin America	419	2.3	9.6
Indian Subcontinent	1,027	2.4	24.6
Middle East	178	2.8	5.0
Africa	583	2.8	16.3
Total[3]	2,621	2.5	65.5

SOURCE: Population Reference Bureau, *1986 World Population Data Sheet* (Washington D.C.: 1986).
[1] Principally China and Japan. [2] Principally Burma, Indonesia, the Philippines, Thailand, and Vietnam.
[3] Numbers may not add up to totals due to rounding.

Table 2-2. Projected Population Size at Stabilization, Selected Countries

Country	Population in 1986 (million)	Annual Rate of Population Growth (percent)	Size of Population at Stabilization (million)	Change from 1986 (percent)
Slow Growth Countries				
China	1,050	1.0	1,571	+ 50
Soviet Union	280	0.9	377	+ 35
United States	241	0.7	289	+ 20
Japan	121	0.7	128	+ 6
United Kingdom	56	0.2	59	+ 5
West Germany	61	− 0.2	52	− 15
Rapid Growth Countries				
Kenya	20	4.2	111	+ 455
Nigeria	105	3.0	532	+ 406
Ethiopia	42	2.1	204	+ 386
Iran	47	2.9	166	+ 253
Pakistan	102	2.8	330	+ 223
Bangladesh	104	2.7	310	+ 198
Egypt	46	2.6	126	+ 174
Mexico	82	2.6	199	+ 143
Turkey	48	2.5	109	+ 127
Indonesia	168	2.1	368	+ 119
India	785	2.3	1,700	+ 116
Brazil	143	2.3	298	+ 108

SOURCE: World Bank, *World Development Report 1985* (New York: Oxford University Press, 1985).

combination of soil erosion and ill-conceived agricultural policies have already led to widespread starvation. Needless to say, these projections are unrealistic for the simple reason that life-support systems will begin to collapse long before the additional numbers materialize.

Population projections for those Third World countries where life-support systems are already disintegrating can only be described as projections of disaster. India's population is expected to more than double, reaching 1.7 billion and making it the world's most populous country, surpassing China, around 2010. During the same period Mexico's population of 82 million is projected to reach 199 million, just over four fifths that of the United States today.

These wide variations in projected population growth suggest that a demographically divided world is likely to become more deeply divided along economic lines as well. Unless this relationship between rapidly multiplying populations and their life-support systems can be stabilized, development policies, however imaginative, are likely to fail. . . .

DIVERGING FOOD AND INCOME TRENDS

Throughout the third quarter of this century, a rising global economic tide was raising incomes everywhere. Between 1950 and 1973, when the world economy expanded at a robust 5 percent per year, incomes were rising in virtually all countries, regardless of their economic system or stage of development.

Since 1973, the global economy has expanded at less than 3 percent per year; the decline is more dramatic in per capita terms, falling from just over 3 percent to scarcely 1 percent. By far the most influential reason for this development was the 1973 oil price hike, reinforced by the 1979 price rise.

Part and parcel of this global economic slowdown was the loss of momentum in agriculture. Even as oil prices were rising, soil erosion and desertification were beginning to take a toll on agriculture. Grain production, expanding at over 3 percent per year before 1973, has increased at only 2.3 percent annually since then. Growth in per capita grain output for the world as a whole since 1973 has been a negligible 0.4 percent per year. If China is excluded, it is almost nonexistent.

When oil prices climbed, political leaders of developing countries were under pressure to keep their economies expanding rapidly so as to maintain per capita gains, and many borrowed heavily to do so. This effort succeeded briefly, but soaring interest rates combined with the slowdown in the global economy to leave many countries heavily indebted and unable to make even their interest payments.

As a result, much of the Third World now devotes the lion's share of export earnings to paying interest on external debts. In extreme cases, such as the Sudan, 80 percent of export earnings are required to service debt. With the weakening of oil prices in early 1986, Mexico's debt rose to $102 billion. With Mexico unable to make all the payments, international lenders began adding the unpaid interest to the outstanding debt.

When the United Nations proclaimed the seventies the Decade of Development, it was scarcely conceivable that half a dozen countries would experience declines in per capita grain production greater than 20 percent over the following 15 years. In three countries—Angola, Haiti, and Iraq—it has fallen by half. Rapid population growth, agricultural mismanagement, environmental degradation, and war or civil unrest have contributed in varying measures to these declines. All too often, the adverse effects of ecological deterioration are abetted by food price policies that favor the cities and starve the countryside of capital needed for investment.

EFFECTS OF POPULATION GROWTH

A comparison of trends in Western Europe, the region with the slowest population growth, and Africa, with the fastest, illustrates graphically how different population growth rates are driving grain production trends in opposite directions. In 1950, Western Europe produced somewhat more grain per capita than Africa (234 kilograms to 157 kilograms), but not a great deal more by international standards. Africa's per capita output edged upward to a peak of 174 kilograms in the mid-sixties, and then began to decline.

By 1985, Western Europe produced 501 kilograms per person and Africa only 150. Total grain production over the 35-year span increased in Western Europe by 164 percent and in Africa by 129 percent. The big difference between the two continents was in population, which increased in Europe by perhaps one fifth at the same time that it easily doubled in Africa.

Closely paralleling these diverging trends are those in per capita income. The patterns in some of the world's more populous countries illustrate the divergence that is becoming the hallmark of this decade. While Mexico's income fell by some 7 percent between 1980 and 1986, that of China increased 58 percent. Per capita income in Nigeria has fallen by nearly a third thus far during the eighties, while South Korea's has increased by that amount. Most of the major countries in Africa and all of the major Latin American ones—Argentina, Brazil, and Mexico—have experienced income declines during this decade.

During the seventies, Africa became the first region to experience a decade-long decline in per capita income during peacetime since the Great Depression. All indications are that during the eighties, the situation in Africa will worsen further. In addition, it is likely to be joined by Latin America, where regional incomes in 1986 were down nearly one tenth from 1980. Barring a miracle, Latin America, like Africa, appears likely to end the decade with a lower per capita income.

Will the forces that have slowed economic growth during the seventies and eighties and reversed the historical rise in per capita income in two regions lead to similar results elsewhere? This could happen on the Indian subcontinent, which now has over 1 billion people, if population growth there is not slowed soon. Bangladesh, India, Nepal, and Pakistan all have population growth rates well in excess of 2 percent per year. And the subcontinent is beset with serious environmental stresses. . . .

GROWING RURAL LANDLESSNESS

In many ways, the most fundamental shift in the population/resource relationship during the demographic transition's middle stage occurs between people and land. Throughout most of human history, the gradual increase in human numbers was accompanied by a slow expansion of the cropland area. As populations grew, forests were cleared for farming. As land pressures built in Europe, the landless migrated to the New World.

By the mid-twentieth century, the amount of new land suitable for cropping was diminished just when population growth was accelerating. Cropland area continued to grow, but not nearly as fast as population. In the more densely populated parts of the Third World, the result was growing rural landlessness—lack of access to land either through ownership or tenancy.

Though fueled by population growth, rural landlessness is exacerbated by the concentration of landownership. In Latin America, the most extreme case, it is not uncommon for 5 percent of the populace to own four fifths of the farmland. Land distribution is at the heart of the civil war in El Salvador, and is undoubtedly the most sensitive political issue that the government of Brazil faces.

The largest landless populations are concentrated in South Asia, principally on the Indian subcontinent. East Asia today has the largest population of any geographic region, but it has benefited from the early postwar land reforms undertaken in China, Japan, and South Korea. In China, although all land is owned by the state, farmers have access to it through long-term leases.

LAND DISTRI-BUTION

Although the degree of landlessness varies among Bangladesh, India, and Pakistan, there are broad similarities. A World Bank study reports that the three countries now have over 30 million landless rural households, consisting of families who neither own nor lease land. Assuming an average of only 6 people per household, the subcontinent's landless rural population is nearly as large as the total U.S. population. In addition, 22 percent of the cultivated holdings are smaller than 0.4 hectares, not enough to support a family, even when intensively farmed. Another group of farmers has between 0.4 and 1.0 hectares, not usually enough to provide an adequate standard of living. A third group, farm families who cultivate between 1.0 and 2.0 hectares of land, accounts for some 21 percent of all cultivated holdings in South Asia.

The 30 million landless rural households, plus the near-landless ones (with less than 0.4 hectares), now represent close to 40 percent of all rural households in South Asia. These people depend heavily on seasonal agricultural employment for their livelihoods, and increasingly on new jobs in the agricultural service industries that are springing up as farming modernizes.

Unfortunately, not nearly enough work exists to employ fully the swelling ranks of the landless and near-landless. As a result, many live at the edge of subsistence. And all indications are that the growth of landlessness in South Asia will continue. In India alone, the number of landless rural households is projected to reach 44 million by the end of the century.

For Africa, landlessness is a relatively new phenomenon, but one that is growing. Land hunger can be seen in the conflicts among people who are migrating from eroded, worn-out fields in search of new areas. It can also be seen in the movement of farmers into wildlife reserves—not because they wish to destroy the habitat, but because the struggle to survive on this famine-ridden continent takes precedence over all other considerations.

Where landownership is heavily concentrated, the growth in landlessness can be curbed or even reversed by initiating land reform. In some countries, the base of landownership can also be broadened through resettlement. Unfortunately, Brazil and Indonesia, the two countries that have invested heavily in resettlement in virgin tropical forests, have done so at great ecological cost. Another way to check the growth in landlessness is to slow population growth through effective family planning. Resettlement (where feasible) and land reform can reduce landlessness in the short run, but in the long run only population stabilization will work.

The rural landless invariably have far higher levels of malnutrition, lower levels of education, and lower life expectancies than others in society. In Bangladesh, for example, those in rural households who own no land or less than 0.2 hectares consume on average 1,924 calories a day. Those who own 1.2 hectares or more consume 2,375 calories per day, 23 percent more. The difference in protein intake is even greater—28 percent on average. To be landless in an agrarian society is thus to be severely disadvantaged in the struggle for survival.

In societies such as Bangladesh, where existing holdings, already divided and subdivided, cannot be divided further, population growth translates into the landlessness that feeds unemployment and worsens income distribution. It is the source of migrants who inhabit the shantytowns surrounding Third World cities and cross national borders in search of work. This landless class, often outside the mainstream of development and bereft of hope, is also a potential source of unrest.

POPULATION GROWTH AND CONFLICT

The relationship between population growth and social conflict has been largely ignored by the social science research community, lost in the gap between demography and political science. Nazli Choucri of the Massachusetts Institute of Technology, a pioneer in research in this area, notes a continued lack of awareness about it within the research community. Howard Wiarda and Iêda Siquiera Wiarda of the University of Massachusetts point out that policymakers also largely neglect this relationship in the formulation of both population and national security policies.

Difficult though they may be to measure, numerous linkages exist between population growth and conflict, both within and among societies. Conflict arises when growing populations compete for a static or shrinking resource base. Inequitable distribution of resources— whether of income, land, or water—complicates the relationship. Increased competition and conflict fray the social fabric that helps to maintain social harmony.

One reason for the dearth of research on how population growth affects social stability is the complexity of the relationship. To begin with, several fields of knowledge are involved— economics and ecology as well as demography and political science. In addition, the relationship between trends in these fields is not a simple matter of cause and effect, but rather of interaction. Any meaningful analysis must take into account a continuous interaction between

SOCIAL CON- FLICT

demographic, economic, environmental, and social or political trends.

The analytical challenge is intimidating, but the issue is a serious one, and an effort must be made. In an analysis of the turmoil in Central America, political analyst Sergio Diaz-Briquets argues that rapid population growth "has added pressure to labor markets already saturated with unemployed and underemployed persons; it increases pressure on the land area, it taxes governments' ability to provide needed social services." Further, it indirectly "plants seeds of discord by continuously increasing the ranks of unemployed youth and creating stiffer competition among those trying to improve their lot in life, particularly in ossified social systems."

When a society's population growth accelerates sharply, the age structure is increasingly dominated by young people. For example, in dozens of developing countries 40 percent of the population is now under the age of 15.

This shift can itself be a source of instability. When young people become so numerous, they are likely to achieve a much higher profile in society. Changing age structures also put pressure on social institutions. Educational systems are inundated with new students, initially for elementary schools and then for colleges. In parts of the Third World, the tidal wave of youngsters has overwhelmed the schools, making a mockery of compulsory education.

POLITICAL EFFECTS

Economic stresses also generate political conflict. As indicated earlier, the difference between a stationary population and a rapidly growing one can spell the difference between societies that are raising their living standards and those that are suffering a sustained decline. A 2-percent rate of economic growth in West Germany or Denmark, which have no population growth, will bring steady progress. But in Kenya or Peru, where population growth is rapid, it leads to a steady decline in living standards and growing social unrest.

For many developing countries, the global economic slowdown has come just as record numbers of young people are entering the job market. The specter of growing numbers of restless unemployed youngsters in the streets does not convey an image of social tranquility. Foreign affairs columnist Georgie Anne Geyer notes, "Given what is coming—unemployed youths roaming the streets in countries where half the population often is under 18 years of age, with no prospect of job formation, hungry, and looking to irregular leaders to lead them in new and as yet unpredictable movements—there is little question that even more political explosions are on the immediate horizon."

When deteriorating environmental support systems can no longer support local populations, conflicts can arise as people are forced to migrate in search of a livelihood. Often these "ecological refugees" cross national borders, a process now widespread within Africa. It is perhaps most noticeable in the movement of nomadic pastoralists being forced southward as a result of desertification. All too often these nomads, with their herds and flocks, come into conflict with farmers in the regions they are trying to enter. . . .

One of the most neglected social issues relating to population growth is the contribution of crowding to human conflict. The scientific literature in this field is weak. Most research has been done on animals. The Wiardas observe that these studies "show a close relationship between crowding and violence, but the relationship is usually indirect . . . crowding does provide a set of conditions, a context in which tension, violence, and various forms of aberrant behavior are more likely to occur." With human populations, the effects of crowding are not easily separated from those of poverty, with which it is usually closely associated. Within societies, crowding and competition for jobs and land may exacerbate long-standing religious, tribal, regional, or ethnic differences.

Mexico and Egypt, two culturally contrasting countries that are beginning to feel the effects of rapid population growth, illustrate the stresses faced in varying degrees throughout the Third World. Mexico's family planning program of the past decade has been rightfully praised for its role in reducing birth rates. Yet, because the problem of rapid growth was recognized too late, the country's population is still growing 2.6 percent annually. Mexico, home to 82 million, adds 2.1 million people each year. Over the remainder of this century, some 15 million youngsters will enter the job market—roughly 1 million annually. The nation needs more new jobs than ever before, but the economy is staggering under an external debt of $102 billion. A broad-based deterioration of land resources and a scarcity of irrigation water are raising the dependence on imported food in the country where the Green Revolution began.

IMPEND-ING CATAS-TROPHE

The basic ingredients for internal political conflict and civil strife are in place. An economic slowdown induced by rising external debt, rising numbers of unemployed youth, and a highly skewed income distribution seem certain to breed social tensions and rising unrest. The wealthiest 10 percent of Mexicans receive 41 percent of total income; the poorest one fifth, less than 3 percent. Real wages have declined at least a fifth during the eighties. Fiscal stringencies have forced the elimination of subsidies on tortillas, the corn meal food staple, at precisely the time when wages were falling, thus weakening the social safety net.

Unemployment is rising. Mexican political scientist Jorge Castaneda believes that Mexican youth who do not find jobs have three options: attempt to migrate to the United States, spend their time idle on the streets, or rise up in revolution. Exposure to the benefits of higher living standards, both through contact with migrants to the United States and through television, gives today's youth higher expectations than their parents had.

Castaneda believes that because of the difficulty in creating enough jobs, average Mexicans may be poorer at the end of the century than they are today. The only way to offset the adverse social effects on the poor is to redistribute wealth. But this is exceedingly difficult, particularly when so much capital is fleeing the country. In looking toward the end of the century, Castaneda believes that Mexico will either be more just and more democratic or "it will be on the verge of splitting asunder—if it has not broken apart already." . . .

Developments within Central America over the past generation illustrate how population growth can contribute to conflict. Following World War II, Central American economies diversified and grew rapidly. Per capita income nearly doubled. Then during the seventies, a number of trends converged to undermine economic progress.

Even before the first oil price shock, deforestation and soil erosion had been accelerating, slowly undermining Central America's agricultural foundation. In effect, population growth began to overwhelm the ecosystems, the educational systems, and the employment-creating capacities of national economies. In some countries, the economic slowdown was aggravated by the inequitable distribution of land and, hence, of income. In Nicaragua, it led to revolution. In El Salvador, where incomes of the richest one fifth of the population are 33 times those of the poorest one fifth, social tensions eventually burst into civil war.

Unfortunately, the conditions giving birth to the tragic recent history of bloodshed in Central America are not unique. In addition to Mexico and Egypt, scores of developing countries are faced with politically destabilizing economic crises. Mounting stresses may cause fragile political institutions to give way, leading to an age of disorder.

THE DEMOGRAPHIC TRAP

For many Third World countries, the demographic trap is becoming the grim alternative to completing the demographic transition. If countries are in the middle of the transition for too long, rapid population growth and the associated ecological and economic deterioration may prevent them from reaching the equilibrium of the final stage. The only long-term alternative then becomes a return to the equilibrium of the first stage—with high birth and death rates. Such a regression is already evident in Africa, where famine has raised death rates twice since 1970.

Most of the Third World entered the second stage of the demographic transition around mid-century. As recently as the forties, world population was growing at scarcely 1 percent per year. At that time, North America and Africa were growing at the same rate, both slightly faster than the world average. Suddenly, as a result of falling Third World death rates, world population growth accelerated sharply in the fifties—approaching 2 percent, where it has since remained.

A typical developing country has thus been in the middle stage of the demographic transition for close to four decades. This high-fertility, low-mortality stage cannot continue for long. After a few decades, countries should have put together a combination of economic policies and family planning programs that reduce birth rates and sustain gains in living standards. If they fail to do so, continuing rapid population growth eventually overwhelms natural support systems, and environmental deterioration starts to reduce per capita food production and income.

Most societies do not know when they are crossing the various biological thresholds that eventually lead to economic decline. Few notice when the topsoil loss begins to exceed new soil formation. Similarly, when firewood harvesting first begins to exceed the sustainable yield, the effects are scarcely visible because the excessive harvesting is so small. But over time it increases and eventually, as population expands and the forested area dwindles, it begins to feed vigorously on itself. By the time the loss of tree cover becomes widely evident, the population growth that is driving the deforestation has so much momentum that the decline becomes difficult to arrest. . . .

The demographic trap is not easily recognized because it involves the interaction of population, environmental, and economic trends, which are monitored by various offices in different governmental ministries. And observers frequently fail to distinguish between triggering events, such as drought, and underlying instability in the population-environment relationship.

The inability to cope with these developments can make political leaders, even capable ones, appear incompetent. Economic stresses begin to generate social stresses. Ethnic and

ON DISASTER'S THRESHOLD

tribal tensions are exacerbated and governments become preoccupied with instability. More and more of their time and energy is required merely to stay in power. Dozens of countries in Africa, Latin America, the Middle East, and South Asia are already enmeshed in this demographic trap.

National governments in the modern era have little experience with a long-term, sustained decline in living standards. Thus countries find themselves caught in a downward spiral with little warning. Figuring out how to arrest the deterioration once it is under way may dwarf in difficulty the other challenges facing governments.

But they are probably not the first to be caught unawares. Archaeologists who have studied the long-term evolution of the Mayan civilization, centered in the Guatemalan lowlands, report that its population increased rather steadily for some 17 centuries before its abrupt collapse in the ninth century. They calculate that the Mayan population was doubling once every 408 years. Kenya's is doubling every 18 years.

Lacking a grounding in ecology and an understanding of carrying capacity, all too many economic planners and population policymakers have failed to distinguish between the need to slow population growth and the need to halt it. If societal demands are far below the sustainable yield of natural systems, then slowing population growth is sufficient. But when they have passed these thresholds, the failure to halt population growth leads to a deterioration of support systems.

Governments are moving into uncharted territory in the population/environment/resources relationship. Most developing countries cannot remain much longer in the middle stage of the demographic transition. Either they must forge ahead with all the energies at their disposal, perhaps even on an emergency basis, to slow and halt population growth. Or they will slide into the demographic trap. For the first time, governments are faced with the monumental task of trying to reduce birth rates as living conditions deteriorate, a challenge that may require some new approaches. If they fail, economic deterioration could eventually lead to social disintegration of the sort that undermined earlier civilizations when population demands became unsustainable.

UNCHARTED
TERRITORY

PROMISE OF AMERICA

William Broyles, Jr.

They come across the South China Sea in tiny boats and brave the Rio Grande in rafts made of automobile hoods welded together. Violence, repression, persecution and poverty may encircle their lives, but they dream of something better—of freedom. Almost 500 years old, the dream still works on the imagination like a magnet. The dream has a magic name: America.

For each new immigrant—as the ordinary and famous attest on the following pages—the dream is born again, fresh and powerful. "Come," it says, "no matter who you are, and be one of us. Come and be free."

"Who is the American, this new man?" asked essayist Michel Crèvecoeur in 1784. Two hundred years later, his question is still as provocative and the answer just as elusive. We are a nation without a nationality, a people without a race. We are an idea. We are Americans because we believe we are.

"Once I thought to write a history of the immigrants in America. Then I discovered that the immigrants *were* American history." So Oscar Handlin began *The Uprooted*, his masterly work on immigration, in words that could have been engraved on the Statue of Liberty. Walter Prescott Webb, no less a historian, wrote in *The Great Frontier* that the history of America "is the history of the frontier"—the vast continent stretching west behind the great statue's back.

It was not enough simply to come to America: Jamestown, the first English colony, perished from "unsufferable hunger." In the New World the old ways didn't work; the immigrants had to change. The parable of the first Thanksgiving is the parable of America. Starving and helpless, the Pilgrims learned from the Indians how to prosper in the wilderness. We are a nation in passage, learning and changing as we cross ocean and continent, bound always toward the setting sun.

Consider America as a play in three acts. First Act: The great immigration. Some 50 million people—the vast majority of them Europeans—abandon their traditional cultures and brave the Atlantic Ocean to begin a new life. Act Two: The great frontier. The vast continent they encounter transforms the immigrants into a new people—Americans. Both acts transpire in the same time frame—from the early 17th century to the beginning of the 20th. Act Three: The new people find their destiny—a tale as yet without end. And at the curtain other immigrants appear, from entirely new quarters, to begin the drama again.

It is tempting to romanticize the immigrant and the pioneer, and no doubt our celebrations of the 100th anniversary of the Statue of Liberty this Fourth of July will do so. Their triumph is all around us, their tragedies by and large distant memories. The great immigration and the great frontier are such powerful themes in our history precisely because they are grounded in tragedy.

Every man who turned his back on the Old World and went to America was, in a way, defeated: If he had been successful where he was, why leave? And every pioneer who left the settled life of the East and went west was re-creating that original immigrant experience. The frontier was where a man could start over—implying that he needed to.

The American dreamed new dreams, yes—but because the old ones had failed. To make new traditions, old traditions had to be destroyed. Each new American is a small death of an old life, born again into a new one.

SURGE OF NEW FACES

Today we are living in a reawakening of the immigrant experience; not since the first decade of the 20th century have so many new immigrants become Americans. Some 7 million legal immigrants are expected this decade, with perhaps millions more entering illegally. New ethnic neighborhoods are transforming our cities; new faces are turning up in our shops and factories; new languages buzz in our schools. This bubbling stew may seem strange to us, but until immigration was all but cut off in 1924 it was the normal condition of America.

In fact, even though the flow of immigrants this decade will be among the largest in history, the annual number of immigrants hovers around only 0.2 percent of the total population; before 1924 the figure was routinely more than 1 percent. The foreign-born population in 1980 was less than half what it was in **1910. In Boston in 1885 almost 70 percent of the population was foreign-born. Today even Los Angeles, where almost a third of the population is foreign-born, does not begin to approach these figures.**

For the first time in our history, however, the majority of immigrants do not come from Europe. The great westward movement that began with Columbus is over. Almost half the new immigrants today are from Asia, with South Korea alone sending more than England, West Germany, Ireland and Italy—the nations that for the past 350 years furnished the great majority of new Americans—put together. The next-largest group is from Mexico, the Caribbean and Latin America.

New York City, the original ethnic metropolis, is being renewed yet again. The older immigrants—the Irish and the Italians—still hold their own in the police and sanitation departments, but coffee shops have long since passed to the Greeks and vegetable stands to the Koreans, who have brought a sense of aesthetics and quality—and a fierce devotion to hard work—back to neighborhoods around the city. Russians and Haitians are transforming Brooklyn and Queens, and the Chinese are overwhelming "Little Italy."

New York remains the classic laboratory of the three-generation immigrant story: The first generation works hard and sacrifices; their children go to college, and their grandchildren, who no longer speak the old language, move to the suburbs. And in come new immigrants to repeat the process.

For all its vibrant immigrant life, New York City is no longer the gateway to America. If the Statue of Liberty were being erected today, it would more likely shine its beacon from Los Angeles International Airport or the Rio Grande.

The melting pot of the new America is Los Angeles. One in 5 of the millions of immigrants since 1970 lives in Southern California. Away from its affluent pockets Los Angeles is like a booming Third World city: "Koreatown," "Little Saigon" and a host of little Philippines, Irans, El Salvadors, Cambodias, Taiwans and Israels stretches for miles. And, of course, everywhere is Mexico: Los Angeles is the third-largest Mexican city.

The downtown market teems with a bewildering variety of ethnic foods, goods and people. Grocery stores do a thriving business in books on how to speak Spanish to the maid. Assembly workers at high-tech plants speak a babel of languages, and the $3-billion-a-year clothing industry survives on immigrant labor, legal and illegal. Beverly Hills High School has a distinctly Iranian look, and everywhere Oriental students are regularly claiming the highest scores in math and sciences and a share of admissions to the best universities far out of proportion to their numbers.

Along the Rio Grande, Texas is being reclaimed by Mexico. This is the most heavily crossed border in the world; the Texas border alone is as long as the line from the Baltic to the Mediterranean that divides the free world from the Communist empire, but it can be crossed casually by a boy on a mule ambling over the dry river bed above Terlingua.

Spanish is the language of the Texas

That immigrants work harder to get ahead is now a well-established American legend. Many of those who came here from humble foreign origins have risen to become paramount figures in the commerce and culture of this nation. These pages bring the voices of four for whom—through their sweat and perseverance and luck—the American dream has come true.

KYUPIN PHILIP HWANG, 50, COMPUTER MAGNATE

"A few years ago [in 1983] Forbes magazine said I was the 28th richest man in the United States—worth 575 million dollars on paper. Can you believe it? An immigrant who came with $50 in his pocket?

"Lately my company has had its troubles. A lot of computer companies have gone bankrupt. We've reorganized and made a strong foundation. I am still a 100-million-dollar guy. I can still laugh.

"You can do that in America. Sometimes you're way up, sometimes down, but you still have the chance to go back up. Most Americans don't appreciate this opportunity.

"I sold pencils and shined shoes in Korea while in high school. I came to the U.S. in 1964 on a student visa, finished a bachelor's degree at Utah State and found a job with Ford Motor as an engineer. They paid the tuition and books for me to get a master's. Fantastic! After working for Ford and Burroughs, I answered an ad that said, 'Sunshine California company looking for engineer.' Two years later I had an opportunity to have my own business. Last year we did 100 million dollars in sales.

"It was not easy. During college summers I washed dishes during the day and cleaned bathrooms at night—16 hours a day, six days a week. The body was aching so much I took aspirin at night to sleep. But with strong determination you can do it.

"I started TeleVideo in 1975 with $9,000—all of our savings. The bank, an investment company, wouldn't give me any money. I put up my car, my furniture to get a loan. We had a hard time. I took out a second mortgage to pay our employes; there were about 15 then.

"We were within two weeks of running out of money again. Then the product started coming out of the factory. We could send out invoices and go to the bank for more credit. Soon we doubled in sales almost every year.

"This is what I call a wonderful country. In many countries you work so hard and have no opportunity. Here there is opportunity for everybody—especially in Silicon Valley. It is all up to you. I never believed I was more talented. I had a vision. I tried hard, and I did my best."

border counties, but Texas is also being transformed by Asians and other new immigrants. The Vietnamese have taken over shrimping on the Gulf of Mexico and in Houston are reclaiming downtown neighborhoods and pushing blacks out of public housing. At times the ethnic mix becomes almost incomprehensible: Houston's best Cuban café is run by Koreans, the best Thai restaurant has a Mexican cook.

Although the sources of most new Americans have changed, the process is still much the same. Samuel Gompers, who created the American Federation of Labor, recalled how in the sweatshops of England in the 1860s the young workers sang a song called "To the West":

To the West, to the West, to the land of the free,
Where mighty Missouri rolls down to the sea,
Where a man is a man if he's willing to toil
And the humblest may gather the fruits of the soil.

A Norwegian immigrant remembered years later how he and his brother heard people in their village talk about a country called America: "This was the first time we had heard that name." Three months later they were on their way there. That story was repeated millions of times—from Sicily to Sichuan, from Galway to Guadalajara. As one Croatian wrote: "America. Suddenly somehow the name appeared in village minds."

First the name began to circulate; then the idea of it took hold, and the flood began. Tens of millions of people forsook the land where their ancestors had lived back into the mists of time—and crossed the ocean. The ones who left were the adventurous, the brave and often the maladjusted. And they were usually the poor. "I want to go to America," wrote a Polish peasant, "but have no means, because I am poor and have nothing but the 10 fingers of my hands, a wife and nine children."

RISKS OF PASSAGE

For most of those who come, the passage to America is the hardest ordeal. For centuries the ocean crossing—the trial by wind and wave, hunger and sickness—was each immigrant's lot. They were fair prey for the elements and unscrupulous captains; it was a voyage that marked them forever and that made the first vision of the Statue of Liberty in New York Harbor so intense an experience that few immigrants ever forgot it.

One example from the records of the New York State Commission of Emigration: The schooner *Leibnitz* left Hamburg on Nov. 2, 1867, and arrived in New York Harbor on Jan. 11, 1868. Its 544 passengers included 395 adults, 103 children and 46 infants. By the time the ship reached New York, 108 of its passengers had died. The commissioners report that they "spoke to some little boys and girls who, when asked where were their parents, pointed to the ocean with sobs and tears and cried, 'Down there!' "

Today the passage can be equally harrowing. Any waiter in a Vietnamese restaurant in Houston or Orange County has a tale of walking across Cambodia or fleeing Vietnam by boat, of attacks by ruthless Thai pirates and long months in a refugee camp. The Cambodians have their holocaust, the Haitians their small boats, the Mexicans their encounters with the feared *La Migra*—the border patrol.

But no danger seems too great, no obstacle too large to stop those who are determined to come. Listen to the Mexican song of the wetbacks, *El Corrido de los Mojados":*

If they kick one out through Laredo,
Ten will come through Mexicali.
If another is kicked out of Tijuana,
Six will come through Nogales.
Long live all the wetbacks! . . .

Each wave of immigrants has had to brave not only the ordeal of uprooting and passage but the resentment of earlier arrivals and their descendants who, all too often, wanted to close the gate behind them. The refrain has always been the same: That "we will lose our 'old' values to the 'new' immigrants"; that the new immigrants won't become proper Americans. "They are the strangers in the land—come to take, not to give."

Anti-immigration sentiment fueled the Immigration Restriction League, the Know-Nothing political party and the Ku Klux Klan, which considered immigration "an attack upon Protestant religion . . . and a menace to American liberties." The American Federation of Labor, although led by immigrants, backed restrictions to protect its hard-won wage-and-bargaining gains. In California the Native Sons of the Golden West became a powerful political force from the turn of the century until World War II. Their creed (ironic to consider today as California becomes a "minority" state) was that "California should

SARA BERMUDEZ, 36, TV PERSONALITY

"One thing I'll always remember about coming to America is how kind people were. When our neighbors saw we had nothing, they began to bring us things. One woman brought a chair; another brought an old television set. It made the first months livable.

"Today my husband and I both work for Channel 34 in Los Angeles. He is a producer; I am hostess on a Spanish-speaking show called 'Mundo Latino,' broadcasting to a potential audience of 30 million from Central America to Alaska. I give viewers in Mexico and Central America a glimpse of American life while giving Americans a look at the Latino world.

"I hope that by seeing me and what I do Hispanic Americans will realize they can be successful. I want to tell them it's time to move on. We have enough busboys and cabdrivers; now we need doctors and lawyers.

"Though my family has less money here than we did in Mexico, we are very happy. In this country, no matter how bad things are, there is always hope."

remain what it has always been and God himself intended it shall always be—the white man's paradise."

BARRING THE GATES

Restriction took two forms: Literacy tests and quotas. In 1882 the Chinese were excluded. Presidents Cleveland, Taft and Wilson all vetoed literacy tests, but in 1917 they were passed over Wilson's veto. In 1921 came the first quotas, which led to the Draconian law of 1924, whose permanent quotas and other provisions ended three centuries of immigration. The quotas were based on the population as of 1890—a blatant ploy to restrict immigrants from Asia and Central and Southern Europe. The quota for Italy was reduced in one year from 42,000 to fewer than 4,000; for Poland, from 31,000 to 6,000; for Turkey, from 2,700 to 100.

After 1930 there were years in which more people left America than came; for the first time the Statue of Liberty lit the way *out* of America. Between 1929 and 1947 we admitted only 1.2 million immigrants—fewer than came in 1906 alone; deducting for those who left America during the same period, the net immigration was only 600,000—or about the number of legal immigrants in 1985. Even the Nazi horror in Europe couldn't reopen the doors. From 1933 to 1944 we let in fewer than 250,000 refugees from the killing fields of Europe, and only 40,000 displaced persons were admitted in 1947 and 1948.

Finally the Immigration Act of 1965 reversed the trend: It repealed the national quotas and opened the way for the great increase in immigrants from Asia, which now accounts for almost 50 percent of all immigrants. The policy on refugees has also changed: In the past 10 years we have admitted more than a million Vietnamese, Cambodians and Cubans, plus hundreds of thousands more from other countries.

Some anti-immigrant feeling still remains. And immigration is still a powerful and divisive issue. Since 1981 the Congress has been deadlocked over passage of a new immigration bill designed to control illegal immigration. The number of illegal aliens apprehended by the Immigration and Naturalization Service is up 50 percent so far this year and should exceed 1.8 million people by year's end.

Facts on how these illegal aliens affect the American economy are hard to come by. Certainly they are overwhelming the schools and hospitals in the poor counties along the Mexican border; El Paso recently sent the State Department a bill for $10 million to cover the hospital costs of treating illegal aliens. Rice University economist Donald Huddle estimates that for every 100 illegal workers, 65 Americans lose their jobs.

But other studies conclude that the illegal aliens pay more in taxes than they draw in services and that they help stimulate economic growth. The INS estimated that a recent pilot program in Houston would show anywhere from 30 to 90 percent of Texas applicants for unemployment benefits were illegal aliens; in fact, fewer than one half of 1 percent were. Los Angeles has absorbed well over a million legal and illegal immigrants in the past 15 years—and during that period its unemployment rate declined to less than the national average. In 1985 the Rand Corporation concluded that "over all, Mexican immigration has probably been an economic asset to California."

And in spite of the common belief that floods of immigrants depress the level of wages, the evidence seems to point to the contrary. During the peak years of immigration into New York City at the turn of the century, average daily wages went up. The President's Council of Economic Advisers argued that immigrants have a net positive effect on the economy in general, but the poor whites and minorities who feel displaced by new immigrants don't think "in general": They see Vietnam-

FELIX ROHATYN, 58, INVESTMENT BANKER

"My family is Jewish and came from a village in Poland called Rogatyn. My father was a brewer, and his business took him to Vienna, where I was born. There was a wave of anti-Semitism in Austria, and we moved to France. The Nazis invaded France, but we were lucky and managed with false papers and all kinds of stratagems to go the classic escape route: Marseilles, Oran, Casablanca, Lisbon, Rio.

"I was 14 when we arrived here in 1942. We lived on our savings, and I got a job in a pharmacy. After attending Middlebury College, I got a summer job in 1949 as a clerk at Lazard Frères, the investment house. I used to work late, and André Meyer, who was the head of the firm, liked young people who worked late. I think I was making $37.50 a week. He raised me to $50 a week. I stayed with the firm, and I'm now a senior partner.

"I think once you've been a refugee, you're always a refugee. But I feel at home here. In fact, this country is the only place I've ever felt at home."

ELIA KAZAN, 76, FILM DIRECTOR

"I was born in Constantinople. My father was Greek and a rug importer. Constantinople was an uncomfortable place for Greeks, and there wasn't much opportunity. America was something that was romantic to us all. I was 4 years old when we came to America, and I never saw the Statue of Liberty. We arrived on the New Jersey side of the river. That's where I made 'On the Waterfront.'

"My English was slow in developing, but I've always worked very hard—maybe out of desperation. I waited on tables for four years at Williams College and attended the Yale Drama School. Always I wanted to be a director. I don't say it's the best film I made, but 'America, America' is the film I'm fondest of. It was about my family and how it got here; it was also about immigrants—something I felt strongly about.

"I think America is the most exciting, marvelous, mixed-up, chaotic, romantic, unusual place. America is the place where anything can happen. It's corny as hell to say it's the land of opportunity, but it's true."

ese fishermen, Cambodian computer assemblers and Mexican carpenters taking their jobs.

Despite the costs—and even the pain—that may be caused by immigration, the benefits are incalculable. Our neighborhoods, our schools, our workplaces are being renewed and invigorated. Each immigrant re-creates the American dream.

For most of us, America is a gift long since given; for each new arrival, it is fresh and dynamic—and not to be squandered. "We came to America thinking the streets were made of gold," recalled Max Lerner, himself an immigrant. "But the gold wasn't here. The immigrants themselves—their talent and their potential—were the gold."

WE ARE ALL IMMIGRANTS

A recent poll in Connecticut found that 83 percent of those surveyed believe that a person "who has just come to this country [can] be every bit as much an American as someone whose ancestors fought in the American Revolution." We now seem agreed on what President Franklin Delano Roosevelt once reminded the Daughters of the American Revolution: "We are all the children of immigrants."

When the Statue of Liberty is rededicated this Fourth of July we shall say similar words. At the end of June came a reminder of just what those words really mean. Several Cubans were found off the coast of Florida. They had made their way across a hundred miles of ocean—on inner tubes. The voyage of the Pilgrims could not have been more dangerous. Those Cubans crossed an ocean on inner tubes for the idea of freedom. They risked their lives to become Americans.

The story never ends.

LIVING DANGEROUSLY

■ Technology was supposed to solve problems, not cause them. To free mankind, not hurt the innocent. But in the span of a few months, the dark side of technology has asserted itself.

Experts still don't know what went wrong at Chernobyl on April 26. More than two weeks later, as small amounts of radiation were settling over parts of the U.S., there was uncertainty over how much the reactor core had melted.

On the frontier of space, the worst series of rocket mishaps in U.S. history has shaken the country's confidence. Not only was the crew of Challenger lost, but in recent weeks, two other spacecraft have exploded and a research rocket misfired. Now a slew of scheduled flights have been grounded, and across America the question is being asked: Why so many disasters? What is happening to the technological fix?

According to a new *USN&WR*-Cable News Network poll, the vast majority of Americans still say that science and technology do more good than harm, but the margin has fallen from 83 percent three years ago to 72 percent today. What's more, nearly a quarter of those surveyed think that over the next 20 years, technology will cause more harm than good for the human race.

The chief source of high-tech anxiety today is nuclear power. In a kind of post-Chernobyl referendum, three Massachusetts towns voted on May 6 against opening the Seabrook, N.H., nuclear power plant, not far from the state line.

At the same time, there is little chance of the nation's turning its back on new technologies. "We have chosen a lifestyle dependent on high technology," says management consultant John Ketteringham of the Arthur D. Little firm in Cambridge, Mass. "To revert to low-tech solutions, we have to be prepared to die young of cold, disease and hunger."

What's gone wrong

Often, major technological disasters occur after bureaucrats take over from scientific pioneers. Then, complacency sets in, or commercial needs are allowed to dominate.

Both these factors took hold of the National Aeronautics and Space Administration in the mid-1970s. Lulled by the exemplary safety record of the lunar flights and pared down by budget cuts, the agency tried to transform itself from a high-tech research operation into a commercial venture.

According to a recent congressional disclosure, a NASA budget squeeze over the last 15 years eliminated 70 percent of engineers who monitor the quality of equipment used for space flight. Al-

---

When the dreams of scientific pioneers come down to earth, they can become nightmares. The most potent technologies tolerate the fewest mistakes

---

though a 1979 memo characterized the seals on the solid-fuel rocket boosters—the main culprit in the Challenger accident—as "completely unacceptable," the space agency stuck to its design.

Critics charge that NASA treated the shuttle as a "space bus" instead of an experimental test vehicle. Teacher Christa McAuliffe was included in the crew even though an Air Force report had recently rated the chances of a fatal accident on the shuttle at 1 in 35—compared with 1 in 10,000 for a nuclear disaster or a dam failure. And more ominous for the general public is the fact that the next shuttle was to carry deadly plutonium as fuel for two space probes—a potential source of lethal radioactivity should a crash occur.

More than space flight, nuclear power is a "mature" technology that has moved from the laboratory into the commercial arena. Yet in the past 15 years, 151

"significant" incidents have been reported in nuclear plants in 14 countries.

"When things become routine, we become very sloppy," explains physicist Frank von Hipple of Princeton University. "The first team of the Nuclear Age has moved on, and now we are trying to contain a technology that we can't handle on a routine basis."

Another unique requirement of managing complex technologies, such as nuclear power and space flight, is a tricky balance of power. According to Charles Perrow, a Yale professor and author of *Normal Accidents,* both managers and technicians must retain enough control to make split-second decisions at the first sign of trouble.

At Chernobyl and Three Mile Island, the combination of "several highly improbable and therefore unforeseen failures" as the Soviet Union's Deputy Prime Minister Boris Y. Shcherbina puts it, led operators to lose control of conditions in the plants. The problems were compounded by management's failure to respond quickly. At Chernobyl, hundreds of lives may eventually be lost because authorities failed to evacuate the nearby population for 36 hours.

In contrast, Perrow argues that the airline industry "became the best example of a near-error-free technology" when it successfully balanced the central control of air-traffic controllers with the local control of pilots.

Technologies at risk

The proliferation of technologies has widened the scope of risk exponentially. With more people flying than ever before, for example, air-traffic safety—despite its former record—is a growing concern. A 33 percent drop in the number of qualified air-traffic controllers has led the independent Flight Safety Foundation to conclude that standards have slipped since 1981, when 11,400 controllers were fired after a strike. All this adds up to what retired airline captain Richard Ortman, director of airline

 Reprinted from *U.S. News & World Report,* May 19, 1986, pp. 19-22. Copyright, 1986, U.S. News & World Report.

MILESTONES ON THE ROCKY ROAD OF PROGRESS

1945 The Atomic Age opens with the mushroom explosion of the first test bomb over the desert skies near Alamogordo, N.M.

1947 The transistor is invented at Bell Laboratories in New Jersey, paving the way for the computer revolution.

1951 The first electric power from a nuclear reactor is produced at the National Reactor Testing Station in Arco, Idaho, heralding the era of nuclear energy.

1953 The chemical structure of genes is revealed by James Watson and Francis Crick at Cambridge University, opening the way for today's biotechnology boom.

1954 The Salk vaccine against polio is tested on nearly a million children, offering the first largely effective protection against the paralyzing disease.

1957 The U.S.S.R. launches Sputnik 1, signaling the dawn of the Space Age.

1958 An accident at a plutonium weapons facility near Sverdlovsk, in the Soviet Urals, contaminates 1,500 square kilometers with radioactive debris.

1959 A patent for the first integrated circuit is filed by Jack Kilby of Texas Instruments, leading to the development of the revolutionary "computer on a chip."

1960 The laser is invented by Theodore Maiman of Hughes Research Laboratories, in California, leading to the creation of new tools for medicine, industry and the military.

1961 Soviet cosmonaut Yuri Gagarin becomes the first human in space, orbiting the earth in his Vostok 1 satellite for 108 minutes.

■ Thalidomide is banned in West Germany and Britain after more than 2,500 deformed babies are born to European women who took the drug during pregnancy.

1967 The three-man crew of what was to have been the first Apollo flight is killed by a fire that erupts during prelaunch tests.

1969 American astronaut Neil Armstrong takes man's first step on the moon.

1971 Soviet three-man crew aboard Soyuz 11 perishes when the spacecraft's cabin decompresses upon re-entry.

1973 The first genetically engineered organism is created by California researchers Stanley Cohen and Herbert Boyer, opening a new age of made-to-order microbes and plants for medicine, agriculture, energy production and the chemical industry.

1976 An explosion at a Swiss-owned chemical plant near Milan throws into the open air a cloud of the highly toxic gas dioxin. Tens of thousands of birds and animals perish, and more than 500 children develop skin rashes.

1978 First test-tube baby, Louise Brown, is delivered by Caesarean section in Oldham, England, by doctors Patrick Steptoe and Robert Edwards.

■ Residents of the Love Canal section of Niagara Falls learn that their neighborhood was a dumping ground for about 21,000 tons of toxic waste in the 1940s and 1950s. Alarmed by studies pointing to high rates of cancer and other illnesses in the community, more than 2,000 residents leave their homes in the next three years. In 1980, Love Canal is declared a federal emergency area.

1979 A near-disastrous accident in the nuclear reactor at Three Mile Island, near Harrisburg, Pa., released a cloud of low-level radioactive gas into the environment.

1981 U.S. space shuttle Columbia makes first orbital test flight, ushering in the era of the re-usable "space plane."

1984 A chemical storage tank explodes at a Union Carbide Plant in Bhopal, India, releasing a cloud of lethal methyl-isocyanate gas. More than 2,000 people are killed, and the number of injured total tens of thousands.

1986 U.S. space shuttle Challenger blows up only moments after takeoff, killing the crew of seven, including the first teacher in space. Within weeks, three more rockets misfire, effectively grounding the U.S. space program.

● Fire burns through the core of a Soviet nuclear reactor at Chernobyl, spewing lethal radioactive debris over the Ukraine, other parts of the U.S.S.R. and Europe.

---

training at Purdue University, calls a lot of "thrashing around up there."

More than 2,000 people were killed on scheduled and chartered flights worldwide last year. On large planes in the U.S. alone, the toll was 526 people, the worst since 1977, when 655 died.

In the past few years, the Federal Aviation Administration (FAA) has stepped up enforcement of airline-maintenance regulations. Last year, the agency slapped carriers with $2.8 million in fines, up from only $298,245 in 1984.

But the agency continually assures the public of aviation safety. "When you consider the numbers we deal with," says Anthony Broderick, the FAA's associate administrator for aviation standards, "the safety record is mind-boggling." Furthermore, a $12 billion modernization of the air-traffic-control system is also under way to increase the amount of traffic that controllers can safely handle.

The chemical industry is another area of worry. Only 18 months ago, a leak at a Union Carbide plant in Bhopal, India, killed more than 2,000 people and injured many thousands. Then, at Union Carbide's plant in Institute, W.Va., a leak last August of the same chemical released in the Bhopal accident—lethal methyl-isocyanate gas—sent six workers and 134 residents to hospital emergency rooms. The Occupational Safety and Health Administration charged Union Carbide with 221 safety violations at the Institute plant—a penalty the company is appealing.

The dangers of a chemical accident are not confined to plants. Hundreds of mishaps occur annually in the storage and transport of hazardous chemicals. In a study made after the Bhopal disaster, the Environmental Protection Agency (EPA) found that between 1980 and 1985, 135 people died and 4,717 were injured in chemical accidents—with roughly a quarter of the accidents involving transport of lethal compounds. Barges that carry dangerous materials, including uranium, have a stunning accident rate worldwide of 1 per day.

Since the Bhopal incident, many companies have become more cautious. Monsanto, for example, has cut its inventory of hazardous chemicals by about 50 percent and increasingly uses ultrasound devices to detect ruptures in steel storage tanks.

Still, the skill of those handling dangerous chemicals is a vexing issue. "I'm not terribly confident about our ability to manage these facilities," says John Henningson, a water-pollution-control expert and vice president of Malcolm-Pirnie, Inc., in New Jersey. "I've always been comfortable with the technologies but not the personnel running them."

Nowhere is the worry so deep as over the handling of the government's arsenal of nuclear weapons.

One concern is the nightmare scenario—dramatized in the 1983 movie "WarGames"—in which the U.S. receives a false warning of an attack by Soviet missiles and nearly sets off World War III with a counterattack. Occasional false alarms have gone off, but there have been no serious responses on the part of the U.S.

Recently, concern has shifted to the military's development of chemical and biological weapons. In 1968, some 6,400 sheep perished mysteriously after the Army secretly tested deadly chemical agents at the Dugway Proving Grounds in Utah. Eleven years later, 45 people near Richmond, Ky., were hospitalized after a toxic cloud formed over the Lexington-Bluegrass Army Depot when the Army tried to destroy some old canisters of nerve gas. Chemical weapons are stored in nine military facilities. The debate over safety is heating up because of Defense Department plans to develop new chemical weapons and destroy its World War II nerve-gas arsenal.

The newest technology with risks potentially as great as those of nuclear energy is genetic engineering. Late this month, the EPA is expected to allow a breakthrough experiment—the outdoor testing of bioengineered bacteria that prevent frost from forming on certain plants.

Biotechnology promises a range of miracle products from drugs for acquired-immune-deficiency syndrome to heartier plants. But critics charge that the risks associated with releasing genetically manipulated organisms into the atmosphere have not been clearly established. "These genetically engineered microbes are alive and are inherently unpredictable," charges leading biotech critic Jeremy Rifkin. "Unlike chemicals, they reproduce, migrate, grow. If something goes wrong, you can't recall them, seal them up, clean them up or do anything about them."

History shows that major accidents often lead to tighter regulations and improved safety standards. Roughly half of the safety standards for nuclear power plants were instituted after the Three Mile Island accident. In the space program, a fire in 1967 that swept through the Apollo spacecraft on a launching-pad ground test, killing three astronauts, led to a complete overhaul of NASA and redesign of the spacecraft—action that many engineers say ultimately guaranteed the lunar program's success.

To keep risks within acceptable bounds, some argue that new ways are needed to regulate the sophisticated technologies such as biotechnology, artificial intelligence, and "smart" satellites that will dominate the next 20 years. "I think there is serious concern these days about whether we're adequately set up to handle today's technology," says Marc Vaucher, program manager of the Center for Space Policy, Inc.

Government regulators are often caught between insuring public safety and promoting new technology. The National Institutes of Health, for example, funds genetic-engineering research and helps regulate it. The FAA, too, regulates air safety and promotes the industry. The Nuclear Regulatory Commission's predecessor, the Atomic Energy Commission, was often accused of being both advocate and arbiter of nuclear power—and some make the same charge against the NRC today.

Critics say that regulators inevitably experience a conflict of interest that leads to a dimmed vigilance. Contends consultant Joseph Coates, former member of the Congress's Office of Technology Assessment: "We've always gotten ourselves into trouble because administrative bodies have conflicting duties."

Technology advocates insist that overzealous regulation has held back important advances and weakened the nation's competitive position vis-à-vis rivals such as the Japanese. Robert

TWENTIETH CENTURY ANXIETIES

Accidents waiting to happen?

In technology we have trusted, but unthinkable, unimaginable accidents do happen, be it in the deafening crash of two airplanes or in a silent chemical leak. The record suggests that the following, and worse, could occur again.

False alert: It looked as if the Soviets were attacking, but it was a computer malfunction at the North American Air Defense complex in Cheyenne Mountain, Colo., in 1979 and 1980. Forces went on low-level alert and bomber engines were fired up, but within minutes the errors were caught.

Bombs away: Crashes of B-52s carrying unarmed nuclear warheads over Spain and Greenland in the late 1960s caused radioactive emissions as well as conventional bomb explosions. Other accidental detonations are unlikely, the Air Force insists, because of improvements in warhead construction.

Leaky landfills: At Love Canal, it took years for poisonous materials dumped by nearby chemical plants in Niagara Falls, N.Y., to leach into back yards. Even state-of-the art disposal systems can fail. A site near Pittston, Pa., was blown apart by Hurricane Gloria last year, spilling 100,000 gallons of waste into the Susquehanna River.

Too close for comfort: Not only do planes have collisions and near-collisions in midair, but they have accidents on the runway. The worst runway collision involved KLM and Pan Am jets in the Canary Islands in 1977 when 583 died. Some accidents are due to pilot error, but others happen when air-traffic controllers mix up directions.

Shaky foundations: Skyscrapers stand tall and bridges straddle rivers and railroads, but collapses do occur. In 1978, the roof of the Hartford Civic Center came tumbling down hours after a basketball game. Above a crowd of dancers at a Kansas City Hyatt Regency in 1981, two concrete skywalks collapsed, killing 114 and injuring more than 200. In 1940, the 5,979-foot Tacoma Narrows Bridge, known to weave in the wind over Puget Sound, fell with a roar.

Looking for a home: The spent fuel rods from 67 nuclear plants sit silently in water-filled storage tanks near reactors, awaiting a decision on potential reprocessing. Experts predict disaster should one of the storage tanks spring a leak, leaving the fuel exposed. Congress wants other nuclear wastes buried by 1998, but critics worry that nuclear leftovers will stay lethal thousands of years.

Computer crashes: The Bank of New York last November found itself taking a $23.6 billion overnight loan from the Federal Reserve Bank of New York to cover a foul-up in the handling of U.S. securities caused by a glitch in a computer program. Other computer problems can be avoided by duplicating data.

Lights out: Twenty-five million people were left in the dark in 1965 when a minor equipment failure in Canada triggered a blackout in the Northeast. Twelve years later, much of metropolitan New York was without power up to 25 hours.

by Cindy Skrzycki with the domestic staff

Gale, for example, who was called to the Soviet Union to perform lifesaving bone-marrow transplants on Chernobyl victims, was censured by the University of California at Los Angeles for conducting bone-marrow transplants in 1980 in violation of NIH guidelines.

To help bolster the spread of technology, the Reagan administration has just changed the rules governing the regulation of new technologies. On April 24, it abolished requirements that "worst case" scenarios be considered in the evaluation of potential hazards.

Warns Senator Albert Gore, Jr. (D-Tenn.): "There's a certain hubris in the Technological Age, tempting us to invest our hopes in dramatic new advances. We have to make choices along the way, instead of ducking tough decisions." Indeed, as Chernobyl, Challenger and Bhopal prove, disaster strikes when nations forget that worst-case scenarios can come true.

by Abigail Trafford and Andrea Gabor with Melissa Healy, Kathleen McAuliffe, Cindy Skrzycki and Ronald A. Taylor

POLL RESULTS

More than just a Soviet problem

The Soviet nuclear accident at Chernobyl has shaken Americans' faith in nuclear energy more deeply than the Three Mile Island accident of 1979, according to a poll for *U.S.News & World Report* and the Cable News Network by the Roper Organization.

The poll was conducted on May 7 and 8.

Fifty-two percent of adults oppose building new nuclear plants, up from 29 percent after the mishap in Pennsylvania. Approval of nuclear power has dropped from 53 percent to 45 percent.

Behind concern lies a belief that the Soviet meltdown illustrates the "inherent danger of nuclear power" rather than weaknesses in Soviet engineering. Four out of 5 now support 24-hour federal inspectors at nuclear plants. Twenty-eight percent favor a permanent shutdown of existing plants, up from 14 percent.

Almost 7 out of 10 people attributed the Chernobyl accident and setbacks in the U.S. space program to accidents that are part of the "price of progress." Yet when asked what risks were acceptable, Americans by better than a 2 to 1 ratio accepted risks in space rather than from nuclear energy. Said one: "With the space shuttle, you don't have the survival of the human race at risk."

Here are key results:

Would you favor not permitting any more new nuclear power plants to be built?
Favor: 52%
Oppose: 38%

Do you think the Soviet nuclear-power-plant accident shows the inherent danger of nuclear power in all countries or only weaknesses in the Soviet Union?
Inherent dangers: 52%
Only Soviet weaknesses: 34%
Both: 2%

Random telephone survey of 1,003 adults was conducted May 7 and May 8. Margin of error is 4 percent. Results do not add to 100 percent because of deletion of "don't knows."

THE THIRD TECHNOLOGICAL REVOLUTION

And Its Possible Socioeconomic Consequences

Daniel Bell

DANIEL BELL is the author of, among other works, *The Cultural Contradictions of Capitalism*, *The Winding Passage*, and *The Coming of Post-Industrial Society*.

We are today on the rising slope of a third technological revolution. It is a rising slope, for we have passed from the plus-minus stage of invention and innovation into the crucial period of diffusion. The rates of diffusion will vary, depending upon the economic conditions and political stabilities of societies. Yet the phenomenon cannot be reversed, and its consequences may be even greater than the previous two technological revolutions that reshaped the West and now, with the spread of industrialization, other parts of the world as well.

NB: I make a distinction between a technological revolution and its socioeconomic consequences. The early phrase "the industrial revolution" obscures two different things: the introduction of steam power as a new form of energy and the creation of factories to apply that energy to machines for the production of goods. The reason for the distinction is that there is no necessary, determinate single path for the use of the new technologies. The ways in which technologies can be organized vary widely, and these are social decisions, which can be made in a conscious way. No one "voted in" the first industrial revolution—in the way that political revolutions, such as the French and the Russian Revolutions, were

shaped by active minorities. The industrial revolution moved along the path of least resistance because it generated profits and provided goods at cheaper prices. Yet the social costs were rarely reckoned or dealt with. Today we have a greater awareness of the forces of change and the possible outcomes; and, given our values, we try to enact policies that will create different social matrices to encapsulate these changes and deal with the transitions they provoke.[1]

What I hope to do in this article is to identify the salient aspects of the "third technological revolution," sketch a number of social frameworks that may allow us to see how this technological revolution may proceed in the reorganization of basic structures, and describe the choices we may have.[2]

Three Technological Revolutions

Any dating or numbering is somewhat arbitrary, yet if we look at the nature of the technological changes and their consequences, we are justified, I believe, in speaking of three major technological revolutions in the Western world in modern times.

The first is the introduction of steam power, more than two hundred years ago, an innova-

From *Dissent*, Spring 1989, pp. 164-176. Copyright © 1989 by Daniel Bell. Reprinted by permission.

tion identified largely with the name of James Watt. The pleasant story goes that as a boy Watt saw the kettle boiling on his mother's hearth and the heavy iron top being raised by the rising steam, and he wondered what would happen if that steam could be enclosed within a chamber and used to push shafts and drives. Yet one cannot underestimate the extraordinary nature of that simple idea.

One can take, as a contrast, the visions of Leonardo da Vinci, who was not only a great painter but, as we know, a civil engineer, a military engineer, and a gifted inventor. In his *Notebooks,* da Vinci imagined an airplane, a submarine, a threshing machine, and refrigeration, and he drew the machines to embody these ideas with extraordinarily painstaking accuracy: the wheels, the gears, the shafts, and so on. Models of these have been made today, and they show how prescient he was. Yet, even with his astonishing imagination, da Vinci could not imagine the one necessary element to make these work: a source of continual and repeatable power strong enough to drive them. He could think of human muscle power, draft animal power, natural wind power, but these were insufficient. Steam provided a quantum jump in our ability to apply energy to machines.

With steam power we could achieve a variety of technological feats impossible before. One was to have steam pumps. England was an island bedded on coal, but one could not dig down very far because of the large pools of underground water, which hand pumps could not extract. With steam pumps, the water could be expelled and coal dug out to create an iron and steel industry. With steam, we could create railroads that could go faster (and longer) than any known animal, steamships that could sail faster, and more steadily, than any wind-driven sails, machines that could card and spin and thus create cloth faster than the nimble fingers of a trained woman. More important than these, the first technological revolution introduced, and made possible, a vast new conception in the creation of wealth: the idea of productivity, the simple proposition of greater output with less effort, as a result of investment. Prior to modern times, wealth had been gained largely by direct exploitation, such as slavery; or by tithes on work, such as in serfdom; or by plunder and conquest; or by direct political levies, such as tax farming, and so on. For the first time, there existed a peaceful means of generating wealth, a means that was not primarily a zero-sum game but one

whereby all might benefit, albeit differentially. That has been the promise of the new methods of production. This is the decisive break with the modes of production of the past. This is the continuing promise of technology.

The second technological revolution, only a hundred years or so ago, can be identified with two innovations: electricity and chemistry. Electricity gives us a new, enhanced form of power that can be transmitted hundreds of miles, as steam cannot, thus permitting new kinds of decentralization that the bunching of machines in a factory, to minimize the loss of steam heat, could not. Electricity gives us a new source of light, which changes our rhythms of night and day. Electricity allows us to code messages on wires or to transform voice electric signals, so as to create telephone and radio. Chemistry, for the first time, allows us to create synthetics, from dyes to plastics, from fibers to vinyls, that are unknown in nature.

And now, the third technological revolution. If we think of the changes that are beginning to occur, we think, inevitably of things and the ways we seek to use them: computers, telecommunications, and the like. But to think in these terms is to confuse applications or instruments with some underlying processes that are the crucial understandings for this revolution, and only by identifying the relevant underlying processes can we begin to "track" the vast number of changes in socioeconomic and political structures that may take place. Four technological innovations underlie this new technological revolution, and I shall describe each briefly:

(1) *The change of all mechanical and electric and electromechanical systems to electronics.* The machines of industrial society were mechanical instruments, powered first by steam and later by electricity. Increasingly, electronic systems have taken over and replaced mechanical parts. A telephone system was basically a set of mechanical parts (e.g. a dial system) in which signals were converted into electricity. Today, the telephone is entirely electronic. Printing was a system in which mechanical type was applied, with inked surfaces, to paper; today, printing is electronic. So is television, with solid-state circuits. The changes mean a reduction in the large number of parts, and an incredible increase in the speed of transmission. In modern computers, we have speeds of nanoseconds, or one-billionth (10^{-9}) of a second (or thirty years of seconds, if one

sought to add these up), and even picoseconds, or one-trillionth (10^{-12}) of a second, permitting "lightning" calculation of problems.

(2) *Miniaturization.* One of the most remarkable changes is the "shrinkage" of units that conduct electricity or switch electrical impulses. Our previous modes were vacuum tubes, each, as in the old-fashioned radios, about two or three inches high. The invention of the transistor is akin to the invention of steam power, for it represented a quantum change in the ability to manufacture microelectronic devices for the hundreds of different functions of control, regulation, direction, and memory that microprocessors perform. We had 4k (k = a thousand) bits on a chip, the size of a thin fingernail, then 32k, 64k, and now we begin to construct megabits, or a million binary digits, or bits, on a chip.

In the past two decades we have seen an exponential growth in components per chip, by a factor of one hundred per decade. Today the limit is almost a million components; by 1990 it will be about five million; and by the year 2000 between ten and one hundred million.

Today a tiny chip of silicon contains an electronic circuit consisting of hundreds of thousands of transistors and all the necessary interconnecting conductors, and it costs only a few dollars. The circuitry on that chip, now made by printed boards, is equivalent to about ten years' work by a person soldering discrete components onto that printed wiring board. A single chip can itself be a microcomputer with input/output processing capability and random-access memory and be, like the AT&T WE* 32100, smaller than an American dime.

(3) *Digitalization.* In the new technology information is represented by digits. Digits are numbers, discrete in their relation to one another, rather than continuous variables. A telephone, for example, was an analogue system, for sound is a wave. Through digital switching a telephone becomes converted to the use of binary systems. One sees this in sound recordings, as on musical discs. The third technological revolution involves the conversion of all previous systems into digital form.

(4) *Software.* Older computers had the instructions or operating systems wired into the machine, and one had to learn a programming language, such as Cobol or Fortran, or the more specialized languages such as Pascal or Lisp, to use the machine. Software, an independent program, frees the user to do various tasks quickly. In distributed processing the software directing the work of a particular computer terminal operates independently of software in other terminals or in the central processing unit. Micro or personal computers have specific software programs—for financial analysis or information data-base retrieval—that tailor the system to particular user needs and become, in the argot of the computer, "user-friendly."

Software—the basis of customization—is still a developing art. It takes a programmer about a year to produce a few thousand lines of code. In telecommunications, large electronic switching machines (to route the hundreds of thousands of calls onto different lines) use more than two million lines. Breaking the "bottleneck" of software programming is the key to the rapid spread of the personal computer into the small business and the home.

(One can point to a significant development that promises the enlargement and enhancement of the new technology: photonics. Photonics is the key technology for transmitting large amounts of digital information through laser and ultrapure glass or optical fibers. Combined, they provide a transmission capability that far exceeds the copper wire and radio. In laboratory experiments, the AT&T Bell laboratories set a "distance record" by transmitting 420 million bits per second over 125 miles without amplification, and two billion bits per second over eighty miles without amplification. The pulse rate can transmit the entire thirty-volume *Encyclopedia Britannica* in a few seconds. But these are still in the development stage, and we are concerned here with already proven technologies that are in the process of marketing and diffusion.)

The most crucial fact about the new technology is that it is not a separate domain (such as the label "high-tech" implies), but a set of changes that pervade all aspects of society and reorganize all older relationships. The industrial revolution produced an age of motors—something we take for granted. Motors are everywhere, from automobiles to boats to power tools and even household devices (such as electric toothbrushes and electric carving knives) that can run on fractional horsepower—motors of one-half and one-quarter horsepower. Similarly, in the coming decades, we shall be "pervaded" by computers—not just the large ones, but the "computer on a chip," the microcomputer, which will transform all our equipment and homes. For automobiles, appliances, tools, home computers and the like, microcomputers will operate with computing power of ten MIPS (millions of instructions per second) per computer.[3]

We can already see the shape of the manifold changes. The old distinctions in communication between telephone (voice), television (image), computer (data), and text (facsimile) have been broken down, physically interconnected by digital switching, and made compatible as a single unified set of teletransmissions. This is what my colleague Anthony Oettinger calls "compunications" and what Simon Nora and Hilary Minc, in their report to the president of France several years ago, called "télématique." The introduction of computer-aided design and simulation has revolutionized engineering and architectural practices. Computer-aided manufacturing and robotics are beginning to transform the production floor. Computers are now indispensable in record-keeping, inventory, scheduling, and other aspects of management information systems in business, firms, hospitals, universities, and any organization. Data-base and information-retrieval systems reshape analysis for decisions and intellectual work. The household is being transformed as digital devices begin to program and control household appliances and, in the newer home designs, all aspects of the household environment. Computers, linked to television screens, begin to change the way we communicate, make transactions, receive and apply information.

The intellectual task is how to "order" these changes in comprehensible ways, rather than just describing the multitude of changes, and thus to provide some basis of analysis rooted in sociological theory. What I intend to do, in the following sections, is to present a number of "social frameworks," or matrices, which may allow us to see how existing social structures come under pressure for change, and the ways in which such changes may occur. I repeat one caveat stated earlier: Technology does not determine social change; technology provides instrumentalities and potentialities. The ways that these are used are social choices. The frameworks that I sketch below, therefore, indicate the "areas" within which relevant changes may occur.

The Postindustrial Society

The postindustrial society is not a projection or extrapolation of existing trends in Western society; it is a new principle of social-technical organization and ways of life, just as the industrial system (e.g., factories) replaced an agrarian way of life. It is, first, a shift in the centrality of industrial production, as it was organized on the basis of standardization and mass production. This does not mean the disappearance of manufacturing or the production of goods; the production of food and products from the soil does not disappear from the Western world (in fact, more food is produced than ever before), but there is a significant change in the way food is produced, and, more significantly, in the number of persons engaged in agricultural production. But more than all these, the idea is a "logical construct," in order to see what is central to the new social forms, rather than an empirical description. Postindustrial developments do not replace previous social forms as "stages" of social development. They often coexist, as a palimpsest, on top of the others, thickening the complexity of society and the nature of social structure.

One can think of the world as divided into three kinds of social organization. One is preindustrial. These are primarily extractive industries: farming, mining, fishing, timber. This is still the lot of most of Africa, Latin America, and Southeast Asia, where 60 percent or more of the labor force is engaged in these activities. These are largely what I call "games against nature," subject to the vicissitudes of the weather, the exhaustion of the soils, the thinning out of forests, or the higher costs of the recovery of minerals and metals.

Similar sections of the world have been industrial, engaged in fabrication, the application of energy to machines for the mass production of goods. These have been the countries around the Atlantic littoral: those of Western Europe and the United States, and then the Soviet Union and Japan. Work, here, is a game against fabricated nature: the hitching of men to machines, the organized rhythmic pacing of work in a highly coordinated fashion.

The third type is postindustrial. These are activities that are primarily processing, control, and information. It is a social way of life that is, increasingly, a "game between persons." More important, there is a new principle of innovation, especially of knowledge and its relation to technology.

Let me describe some of the lineaments of the postindustrial society. It is, first, a society of services. In the United States today, more than 70 percent of the labor force is engaged in services. Yet "services" is inherently an ambiguous term and, in economic analysis, one without shape because it has been used primarily as a "residual" term.

In every society there is a high component of services. In preindustrial society, it is primarily domestic or personal service. In a country such as India, most persons with a middle-class income would have one or two servants, because many persons simply wish for a roof to sleep and a place to eat. (In England, until 1870, the largest single occupational class was that of domestic servants.)

In an industrial society services are those activities auxiliary to industry: utilities, transportation (including garages and repairs), finance, and real estate.

In a postindustrial society there is an expansion of new kinds of service. These are human services—education, health, social work, social services—and professional services—analysis and planning, design, programming, and the like. In the older conceptions of classical economics (including Marxism), services were thought of as inherently unproductive, since wealth was identified with goods, and lawyers and priests or barbers or waiters did not contribute to the national wealth. Yet surely education and health services contribute to the increased skills and strengths of a population, while professional services (such as linear programming in the organization of production, or new modes of layout of work and social interaction) contribute to the productivity of an enterprise and society. And the important fact is that the expansion of a postindustrial sector of a society requires the expansion of higher education and the education of many more in the population in abstract conceptual, technical, and alphanumeric skills.

In the United States today more than 30 percent of the labor force (of more than one hundred million persons) is professional, technical, and managerial, an amazing figure in social history. About 17 percent of the labor force does factory work (the industrial proletariat, in the older Marxian sense of the term), and it is likely that this will shrink to about 10 percent within a decade. If one thinks this is small, consider the fact that fewer than 4 percent of the labor force are farmers, producing a glut of food for the United States—as against 50 percent in 1900.

An equally important change is in the role of women. In 1950 the "typical" picture for 70 percent of the labor force was a husband at work and his wife and two children at home. Today that is true of only 15 percent of the labor force. Today more than 50 percent of all wives are working outside the home.

Any social change is an intersection of cultural attitudes with the ability to institutionalize those attitudes in market terms. The cultural attitudes regarding equal rights of women go back a hundred years. But the ability to institutionalize those sentiments in market terms goes back only to the past twenty-five or so years—with the expansion of postindustrial employments, particularly in the "quinary" sector of services (health, education, research) and then back into the "quaternary" areas (trade, finance, real estate). The reason is, broadly, that industrial work has been largely considered men's work (including the corporate sectors of management). Postindustrial employments are open, in skills and capacities, to women.

The decisive change—what I call the axial principle of organization—is a change in the character of knowledge. Now, every human society has always existed on the basis of knowledge. The sources go far back, lost in the vistas of time, when the human animal was able, because of the voice box in the larynx, to take the sounds of communication made by all birds and animals, and to codify these into distinct vocables that could be combined, differentiated, and organized into complex meanings, and, through voice, to make intelligible signals that could be transmitted through an oral tradition. With the creation of alphabets we could take a few ideographic scratches and combine these into thousands of words that could be written in stylized forms, to be learned and read by others.

But what is radically new today is the codification of theoretical knowledge and its centrality for innovation, both of new knowledge and for economic goods and services. In his pathbreaking book, *Invention, Growth and Welfare: A Theoretical Treatment of Technological Change* (M.I.T. Press, 1969), William Nordhaus lays out an analytical framework in which, "for the purposes of economic analysis, it is important to distinguish two kinds of knowledge, general and technical. The distinction refers to the usefulness of knowledge in producing either more knowledge or more goods." On the higher level, there is general knowledge, such as the laws of nature, liberal arts, and language, knowledge "not particularly useful for the specialized problems of producing goods." And there is a second tier of technical knowledge, in which he includes computer programs and engineering formulas, which is useful in producing goods but not additional knowledge.

Whatever utility that distinction may have had for the measurement of inventions and the rate of technological change, it is increasingly diminished and even misleading in understanding the way innovation now increasingly proceeds with the new technology. Let us take the relation of technological invention to science in the major sectors of industrial society. If we look at the major industries that were developed then and that still carry over today—steel, electricity, telephone, radio, aviation—we can see that they are all "nineteenth-century" industries (though steel was begun in the eighteenth century by Darby with the invention of the coking process and aviation in the twentieth century by the Wright brothers) created by "talented tinkerers," men who were adroit with the nature of equipment, but who knew little about, or were indifferent to, the developments of science, and in particular the theoretical aspects taking place at the time.

Sir Henry Bessemer, who invented an oxidation process to reduce the impurities in molten metal and to produce stronger structure steel (and to win a prize from Louis Napoleon for a better cannon), knew little of the work of the metallurgist Henry Sorby on the properties of metals. Alexander Graham Bell, one of the inventors of the telephone, was originally a speech teacher who sought to transmit amplified voice on a wire in order to enable deaf people to hear better. Thomas Alva Edison, one of the great geniuses among inventors—he invented the long-lasting filament for the electric-light bulb, the phonograph, and the motion picture—was a mathematical illiterate who cared little about the work of Clerk Maxwell in uniting electricity and magnetism into a combined theoretical set of equations. (It was Maxwell who started us off, thus, on the search that continues today for the unification of all the forces that hold matter together in the universe.) When Edison became head of the U.S. Navy Consulting Board during World War I, he said that there ought to be someone on the board who knew some mathematics, in the event they encountered some problems that had numbers or equations, and the Navy hired a physicist; but since the Navy personnel slots had no designation at that time for a physicist, the man was paid

as a chemist. This gives us some indication of the magnitudes of change from World War I to the present. Similarly, Guglielmo Marconi, who invented wireless communication, knew little of the work of Hertz on radio waves.

But all of that has now changed radically. Let me take three instances for dramatic effect:

In 1905 Albert Einstein, at age twenty-eight, wrote three papers for *Annalen der Physik* (plus his Ph.D. thesis on a new theoretical method for determining molecular radia and Avogadro's number), any one of which would have won him eponymous fame in the history of science. One paper was on the Brownian motion, which not only "proved" the "reality of molecules," but provided exact computations that demonstrated the correctness of Boltzmann's interpretation of thermodynamic laws. The second paper dealt with "special relativity" and described how the invariance of the velocity of light held in different moving frames of reference, thus showing the limiting nature of the Newtonian view of the universe, putting space and time into a single continuum and the pregnant equation $E = mc^2$, which exploded into the atomic age. And the third paper was on the so-called "photo-electric effect." In many respects, the latter paper has been of lesser importance in the arcane theoretical literature of physics (quoted less than the others), yet it has had the most extraordinary technological importance and, in 1922, was the basis for Einstein's Nobel Prize.

Einstein's paper on the photoelectric effect flouted the concepts of classical physics, which held that light (like sound) was a wave. The paper postulated, hypothetically, that light was a *quanta*, or a stream of discontinuous particles. This paper met with extraordinary resistance among experimental physicists, was not vindicated experimentally until a decade later, and was finally resolved theoretically by the complementary principle of wave-particle dualism. Yet the crucial point is that Einstein's paper was the starting point for much twentieth-century work in optics, from such simple things as we now see in the application of photoelectric effects, in breaking light beams, to the work of Charles Townes in creating lasers (an acronym for "light amplification stimulated by the emission of radiation"), Dennis Gabor on holography, and the development of photonics as the new frontier for telecommunications.

The second illustration is the revolution in solid-state physics. The contemporary conceptions of solid-state physics play no role, and to some extent are unthinkable, within the purview of classical physics. Our shifts in the conception of matter go back to the model of the hydrogen atom that Niels Bohr constructed in 1912, with the idea of the nucleus and the orbits of electrons around the nucleus. The basic step forward was taken in 1927 with the picture of the lattice structure of matter, by Felix Bloch, in which one could show how electrons, in their spins, "jumped" from orbit to orbit as energy is given off. These "pictures" of the structures of matter led to the discovery of the transistor at Bell Labs by Bardeen, Brittain, and Shockley in the late 1940s and to the revolution in solid-state technology that is the basis of modern-day electronics and the computer.

And, finally, an innovation of an entirely different sort, Alan Turing's mathematical paper in 1937, "On Computable Numbers," which is the fundamental basis for programming, storage, and the creation of the digital computer. In 1928, the great German mathematician David Hilbert, at the World Congress of Mathematics, had laid down three questions in order to see whether a complete formulization of mathematics was possible. He asked whether mathematics could be complete, consistent, and decidable. Two years later, in 1930, the Czech mathematician Kurt Gödel had produced his theorems, which showed that, given the problems of providing a complete and consistent set of axioms, if mathematics was complete it could not be consistent, and if consistent it could not be complete.

When Alan Turing wrote his paper, which showed that there could be a principle of decidability (whether in principle a problem was solvable or not) if the numbers were computable, he invented a tape that would be a "table of behavior" that could through binary rules compute any possible configuration of finite numbers. The idea of a computer goes back to the work of an earlier Cambridge mathematician, Charles Babbage, who in 1837 conceived of a "difference engine" that could mechanize any mechanical operation. What Turing's innovation did was utilize binary numbers (Boolean algebra) with internal program storage, to allow for the development of an automatic electronic digital computer. Thus, theory preceded artifice.*

One consequence of this is that invention, or the "talented tinkerer," disappears from the

horizon. There will always be innovations and changes in "things" that will create new products. But the basic point remains that fundamental innovations in theoretical knowledge—not just in physics, as in the illustrations above, but in biology (going back to the discovery of the double helix of the DNA molecule by Crick and Watson, and to the branching structure of molecular biology by Monod, Jacobs, and Lwoff) or in cognitive psychology (as the basis for expert inference systems)—become the new principle of innovation in society.

I said before that one has to distinguish technological changes (even when they are now not only in machine technology but in intellectual technology) from the more valuable changes in social structure. Changes in technology, as I have insisted, do not determine social changes; they pose problems that the political controllers of society have to deal with. It would take a book to begin to explore the many problems suggested by the possible changes we have seen. Some of these are explored in the following two sections on changes in infrastructure, or the social geography of societies, and changes in the nature of production systems. Let me briefly, however, with the more delimited framework of a postindustrial hypothesis, pose a number of questions.

1. The shrinkage of the traditional manufacturing sectors—augmented, in these instances, by the rising competition from Asia and the ease whereby the routinized, low-value-added production can be taken up by some of the Third World societies—raises the question whether Western societies (all or some) can reorganize their production to move toward the new "high-tech, high-value-added" kinds of specialized production, or whether they will be "headquarter economies" providing investment and financial services to the rest of the world.

2. The costs of transition. Can these be managed? And if so, by the "market," or by some kind of "industrial policy"?

3. The reorganization of an educational system to provide a greater degree of "alphanumeric" fluency in larger portions of the population who would be employed in these postindustrial sectors.

4. The character of "work." If character is defined by work, then we shall see a society where "nature" is largely excluded and "things" are largely excluded within the experience of persons. If more and more individuals are in

---

* One should distinguish this innovation of Turing's from his later creation of the "Turing Machine problem": Could a human being distinguish an answer to any set of problems whether given by another human being or by a "computer"?

work situations that involve a "game between persons," clearly more and more questions of equity and "comparable worth" will arise. The nature of hierarchy in work may be increasingly questioned, and new modes of participation may be called for. All of these portend huge changes in the structures of organization from those we have seen in the older models of the army and the church, or the industrial-factory organization, which have been the structures of organization (if not domination) until now.

Societal Geography and Infrastructures

Historically every society has been tied together by three kinds of infrastructure: These have been the nodes and highways of trade and transactions, of the location of cities and the connections between peoples. The first has been transportation: rivers, roads, canals, and, in modern times, railroads, highways, and airplanes. The second is energy systems: hydropower, electricity grids, oil pipelines, gas pipelines, and the like. And the third has been communications: postal systems (which moved along highways), then telegraph (the first break in that linkage), telephone, radio, and now the entire panoply of new technological means from microwave to satellites.

The oldest system has been transportation. The breakdown between isolated segments of a society comes when roads are built to connect these, so that trade can commence. The location of human habitats has come with the crossing of roads or the merging of rivers and arms of lakes: traders stop with their wares, farmers bring their food, artisans settle down to provide services, and towns and cities develop.

Within the system of transport, the most important has been water routes. They are the easiest means for carrying bulk items; waterways weave around natural obstacles; tides and currents provide means of additional motion. It is striking to realize that almost every major city in the world, in the last millennia (leaving aside the fortified hill towns that arose during the breakdown of commerce and provided a means of protection against marauders) is located on water: Rome on the Tiber, Paris on the Seine, London on the Thames, not to mention the great cities located on the oceans, seas, and great lakes.

If one looks at industrial societies, the location of cities and the hubs of production come from the interplay of water and resources. Consider a map of the United States and look at the north-central area of the country. In the Mesabi range of Minnesota there was iron ore; in the fields of southern Illinois and western Pennsylvania there was coal. And these were tied together by a Great Lakes and river-valley system that connected them with ports on the oceans: the lakes of Superior, Huron, Michigan, Ontario, and Erie, the St. Lawrence waterway through Canada reaching out to the Atlantic, the Erie Canal across New York reaching down the Hudson River, and the Ohio River wending its way down to the Mississippi and the Gulf of Mexico.

Given the iron ore and coal, one has a steel industry and from it an automobile industry, a machine-tool industry, a rubber industry, and the like. And given the water-transport system tying these together, we get the locational reasons for the great industrial heartland of the United States, the bands of cities along the lakes and rivers of Chicago, Detroit, Cleveland, Buffalo, and Pittsburgh. Thus the imprint of economic geography.

Now all this is changing, as industrial society begins to give way. Communication begins to replace transportation as the major node of connection between people and as the mode of transaction.

Water and natural resources become less important as locational factors for cities, particularly as, with the newer technology, the size of manufacturing plants begins to shrink. Proximity to universities and culture becomes more important as a locational factor. If we look at the major development of high-tech in the United States, we see that the four major concentrations respond to these elements: Silicon Valley, in relation to Stanford University and San Francisco; the circumferential Route 128 around Boston, in relation to M.I.T. and Harvard; Route 1 in New Jersey, from New Brunswick to Trenton, with Princeton University at its hub; and Minneapolis-St. Paul in Minnesota, clustering around the large state university and the Twin City metropolis.

What we see, equally, with communication networks becoming so cheap, is a great pull toward decentralization. In the past, central business districts concentrated the headquarters of large enterprises because of the huge "external economies" available through the bunching of auxiliary services. One could "walk across the street" and have easily available legal services, financial services, advertising services, printing and publishing, and the like. Today, with the increasing cheapness of communication and the high cost of land, density and the external economies become less critical. So we find that dozens of the major U.S. corporations, in the last decade or so, have moved their basic headquarters from New York to the suburban areas where land is cheaper, and transport to and from work easier: northeast to Fairfield County in Connecticut; north to Westchester County in New York; and west and southwest to Mercer County in New Jersey.

In Japan we see a major effort now under way, the Technopolis project, to create large, far-flung regional centers for the new computer and telecommunications industries. For status reasons, many corporations maintain a display building in New York or Tokyo; but the major managerial activities are now decentralized.

As geography is no longer the controller of costs, distance becomes a function not of space but of time; and the costs of time and rapidity of communication become the decisive variables. And, with the spread of mini- and microcomputers, the ability to "down-load" databases and memories, and to place these in the small computers (as well as give them access to the large mainframes) means there is less of a necessary relation to fixed sites in the location of work.

As with habitats, so with markets. What is a market? Again, it is a place where roads crossed and rivers merged and individuals settled down to buy and sell their wares. Markets were places. Perhaps no longer.

Take the Rotterdam spot market for oil. It was the place where tankers carrying surplus oil would come so that oil could be sold "on the spot." They came to Rotterdam because it was a large, protected port, close to the markets of Western Europe; it had large storage capacity; there was a concentration of brokers who would go around and make their deals. It is still called the Rotterdam spot market for oil, but it is no longer in Rotterdam. But if not in Rotterdam, where? Everywhere. It is a telex-and-radio system whereby brokers in different parts of the world can make their deals and redirect the ships on the high seas to different ports for the sales they have made. In effect, markets are no longer places but networks.

And this is true for most commodities, especially for capital and currency markets. Today one can get in "real time" quotations for dollars, D-marks, Swiss francs, yen, French francs, sterling, Italian lire, in Tokyo, Singapore, Hong Kong, Milan, Frankfurt, Paris, London, New York, Chicago, San Francisco, and money moves swiftly across national lines. Capital flows in response to differential interest rates or in reaction to news of political disturbances.

What we have here, clearly, are the nerves, nodes, and ganglia of a genuine international economy tied together in ways the world has never seen before. What this means—and I shall return to the question at the close of this article—is a widening of the arenas, the multiplication of the numbers of actors, and an increase in the velocity and volatility of transactions and exchanges. The crucial question is whether the older institutional structures are able to deal with this extraordinary volume of interactions.

The Social Organization of Production

The modern corporation—I take the United States as the model—is less than a hundred years old. Business, the exchange of goods and services, is as old as human civilization itself. But the modern corporation, as a social form to coordinate men, materials and markets for the mass production and mass consumption of goods, is an institution that has taken shape only in the past century.

There are three kinds of innovators who conjoined to create the modern industrial system. The greatest attention has been paid to those who have been the organizers of the production system itself: Eli Whitney, who created standardized forms and interchangeable parts in production; Frederick Taylor, who designed the measurement of work; and Henry Ford, who created the assembly line and mass production. (There were of course other forebears, and there were European counterparts: Siemens, Bedaux, Renault, etc.)

Those who achieved the greatest notoriety were the capitalists, the men who by ruthless means put together the great enterprises: the Carnegies, the Rockefellers, Harriman, the men who initiated the large quasi-monopoly organizations, and the financiers, such as J. P. Morgan, who assembled the monies for the formation of such great corporations as U.S. Steel, General Electric, and the like.

But there was also a different social role, often unnoticed even in the history of business, played by men who, curiously, were probably just as important, and perhaps more so: the organizers of the corporate form, those who rationalized the system and gave it an ongoing structural continuity. I will discuss three individuals who symbolize the three crucial structural changes: one was Walter Teagle, of Standard Oil of New Jersey, who created vertical integration; another was Theodore N. Vail, who fashioned the American Telephone and Telegraph Co. and imposed the idea of a single uniform system; and the third was Alfred P. Sloan, of General Motors, who created the system of financial controls and budgetary accounting that still rules the corporate world today.

These three men created modern industrial capitalism. It is my thesis, implicit in this article and which can be stated only schematically here, that this system, marvelously adaptive to a mass-production society, is increasingly dysfunctional in today's postindustrial world.

Vertical integration, the control of all aspects of a product—in the case of Teagle, from oil in the ground, to shipping, refining, and distribution to industrial customers and retail outlets—was created for the clear reasons of economies of scale, reduction of transaction costs, the utilization of information within the entire process, and the control of prices, from raw materials to finished goods. What vertical integration did, as Alfred Chandler has pointed out in his book *The Visible Hand*, was to destroy "producer markets" within the chain of production and impose uniform controls. In the previous system, one of merchant capitalism, production was in the hands of independent artisans or small-business companies, and all of this was funneled through the matrix of the merchant capitalist, who ordered the goods he needed, or contracted production to the small workshop, and sold finished products to the customers. But the creation of large-scale, mass-produced, identical goods made vertical integration a functional necessity.

The idea of a single system arose when Vail, seeking to build a telephone utility, beheld the railroad system in the United States, where railroad systems grew "higgledy-piggledy," without plan, and often for financial reasons, to sell inflated stock. Franchises were obtained from corrupt legislatures or from congressional land grants, and the roads were built in sprawling ways. Before the advent of coast-to-coast air flight, if a traveler wanted to go from

New York to the West Coast by train, he could not do so on a single system. He could take one of two competitive railroads from New York to Chicago, where he changed trains and then took one of three competitive systems to the Coast. (If one wished to ship a hog, or freight, it was not necessary to change trains. Animals or freight goods, unlike human beings, could not pick themselves up and move to another freight car; it was cheaper to shuttle the freight car onto different lines.) Even today there is no unified rational rail system in the United States.

Vail, in building a telephone network, decided that if there was to be efficient service between a person calling from any point in the United States to any other point, there would have to be a single set of "long lines" connecting all the local telephones to one another. Until the recent federal court decision which broke up the American Telephone and Telegraph Co., it was a unified, single system.

Alfred P. Sloan's innovations came about when he took over the sprawling General Motors from William C. Durant, a Wall Street speculator who had put together the different automobile companies (named for their early founders: Chevrolet, Olds, Cadillac, and the like) into a single firm, General Motors. But Durant had little talent for creating a rational structure. Alfred P. Sloan, the MIT-trained engineer who was installed as head of the company by the Du Pont interests (the largest block of stockholders until the courts forced them to divest their holdings about twenty-five years ago), installed unit cost accounting and financial controls with a single aim: to obtain a clear return on investment for the monies given to the different divisions. Durant never knew which of the companies was making money, and which not; he did not know whether it was cheaper to make his own steel or buy outside, make his own parts or buy outside. Sloan rationalized the company. His key innovation was a pricing system for the different lines of automobiles that would provide a 20 percent return on investment based on a stipulated capacity, a break-even point based on overhead and fixed costs, and a market share for the particular line of car.

Together, these innovations were the corporate principles of modern industrial capitalism. Why are they now dysfunctional?

In the case of production, the older standardized, routinized, low-value-added forms of production are being increasingly taken over by the newly industrializing societies, where cheap wages provide the crucial cost differential in competition. More than that, the newer technologies—particularly computer-aided design (CAD), numerical-control machine tools (NC), and computer-aided manufacturing (CAM)—now make possible *flexible*, shorter-run, batch productions that can be easily adapted to different kinds of markets, and which can be responsive to specialized products and customized demands.

One of the great success stories in this respect is Italy, in such an "old-fashioned" industry as textiles. The textile district of Prato—the group of towns in Central Italy in the provinces of Florence and Pistoia—was able to survive and flourish because it could adapt. As two MIT scholars have pointed out (relying, of course, on Italian studies), "Prato's success rests on two factors: a long-term shift from standard to fashionable fabrics and a corresponding reorganization of production from large integrated mills to technologically sophisticated shops specializing in various phases of production—a modern *systeme Motte*."[4]

But what holds true for textiles is true for a wide variety of industries as well. In steel, integrated production is now cumbersome and costly, and it is the minimills, with their specialized, flexible production, and the specialty steels that have become the basis for survival in the Western world. It is not, thus, deindustrialization, but a new form of industrialization, which is taking place.

In the case of telecommunications—to be brief—the breakdown of the old distinctions between telephone, computer, television, and facsimile (Xerox) means that new, highly differentiated systems—private branch exchanges, local area networks, "internal" communication networks between firms, international satellite communication—all emphasize diversity rather than uniformity, with many specialized systems rather than a single product such as the telephone.

In the case of Sloan's system of a return on investment through budgetary controls, the assumptions he made were those of a quasi monopoly or oligopoly in a "steady-state" market, and that kind of financial planning can scarcely adapt to a changing world where old product lines are breaking down (one need simply consider the old distinctions between banks, insurance companies, brokerage houses, credit firms, real estate investment, all of which become to some extent interchangeable under the rubric of financial-asset management), where substitutions of products provide price challenges, where market share and cash flow may be more important momentarily, and a long-term commitment necessary technologically, than the simple unit-cost accounting that Alfred Sloan introduced.

In effect, the world of the postindustrial society requires new modes of social organization, and these are only now being fashioned by the new entrepreneurs of the new technology.

The Question of Scale

The crucial question, as I have indicated, is how new social structures will be created in response to the different values of societies, to the new technological instruments of a postindustrial world. Beyond the structural frameworks I have tried to identify, there is one crucial variable that must be taken into account—the change in scale.

It is a cliché of our time that ours is an era of acceleration in the pace of change. I must confess that I do not understand what this actually means. If we seek to use this concept analytically, we find a lack of boundary and meaning. To speak of "change" is in itself meaningless, for the question remains: change of what? To say that "everything" changes is hardly illuminating. And if one speaks of a pace, or of an acceleration in pace, the words imply a metric—a unit of measurement. But what is being measured?

However, one can gain a certain perspective about what is happening by thinking of the concept of scale. A change in the scale of an institution is a change of form. Metaphorically, this goes back to Galileo's square-cube law: If you double the size of an object, you triple its volume. There is consequently a question of shape and proportion. A university with fifty thousand students may still be called by the same name it had thirty years before, with five thousand students, but the increase in numbers calls for a change in the institutional structure. And this is true of all social organizations.

What the revolutions in communication are doing is changing the scale of human activities. Given the nature of "real time" communication, we are for the first time forging an interdependent international economy with more and more characteristics of an unstable system in which changes in the magnitudes of some variables, or shocks and disturbances in some of the units, have immediate repercussions in all the others.

The management of scale has been one of

the oldest problems in social institutions, whether it be the church, the army, or economic enterprise, let alone the political order. Societies have tended to function reasonably well when there is a congruence of scale between economic activities, social units and organization, and political and administrative control. But increasingly what is happening is a mismatch of scale. As I stated in an essay several years ago,[5] the national state has become too small for the big problems of life, and too big for the small problems. The national state, with its political policies, is increasingly ineffective in dealing with the tidal waves of the international economy (coordination through economic summitry is only a charade) and too big, when political decisions are concentrated in a bureaucratic center, for the diversity and initiative of the varied local and regional units under its control. To that extent, if there is a single overriding sociological problem in the postindustrial society—particularly in the management of transition—it is the management of scale.

Notes

[1] There are important consequences for sociological theory in these distinctions. My division can be seen as corresponding to the Marxist distinction between "forces of production" (technology or technique) and the "social relations of production" (property, organization of work, etc.). Yet in Marxist theory the two are yoked into a single form, the "mode of production." Social change is seen as "holistic" changes from one form of production to another.

Yet this is patently not true. In *The Poverty of Philosophy*, Marx remarks that the hand mill or windmill gives us feudalism and the steam mill capitalism. But the technologies of wind and steam are compatible with many different kinds of social formation. To couple the two terms is to distort social analysis.

In my book *The Coming of Post-Industrial Society* (New York: Basic Books, 1976; original edition 1973), what I sought to do was to "de-couple" the two terms, and to treat them analytically, as two independent variables. Given that distinction, we can then see, along the axis of technology, societies that we can call preindustrial, industrial, and postindustrial. Along the axis of social relations, we can have feudal, capitalist, and state-collectivist societies. (I reserve the term "socialism" for more humane societies.) None of the social forms is complete or is a "total" description of a society. Any particular society would be a combination of several forms, depending on its own historical evolution. Yet if we treat these as "ideal types," we can make relevant comparisons, depending on which axis we use.

When one speaks of the "convergence" of societies, one would have to ask, along which axis? On the axis of technology, both the United States and the Soviet Union are industrial societies, as against, say, Indonesia and China, which are preindustrial. But along the axis of social relations, the Soviet Union and China are state-collectivist societies while the United States and Indonesia are capitalist.

[2] A simple methodological point: Most discussions of technological change have focused on a single, major item and then sought to trace the social effects. Thus we have had many studies of "The Social Effects of the Railroad," of radio, of the automobile, of aviation, etc. The problem with such a strategy is that it is increasingly difficult to understand the technological changes in terms of single major innovations, and even more difficult to trace the multiple effects. It is clearly quite different to trace the effects, say, of the plough on medieval agriculture or the stirrup on war, than the interacting ways that automobiles, trucks, railroads, ships, and airplanes change a transportation system. For this reason, I begin with social matrices and try to see how they may change with the introduction of the new technologies. (For a contrast with the older modes of analysis and the hazards of their contemporary use, see Lynn White, Jr., *Medieval Technology and Social Change* [Oxford: Clarendon Press, 1962] and W. F. Ogburn, *The Social Effects of Aviation* [Boston and New York: Houghton Mifflin, 1946].)

[3] For a convenient summary of these technologies, see *Information Technologies and Social Transformation,*" The National Academy of Engineering (Washington D.C.: National Academy of Science, 1985).

[4] Michael J. Piore and Charles Sabel, *The Second Industrial Divide* (New York: Basic Books, 1984). Piore and Sabel cite the various studies of Gianni Lorenzi, Ezio Avigdor, Danielle Mazzonis, and others, and the OECD study of textile and clothing, 1983.

[5] "The Future World Disorders," reprinted in my book of essays, *The Winding Passage* (Cambridge, Mass.: Abt Books, 1980).

Earth's Vital Signs

The earth's vital signs reveal a patient in declining health. Policy makers can ill afford to postpone making the investments needed for a preventive health-care plan for the planet.

Lester R. Brown, Christopher Flavin, and Edward C. Wolf

Lester R. Brown is president of the Worldwatch Institute (1776 Massachusetts Avenue, N.W., Washington, D.C. 20036), and Christopher Flavin and Edward C. Wolf are senior researchers.

In giving the earth a physical examination, checking its vital signs, we find that the readings are not reassuring: The planet's forests are shrinking, its deserts expanding, and its soils eroding — all at record rates.

Each year, thousands of plant and animal species disappear, many before they are named or cataloged. The ozone layer in the upper atmosphere that protects us from ultraviolet radiation is thinning. The temperature of the earth appears to be rising, posing a threat of unknown dimensions to virtually all the life-support systems on which humanity depends.

All human activities affect the earth's physical condition, but two are disproportionately important: energy use and population growth. Heavy dependence on fossil fuels has caused a buildup of carbon dioxide in the atmosphere that threatens to warm the earth. Pollutants from fossil-fuel burning have also led to acidification and the death of lakes and forests. Advances in human health have led to unprecedented reproductive success and a growth of population that in many countries is overwhelming local life-support systems.

Many of the world's problems, including ozone depletion and climate protection, cannot be solved without international action. In these areas, any one country's efforts to change would be overwhelmed without global cooperation. This sense of international responsibility marked the September 1987 signing in Montreal of international accords to limit the production of chlorofluorocarbons to protect the earth's ozone layer.

These accords, although modest in scope, were a signal achievement and could become a model for future agreements.

The world has come a long way from the mid-1970s, when environmental concerns were considered something that only the rich could afford to worry about. Today, they are concerns no one can afford to ignore.

The Earth's Annual Physical

Table 1 depicts the earth's vital signs — the current state of the world's physical health.

Tree cover is one of the most visible indicators of the earth's health and, because trees are an integral part of basic life-support systems, one of the most vital. The loss of trees on sloping land can accelerate rainfall runoff and increase soil erosion, diminishing land productiv-

From *The Futurist*, July/August 1988, pp. 13-20. The Futurist, published by The World Future Society, 4916 St. Elmo Avenue, Bethesda, MD 20814. Reprinted by permission.

Table 1 Vital Signs

Indicator	Reading
Forest Cover	Tropical forests shrinking by 11 million hectares per year; 31 million hectares in industrial countries damaged, apparently by air pollution or acid rain.
Topsoil on Cropland	An estimated 26 billion tons lost annually in excess of new soil formation.
Desert Area	Some 6 million hectares of new desert formed annually by land mismanagement.
Lakes	Thousands of lakes in the industrial north now biologically dead; thousands more dying.
Fresh Water	Underground water tables falling in parts of Africa, China, India, and North America as demand for water rises above aquifer recharge rates.
Species Diversity	Extinctions of plant and animal species together now estimated at several thousand per year; one-fifth of all species may disappear over next 20 years.
Groundwater Quality	Some 50 pesticides contaminate groundwater in 32 American states; some 2,500 U.S. toxic waste sites need cleanup; extent of toxic contamination unknown.
Climate	Mean temperature projected to rise between 1.5° and 4.5° C between now and 2050.
Sea Level	Projected to rise between 1.4 meters (4.7 feet) and 2.2 meters (7.1 feet) by 2100.
Ozone Layer in Upper Atmosphere	Growing "hole" in the earth's ozone layer over Antarctica each spring suggests annual global depletion could be starting.

SOURCE: Compiled by Worldwatch Institute from various sources.

ity and aggravating local flooding. Where tree cutting exceeds regrowth, deforestation releases carbon that contributes to the buildup of atmospheric CO_2 and a warming of the earth.

One consequence of declining tree cover and expanding agriculture is accelerated soil erosion. Despite topsoil's essential economic role, only a few countries regularly monitor these losses. As erosion continues, land gradually loses its inherent productivity, threatening the livelihood of those who depend on it.

The health of the earth's inhabitants cannot be separated from that of the planet itself. Contaminations by industrial chemicals in communities such as Love Canal in the United States and Seveso in Italy have led to permanent evacuations. In Brazil, where concentrations of industrial wastes along the southern coast have reached life-threatening levels, the industrial city of Cubatão is locally referred to as the "Valley of Death."

Another of the earth's vital indicators, the amount of carbon dioxide and other greenhouse gases in the atmosphere, can be measured rather precisely. Since 1958, careful recordings have shown that the atmospheric CO_2 concentration is rising each year. This increase, combined with that of trace gases, may be warming the earth more rapidly than had been anticipated.

As forests disappear, as soils erode, and as lakes and soil acidify and become polluted, the number of plant and animal species diminishes. This reduction in the diversity of life on earth may well have unforeseen long-term consequences.

Population Growth and Land Degradation

The annual increment of births over deaths has climbed from 74 million in 1970 to 83 million in 1987. During the 1990s, it is projected to surpass 90 million before moderating as the next century begins. Most of the annual increment has been concentrated in the Third World, where human demands often overtax local life-support systems already.

When annual population additions are coupled with heightened stress on local life-support systems, shortages of food, fodder, and fuel can emerge almost overnight. Development economists typically focus on changes in the rate of population growth, but a more vital sign is the relationship between population size and the sustainable yield of local forests, grasslands, and croplands. If the demands of a local population surpass these sustainable yields, the systems will continue to deteriorate even if population growth stops.

In the Third World, continuous population growth and skewed land distribution drive land-hungry farmers onto marginal land that is highly erodible and incapable of sustaining cultivation over the long term.

A Destructive Energy Path

Energy trends are an important indicator of the world's economic and ecological health. The trends since early 1986 point to a partial resurgence of growth in world oil consumption and continued growth in coal use. Although oil ministers and coal operators are undoubtedly cheered by this turn of events, it is in fact an ominous one. Any additional energy growth will add to the dangerous chemistry experiment we are conducting on the earth's atmosphere. Lakes, estuaries, forests, human health, and the climate itself are now at risk.

By the early 1980s, activities such as generating electricity, driving automobiles, and producing steel were releasing into the atmosphere over 5 billion tons of carbon, close to 10 million tons of sulfur, and lesser quantities of nitrogen oxides each year. Carbon emissions closely track world energy trends, but, because coal releases more carbon than does either oil or natural gas, the shift to coal accelerates the rise in carbon emissions. At a time when climatological evidence

"Where tree cutting exceeds regrowth, deforestation releases carbon that contributes to the buildup of atmospheric CO_2 and a warming of the earth."

Villagers of Douentza, Mali, cart firewood from long distance.   FAO

points to a need to reduce carbon emissions, they are actually rising.

Developing countries are also among the victims of environmental damage from the use of fossil fuels. China, for instance, is suffering from its massive use of coal. Since China generally lacks both tall smokestacks and pollution-control equipment, cities and surrounding farmland will likely suffer severe damage from coal-fired air pollution. The Third World as a whole will have to exert enormous effort in order to avoid the apparent environmental fate of Eastern Europe.

In developing energy strategies, policy makers should consider the benefits of reducing acidification and CO_2 emission together. The combined societal cost of acidification and climate warming of the sort projected may justify a more fundamental redirection of the world's energy systems than any seriously considered to date.

The Climatic Consequences

As indicated in Table 1, the earth's mean temperature will rise over the next decades. Two of the most serious effects of the projected warming would be the impact on agriculture and sea level. Meteorological models, though they remain sketchy, suggest that two of the world's major food-producing regions — the North American heartland and the grain-growing regions of the Soviet Union — are likely to experience a decline in soil moisture during the summer growing season as a result of increased evaporation.

A somewhat more predictable result of a hotter earth is a rise in sea level. This would hurt most in Asia, where rice is produced on low-lying river deltas and floodplains. Without heavy investments in dikes and seawalls to protect the rice fields from saltwater intrusion, even a relatively modest one-meter rise would markedly reduce harvests.

The detailed effects of climate change cannot be predicted with great accuracy. We do know, however, that human civilization has evolved within a narrow range of climate conditions. Any major departure from those conditions will cause enormous hardship and require incalculable investments during the adjustment. Because some of the most important changes could occur abruptly, with little warning, most of the costs would simply have to be borne by an unwitting society. Ways to avoid massive climate change now deserve serious consideration.

Reclaiming the Future

Assessing the threats to the future of the planet's life-support systems can easily lead to apathy or despair, particularly in view of policy makers' preoccupation with the East–West political conflict and global economic issues. Yet, we can do something about the planet's deteriorating physical condition. Some of the steps needed to restore its health, including investment in energy efficiency, reforestation, and population stabilization, can be sketched out.

A sustainable future requires that a series of interlocking issues be dealt with simultaneously. For instance, it may be impossible to avoid a mass extinction of species as long as the Third World is burdened with debt. And the resources needed to arrest the physical deterioration of the planet may not be available unless the international arms race can be reversed.

The immediate effects of population growth and land degradation are largely local, but the climate alteration linked to fossil-fuel combustion is incontestably global. Just as land degradation can threaten local efforts to raise living standards, so, too, climate alteration can overwhelm progress at the global level. Efforts to adjust the global economy to a much warmer earth — with the accompanying changes in rainfall patterns, evaporation rates, and sea level — eventually could absorb all available investment capital.

Conserving Soil

Restoring two of the earth's life-support systems — its soil and trees — will require heavy capital investments and strong commitments by political leaders. The expenditures sketched here are rough estimates at best, intended

Orca whales accompany *Greenpeace* en route to Antarctica. "Greenhouse gases" causing global warming have contributed to increased melting of the unstable West Antarctic ice sheet.

only to convey the magnitude of the effort needed.

As of the early 1980s, American farmers and the U.S. Department of Agriculture together were spending just over $1 billion per year to control erosion on cropland. Despite this effort, a detailed soil survey conducted in 1982 showed farmers were losing 3.1 billion tons of topsoil annually from water and wind erosion, some 2 billion tons in excess of tolerable levels of soil loss. For every ton of grain they produced, American farmers were losing six tons of their topsoil.

Congress responded to this clearly documented threat and the runaway costs of farm price-support programs with the landmark Conservation Reserve program. For the first time, policy was designed to control excessive production *and* to cut soil losses by idling land. The USDA agreed to pay farmers an average of $48 per acre each year for land enrolled in the reserve to compensate them for net income from the crops the land would otherwise have produced.

Reaching a goal of converting 40 million acres of highly erodible cropland to grassland or woodland by 1990 will cost the U.S. Treasury $2 billion per year once the full area is retired.

Erosion on the land planted to grass or trees during the first year of the cropland-conversion pro-

gram was estimated to decline from an average of 29 tons per acre to two tons. If this rate prevailed on all the land to be enrolled in the reserve, excessive erosion would be reduced by over 1 billion tons. This would leave just under 1 billion tons to be eliminated on the remaining 30% of the cropland still eroding excessively.

In summary, annual expenditures of roughly $3 billion would be required for the United States to stabilize the soils on its cropland once the program is fully in place by 1990.

Extrapolating these data, we estimate that global expenditures to protect the cropland base would total some $24 billion per year. Although this is obviously a large sum, it is less than the U.S. government paid farmers to support crop prices in 1986. As an investment in future food supplies for a world expecting 3–5 billion more people, $24 billion is one that humanity can ill afford not to make.

Planting Trees

Adding trees to the global forest stock is a valuable investment in our economic future, whether to satisfy growing firewood needs in the Third World or to stabilize soil and water regimes in watersheds where land degradation and disruptions of the hydrological cycle are undermining local economies.

Considering that some trees

6. THE FUTURE: Choices Ahead

"The immediate effects of population growth and land degradation are largely local, but the climate alteration linked to fossil-fuel combustion is incontestably global."

would serve both ecological and fuelwood objectives, a total of 120 million hectares might need to be planted. An additional 30 million hectares will be needed to satisfy demand for lumber, paper, and other forest products. If this tree-planting goal is to be achieved by the end of the century, the effort would need to reach total plantings of 17 million hectares, at a cost of $6.8 billion, per year.

It should be noted that tree planting which restores watersheds, thereby conserving soil and water, complements the expenditures on soil erosion by farmers on their cropland.

Slowing Population Growth

The success of efforts to save topsoil and restore tree cover both depend heavily on slowing population growth. Indeed, countries with populations expanding at 2%–4% per year may find it almost impossible to restore tree cover, protect their soils, and take other steps toward a sustainable development path.

Providing family-planning services in response to unsatisfied demand is often the quickest and most cost-effective step countries can take to secure life-support systems. World Bank surveys show that 50%–90% of the Third World women interviewed want either to stop childbearing altogether or to delay the birth of another child. This suggests an enormous unsatisfied demand for contraceptive services. The Bank estimates that providing family-planning services to all those in need would entail expenditures of roughly $8 billion per year by the end of the century.

Fertility declines most rapidly when family-planning services are introduced into a society already enjoying broad-based economic and social gains. The social indicator that correlates most closely

with fertility decline is the education of women. Providing elementary education for the estimated 120 million school-age children not now in school would cost roughly $50 each, or $6 billion per year. Providing literacy training for those women who are illiterate and beyond school age would require an additional estimated $2 billion per year.

A second social indicator that closely correlates with declines in birth rates is infant mortality. It is rare for birth rates to drop sharply if infant survival remains low. Substantial gains in reducing infant mortality can be achieved with relatively modest investments. Immunizing the 55% of the world's

children not now protected from diphtheria, measles, polio, and tuberculosis would cost roughly $2 billion per year. Training mothers in oral rehydration therapy (used to treat infants with diarrhea), in basic hygiene, and in the health advantages of breastfeeding would cost another $1 billion per year. These efforts would markedly lower infant death and in the process stimulate interest in reducing family size.

Stabilizing the Earth's Climate

The central issue for policy makers is whether to follow a business-as-usual energy policy and risk having to adapt the global economy to the changed climate, or to

Mother in Bangladesh receives loan. Achieving a sustainable future may depend to a great extent on meeting the family-planning needs of women in the Third World, as well as investing in education for women and in reducing infant mortality.

IFAD

Table 2 Investments Needed for Sustainability

Year	Protecting Topsoil on Cropland	Reforesting the Earth	Slowing Population Growth	Raising Energy Efficiency	Developing Renewable Energy	Retiring Third World Debt	Total	Billion Dollars
1990	4	2	13	5	2	20	46	
1991	9	3	18	10	5	30	75	
1992	14	4	22	15	8	40	103	
1993	18	5	26	20	10	50	129	
1994	24	6	28	25	12	50	145	
1995	24	6	30	30	15	40	145	
1996	24	6	31	35	18	30	144	
1997	24	6	32	40	21	20	143	
1998	24	7	32	45	24	10	142	
1999	24	7	32	50	27	10	150	
2000	24	7	33	55	30	0	149	

take steps to slow the warming. Unfortunately, the costs of adapting to the global warming could one day siphon off so much investment capital that economic progress would come to a halt and living standards would begin to decline.

The most-costly adjustments now anticipated would be those needed to protect coastal areas from the rising sea. Some sense of the magnitude of these expenses is offered by Bangladesh.

Unlike the Netherlands, which spends 6% of its gross national product to maintain a complex set of dikes, seawalls, and other structures to protect the nation from the sea, Bangladesh cannot afford this approach. Consequently, it has paid a heavy toll in human lives. In 1970, some 300,000 people were killed in a single cyclone; 10,000 people were killed and 1.3 million affected by a storm surge in 1985. The willingness of Bangladeshis to resettle in such high-risk areas reflects a keen land hunger — one that will intensify if the population increases, as projected, from 106 million in 1988 to 305 million late in the next century.

One thing is clear: If the projected warming is to be minimized, the buildup of CO_2 and the trace gases that contribute to the greenhouse effect must be slowed, and quickly, by raising the efficiency of energy use, shifting from fossil fuels to renewable energy sources, and reversing deforestation.

The United States uses twice as much energy to produce a dollar's worth of goods and services as Japan does. If the United States were to double fuel-efficiency standards for vehicles to over 50 miles per gallon by the end of the century — a level that can be achieved with cars now on the market — global carbon emissions would drop measurably.

Replacing existing technologies with more-efficient ones is merely the first step. Beyond this, economic systems can be redesigned

Table 3   Alternative Global-Security Budgets

Billion Dollars	Year	Global Security Defined in Military Terms	Global Security Defined in Sustainable Development Terms		
		Current Military Expenditures Continued	Military Expenditures	Expenditures to Achieve Sustainable Development	Total Security Expenditures
	1990	900	854	46	900
	1991	900	825	75	900
	1992	900	797	103	900
	1993	900	771	129	900
	1994	900	755	145	900
	1995	900	755	145	900
	1996	900	756	144	900
	1997	900	757	143	900
	1998	900	758	142	900
	1999	900	750	150	900
	2000	900	751	149	900

so that some sectors can be sustained with relatively little energy. For example, although fuel-inefficient cars can be replaced with more-efficient ones, the large gains in transport efficiency will come from designing communities where residents do not depend on automobiles.

Countries that rely heavily on renewable energy typically use several different sources. Among the largest is Brazil, a country that relies heavily on hydropower for electricity, alcohol fuels for transport, and charcoal for steel smelting. Altogether, renewable energy sources account for some 60% of Brazil's total energy use, making it the first large industrializing economy to rely primarily on renewables.

But Brazil ranks fourth in CO_2 emissions. The reason is not because it is a heavy user of fossil fuels, but because it is burning its rain forest to make way for cattle ranching and crop production. The vast Amazon rain forest helps shape continental climate patterns; unrestrained forest clearing would therefore adversely affect rainfall and temperatures in the important agricultural regions to the south.

Expenditures in energy efficiency and renewable energy sufficient to head off the global warming cannot easily be estimated, in contrast to those on soil conservation and population stabilization. Having only a sense that the costs of climate change are enormous, we recommend a tripling in the annual investment in energy efficiency during the 1990s and a doubling in investment in developing renewable energy resources.

These investment levels, which offer immediate environmental and economic gains, should be viewed as minimal. If the economic disruption associated with the global warming passes the threshold of political acceptability, then investments far greater than those outlined here will be made to reduce fossil-fuel use.

Investing in Environmental Security

To continue with a more or less business-as-usual attitude — to accept the loss of tree cover, the erosion of soil, the expansion of deserts, the loss of plant and animal species, the depletion of the ozone layer, and the buildup of greenhouse gases — implies acceptance of economic decline and social disintegration. In a world where progress depends on a complex set of national and international economic ties, such disintegration would bring human suffering on a scale that has no precedent. The threat posed by continuing environmental deterioration is no longer a hypothetical one. Dozens of countries will have lower living standards at the end of the 1980s than at the beginning.

The momentum inherent in population growth, the forces of land degradation, and the changing chemistry of the atmosphere make it difficult to get the world on a sustainable development path. The scale of these challenges and the urgency with which they must be addressed require that they be moved to the center of governmental agendas.

Through decisions about existing and prospective technologies, humanity has far more control over the rate of global warming than is commonly recognized. In addition to direct influence over the activities that produce CO_2 and the land uses that sequester carbon from the atmosphere, accelerating progress toward population stabilization can reduce the numbers dependent on activities that put climate stability at risk. The many factors that will shape future energy demand and the pattern of human activities in generations to come cannot be forecast with any certainty, but investing some $150 billion per year in areas that broaden human options in the face of enormous uncertainty would be a reasonable down payment on an environmentally sustainable global economy. (See Table 2.)

Two barriers now stand in the

Bangladeshis carry loads of earth to complete damming project. A rise in sea levels, caused by the warming of the earth, would hit low-lying nations such as Bangladesh especially hard.

way of ensuring that capital and political will are available on the scale needed. One is the profound misallocation of capital implicit in global military expenditures of $900 billion each year. (See Table 3.) The other is the unmanageable Third World debt that burdens the world economy. Unless these obstacles are overcome, funds on the scale needed to ensure sustainable development will not be available.

Entering a New Era

In some important respects, the world situation today resembles that during the mid-1940s. The scale of human suffering as a result of the Great Depression and World War II gave the international community the resolve to address the weaknesses inherent in the global system.

This period of crisis produced some visionaries — leaders who were able to engineer an effective response to the new threats to progress. One was General George Marshall, U.S. Secretary of State from 1947 to 1949. When he proposed in 1947 that the United States launch a massive international assistance plan to rebuild Europe, including Germany, the conventional image of postwar relationships was turned upside down. In-

stead of plundering the defeated enemy, the United States held out a helping hand, launching a massive reconstruction of victors and vanquished alike, an effort that led to a generation of European prosperity.

Initiatives of comparable boldness are needed in the late 1980s. The world may not have the financial resources both to sustain the arms race and to make the investments needed to return the world to a sustainable development path. The deterioration of the earth's life-support systems is threatening, but the psychological toll of failing to reverse it could also be high. Such a failure would lead to a loss of confidence in political institutions and would risk widespread demoralization — a sense that our ability to control our destiny is slipping away.

If, on the other hand, the world can mobilize along the lines discussed here, the trends that threaten to undermine the human future can be reversed. If widespread concern motivates political action, and if the needed changes in national priorities, national policies, and individual lifestyles take root, then — and only then — can we expect sustained improvements in the human condition.

America's Rising Sun

The doomsayers ignore unique strengths that could spark a resurgence in our third century of independence.

JOEL KOTKIN

Joel Kotkin is West Coast editor of Inc. *magazine and coauthor, with Yoriko Kishimoto, of the new book* The Third Century: America's Resurgence in the Asian Era *(Crown).*

Over the past year America has become a nation obsessed with forebodings of decline. A perceptible gloom grips the nation's political, corporate, and media elites. We have seen one bestseller, Paul Kennedy's *Rise and Fall of the Great Powers*, chart America's progress down the road to relative insignificance and another, Allan Bloom's *Closing of the American Mind*, paint America's future—its young people—as essentially anti-intellectual, Philistine, and in conflict with the basic values of our civilization.

Yet even as they point out serious deficiencies—the primacy of consumption over production and military spending over the generation of wealth—the apostles of decline are distorting the objective reality of America's actual situation in the world. In their passion to explode the Norman Rockwellesque mythology of Reaganism, the decliners ignore the assets that can help America reclaim its message to the world.

One common fallacy is to compare the United States to the fading empires of the past, most particularly Great Britain. But unlike Britain, or any of the other past empires, the United States remains a relatively young nation, still in the process of establishing its own identity. Even after the debacles of the last 15 years, including the disaster in Vietnam and widespread stagnation on the industrial front, this youthfulness gives us what Fuji Kamiya, a leading social commentator and professor at Tokyo's Keio University, describes as *sokojikara*—a resiliency and ability to recover in new and often unexpected ways.

America's *sokojikara* rests upon three pillars—massive immigration, an entrepreneurial open economy, and vast natural resources. At a time when many critics suggest we refashion our national character to European or Japanese standards, we would be far better served by finding ways to build upon these unique advantages. In the process we can best find the strategy for America's resurgence in our third century of independence.

BY CHANGING THE VERY CORE OF AMERICA, its people and their racial identity, immigration has the potential to play the most revolutionary role in this resurgence. Since the 1970s the United States has accepted more *legal* immigrants than the rest of the world combined. Due largely to their presence, America by the 1990s will have a younger population than any of our rivals; in Japan, for instance, by the end of the century, the percentage of retirees will be nearly twice ours. In Europe, where anti-immigration sentiment has been growing, some national populations are already beginning to shrink, with Germany's expected to fall nearly 50 percent by the middle of the 21st century.

Perhaps more important than mere numbers, however, is the racial makeup of America's new immigrants, the vast majority of whom hail from Latin America and Asia. Due largely to their presence and to their higher birth rates, by the middle of the 21st century the majority of Americans will no longer trace their ancestry to Europe. We are moving from being a "melting pot" of Europeans to a "world nation" with links to virtually every part of the inhabited globe.

In a world where the economic center of gravity is rapidly shifting away from the Atlantic toward the Pacific Basin, the emergence of the American world nation provides a major advantage in adjusting to the new world reality. As a world nation, the United States can transcend its European identity and emerge as a multiracial role model in an increasingly nonwhite world economic order.

Some may see in this concept of the world nation a contradiction of the traditional America. Yet it rests solidly upon the basic ideological firmament of our republic. Never a racial or cultural motherland in the sense of *La France* or *Dai Nippon*, America at its best represents a universal idea, a conception of humanity that transcends narrow racial classifications.

This idea has its roots in the earliest days of the republic. Thomas Paine, writing in 1776, rejected the notion of America as a purely Anglo-Saxon nation. In revolutionary Pennsylvania, for instance, Germans represented a majority of the population and Englishmen less than a third. In 1790, before the final ratification of the Constitution, Anglo-Saxons constituted slightly less than 50 percent of the population. Far from being merely an offshoot of English civilization, America, in the conception of revolutionaries such as Paine, was destined to be "an asylum for mankind."

Today, Paine's notion has expanded to include not only other Europeans but people of other races as well. The growing appreciation of nonwhite contributions—from the celebration of Martin Luther King's birthday to the academic study of Hispanic and Asian roles in developing the American West—reflects the continuing development of the original revolutionary idea. Today we more fully embody what Walt Whitman wrote over a century ago: "America is the race of races."

The power of this new identity can already be seen in the growing hegemony of multiracial American culture—epitomized by nonwhite stars such as Eddie Murphy and Michael Jackson—throughout various nations of the world. Already the second-largest source of American exports, our entertainment industry dominates virtually every market in which it is allowed to operate. But it is more than movies and music. It is the appeal of our individualist lifestyle that is leading to "the Californianization of the free world," in Japanese consultant Kenichi Ohmae's phrase.

The emergence of the American world nation also has profound ideological implications. The American message—stressing individual rights and private initiative—is gradually becoming universal and less linked to "white" ideology. Nowhere is this clearer than in China, where American cultural and political influence has a powerful appeal, particularly among the young. When 50,000 Chinese students demonstrated in Shanghai's People's Square in December 1986, they waved banners depicting the Statue of Liberty and a dragon bound in chains. Emblazoned on the banners were calls for such American-style values as democracy, human rights, and freedom.

None of this means to suggest that these foreign movements identify with the defense or foreign policy positions of U.S. administrations. But it does suggest that our cultural forms and ideals, if not our policies, still possess a revolutionary appeal to those non-Europeans who constitute the overwhelming majority of the planet's inhabitants.

But we do not have to look abroad for the positive impact of immigration. Hispanic influence has transformed Miami into the banking capital of Latin America, while on a smaller scale boosting San Antonio and San Diego into business centers for rapidly industrializing northern Mexico. Asian immigrants have turned Los Angeles and San Francisco into dynamic centers of Oriental capitalism.

Indeed, wherever they have clustered, immigrants have injected new dynamism into local economies. In the Santa Clara Valley near San Francisco, for instance, nearly 70 companies have been formed by Chinese-Americas. And, notes Robert Kelley, president of the Southern California Technology Executives Network, an association of 170 local technology firms, "Without the movement of Asians, particularly Vietnamese, there would not have been the sort of explosion you had in Orange County."

An example of that explosive growth is AST Research, a leading personal computer firm. It was founded in 1980 by a typical group of new American entrepreneurs: Tom Yuen and Albert Wong, hailed from the crowded tenements of Hong Kong; Safi Qureshey was the son of a Pakistani foreign service officer, raised in Karachi. Although they had been brought up in the backwaters of Asia's colonial past, their aspirations were American. "My school was British, but it seemed foreign to me," says Wong, who emigrated in 1970. "But America was different. It was *our* culture; the movies, TV, and Pepsi were everywhere. The Gemini program, Apollo—they were what we talked about back home."

When AST's sales broke $400,000 in 1982, the young company resorted to traditional Chinese methods. Albert Wong called in members of his sprawling family, who in turn recruited their friends. When the production runs got larger than the family could handle, they recruited hundreds of Vietnamese, Chinese, and Latinos who had begun to concentrate in the poorer sections of the county. Today, AST, with sales in excess of $206 million, stands as the world's leading independent producer of add-on boards for personal computers. With sparkling new plants in Hong Kong and Irvine, California, it makes over one-quarter of its sales overseas, mostly in Europe and Asia.

Similarly, Hispanic immigrants play a crucial role in the garment, leather, textile, furniture, and lumber industries in Southern California. During the 1970s, all these California businesses grew by more than 50 percent, while the same industries declined in the rest of the country. Rather than taking jobs from "native" Americans, note Rand Corp. researchers Kevin P. McCarthy and R. Burciaga Valdez, the massive influx of Mexicans into California has actually boosted employment. As Richard Rothstein, former manager of the Amalgamated Clothing and Textile Workers Union in Los Angeles puts it: "Prohibiting employment of immigrants, the only workers willing to labor in minimum and near-minimum garment jobs, will only accelerate the destruction of domestic industry."

THE ECONOMIC CONTRIBUTION BY OUR IMMIGRANTS reflects a greater source of American strength—the openness of our economic system. This flexibility, allowing for the birth and death of companies on a massive scale, has produced in the past decade a resurgence of entrepreneurial enterprise admired around the world. As Peter Drucker has noted, "America shares equally in the crisis that afflicts all developed countries. But in entrepreneurship—in creating the different and the new—the United States is way out in front."

Drucker's observation, of course, flies in the face of many of the leading economic gurus, such as Harvard's Robert Reich, who reject the entrepreneurial model for the more closed and controlled corporatist system common in Europe and, to a lesser extent, some Far Eastern nations. It also contradicts the notion advanced by Reich that our addiction to "individualism" and "the myth of the self-made man" lies at the heart of America's economic problems.

In reality, it is precisely this individualism, as expressed in entrepreneurial activity, that provides the economic basis for America's resurgence. Due almost totally to small and mid-sized firms, the United States in the 1980s has created nearly 15 times as many jobs as the more closed and controlled systems of Europe.

In fact, the European model—with its much-ballyhooed stress on cooperation among government, labor, and business—has proved almost totally incapable of meeting the economic challenges of the 1980s. Unemployment rates in these countries, once far lower than in the United States, are now as much as two to three times the U.S. level—despite stagnant or even decreasing populations. Even as the economic gurus urge us to adopt the corporatist model, many European leaders, from Margaret Thatcher to members of France's Socialist Party, are seeking ways to emulate the American model.

Equally important, entrepreneurs are emerging as key players in the reindustrialization of the United States. Falsely linked by such pundits as John Naisbitt with the rise of a "post-industrial" society, entrepreneurs are manning the manufacturing battlements all too often abandoned by our large corporations.

While large firms shed nearly 1.4 million factory jobs between 1974 and 1984, nearly 41,000 *new* industrial companies have offset almost all this loss. As a result, companies employing fewer than 250 employees have increased their share of American manufacturing employment to 46 percent, up from 42 percent a decade ago. If this trend continues, small firms could employ 50 percent of our industrial workforce by the 1990s.

The success of these firms springs from superior execution. For instance, Nucor Corp., based in Charlotte, North Carolina, now produces twice as much steel per hour as its giant U.S. counterparts. From its new Pilgrim, Utah, plant, Nucor is also penetrating the West Coast markets dominated by the Japanese and other Asian steelmakers. In 1986, the company began an assault on the steel-fastener market, at present 90 percent dominated by foreign firms, and in the following year started construction of a technically advanced plant outside Indianapolis to produce flat rolled steel, thus threatening one of the last bastions of the big steel companies.

Nucor president Ken Iverson, who took over the company in its infancy back in 1965, believes in economic *sokojikara*, even in one of the world's most overbuilt, fiercely competitive industries. Convinced that free competition can lead to renewal, he opposes protectionist measures. "Unless you're under intense competitive pressure and it becomes a question of the survival of the business to do it, you're just going to lapse back into your old ways," Iverson says. "There's no other answer. But out of all this will come a lot of things that are beneficial: more of an orientation toward technology, greater productivity, certainly a lot of changes in management structure." Such manufacturing companies, with their internal flexibility and emphasis on niche markets, will become increasingly crucial in America's struggle to regain international competitiveness.

THIS LEADS TO THE MOST IMPORTANT CHALLENGE of all, meeting the competition from Japan and other rising economic powers in Asia. Of course, here again the economic gurus have their European guidebook ready, urging an industrial policy based on close cooperation among organized labor, government bureaucrats, and, most particularly, the *Fortune 500* corporations—the very forces that have led us to the current abyss.

Fortunately, there are signs that some large U.S. companies—notably Xerox, IBM, and Cummins Engine—are recommitting themselves to the "blocking and tackling" of the production process. Product-oriented executives, such as Ford's Don Peterson and IBM Executive Vice President Jack Kuehler, are emerging as the new corporate role models, replacing the discredited green eyeshade managers typified by David Roderick of USX and Roger Smith of GM.

But the most significant challenge to the Japanese will likely come not from the renewal of large companies but from a new breed of American industrialists. These executives, hardened by the humiliations of the past 15 years, represent something of a "post-Vietnam" generation. Unlike the prototypical managers of the 1960s and 1970s, they have gained the wisdom not to assume American supremacy. At the same time, these executives—many only in their 20s and 30s—have no desire to hand the keys of the future to Asian competitors.

This post-Vietnam mentality can be seen at work in companies all across the spectrum of American industry. Steel minimills, such as Nucor, now represent over one-fifth of the nation's steel production, winning market share not only from U.S. giants but also from Japanese and Korean steelmakers. And while Japan's vertically integrated electronics houses have "taken over" the high-volume, low-margin DRAM market, smaller American firms—such as LSI Logic, Cypress Semiconductor, and Linear Technologies—have continued to dominate many of the cutting-edge, high-margin parts of the chip business.

But perhaps the most interesting example of the post-Vietnam managers can be seen in the microcomputer field. Several years ago, many analysts predicted that only giant firms, such as IBM and AT&T, would be able to withstand the onslaught of the Japanese and Korean conglomerates. Yet since 1986 the gainers in market share and profitability have been the new breed of entrepreneurial industrial firms—such as Compaq, AST Research, Everex, and Dell Computers—all of whom started within the past decade.

The failure of Japanese companies to win in the personal computer business reflects a growing problem for the island nation. While the Japanese have done well in projecting themselves into already established industries, often with the assistance of their brain-dead American competitors, they have had little success in creating the new growth companies—the modern-day equivalents of the Hondas and Sonys of the 1950s—who tend to provide leadership in cutting-edge industries.

Such trends, of course, rarely impress our politicians, corporate lobbyists, and economic gurus, but the Japanese themselves are profoundly aware of these problems. Although currently buoyed by low oil prices and an orgy of domestic spending, Japan's rate of economic growth, once among the highest in the world, has in recent years been roughly even with that of the United States and below that of such places as California.

Equally important, the current *endaka*, or yen shock, has sent Japan, the prototypical industrial superpower, speeding toward a more service-based and financially driven economy. Over the past few years, new investment in plant and equipment has generally slowed, and the largest source of profits for many Japanese firms last year was not products but *zaitech*, money made through financial and real estate transactions. While American MBAs are rethinking their commitment to Wall Street, Japanese financial institutions, now the world's largest, are becoming "hot" among that nation's top college graduates. And without a pool of immigrants to take up the slack, Japanese industry is having problems finding young motivated workers to man its assembly lines.

IF THESE PATTERNS SEEM FAMILIAR to Americans, they

should be—the United States has undergone a similar process in the past 25 years. But Japan's transition from an industrial to a financial paradigm is likely to be more lasting. This is because Japan lacks that third pillar of *sokojikara*, a large continental landmass.

Growing up in a huge country, we Americans often forget the advantages of our natural endowment. Our prime industrial competitors—Japan, the newly industrializing nations of Asia, and Western Europe—are fundamentally land and resource poor. Many of these nations, notably Japan and Germany, spent much of the first half of this century attempting to achieve what the Japanese call *tairiku*, or continental power, ultimately failing at terrible cost.

Rather than some dark conspiracy to "take over" an America beset with a weak currency, the recent upsurge in foreign investment reflects foreigners' often greater appreciation of our natural advantages, as well as U.S. demographic and entrepreneurial vitality. A poll of Western European executives in 1984—at the height of the strong dollar—found that 45 percent preferred the United States as their first choice for expansion. Similarly, the majority of all capital exported from the cash-rich Chinese diaspora, notably Taiwan and Hong Kong, is flowing toward the United States.

But in the long run, no nation more appreciates American *tairiku* power than Japan. Within its borders the United States possesses 30 times Japan's arable land, 1,300 times its oil reserves, and 327 times its coal deposits. Viewed from the Japanese perspective, the United States simply represents what Max Weber once called "the area of optimal economic opportunities."

Japan's could be a crucial role—in terms both of capital and of technology—in rebuilding our nation's industrial plant. Increasingly, for instance, many of our imports from Japan are in the form, not of consumer products such as cars and VCRs, but of capital goods, such as machine tools and textile-making machinery, that are used to make products here at home. Sometimes these goods find their way into Japanese-financed industrial expansions—from the car plants in Ohio to cotton mills in California.

Indeed, so great is Japan's role in refinancing America—accounting for roughly 45 percent of that nation's worldwide direct foreign investment in 1986—that some Japanese are afraid it might eventually threaten Japan's own economic position. Capital-rich nations have tended to lay "the secret foundations," in Karl Marx's words, for the next economic ascendancy. As Venice financed Holland, and Holland Great Britain, and Great Britain America, some Japanese fear the new outflows of capital and producer goods could in the long term hand the keys to future ascendancy to its great competitor.

"United States society is very strong, with all your immigration from other countries. You have the scale and the resources that we simply will never possess," Hiroshi Takeuchi, chief economist for the Long Term Credit Bank of Japan, says resignedly. "The Japanese role will be to assist the United States by exporting our money to rebuild your economy. This is the evidence that our economy is fundamentally weak. The money goes to America because you are fundamentally strong."

"THE EMPIRES OF THE FUTURE," wrote Winston Churchill, "are the empires of the mind." In this context, American greatness does not mean attempting to recreate the artificial, war-induced hegemony of 1945. Nor does it mean bankrupting ourselves for our competitors' sake, most lavishly in the case of Europe, in order to achieve military control of the planet. And most importantly of all, the American empire cannot preserve itself—as Gore Vidal among others has advocated—by lining up with the other white powers, including the Soviet Union, to defend European civilization against the rising forces of Asia.

To retain its preeminence, America must instead hasten its transition into a world nation. Rather than submitting to the great angst of the Atlantic world, we must begin to identify ourselves more with the Asians, Latins, and Africans, who every day become a greater part of America. They, together with Americans of European descent, are the true sources of our nation's unparalleled technological, cultural, and economic dynamism—the human basis for our "empire of the mind." Similarly, in our foreign affairs, we must turn from our historical obsession with Europe and shift our prime attention to the Pacific that is our future and to a Latin America with which we share growing economic, cultural, linguistic, and ethnic ties.

Pacific and North American countries now represent our largest markets, while Europe's share of U.S. trade has fallen from 36 percent to 22 percent over the past decade. Today our three leading trading partners and export markets are Canada, Japan, and Mexico. Our fastest-growing export markets are Taiwan and the People's Republic of China. Today we already sell more products in Taiwan than we do in Italy; by the beginning of the 1990s it is likely that Taiwan and South Korea will become bigger markets for U.S. products than France, perhaps even larger than West Germany and the United Kingdom.

But more than economic necessity drives us to the Pacific. It is indeed our national destiny. Some such as Allan Bloom see the embrace of a post-European reality as a denial of our fundamental values. But by extending the nation's mission beyond the confines of the narrowly defined "West," the United States, for the first time, could begin to fulfill the aspirations of the 18th- and 19th-century visionaries who saw our destiny as something greater than the western expansion of European history. "We are the heirs of all mankind," wrote Herman Melville, "and with all people we share our inheritance."

We should never forget that America's revolutionary message—its promise of an open economic and political system based on individuals freely associating—remains as relevant and powerful as in any epoch. In Asia, in Latin America, even the Soviet Union, millions seek those very liberties that Paine, Jefferson, and Adams created from revolution two centuries ago.

For in the end, the greatness of America depends not so much on its force of arms, or even the opulence of its economy, but upon the power of its message to the world. Lacking a sense of mission, the nation will likely continue to flounder, unsure even of its true identity. Only by rediscovering our revolutionary charter and applying it to the realities of the post-European world can the United States in its third century enjoy a renaissance equal to the great vision of its founders and the uniqueness of its people.

Glossary

This glossary of 459 sociology terms is included to provide you with a convenient and ready reference as you encounter general terms in your study of sociology which are unfamiliar or require a review. It is not intended to be comprehensive but taken together with the many definitions included in the articles themselves it should prove to be quite useful.

Absolute Poverty A condition in which one lacks the essentials of life such as food, clothing, or shelter. *See* Relative Poverty.

Achieved Status The position of an individual within a system of social stratification based on changeable factors such as occupations, high income, or marriage into hgiher social strata. *See* Ascriptive Status.

Agents of Socialization The people, groups, and organizations who socialize the individual. *See* Socialization.

Alienation A sense of separation from society. In the context of the bureacracy, one's feeling of not having control over or responsibility for one's own behavior at work. *See* Bureaucracy.

Altruism Behavior motivated by a desire to benefit another individual, or sacrifice by individuals for the benefit of the group as a whole.

Androgyny A combination of male and female characteristics. The term may be used in a strictly physical sense or it may apply to a wider, social ideal.

Anomie The loosening of social control over individual behavior that occurs when norms become ineffective.

Ascriptive Status The position of an individual within a system of social stratification based on factors such as sex, age, race, over which the individual has no control. *See* Achieved Status, Social Stratification, Status.

Assimilation The absorption of a subordinate group into the dominant culture.

Authority Power that people recognize as just, legitimate, and necessary; the basis for compliance with a government's laws.

Authority Systems Systems by which authority is legitimated. According to Max Weber, in a traditional system, positions of authority are obtained by heredity. In a charismatic system, leaders are followed because of some extraordinarily appealing personal quality. In a legal-rational system, the office is the source of authority, rather than the officeholder.

Autocratic Leader The type of group leader who is authoritarian and impersonal and who does not participate in group projects. *See* Democratic Leader, Laissez-Faire Leader.

Awareness Context The "total combination of what each interactant in a situation knows about the identity of the other and [about his or her] own identity in the eyes of the other."

Belief System Groups of basic assumptions about general concepts such as the existence and nature of God, the meaning of life, or the relationship of the individual and the state held by a culture.

Bilineal Kinship Kinship system in which descent is traced through both parents and all grandparents. *See* Kinship, Lineal Kinship.

Biological Determinism The view of behavior as a product of genetic makeup.

Biological-Instinctual Theories Theories of behavior that stress the importance of instinct. *See* Environmental Theories.

Biosocial Interaction The ways in which interrelationships with society influence and are influenced by biological factors. *See* Biosociologists.

Biosocial Systems Systems of social organization such as those among insects, which survive because behavior patterns are biologically controlled.

Biosociologists Sociologists who are concerned with the implications of biology in the study of society. They study the genotype-environment interactions in the production of behavior. *See* Genotype/Phenotype, Sociobiology.

Birth Rate (Crude) The number of people born in a single year per 1,000 persons in the population.

Bourgeoisie The class that owns the means of production. *See* Proletariat.

Bureaucracy An authority structure arranged hierarchically for the purpose of efficient operation.

Case Study A research method which involves intensive examination of a particular social group over time. *See* Sample Survey, Participant Observation, Research.

Caste A rigid form of social stratification, rooted in religious standards, in which individuals spend their lives in the stratum into which they were born. *See* Class, Estate, Social Stratification.

Census A periodic count and collection of demographic information about an entire population. *See* Demography.

Central City The core unit of a metropolitan area. The term is also used to mean "inner city" or "ghetto," with its urban problems of poverty, crime, racial discrimination, poor schools and housing, and so on.

Centrality of the Leader A concept of group interaction formulated by Sigmund Freud which considers the group leader's power and authority to be centrally important to the group.

Charisma Exceptional personal leadership qualities which command authority as contrasted to legal or formal authority. A driving, creative force that attaches both to individuals and to social movements.

Clan A lineal kinship group. *See* Kinship, Lineal Kinship.

Class A form of social stratification in which groups are divided primarily by economic positions. According to Weber, people with the same amount of property belong to the same class. *See* Caste, Estate, Social Stratification.

Class Conflict According to Marxist theory, the dynamics for change created by the conflict between ruling classes and subordinate classes in society.

Class Consciousness According to Marxist theory, the awareness of what it means to be a member of a certain class.

Classless Society According to Marxist theory, the goal of socialism and the state in which all social stratification on the basis of class is eliminated. *See* Class, Social Stratification.

Cliques Tight clusters of friends and acquaintances who share relatively intense feelings of belonging. Cliques are primary groups. *See* Primary Groups.

Closed Community A type of community in which families within tight kinship groups cooperate closely and are closed to non-relatives. *See* Open Community.

Closed System A social stratification system which offers an individual no way to rise to a higher position; based on ascriptive status. *See* Ascriptive Status, Open System.

Coercion The power to compel people to act against their will, by using force or the threat of force. The constraint of some people by others. According to conflict theorists, it is that glue that binds society together. *See* Conflict Model, Power.

Coercive Organization According to Amitai Etzioni, an organization in which force is the major means of control. Examples include prisons and custodial mental hospitals. *See* Normative and Utilitarian Organizations, Compliance Patterns.

Cognitive Category Category of knowledge and experience into which people organize their perceptions of the world.

Cognitive Development A theory of psychology which states that cognitive processes such as thinking, knowing, perceiving, develop in stages although they function and influence even newborns' behavior. *See* Behaviorist.

Collective Behavior The behavior of a loosely associated group which is responding to the same stimulus. The concept embraces a wide range of group phenomena, including riots, social movements, revolutions, fads, crazes, panics, public opinion, and rumors. All are responses to as well as causes of social change. Elementary forms of collective behavior (panics, rumors) are relatively spontaneous and unstructured, but longer-lasting activities (social movements) require more planning and coordination. *See* Social Aggregate.

Communalism The need for scientific discoveries to be made available to the whole community. *See* Universalism.

Communism A political-economic system in which wealth and power are shared harmoniously by the whole community. The concept today refers mainly to the revolutionary socialism of Karl Marx and to the political systems that adhere to his principles. *See* Socialism.

Community The spatial, or territorial, unit in social organization; also the psychological feeling of belonging associated with such units. *See* Metropolis.

Competitive Social System A social system in which the dominant group views the subordinate group as aggressive and dangerous and thereby in need of suppression. *See* Paternalistic Social System.

Compliance Patterns According to Amitai Etzioni, the (three) ways in which formal organizations exercise control over members. *See* Coercive, Normative, Utilitarian Organizations.

Comte, Auguste (1798-1857) French philosopher who coined the term "sociology" and is considered the founder of the modern discipline.

Concentric Zone Theory A proposal by the Chicago School founders, Park and Burgess, saying that cities grew from a central business district outward in a series of concentric circles. Each zone was inhabited by different social classes and different types of homes and businesses. *See* Multiple-Nuclei Theory, Sector Theory.

Conflict Model The view of society that sees social units a sources of competing values and norms. *See* Equilibrium Model.

Conforming Behavior Behavior that follows the accepted standards of conduct of a group or society. *See* Deviance.

Conjugal Family A family type in which major emphasis is placed on the husband-wife relationship. *See* Consanguine Family.

Consanguine Family The family type in which the major emphasis is on the blood relationships of parents and children or brothers and sisters.

Contagion Theory A theory of collective behavior, originated by Gustave LeBon, which states that the rapid spread of a common mood among a large number of people is what forms a crowd.

Conventional Morality According to Lawrence Kohlberg, the second level of moral development, at which most adults remain. This level involves conformity to cultural or family norms, maintenance of, and loyalty to, the social order. *See* Preconventional, Postconventional Morality.

Convergence Theory A theory of collective behavior which states that people with certain tendencies are most likely to come together in a crowd. This theory assumes that crowd behavior is uniform.

Core of the Aggregate People in a particularly visible location within a social aggregate who may induce action by the aggregate. *See* Social Aggregate.

Crimes Without Victims Violations of criminal law, such as homosexuality, drug addiction, prostitution, or abortion, which raise questions about the enforcement of morality by legal controls. *See* Crime, Sin.

Criminality Deviant behavior that is punishable through formal sanctions, or penalties, applied by political authorities. *See* Crime, Deviance.

Criminalization The labeling of individuals as criminals, especially by the criminal justice system. *See* Criminal Justice System, Stigmatization.

Criminal Justice System Authorities and institutions in a society concerned with labeling and punishing criminals according to formal social sanctions.

Criminology The social science that analyzes crime as a social occurrence; the study of crime, criminality, and the operation of the criminal justice system. *See* Crime.

Crowd A type of social aggregate in which all participants are in the same place at the same time, and they interact in a limited way. *See* Social Aggregate.

Cults Small groups whose teachings stress ritual, magic, or beliefs widely regarded as false by the dominant culture. *See* Religion.

Cultural Adaptation The flexibility of a culture that allows it to change as the environment changes.

Cultural Diffusion The adaptation of a culture as it encounters another and undergoes social change.

Cultural Lag The condition that exists when values or social institutions do not change as rapidly as social practices.

Cultural Relativism The principle of judging a culture on its own terms. *See* Ethnocentrism.

Culture The knowledge people need to function as members of the particular groups they belong to; our shared beliefs, customs, values, norms, language, and artifacts.

Culture of Poverty As defined by Oscar Lewis, "an effort to cope with the feelings of hopelessness and despair that arise [when the poor realize] the improbability of their achieving success in terms of the prevailing values and goals."

Death Traditionally defined as the end of all vital functions. Some states define the cessation of breathing and absence of heartbeat as death. Others say death occurs when brain activity stops.

Death Rate (Crude) The number of deaths in a single year per 1,000 persons in the population. *See* Demography.

Democratic Leader A type of group leader who encourages group decision-making rather than giving orders. *See* Autocratic and Laissez-Faire Leader.

Democratization The process of making something democratic. According to Max Weber, political democratization is related to the growth of the bureaucratic state.

Demographic Transition The pattern in which death rates fall with industrialization, causing a rise in population and ensuing drop in birth rate which returns the rate of population growth to nearly the same level as before industrialization.

Demography The study of human population, focusing on birth rate, death rate, and migration patterns.

Dependent Variable The factor that varies with changes in the independent variable. *See* Independent Variable.

Desegregation Elimination of racial segregation in a society. *See* Discrimination.

Determinism The view of social change proposing that an inevitable pattern of change occurs in societies because of a universal principle, or dynamic, of the historic process. *See* Deterministic.

Deterministic Any theory that sees natural, social, or psychological factors as determined by preceding causes.

Deterrence Theory A theory held by some criminologists that punishment will prevent as well as control crime.

Deviance The label for all forms of behavior that are considered unacceptable, threatening, harmful, or offensive in terms of the standards or expectations of a particular society or social group. *See* Conforming Behavior, Norm, Secondary Deviance.

Dewey, John (1859-1952) American philosopher and educator, a functionalist, whose ideas about education had a strong effect on schooling. He pressed for a science of education and believed in learning by doing. Individualized instruction and experimental learning can be traced to his theories.

Dialectical Materialism The philosophical method of Karl Marx, who considered knowledge and ideas as reflections of material conditions. Thus the flow of history, for example, can be understood as being moved forward by the conflict of opposing social classes. *See* Communism.

Discrimination Unfavorable treatment, based on prejudice, of groups to which one does not belong. *See* Prejudice.

Disinterestedness The quality of not allowing personal motives or commitments to distort scientific findings or evaluations of scientific work. *See* Communalism, Organized Skepticism.

Division of Labor The separation of tasks or work into distinct parts that are to be done by particular individuals or groups. Division of labor may be based on many factors, including sex, level of technology, and so on. *See* Task Segregation.

Double Standard A moral judgment by which sexual activity of men is considered appropriate or excused while that of women is considered immoral. *See* Sex Role.

Doubling Time The time it takes a population to double its size.

Dramaturgical Perspective The point of view, favored by Erving Goffman, that social interaction can be compared to a dramatic presentation.

Durkheim, Emile (1858-1917) French sociologist and one of the founders of modern sociology. Deeply influenced by the positivism of Auguste Comte, Durkheim's major concern was with social order, which he believed to be the product of a cohesion stemming from a common system of values and norms.

Dying Trajectory A graph that plots the time span from the terminally ill patient's hosptial admission until the moment of death, and the course of the patient's physical deterioration. *See* Thanatology.

Ecological Determinism The point of view stressing how environment affects behavior. *See* Urbanism.

Economic Determinism The doctrine, supported by Karl Marx, that economic factors are the only bases for social patterns.

Economic Modernization Shift from an agricultural-based economy to an industrial one.

Education The social institution by which a culture is transmitted from one generation to the next. *See* Institutions, Sociology of Education.

Egalitarianism Emphasis within a society on the concept of equality among members of social systems.

Egocentricity The characteristic quality of very young children, their awareness of only their own point of view.

Elaborated Code According to Basil Bernstein, the formal type of language available to the middle class only. *See* Restricted Code.

Elements of Culture Factors such as customs, language, symbols, and values shared by members of a cultural group.

Elite Those at the top of a hierarchy based on status and on economic, social, or political power. *See* Hierarchy.

Elite Groups Members of the top ranks of society in terms of power, prestige, and economic or intellectual resources. *See* Power Elite.

Emergent Norm Theory A theory of collective behavior stating that social aggregates form in response to specific problems that cannot be solved through institutionalized action. *See* Crowd, Social Aggregate.

Encounter Groups Groups of individuals who meet to change their personal lives by confronting each other, discussing personal problems, and talking more honestly and openly than in everyday life. *See* Group Therapy.

Endogamy Marriage within one's social group. *See* Exogamy.

Environmental Theories Theories of behavior that stress the influence of learning and environment. *See* Biological-Instinctual Theories.

Equilibrium Model A view of society as a system of interdependent parts which function together to maintain the equilibrium of the whole system. *See* Conflict Model, Functionalism.

Erikson, Erik (1902-   ) Danish-born psychoanalytic theorist who lives in the United States. He supplemented Freud's theory of psychosexual development with a separate theory of psychosocial development. He theorized that individuals move through a series of psychosocial stages throughout life, with the integrity of the personality depending largely on the individual's success in making appropriate adaptations at previous stages.

Estate A form of social stratification based on laws, usually about one's relationship to land. *See* Social Stratification.

Ethnic Group A social group distinguished by various traits, including language, national or geographic origin, customs, religion, and race.

Ethnicity The act or process of becoming or being a religious, racial, national, cultural, or subcultural ethnic group. *See* Ethnic Group.

Ethnocentrism The tendency to judge other groups by the standards of one's own culture and to believe that one's own group values and norms are better than others'. *See* Cultural Relativism.

Ethology The comparative study of animal behavior patterns as they occur in nature.

Eugenics The science of controlling heredity.

Evolution A process of change by which living organisms develop, and each succeeding generation is connected with its preceding generation.

Evolutionary Change A gradual process of social change. *See* Revolutionary Change.

Exchange Theory The viewpoint that stresses that individuals judge the worth of particular interactions on the basis of costs and profits to themselves.

Exogamy Marriage outside one's social group. *See* Endogamy.

Experiment A research method in which only one factor is varied at a time and efforts are made to keep other variables constant in order to isolate the causal or independent variable. *See* Research, Independent Variable.

Extended Family A family type consisting of two or more nuclear families. Also characterized as three or more generations who usually live together. *See* Modified Extended Family System.

Facilitating Conditions In a model of suburban growth, those factors that make movement from city to suburb possible. Such factors include commuter transportation systems and communications technology. *See* Motivating Conditions.

Family A set of people related to each other by blood, marriage, or adoption. Family membership is determined by a combination of biological and cultural factors that vary among societies.

Family Life Cycle The process of characteristic changes that a family's task (such as child-rearing) undergo over time.

Family Planning The theory of population control that assumes that parents should be able to determine and produce the number of children they want, spaced at the intervals they think best. *See* Population Control.

Fashioning Effect The tendency for role categories to determine people's behavior and thus to help shape their self-concepts. *See* Role Selection.

Feral Children Children who are not socialized because they have been, according to unconfirmed reports, brought up by wild animals. *See* Social Isolates.

Fertility Rate The number of births in relation to the number of women of childbearing age in a population.

Folk Taxonomy Classification system used by a culture to organize its cognitive categories.

Formal Organization A large social unit purposely set up to meet specific, impersonal goals. *See* Informal Organization.

Freud, Sigmund (1856-1939) Viennese founder of modern psychology and originator of psychoanalysis. Basic to Freud's theories are the beliefs that much of human behavior is unconsciously motivated and that neuroses often have their origins in early childhood wishes or memories that have been repressed. He developed an account of psychosexual development in which he said that sexuality was present even in infants, although the nature of this sexuality changed as the individual progressed through a sequence of stages to mature adult sexuality.

Freud also proposed a division of the self into the *id* (instinctual desires), the *ego* (the conscious self), and the *superego* (conscience). The ego mediates between the pressures of the other two parts in an effort to adapt the individual to the demands of society, and personality formation is largely the result of this process. *See* Psychoanalytic Theory.

Functionalism A dominant school in modern sociology which assumes that each part of the social structure functions to maintain the society and which views social change according to the equilibrium model; also called structural-functionalism. *See* Equilibrium Model.

Game Theory The study of situations in which the outcome of interaction depends on the joint action of the partners.

Gemeinschaft/Gesellschaft Simple, close-knit communal form of social organization/impersonal bureaucratic form. Typology of social organization devised by Tönnies and used to understand variety and changes in societies' social structure. *See* Tönnies.

Gender Identity A child's awareness of being either male or female. *See* Sex Role.

Gene Pool The total of genes present in the population.

Generalized Others According to George Herbert Mead, the developmental stage in which children adopt the viewpoint of many other people or, in short, of society in general. *See* Significant Others.

Genetic Engineering Altering the reproductive process in order to alter the genetic structure of the new organism.

Genetic Load The presence of genes in a population that are capable of reducing fitness. *See* Adaptive.

Genocide Deliberate destruction of a racial or ethnic group.

Genotype/Phenotype Genotype is the entire structure of genes that are inherited by an organism from its parents. Phenotype is the observable result of interaction between the genotype and the environment.

Gerontology The study of the problems of aging and old age.

Group Two or more people who know each other, interact regularly or systematically, share ideas or goals, and think of themselves as a unit.

Group Marriage Marriage among two or more women and two or more men at the same time.

Group Processes The dynamics of group functioning and decision-making and of the interactions of group members.

Group Space A concept of Robert Bales, from his research on social groups. Bales correlated many factors and then constructed dimensions, such as dominance, likeability, task orientation, along which group members could be placed. When these dimensions are combined in three dimensions, they form the group space.

Group Therapy A form of psychotherapy in which interaction among group members is the main therapeutic mode. Group therapy takes many forms but essentially requires a sense of community, support, increased personal responsibility, and a professionally trained leader.

Hierarchy The relative positions of individuals or groups within a body or society and their relationship to power and control. *See* Social Sciences.

Hobbesian Question The term referring to the question of the 17th-century philosopher Thomas Hobbes, who asked how society could establish and maintain social order. Today, sociologists apply this question to the problem of conformity within the social order.

Hobbes, Thomas (1588-1679) British philosopher and writer who theorized about social order and social conflict. He was the first social conflict theorist.

Human Ecology Term used by geographers to define the impact of changes in human populations in the broader environment; refers to the relationship between humans and their environment.

Hypothesis An "educated guess," a statement of a probable relationship between variables in a research design. *See* Research, Scientific Method, Theory.

Ideal Type A conceptual model or tool used to help analyze social occurrences. It is an abstraction based on reality, although it seldom, if ever, occurs in exactly that form.

Identity According to Erik Erikson, a person's sense of who and what he or she is.

I/Me According to George Herbert Mead, the I is the spontaneous, natural, self-interested aspect of the self. The me is the socialized part that has adopted the norms of the community.

Imperialism According to Lenin, a nation's policy of building empires by extending its power and domination.

Independent Variable The causal variable, or factor that changes. *See* Dependent Variable.

Individuation The development and recognition of the individual as a distinct being in the group.

Industrialization The systematic organization of production through the use of machinery and a specialized labor force.

Industrial Society Society characterized by mechanized means of production for its goods and services, a high degree of economic development, and a specialized labor force. *See* Postindustrial Society, Traditional Society.

Infant Mortality Rate The number of children per 1,000 dying in the first year of life.

Influence A subtle form of power involving the ability to sway people to do what they might not otherwise do. *See* Power.

Informal Norms The rules governing behavior generally set by an informal group instead of the formal requirements of an organization. *See* Informal Organization.

Informal Organization In contrast to and within a formal organization, those groups of people or roles they play that cut across the official bureaucratic pattern. *See* Formal Organization.

Instinct An unlearned fixed action pattern that occurs in response to specific stimuli as a result of complex hormonal and neurological processes.

Institutions Complex and well-accepted ways of behaving aimed at meeting broad social goals. The major social institutions are government, family, religion, education, and the economy. *See* Organization.

Intelligence A capacity for knowledge. There is not agreement on a precise definition, although intelligence has come to refer to higher-level abstract processes.

Intelligence Quotient (IQ) A measurement of intelligence, defined as a relation between chronological and mental ages. Measured IQ is a good indicator of school performance. Relative contributions of genetic inheritance and environment are not known.

Interest Groups Political factions made up of citizens who associate voluntarily and who aim to influence communal action. *See* Pluralism.

Intergenerational Learning Learning by one generation from another. It is found generally among nonhuman primates as well as among humans.

Intergenerational Status Transmission The passing of the parents' socioeconomic status onto their children.

Internalization In the process of socialization, the taking into oneself of attitudes, values, and norms so that they are part of one's personality. *See* Socialization.

Interpersonal Space The physical distance between people. Cultures vary in the amount of space people leave between themselves when they interact in various ways.

Iron Law of Oligarchy According to Robert Michels, the tendency of formal organizations to give their officers a near monopoly of power. *See* Formal Organization.

Kin Selection A process in which individuals cooperate, sacrifice themselves, or do not reproduce so that their kin can survive and reproduce.

Kinship A system of organizing and naming relationships that arise through marriage (affinal kinship) and through birth (consanguine kinship). *See* Lineal Kinship, BIlineal Kinship.

Kinship Networks Family systems.

Labeling Theory The school of thought that sees deviance or criminality as a status imposed by societal reaction. *See* Criminality, Opportunity Theory, Secondary Deviance, Status.

Laissez-faire Leader A type of group leader who makes few suggestions and allows the group great freedom to do what it wants. *See* Autocratic Leader, Democratic Leader.

Language A means of communication using vocal sounds that make up units of meaning (words) and arranged according to rules of usage and order (grammar and syntax).

Leisure Class The social stratum which exists on inherited wealth. *See* Social Stratification.

Level of Interaction The way in which people relate to one another. Interactions may be subtle and nearly undetectable, or they may be clear and obvious. People may relate on a number of different levels with each statement or gesture. *See* Group Processes.

Lineal Kinship Kinship traced through one parent only. *See* Clan, Kinship, Bilineal Kinship.

Linguistic Relativity The concept that different languages analyze and portray the universe in different ways.

Locke, John (1632-1700) British philosopher and political theorist who put forward a social contract theory of government, which saw people as rational and dignified and entitled to overthrow any government that grew tyrannical. *See* Social Contract.

Macrosociology The sociological study of relations between groups. Some sociologists consider it the study of the entire society or social system. *See* Microsociology.

Malthusian Theory Pessimistic pronouncements by Thomas Malthus (1766-1834) about population growth outstripping increases in food production, thus resulting in starvation. *See* Demography, Thomas Malthus.

Malthus, Thomas (1766-1834) British economic and demographic theorist who predicted that population increases would outrun increases in food production, with starvation as a result.

Marriage The social institution that sanctions, or gives approval to, the union of husband and wife and assumes some permanence and conformity to social custom. Marriage patterns differ among societies.

Marx, Karl (1818-1883) The German-born economic, political, and social thinker whose ideas provided the inspiration for modern communism. Marx's social theory is based on a determinist view of history: according to the "materialist method" that Marx elaborated, the mode of production in any particular society determines the character of the economy of the society and hence the society's cultural characteristics. The economic base constitutes the substructure of society, and all other social and cultural phenomena, such as law, religion, or art, form a superstructure that is ultimately conditioned by the economic base. Social change comes about through a dialectical process of conflict between opposing classes; all history is but the history of class conflict. In capitalist society, class conflict reaches its most antagonistic form; the struggle between the bourgeoisie and proletariat will result ultimatley in the creation of a classless society. In such a society people will finally realize their own potential, no longer feeling themselves alien in the social world they have created.

Mass A type of social aggregate in which separate individuals respond to a common stimulus, but with little or no communication or interaction. For example, all of the people who watch the same television program constitute a mass. *See* Mass Society, Social Aggregate.

Mass Communications Those forms of communication, including especially the mass media, which involve the transmission of ideas and attitudes from a communications center to a diverse mass of people. *See* Mass, Mass Media.

Mass Media The press (newspapers and magazines) and broadcasting (radio and television). The mass media are important agents of socialization. *See* Agent of Socialization.

Mass Society The complex, industrialized society that displays a basic uniformity of material goods, ideas, roles, and lifestyles. Also used in the sense of those at the bottom of the social scale who produce a nation's goods and perform its services. *See* Mass, Mass Media.

Matrilineal Kinship The tracing of one's descent through the mother and her side of the family. *See* Patrilineal Kinship.

Matrilocal A pattern of residence in which a married couple lives with or near the wife's family. *See* Patrilocal.

Mead, George Herbert (1863-1931) American social psychologist and philosopher whose theories of mind, self, and society had a major influence on sociological approaches such as role theory and symbolic interactionism. *See* I/Me, Significant Others.

Measures of Central Tendency Descriptive statistical techniques used to measure the central tendency of distribution of group scores or results.

Mechanisms of Perpetuation In a model of suburban growth, factors that assure that successive generations of target populations will exist and will be drawn to the suburbs. Such factors include movement of industry from city to suburbs and cheaper land, taxes, and facilities in the suburbs. *See* Target Population.

Median Age The age that divides the population in half. Half of the population is older and half younger than the median age.

Megalopolis Urban areas made up of more than one metropolis, "supercities." The area between New Hampshire and nortnern Virginia is one megalopolis. *See* Metropolis.

Methodology The logic of applying the scientific perspective and the set of rules for conducting research. *See* Scientific Method.

Metropolis Urban area made up of separate cities, towns, and unincorporated areas which are interrelated. *See* Standard Metropolitan Statistical Area.

Microsociology The sociological study of interaction between individuals. *See* Macrosociology.

Migration The movement of people, a variable affecting the size and composition of population. Migration may be internal, within a country, or international, between countries. *See* Demography.

Milling The physical moving about of people in a crowd who spread emotions as their contact increases. Milling is an important factor in the escalation of excitement in collective behavior. *See* Collective Behavior.

Mills, C. Wright (1916-1962) The leader of mid-20th-century American sociological thought, who attempted to develop a radical sociological critique of capitalist society. His social-interactionist position, derived from Max Weber and Herbert Spencer, also influenced his thinking.

Miscegenation Mingling of races, particularly marriage or cohabitation between whites and other races. *See* Race.

Modernization The process of gradual change in a society from traditional social, economic, and political institutions to those characteristic of modern urban, industrial societies. *See* Industrialization, Social Modernization.

Modified Extended Family System A middle-class urban family pattern of related nuclear families participating in a kinship structure based on ties of affection rather than ties demanded by tradition. *See* Extended Family.

Monasticism An organized system of withdrawal from everyday life and devotion to religous principles.

Monogamy Marriage of one woman and one man. *See* Polygamy.

Moral Absolutism The idea that one's own moral values are the only true ones and that they are the proper basis for judging all others. *See* Cultural Relativism.

Moral Development The growth of a child into an adult who is willing to make the sacrifices necessary for social living. Study of moral development has focused on how people come to adopt their culture's standards of right and wrong and how they resist the temptation to defy the rules of acceptable conduct.

Mores Folkways or customs to which group members attach social importance or necessity; standards of behavior that carry the force of right and wrong. *See* Socialization.

Motivating Conditions In a model of suburban growth, factors that stimulate the shift of population from city to suburb. Such factors include deteriorating conditions in the cities and rising economic productivity. *See* Facilitating Conditions.

Multiple-Nuclei Theory Theory of urban development stating that a city grows from a number of centers rather than from a single point. *See* Concentric Zone Theory, Sector Theory.

Natural Increase Births minus deaths per 1,000 population.

Natural Selection The evolutionary process by which those individuals of a species with the best-adapted genetic endowment tend to survive to become parents of the next generation. *See* Evolution.

Negative Rites According to Emile Durkheim, rites which maintain taboos or prohibitions. *See* Piacular Rites.

Neoidealism A philosophy that rejects the positivist approach to social phenomena as inadequate. Neoidealists believe that a full explanation must take into account the experience and subjective values of the social actors. *See* Positivism, *Verstehen*.

Non-participant Observations A research method used in case studies by social scientists who come into contact with others but do not interact and behave primarily as a trained observer. *See* Participant Observation.

Nonperiodic Assemblies Gatherings that occur sporadically and whose membership is rarely the same over a period of time. Parades, protest demonstrations, and rallies are examples. *See* Periodic Assemblies.

Norm A shared standard for judging the behavior of an individual. Norms are elements of culture.

Normative Organization According to Amitai Etzioni, a formal organization to which people belong because of personal interest or commitment to the organization's goals. Examples include religious, political, and professional organizations. *See* Coercive and Utilitarian Organizations.

Nuclear Family The smallest family type, consisting of parents and their children. In Western society, custom has broadened the basic definition to include childless couples and single parents.

Open Community A type of community in which families interact with relatives and friends and have selective attachments to a variety of associations and secondary social groups which offer relatively impersonal relationships. *See* Closed Community.

Open System A social stratification system which allows an individual to rise to a higher position; based on achieved status. *See* Achieved Status, Closed System.

Opportunity Theory The school of criminology that sees criminality as conduct. It is based on the writings of Robert Merton, who reasoned that deviance results from pressures within the social structure. *See* Criminology, Labeling Theory.

Organization A deliberately formed group of people who achieves the aims of a social institution. For example, the aims of the educational institution are carried out by organizations such as schools and colleges. *See* Institution.

Organization Development A field of endeavor that seeks to help organizations adapt to a difficult and changing environment by techniques such as sensitivity training, and which aims to humanize and democratize bureaucracies. *See* Formal Organization, Sensitivity Training.

Organized Skepticism The suspension of judgment until all relevant facts are at hand and the analysis of all such facts according to established scientific standards. *See* Communalism, Disinterestedness.

Parsons, Talcott (1902-1979) An American sociologist and one of the most controversial and influential of social theorists. Although clearly identified with the functionalist approach to social analysis, Parsons avoided becoming personally involved in the debates surrounding that concept. His career has passed through a number of phases, ranging from a substantive approach to social data involving a moderate level of abstraction to an analytic approach of almost metaphysical abstraction. *See* Functionalism.

Participant Observation A research method used in case studies by social scientists who interact with other people and record relatively informal observations. *See* case study, Non-Participant Observations.

Party According to Max Weber, made up of people who share political interests. Parties are goal-oriented, and they aim to acquire social power.

Paternalistic Social System A social system in which people or groups are treated in the manner in which a father controls his children. *See* Competitive Social System.

Passive Euthanasia The practice of letting a very ill person die naturally when there is no hope of recovery.

Pathological Behavior Conduct that results from some form of physical or mental illness or psychological problem. *See* Deviance.

Patrilineal Kinship The tracing of one's descent through the father and his side of the family. *See* Matrilineal Kinship.

Patrilocal A pattern of residence by which married couples reside with or near the husband's family. *See* Matrilocal.

Pecking Order A hierarchical relationship of dominance and submission within a flock, herd, or community.

Peer Group Group of people with whom one has equal standing.

Periodic Assemblies Gatherings that are scheduled in advance, have a preset time and place, and draw repeated attendance if they are part of a series. *See* Nonperiodic Assemblies.

Personality The individual's pattern of thoughts, motives, and self-concepts.

Phenomenology A scientific method that attempts to study an individual's awareness of experience without making assumptions, theories, or value judgments that would prejudice the study. *See* Relativism.

Piacular Rites According to Emile Durkheim, religious rites which comfort or console individuals, help the community in times of disaster, and ensure the piety of the individual. *See* Negative Rites.

Piaget, Jean (1896-1980) Swiss biologist and psychologist who has demonstrated the developmental nature of children's reasoning processes. He believes that humans pass through a universal, invariant development sequence of cognitive stages. Intelligence is at first a purely sensorimotor phenomenon. But it develops through a hierarchical process until it can finally be applied to formal, hypothetical thinking.

Pluralism A state of society in which a variety of groups and institutions retain political power and distinctive cultural characteristics.

Pluralistic Society A society in which power is distributed among a number of interest groups which are presumed to counterbalance each other.

Political Modernization The shift in loyalty or administrative structure from traditional authorities, such as tribal and religious leaders, to large-scale government organizations or from regional to national government. *See* Social Modernization.

Political Socialization The social process by which political values are acquired, particularly by young children. *See* Socialization.

Political Sociology The sociological study of politics, which, in turn, involves the regulation and control of citizens; closely related to political science. Traditionally, politcal scientists have been concerned with the abstract qualities of the political order and the formal behavior of citizens, especially in voting and political party participation. Sociologists generally claim that they are more inclined to focus on the actual power relations cloaked by the formal political structure. *See* Political Science.

Polyandry The marriage of one woman to several men. *See* Polygamy, Polygyny.

Polygamy The marriage of one woman to several men. *See* Monagamy.

Polygyny The marriage of one man to several women. *See* Polygamy, Polyandry.

Population Control Lowering the rate of natural increase of population. *See* Natural Increase.

Population Explosion A sudden, dramatic growth in the rate of natural increase of population. *See* Natural Increase.

Positivism A philosophy that rejects abstract ideas in favor of a factual, scientific orientation to reality. *See* Neoidealism.

Postconventional Morality According to Lawrence Kohlberg, the final level of moral development, which few people ever attain. This level is concerned with the moral values and individual rights apart from the group or society. *See* Conventional, Preconventional Morality.

Postindustrial Society A "service" economy of relatively recent development, in which the principal economic activity has advanced from industrial production to services that depend on significant inputs of knowledge. *See* Industrial Society.

Power The ability of people to realize their will, even against others' opposition. *See* Coercion, Influence.

Power Elite According to C. Wright Mills, the leaders in an organization or society who have a near monopoloy on policy making. *See* Elite Groups.

Preconventional Morality According to Lawrence Kohlberg, the first level of moral development. At this level, children know cultural labels of good and bad, although they judge behavior only in terms of consequences. *See* Conventional, Post Convention Morality.

Prejudice A biased prejudgment; an attitude in which one holds a negative belief about members of a group to which one does not belong. Prejudice is often directed at minority ethnic or racial groups. *See* Stereotype.

Primary Groups Groups such as the family, work group, gang, or neighborhood, which are characterized by face-to-face contact of members and which are thought to significantly affect members' personality development. *See* Secondary Group.

Products of Culture Religion, art, law, architecture, and all the many material objects used and produced by a given cultural group.

Projection According to Sigmund Freud, the tendency for people to attribute to others beliefs or motives that they have but cannot bring themselves to recognize or admit consciously. *See* Prejudice.

Proletariat According to Karl Marx, the working class. *See* Bourgeoisie.

Protestant Ethic According to Max Weber, the belief that hard work and frugal living would ensure future salvation.

Psychoanalytic Theory A theory of personality development, based on the work of Sigmund Freud, which maintains that the personality develops through a series of psychosexual stages as it experiences tension between demands of society and individual insticts for self-indulgence and independence. *See* Personality.

Public A loose, heterogenous social aggregate held together for a specific period by a shared interest in a public event or issue. Participants are not usually in the same physical location. *See* Social Aggregate.

Public Opinion Open verbal or nonverbal expressions by members of a social aggregate who are giving attention to a particular controversial point at a particular time. *See* Collective Behavior, Public, Social Aggregate.

Race Biologically, the classificiation of people by observed physical characteristics; culturally, the meaning we give to physical characteristics and behavior traits when identifying in- and outgroups.

Race Relations Social interactions among members of different groups that are based on, or affected by, an awareness of real or imagined racial or ethnic differences. *See* Race.

Racial Group As defined sociologically, any collection of people that other groups treat as a distinct race. *See* Race.

Racism A belief in racial superiority that leads to discrimination and prejudice toward those races considered inferior. *See* Discrimination, Prejudice, Race.

Rationalization According to Max Weber, the systematic application of impersonal and specific rules and procedures to obtain efficient coordination within modern organizations. *See* Formal Organization.

Recidivism The return to criminal behavior after punishment has been administered. *See* Deterrence Theory.

Relative Poverty Poverty of the lower strata of society as compared to the abundance enjoyed by members of higher strata. *See* Absolute Poverty.

Relativsm The idea that different people will have different experiences and interpretations of the same event. *See* Phenomenology.

Reliability A criterion for evaluating research results that refers to how well the study was done. A reliable study can be duplicated and its results found by other researchers. *See* Validity.

Religion A communally held system of beliefs and practices that are associated with some transcendent supernatural reality. *See* Sect.

Replacement Level The rate of population increase at which individuals merely replace themselves. *See* Zero Population Growth.

Research In the application of scientific method, the process by which an investigator seeks information to verify a theory. *See* Scientific Method, Theory.

Resocialization Major changes of attitudes or behavior, enforced by agents of socialization, that are likely to occur in institutions in which people are cut off from the outside world, spend all day with the same people, shed all possessions and identity, break with the past, and lose their freedom of action. *See* Socialization.

Restricted Code According to Basil Bernstein, the kind of ungrammatical, colloquial speech available to both middle-class and working-class people. *See* Elaborated Code.

Revolutionary Change Violent social change, most likely to occur when the gap between rising expectations and actual attainments becomes too frustrating for people to bear. *See* Evolutionary Change, Rising Expectations.

Rising Expectations The tendency of people to expect and demand improved social, economic, and political conditions as social change progresses within a society.

Rite of Passage A ceremony that dramatizes a change in an individual's status. Weddings and funerals are examples.

Role The behavior of an indivdiual in relations with others. Also, the behavior considered acceptable for an individual in a particular situation or in the performance of a necessary social function. *See* Role Allocation, Role Label, Role Performance.

Role Allocation Assignment of people to separate jobs, such as cook, table setter, and dishwasher. *See* Division of Labor.

Role Convergence A growing similarity in roles that were formerly segregated and distinct. As men and women come to share domestic tasks, for example, their roles converge. *See* Sex Role.

Role Label The name assigned to an individual who acts in a particular way. Role labels may be broad ("laborer") or specific ("people who get colds easily").

Role Performance The actual behavior of individuals in a particular role.

Role Portrayal The adapting of roles to fit one's style of interaction. *See* Fashioning Effect, Role Selection.

Role Selection The process of choosing a role that allows one to fulfill one's self-concept. *See* Fashioning Effect, Role Portrayal.

Rumor Unconfirmed stories and interpretations. They are the major form of communication during the milling process in collective behavior. *See* Collective Behavior, Milling.

Rural Areas Settlements of fewer than 2,500 residents or areas of low population density, such as farmlands. *See* Urban Areas.

Salience The degree of importance of a group to its members; its impact on members. Generally, the smaller the group, the more salient it can become. *See* Small Groups.

Sample Survey A research method in which a representative group of people is chosen from a particular population. Sample surveys may be conducted by interview or questionnaire. *See* Case Study, Experiment.

Scapegoat A person or community that is made the undeserving object of aggression by others. The aggression derives from the need to allocate blame for any misfortune experienced by the aggressors. *See* Prejudice.

Scientific Method The process used by scientists to analyze phenomena in a systematic and complete way. It is based on an agreement that criteria must be established for each set of observations referred to as fact and involves theory, research, and application. *See* Research, Theory.

Secondary Group A social group characterized by limited face-to-face interaction, relatively impersonal relationships, goal-oriented or task-oriented behavior, and possibly formal organization. *See* Primary Group.

Sect A relatively small religious movement that has broken away from a larger church. A sect generally is in opposition to the larger society's values and norms.

Sectarianism Having characteristics of sects, such as opposition to and withdrawal from, the larger society. *See* Sect.

Sector Theory Theory of urban development which states that urban growth tends to occur along major transportation routes and that new residential areas are created at the edges of older areas of the same class. These developments produce more or less homogeneous pie-shaped sectors. *See* Concentric Zone Theory, Multiple-Nuclei Theory.

Secularization The displacement of religious beliefs and influences by worldly beliefs and influences.

Segmental Roles Specialized duties by people in a bureaucratic society and over which they have little control. *See* Role, Specialization.

Segregation Involuntary separation of groups, on the basis of race, religion, sex, age, class, nationality, or culture.

Sex Role The culturally determined set of behavior and attitudes considered appropriate for males and females. *See* Gender Identity.

Shaman The individual in a tribal or nonliterate society who is priest, sorcerer, and healer all in one. The shaman treats diseases, exorcizes evil spirits, and is considered to have supernatural powers.

Significant Others According to George Herbert Mead, parents and other relatives or friends whose viewpoints children learn to adopt. *See* Generalized Others.

Simmel, Georg (1858-1918) German sociologist and conflict theorist who proposed that a small number of stable forms of interaction underlie the superficial diversity of manifest social occurrences. *See* Conflict Model.

Small Group An interaction system in which members have face-to-face contact and which tend to have important effects on members' behavior. *See* Primary Group.

Social Aggregate A relatively large number of people who do not know one another or who interact impersonally. Aggregates have loose structures and brief lives. There are basically three types of aggregates: the crowd, the mass, and the public. *See* Collective Behavior, Crowd, Mass, Public.

Social Bonding The quality of forming relatively permanent associations, found in both human and some animal and insect societies.

Social Change An alteration of stable patterns of social organization and interaction, preceded or followed by changes in related values and norms.

Social Conflict Disagreement over social values and competing interests. *See* Conflict Model.

Social Constraints Factors that produce conformity to the behavioral expectations of society, such as ridicule, expulsion from a group, or punishments. Knowledge of social constraints is taught during socialization. *See* Socialization.

Social Contract An agreement binding all parties that sets up rights, responsibilities, powers, and privileges and forms a basis for government.

Social Control Techniques and strategies for regulating human behavior.

Social Darwinism The view which sees society as an organism that grows more perfect through the natural selection of favored individuals. In this view, the wealthier and better-educated classes are more "fit" because they have competed their way to success. Social Darwinism applies Darwin's theory of biological evolution to social groups. *See* Evolution, Natural Selection.

Social Disorganization The breakdown of institutions and communities, which results in dislocation and breakdown of ordinary social controls over behavior.

Social Distance The relative positions of members or groups in a stratified social system; the degree of social acceptance that exists between certain social groups in a society.

Social Dynamics All the forces and processes involved in social change.

Social Engineering Systematic planning to solve social problems.

Social Epidemiology The study of illness rate in a population within a specific geographic area. *See* Sociology of Medicine.

Social Group A collection of interrelating human beings. A group may consist of two or more people. The interaction may involve performing a complex task—a surgical team—or simple proximity—all the drivers on a road during rush hour. Groups may be classified as primary or secondary. *See* Primary Group, Secondary Group, Small Groups.

Social Interaction The effect that two or more people have on each other's behavior, thoughts, and emotions through symbolic and nonsymbolic modes of expression.

Socialism An economic system in which means of production (land, equipment, materials) are collectively owned and controlled by the state rather than by private individuals. *See* Capitalism, Communism.

Social Isolates Children who have had minimal human contact because of abandonment or parental neglect. Also refers to people cut off from social contact voluntarily or involuntarily. *See* Feral Children.

Socialization The complex process by which individuals learn and adopt the behavior patterns and norms that enable them to function appropriately in their social environments. *See* Agents of Socialization, Personality.

Social Mobility The movement of people up or down a social hierarchy based on wealth, power, and education.

Social Modernization A process of change in social institutions, usually viewed as a movement from traditional or less-developed institutions to those characteristic of developed societies. *See* Economic Modernization.

Social Movement A long-term collective effort to resist or to promote social change. See collective behavior.

Social Organization A general term used in different ways in different contexts, but usually referring to organizational aspects of societies, communities, institutions, and groups. Perhaps the most basic aspect of social organization is a common understanding among members of the organization about the interpretation of social reality.

Social Relations Perspectives A view which emphasizes factors other than intelligence, such as family, in determining an individual's economic positions. *See* Technocratic Perspective.

Social Sciences Branches of learning concerned with the institutions of human societies and with human behavior and interrelationships. Social sciences draw their subject matter from the natural sciences.

Social Stratification A system of social inequality in which groups are ranked according to their attainment of socially valued rewards.

Social System The arrangement or pattern of organization of any social group. A system is a whole made up of interacting parts.

Society A social group that is relatively large, self-sufficient, and continues from generation to generation. Its members are generally recruited through the process of socialization. *See* Conflict Model, Functionalism, Socialization, Sociology.

Sociobiology A realtively new field which is a branch of behavioral biology that studies the biological bases of the social behavior and social organization of all animal species. *See* Biosociology.

Sociocultural Social organization in which patterns of behavior are largely governed by a network of learned values, norms, and beliefs. *See* Culture, Norm.

Sociogram A diagram showing the interaction among group members. A sociogram of a group might show, for example, who is most liked and who is least liked. *See* Group Processes.

Sociological Perspective The point of view of the sociologist. It aims at precision and objectivity through the scientific method. *See* Scientific Method.

Sociology The social science concerned with the systematic study of human society and human social interaction. *See* Society.

Sociology of Death The inquiry into the impact of dying on a patient's relationship to self, to others, and to the social structure as a whole. *See* Thanatology.

Sociology of Education The scientific analysis of both formal and informal learning in a society. *See* Education.

Sociology of Medicine The study of the definition, causes, and cure of disease in different societies and social groups. The sociology of medicine also studies the social organization of modern medical care and the social roles of staff and patients at various medical facilities.

Sociology of Work A study of the relations of production and consumption and the influence of work on social organization and social change. *See* Social Change.

Specialization A concentration of work in a specific area. According to Max Weber, specialization is a characteristic of an ideal type of bureaucratic organization. *See* Bureaucracy, Ideal Type.

Spencer, Hebert (1820-1913) British philosopher whose descriptive sociology was very influential and formed the basis for Social Darwinism. *See* Social Darwinism.

Standard Metropolitan Statistical Area (SMSA) A Census Bureau concept for counting population in core cities, their suburbs, satellite communities, and other closely related areas. SMSAs ignore usual political divisions, such as state boundaries. *See* Metropolis.

State The political-legal system that represents a whole country, its territory, and people. A state is a more formal legal and technical entity than the broader concept, "society." *See* Society.

Statistics A method for analyzing data gathered from samples of observations in order to: describe the amount of variation in each of the variables; describe hypothetical relationships among variables; to make inferences from the results to the larger population from which the sample was drawn.

Status The position of the individual (actor) in a system of social relationships. *See* Achieved Status, Ascribed Status.

Status Group According to Max Weber, people with similar lifestyles and social standing.

Stereotype An exaggerated belief associated with some particular category, particularly of a national, ethnic, or racial group. *See* Racial Group, Sex Role.

Stigmatization The labeling of individuals in such a way that they are disqualified from full social acceptance and participation. Criminalization is part of this process. *See* Criminalization, Deviance.

Structural Differentiation The specialization of institutions, social roles, and functions that accompanies social change.

Structural-functionalism *See* Functionalism.

Structuralism An intellectual approach which emphasizes studying the underlying structures of human behavior rather than obvious, surface events.

Subcultures Various groups within the society who share some elements of the basic culture but who also possess some distinctive folkways and mores. *See* Culture.

Surrogate Religion A belief system that substitutes for a traditional religion. Communism is an example.

Symbol Anything that stands for something else. For example, words may be symbols of objects, ideas, or emotions.

Symbolic Interactionism A theory in academic sociology founded by George Herbert Mead that says humans communicate through symbols—words and gestures—and develop self-images through others' responses.

Symbolic Interactions Interactions conducted through the use of symbols.

Target Population In a model of suburban growth, a group of people who are affected both by facilitating and motivating conditions. This population consisted of young to middle-age white married couples. *See* Facilitating and Motivating Conditions.

Task Segregation A division of labor based on a feature such as the sex or age of the participants. Task segregation is common in most societies. *See* Division of Labor.

Taxonomy A classification system of cognitive categories. *See* Folk Taxonomy.

Technocracy The domination of an industrial society by a technical elite. *See* Elite Groups, Technocratic Perspective.

Technocratic Perspective The view which sees the hierarchical division of labor as a result of the need to motivate the ablest individuals to undertake the most extensive training, which will allow them to perform the most difficult and important occupations in a society. *See* Technocracy.

Thanatology The study of theories, causes, and conditions of death.

Theory A set of generalized, often related, statements about some phenomenon. A theory is useful in generating hypotheses. Middle-range theories interrelate two or more empirical generalizations. Grand theory organizes all concepts, generalizations, and middle-range theories into an overall explanation. *See* Hypothesis, Research.

Tönnies, Ferdinand (1855-1936) Classical German sociologist who was the first to recognize the impact of the organic point of view on positivism. He identified the social organization concepts of *Gemeinschaft* and *Gesellschaft*. *See Gemeinschaft/Gesellschaft.*

Totemism Religious belief in which a totem—a representation of some natural object in the environment—figures prominently. Totems serve as symbols of clans and sacred representations. *See* Clan.

Traditional Society Rural, agricultural, homogeneous societies characterized by relatively simple means of production. *See* Industrial Society.

Tylor, Sir Edward Burnett (1832-1917) British pioneer anthropologist upon whose central ideas about culture all modern definitions are based.

Typology A classification system of characteristics. An example is *Gemeinschaft/Gesellschaft*, two types of social organization.

Universalism A rule for scientific innovation, according to Robert Merton. It refers to an objectivity which does not allow factors such as race, religion, or national origin to interfere with scientific inquiry. *See* Communalism, Disinterestedness, Organized Skepticism.

Urban Area According to Census Bureau definitions, a settlement of 2,500 or more persons. *See* Rural Area.

Urbanism The ways in which the city affects how people feel, think, and interact.

Urbanization The movement of people from country to city as well as the spread of urban influence and cultural patterns to rural areas. Also refers to the greater proportion of the population in urban areas than in rural areas. *See* Urban Society.

Urban Society A form of social organization in which: (1) economic exchange and markets are very important; (2) social roles are highly specialized; (3) centralized administrative and legal agencies provide political direction; and (4) interaction tends to be impersonal and functional. *See* Urbanization.

Utilitarian Organization According to Amitai Etzioni, a formal organization that people join for practical reasons, mainly jobs and salaries. Examples include blue-collar and white-collar industries. *See* Coercive and Normative Organizations.

Validity A criterion for evaluating research results that refers to how well the data actually reflect the real world. *See* Reliability, Research.

Value-added Theory Neil Smelser's theory which postulates five stages in the development of collective behavior. *Social conduciveness* describes situations that permit collective behaviors to occur. *Structural strain* refers to problems in the social environment. The growth of a *generalized belief* involves the interpretation of structural conduciveness and strain in a way that favors collective behavior. *Precipitating factors* are events that trigger collective behavior. *Mobilization for action* is the "organizational" component and usually involves explicit instruction and/or suggestions. *See* Collective Behavior.

Values Individual or collective conceptions of what is desirable. This conception usually has both emotional and symbolic components. *See* Norm.

Variables Factors that can change. Researchers must state the specific variables they intend to measure. An independent variable is causal. A dependent variable changes according to the independent variable's behavior. *See* Research, Scientific Method.

Verstehen Subjective understanding which, according to Max Weber, must be employed in sociological investigation. *See* Neoidealism, Positivism.

Weber, Max (1864-1920) German sociologist whose work profoundly influenced Western sociological thought and method. The key to Weber's analysis of the modern world is his concept of *rationalization*—the substitution of explicit formal rules and procedures for earlier spontaneous, rule-of-thumb methods and attitudes. The result of this process was a profound "disenchantment of the world," which had been carried to its ultimate form in capitalist society, where older values were being subordinated to technical methods. The prime example of the rationalized insitution was bureaucracy.

Weber's writings on methodology have been singularly influential. He argued that the social sciences were inherently different from the natural sciences, for a full understanding of social action must involve *Verstehen* (empathetic understanding). He firmly believed that, although true objectivity was impossible, the sociologist should attempt to remain value-free. *See* Rationalization, *Verstehen*.

Woman Suffrage The right of women to vote. *See* Women's Movement.

Women's Movement A social movement by women to gain equal social, economic, and legal status with men. *See* Feminists, Social Movement.

Zero Population Growth The point at which population stops increasing. *See* Population Control, Replacement Level.

Source for the Glossary:
This glossary of 459 terms is reprinted from *The Study of Society, Second Edition.* ©The Dushkin Publishing Group, Inc. Guilford, CT 06437.

Index

Credits/ Acknowledgments

Cover design by Charles Vitelli

1. Culture
Facing overview—United Nations photo by John Isaac.
23-26—Photos by Colin M. Turnbull.

2. Socialization and Biology
Facing overview—United Nations photo. 68—Clemens Kalischer.

3. Groups and Roles
Facing overview—United Nations photo by John Isaac.
83—Illustrations by Paul Meisel. 86-87, 89—Illustrations by Laurel Daunis.

4. Social Institutions
Facing overview—Congressional News photo by K. Jewell.
127—NASA.

5. Social Inequalities
Facing overview—United Nation photo by D. Otfinowski.
182—Photo by Lester Sloan/Newsweek.

6. The Future
Facing overview—General Motors photo. 229—Agency for International Development.

We Want Your Advice

ANNUAL EDITIONS: SOCIOLOGY 90/91
Article Rating Form

Here is an opportunity for you to have direct input into the next revision of this volume.
We would like you to rate each of the 45 articles listed below, using the following scale:

1. **Excellent: should definitely be retained**
2. **Above average: should probably be retained**
3. **Below average: should probably be deleted**
4. **Poor: should definitely be deleted**

Your ratings will play a vital part in the next revision. So please mail this prepaid form to us just as soon as you complete it.
Thanks for your help!

Annual Editions revisions depend on two major opinion sources: one is our Advisory Board, listed in the front of this volume, which works with us in scanning the thousands of articles published in the public press each year; the other is you—the person actually using the book. Please help us and the users of the next edition by completing the prepaid article rating form on this page and returning it to us. Thank you.

Rating	Article	Rating	Article
	1. Invitation to Sociology: A Humanistic Perspective		24. Will America Become # 2
	2. Why I Love America		25. As the World Turns
	3. Is Greed Dead?		26. Post-Crash Institutions
	4. How America Has Run Out of Time		27. From Ouagadougo to Cape Canaveral: Why the Bad News Doesn't Travel Up
	5. The Mountain People		28. It's Money That Matters
	6. Shakespeare in the Bush		29. Corporate Teams and Totems
	7. What's American About America? Toward Claiming Our Multicultural Heritage		30. Back to Basics
	8. A People's History, One Child's Future		31. How to Kill a Company
	9. Young, Black, Male, and Trapped		32. Technology as Destiny
	10. Childhood Through the Ages		33. Television and the Communications Revolution
	11. Wilding in the Night		34. A Talent for Disorder
	12. Men vs. Women		35. Helping and Hating the Homeless
	13. Erik Erikson's Eight Ages of Man		36. What About America's Underclass?
	14. Why We're Losing the War on Crime		37. Children of the Underclass
	15. Crime in the Suites		38. The Two Black Americas
	16. Is Rehabilitation a Waste of Time?		39. The Global War Against Women
	17. Working Parents		40. Divided by Demography: Analyzing the Demographic Trap
	18. The Mommy Track		41. Promise of America
	19. The Changing Role of Fathers		42. Living Dangerously
	20. For Goodness' Sake		43. The Third Technological Revolution
	21. They Can't Stop Us Now		44. Earth's Vital Signs
	22. Further Thoughts on a "Sociology of Acceptance" for Disabled People		45. America's Rising Sun
	23. The Third Age		

(Continued on next page)

ABOUT YOU

Name_____ Date_____

Are you a teacher? ☐ Or student? ☐

Your School Name _____

Department _____

Address _____

City _____ State _____ Zip _____

School Telephone # _____

YOUR COMMENTS ARE IMPORTANT TO US!

Please fill in the following information:

For which course did you use this book? _____

Did you use a text with this Annual Edition? ☐ yes ☐ no

The title of the text? _____

What are your general reactions to the Annual Editions concept?

Have you read any particular articles recently that you think should be included in the next edition?

Are there any articles you feel should be replaced in the next edition? Why?

Are there other areas that you feel would utilize an Annual Edition?

May we contact you for editorial input?

May we quote you from above?

ANNUAL EDITIONS: SOCIOLOGY 90/91